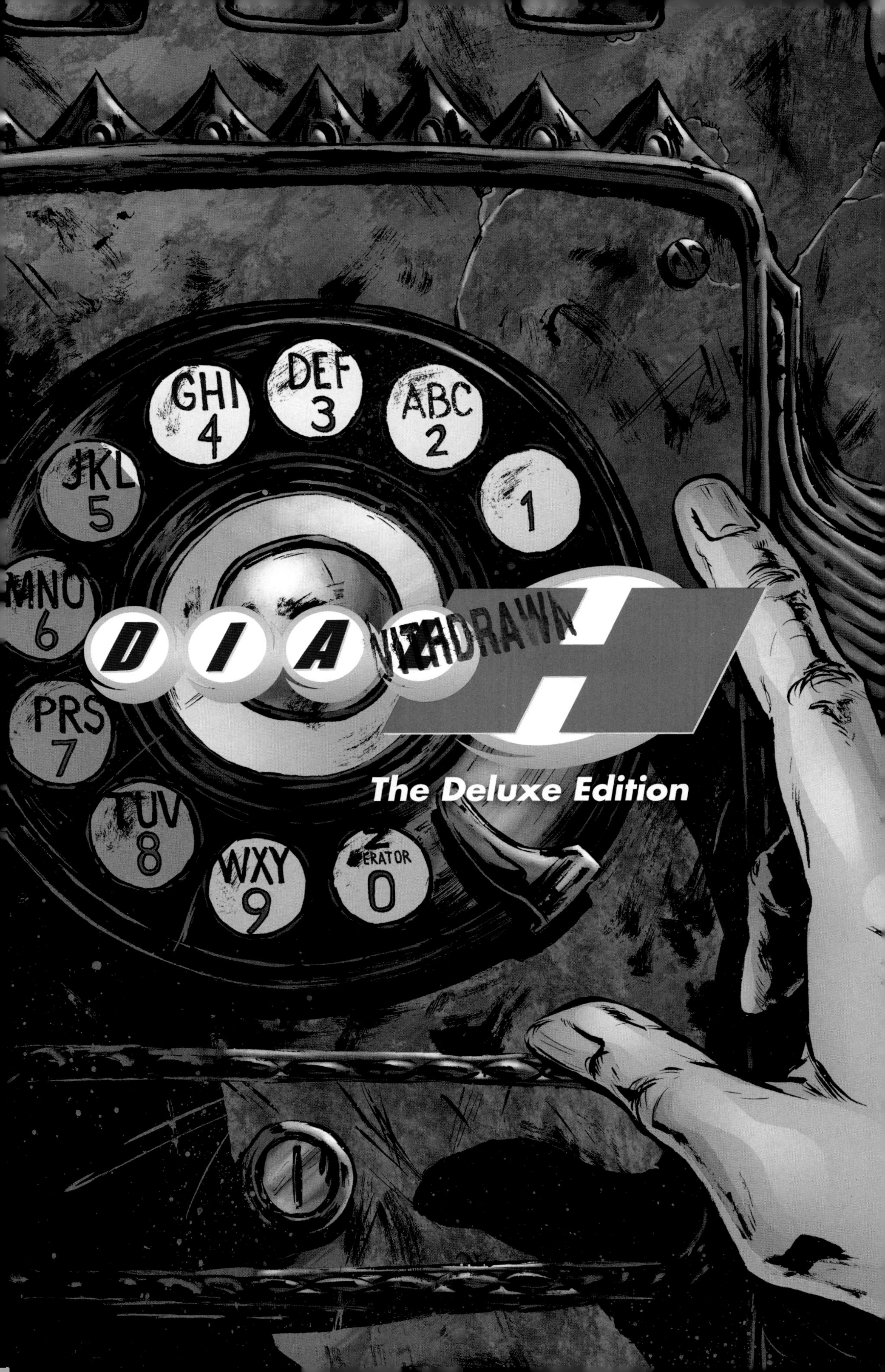
DIAL H
The Deluxe Edition
GHI 4
DEF 3
ABC 2
1
JKL 5
MNO 6
PRS 7
TUV 8
WXY 9
0

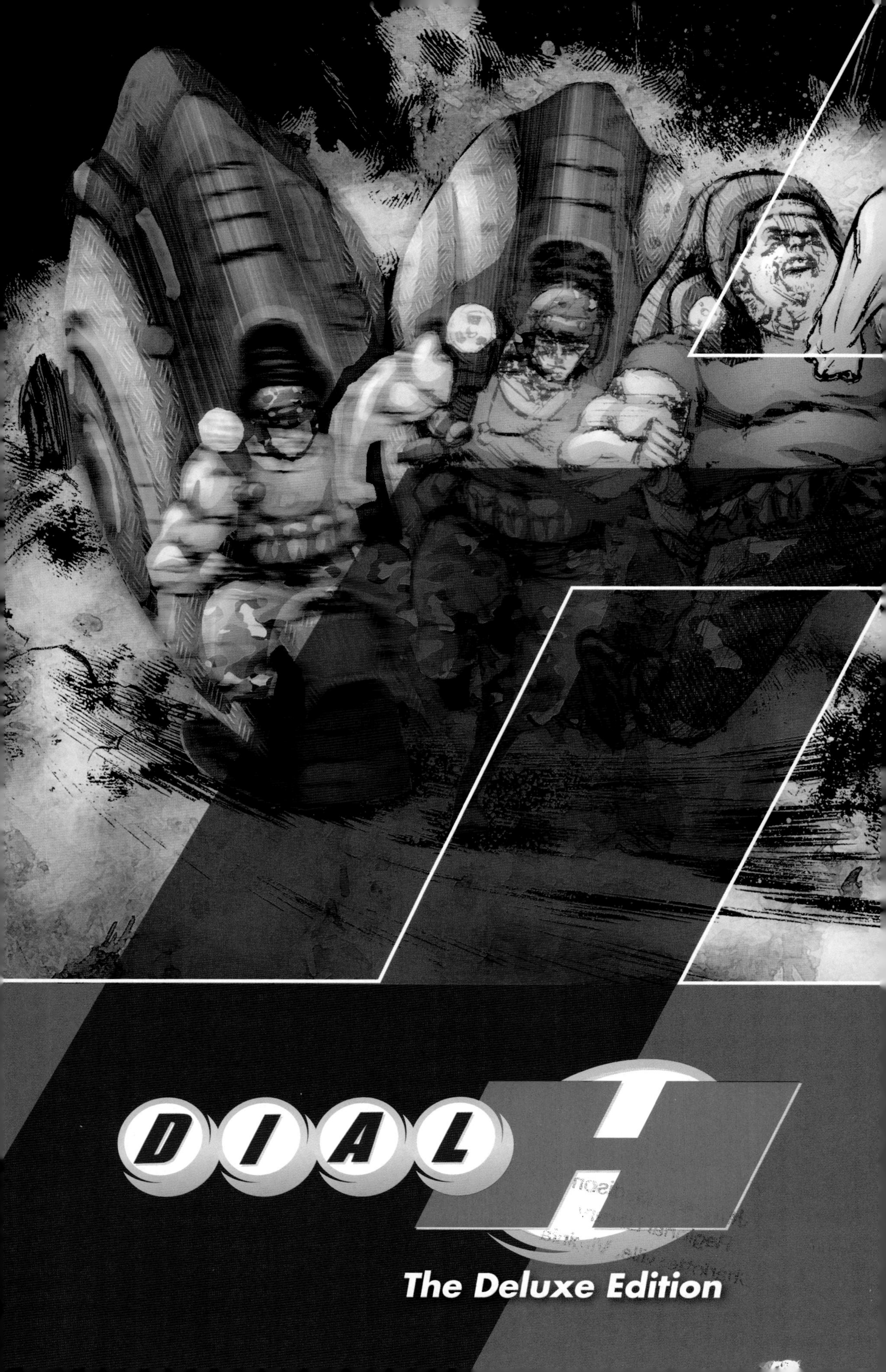

DIAL H

The Deluxe Edition

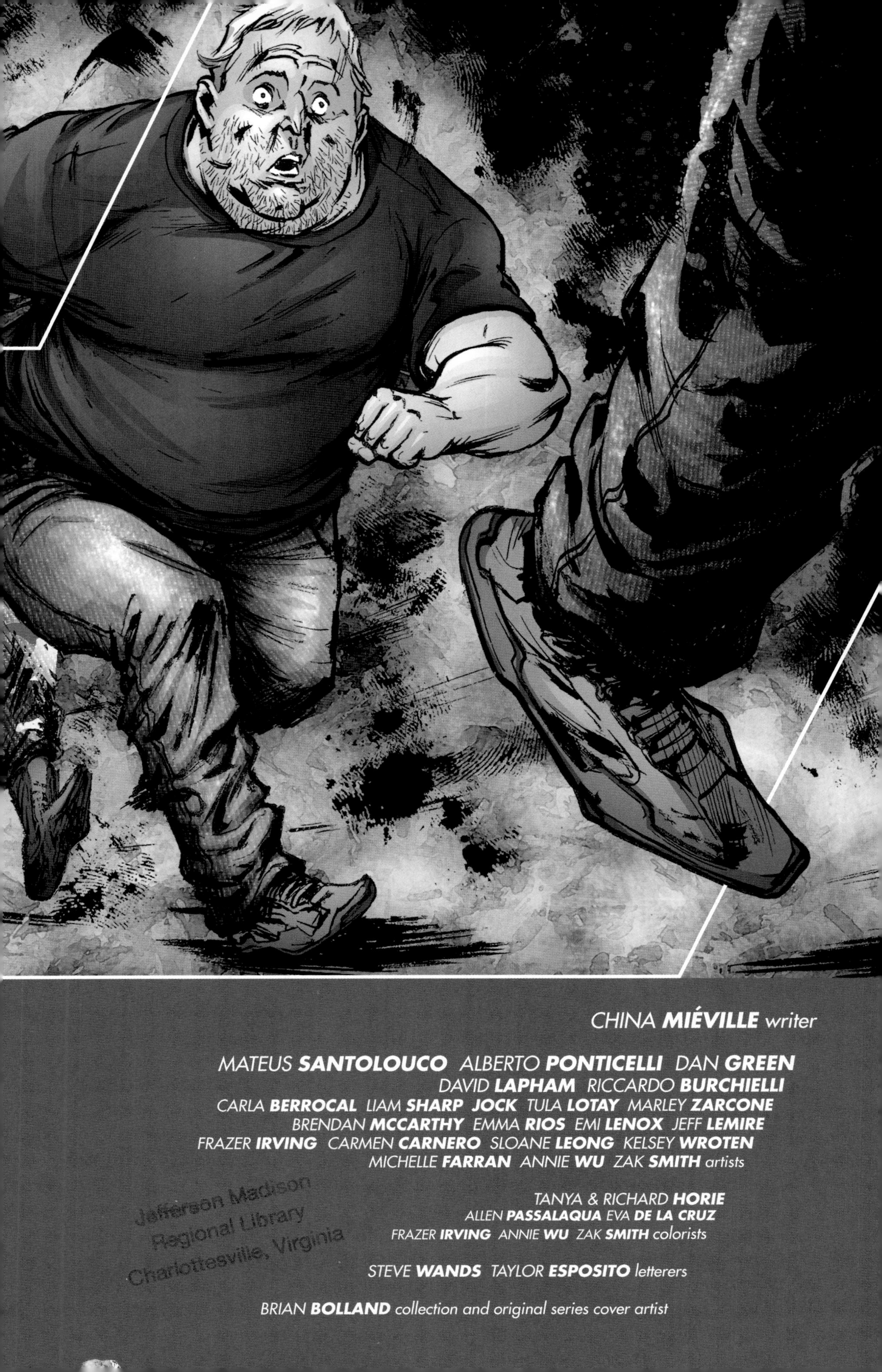

CHINA **MIÉVILLE** writer

MATEUS **SANTOLOUCO** ALBERTO **PONTICELLI** DAN **GREEN**
DAVID **LAPHAM** RICCARDO **BURCHIELLI**
CARLA **BERROCAL** LIAM **SHARP** **JOCK** TULA **LOTAY** MARLEY **ZARCONE**
BRENDAN **McCARTHY** EMMA **RIOS** EMI **LENOX** JEFF **LEMIRE**
FRAZER **IRVING** CARMEN **CARNERO** SLOANE **LEONG** KELSEY **WROTEN**
MICHELLE **FARRAN** ANNIE **WU** ZAK **SMITH** artists

TANYA & RICHARD **HORIE**
ALLEN **PASSALAQUA** EVA **DE LA CRUZ**
FRAZER **IRVING** ANNIE **WU** ZAK **SMITH** colorists

STEVE **WANDS** TAYLOR **ESPOSITO** letterers

BRIAN **BOLLAND** collection and original series cover artist

KAREN **BERGER**
GREGORY **LOCKARD**
WILL **DENNIS**
Editors – Original Series

JOE **HUGHES**
Assistant Editor – Original Series

ROBIN **WILDMAN**
Editor

ROBBIN **BROSTERMAN**
Design Director – Books

CHRIS **GRIGGS**
Publication Design

BOB **HARRAS**
Senior VP – Editor-in-Chief, DC Comics

DIANE **NELSON**
President

DAN **DIDIO** AND JIM **LEE**
Co-Publishers

GEOFF **JOHNS**
Chief Creative Officer

AMIT **DESAI**
Senior VP – Marketing and
Franchise Management

AMY **GENKINS**
Senior VP – Business and Legal Affairs

NAIRI **GARDINER**
Senior VP – Finance

JEFF **BOISON**
VP – Publishing Planning

MARK **CHIARELLO**
VP – Art Direction and Design

JOHN **CUNNINGHAM**
VP – Marketing

TERRI **CUNNINGHAM**
VP – Editorial Administration

LARRY **GANEM**
VP – Talent Relations and Services

ALISON **GILL**
Senior VP – Manufacturing and Operations

HANK **KANALZ**
Senior VP – Vertigo and
Integrated Publishing

JAY **KOGAN**
VP – Business and Legal Affairs, Publishing

JACK **MAHAN**
VP – Business Affairs, Talent

NICK **NAPOLITANO**
VP – Manufacturing Administration

SUE **POHJA**
VP – Book Sales

FRED **RUIZ**
VP – Manufacturing Operations

COURTNEY **SIMMONS**
Senior VP – Publicity

BOB **WAYNE**
Senior VP – Sales

DIAL H: THE DELUXE EDITION

Published by DC Comics. Compilation Copyright © 2015 DC Comics.
All Rights Reserved.

Originally published in single magazine form as **DIAL H** #0-15,
JUSTICE LEAGUE #23.3 © 2012, 2013 DC Comics. All Rights Reserved.
All characters, their distinctive likenesses and related elements featured in this
publication are trademarks of DC Comics. The stories, characters and incidents
featured in this publication are entirely fictional. DC Comics does not read or
accept unsolicited ideas, stories or artwork.

DC Comics, 4000 Warner Blvd., Burbank, CA 91522
A Warner Bros. Entertainment Company.
Printed by Transcontinental Interglobe, Beauceville, QC, Canada.
4/3/15. First Printing.
ISBN: 978-1-4012-5520-6

Library of Congress Cataloging-in-Publication Data is available.

SUSTAINABLE
FORESTRY
INITIATIVE

Certified Chain of Custody
Promoting Sustainable Forestry
www.sfiprogram.org
SFI-00507

This label only applies to the text section.

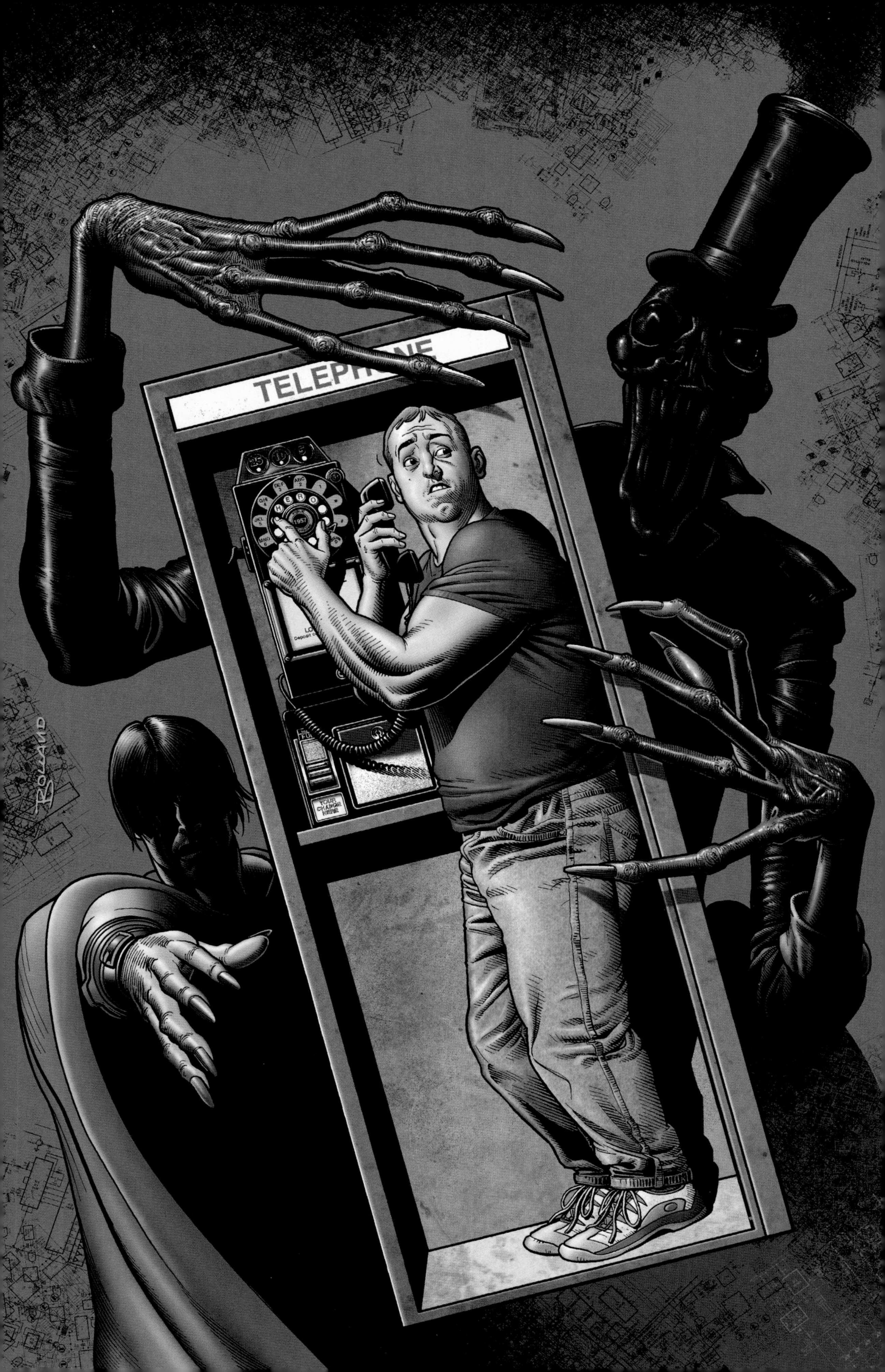
YOUR CHANGE HERE

DIAL H #1 Variant cover by David Finch, Richard Friend and Jeromy Co

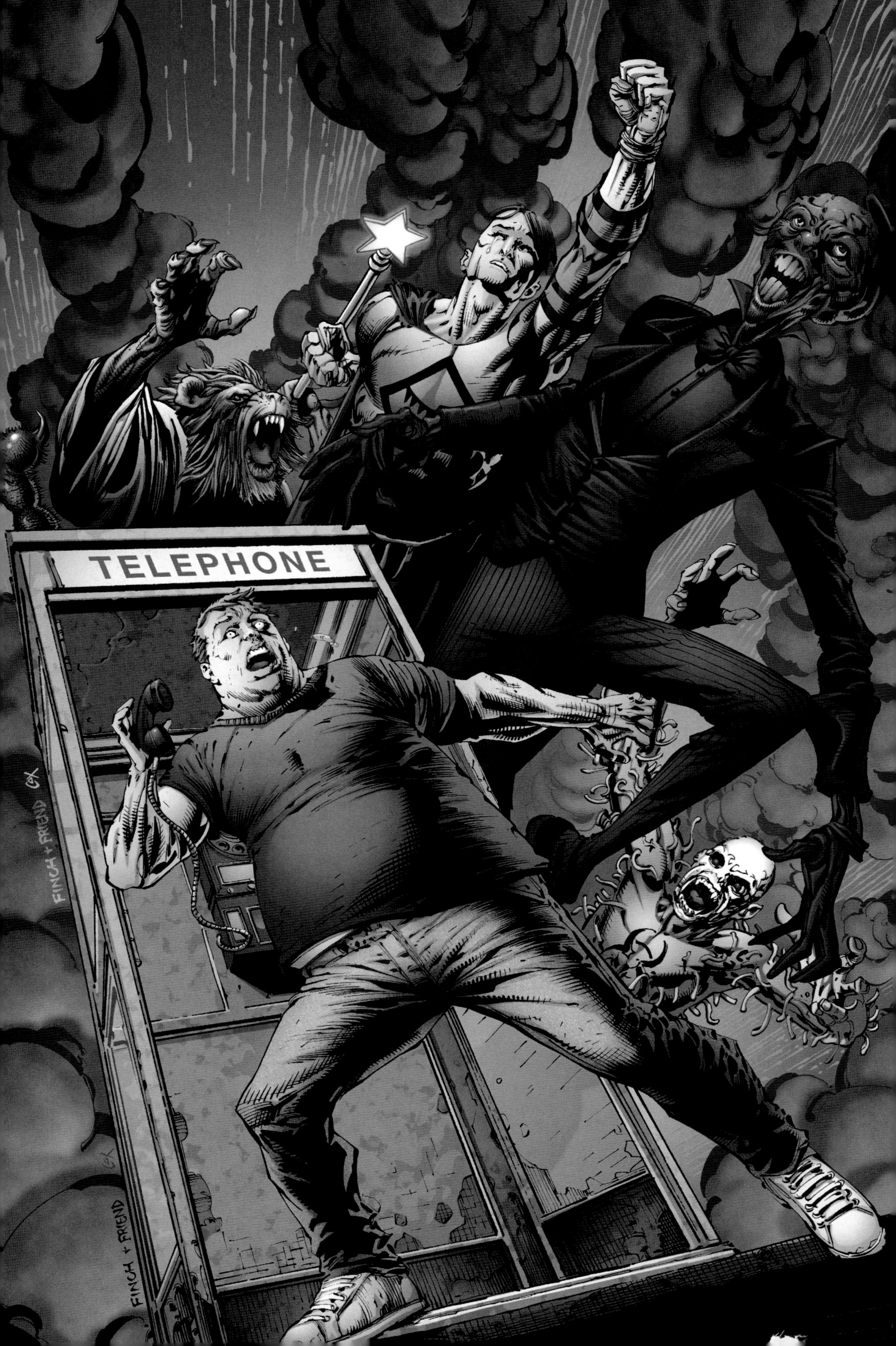
TELEPHONE
FINCH + FRIEND
CX

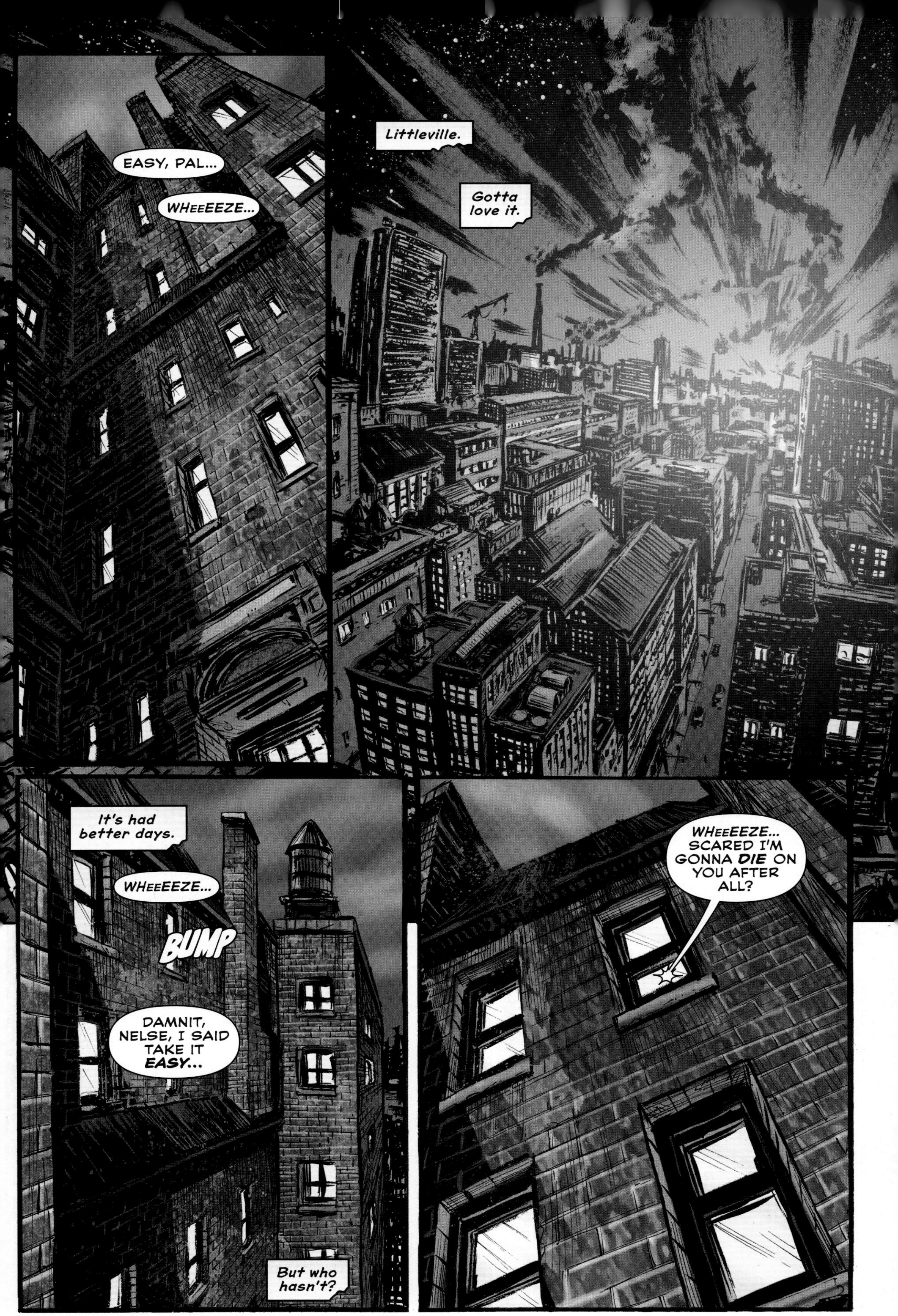
EASY, PAL...
WHeeEEZE...
Littleville.
Gotta love it.
It's had better days.
WHeeEEZE...
BUMP
DAMNIT, NELSE, I SAID TAKE IT EASY...
But who hasn't?
WHeeEEZE... SCARED I'M GONNA DIE ON YOU AFTER ALL?

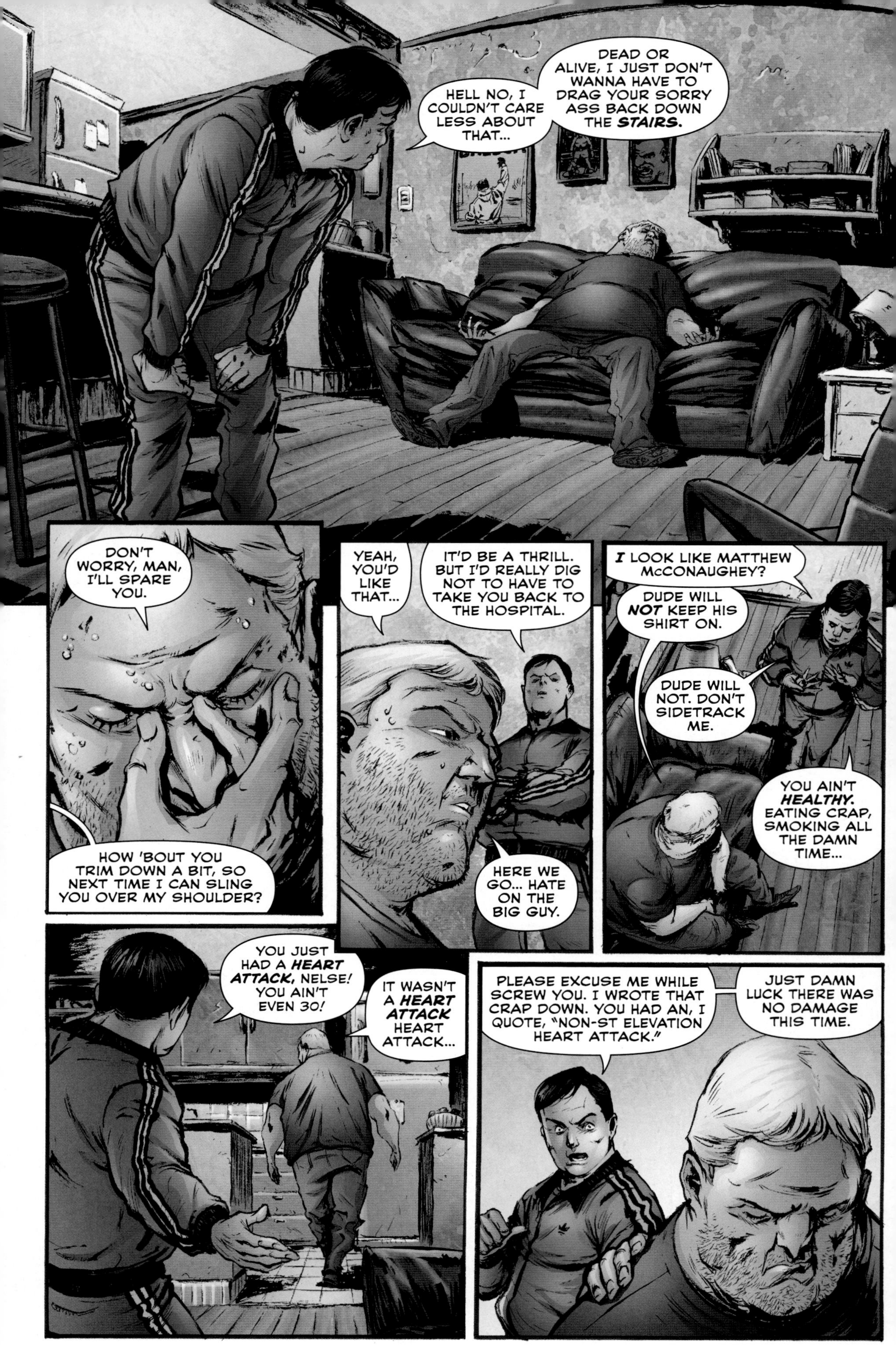
HELL NO, I COULDN'T CARE LESS ABOUT THAT...
DEAD OR ALIVE, I JUST DON'T WANNA HAVE TO DRAG YOUR SORRY ASS BACK DOWN THE STAIRS.
DON'T WORRY, MAN, I'LL SPARE YOU.
HOW 'BOUT YOU TRIM DOWN A BIT, SO NEXT TIME I CAN SLING YOU OVER MY SHOULDER?
YEAH, YOU'D LIKE THAT...
IT'D BE A THRILL. BUT I'D REALLY DIG NOT TO HAVE TO TAKE YOU BACK TO THE HOSPITAL.
HERE WE GO... HATE ON THE BIG GUY.
I LOOK LIKE MATTHEW McCONAUGHEY?
DUDE WILL NOT KEEP HIS SHIRT ON.
DUDE WILL NOT. DON'T SIDETRACK ME.
YOU AIN'T HEALTHY. EATING CRAP, SMOKING ALL THE DAMN TIME...
YOU JUST HAD A HEART ATTACK, NELSE! YOU AIN'T EVEN 30!
IT WASN'T A HEART ATTACK HEART ATTACK...
PLEASE EXCUSE ME WHILE SCREW YOU. I WROTE THAT CRAP DOWN. YOU HAD AN, I QUOTE, "NON-ST ELEVATION HEART ATTACK."
JUST DAMN LUCK THERE WAS NO DAMAGE THIS TIME.

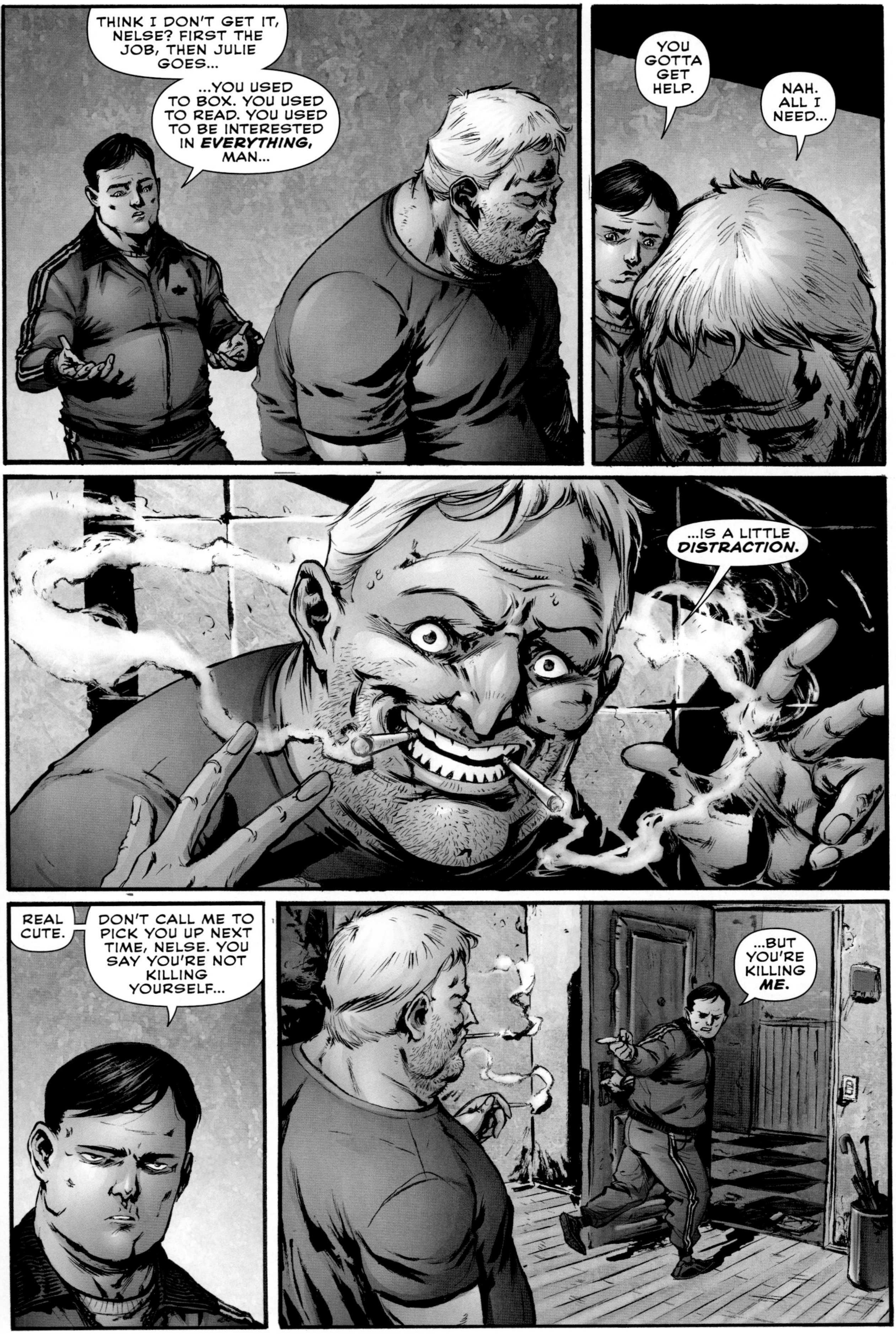
THINK I DON'T GET IT, NELSE? FIRST THE JOB, THEN JULIE GOES...
...YOU USED TO BOX. YOU USED TO READ. YOU USED TO BE INTERESTED IN EVERYTHING, MAN...
YOU GOTTA GET HELP.
NAH. ALL I NEED...
...IS A LITTLE DISTRACTION.
REAL CUTE.
DON'T CALL ME TO PICK YOU UP NEXT TIME, NELSE. YOU SAY YOU'RE NOT KILLING YOURSELF...
...BUT YOU'RE KILLING ME.

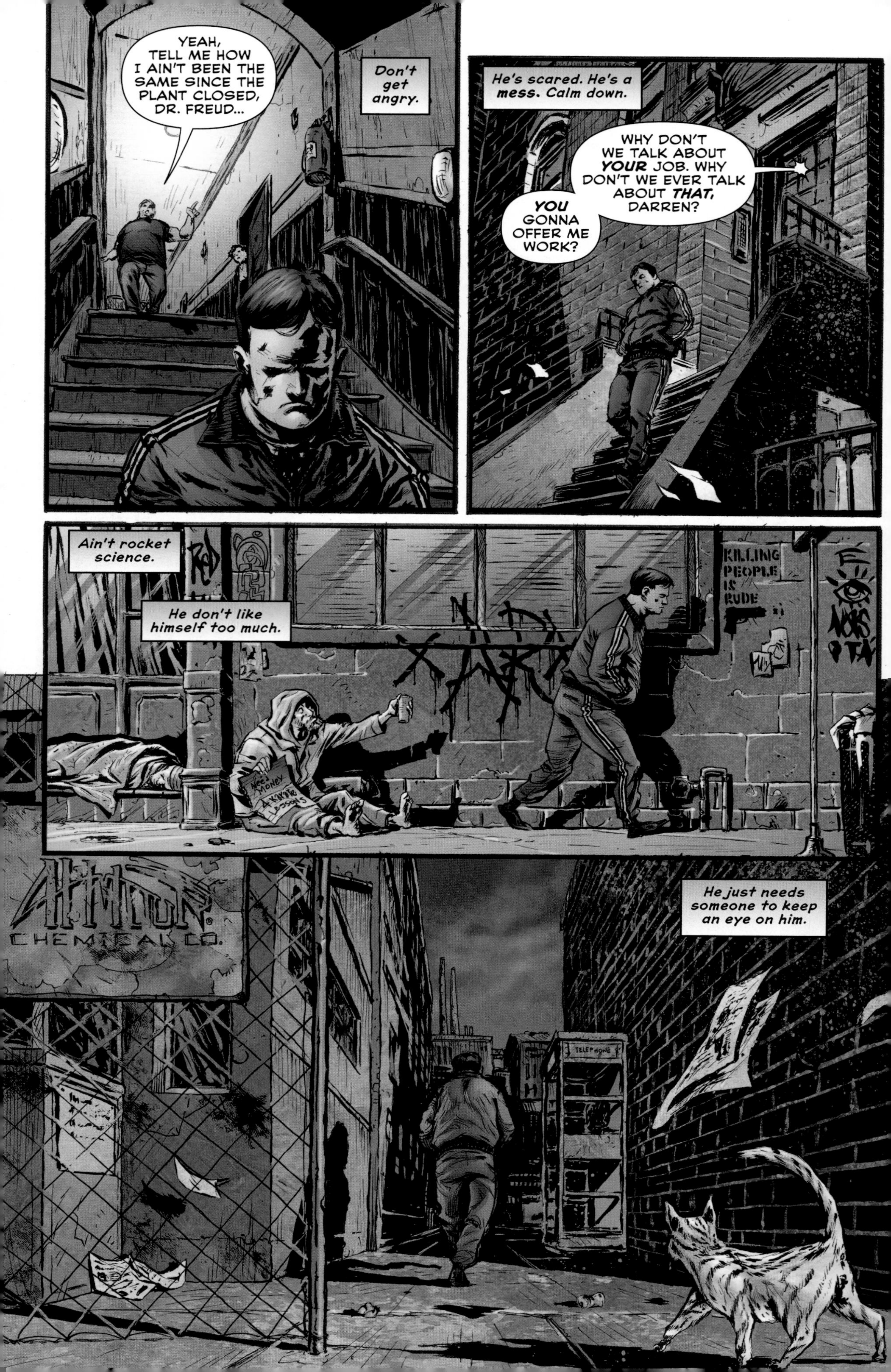

YEAH, TELL ME HOW I AIN'T BEEN THE SAME SINCE THE PLANT CLOSED, DR. FREUD...
Don't get angry.
He's scared. He's a mess. Calm down.
WHY DON'T WE TALK ABOUT YOUR JOB. WHY DON'T WE EVER TALK ABOUT THAT, DARREN?
YOU GONNA OFFER ME WORK?
Ain't rocket science.
He don't like himself too much.
KILLING PEOPLE IS RUDE
He just needs someone to keep an eye on him.
CHEMICAL CO.
TELEPHONE

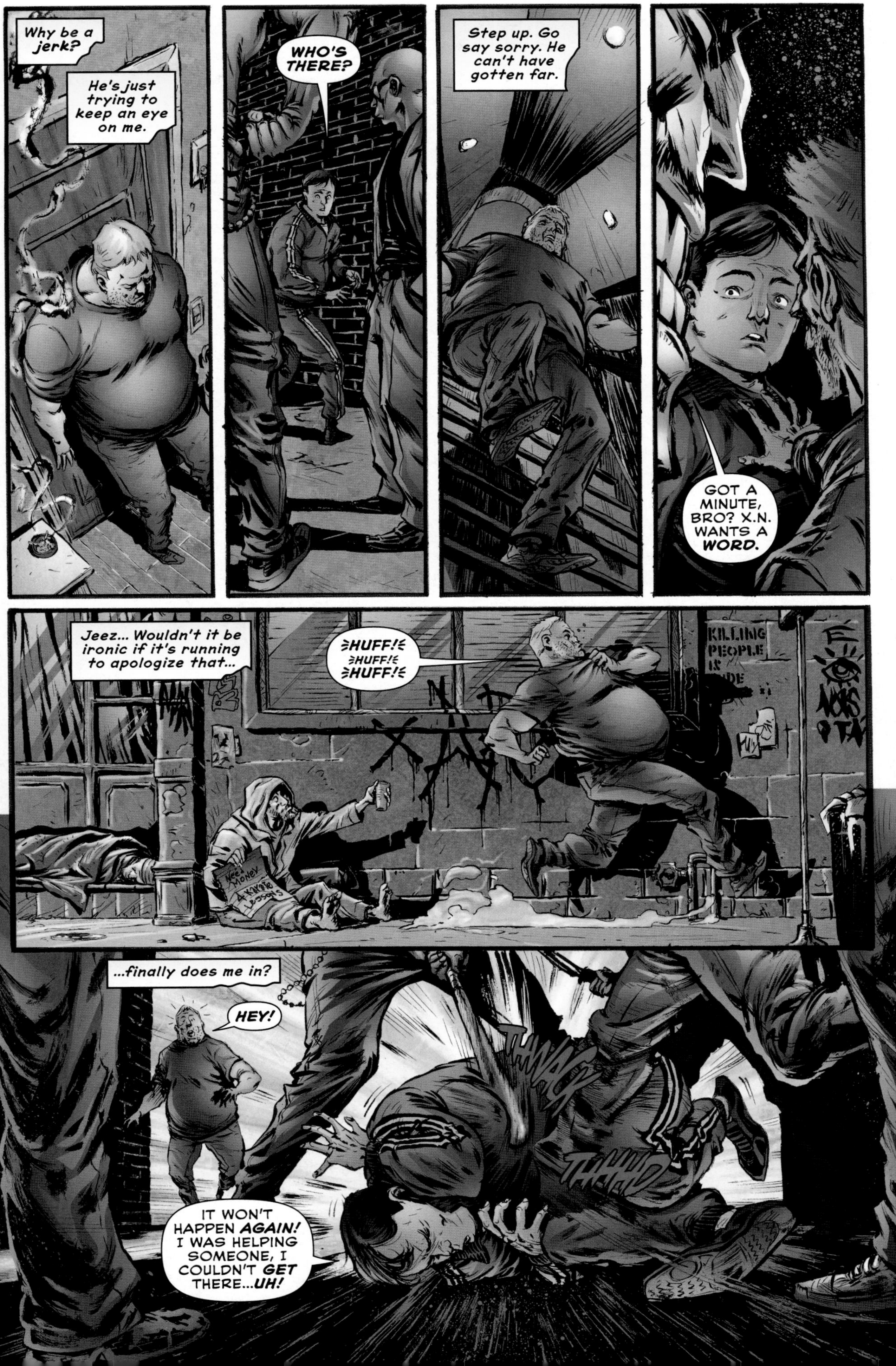
Why be a jerk?
He's just trying to keep an eye on me.
WHO'S THERE?
Step up. Go say sorry. He can't have gotten far.
GOT A MINUTE, BRO? X.N. WANTS A WORD.
Jeez... Wouldn't it be ironic if it's running to apologize that...
HUFF! HUFF! HUFF!
KILLING PEOPLE IS
...finally does me in?
HEY!
THWACK
THHUD
IT WON'T HAPPEN AGAIN! I WAS HELPING SOMEONE, I COULDN'T GET THERE...UH!

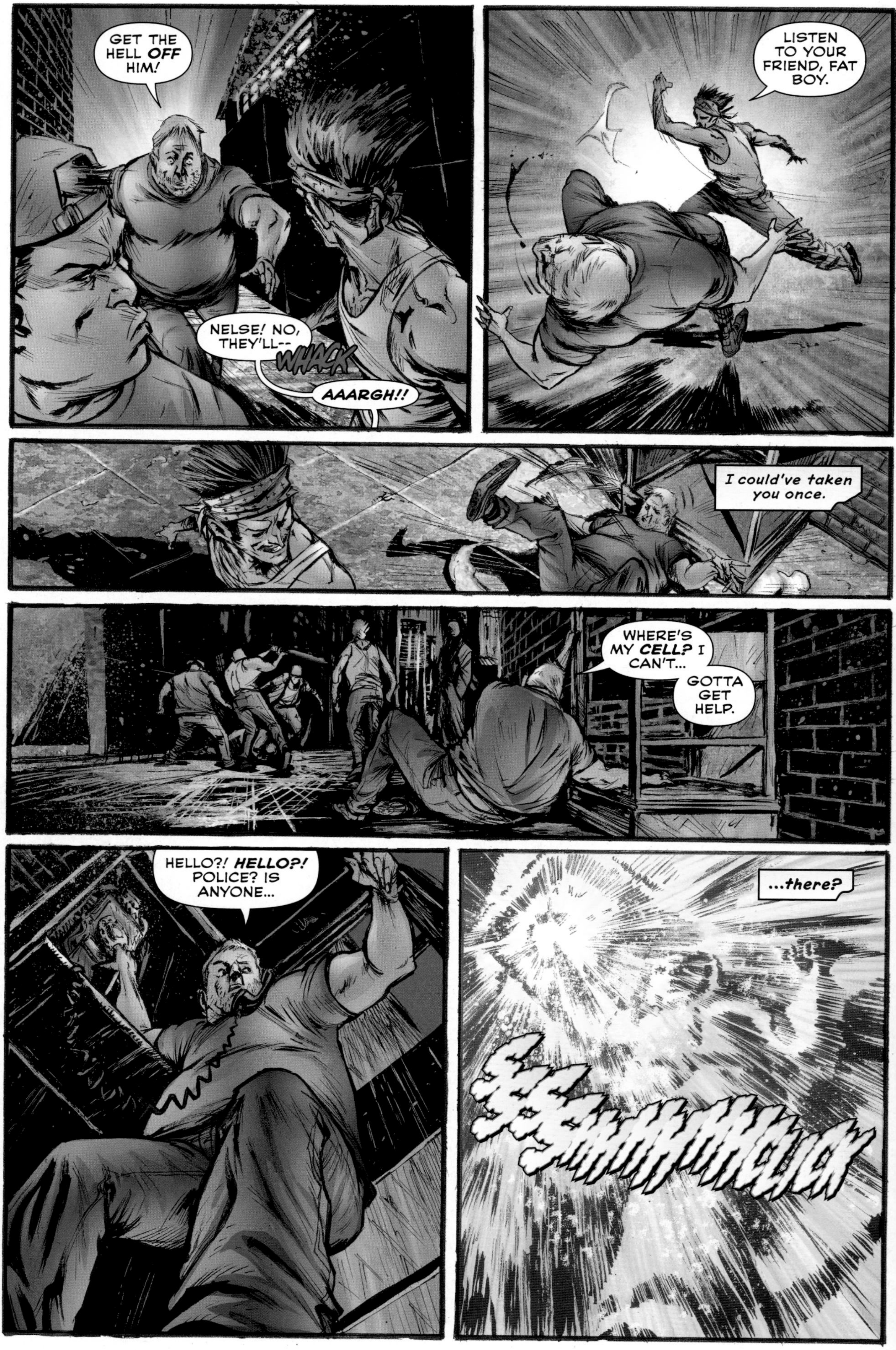
GET THE HELL **OFF** HIM!
NELSE! NO, THEY'LL--
WHACK
AAARGH!!
LISTEN TO YOUR FRIEND, FAT BOY.
I could've taken you once.
WHERE'S MY **CELL?** I CAN'T...
GOTTA GET HELP.
HELLO?! **HELLO?!** POLICE? IS ANYONE...
...there?

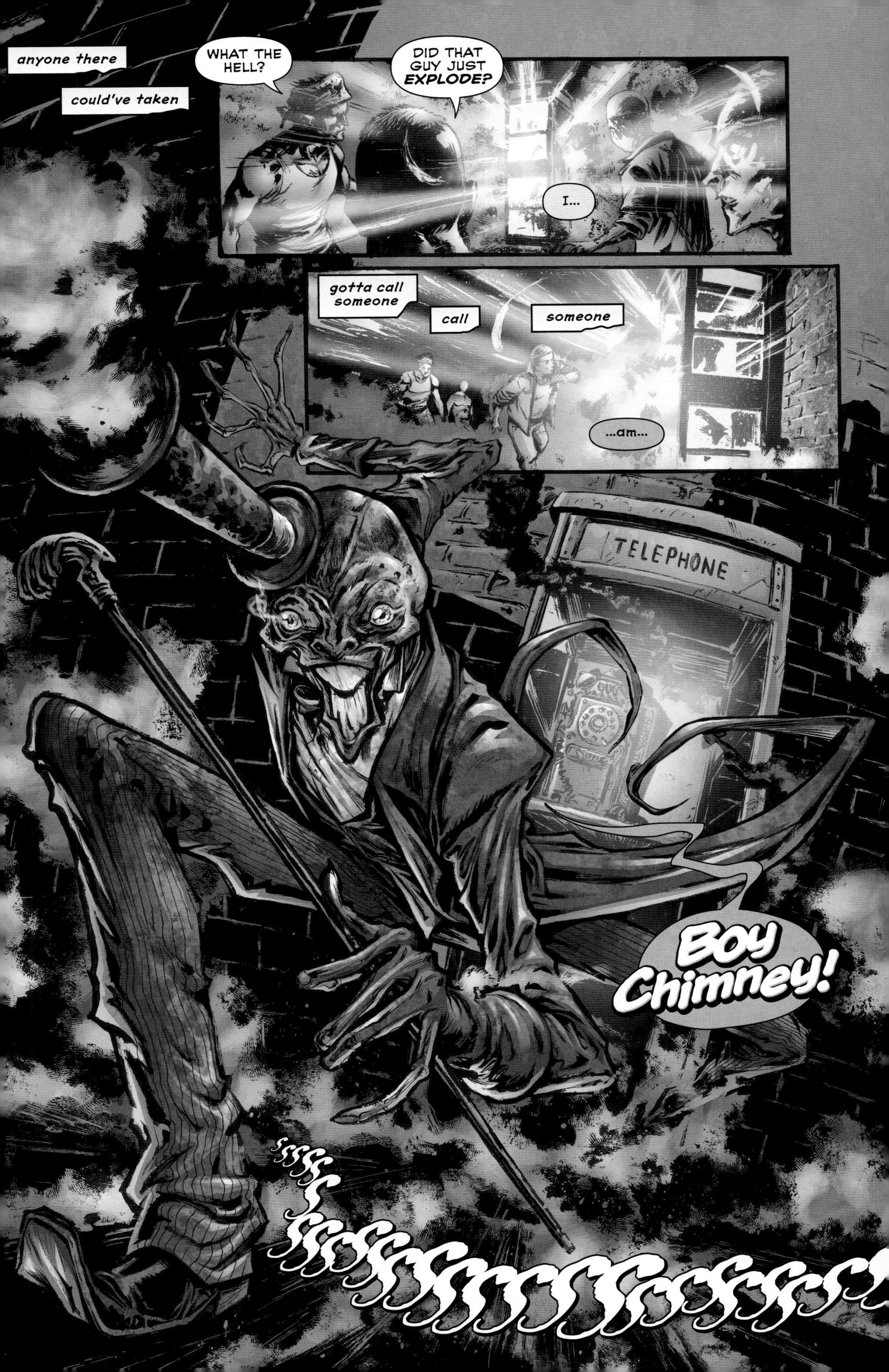
anyone there
could've taken
WHAT THE HELL?
DID THAT GUY JUST EXPLODE?
I...
gotta call someone
call
someone
...am...
TELEPHONE
Boy Chimney!
SSSSSSSSSSSSSSSSSSSSSSSSS

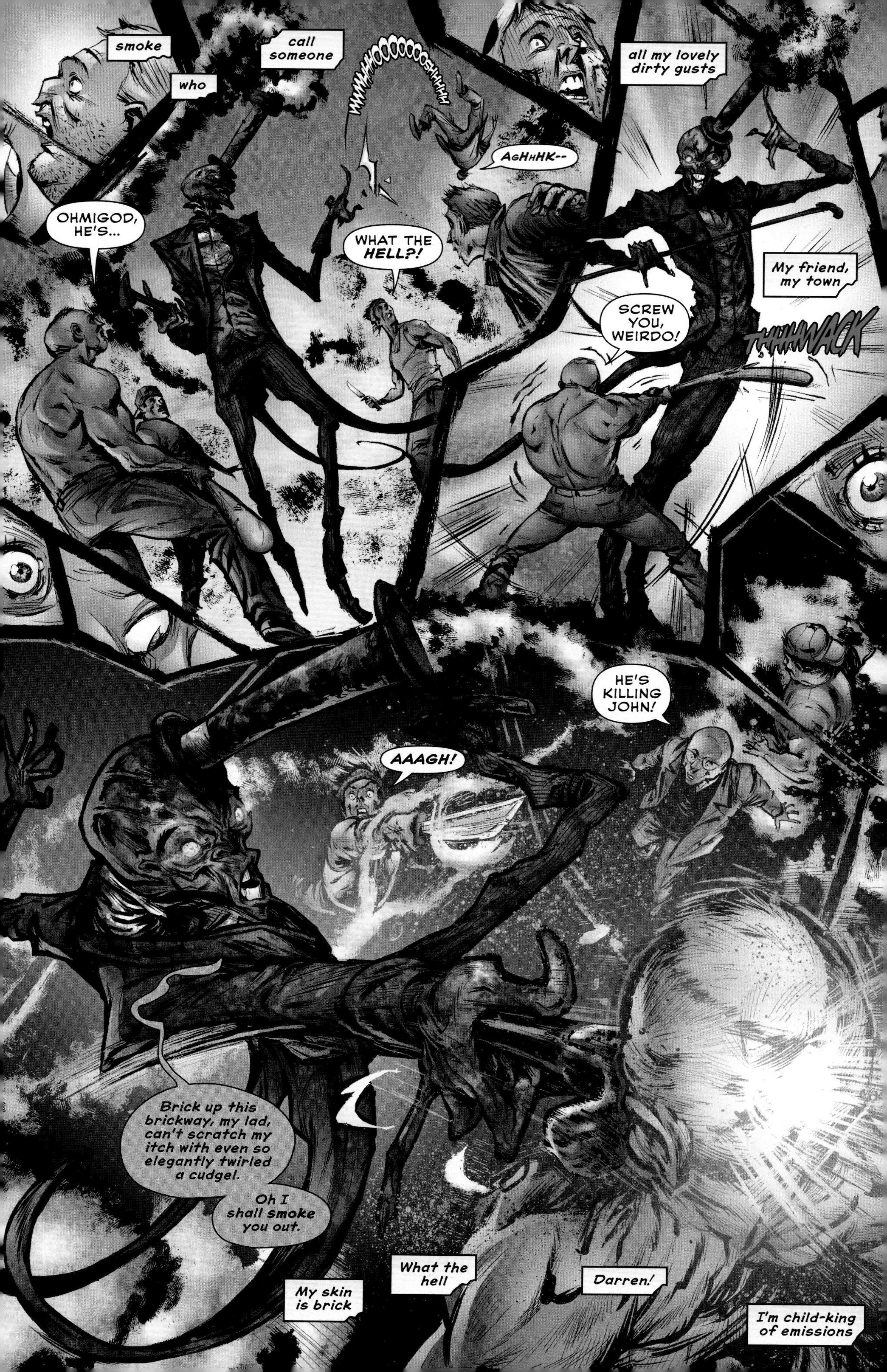

smoke
who
call someone
AGHHHK--
all my lovely dirty gusts
OHMIGOD, HE'S...
WHAT THE HELL?!
SCREW YOU, WEIRDO!
My friend, my town
THHHWACK
HE'S KILLING JOHN!
AAAGH!
Brick up this brickway, my lad, can't scratch my itch with even so elegantly twirled a cudgel.
Oh I shall smoke you out.
My skin is brick
What the hell
Darren!
I'm child-king of emissions

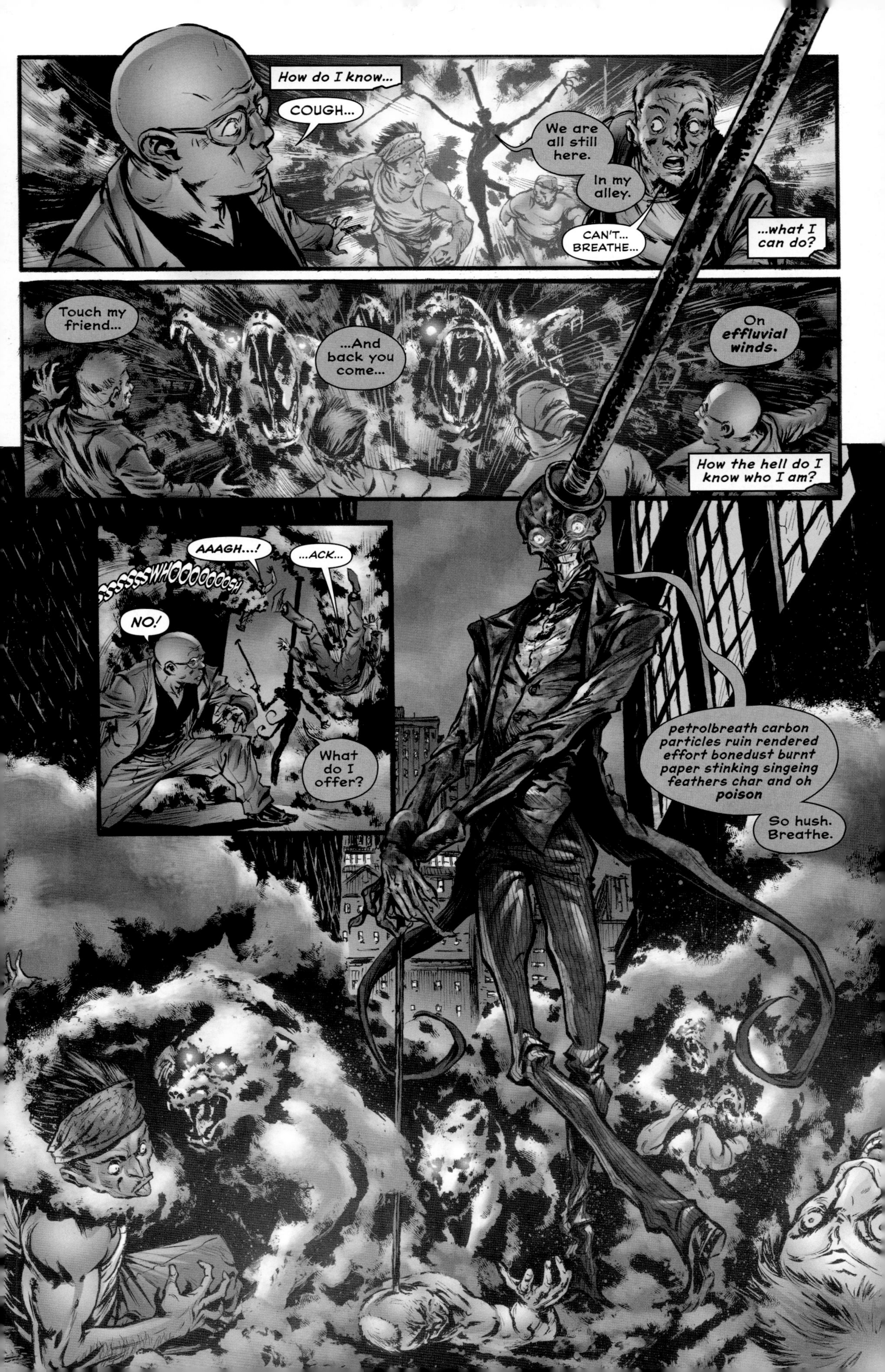

How do I know...
COUGH...
We are all still here.
In my alley.
CAN'T... BREATHE...
...what I can do?
Touch my friend...
...And back you come...
On effluvial winds.
How the hell do I know who I am?
AAAGH...!
...ACK...
SSSSSSWHOOOOOOOSH
NO!
What do I offer?
petrolbreath carbon particles ruin rendered effort bonedust burnt paper stinking singeing feathers char and oh poison
So hush. Breathe.

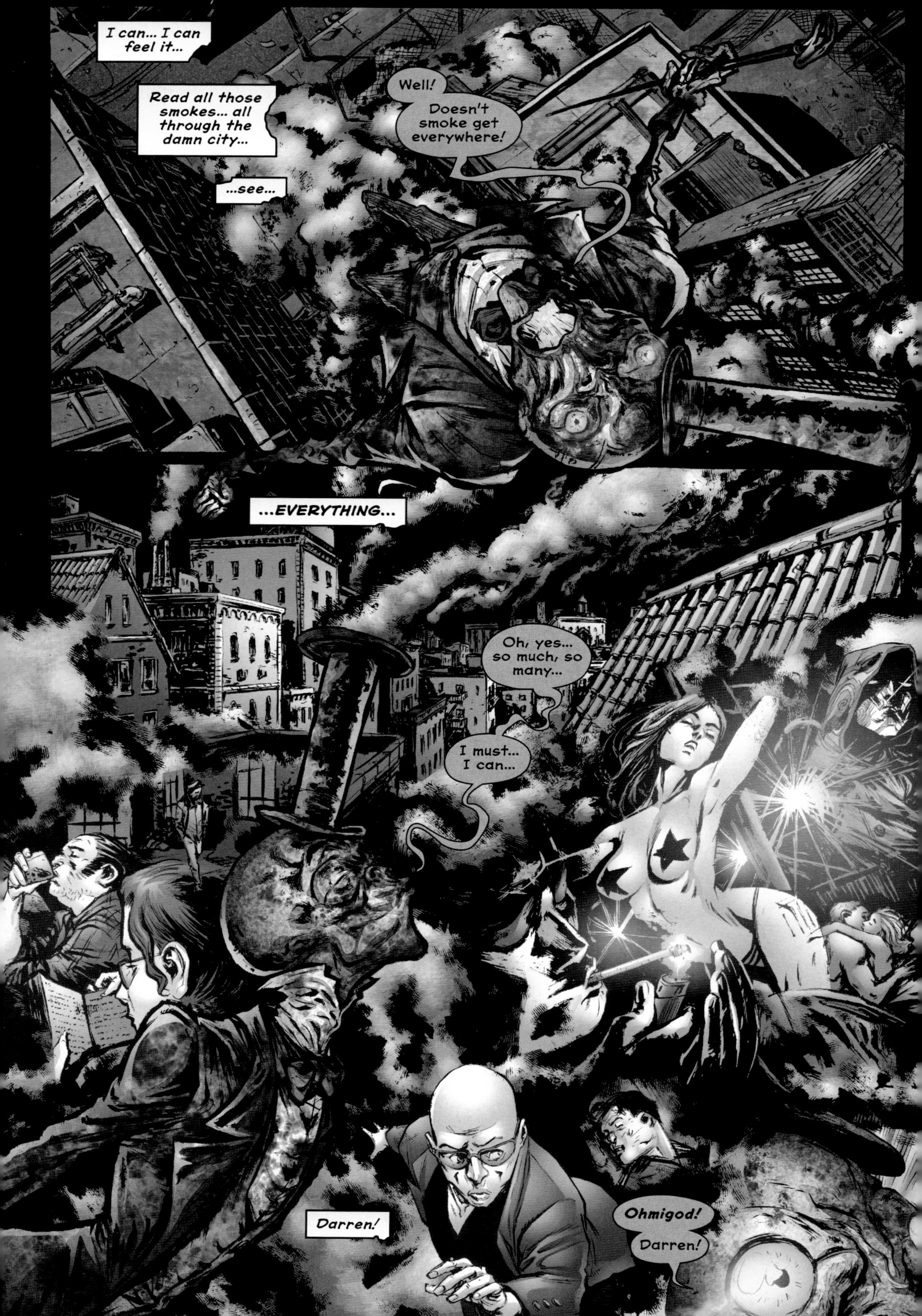
I can... I can feel it...
Read all those smokes... all through the damn city...
Well!
Doesn't smoke get everywhere!
...see...
...EVERYTHING...
Oh, yes... so much, so many...
I must... I can...
Darren!
Ohmigod!
Darren!

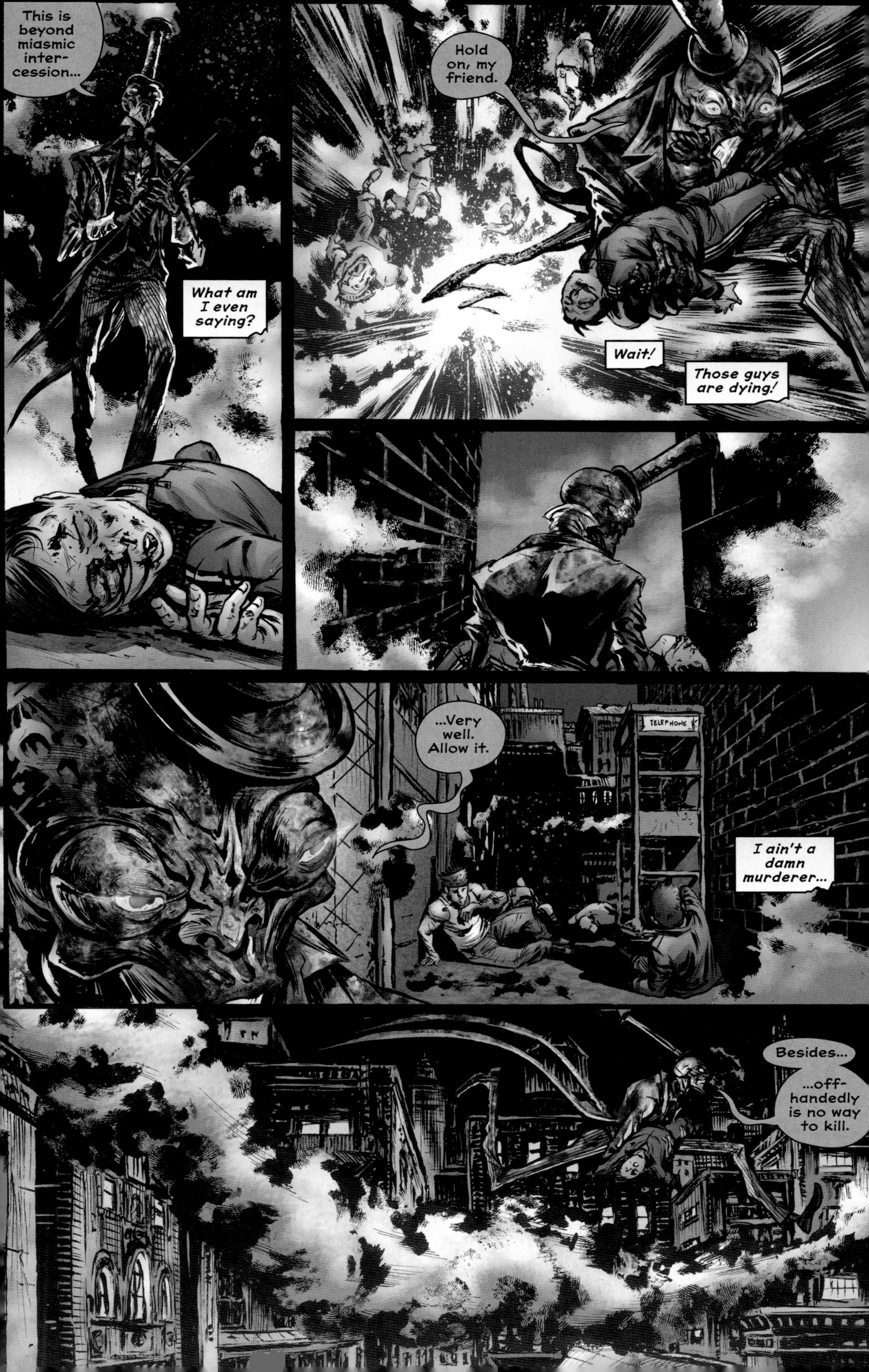
This is beyond miasmic inter-cession...
What am I even saying?
Hold on, my friend.
Wait!
Those guys are dying!
...Very well. Allow it.
TELEPHONE
I ain't a damn murderer...
Besides...
...off-handedly is no way to kill.

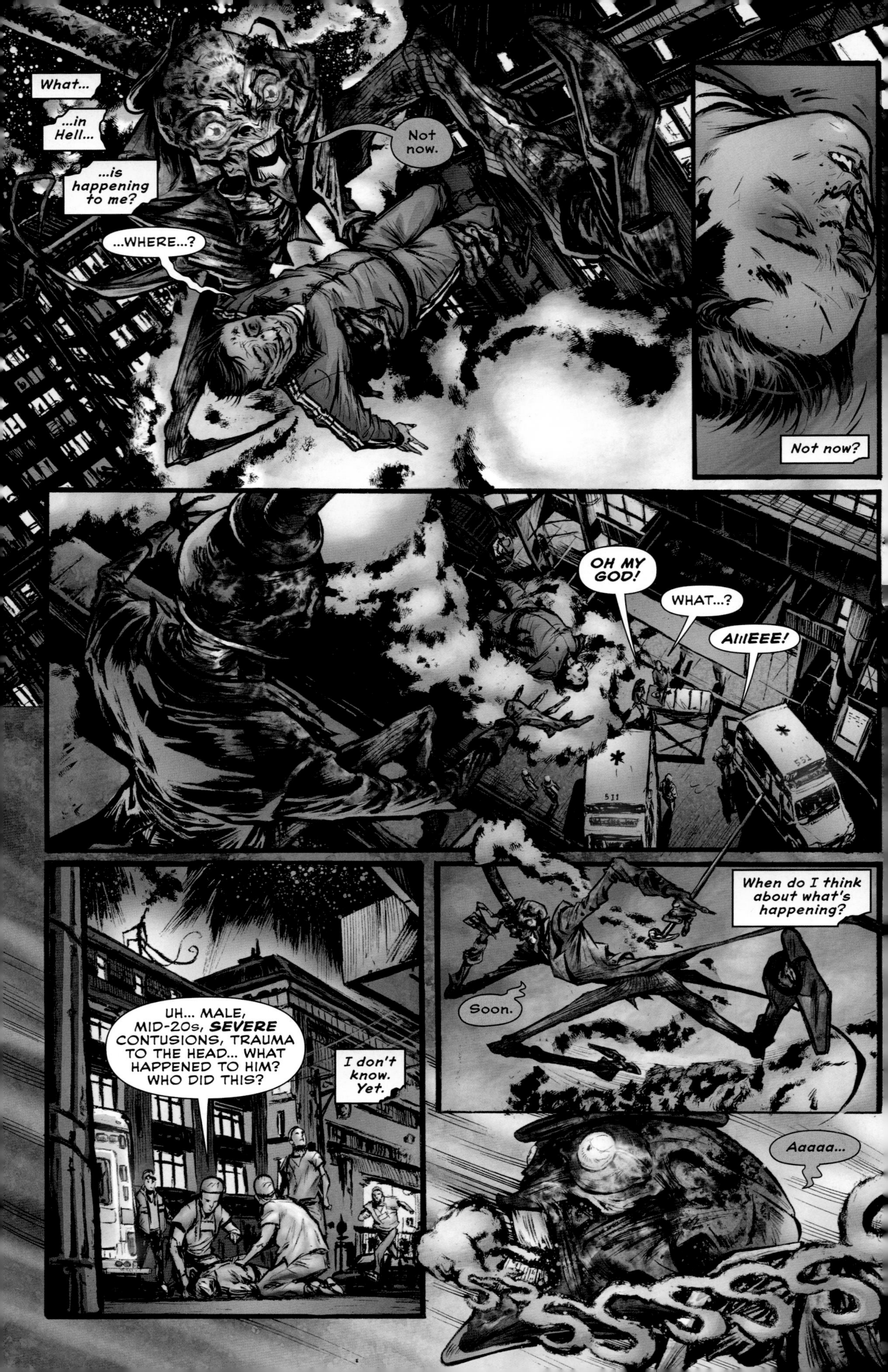
What...
...in Hell...
...is happening to me?
Not now.
...WHERE...?
Not now?
OH MY GOD!
WHAT...?
AIIIEEE!
UH... MALE, MID-20s, SEVERE CONTUSIONS, TRAUMA TO THE HEAD... WHAT HAPPENED TO HIM? WHO DID THIS?
I don't know. Yet.
When do I think about what's happening?
Soon.
Aaaaa...
SSSSSS

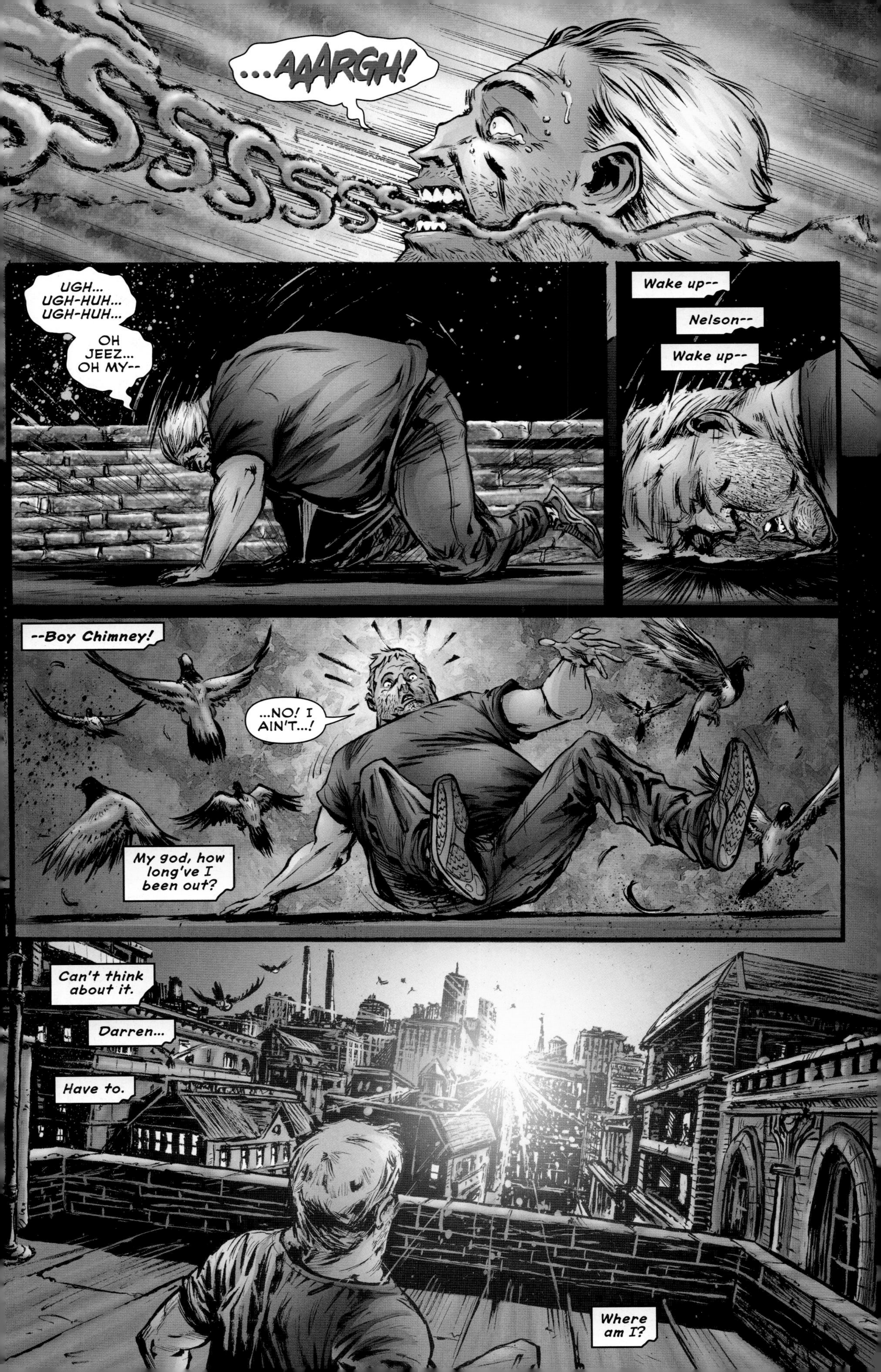
...AAARGH!
UGH... UGH-HUH... UGH-HUH...
OH JEEZ... OH MY--
Wake up--
Nelson--
Wake up--
--Boy Chimney!
...NO! I AIN'T...!
My god, how long've I been out?
Can't think about it.
Darren...
Have to.
Where am I?

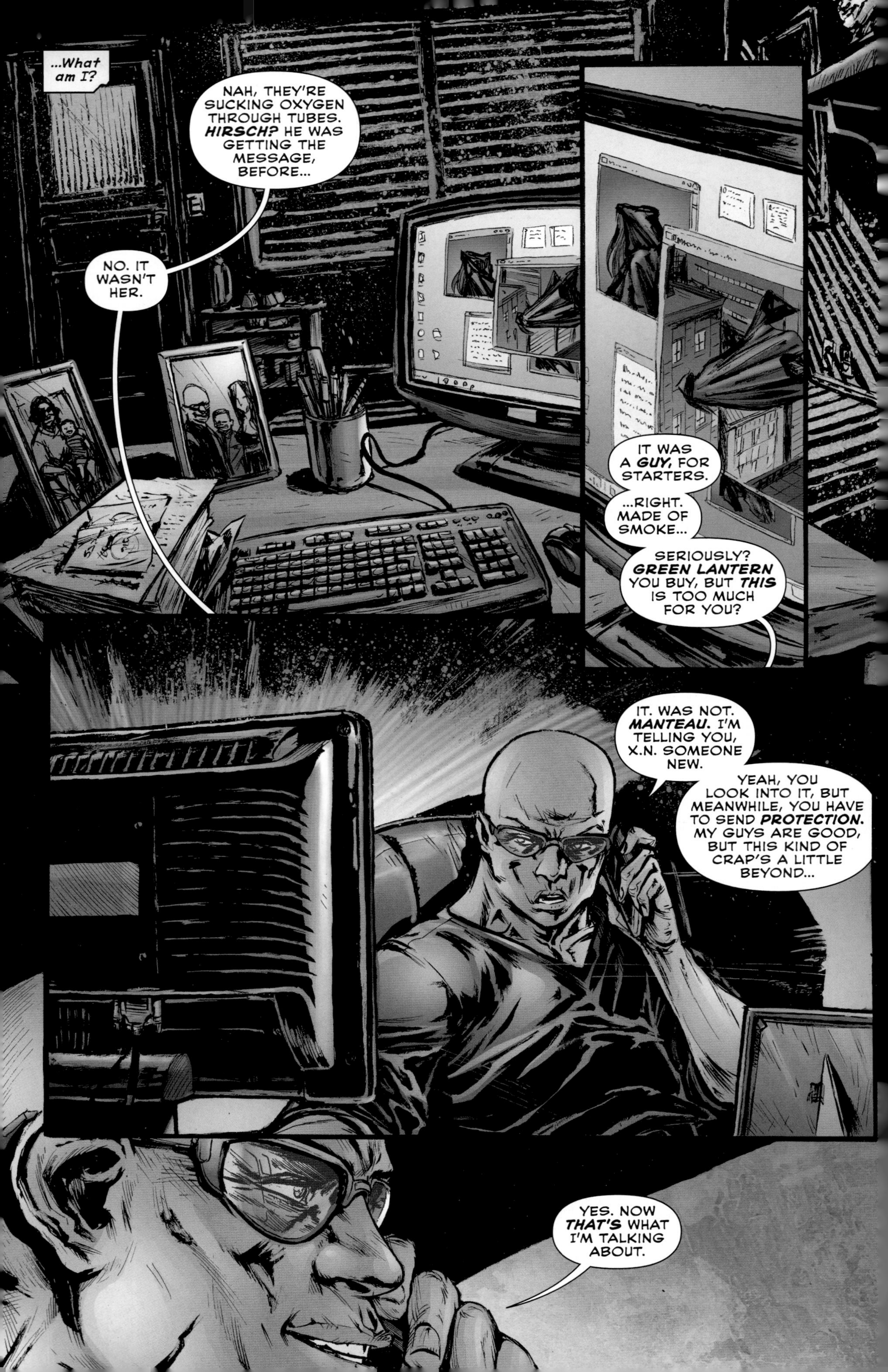

...What am I?
NAH, THEY'RE SUCKING OXYGEN THROUGH TUBES. HIRSCH? HE WAS GETTING THE MESSAGE, BEFORE...
NO. IT WASN'T HER.
IT WAS A GUY, FOR STARTERS.
...RIGHT. MADE OF SMOKE...
SERIOUSLY? GREEN LANTERN YOU BUY, BUT THIS IS TOO MUCH FOR YOU?
IT. WAS NOT. MANTEAU. I'M TELLING YOU, X.N. SOMEONE NEW.
YEAH, YOU LOOK INTO IT, BUT MEANWHILE, YOU HAVE TO SEND PROTECTION. MY GUYS ARE GOOD, BUT THIS KIND OF CRAP'S A LITTLE BEYOND...
YES. NOW THAT'S WHAT I'M TALKING ABOUT.

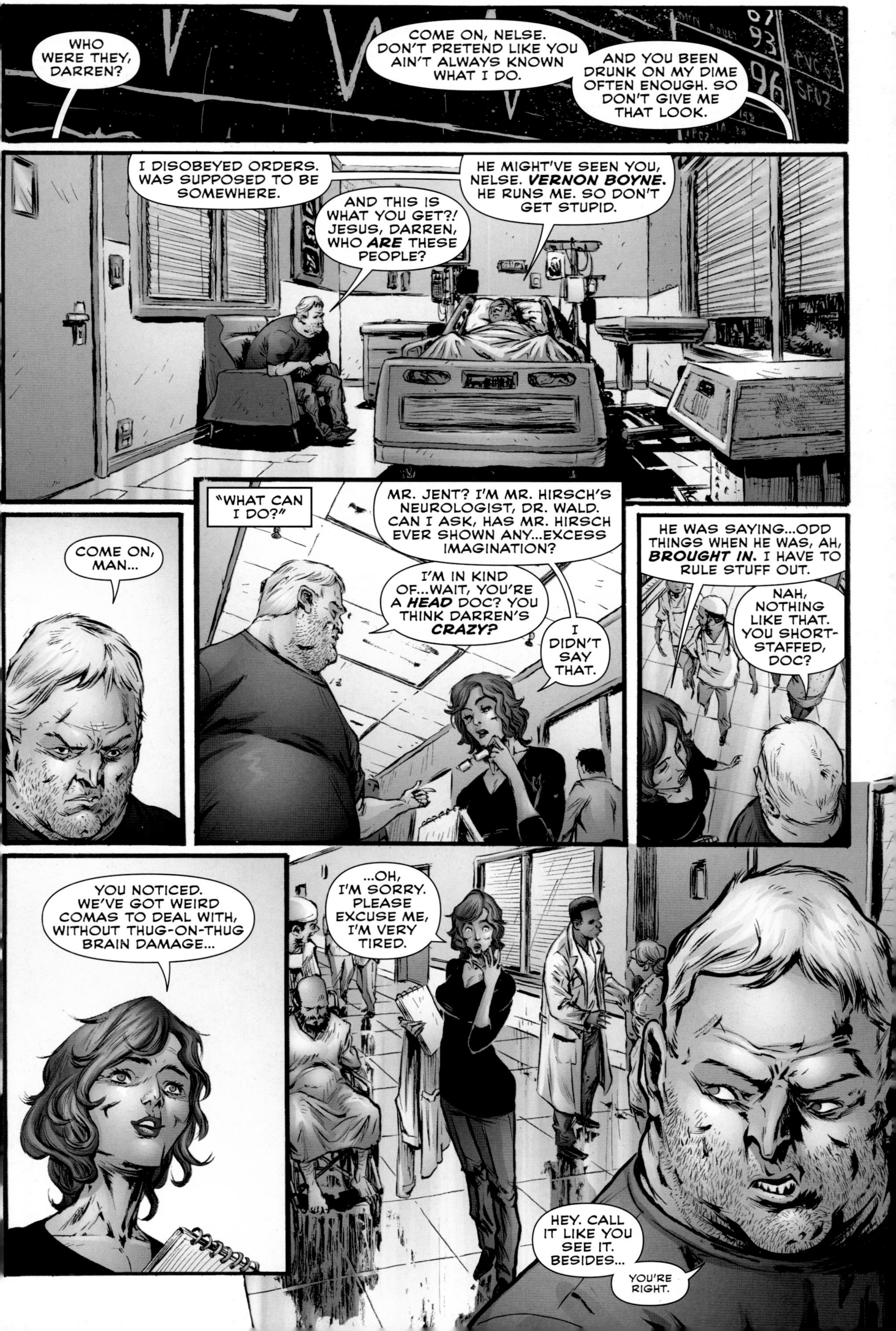
WHO WERE THEY, DARREN?
COME ON, NELSE. DON'T PRETEND LIKE YOU AIN'T ALWAYS KNOWN WHAT I DO.
AND YOU BEEN DRUNK ON MY DIME OFTEN ENOUGH. SO DON'T GIVE ME THAT LOOK.
I DISOBEYED ORDERS. WAS SUPPOSED TO BE SOMEWHERE.
AND THIS IS WHAT YOU GET?! JESUS, DARREN, WHO ARE THESE PEOPLE?
HE MIGHT'VE SEEN YOU, NELSE. VERNON BOYNE. HE RUNS ME. SO DON'T GET STUPID.
COME ON, MAN...
"WHAT CAN I DO?"
MR. JENT? I'M MR. HIRSCH'S NEUROLOGIST, DR. WALD. CAN I ASK, HAS MR. HIRSCH EVER SHOWN ANY...EXCESS IMAGINATION?
I'M IN KIND OF...WAIT, YOU'RE A HEAD DOC? YOU THINK DARREN'S CRAZY?
I DIDN'T SAY THAT.
HE WAS SAYING...ODD THINGS WHEN HE WAS, AH, BROUGHT IN. I HAVE TO RULE STUFF OUT.
NAH, NOTHING LIKE THAT. YOU SHORT-STAFFED, DOC?
YOU NOTICED. WE'VE GOT WEIRD COMAS TO DEAL WITH, WITHOUT THUG-ON-THUG BRAIN DAMAGE...
...OH, I'M SORRY. PLEASE EXCUSE ME, I'M VERY TIRED.
HEY. CALL IT LIKE YOU SEE IT. BESIDES...
YOU'RE RIGHT.

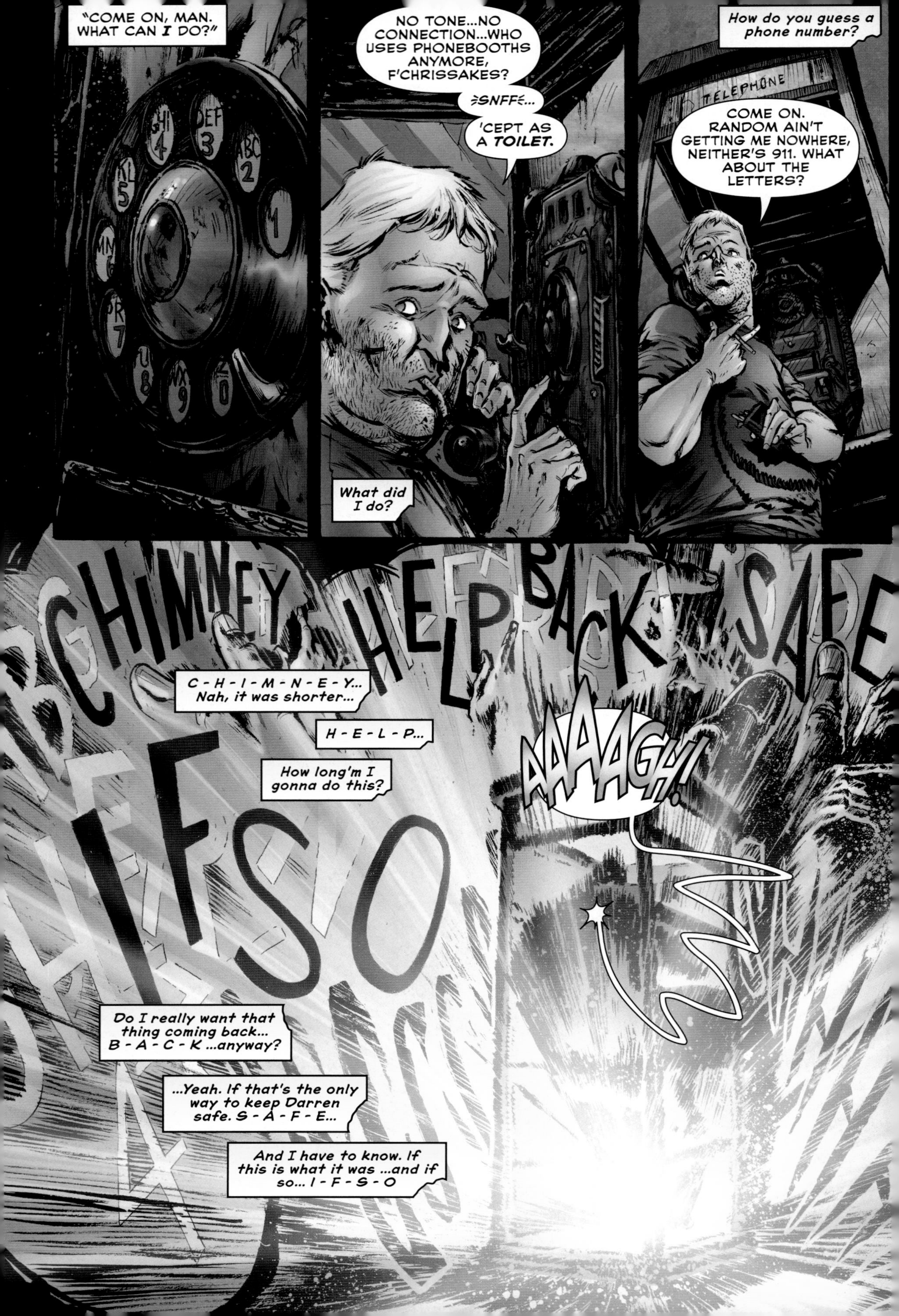
"COME ON, MAN. WHAT CAN I DO?"
NO TONE...NO CONNECTION...WHO USES PHONEBOOTHS ANYMORE, F'CHRISSAKES?
SNFF...
'CEPT AS A TOILET.
What did I do?
How do you guess a phone number?
TELEPHONE
COME ON. RANDOM AIN'T GETTING ME NOWHERE, NEITHER'S 911. WHAT ABOUT THE LETTERS?
CHIMNEY
HELP
BACK
SAFE
C-H-I-M-N-E-Y... Nah, it was shorter...
H-E-L-P...
How long'm I gonna do this?
AAAAGH!
IFSO
Do I really want that thing coming back... B-A-C-K ...anyway?
...Yeah. If that's the only way to keep Darren safe. S-A-F-E...
And I have to know. If this is what it was ...and if so... I-F-S-O

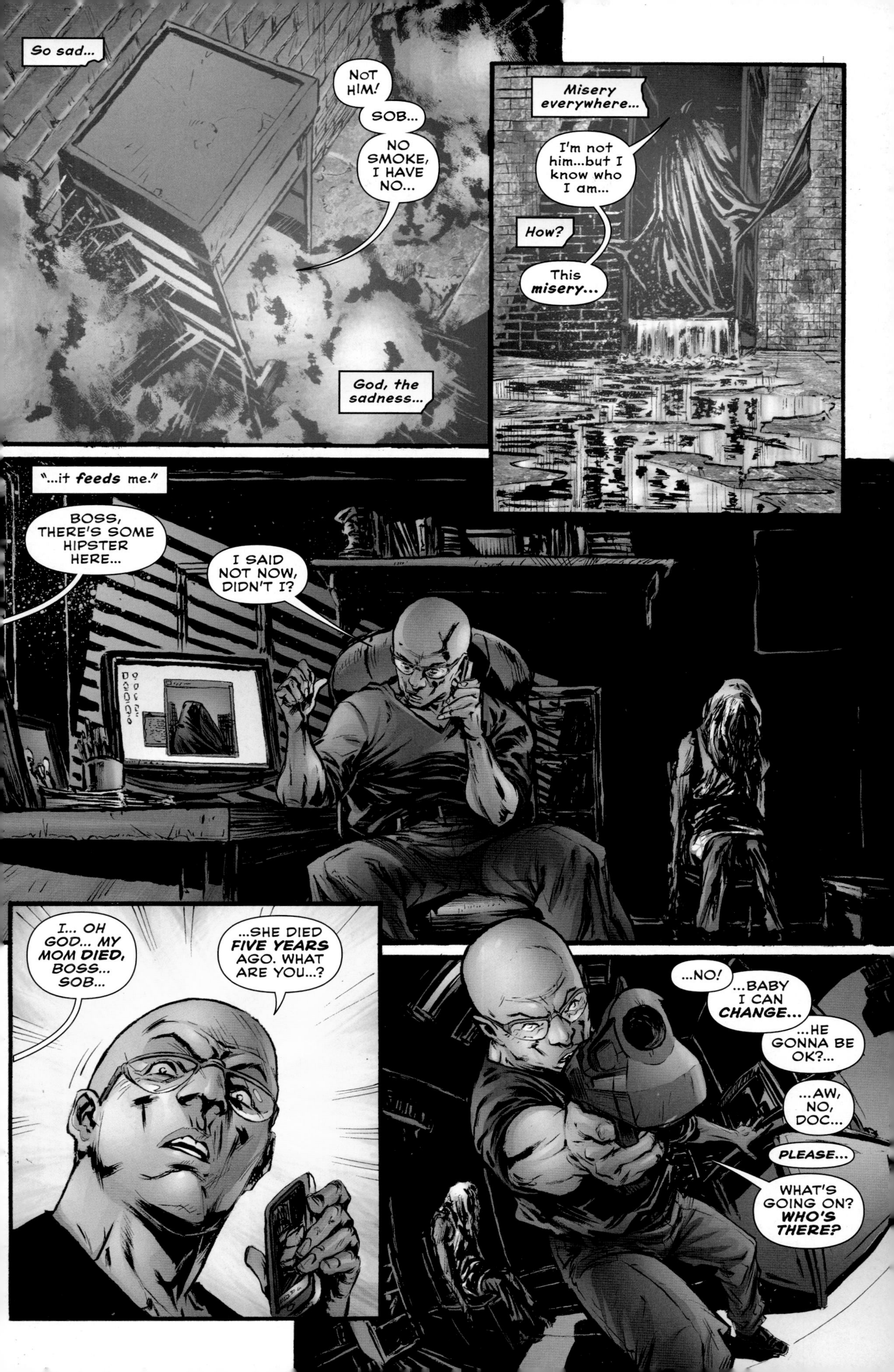

So sad...
NOT HIM!
SOB...
NO SMOKE, I HAVE NO...
God, the sadness...
Misery everywhere...
I'm not him...but I know who I am...
How?
This misery...
"...it feeds me."
BOSS, THERE'S SOME HIPSTER HERE...
I SAID NOT NOW, DIDN'T I?
I... OH GOD... MY MOM DIED, BOSS... SOB...
...SHE DIED FIVE YEARS AGO. WHAT ARE YOU...?
...NO!
...BABY I CAN CHANGE...
...HE GONNA BE OK?...
...AW, NO, DOC...
PLEASE...
WHAT'S GOING ON? WHO'S THERE?

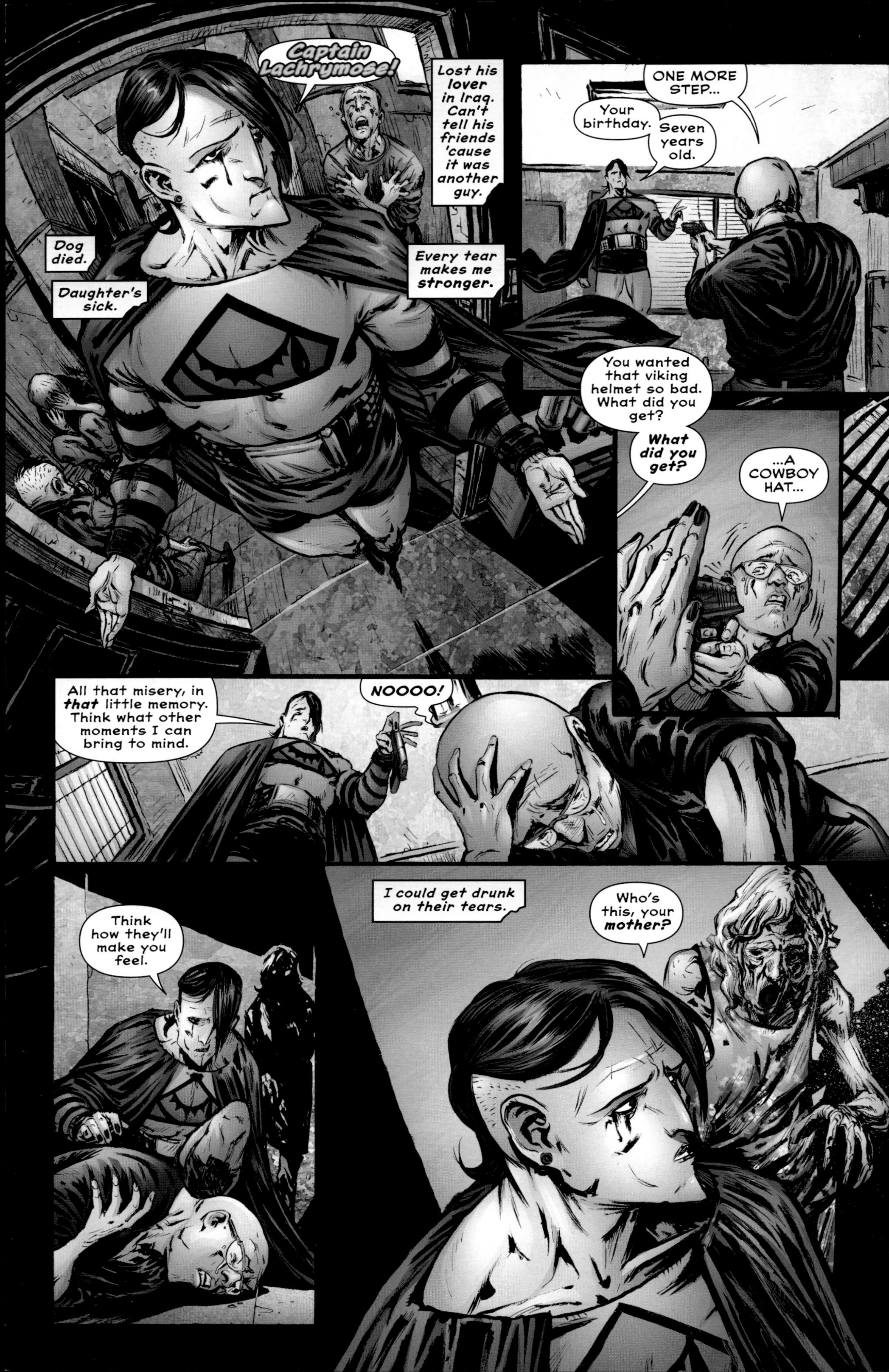
Captain Lachrymose!
Lost his lover in Iraq. Can't tell his friends 'cause it was another guy.
Dog died.
Daughter's sick.
Every tear makes me stronger.
ONE MORE STEP...
Your birthday.
Seven years old.
You wanted that viking helmet so bad. What did you get?
What did you get?
...A COWBOY HAT...
All that misery, in that little memory. Think what other moments I can bring to mind.
NOOOO!
Think how they'll make you feel.
I could get drunk on their tears.
Who's this, your mother?

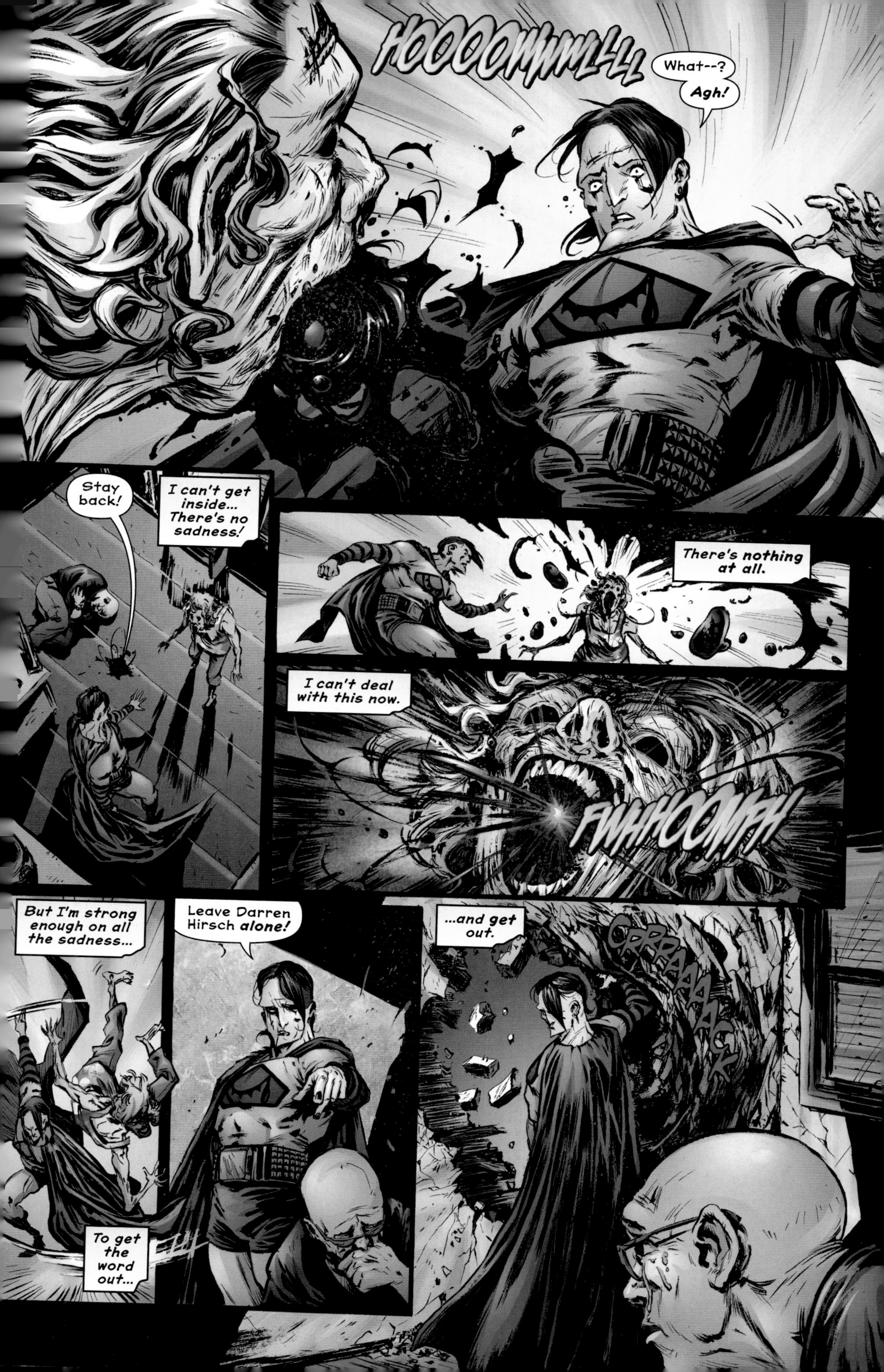
HOOOOMMMLLL
What--?
Agh!
Stay back!
I can't get inside... There's no sadness!
There's nothing at all.
I can't deal with this now.
FWAHOOMPH
But I'm strong enough on all the sadness...
To get the word out...
Leave Darren Hirsch alone!
...and get out.
CRRRAAAACK

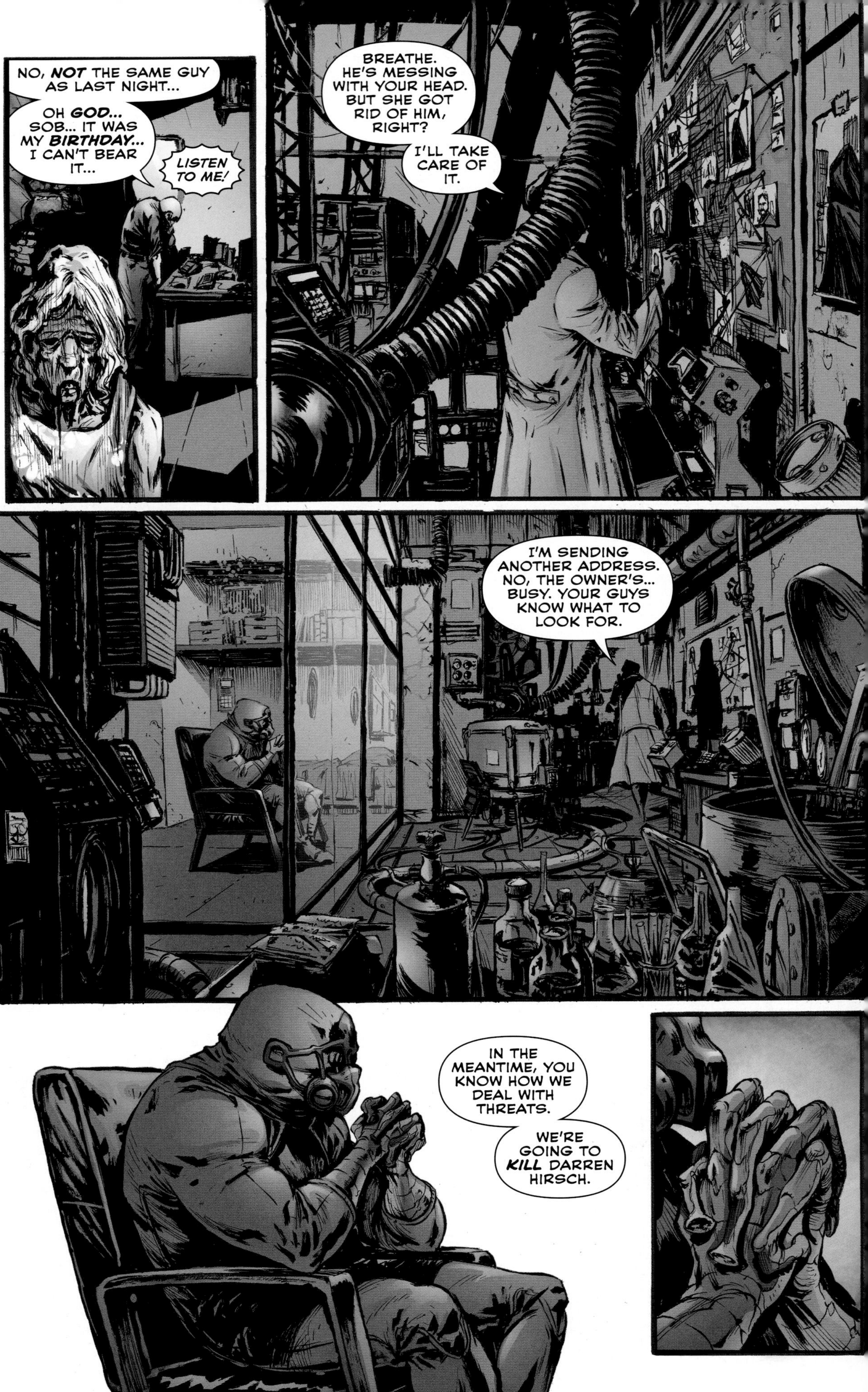
NO, NOT THE SAME GUY AS LAST NIGHT...
OH GOD... SOB... IT WAS MY BIRTHDAY... I CAN'T BEAR IT...
LISTEN TO ME!
BREATHE. HE'S MESSING WITH YOUR HEAD. BUT SHE GOT RID OF HIM, RIGHT?
I'LL TAKE CARE OF IT.
I'M SENDING ANOTHER ADDRESS. NO, THE OWNER'S... BUSY. YOUR GUYS KNOW WHAT TO LOOK FOR.
IN THE MEANTIME, YOU KNOW HOW WE DEAL WITH THREATS.
WE'RE GOING TO KILL DARREN HIRSCH.

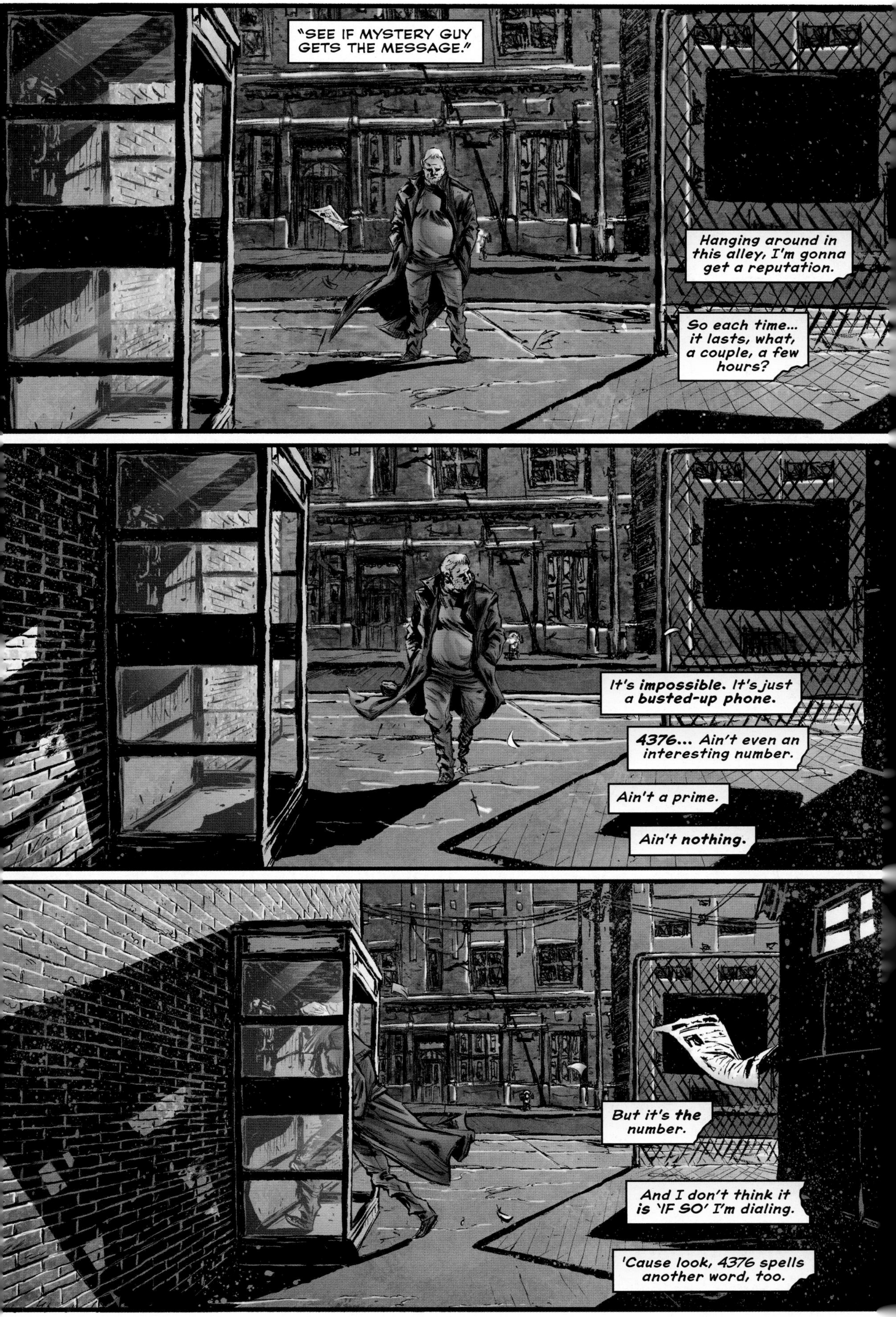
"SEE IF MYSTERY GUY GETS THE MESSAGE."
Hanging around in this alley, I'm gonna get a reputation.
So each time... it lasts, what, a couple, a few hours?
It's impossible. It's just a busted-up phone.
4376... Ain't even an interesting number.
Ain't a prime.
Ain't nothing.
But it's the number.
And I don't think it is 'IF SO' I'm dialing.
'Cause look, 4376 spells another word, too.

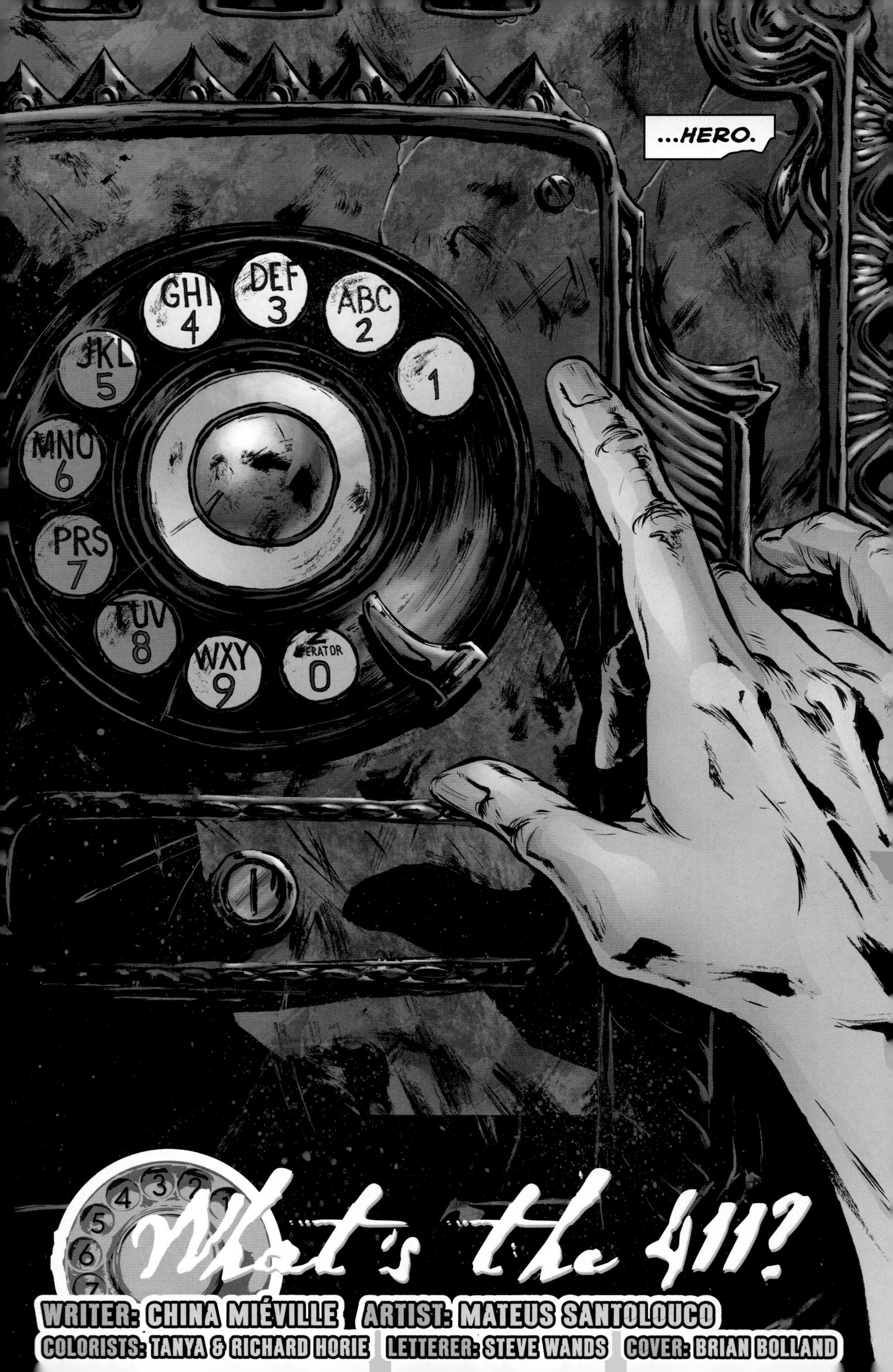
...HERO.
What's the 411?
WRITER: CHINA MIÉVILLE ARTIST: MATEUS SANTOLOUCO
COLORISTS: TANYA & RICHARD HORIE LETTERER: STEVE WANDS COVER: BRIAN BOLLAND

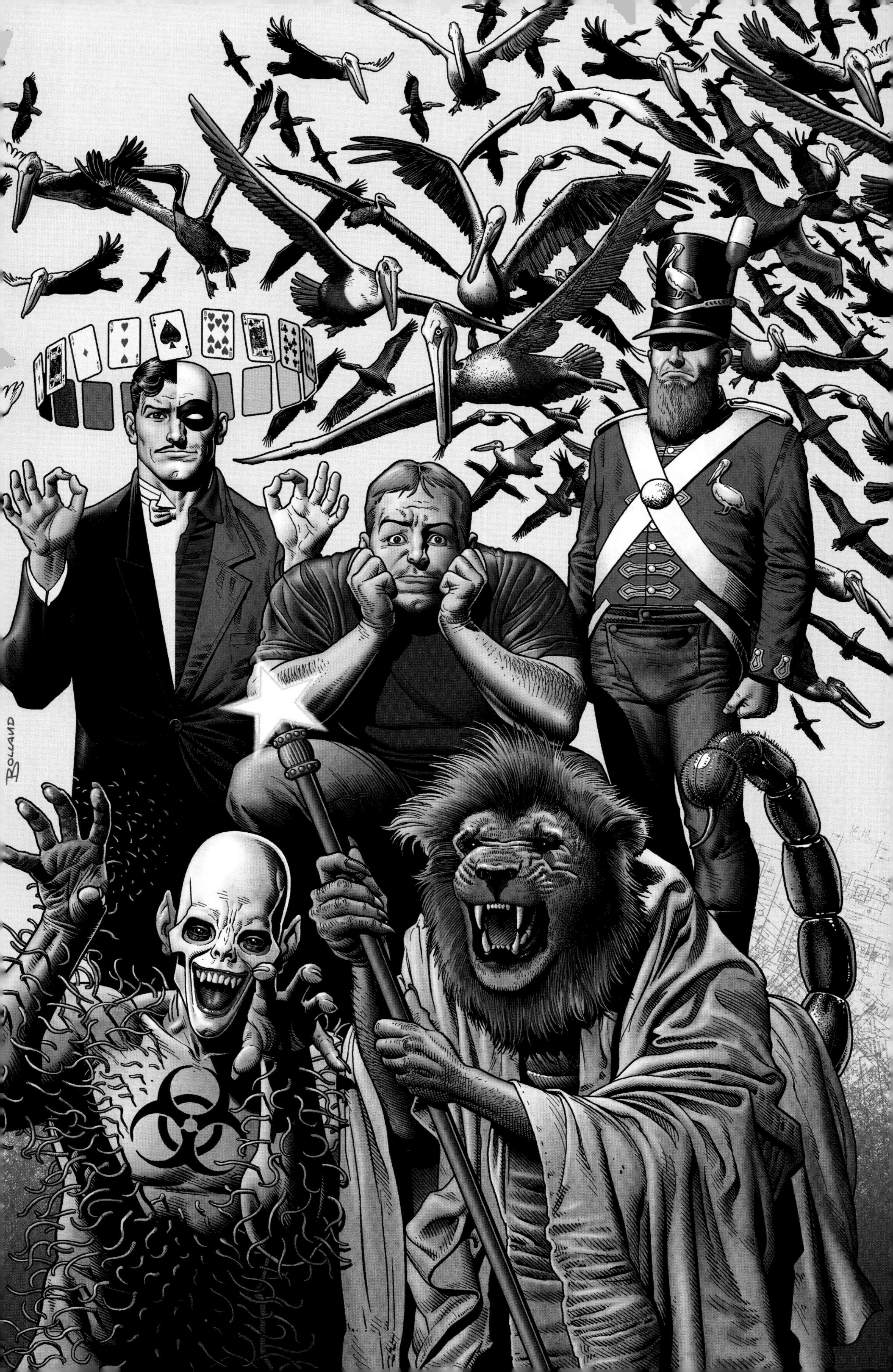
BOLLAND

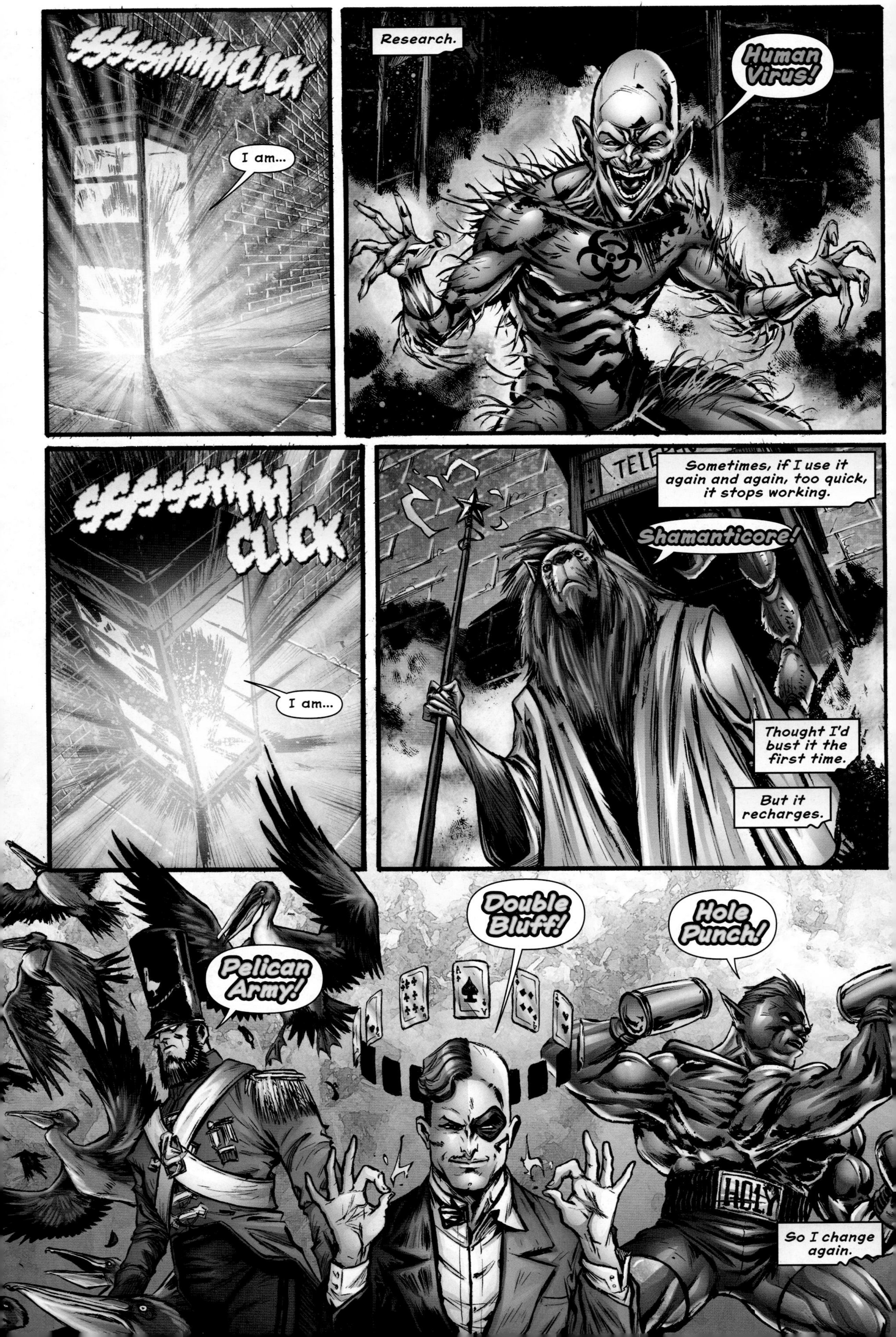
SSSSSHHHHCLICK
I am...
Research.
Human Virus!
SSSSSHHH CLICK
I am...
Sometimes, if I use it again and again, too quick, it stops working.
Shamanticore!
Thought I'd bust it the first time.
But it recharges.
Pelican Army!
Double Bluff!
Hole Punch!
HOLY
So I change again.

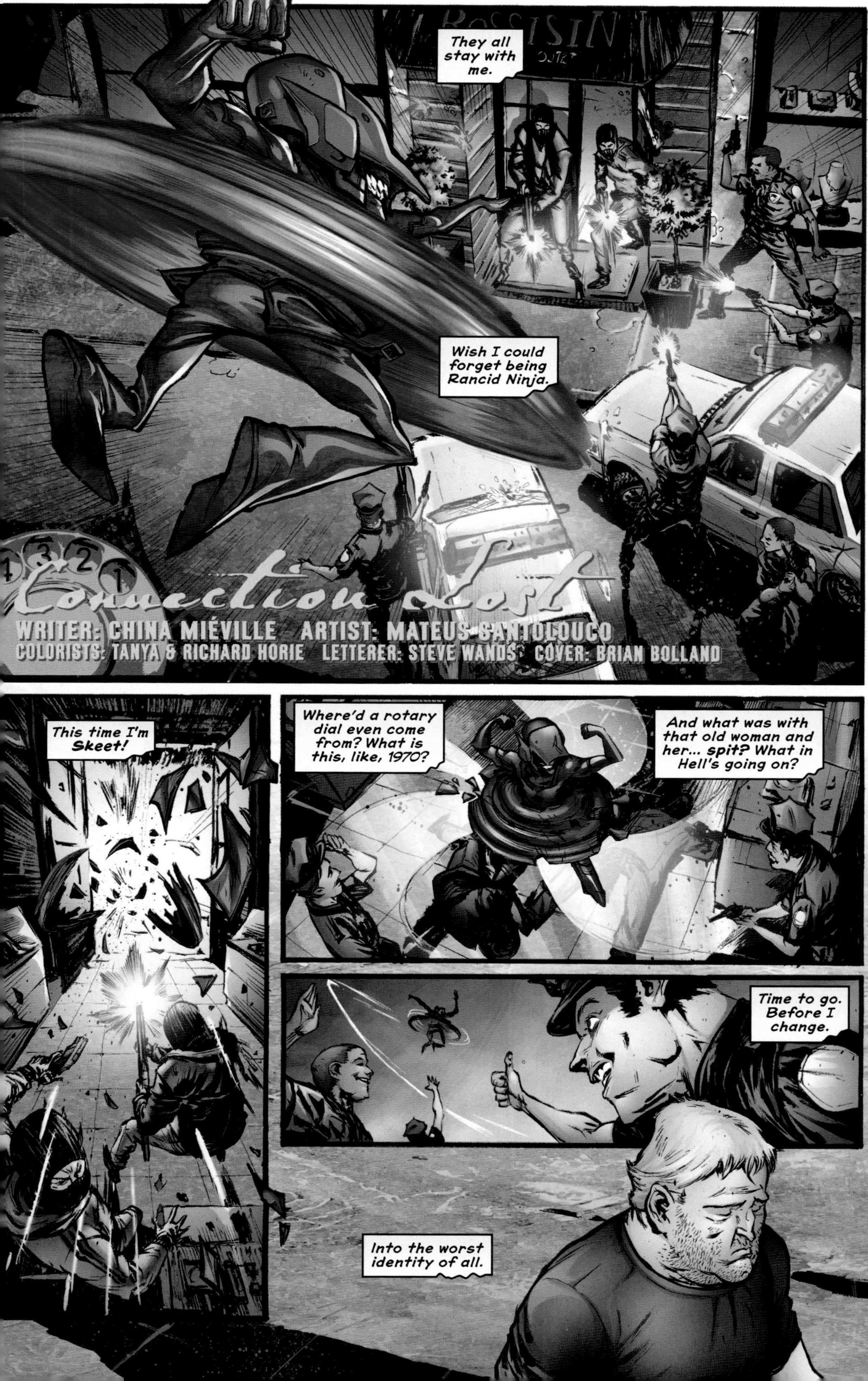

They all stay with me.
Wish I could forget being Rancid Ninja.
Connection Lost
WRITER: CHINA MIÉVILLE ARTIST: MATEUS SANTOLOUCO
COLORISTS: TANYA & RICHARD HORIE LETTERER: STEVE WANDS COVER: BRIAN BOLLAND
This time I'm Skeet!
Where'd a rotary dial even come from? What is this, like, 1970?
And what was with that old woman and her... spit? What in Hell's going on?
Time to go. Before I change.
Into the worst identity of all.

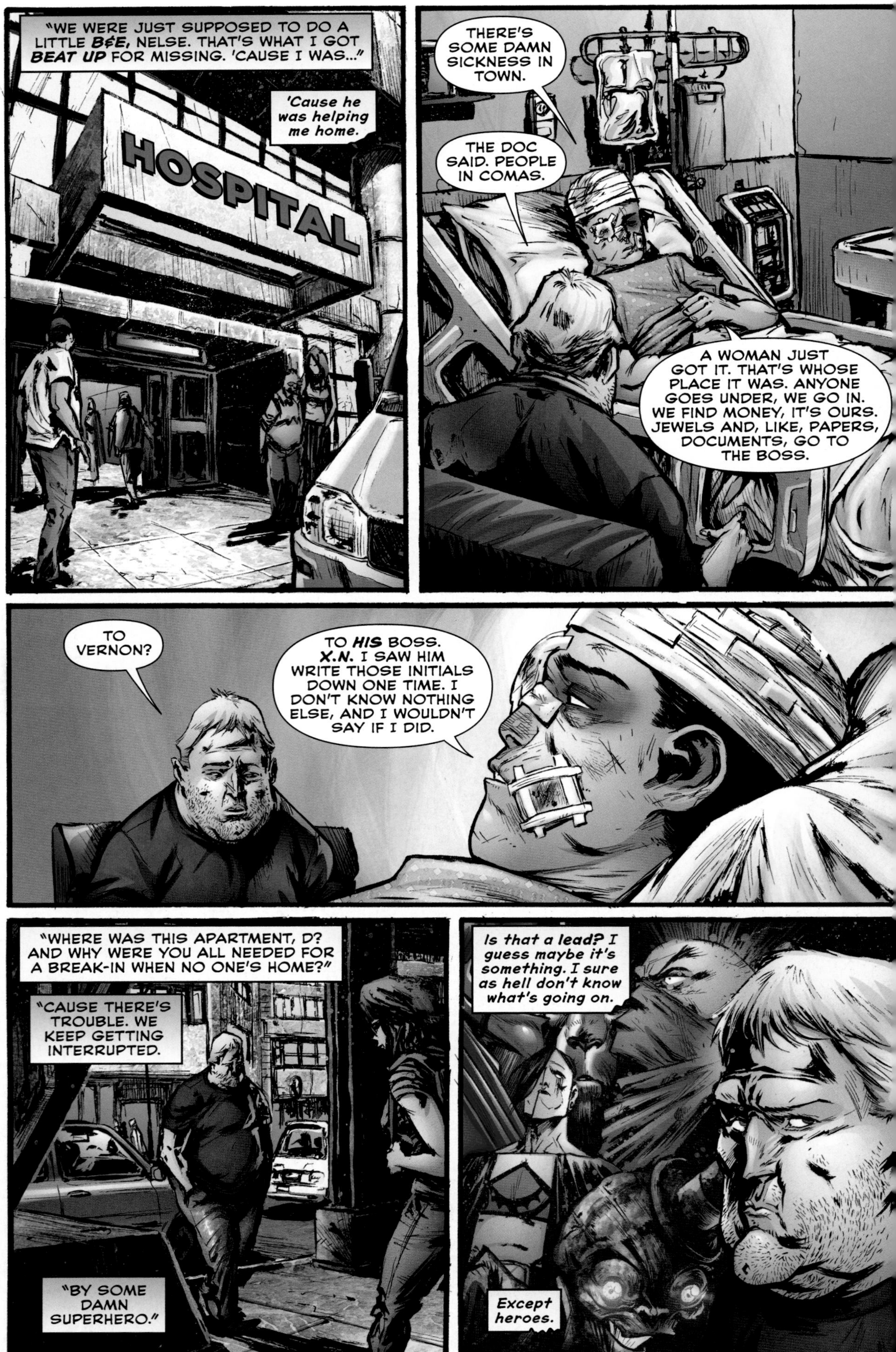
"WE WERE JUST SUPPOSED TO DO A LITTLE B&E, NELSE. THAT'S WHAT I GOT BEAT UP FOR MISSING. 'CAUSE I WAS..."
'Cause he was helping me home.
HOSPITAL
THERE'S SOME DAMN SICKNESS IN TOWN.
THE DOC SAID. PEOPLE IN COMAS.
A WOMAN JUST GOT IT. THAT'S WHOSE PLACE IT WAS. ANYONE GOES UNDER, WE GO IN. WE FIND MONEY, IT'S OURS. JEWELS AND, LIKE, PAPERS, DOCUMENTS, GO TO THE BOSS.
TO VERNON?
TO HIS BOSS. X.N. I SAW HIM WRITE THOSE INITIALS DOWN ONE TIME. I DON'T KNOW NOTHING ELSE, AND I WOULDN'T SAY IF I DID.
"WHERE WAS THIS APARTMENT, D? AND WHY WERE YOU ALL NEEDED FOR A BREAK-IN WHEN NO ONE'S HOME?"
"CAUSE THERE'S TROUBLE. WE KEEP GETTING INTERRUPTED.
"BY SOME DAMN SUPERHERO."
Is that a lead? I guess maybe it's something. I sure as hell don't know what's going on.
Except heroes.

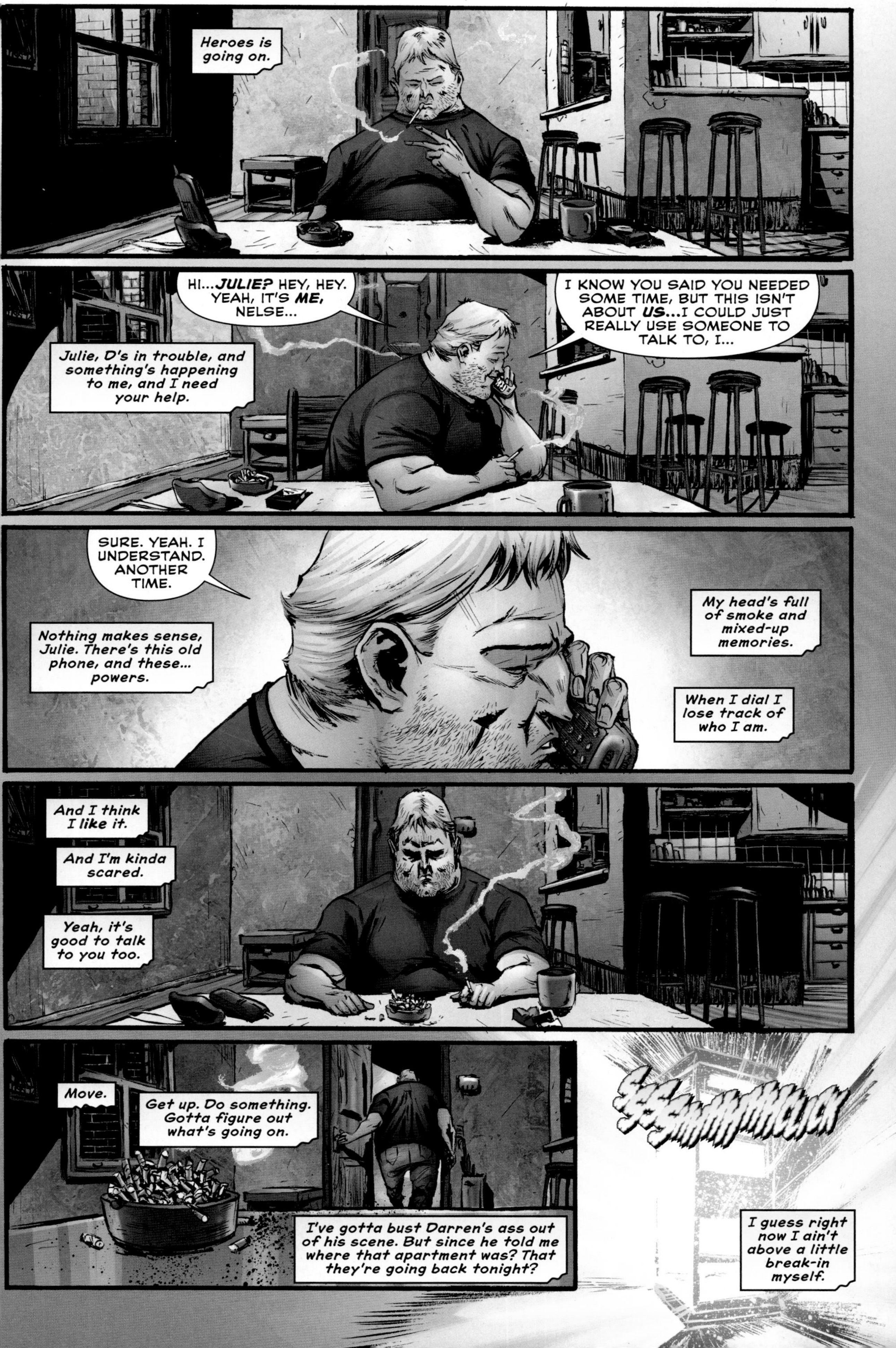
Heroes is going on.
HI...JULIE? HEY, HEY. YEAH, IT'S ME, NELSE...
Julie, D's in trouble, and something's happening to me, and I need your help.
I KNOW YOU SAID YOU NEEDED SOME TIME, BUT THIS ISN'T ABOUT US...I COULD JUST REALLY USE SOMEONE TO TALK TO, I...
SURE. YEAH. I UNDERSTAND. ANOTHER TIME.
Nothing makes sense, Julie. There's this old phone, and these... powers.
My head's full of smoke and mixed-up memories.
When I dial I lose track of who I am.
And I think I like it.
And I'm kinda scared.
Yeah, it's good to talk to you too.
Move.
Get up. Do something. Gotta figure out what's going on.
I've gotta bust Darren's ass out of his scene. But since he told me where that apartment was? That they're going back tonight?
SSSHHHHHHCLICK
I guess right now I ain't above a little break-in myself.

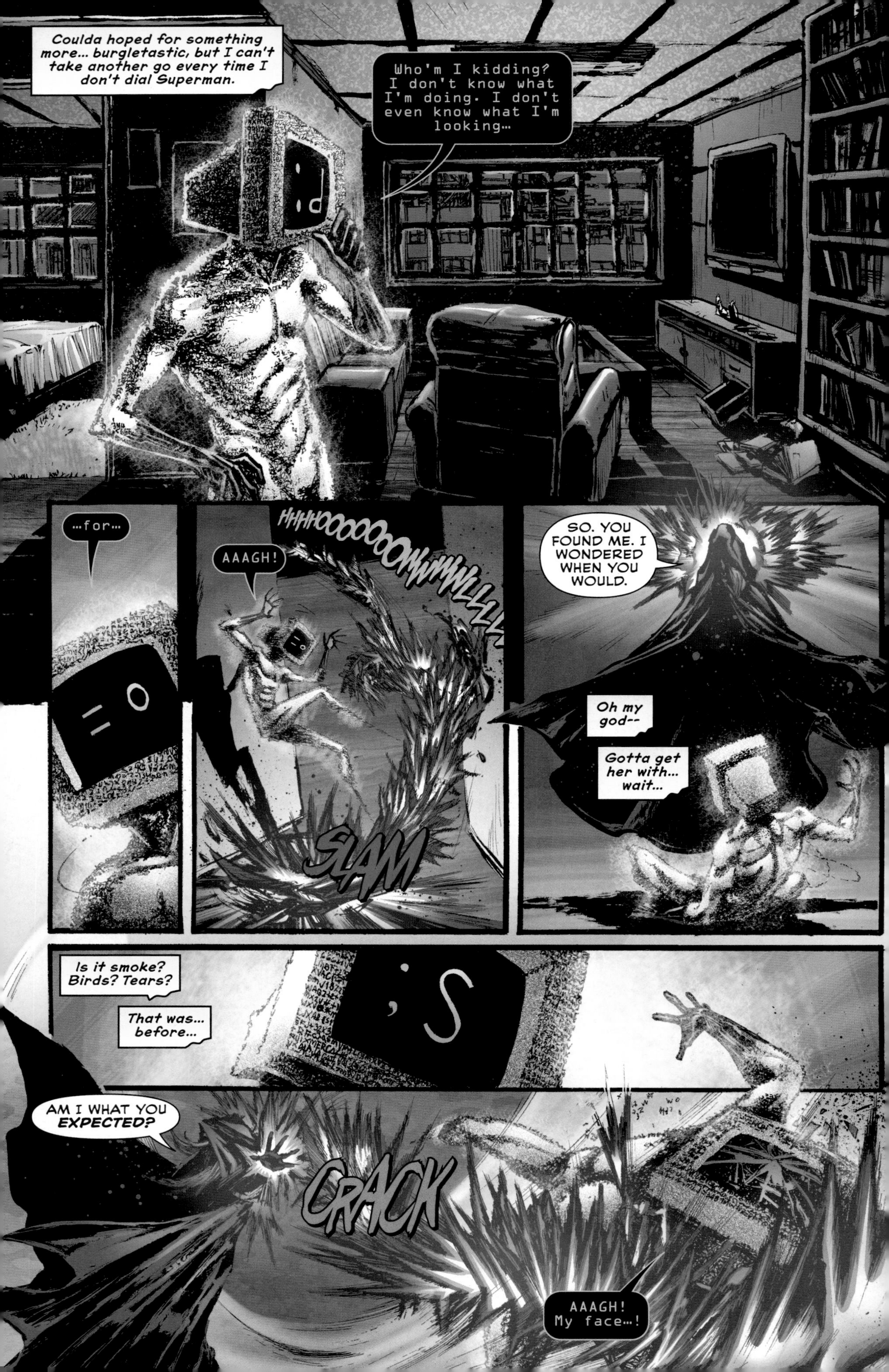

Coulda hoped for something more... burgletastic, but I can't take another go every time I don't dial Superman.
Who'm I kidding? I don't know what I'm doing. I don't even know what I'm looking…
…for…
AAAGH!
HHHHOOOOOOOOWWWLLLLL
SLAM
SO. YOU FOUND ME. I WONDERED WHEN YOU WOULD.
Oh my god--
Gotta get her with... wait...
Is it smoke? Birds? Tears?
That was... before...
AM I WHAT YOU EXPECTED?
CRACK
AAAGH! My face…!

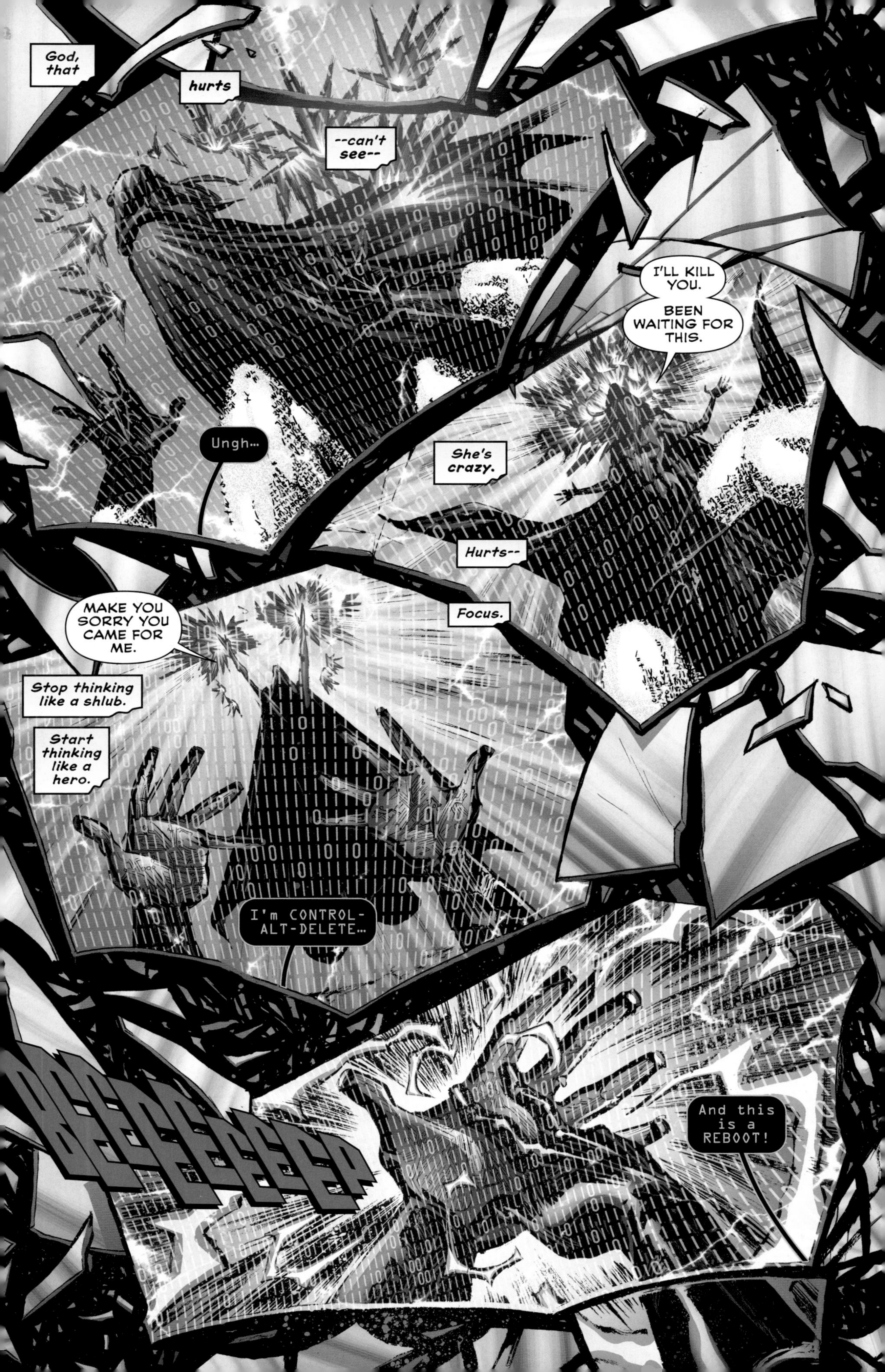
God, that
hurts
--can't see--
I'LL KILL YOU.
BEEN WAITING FOR THIS.
Ungh...
She's crazy.
Hurts--
Focus.
MAKE YOU SORRY YOU CAME FOR ME.
Stop thinking like a shlub.
Start thinking like a hero.
I'm CONTROL-ALT-DELETE...
BEEEEEEP
And this is a REBOOT!

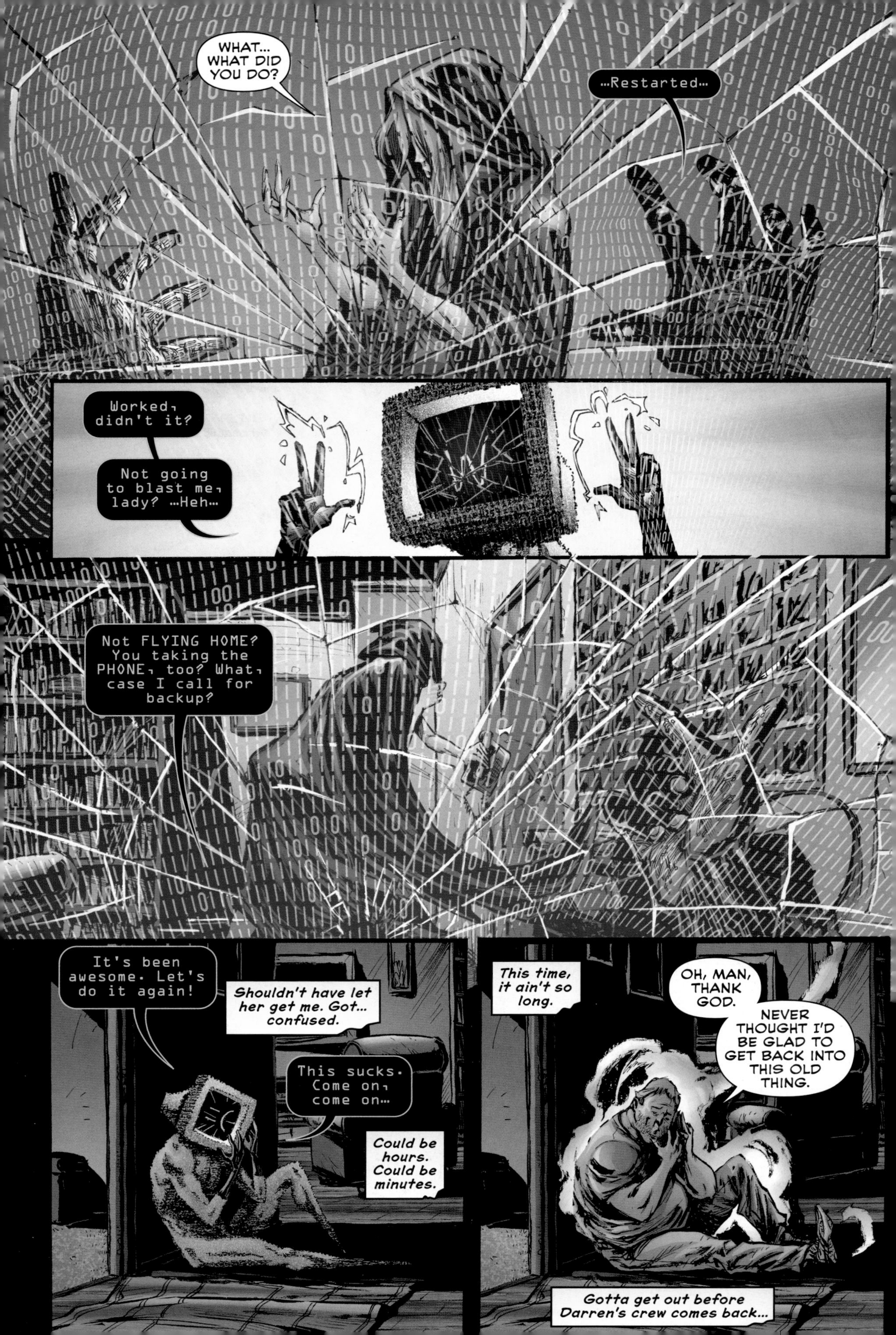
WHAT... WHAT DID YOU DO?
...Restarted...
Worked, didn't it?
Not going to blast me, lady? ...Heh...
Not FLYING HOME? You taking the PHONE, too? What, case I call for backup?
It's been awesome. Let's do it again!
Shouldn't have let her get me. Got... confused.
This sucks. Come on, come on...
Could be hours. Could be minutes.
This time, it ain't so long.
OH, MAN, THANK GOD.
NEVER THOUGHT I'D BE GLAD TO GET BACK INTO THIS OLD THING.
Gotta get out before Darren's crew comes back...

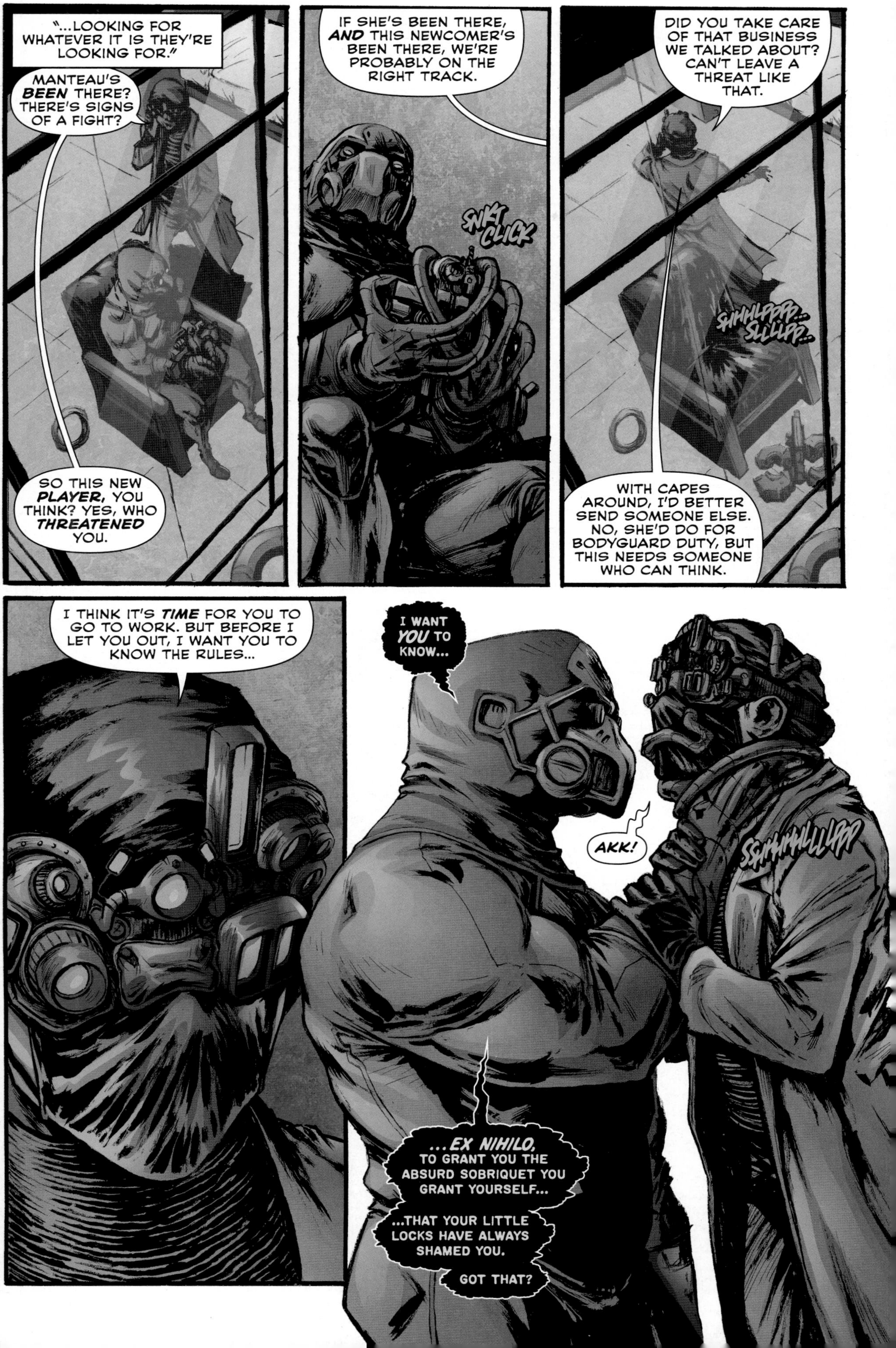
"...LOOKING FOR WHATEVER IT IS THEY'RE LOOKING FOR."
MANTEAU'S ***BEEN*** THERE? THERE'S SIGNS OF A FIGHT?
SO THIS NEW ***PLAYER,*** YOU THINK? YES, WHO ***THREATENED*** YOU.
IF SHE'S BEEN THERE, ***AND*** THIS NEWCOMER'S BEEN THERE, WE'RE PROBABLY ON THE RIGHT TRACK.
SNKT CLICK
DID YOU TAKE CARE OF THAT BUSINESS WE TALKED ABOUT? CAN'T LEAVE A THREAT LIKE THAT.
SHHHLPPP... SLLLPP...
WITH CAPES AROUND, I'D BETTER SEND SOMEONE ELSE. NO, SHE'D DO FOR BODYGUARD DUTY, BUT THIS NEEDS SOMEONE WHO CAN THINK.
I THINK IT'S ***TIME*** FOR YOU TO GO TO WORK. BUT BEFORE I LET YOU OUT, I WANT YOU TO KNOW THE RULES...
I WANT ***YOU*** TO KNOW...
AKK!
SSHHHHLLLPPP
...EX NIHILO, TO GRANT YOU THE ABSURD SOBRIQUET YOU GRANT YOURSELF...
...THAT YOUR LITTLE LOCKS HAVE ALWAYS SHAMED YOU.
GOT THAT?

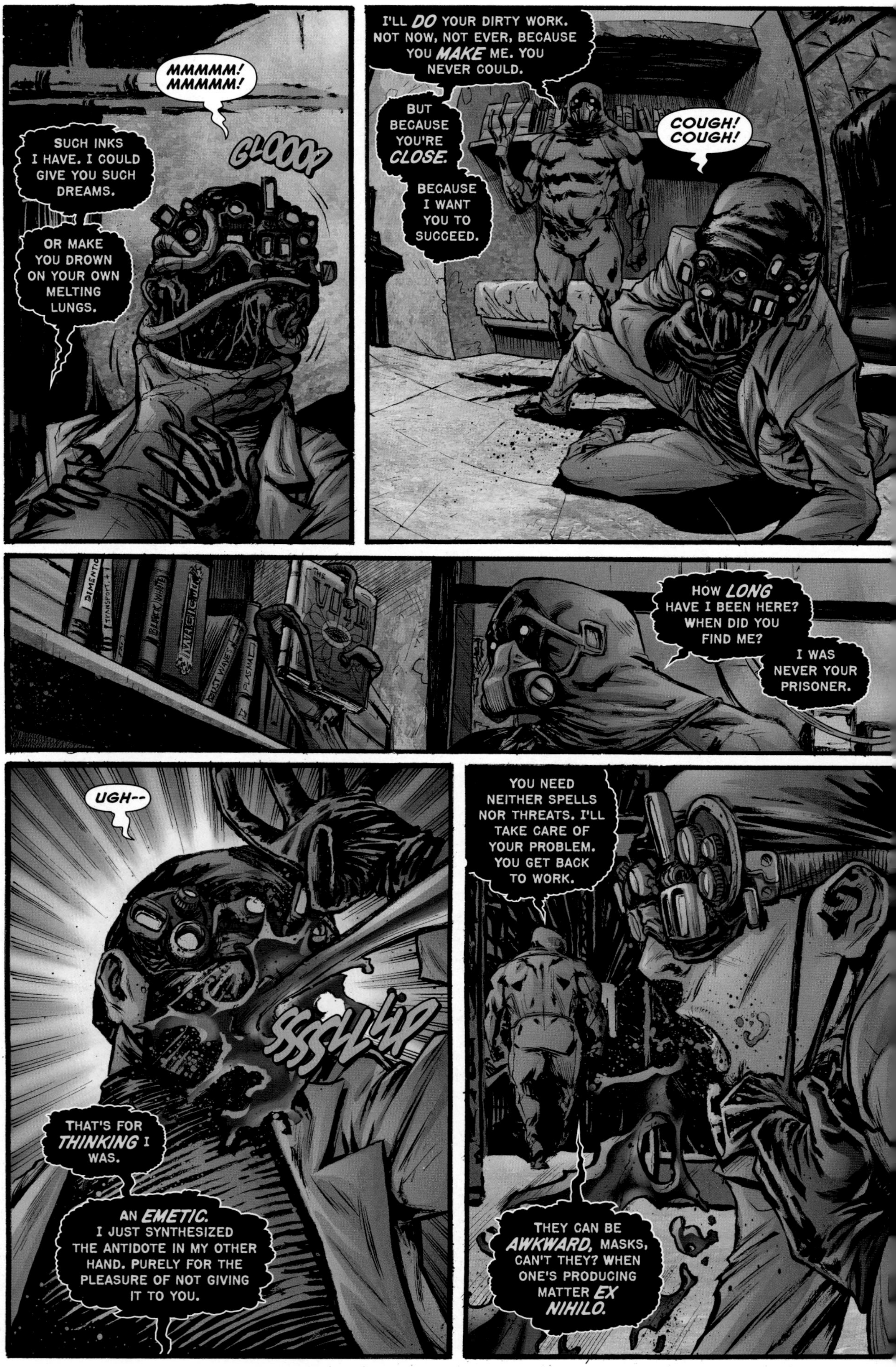
MMMMM! MMMMM!
SUCH INKS I HAVE. I COULD GIVE YOU SUCH DREAMS.
OR MAKE YOU DROWN ON YOUR OWN MELTING LUNGS.
GLOOOP
I'LL DO YOUR DIRTY WORK. NOT NOW, NOT EVER, BECAUSE YOU MAKE ME. YOU NEVER COULD.
BUT BECAUSE YOU'RE CLOSE.
BECAUSE I WANT YOU TO SUCCEED.
COUGH! COUGH!
HOW LONG HAVE I BEEN HERE? WHEN DID YOU FIND ME?
I WAS NEVER YOUR PRISONER.
UGH--
SSSSLLLLIP
THAT'S FOR THINKING I WAS.
AN EMETIC. I JUST SYNTHESIZED THE ANTIDOTE IN MY OTHER HAND. PURELY FOR THE PLEASURE OF NOT GIVING IT TO YOU.
YOU NEED NEITHER SPELLS NOR THREATS. I'LL TAKE CARE OF YOUR PROBLEM. YOU GET BACK TO WORK.
THEY CAN BE AWKWARD, MASKS, CAN'T THEY? WHEN ONE'S PRODUCING MATTER EX NIHILO.

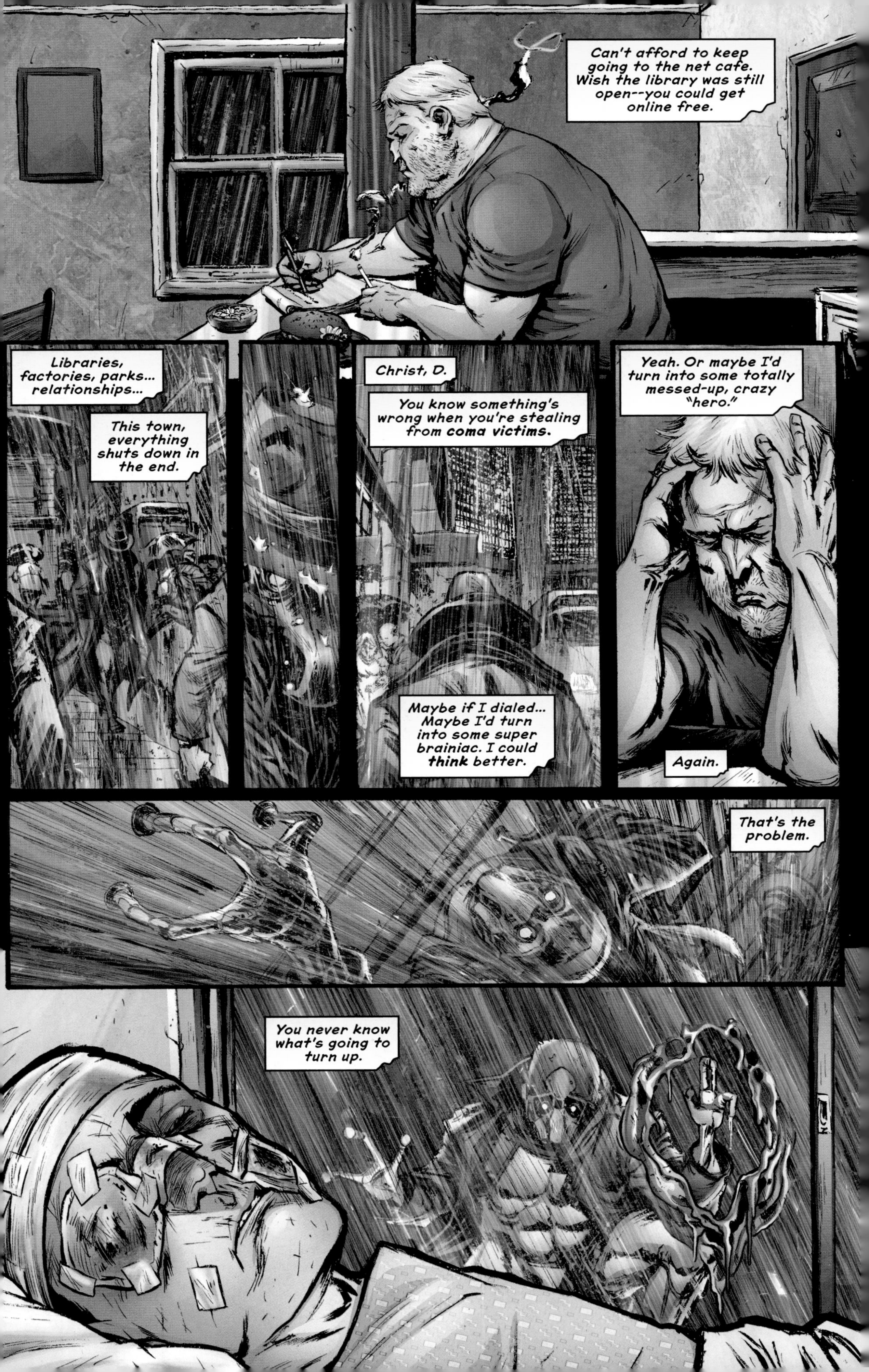
Can't afford to keep going to the net cafe. Wish the library was still open--you could get online free.
Libraries, factories, parks... relationships...
This town, everything shuts down in the end.
Christ, D.
You know something's wrong when you're stealing from **coma victims.**
Maybe if I dialed... Maybe I'd turn into some super brainiac. I could **think** better.
Yeah. Or maybe I'd turn into some totally messed-up, crazy "hero."
Again.
That's the problem.
You never know what's going to turn up.

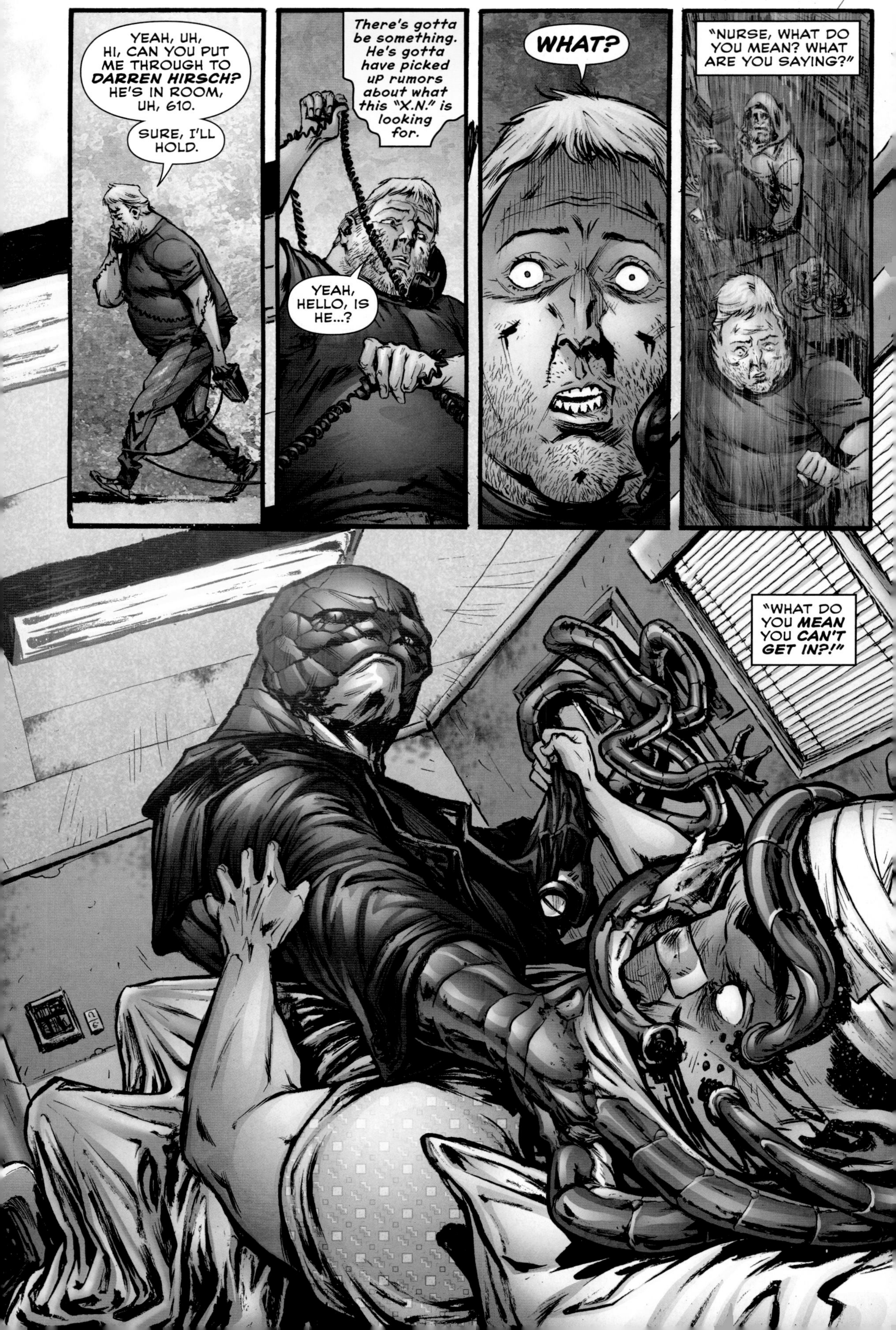
YEAH, UH, HI, CAN YOU PUT ME THROUGH TO DARREN HIRSCH? HE'S IN ROOM, UH, 610.
SURE, I'LL HOLD.
There's gotta be something. He's gotta have picked up rumors about what this "X.N." is looking for.
YEAH, HELLO, IS HE...?
WHAT?
"NURSE, WHAT DO YOU MEAN? WHAT ARE YOU SAYING?"
"WHAT DO YOU MEAN YOU CAN'T GET IN?!"

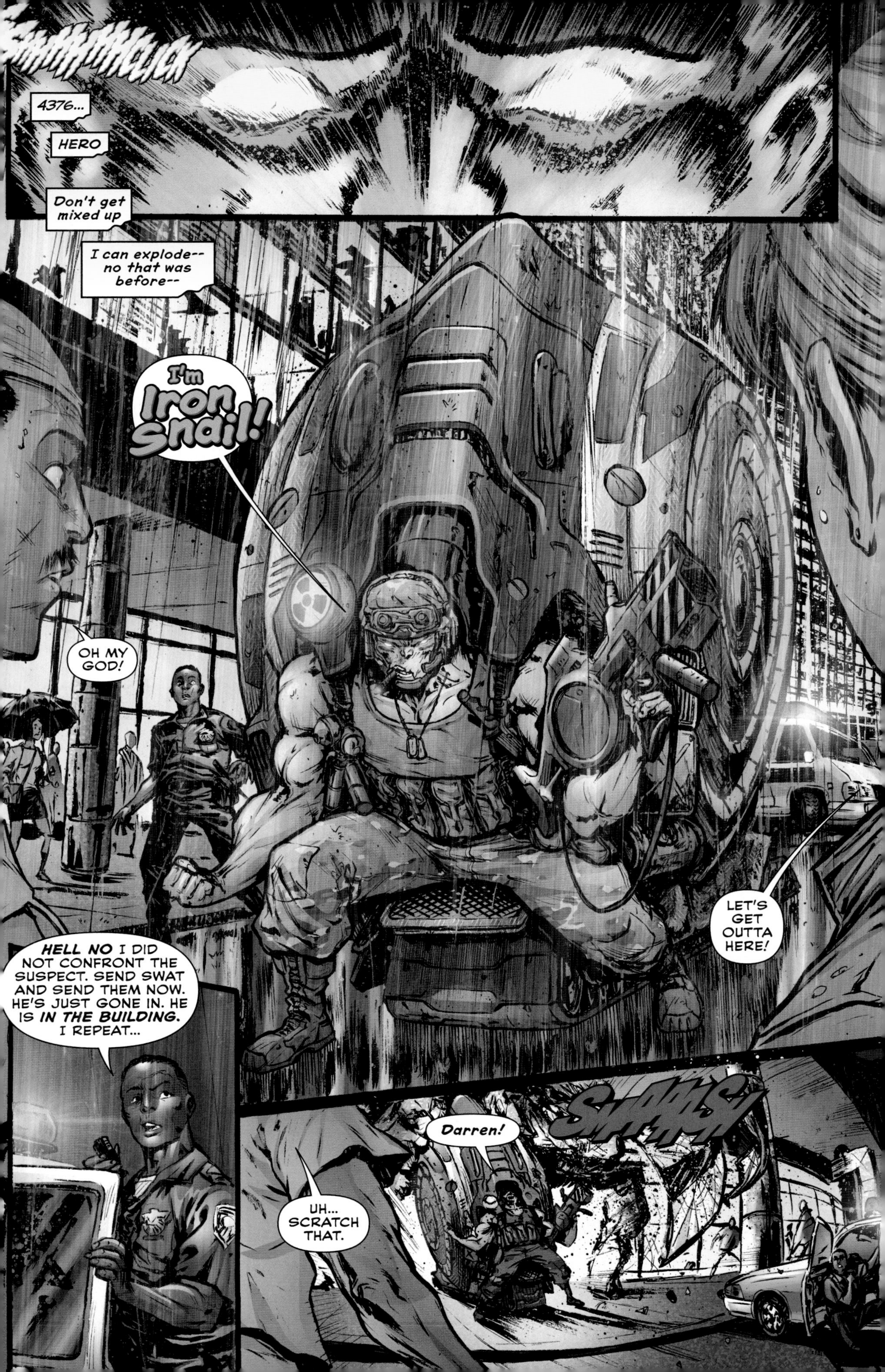
4376...
HERO
Don't get mixed up
I can explode-- no that was before--
I'm Iron Snail!
OH MY GOD!
LET'S GET OUTTA HERE!
HELL NO I DID NOT CONFRONT THE SUSPECT. SEND SWAT AND SEND THEM NOW. HE'S JUST GONE IN. HE IS IN THE BUILDING. I REPEAT...
Darren!
UH... SCRATCH THAT.

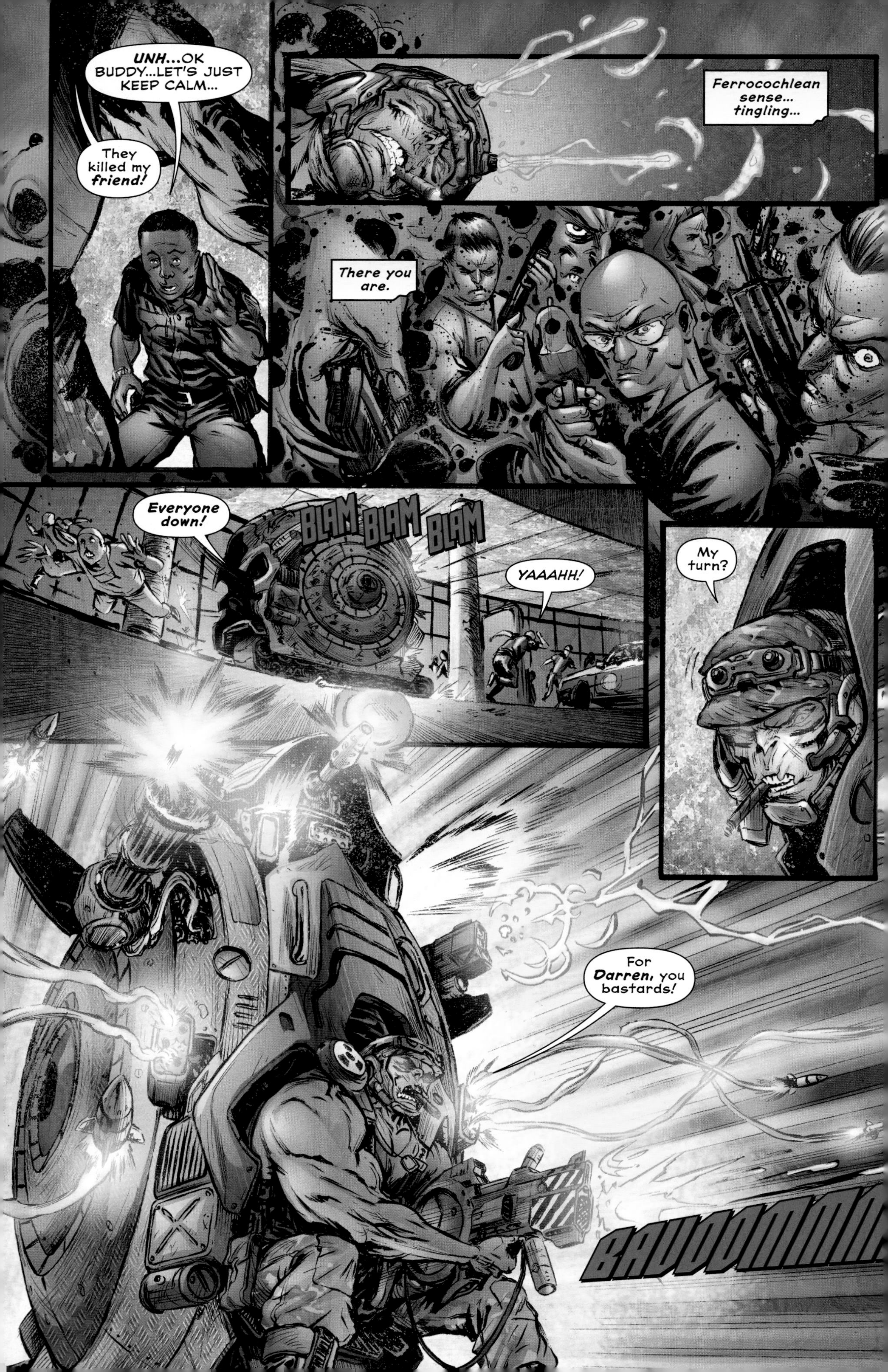

UNH...OK BUDDY...LET'S JUST KEEP CALM...
They killed my friend!
Ferrocochlean sense... tingling...
There you are.
Everyone down!
BLAM BLAM BLAM
YAAAHH!
My turn?
For Darren, you bastards!

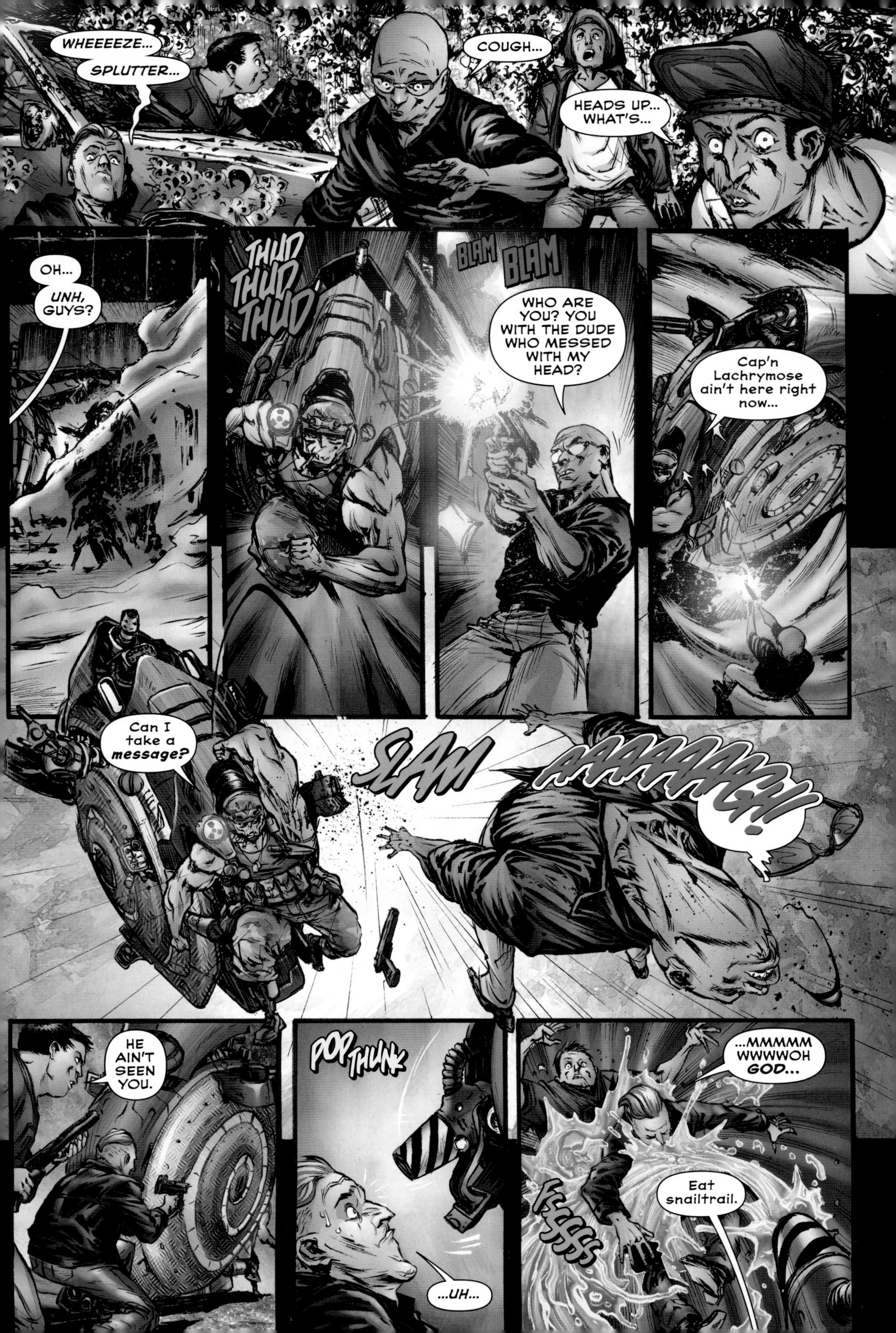
WHEEEEZE...
SPLUTTER...
COUGH...
HEADS UP... WHAT'S...
OH...
UNH, GUYS?
THUD THUD THUD
BLAM BLAM
WHO ARE YOU? YOU WITH THE DUDE WHO MESSED WITH MY HEAD?
Cap'n Lachrymose ain't here right now...
Can I take a message?
SLAM
AAAAAAAGH!
HE AIN'T SEEN YOU.
POP THUNK
...UH...
...MMMMM WWWWOH GOD...
Eat snailtrail.

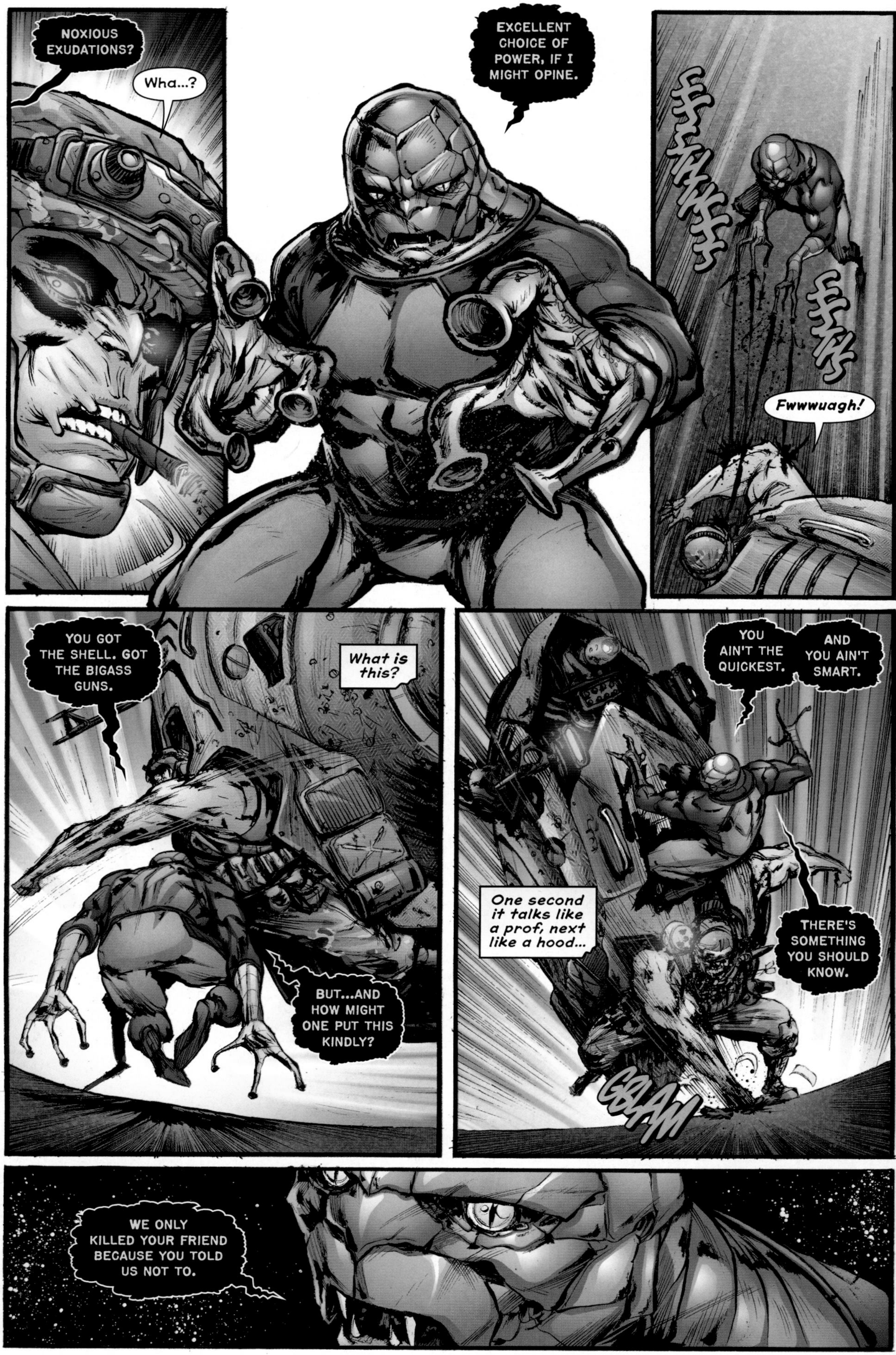
NOXIOUS EXUDATIONS?
Wha...?
EXCELLENT CHOICE OF POWER, IF I MIGHT OPINE.
FSSSHHKKKSSSH
FSSHKS
Fwwwuagh!
YOU GOT THE SHELL. GOT THE BIGASS GUNS.
What is this?
BUT...AND HOW MIGHT ONE PUT THIS KINDLY?
YOU AIN'T THE QUICKEST.
AND YOU AIN'T SMART.
One second it talks like a prof, next like a hood...
THERE'S SOMETHING YOU SHOULD KNOW.
GBLAM
WE ONLY KILLED YOUR FRIEND BECAUSE YOU TOLD US NOT TO.

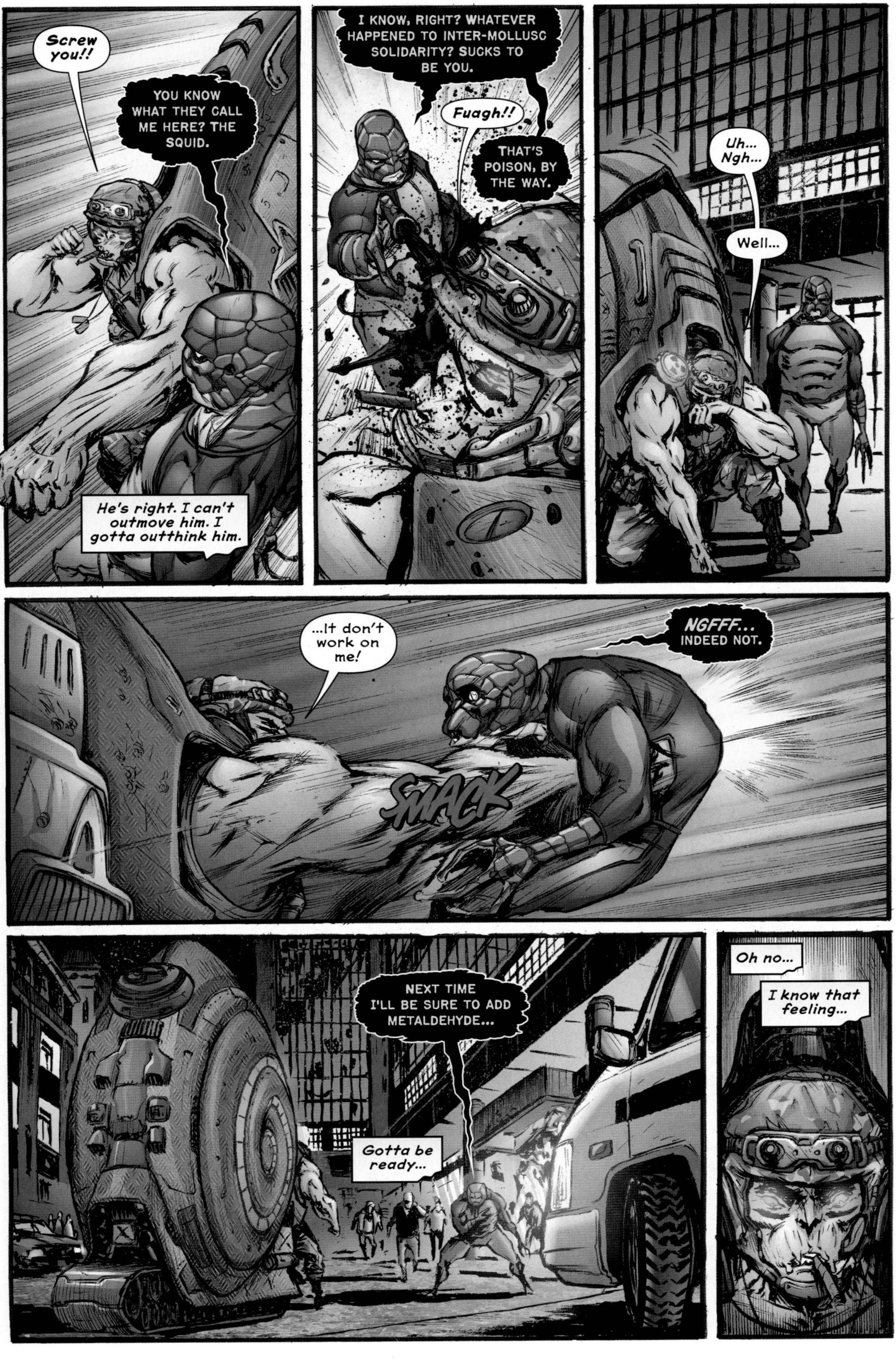
Screw you!!
YOU KNOW WHAT THEY CALL ME HERE? THE SQUID.
He's right. I can't outmove him. I gotta outthink him.
I KNOW, RIGHT? WHATEVER HAPPENED TO INTER-MOLLUSC SOLIDARITY? SUCKS TO BE YOU.
Fuagh!!
THAT'S POISON, BY THE WAY.
Uh... Ngh...
Well...
...It don't work on me!
NGFFF... INDEED NOT.
SMACK
NEXT TIME I'LL BE SURE TO ADD METALDEHYDE...
Gotta be ready...
Oh no...
I know that feeling...

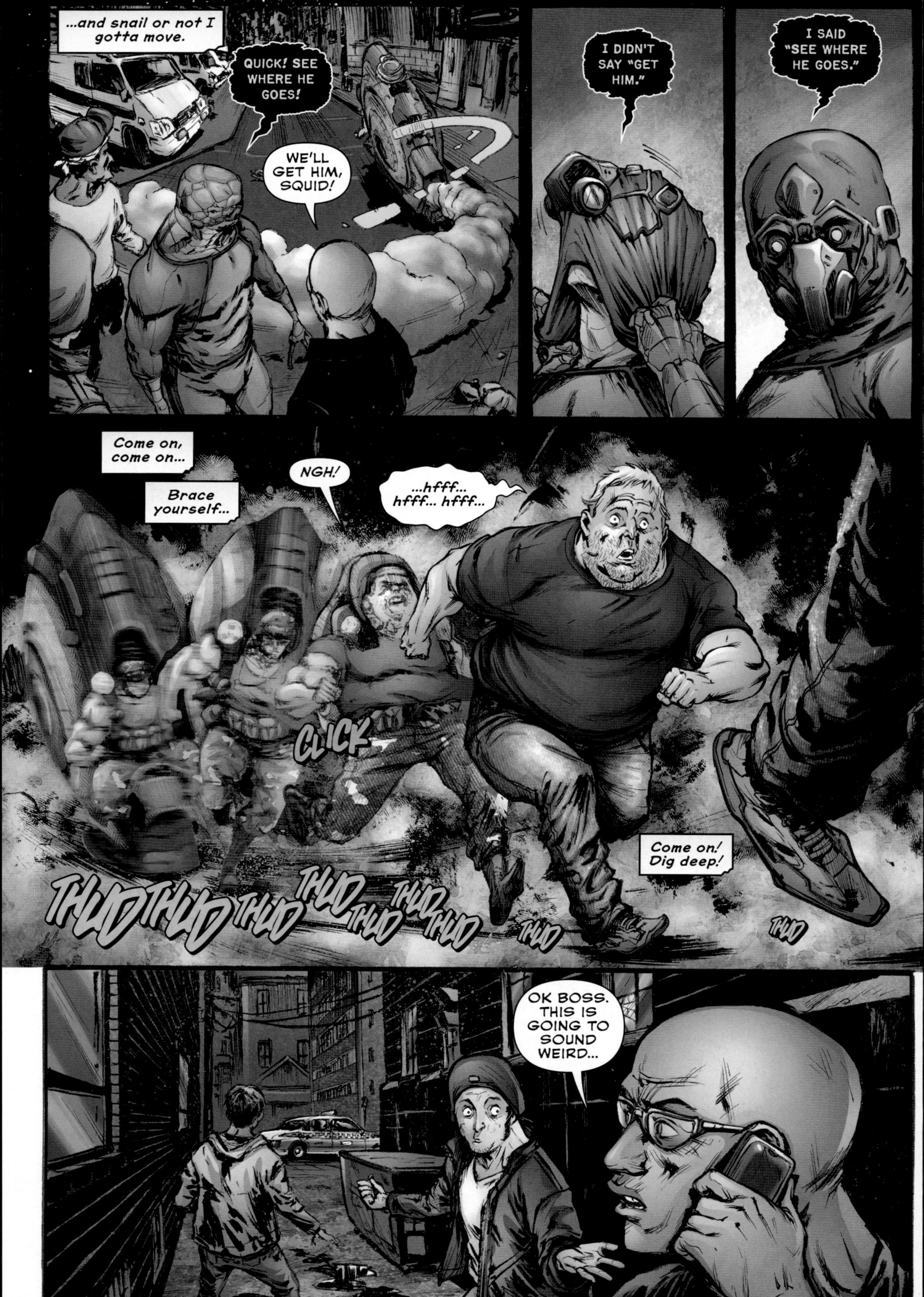

...and snail or not I gotta move.
QUICK! SEE WHERE HE GOES!
WE'LL GET HIM, SQUID!
I DIDN'T SAY "GET HIM."
I SAID "SEE WHERE HE GOES."
Come on, come on...
Brace yourself...
NGH!
...hfff... hfff... hfff...
CLICK
Come on! Dig deep!
THUD THUD THUD THUD THUD THUD THUD THUD THUD
OK BOSS. THIS IS GOING TO SOUND WEIRD...

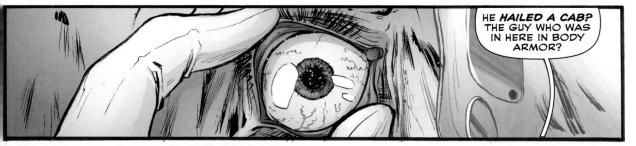

HE *HAILED A CAB?* THE GUY WHO WAS IN HERE IN BODY ARMOR?

HOW DID HE EVEN FIT INSIDE?

BECAUSE IT AIN'T HIM, *EX NIHILO.* AT LEAST...NOT QUITE.

TELL VERN TO FOLLOW HIM. OUTTA SIGHT.

TAIL HIM. DON'T LET HIM SEE YOU. CALL ME WHEN HE'S GOT WHERE HE'S GOING.

GOOD.

YOU... I'M WARNING YOU...

WHATEVER SPECIAL WEAPON THAT IS, KEEP IT IN YOUR POCKET.

I DON'T LIKE YOU, DOCTOR. BUT I NEED YOU. YOU'VE NEARLY DONE IT.

LOOK TO YOUR PATIENT.

I'VE BEEN YOUR...GUEST... BECAUSE OF WHAT I KNOW.

AND I'LL HELP YOU.

WITH INFORMATION. TECHNIQUES. WITH THESE IDIOTS IN COSTUME. BECAUSE I DON'T WANT THEM CAUSING TROUBLE. NOT NOW.

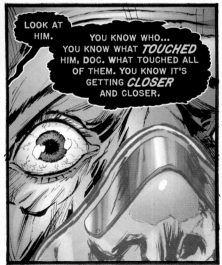

LOOK AT HIM.

YOU KNOW WHO... YOU KNOW WHAT *TOUCHED* HIM, DOC. WHAT TOUCHED ALL OF THEM. YOU KNOW IT'S GETTING *CLOSER* AND CLOSER.

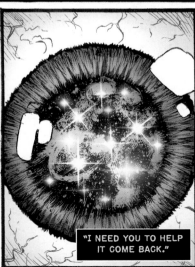

"I NEED YOU TO HELP IT COME BACK."

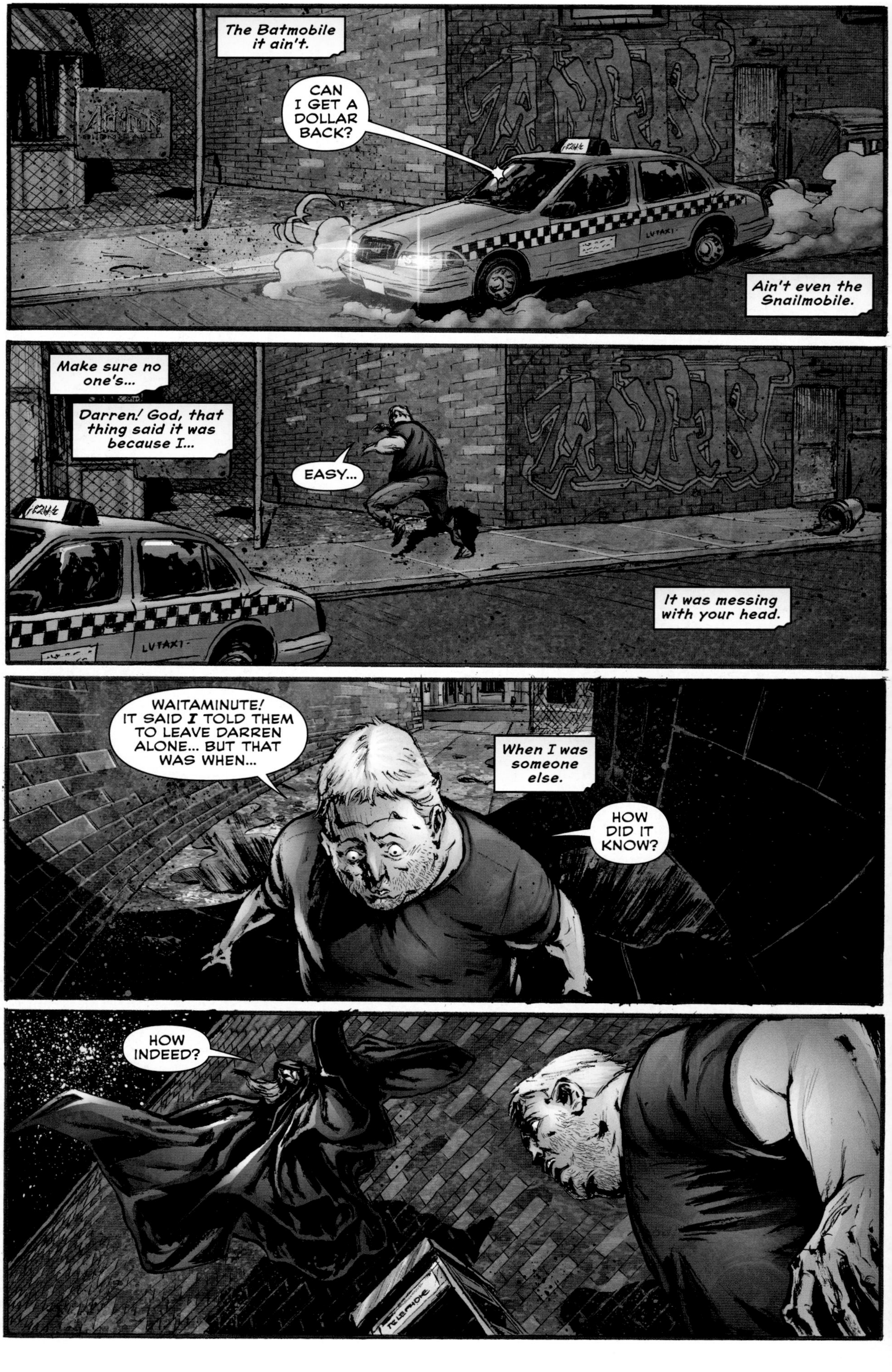
The Batmobile it ain't.
CAN I GET A DOLLAR BACK?
Ain't even the Snailmobile.
Make sure no one's...
Darren! God, that thing said it was because I...
EASY...
It was messing with your head.
WAITAMINUTE! IT SAID I TOLD THEM TO LEAVE DARREN ALONE... BUT THAT WAS WHEN...
When I was someone else.
HOW DID IT KNOW?
HOW INDEED?

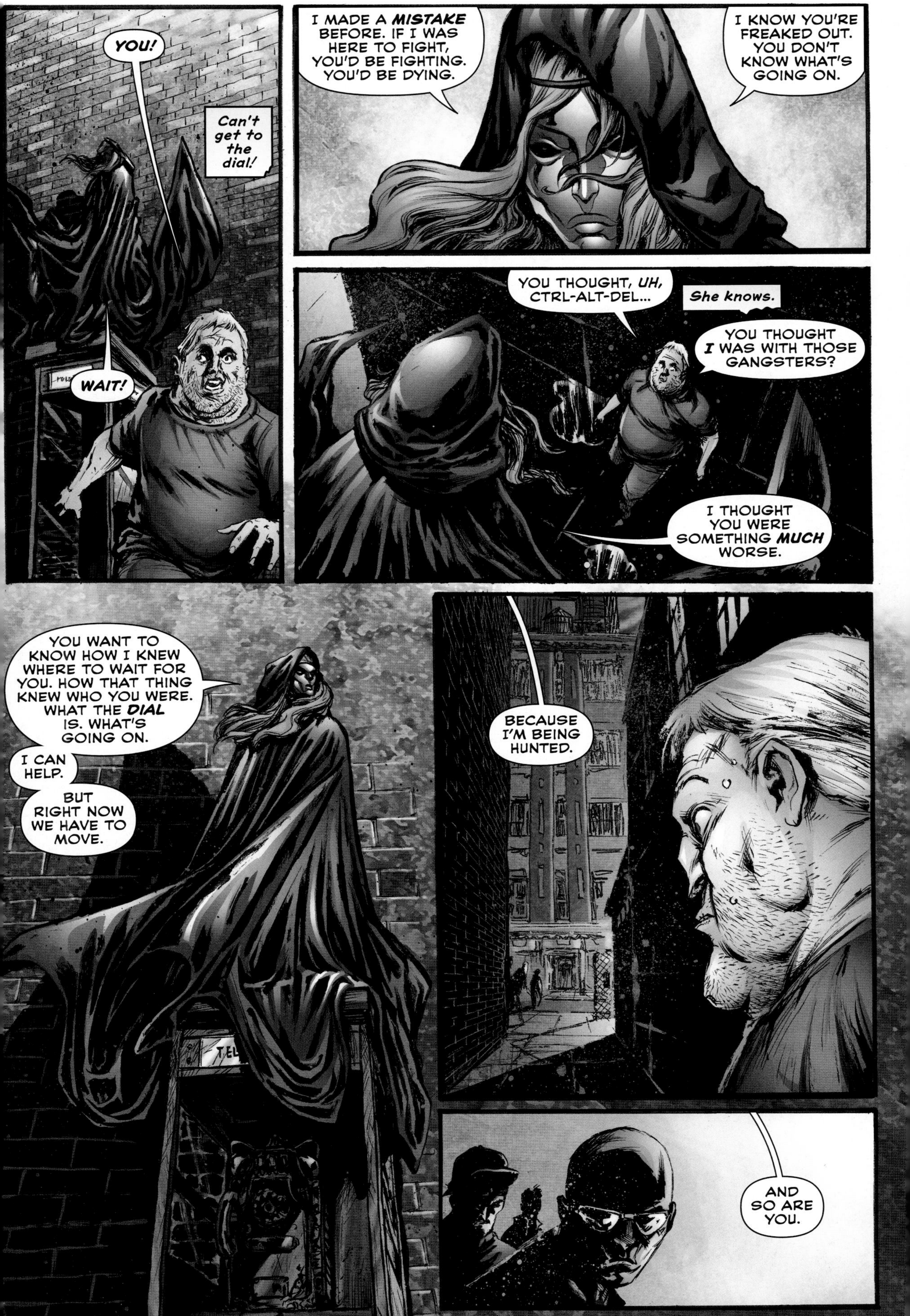
YOU!
Can't get to the dial!
WAIT!
I MADE A MISTAKE BEFORE. IF I WAS HERE TO FIGHT, YOU'D BE FIGHTING. YOU'D BE DYING.
I KNOW YOU'RE FREAKED OUT. YOU DON'T KNOW WHAT'S GOING ON.
YOU THOUGHT, UH, CTRL-ALT-DEL...
She knows.
YOU THOUGHT I WAS WITH THOSE GANGSTERS?
I THOUGHT YOU WERE SOMETHING MUCH WORSE.
YOU WANT TO KNOW HOW I KNEW WHERE TO WAIT FOR YOU. HOW THAT THING KNEW WHO YOU WERE. WHAT THE DIAL IS. WHAT'S GOING ON.
I CAN HELP.
BUT RIGHT NOW WE HAVE TO MOVE.
BECAUSE I'M BEING HUNTED.
AND SO ARE YOU.

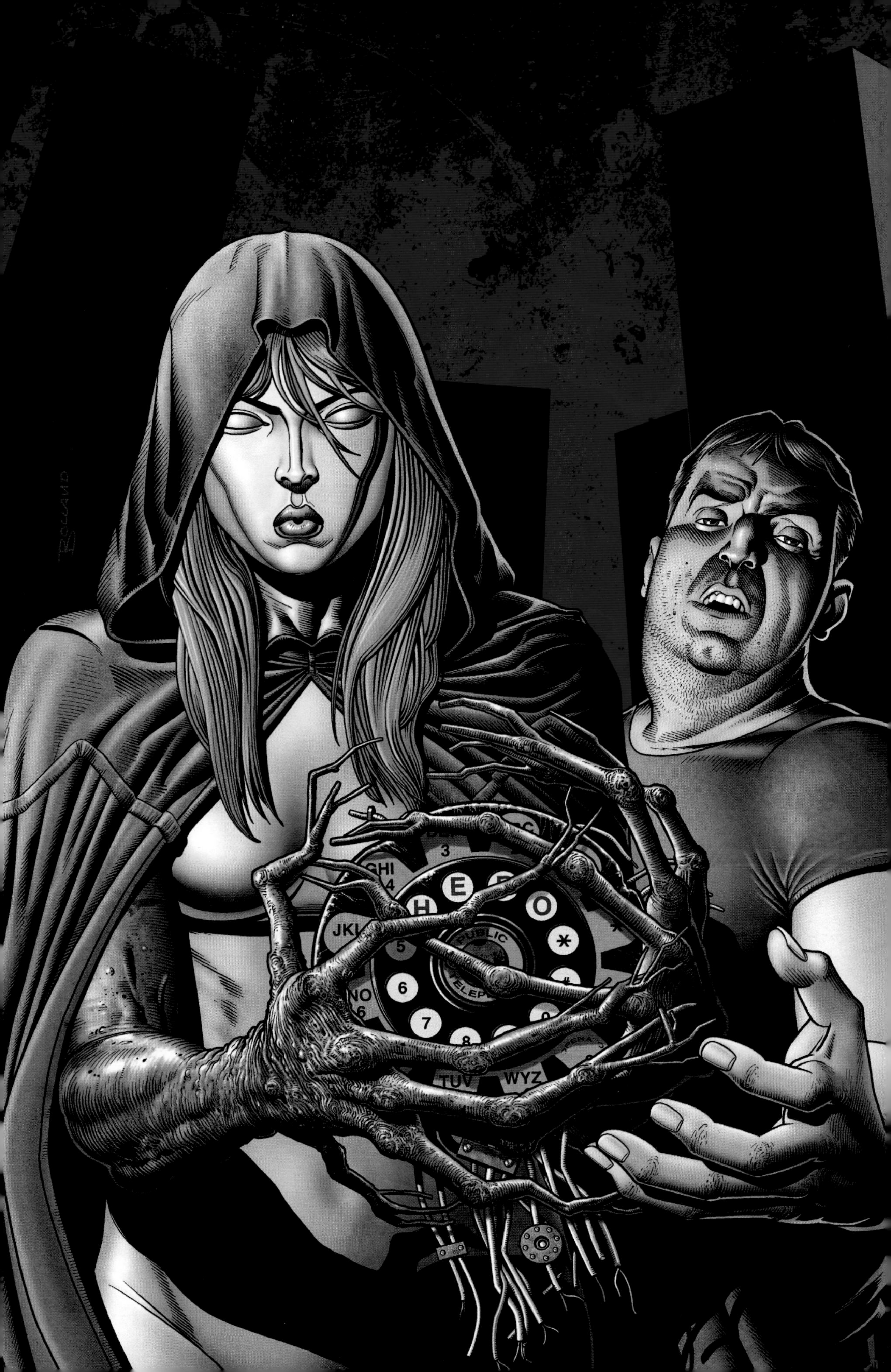

GHI
JKL
PUBLIC
TUV
WYZ

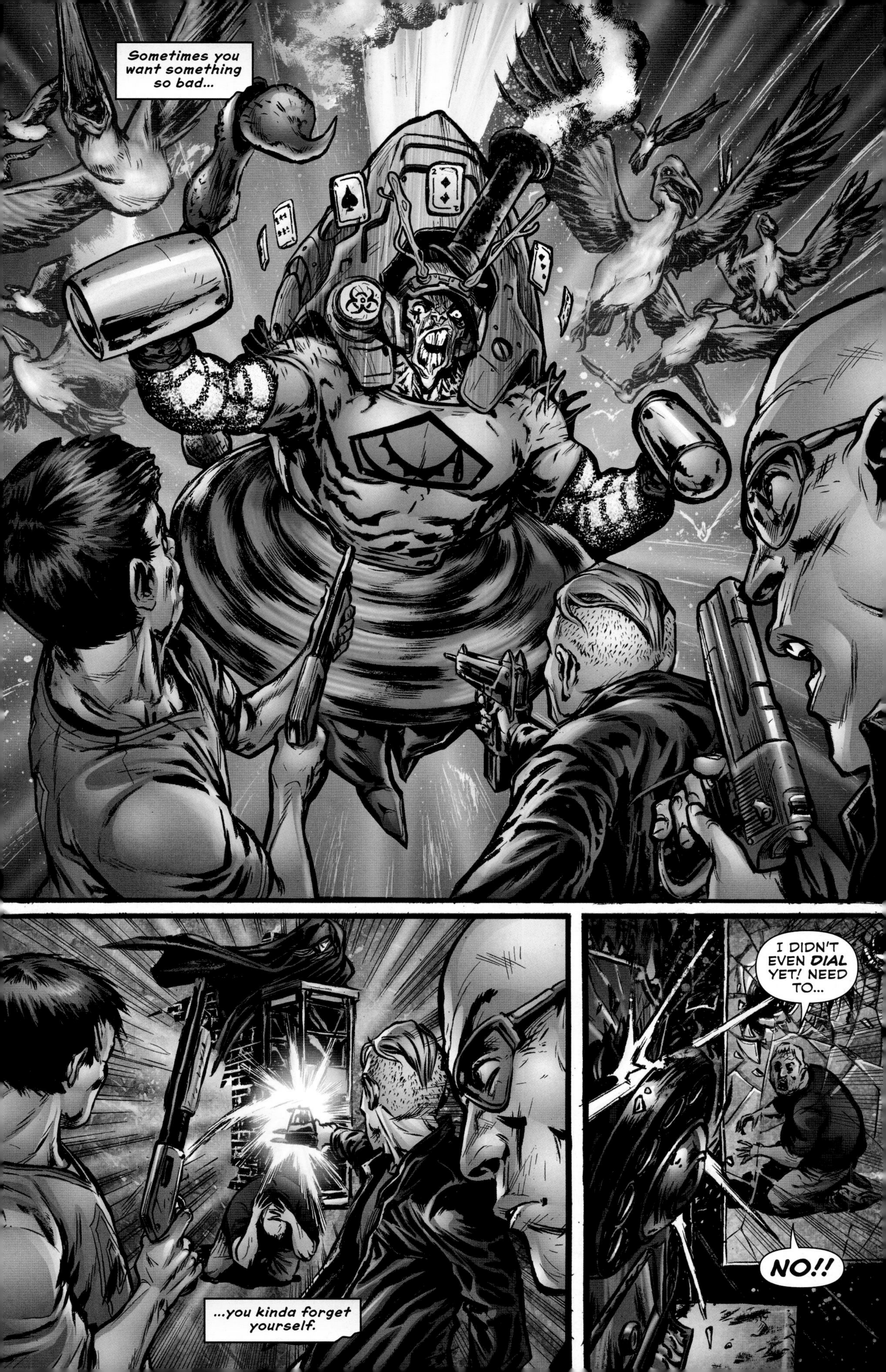
Sometimes you want something so bad...
...you kinda forget yourself.
I DIDN'T EVEN DIAL YET! NEED TO...
NO!!

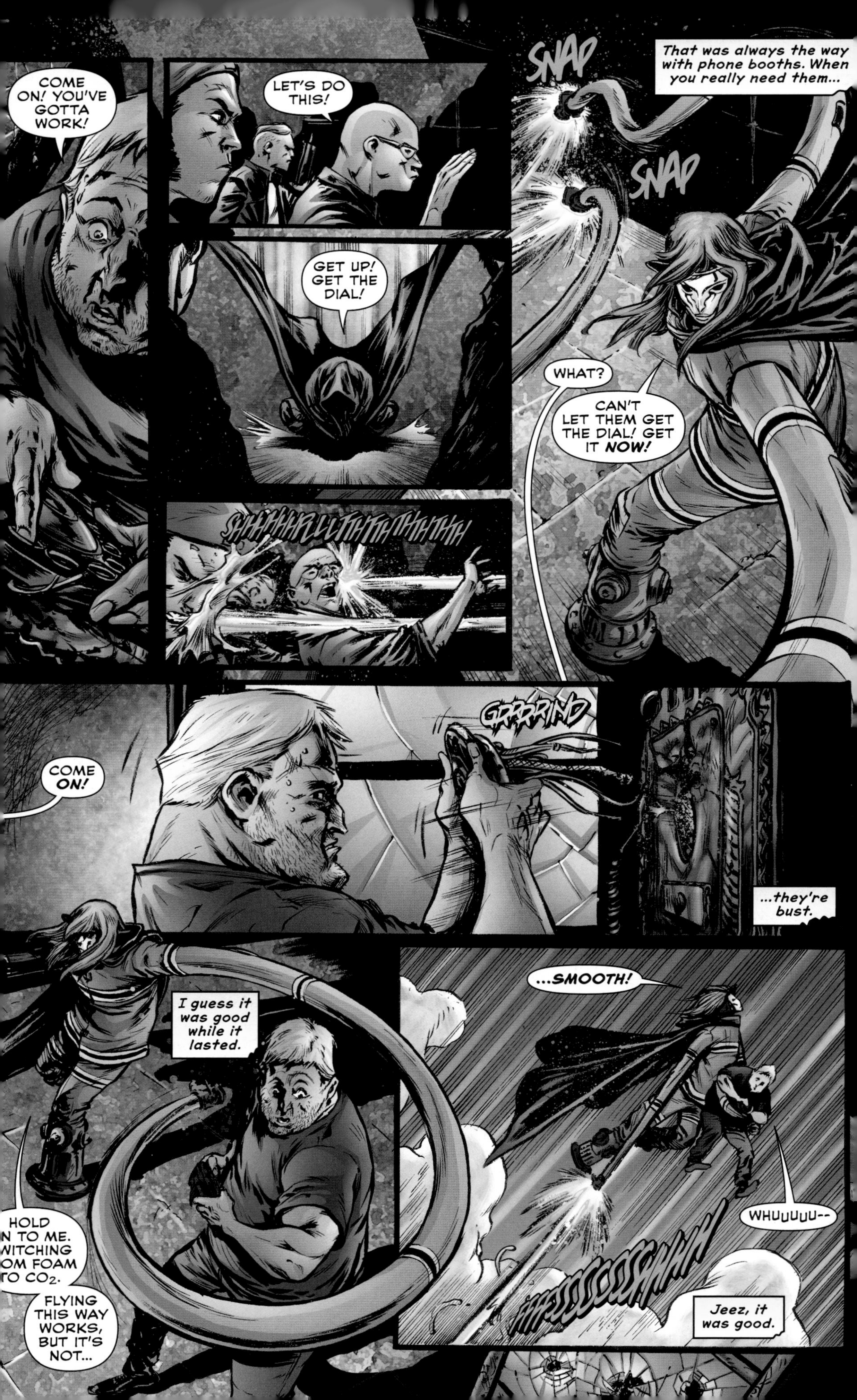
COME ON! YOU'VE GOTTA WORK!
LET'S DO THIS!
SNAP
That was always the way with phone booths. When you really need them...
SNAP
GET UP! GET THE DIAL!
WHAT?
CAN'T LET THEM GET THE DIAL! GET IT NOW!
GRRRRIND
COME ON!
...they're bust.
I guess it was good while it lasted.
HOLD
N TO ME.
WITCHING
OM FOAM
TO CO_2.
FLYING THIS WAY WORKS, BUT IT'S NOT...
...SMOOTH!
WHUUUUU--
Jeez, it was good.

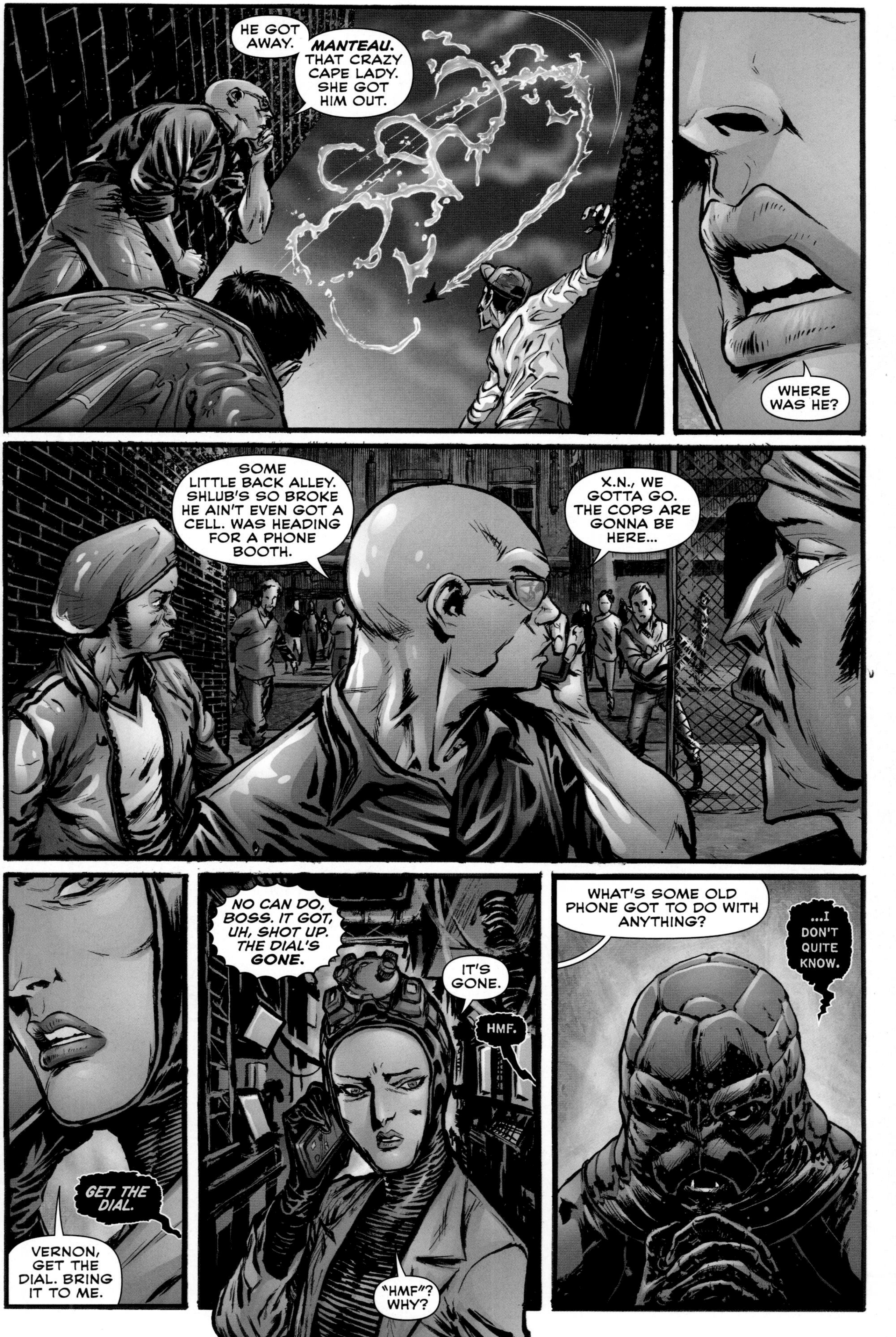
HE GOT AWAY.
MANTEAU. THAT CRAZY CAPE LADY. SHE GOT HIM OUT.
WHERE WAS HE?
SOME LITTLE BACK ALLEY. SHLUB'S SO BROKE HE AIN'T EVEN GOT A CELL. WAS HEADING FOR A PHONE BOOTH.
X.N., WE GOTTA GO. THE COPS ARE GONNA BE HERE...
GET THE DIAL.
VERNON, GET THE DIAL. BRING IT TO ME.
*NO CAN DO, BOSS. IT GOT, UH, SHOT UP. THE DIAL'S **GONE**.*
IT'S GONE.
HMF.
"HMF"? WHY?
WHAT'S SOME OLD PHONE GOT TO DO WITH ANYTHING?
...I DON'T QUITE KNOW.

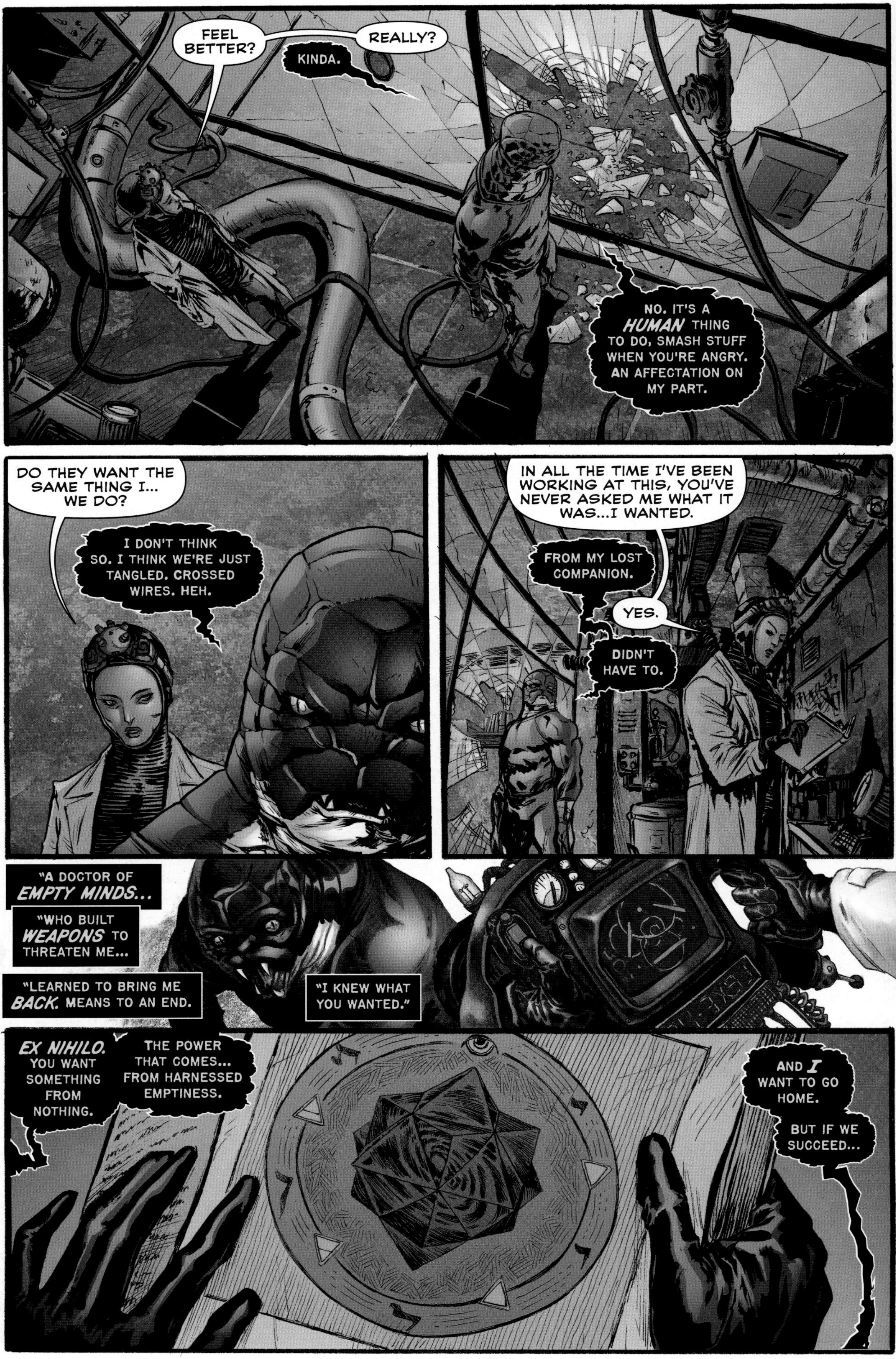
FEEL BETTER?
KINDA.
REALLY?
NO. IT'S A HUMAN THING TO DO, SMASH STUFF WHEN YOU'RE ANGRY. AN AFFECTATION ON MY PART.
DO THEY WANT THE SAME THING I... WE DO?
I DON'T THINK SO. I THINK WE'RE JUST TANGLED. CROSSED WIRES. HEH.
IN ALL THE TIME I'VE BEEN WORKING AT THIS, YOU'VE NEVER ASKED ME WHAT IT WAS...I WANTED.
FROM MY LOST COMPANION.
YES.
DIDN'T HAVE TO.
"A DOCTOR OF EMPTY MINDS...
"WHO BUILT WEAPONS TO THREATEN ME...
"LEARNED TO BRING ME BACK. MEANS TO AN END.
"I KNEW WHAT YOU WANTED."
EX NIHILO. YOU WANT SOMETHING FROM NOTHING.
THE POWER THAT COMES... FROM HARNESSED EMPTINESS.
AND I WANT TO GO HOME.
BUT IF WE SUCCEED...

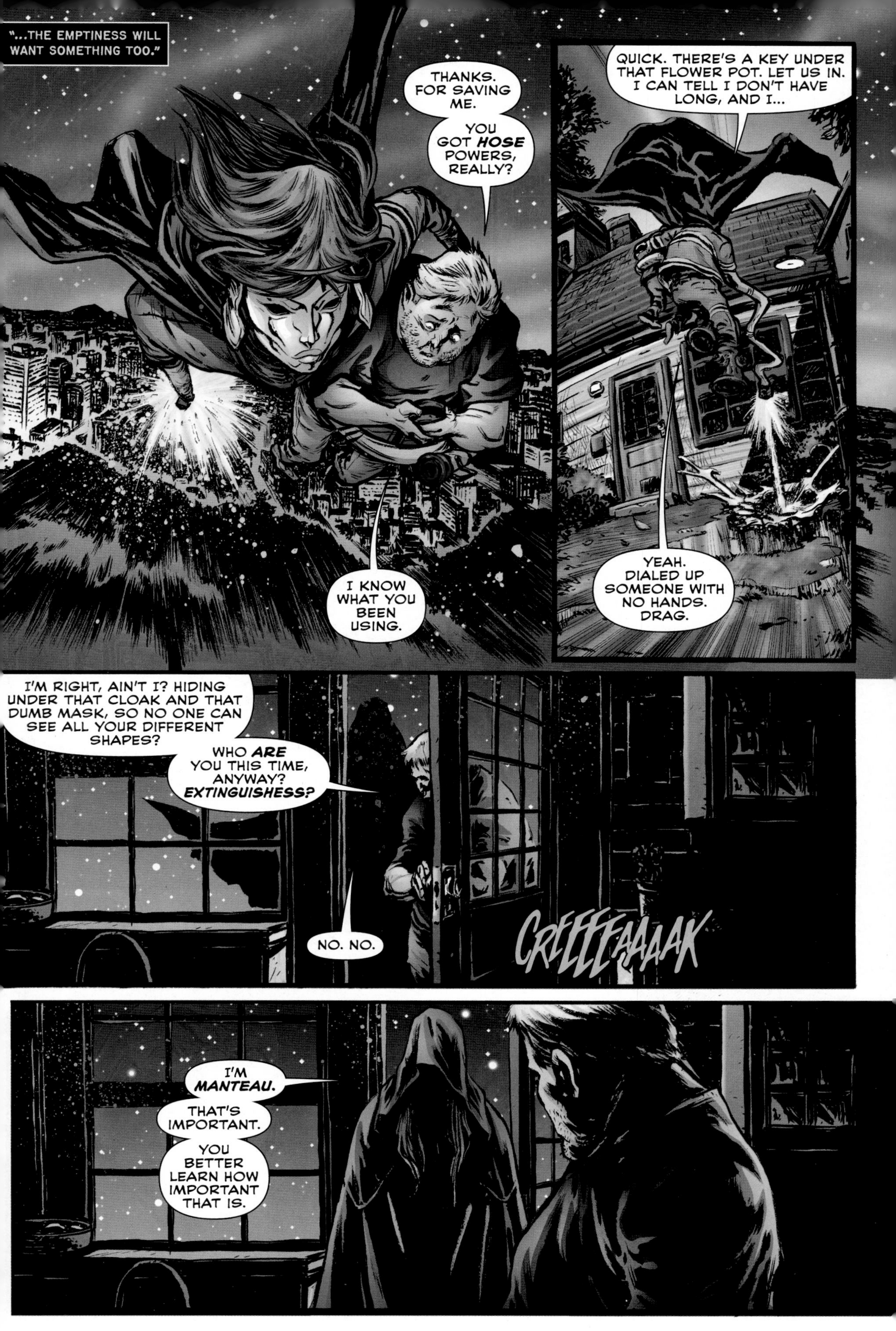
"...THE EMPTINESS WILL WANT SOMETHING TOO."
THANKS. FOR SAVING ME.
YOU GOT HOSE POWERS, REALLY?
I KNOW WHAT YOU BEEN USING.
QUICK. THERE'S A KEY UNDER THAT FLOWER POT. LET US IN. I CAN TELL I DON'T HAVE LONG, AND I...
YEAH. DIALED UP SOMEONE WITH NO HANDS. DRAG.
I'M RIGHT, AIN'T I? HIDING UNDER THAT CLOAK AND THAT DUMB MASK, SO NO ONE CAN SEE ALL YOUR DIFFERENT SHAPES?
WHO ARE YOU THIS TIME, ANYWAY? EXTINGUISHESS?
NO. NO.
CREEEEAAAAK
I'M MANTEAU.
THAT'S IMPORTANT.
YOU BETTER LEARN HOW IMPORTANT THAT IS.

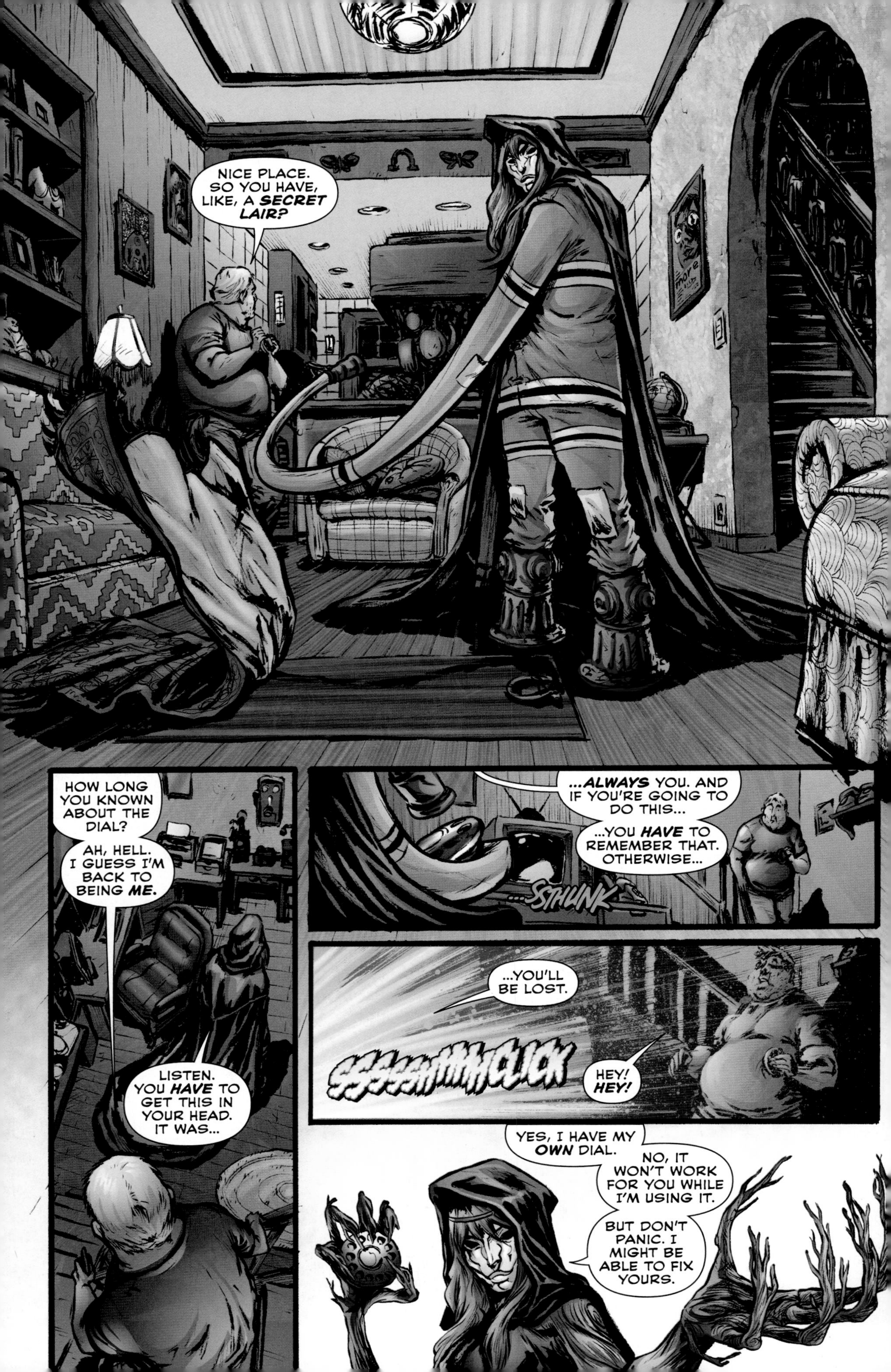
NICE PLACE. SO YOU HAVE, LIKE, A ***SECRET LAIR?***
HOW LONG YOU KNOWN ABOUT THE DIAL?
AH, HELL. I GUESS I'M BACK TO BEING ***ME.***
LISTEN. YOU ***HAVE*** TO GET THIS IN YOUR HEAD. IT WAS...
...ALWAYS YOU. AND IF YOU'RE GOING TO DO THIS...
...YOU ***HAVE*** TO REMEMBER THAT. OTHERWISE...
...SSTHUNK
...YOU'LL BE LOST.
SSSSSHHHHCLICK
HEY! ***HEY!***
YES, I HAVE MY ***OWN*** DIAL.
NO, IT WON'T WORK FOR YOU WHILE I'M USING IT.
BUT DON'T PANIC. I MIGHT BE ABLE TO FIX YOURS.

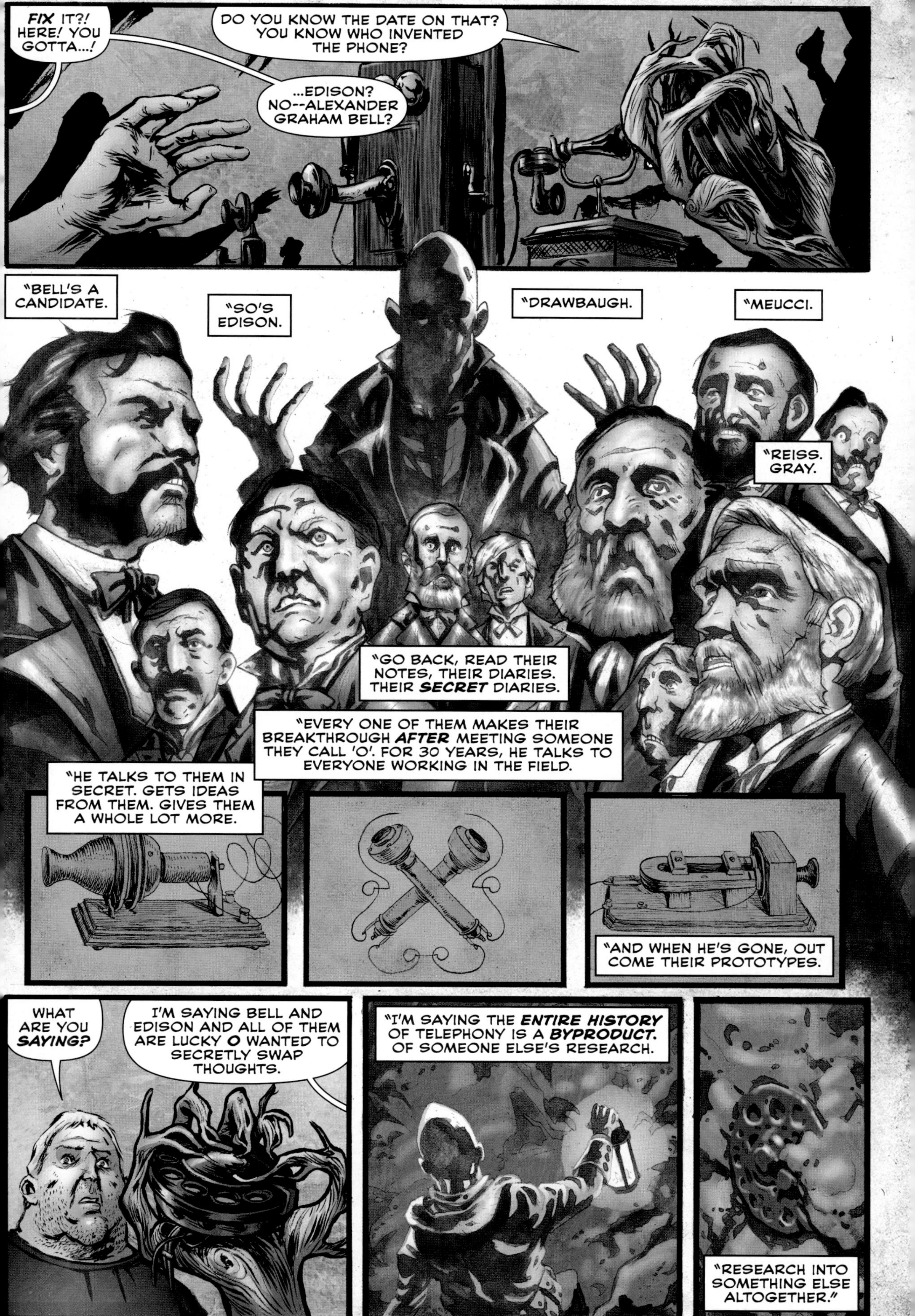

FIX IT?! HERE! YOU GOTTA...!
DO YOU KNOW THE DATE ON THAT? YOU KNOW WHO INVENTED THE PHONE?
...EDISON? NO--ALEXANDER GRAHAM BELL?
"BELL'S A CANDIDATE.
"SO'S EDISON.
"DRAWBAUGH.
"MEUCCI.
"REISS. GRAY.
"GO BACK, READ THEIR NOTES, THEIR DIARIES. THEIR SECRET DIARIES.
"EVERY ONE OF THEM MAKES THEIR BREAKTHROUGH AFTER MEETING SOMEONE THEY CALL 'O'. FOR 30 YEARS, HE TALKS TO EVERYONE WORKING IN THE FIELD.
"HE TALKS TO THEM IN SECRET. GETS IDEAS FROM THEM. GIVES THEM A WHOLE LOT MORE.
"AND WHEN HE'S GONE, OUT COME THEIR PROTOTYPES.
WHAT ARE YOU SAYING?
I'M SAYING BELL AND EDISON AND ALL OF THEM ARE LUCKY O WANTED TO SECRETLY SWAP THOUGHTS.
"I'M SAYING THE ENTIRE HISTORY OF TELEPHONY IS A BYPRODUCT. OF SOMEONE ELSE'S RESEARCH.
"RESEARCH INTO SOMETHING ELSE ALTOGETHER."

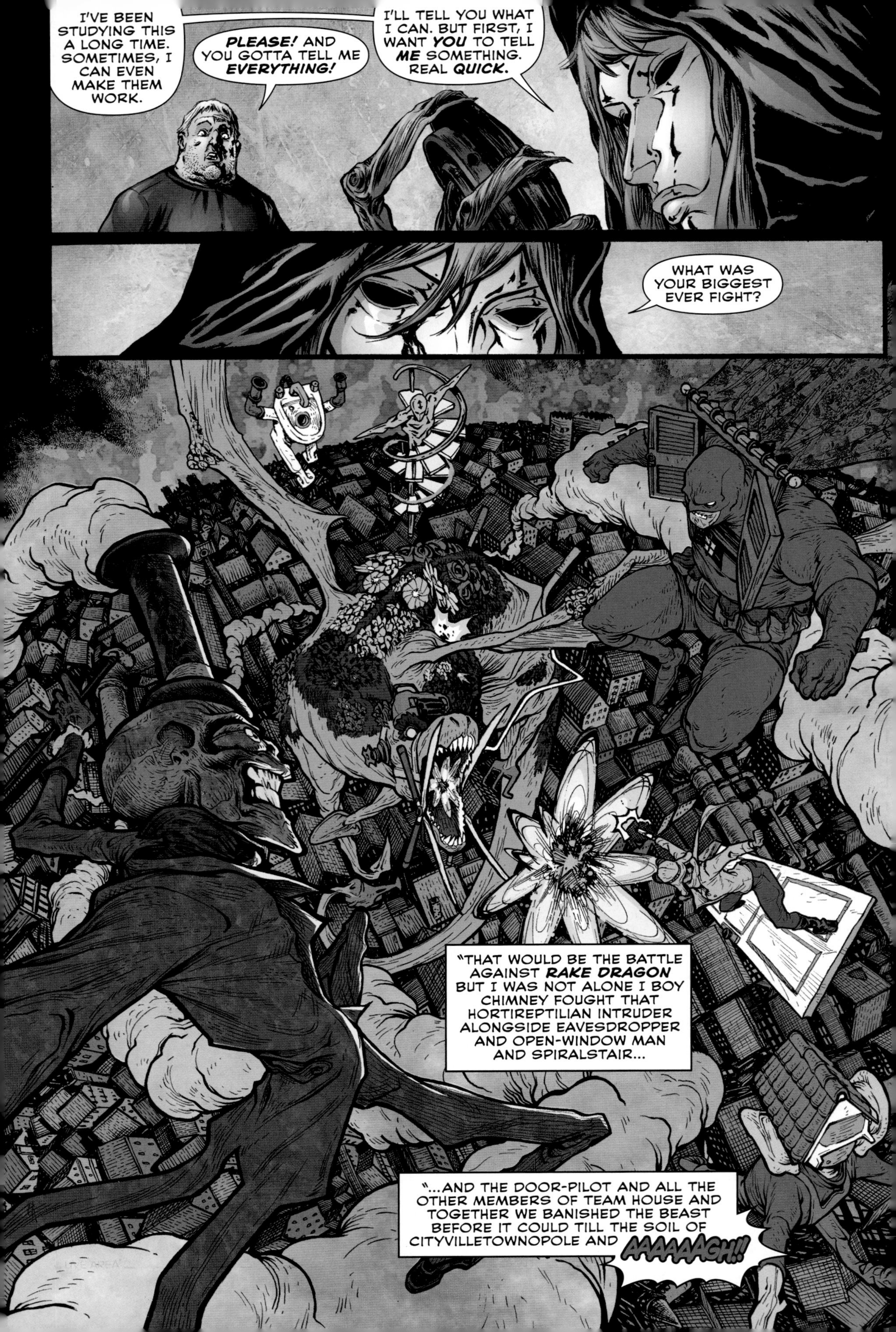
I'VE BEEN STUDYING THIS A LONG TIME. SOMETIMES, I CAN EVEN MAKE THEM WORK.
PLEASE! AND YOU GOTTA TELL ME EVERYTHING!
I'LL TELL YOU WHAT I CAN. BUT FIRST, I WANT YOU TO TELL ME SOMETHING. REAL QUICK.
WHAT WAS YOUR BIGGEST EVER FIGHT?
"THAT WOULD BE THE BATTLE AGAINST RAKE DRAGON BUT I WAS NOT ALONE I BOY CHIMNEY FOUGHT THAT HORTIREPTILIAN INTRUDER ALONGSIDE EAVESDROPPER AND OPEN-WINDOW MAN AND SPIRALSTAIR...
"...AND THE DOOR-PILOT AND ALL THE OTHER MEMBERS OF TEAM HOUSE AND TOGETHER WE BANISHED THE BEAST BEFORE IT COULD TILL THE SOIL OF CITYVILLETOWNOPOLE AND AAAAAAGH!!

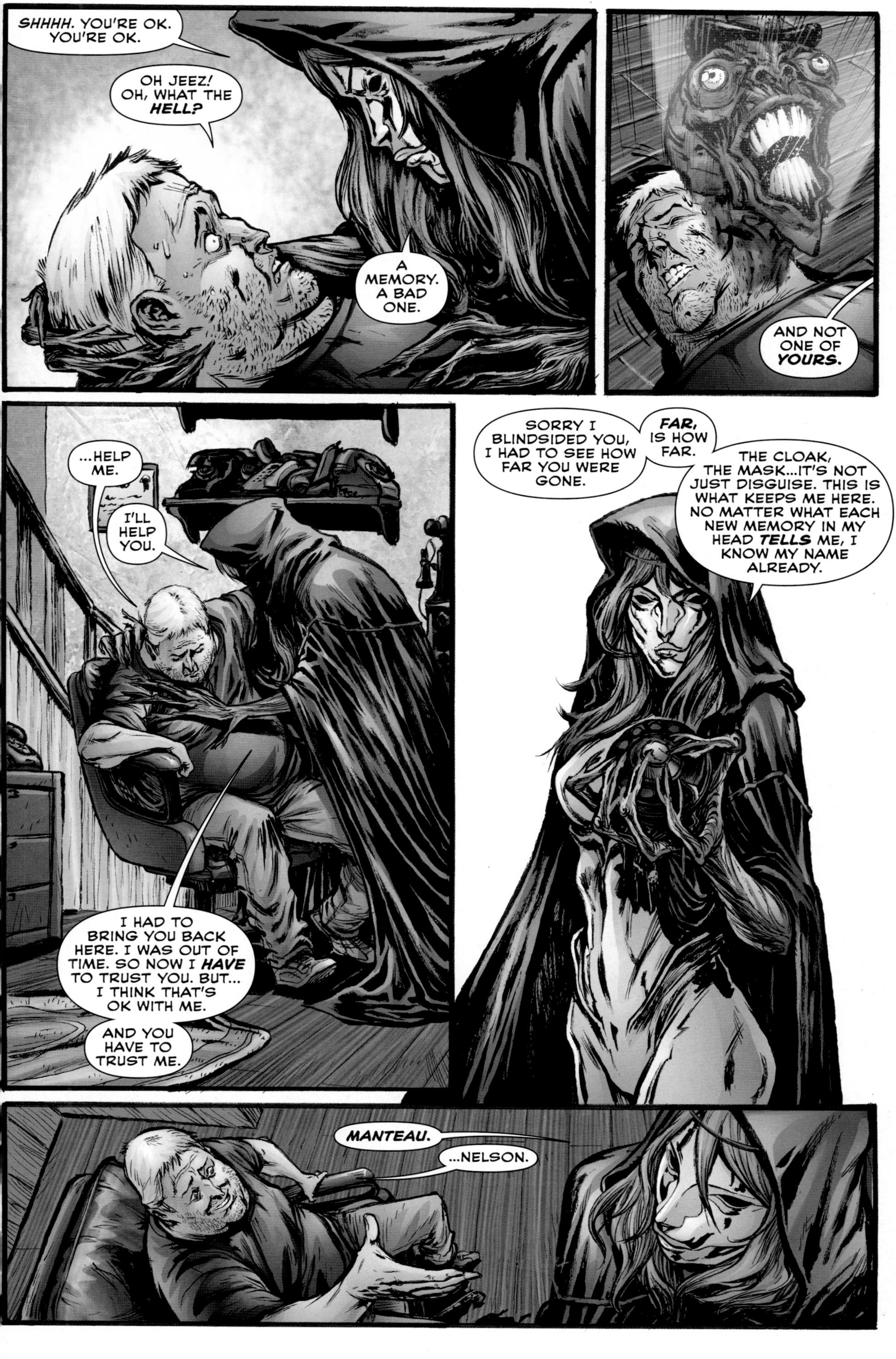
SHHHH. YOU'RE OK. YOU'RE OK.
OH JEEZ! OH, WHAT THE HELL?
A MEMORY. A BAD ONE.
AND NOT ONE OF YOURS.
...HELP ME.
I'LL HELP YOU.
I HAD TO BRING YOU BACK HERE. I WAS OUT OF TIME. SO NOW I HAVE TO TRUST YOU. BUT... I THINK THAT'S OK WITH ME.
AND YOU HAVE TO TRUST ME.
SORRY I BLINDSIDED YOU, I HAD TO SEE HOW FAR YOU WERE GONE.
FAR, IS HOW FAR.
THE CLOAK, THE MASK...IT'S NOT JUST DISGUISE. THIS IS WHAT KEEPS ME HERE. NO MATTER WHAT EACH NEW MEMORY IN MY HEAD TELLS ME, I KNOW MY NAME ALREADY.
MANTEAU.
...NELSON.

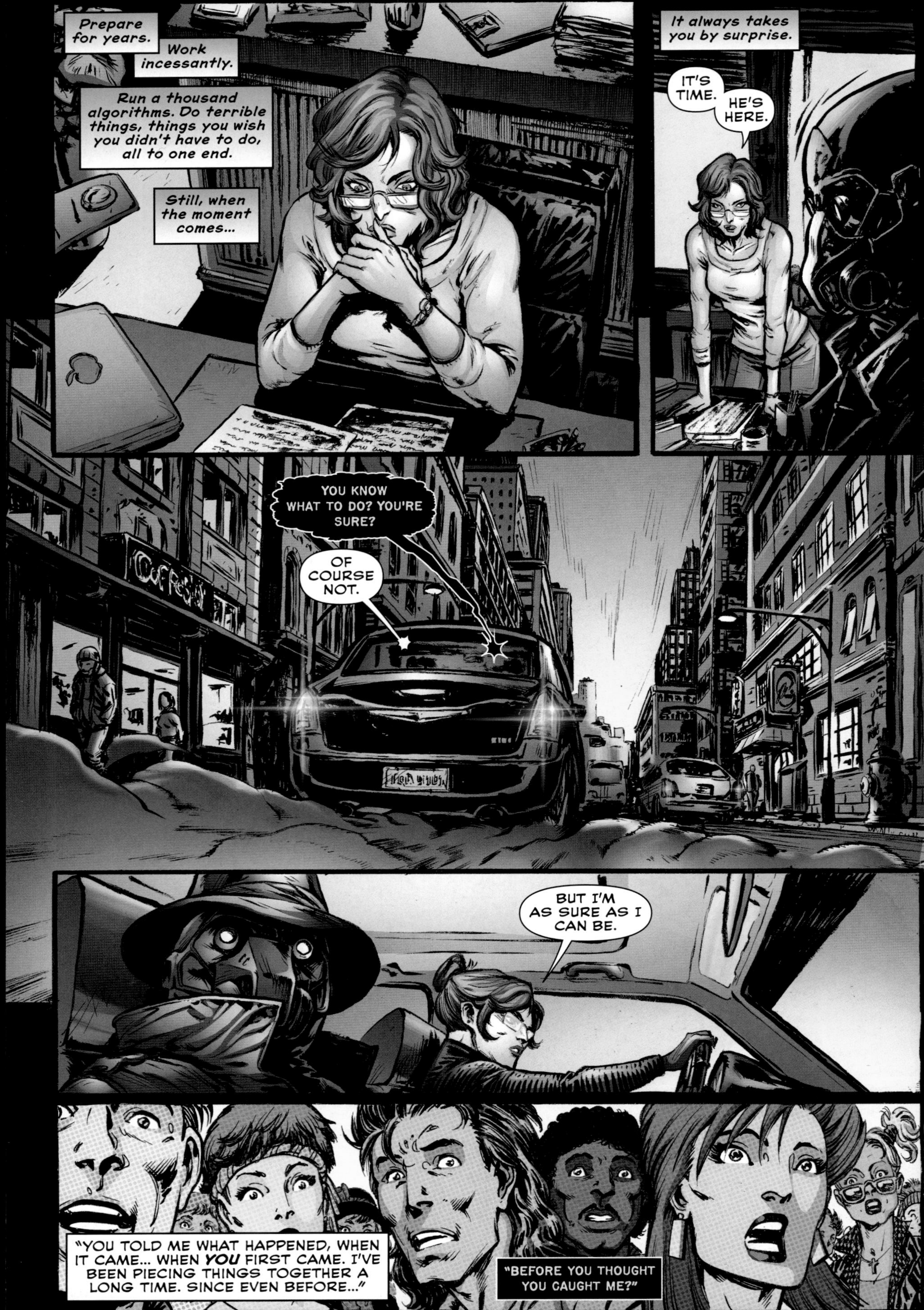
Prepare for years.
Work incessantly.
Run a thousand algorithms. Do terrible things, things you wish you didn't have to do, all to one end.
Still, when the moment comes...
It always takes you by surprise.
IT'S TIME.
HE'S HERE.
YOU KNOW WHAT TO DO? YOU'RE SURE?
OF COURSE NOT.
BUT I'M AS SURE AS I CAN BE.
"YOU TOLD ME WHAT HAPPENED, WHEN IT CAME... WHEN YOU FIRST CAME. I'VE BEEN PIECING THINGS TOGETHER A LONG TIME. SINCE EVEN BEFORE..."
"BEFORE YOU THOUGHT YOU CAUGHT ME?"

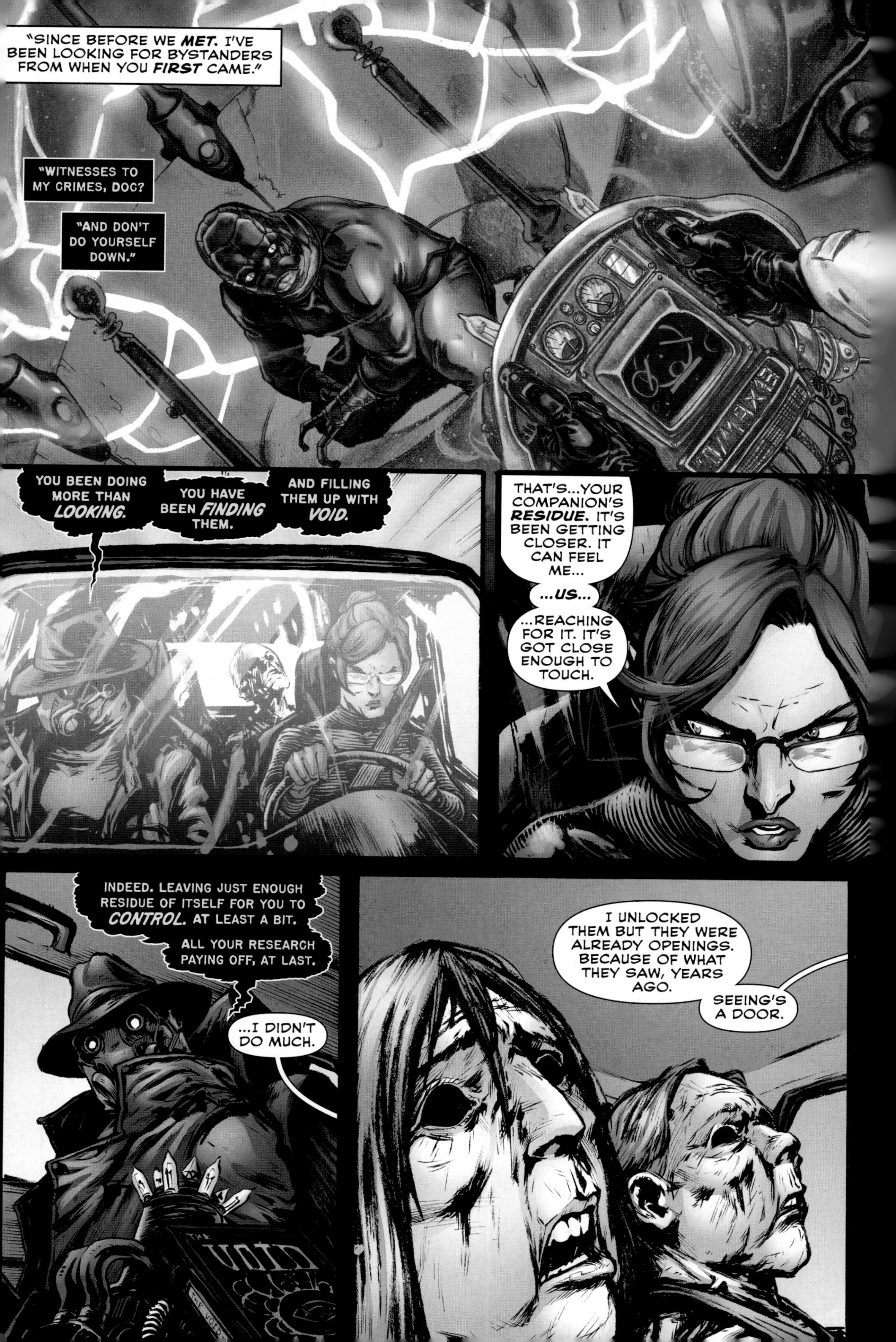
"SINCE BEFORE WE MET. I'VE BEEN LOOKING FOR BYSTANDERS FROM WHEN YOU FIRST CAME."
"WITNESSES TO MY CRIMES, DOC?
"AND DON'T DO YOURSELF DOWN."
YOU BEEN DOING MORE THAN LOOKING.
YOU HAVE BEEN FINDING THEM.
AND FILLING THEM UP WITH VOID.
THAT'S...YOUR COMPANION'S RESIDUE. IT'S BEEN GETTING CLOSER. IT CAN FEEL ME...
...US...
...REACHING FOR IT. IT'S GOT CLOSE ENOUGH TO TOUCH.
INDEED. LEAVING JUST ENOUGH RESIDUE OF ITSELF FOR YOU TO CONTROL. AT LEAST A BIT.
ALL YOUR RESEARCH PAYING OFF, AT LAST.
...I DIDN'T DO MUCH.
I UNLOCKED THEM BUT THEY WERE ALREADY OPENINGS. BECAUSE OF WHAT THEY SAW, YEARS AGO.
SEEING'S A DOOR.

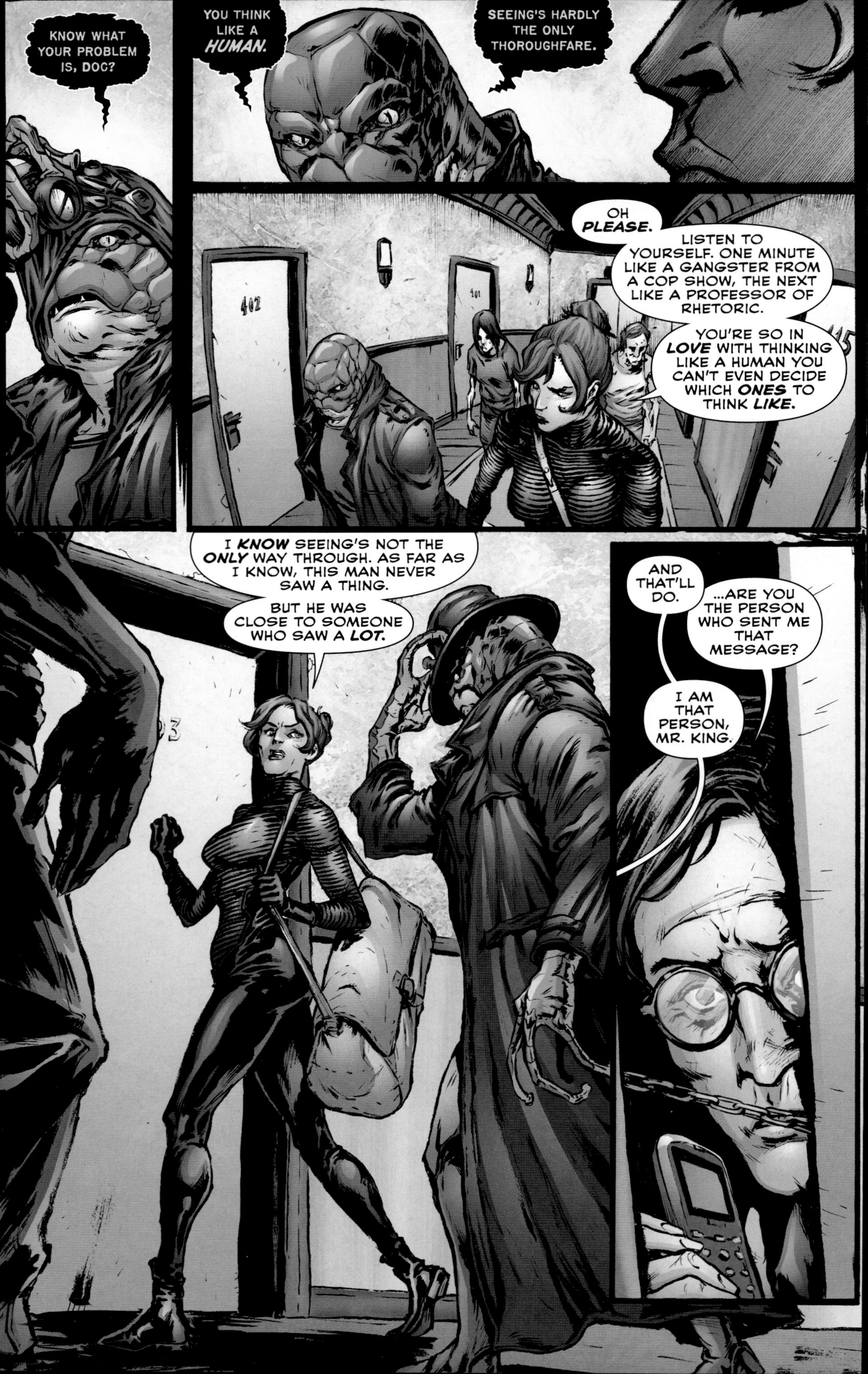
KNOW WHAT YOUR PROBLEM IS, DOC?
YOU THINK LIKE A *HUMAN.*
SEEING'S HARDLY THE ONLY THOROUGHFARE.
OH *PLEASE.*
LISTEN TO YOURSELF. ONE MINUTE LIKE A GANGSTER FROM A COP SHOW, THE NEXT LIKE A PROFESSOR OF RHETORIC.
YOU'RE SO IN *LOVE* WITH THINKING LIKE A HUMAN YOU CAN'T EVEN DECIDE WHICH *ONES* TO THINK *LIKE.*
I *KNOW* SEEING'S NOT THE *ONLY* WAY THROUGH. AS FAR AS I KNOW, THIS MAN NEVER SAW A THING.
BUT HE WAS CLOSE TO SOMEONE WHO SAW A *LOT.*
AND THAT'LL DO.
...ARE YOU THE PERSON WHO SENT ME THAT MESSAGE?
I AM THAT PERSON, MR. KING.

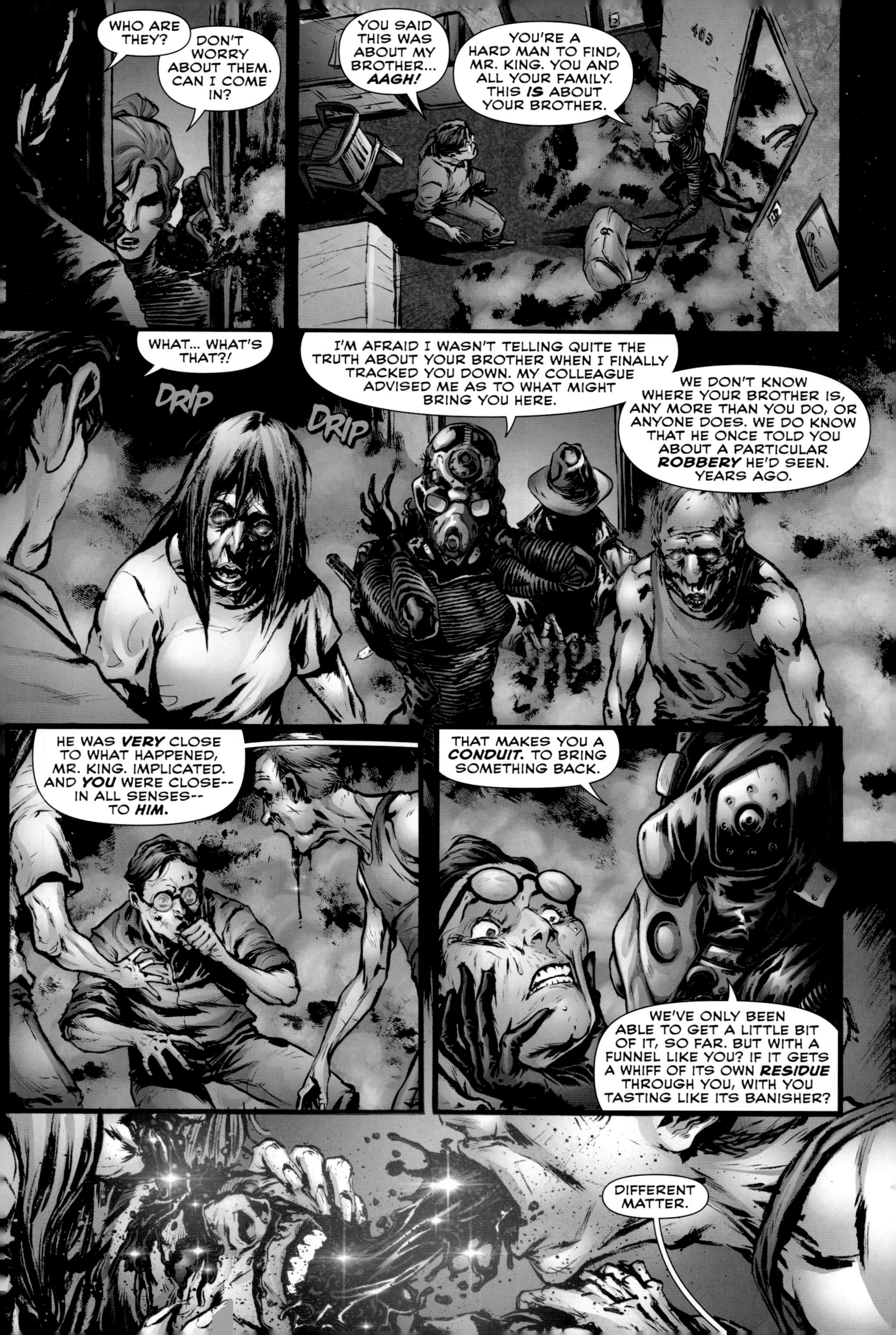
WHO ARE THEY?
DON'T WORRY ABOUT THEM. CAN I COME IN?
YOU SAID THIS WAS ABOUT MY BROTHER... AAGH!
YOU'RE A HARD MAN TO FIND, MR. KING. YOU AND ALL YOUR FAMILY. THIS IS ABOUT YOUR BROTHER.
403
WHAT... WHAT'S THAT?!
DRIP
DRIP
I'M AFRAID I WASN'T TELLING QUITE THE TRUTH ABOUT YOUR BROTHER WHEN I FINALLY TRACKED YOU DOWN. MY COLLEAGUE ADVISED ME AS TO WHAT MIGHT BRING YOU HERE.
WE DON'T KNOW WHERE YOUR BROTHER IS, ANY MORE THAN YOU DO, OR ANYONE DOES. WE DO KNOW THAT HE ONCE TOLD YOU ABOUT A PARTICULAR ROBBERY HE'D SEEN. YEARS AGO.
HE WAS VERY CLOSE TO WHAT HAPPENED, MR. KING. IMPLICATED. AND YOU WERE CLOSE-- IN ALL SENSES-- TO HIM.
THAT MAKES YOU A CONDUIT. TO BRING SOMETHING BACK.
WE'VE ONLY BEEN ABLE TO GET A LITTLE BIT OF IT, SO FAR. BUT WITH A FUNNEL LIKE YOU? IF IT GETS A WHIFF OF ITS OWN RESIDUE THROUGH YOU, WITH YOU TASTING LIKE ITS BANISHER?
DIFFERENT MATTER.

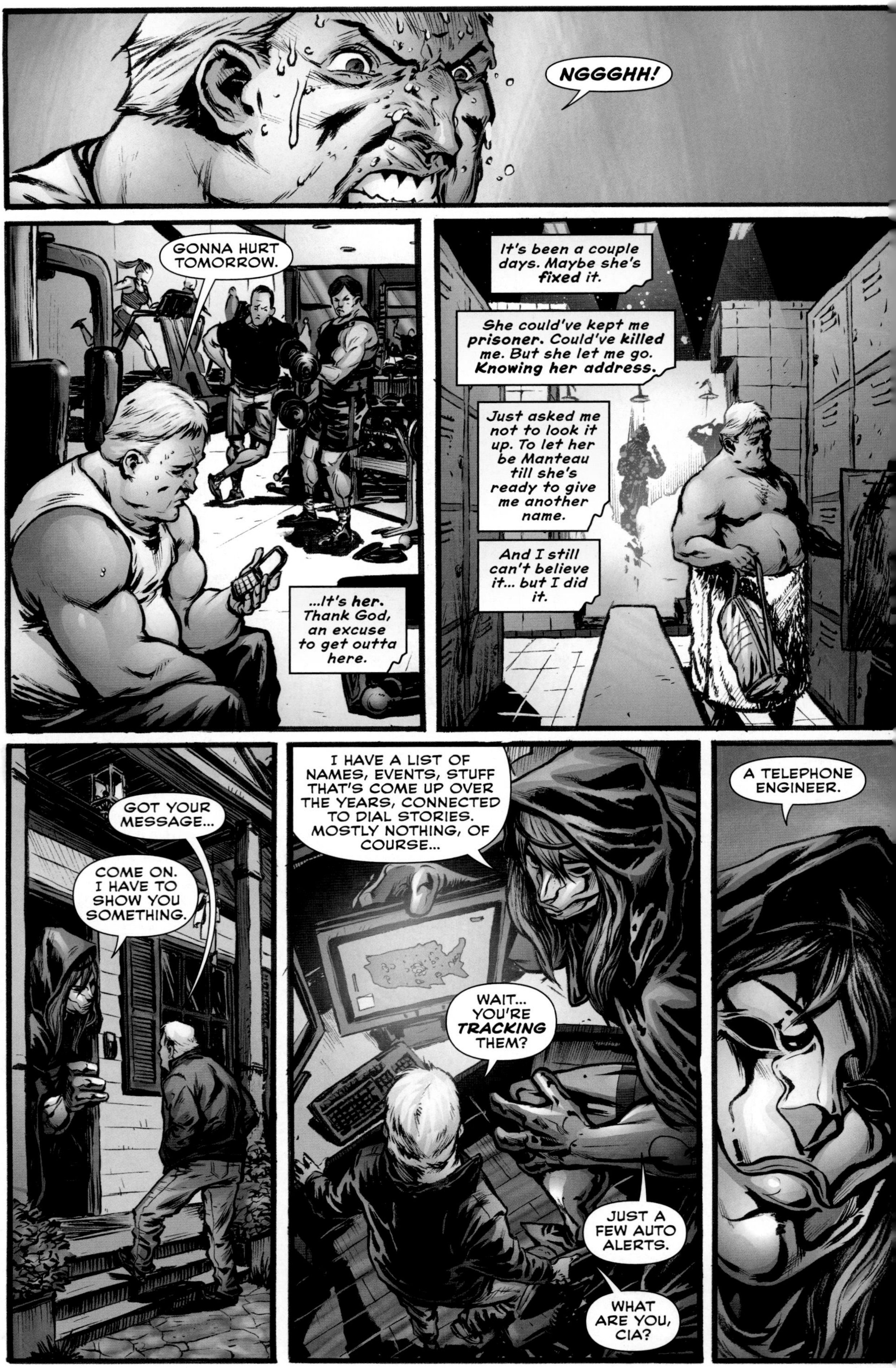
NGGGHH!
GONNA HURT TOMORROW.
...It's her. Thank God, an excuse to get outta here.
It's been a couple days. Maybe she's fixed it.
She could've kept me prisoner. Could've killed me. But she let me go. Knowing her address.
Just asked me not to look it up. To let her be Manteau till she's ready to give me another name.
And I still can't believe it... but I did it.
GOT YOUR MESSAGE...
COME ON. I HAVE TO SHOW YOU SOMETHING.
I HAVE A LIST OF NAMES, EVENTS, STUFF THAT'S COME UP OVER THE YEARS, CONNECTED TO DIAL STORIES. MOSTLY NOTHING, OF COURSE...
WAIT... YOU'RE TRACKING THEM?
JUST A FEW AUTO ALERTS.
WHAT ARE YOU, CIA?
A TELEPHONE ENGINEER.

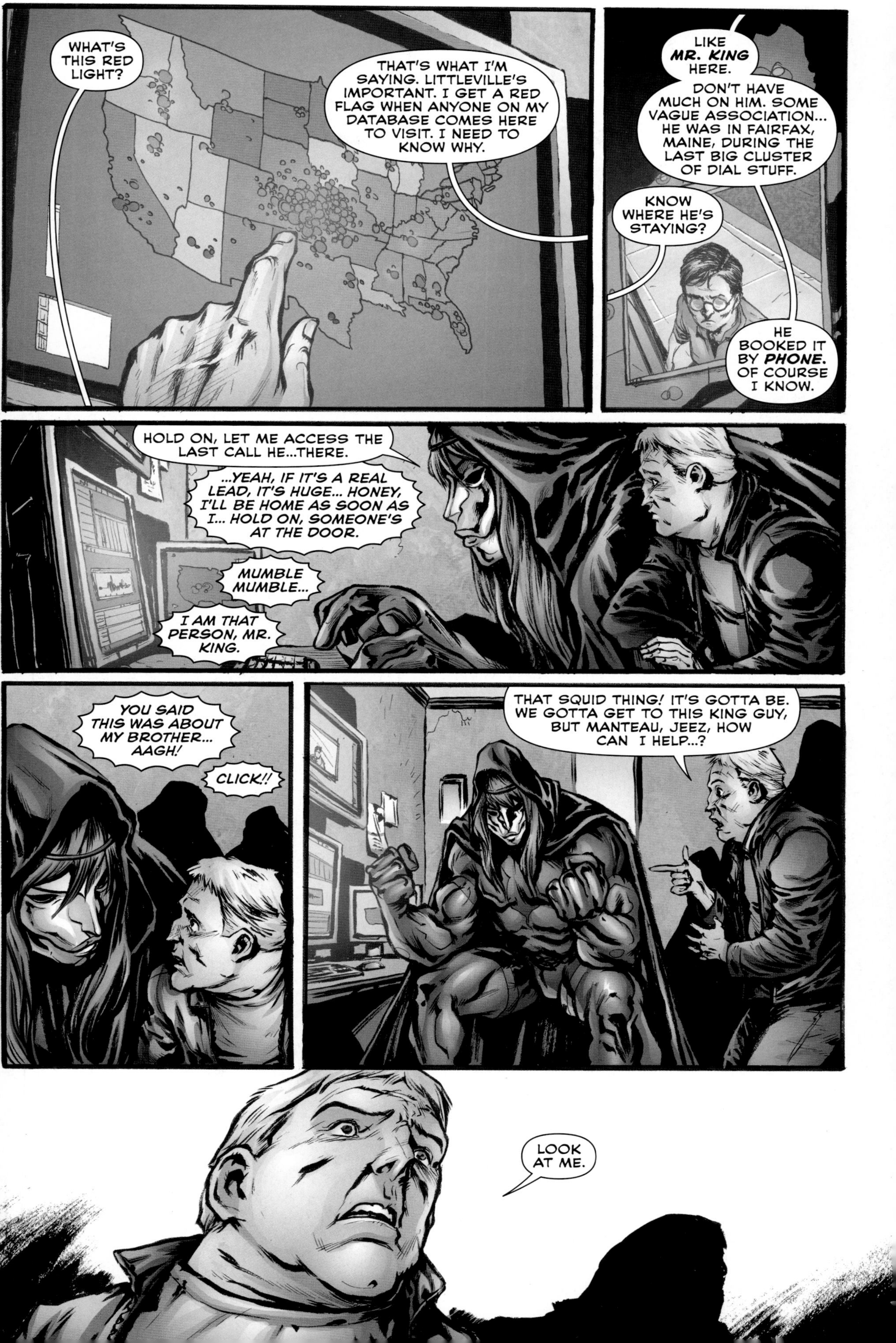
WHAT'S THIS RED LIGHT?
THAT'S WHAT I'M SAYING. LITTLEVILLE'S IMPORTANT. I GET A RED FLAG WHEN ANYONE ON MY DATABASE COMES HERE TO VISIT. I NEED TO KNOW WHY.
LIKE **MR. KING** HERE.
DON'T HAVE MUCH ON HIM. SOME VAGUE ASSOCIATION... HE WAS IN FAIRFAX, MAINE, DURING THE LAST BIG CLUSTER OF DIAL STUFF.
KNOW WHERE HE'S STAYING?
HE BOOKED IT BY ***PHONE.*** OF COURSE I KNOW.
HOLD ON, LET ME ACCESS THE LAST CALL HE...THERE.
...YEAH, IF IT'S A REAL LEAD, IT'S HUGE... HONEY, I'LL BE HOME AS SOON AS I... HOLD ON, SOMEONE'S AT THE DOOR.
MUMBLE MUMBLE...
I AM THAT PERSON, MR. KING.
YOU SAID THIS WAS ABOUT MY BROTHER... AAGH!
CLICK!!
THAT SQUID THING! IT'S GOTTA BE. WE GOTTA GET TO THIS KING GUY, BUT MANTEAU, JEEZ, HOW CAN I HELP...?
LOOK AT ME.

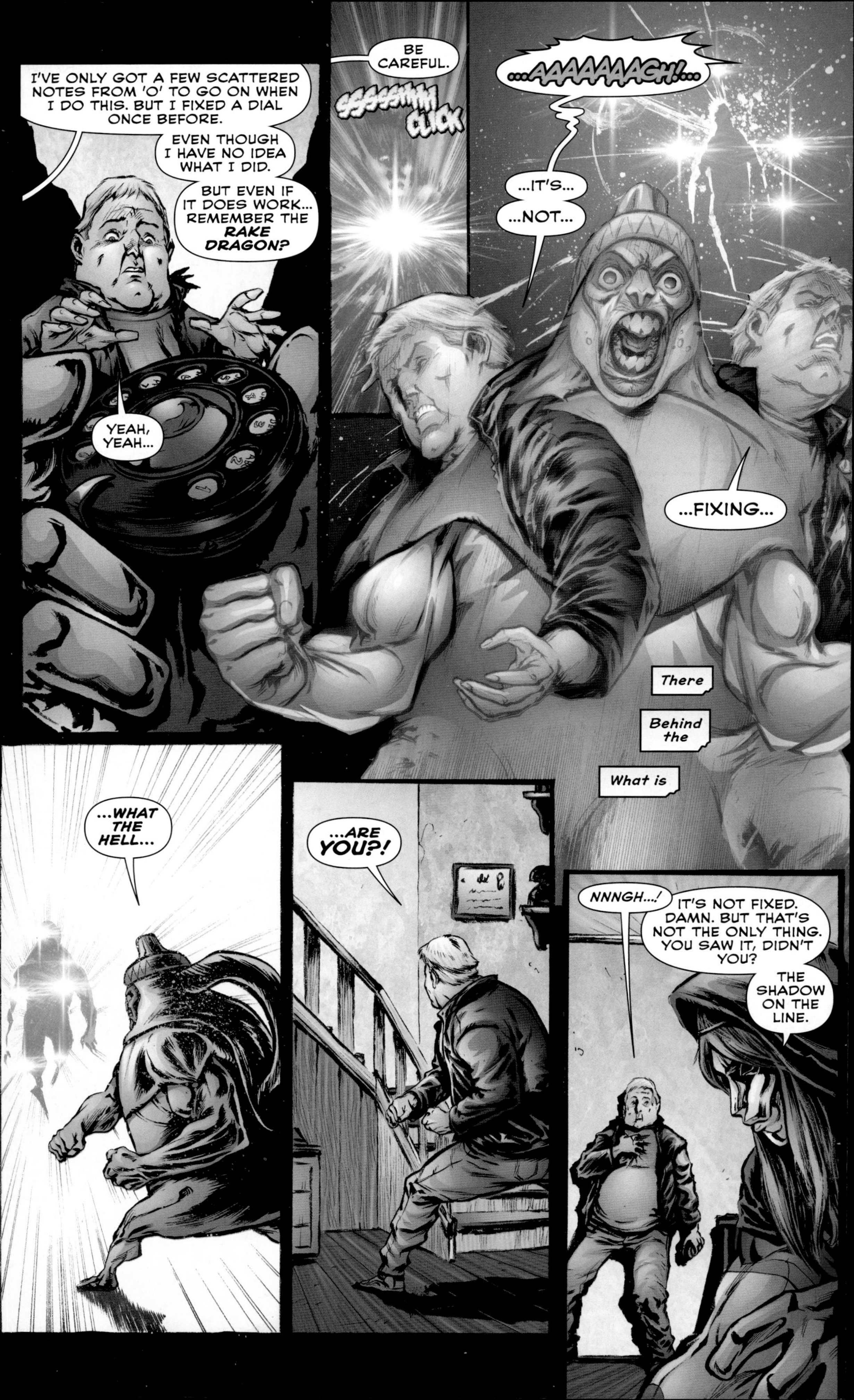
I'VE ONLY GOT A FEW SCATTERED NOTES FROM 'O' TO GO ON WHEN I DO THIS. BUT I FIXED A DIAL ONCE BEFORE.
EVEN THOUGH I HAVE NO IDEA WHAT I DID.
BUT EVEN IF IT DOES WORK... REMEMBER THE RAKE DRAGON?
YEAH, YEAH...
BE CAREFUL.
SSSSSHHH
CLICK
...AAAAAAAGH!...
...IT'S...
...NOT...
...FIXING...
There
Behind the
What is
...WHAT THE HELL...
...ARE YOU?!
NNNGH...!
IT'S NOT FIXED. DAMN. BUT THAT'S NOT THE ONLY THING. YOU SAW IT, DIDN'T YOU?
THE SHADOW ON THE LINE.

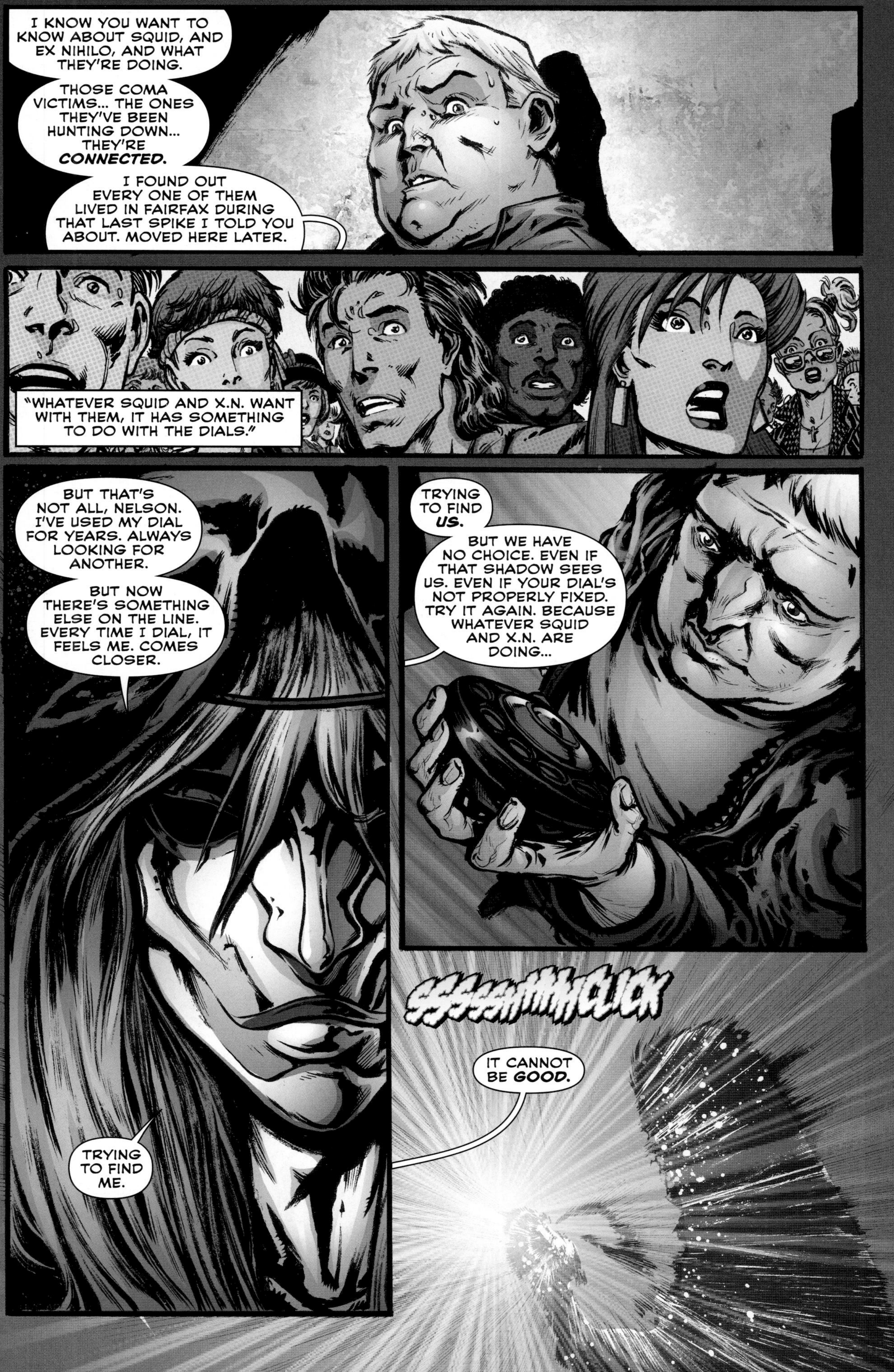

I KNOW YOU WANT TO KNOW ABOUT SQUID, AND EX NIHILO, AND WHAT THEY'RE DOING.
THOSE COMA VICTIMS... THE ONES THEY'VE BEEN HUNTING DOWN... THEY'RE ***CONNECTED.***
I FOUND OUT EVERY ONE OF THEM LIVED IN FAIRFAX DURING THAT LAST SPIKE I TOLD YOU ABOUT. MOVED HERE LATER.
"WHATEVER SQUID AND X.N. WANT WITH THEM, IT HAS SOMETHING TO DO WITH THE DIALS."
BUT THAT'S NOT ALL, NELSON. I'VE USED MY DIAL FOR YEARS. ALWAYS LOOKING FOR ANOTHER.
BUT NOW THERE'S SOMETHING ELSE ON THE LINE. EVERY TIME I DIAL, IT FEELS ME. COMES CLOSER.
TRYING TO FIND ME.
TRYING TO FIND ***US.***
BUT WE HAVE NO CHOICE. EVEN IF THAT SHADOW SEES US. EVEN IF YOUR DIAL'S NOT PROPERLY FIXED. TRY IT AGAIN. BECAUSE WHATEVER SQUID AND X.N. ARE DOING...
SSSSSHHHHCLICK
IT CANNOT BE ***GOOD.***

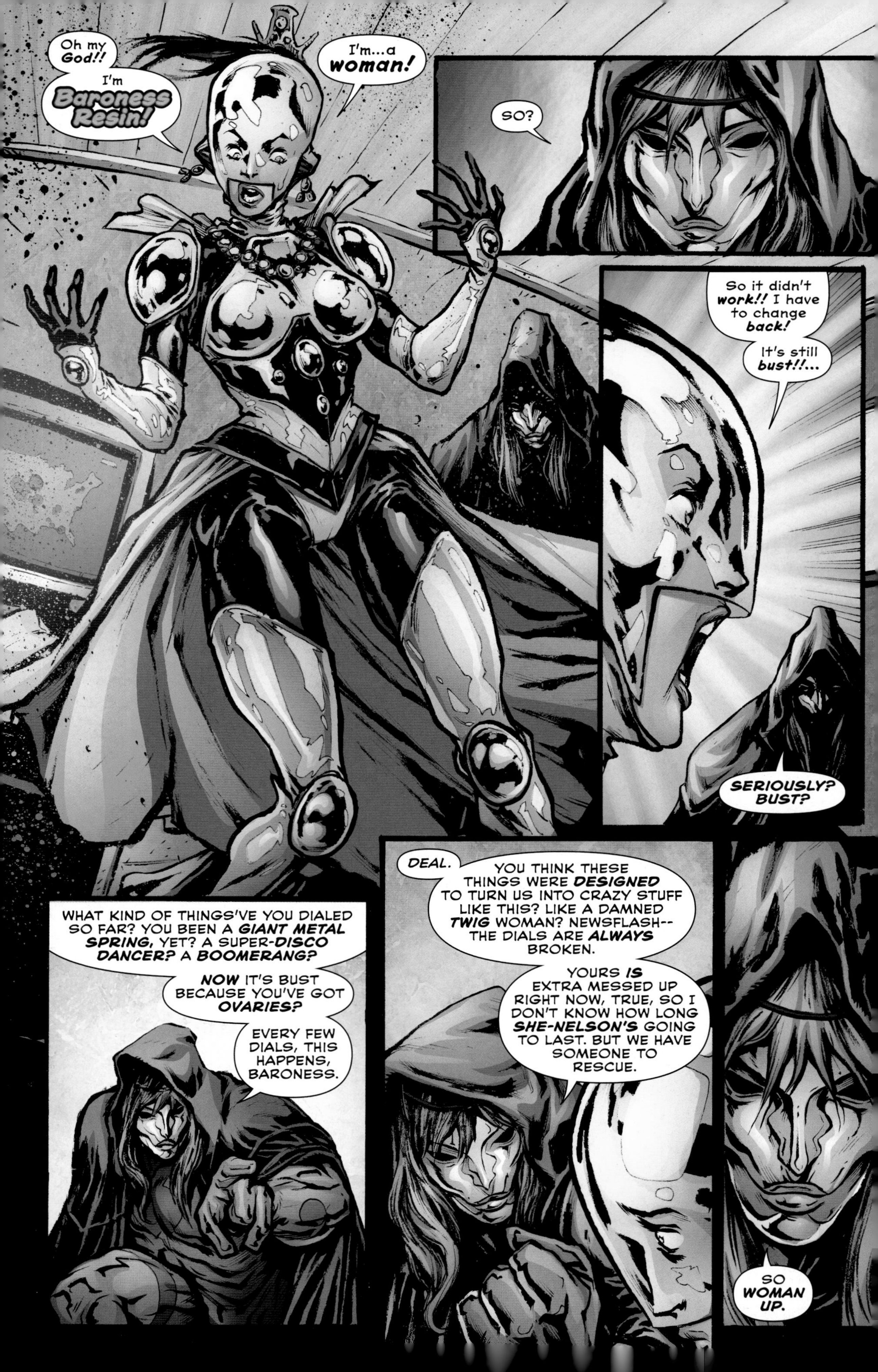
Oh my God!! I'm
Baroness Resin!
I'm...a woman!
SO?
So it didn't work!! I have to change back!
It's still bust!!...
SERIOUSLY? BUST?
WHAT KIND OF THINGS'VE YOU DIALED SO FAR? YOU BEEN A GIANT METAL SPRING, YET? A SUPER-DISCO DANCER? A BOOMERANG?
NOW IT'S BUST BECAUSE YOU'VE GOT OVARIES?
EVERY FEW DIALS, THIS HAPPENS, BARONESS.
DEAL.
YOU THINK THESE THINGS WERE DESIGNED TO TURN US INTO CRAZY STUFF LIKE THIS? LIKE A DAMNED TWIG WOMAN? NEWSFLASH-- THE DIALS ARE ALWAYS BROKEN.
YOURS IS EXTRA MESSED UP RIGHT NOW, TRUE, SO I DON'T KNOW HOW LONG SHE-NELSON'S GOING TO LAST. BUT WE HAVE SOMEONE TO RESCUE.
SO WOMAN UP.

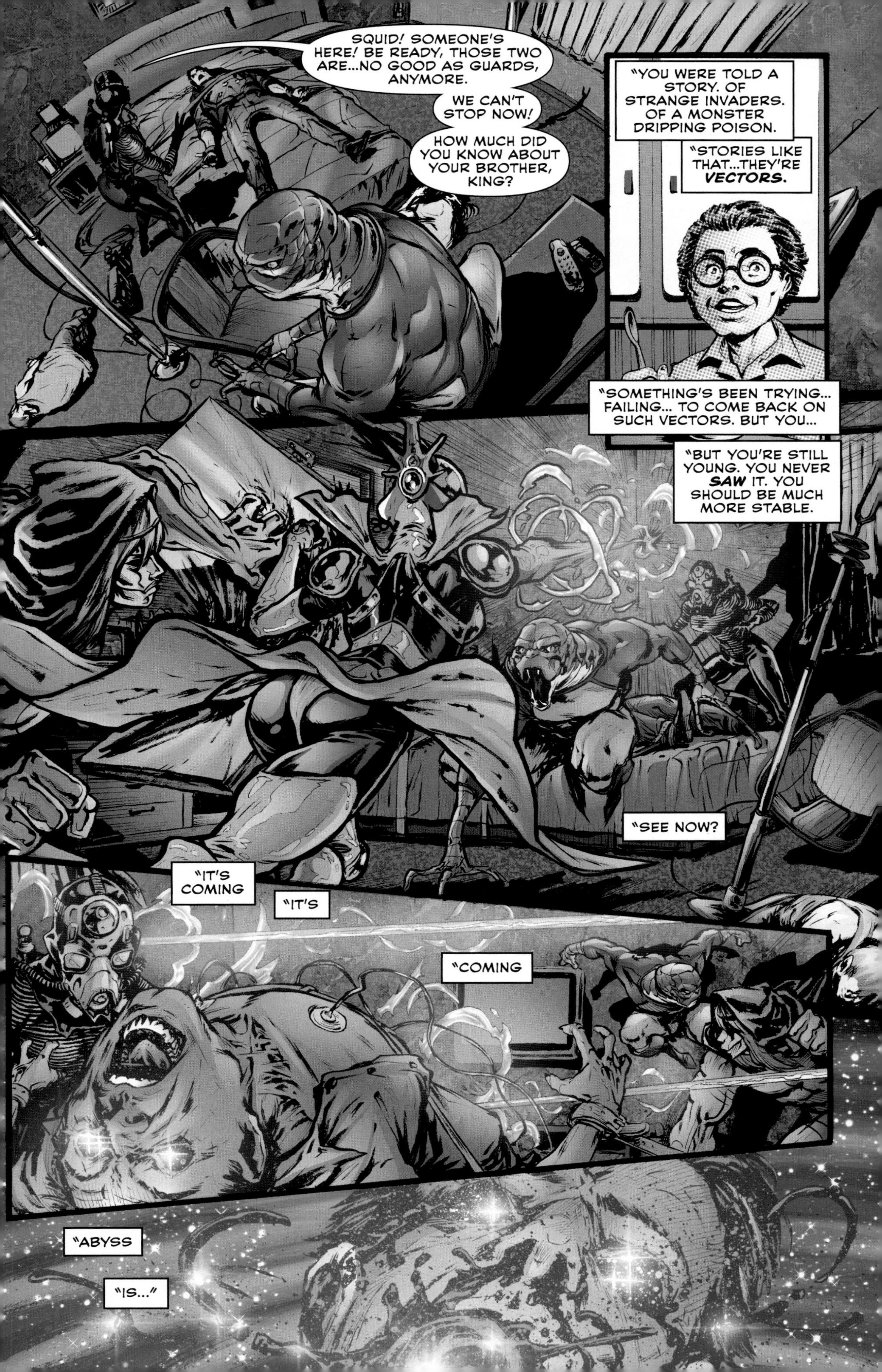
SQUID! SOMEONE'S HERE! BE READY, THOSE TWO ARE...NO GOOD AS GUARDS, ANYMORE.
WE CAN'T STOP NOW!
HOW MUCH DID YOU KNOW ABOUT YOUR BROTHER, KING?
"YOU WERE TOLD A STORY. OF STRANGE INVADERS. OF A MONSTER DRIPPING POISON.
"STORIES LIKE THAT...THEY'RE VECTORS.
"SOMETHING'S BEEN TRYING... FAILING... TO COME BACK ON SUCH VECTORS. BUT YOU...
"BUT YOU'RE STILL YOUNG. YOU NEVER SAW IT. YOU SHOULD BE MUCH MORE STABLE.
"SEE NOW?
"IT'S COMING
"IT'S
"COMING
"ABYSS
"IS..."

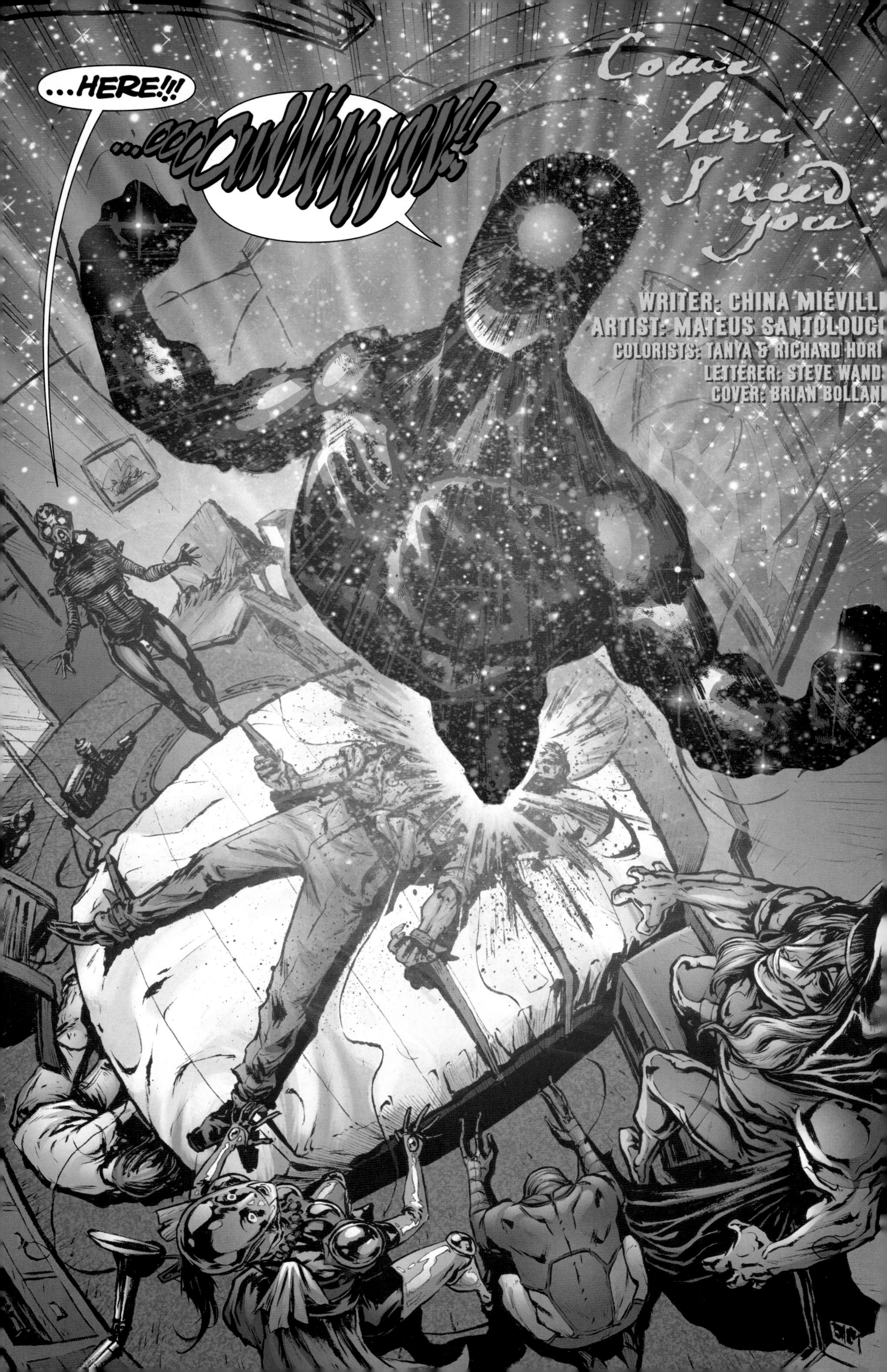
...HERE!!!
Come here! I need you!
WRITER: CHINA MIÉVILL
ARTIST: MATEUS SANTOLOUC
COLORISTS: TANYA & RICHARD HORI
LETTERER: STEVE WAND
COVER: BRIAN BOLLAN

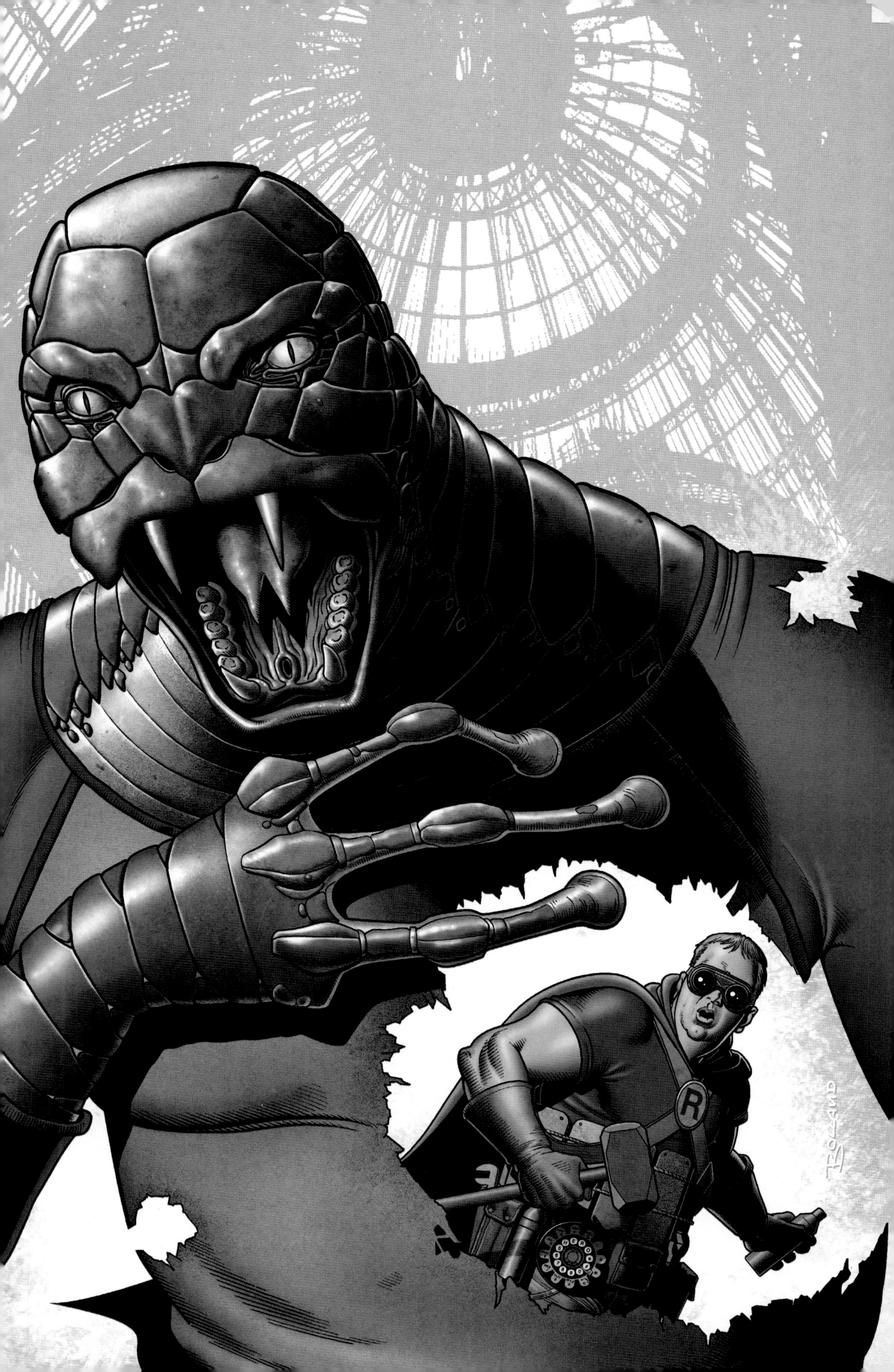
BOLLAND

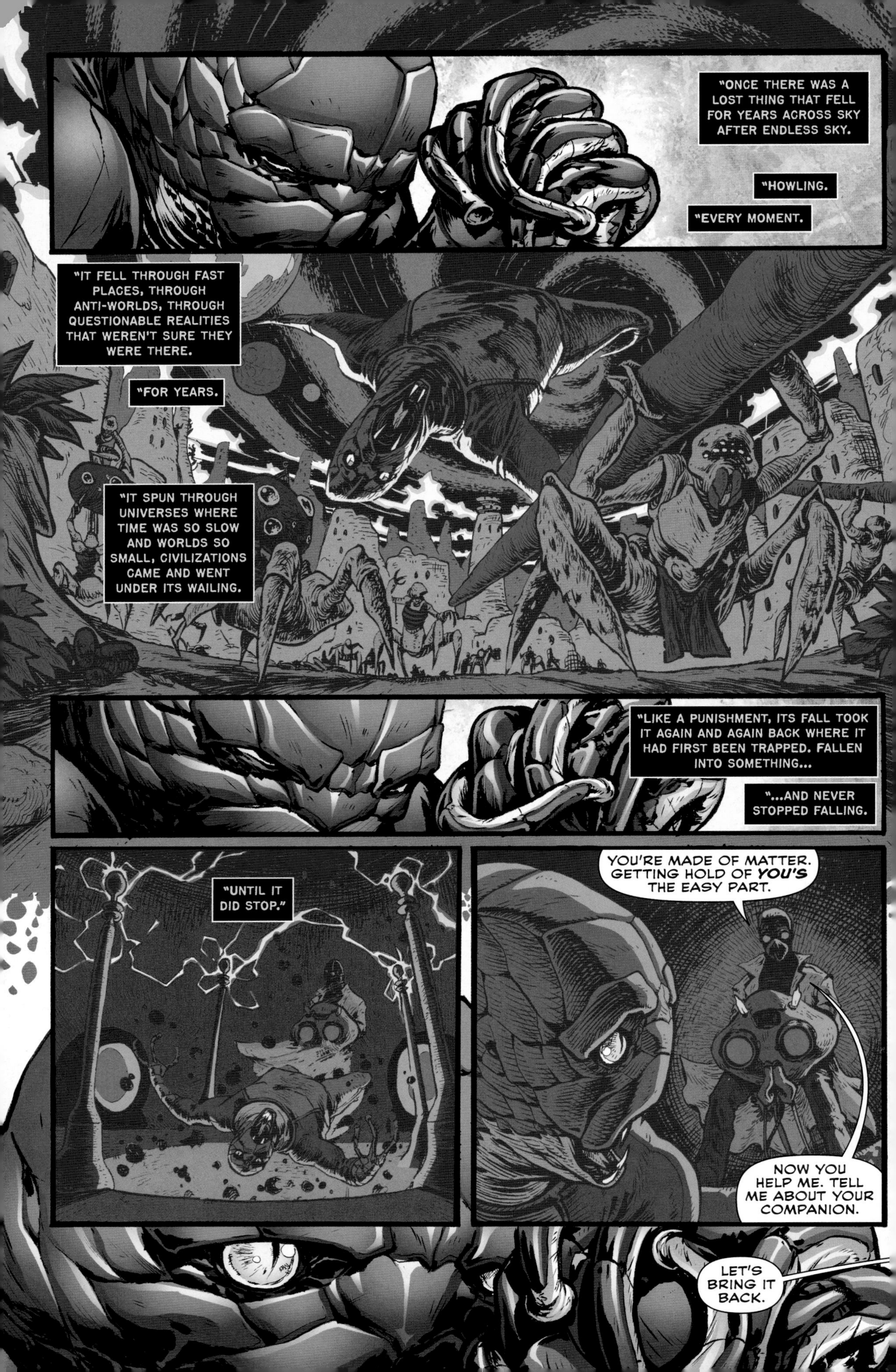
"ONCE THERE WAS A LOST THING THAT FELL FOR YEARS ACROSS SKY AFTER ENDLESS SKY.
"HOWLING.
"EVERY MOMENT.
"IT FELL THROUGH FAST PLACES, THROUGH ANTI-WORLDS, THROUGH QUESTIONABLE REALITIES THAT WEREN'T SURE THEY WERE THERE.
"FOR YEARS.
"IT SPUN THROUGH UNIVERSES WHERE TIME WAS SO SLOW AND WORLDS SO SMALL, CIVILIZATIONS CAME AND WENT UNDER ITS WAILING.
"LIKE A PUNISHMENT, ITS FALL TOOK IT AGAIN AND AGAIN BACK WHERE IT HAD FIRST BEEN TRAPPED. FALLEN INTO SOMETHING...
"...AND NEVER STOPPED FALLING.
"UNTIL IT DID STOP."
YOU'RE MADE OF MATTER. GETTING HOLD OF *YOU'S* THE EASY PART.
NOW YOU HELP ME. TELL ME ABOUT YOUR COMPANION.
LET'S BRING IT BACK.

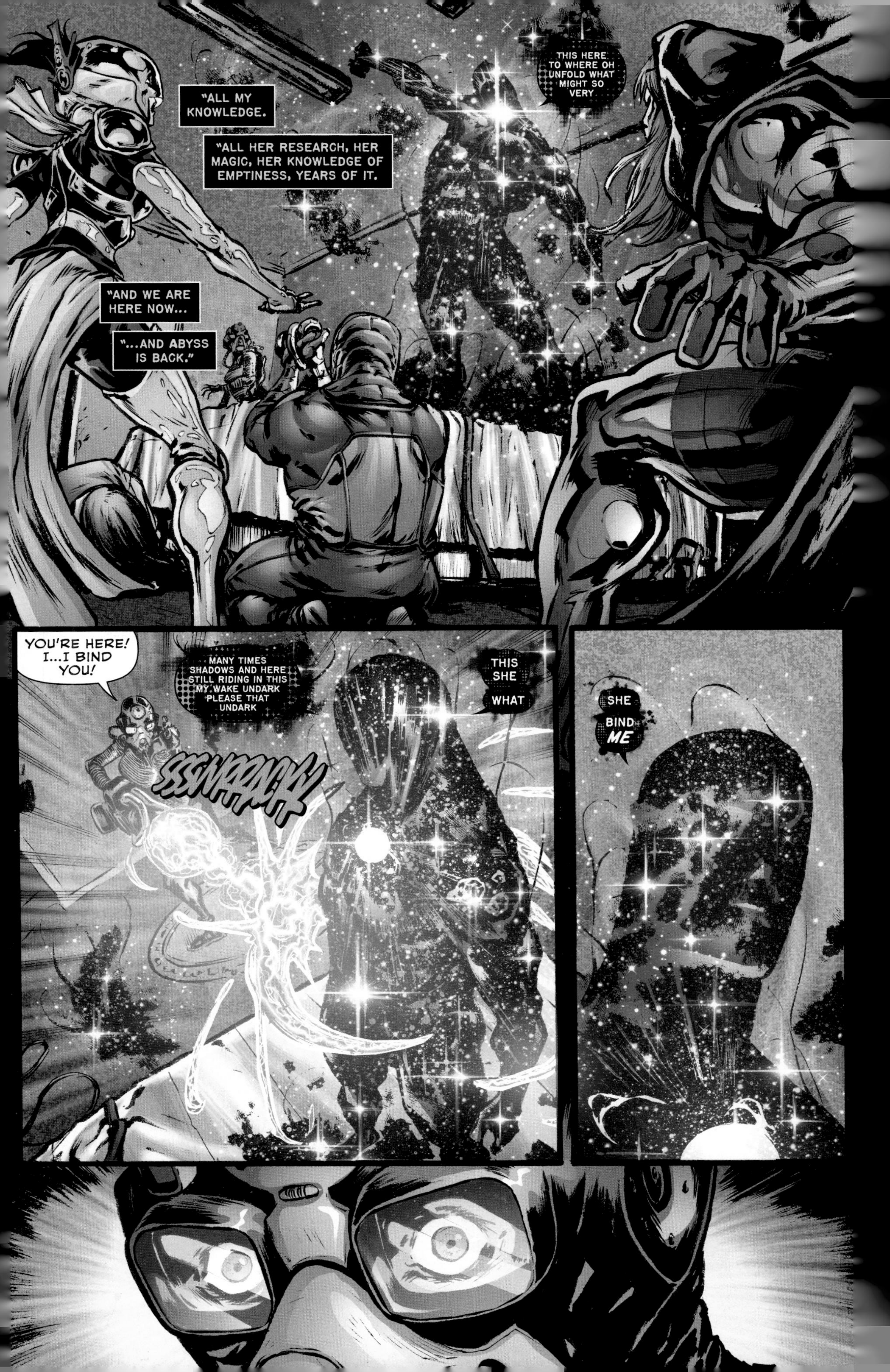

"ALL MY KNOWLEDGE.
"ALL HER RESEARCH, HER MAGIC, HER KNOWLEDGE OF EMPTINESS, YEARS OF IT.
THIS HERE TO WHERE OH UNFOLD WHAT MIGHT SO VERY
"AND WE ARE HERE NOW...
"...AND ABYSS IS BACK."
YOU'RE HERE! I...I BIND YOU!
MANY TIMES SHADOWS AND HERE STILL RIDING IN THIS MY WAKE UNDARK PLEASE THAT UNDARK
THIS SHE
WHAT
SSSNARRACKK
SHE
BIND ME

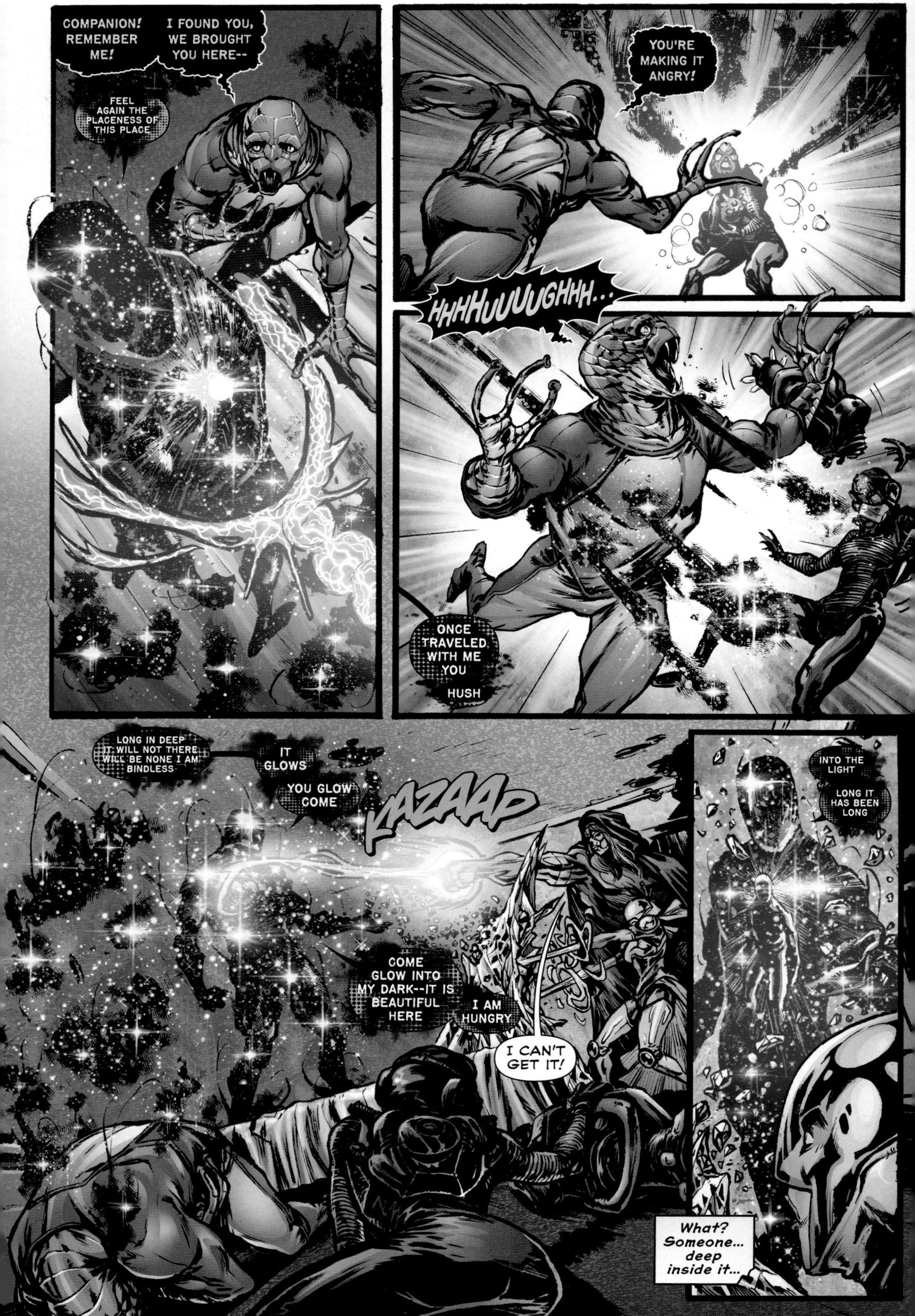
COMPANION! REMEMBER ME!
I FOUND YOU, WE BROUGHT YOU HERE--
FEEL AGAIN THE PLACENESS OF THIS PLACE
YOU'RE MAKING IT ANGRY!
HHHHUUUUGHHH...
ONCE TRAVELED WITH ME YOU
HUSH
LONG IN DEEP IT WILL NOT THERE WILL BE NONE I AM BINDLESS
IT GLOWS
YOU GLOW COME
KAZAAP
COME GLOW INTO MY DARK--IT IS BEAUTIFUL HERE
I AM HUNGRY
I CAN'T GET IT!
INTO THE LIGHT
LONG IT HAS BEEN LONG
What? Someone... deep inside it...

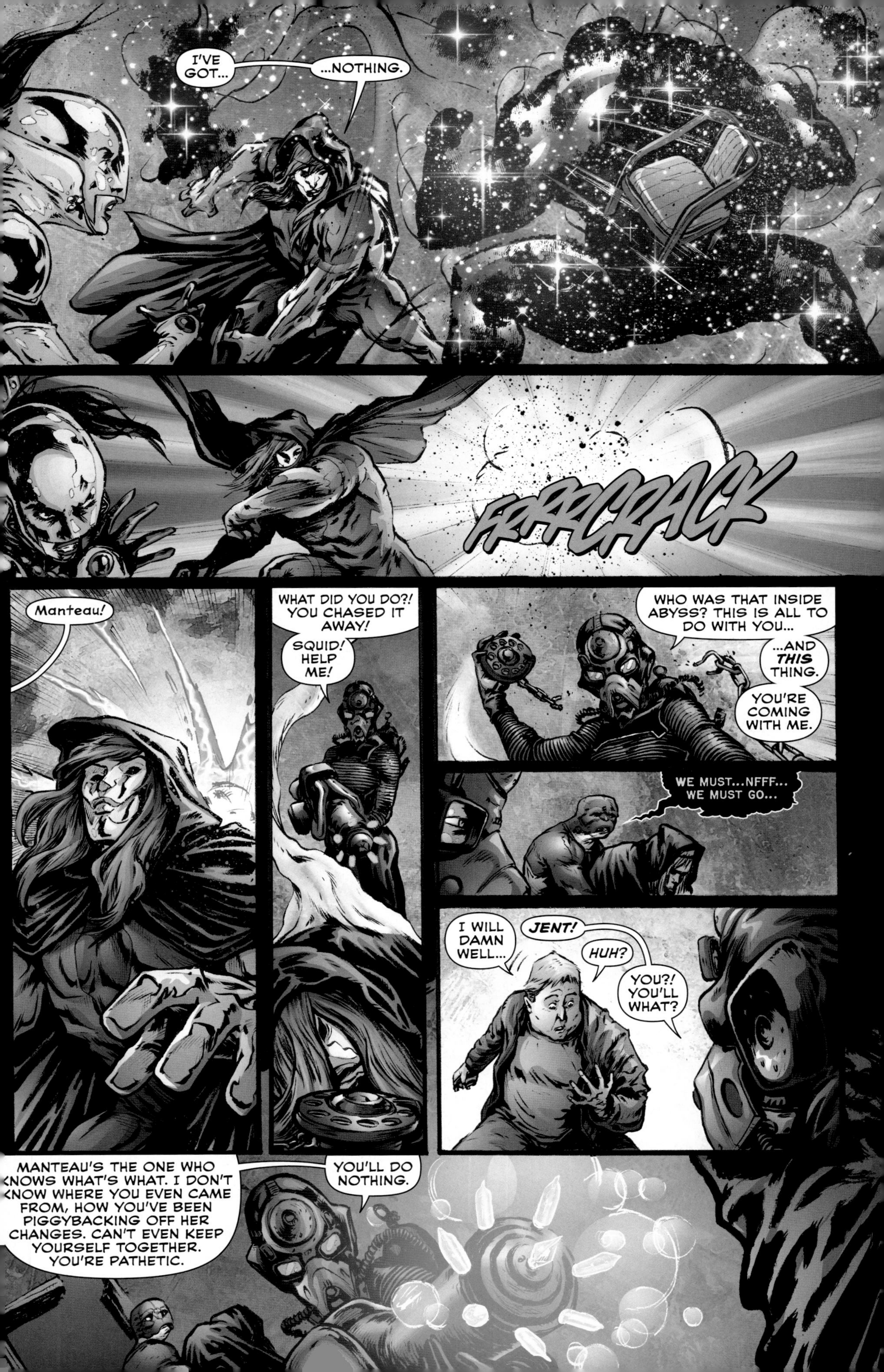

I'VE GOT...
...NOTHING.
FRRRCRACK
Manteau!
WHAT DID YOU DO?! YOU CHASED IT AWAY!
SQUID! HELP ME!
WHO WAS THAT INSIDE ABYSS? THIS IS ALL TO DO WITH YOU...
...AND THIS THING.
YOU'RE COMING WITH ME.
WE MUST...NFFF... WE MUST GO...
I WILL DAMN WELL...
JENT!
HUH?
YOU?! YOU'LL WHAT?
YOU'LL DO NOTHING.
MANTEAU'S THE ONE WHO KNOWS WHAT'S WHAT. I DON'T KNOW WHERE YOU EVEN CAME FROM, HOW YOU'VE BEEN PIGGYBACKING OFF HER CHANGES. CAN'T EVEN KEEP YOURSELF TOGETHER. YOU'RE PATHETIC.

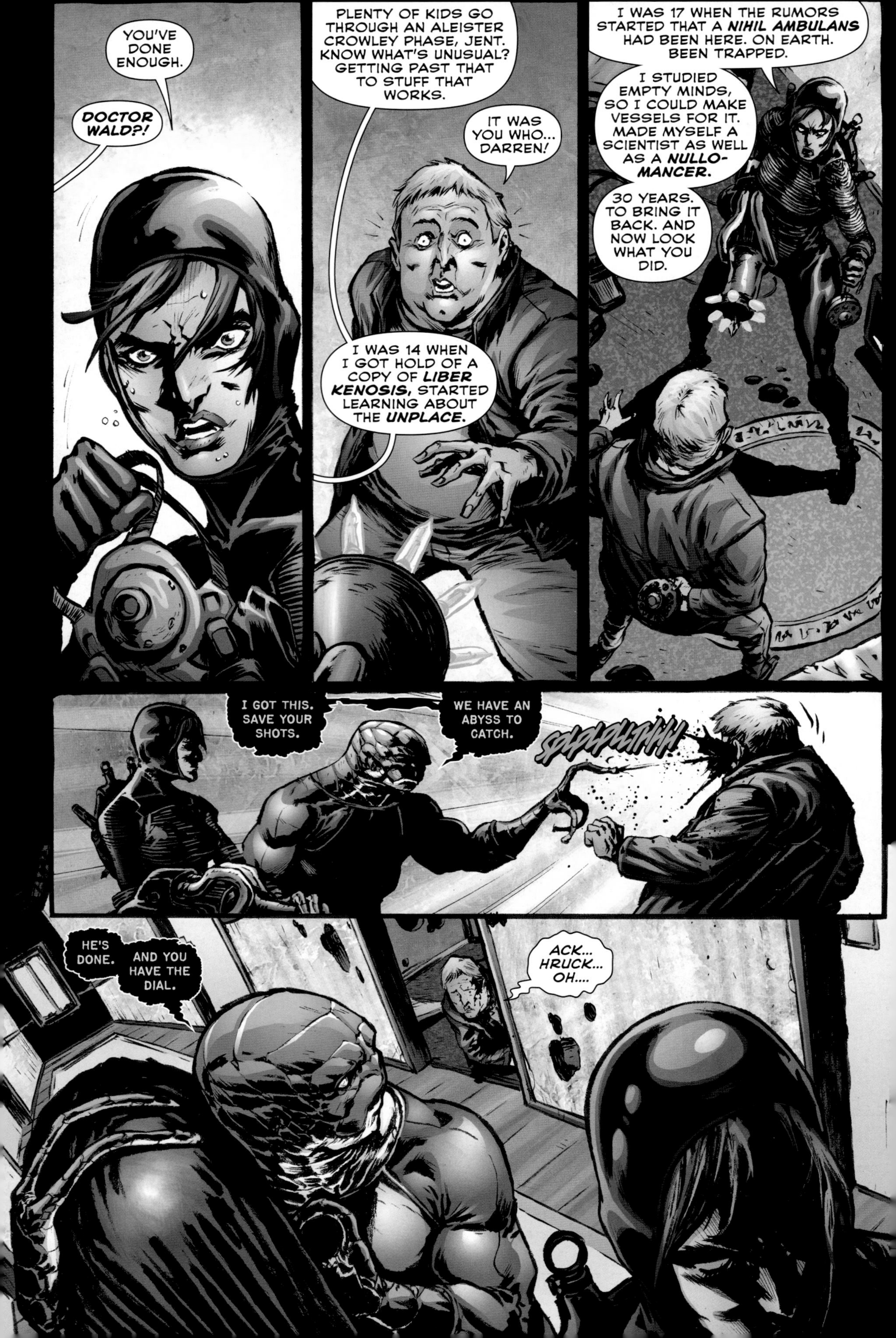
YOU'VE DONE ENOUGH.
DOCTOR WALD?!
PLENTY OF KIDS GO THROUGH AN ALEISTER CROWLEY PHASE, JENT. KNOW WHAT'S UNUSUAL? GETTING PAST THAT TO STUFF THAT WORKS.
IT WAS YOU WHO... DARREN!
I WAS 14 WHEN I GOT HOLD OF A COPY OF LIBER KENOSIS, STARTED LEARNING ABOUT THE UNPLACE.
I WAS 17 WHEN THE RUMORS STARTED THAT A NIHIL AMBULANS HAD BEEN HERE. ON EARTH. BEEN TRAPPED.
I STUDIED EMPTY MINDS, SO I COULD MAKE VESSELS FOR IT. MADE MYSELF A SCIENTIST AS WELL AS A NULLO-MANCER.
30 YEARS. TO BRING IT BACK. AND NOW LOOK WHAT YOU DID.
I GOT THIS. SAVE YOUR SHOTS.
WE HAVE AN ABYSS TO CATCH.
SPLPLPLUTHHH!
HE'S DONE.
AND YOU HAVE THE DIAL.
ACK... HRUCK... OH....

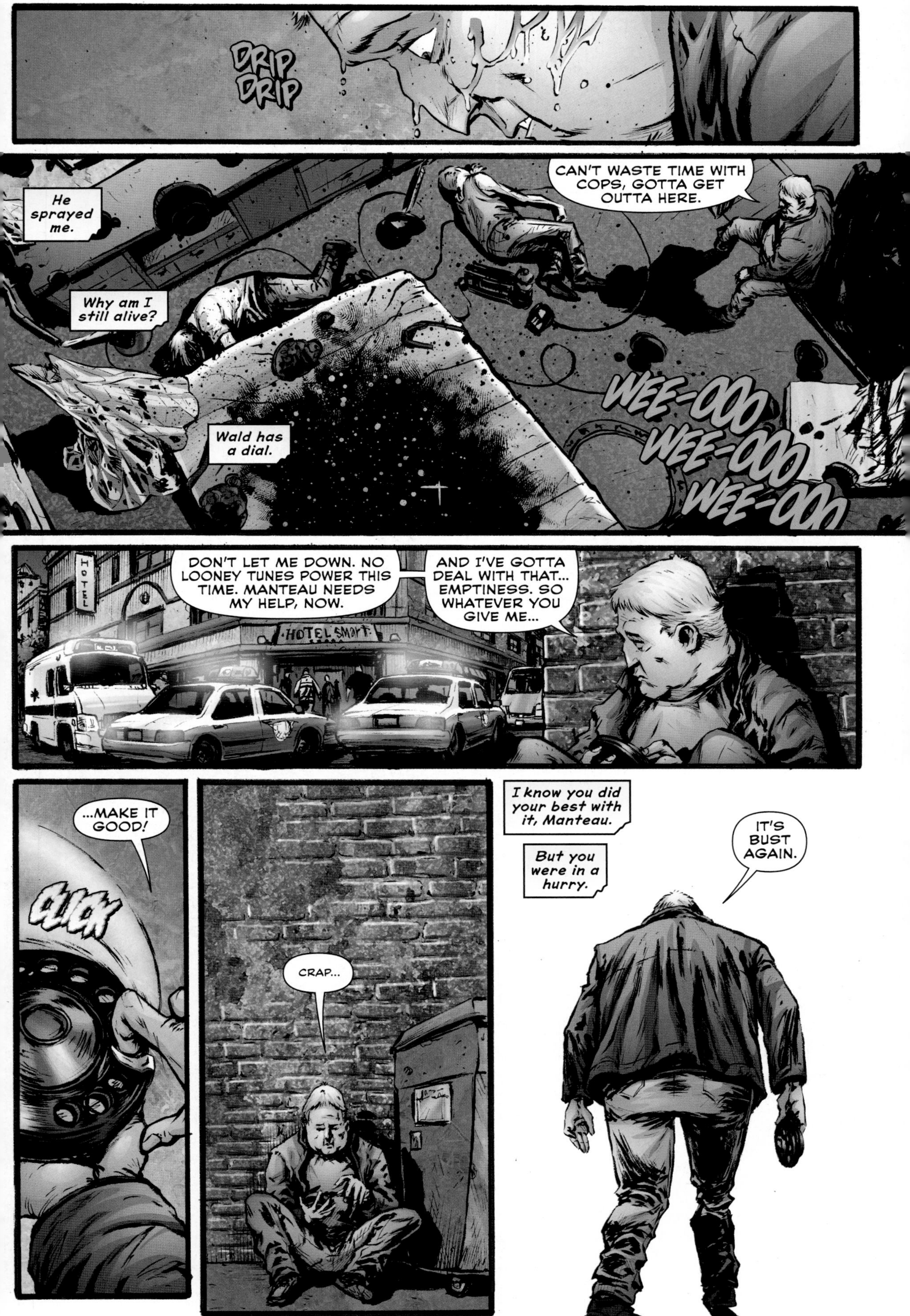
DRIP DRIP
He sprayed me.
Why am I still alive?
Wald has a dial.
CAN'T WASTE TIME WITH COPS, GOTTA GET OUTTA HERE.
WEE-OOO WEE-OOO WEE-OOO
HOTEL
HOTEL SMART
DON'T LET ME DOWN. NO LOONEY TUNES POWER THIS TIME. MANTEAU NEEDS MY HELP, NOW.
AND I'VE GOTTA DEAL WITH THAT... EMPTINESS. SO WHATEVER YOU GIVE ME...
...MAKE IT GOOD!
CLICK
CRAP...
I know you did your best with it, Manteau.
But you were in a hurry.
IT'S BUST AGAIN.

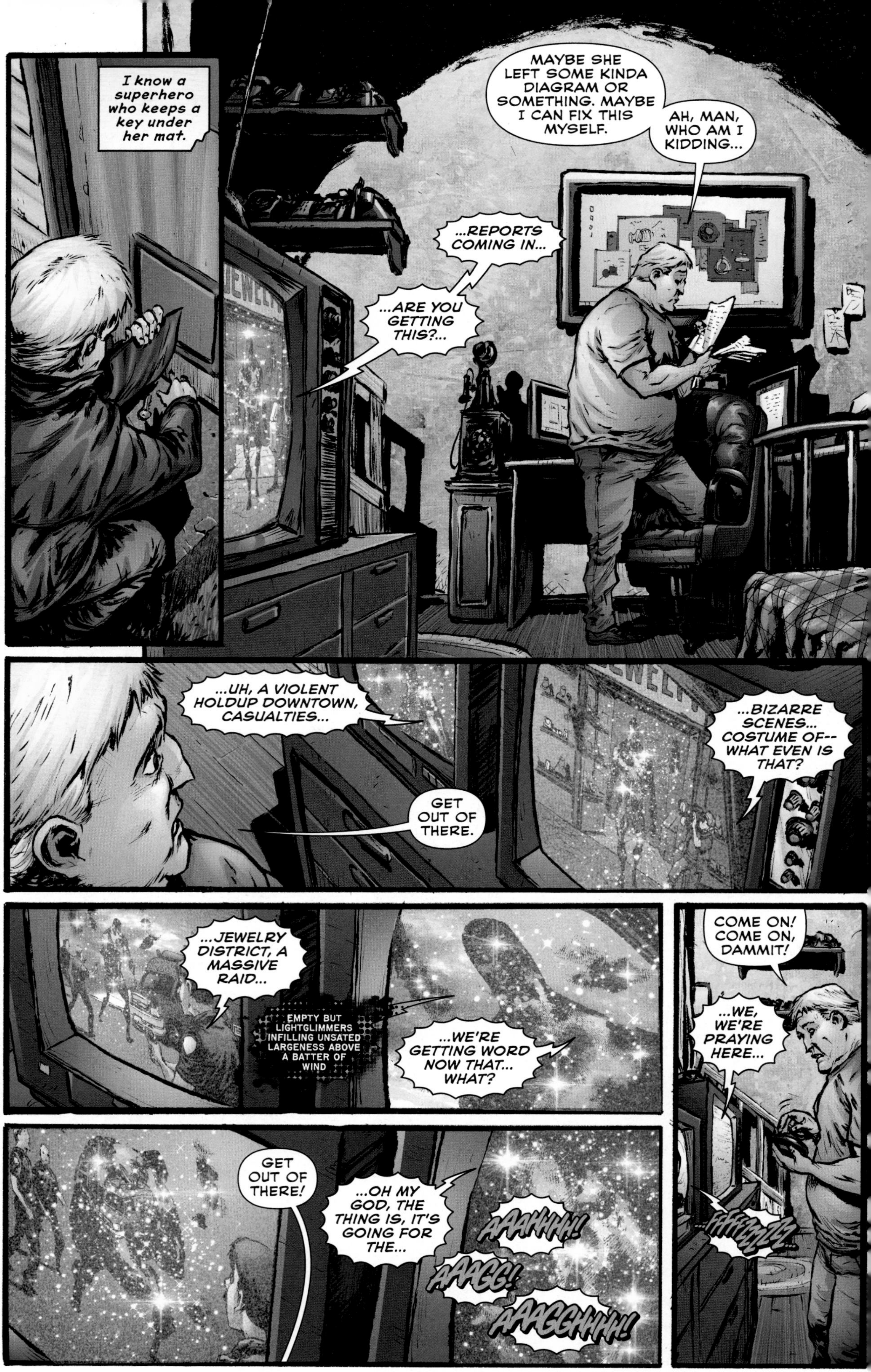
I know a superhero who keeps a key under her mat.
MAYBE SHE LEFT SOME KINDA DIAGRAM OR SOMETHING. MAYBE I CAN FIX THIS MYSELF.
AH, MAN, WHO AM I KIDDING...
...REPORTS COMING IN...
...ARE YOU GETTING THIS?...
...UH, A VIOLENT HOLDUP DOWNTOWN, CASUALTIES...
GET OUT OF THERE.
...BIZARRE SCENES... COSTUME OF-- WHAT EVEN IS THAT?
...JEWELRY DISTRICT, A MASSIVE RAID...
EMPTY BUT LIGHTGLIMMERS INFILLING UNSATED LARGENESS ABOVE A BATTER OF WIND
...WE'RE GETTING WORD NOW THAT... WHAT?
COME ON! COME ON, DAMMIT!
...WE, WE'RE PRAYING HERE...
GET OUT OF THERE!
...OH MY GOD, THE THING IS, IT'S GOING FOR THE...
AAAHHHH!
AAAGG!
AAAGGHHHH!

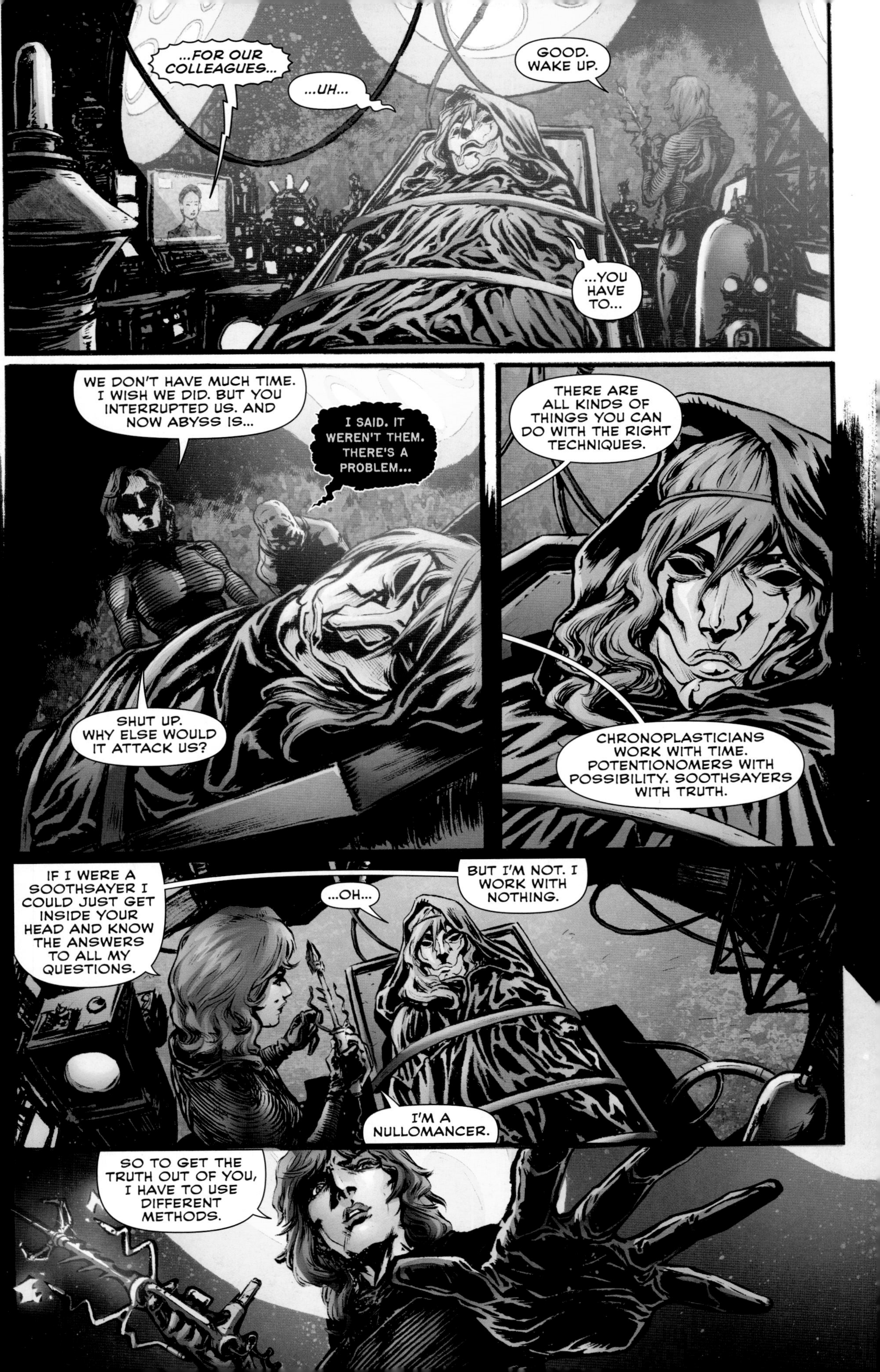
...FOR OUR COLLEAGUES...
...UH...
GOOD. WAKE UP.
...YOU HAVE TO...
WE DON'T HAVE MUCH TIME. I WISH WE DID. BUT YOU INTERRUPTED US. AND NOW ABYSS IS...
I SAID. IT WEREN'T THEM. THERE'S A PROBLEM...
SHUT UP. WHY ELSE WOULD IT ATTACK US?
THERE ARE ALL KINDS OF THINGS YOU CAN DO WITH THE RIGHT TECHNIQUES.
CHRONOPLASTICIANS WORK WITH TIME. POTENTIONOMERS WITH POSSIBILITY. SOOTHSAYERS WITH TRUTH.
IF I WERE A SOOTHSAYER I COULD JUST GET INSIDE YOUR HEAD AND KNOW THE ANSWERS TO ALL MY QUESTIONS.
...OH...
BUT I'M NOT. I WORK WITH NOTHING.
I'M A NULLOMANCER.
SO TO GET THE TRUTH OUT OF YOU, I HAVE TO USE DIFFERENT METHODS.

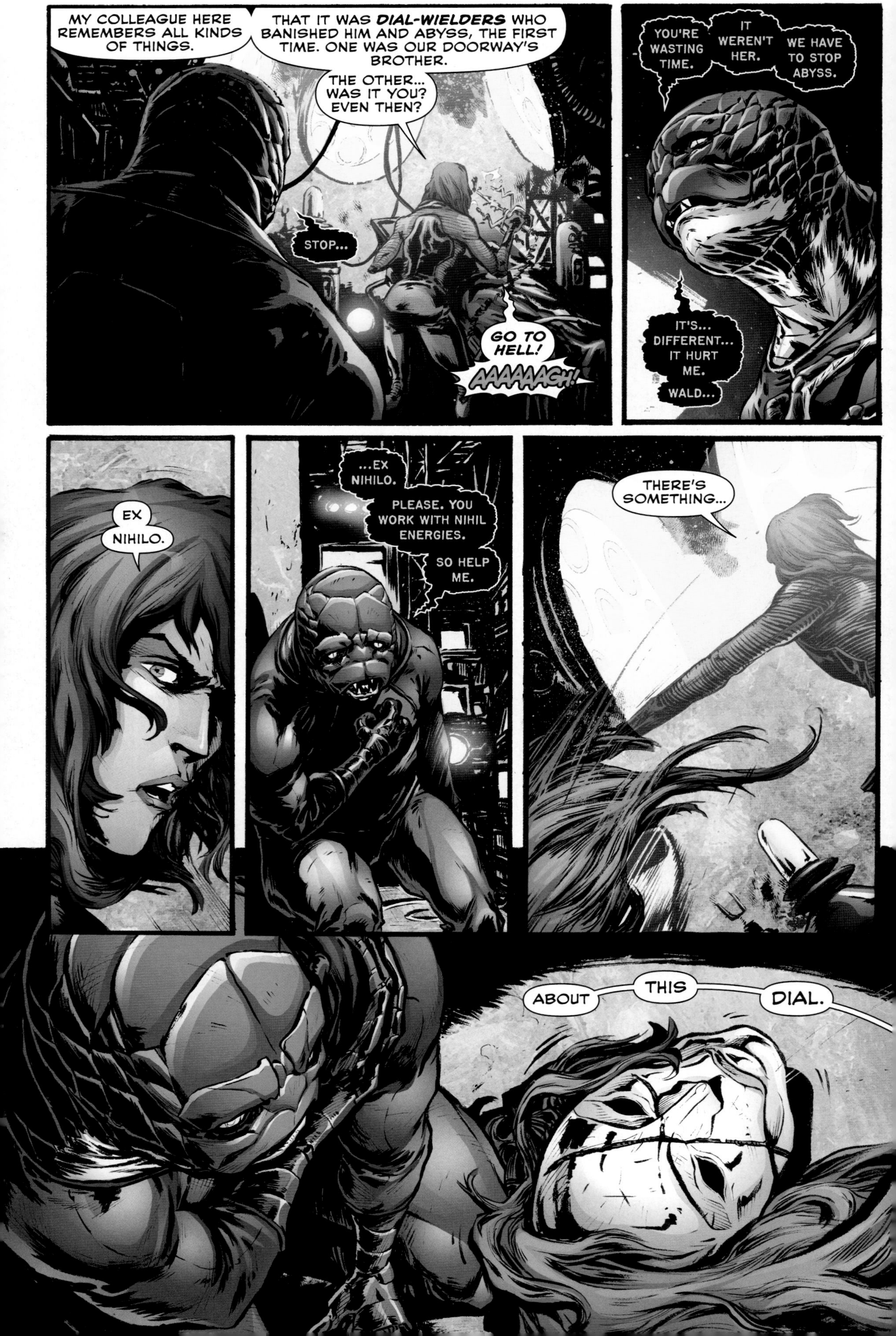
MY COLLEAGUE HERE REMEMBERS ALL KINDS OF THINGS.
THAT IT WAS *DIAL-WIELDERS* WHO BANISHED HIM AND ABYSS, THE FIRST TIME. ONE WAS OUR DOORWAY'S BROTHER.
THE OTHER... WAS IT YOU? EVEN THEN?
STOP...
GO TO HELL!
AAAAAAGH!
YOU'RE WASTING TIME.
IT WEREN'T HER.
WE HAVE TO STOP ABYSS.
IT'S... DIFFERENT... IT HURT ME.
WALD...
EX NIHILO.
...EX NIHILO.
PLEASE. YOU WORK WITH NIHIL ENERGIES.
SO HELP ME.
THERE'S SOMETHING...
ABOUT
THIS
DIAL.

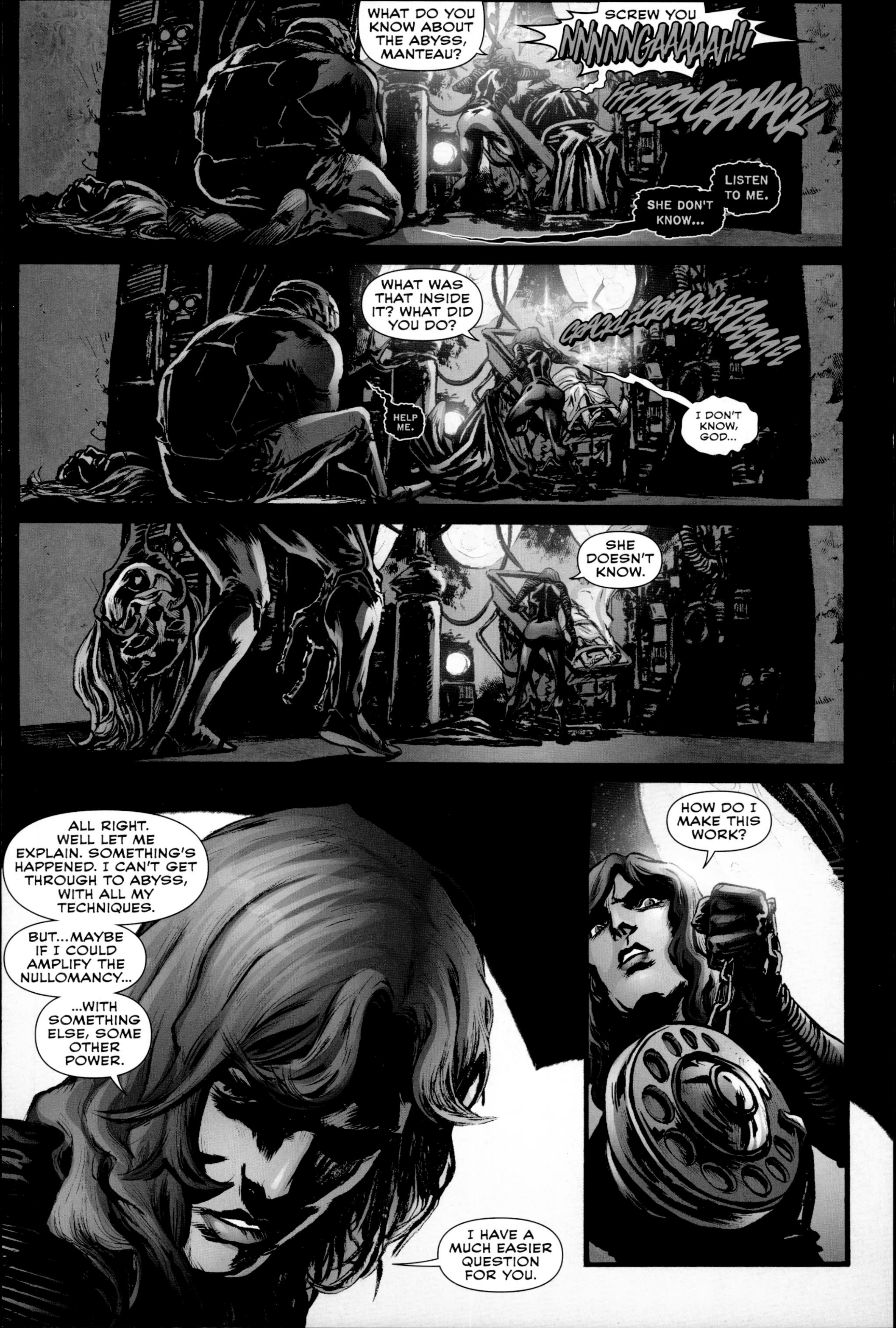
WHAT DO YOU KNOW ABOUT THE ABYSS, MANTEAU?
SCREW YOU
NNNNNGAAAAAH!!
FFEEEZZZCRAAACK
LISTEN TO ME.
SHE DON'T KNOW...
WHAT WAS THAT INSIDE IT? WHAT DID YOU DO?
HELP ME.
I DON'T KNOW, GOD...
SHE DOESN'T KNOW.
ALL RIGHT. WELL LET ME EXPLAIN. SOMETHING'S HAPPENED. I CAN'T GET THROUGH TO ABYSS, WITH ALL MY TECHNIQUES.
BUT...MAYBE IF I COULD AMPLIFY THE NULLOMANCY...
...WITH SOMETHING ELSE, SOME OTHER POWER.
HOW DO I MAKE THIS WORK?
I HAVE A MUCH EASIER QUESTION FOR YOU.

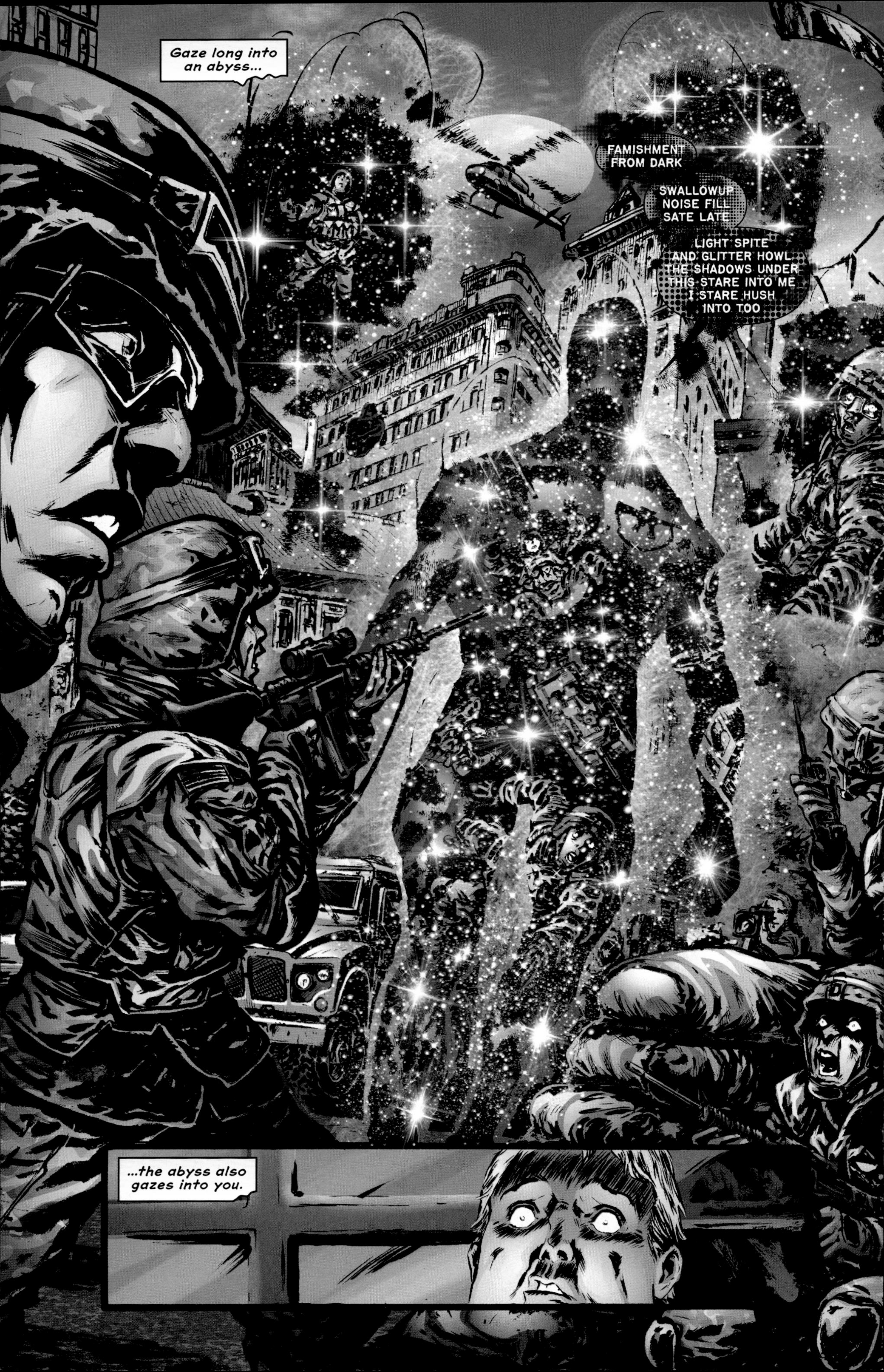
Gaze long into an abyss...
FAMISHMENT FROM DARK
SWALLOWUP NOISE FILL SATE LATE
LIGHT SPITE AND GLITTER HOWL THE SHADOWS UNDER THIS STARE INTO ME I STARE HUSH INTO TOO
...the abyss also gazes into you.

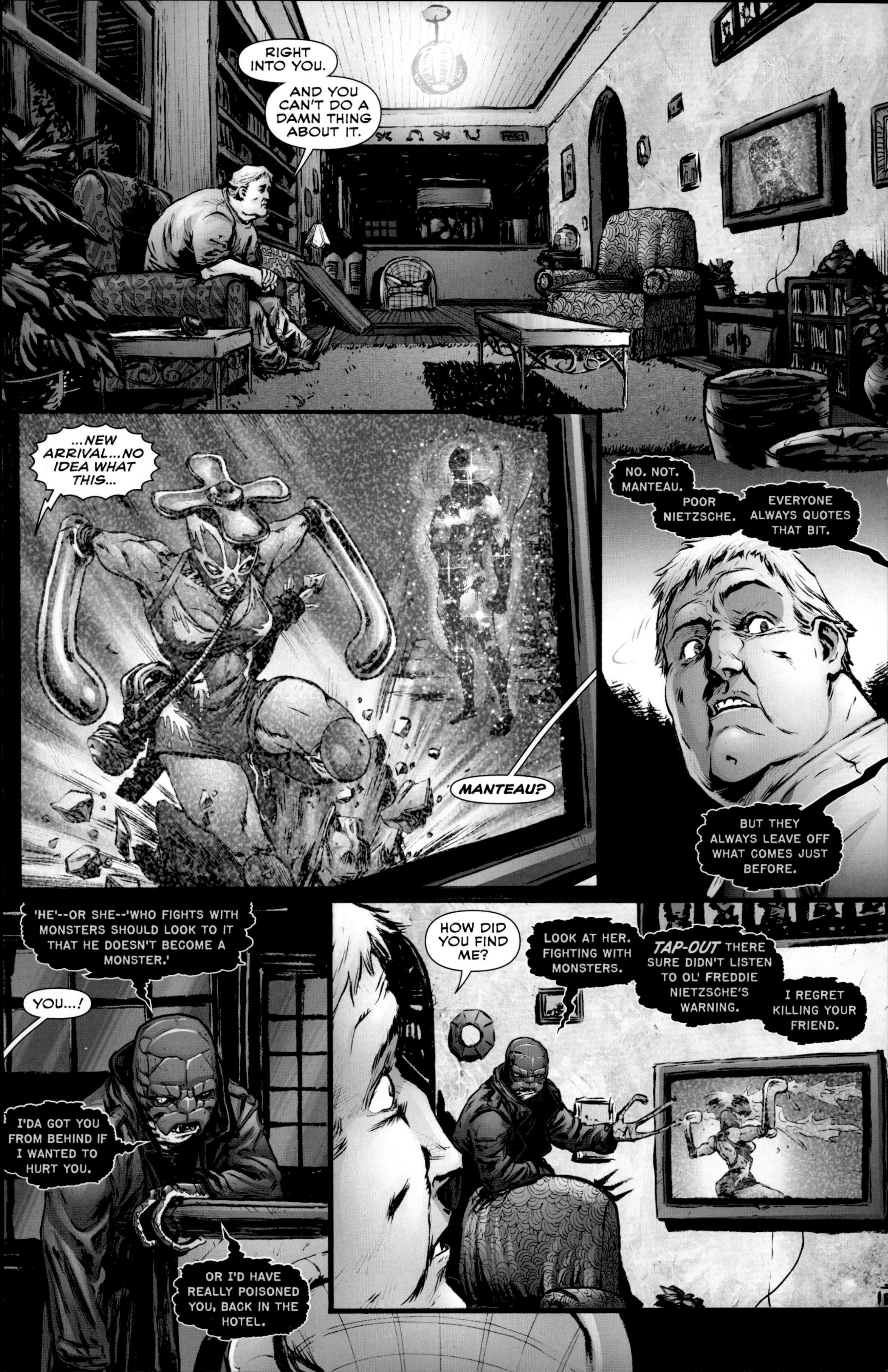
RIGHT INTO YOU.
AND YOU CAN'T DO A DAMN THING ABOUT IT.
...NEW ARRIVAL...NO IDEA WHAT THIS...
MANTEAU?
NO. NOT. MANTEAU.
POOR NIETZSCHE.
EVERYONE ALWAYS QUOTES THAT BIT.
BUT THEY ALWAYS LEAVE OFF WHAT COMES JUST BEFORE.
'HE'--OR SHE--'WHO FIGHTS WITH MONSTERS SHOULD LOOK TO IT THAT HE DOESN'T BECOME A MONSTER.'
YOU...!
I'DA GOT YOU FROM BEHIND IF I WANTED TO HURT YOU.
OR I'D HAVE REALLY POISONED YOU, BACK IN THE HOTEL.
HOW DID YOU FIND ME?
LOOK AT HER. FIGHTING WITH MONSTERS.
TAP-OUT THERE SURE DIDN'T LISTEN TO OL' FREDDIE NIETZSCHE'S WARNING.
I REGRET KILLING YOUR FRIEND.

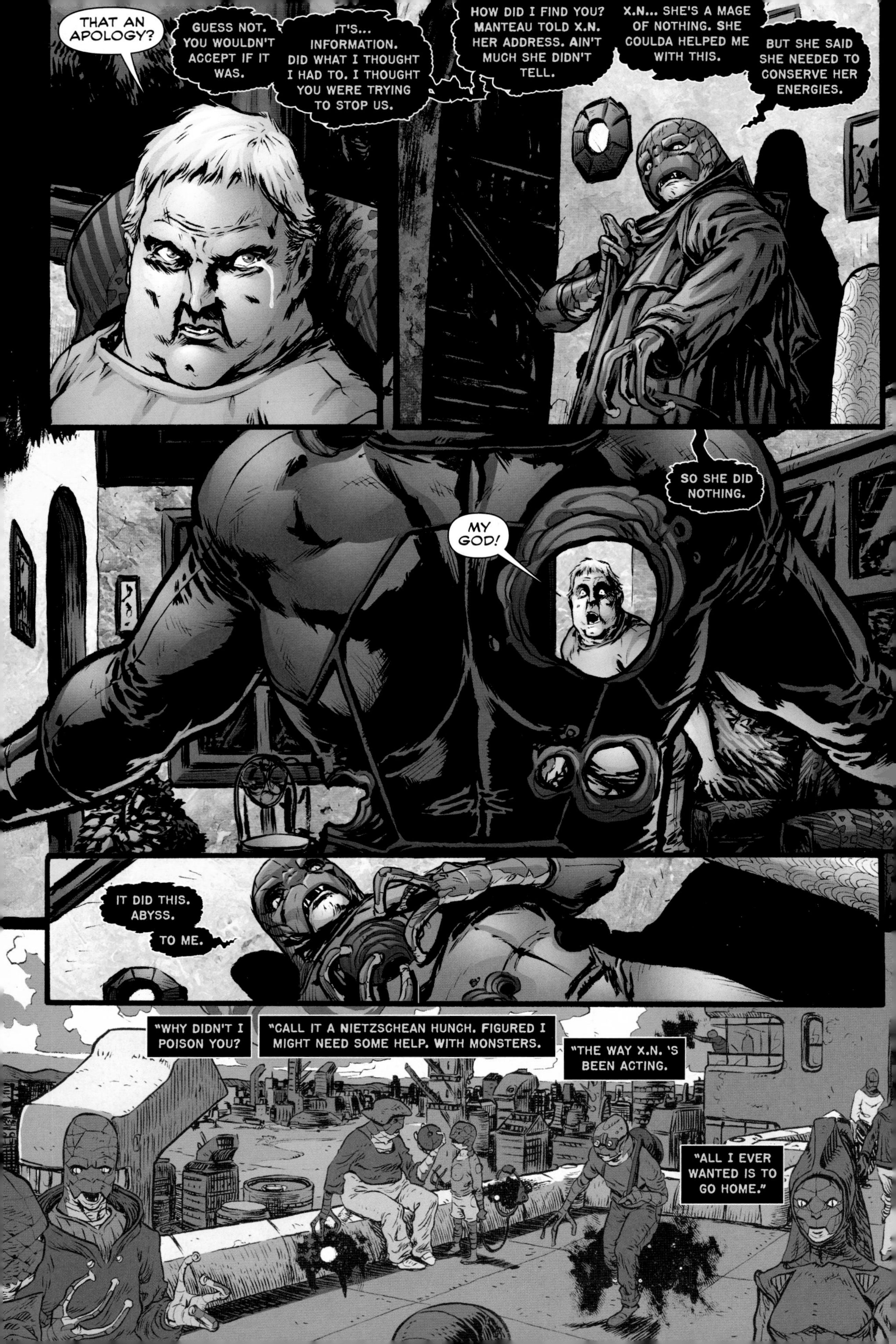
THAT AN APOLOGY?
GUESS NOT. YOU WOULDN'T ACCEPT IF IT WAS.
IT'S... INFORMATION. DID WHAT I THOUGHT I HAD TO. I THOUGHT YOU WERE TRYING TO STOP US.
HOW DID I FIND YOU? MANTEAU TOLD X.N. HER ADDRESS. AIN'T MUCH SHE DIDN'T TELL.
X.N... SHE'S A MAGE OF NOTHING. SHE COULDA HELPED ME WITH THIS.
BUT SHE SAID SHE NEEDED TO CONSERVE HER ENERGIES.
SO SHE DID NOTHING.
MY GOD!
IT DID THIS. ABYSS.
TO ME.
"WHY DIDN'T I POISON YOU?
"CALL IT A NIETZSCHEAN HUNCH. FIGURED I MIGHT NEED SOME HELP. WITH MONSTERS.
"THE WAY X.N. 'S BEEN ACTING.
"ALL I EVER WANTED IS TO GO HOME."

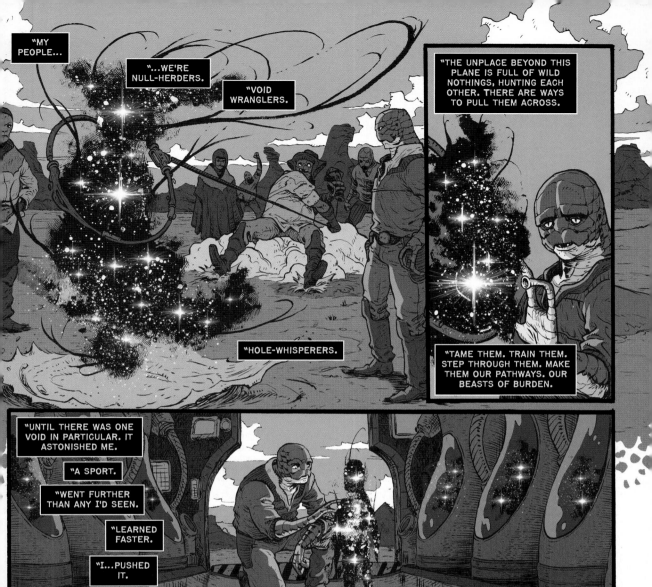

"MY PEOPLE...

"...WE'RE NULL-HERDERS.

"VOID WRANGLERS.

"HOLE-WHISPERERS.

"THE UNPLACE BEYOND THIS PLANE IS FULL OF WILD NOTHINGS, HUNTING EACH OTHER. THERE ARE WAYS TO PULL THEM ACROSS.

"TAME THEM. TRAIN THEM. STEP THROUGH THEM. MAKE THEM OUR PATHWAYS. OUR BEASTS OF BURDEN.

"UNTIL THERE WAS ONE VOID IN PARTICULAR. IT ASTONISHED ME.

"A SPORT.

"WENT FURTHER THAN ANY I'D SEEN.

"LEARNED FASTER.

"I...PUSHED IT.

"ITS DEEPS REACHED TO THE OTHER END OF THE UNIVERSE.

"AND BROUGHT BACK TREASURE.

"I RODE IT. EVERYWHERE. EXPLORED.

"WHILE IT GOT HUNGRIER AND HUNGRIER.

"TILL ONE DAY *IT* WAS TELLING *ME* WHERE TO GO.

HUNGRY? FOR WHAT?

IT IS THE DARK BETWEEN STARS.

IT'S HUNGRY FOR LIGHT.

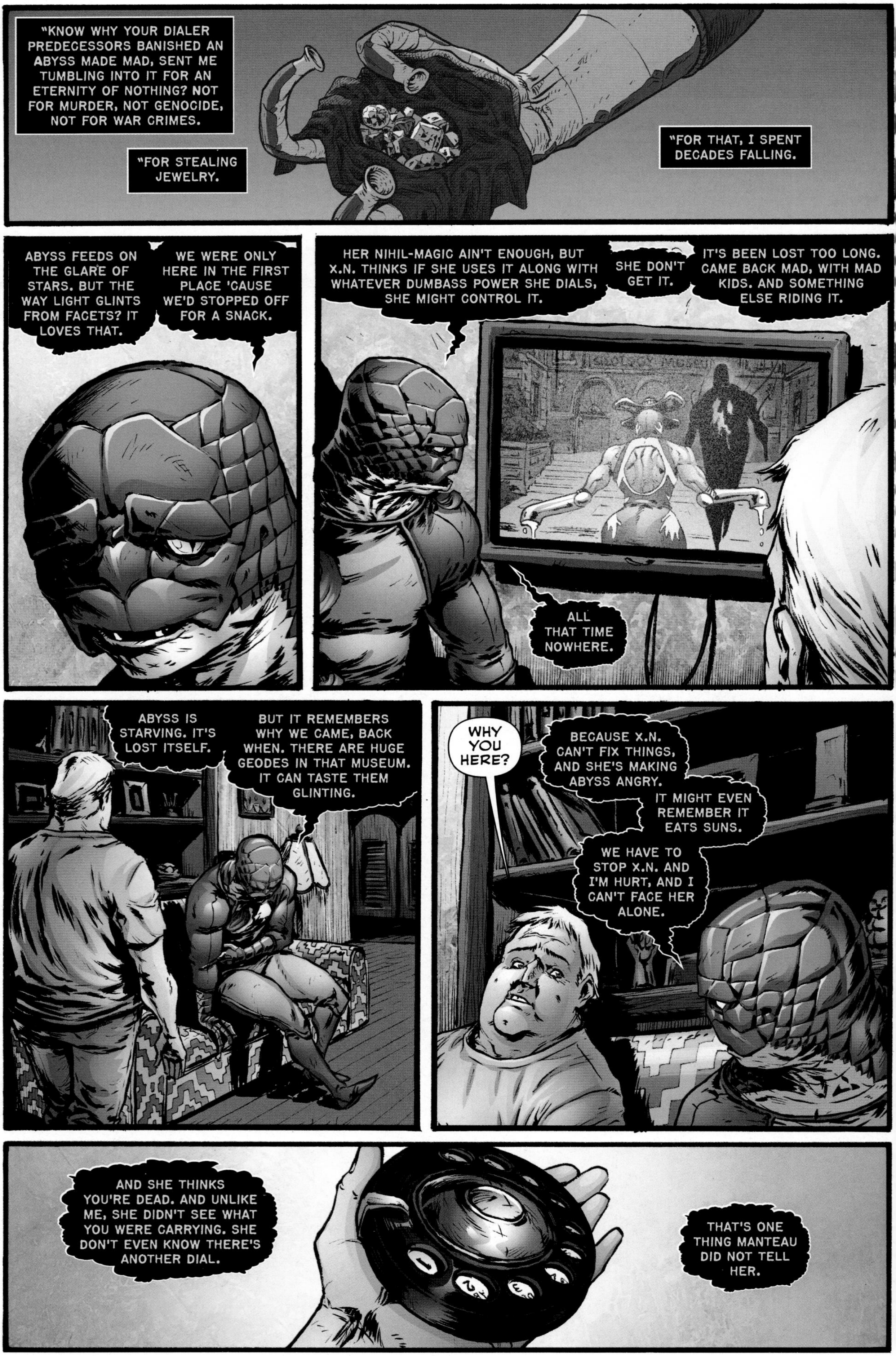
"KNOW WHY YOUR DIALER PREDECESSORS BANISHED AN ABYSS MADE MAD, SENT ME TUMBLING INTO IT FOR AN ETERNITY OF NOTHING? NOT FOR MURDER, NOT GENOCIDE, NOT FOR WAR CRIMES.
"FOR STEALING JEWELRY.
"FOR THAT, I SPENT DECADES FALLING.
ABYSS FEEDS ON THE GLARE OF STARS. BUT THE WAY LIGHT GLINTS FROM FACETS? IT LOVES THAT.
WE WERE ONLY HERE IN THE FIRST PLACE 'CAUSE WE'D STOPPED OFF FOR A SNACK.
HER NIHIL-MAGIC AIN'T ENOUGH, BUT X.N. THINKS IF SHE USES IT ALONG WITH WHATEVER DUMBASS POWER SHE DIALS, SHE MIGHT CONTROL IT.
SHE DON'T GET IT.
IT'S BEEN LOST TOO LONG. CAME BACK MAD, WITH MAD KIDS. AND SOMETHING ELSE RIDING IT.
ALL THAT TIME NOWHERE.
ABYSS IS STARVING. IT'S LOST ITSELF.
BUT IT REMEMBERS WHY WE CAME, BACK WHEN. THERE ARE HUGE GEODES IN THAT MUSEUM. IT CAN TASTE THEM GLINTING.
WHY YOU HERE?
BECAUSE X.N. CAN'T FIX THINGS, AND SHE'S MAKING ABYSS ANGRY.
IT MIGHT EVEN REMEMBER IT EATS SUNS.
WE HAVE TO STOP X.N. AND I'M HURT, AND I CAN'T FACE HER ALONE.
AND SHE THINKS YOU'RE DEAD. AND UNLIKE ME, SHE DIDN'T SEE WHAT YOU WERE CARRYING. SHE DON'T EVEN KNOW THERE'S ANOTHER DIAL.
THAT'S ONE THING MANTEAU DID NOT TELL HER.

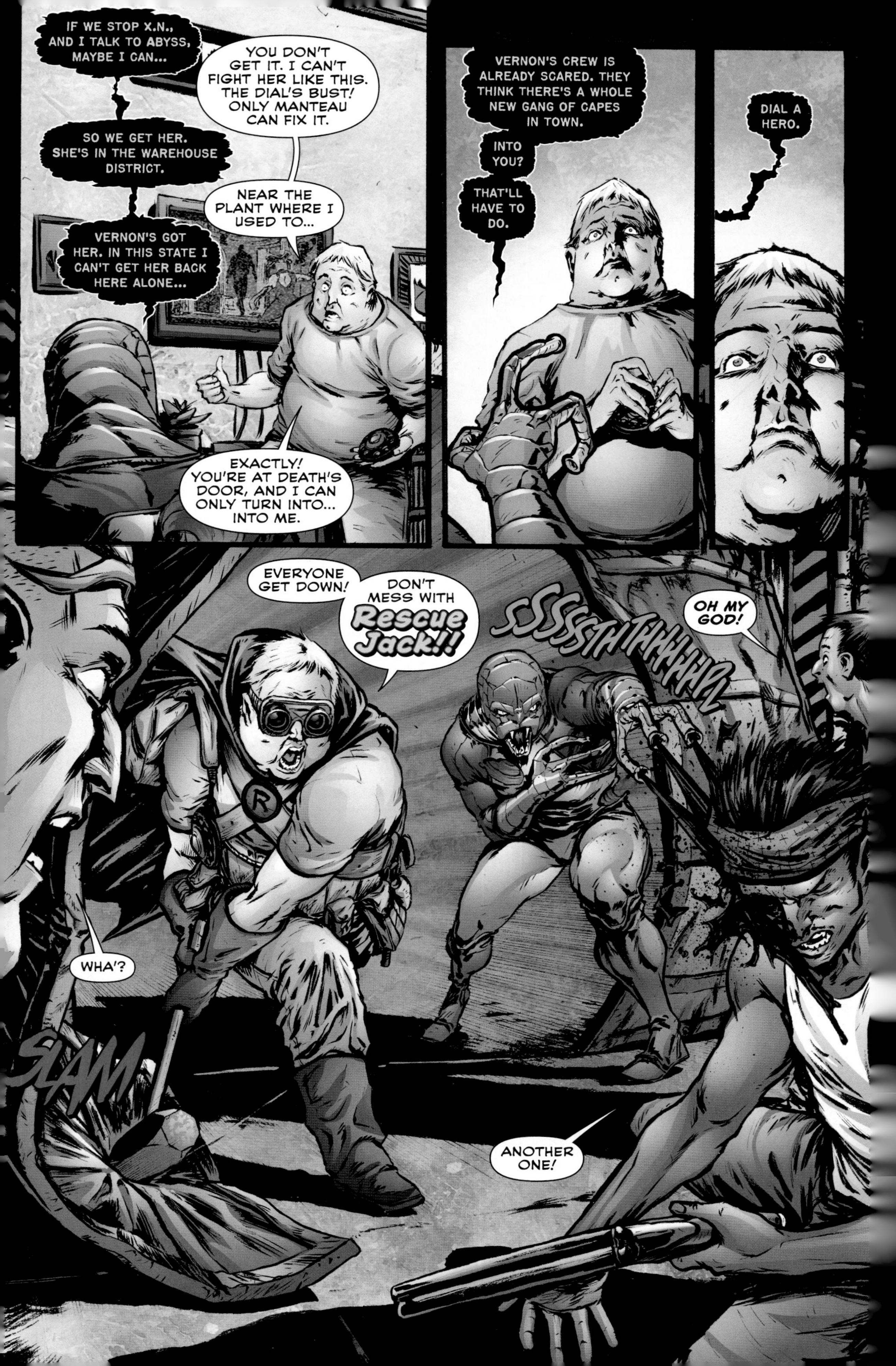
IF WE STOP X.N., AND I TALK TO ABYSS, MAYBE I CAN...
YOU DON'T GET IT. I CAN'T FIGHT HER LIKE THIS. THE DIAL'S BUST! ONLY MANTEAU CAN FIX IT.
SO WE GET HER. SHE'S IN THE WAREHOUSE DISTRICT.
NEAR THE PLANT WHERE I USED TO...
VERNON'S GOT HER. IN THIS STATE I CAN'T GET HER BACK HERE ALONE...
EXACTLY! YOU'RE AT DEATH'S DOOR, AND I CAN ONLY TURN INTO... INTO ME.
VERNON'S CREW IS ALREADY SCARED. THEY THINK THERE'S A WHOLE NEW GANG OF CAPES IN TOWN.
INTO YOU?
THAT'LL HAVE TO DO.
DIAL A HERO.
EVERYONE GET DOWN!
DON'T MESS WITH Rescue Jack!!
SSSSSTHTHHHHN
OH MY GOD!
WHA'?
SLAM
ANOTHER ONE!

SPLITHH!

NGHAAGH!

THIS WAY.

UNGH!

YOU MET MY PARTNERS.

NOW MEET ME.

BOY CHIMNEY SAYS HI.

AIN'T YOU GLAD I MADE YOU STOP AT THE PLANT FOR THIS GET-UP, SQUID?

BETTER SHE SEES YOU BEFORE SHE SEES ME.

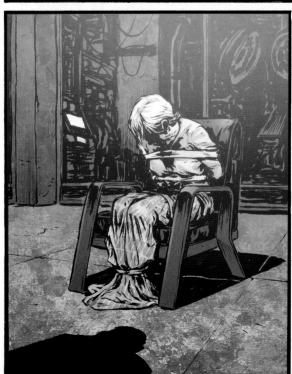

...MA'AM...?

OH...

MANTEAU.

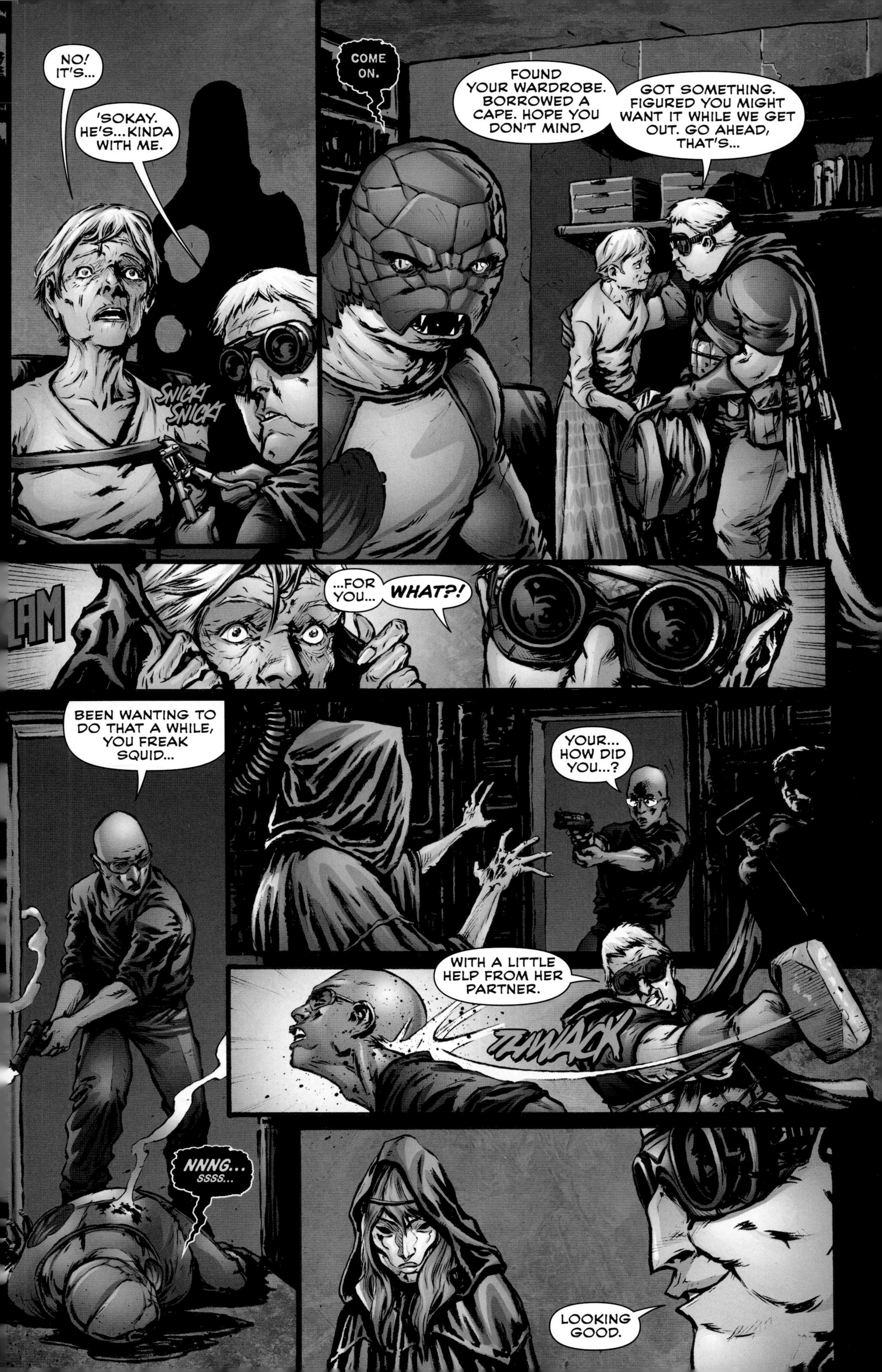
NO! IT'S...
'SOKAY. HE'S...KINDA WITH ME.
SNICK! SNICK!
COME ON.
FOUND YOUR WARDROBE. BORROWED A CAPE. HOPE YOU DON'T MIND.
GOT SOMETHING. FIGURED YOU MIGHT WANT IT WHILE WE GET OUT. GO AHEAD, THAT'S...
LAM
...FOR YOU...
WHAT?!
BEEN WANTING TO DO THAT A WHILE, YOU FREAK SQUID...
YOUR... HOW DID YOU...?
WITH A LITTLE HELP FROM HER PARTNER.
THWACK
NNNG... SSSS...
LOOKING GOOD.

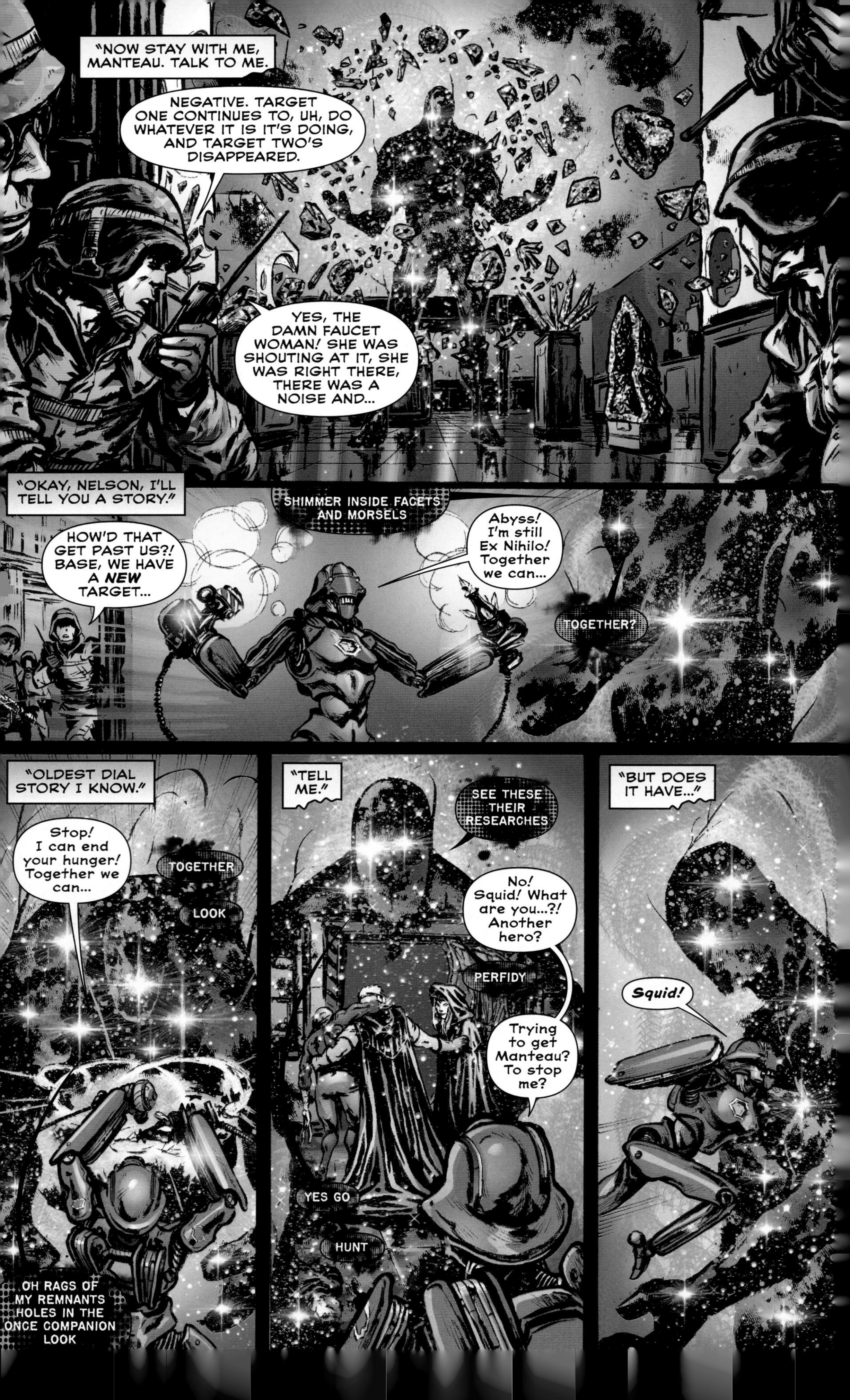
"NOW STAY WITH ME, MANTEAU. TALK TO ME.
NEGATIVE. TARGET ONE CONTINUES TO, UH, DO WHATEVER IT IS IT'S DOING, AND TARGET TWO'S DISAPPEARED.
YES, THE DAMN FAUCET WOMAN! SHE WAS SHOUTING AT IT, SHE WAS RIGHT THERE, THERE WAS A NOISE AND...
"OKAY, NELSON, I'LL TELL YOU A STORY."
SHIMMER INSIDE FACETS AND MORSELS
HOW'D THAT GET PAST US?! BASE, WE HAVE A NEW TARGET...
Abyss! I'm still Ex Nihilo! Together we can...
TOGETHER?
"OLDEST DIAL STORY I KNOW."
Stop! I can end your hunger! Together we can...
TOGETHER
LOOK
OH RAGS OF MY REMNANTS HOLES IN THE ONCE COMPANION LOOK
"TELL ME."
SEE THESE THEIR RESEARCHES
No! Squid! What are you...?! Another hero?
PERFIDY
Trying to get Manteau? To stop me?
YES GO
HUNT
"BUT DOES IT HAVE..."
Squid!

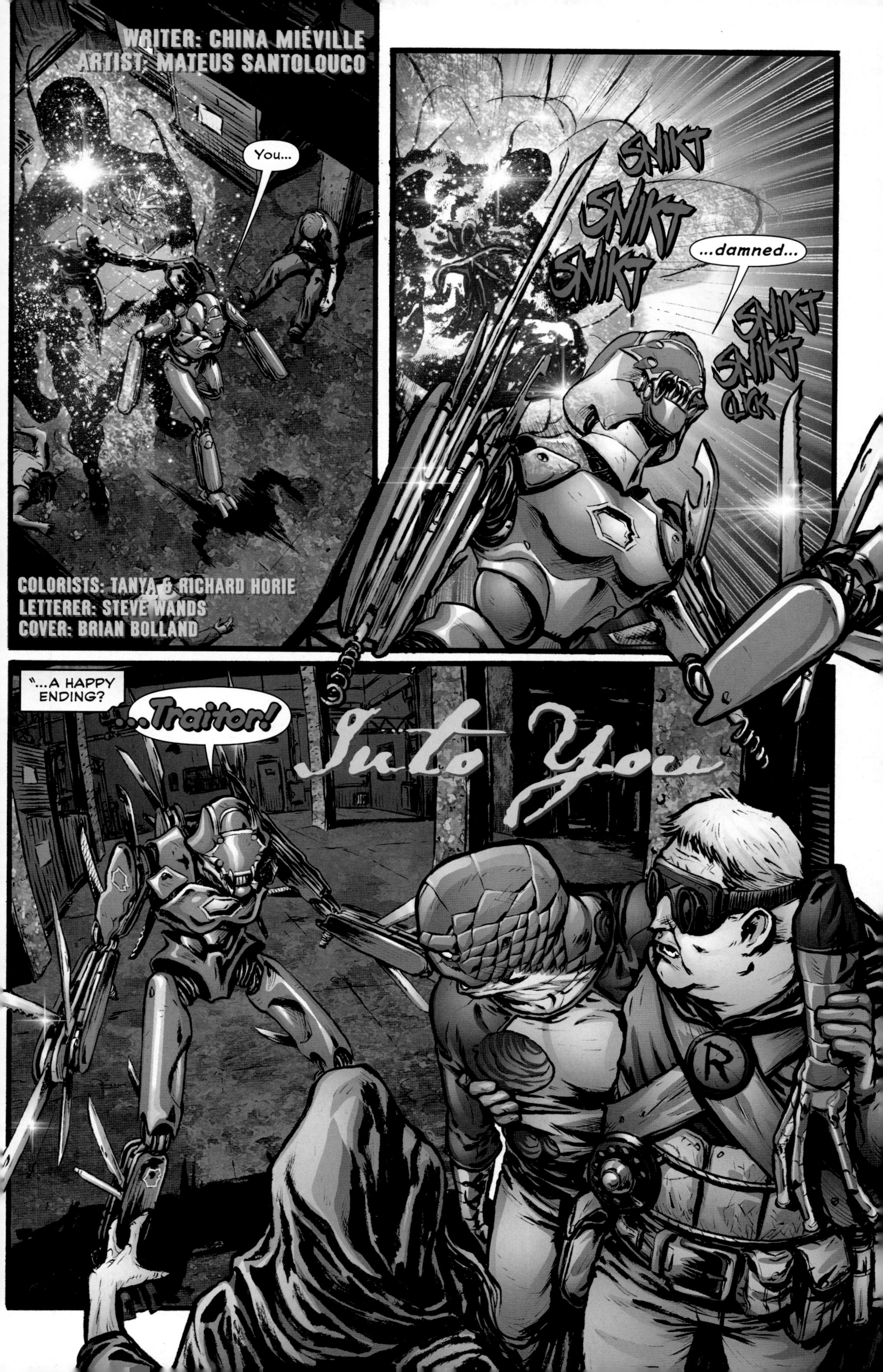
WRITER: CHINA MIÉVILLE
ARTIST: MATEUS SANTOLOUCO
You...
COLORISTS: TANYA & RICHARD HORIE
LETTERER: STEVE WANDS
COVER: BRIAN BOLLAND
SNIKT
SNIKT
SNIKT
...damned...
SNIKT
SNIKT
CLICK
"...A HAPPY ENDING?
...Traitor!
Into You

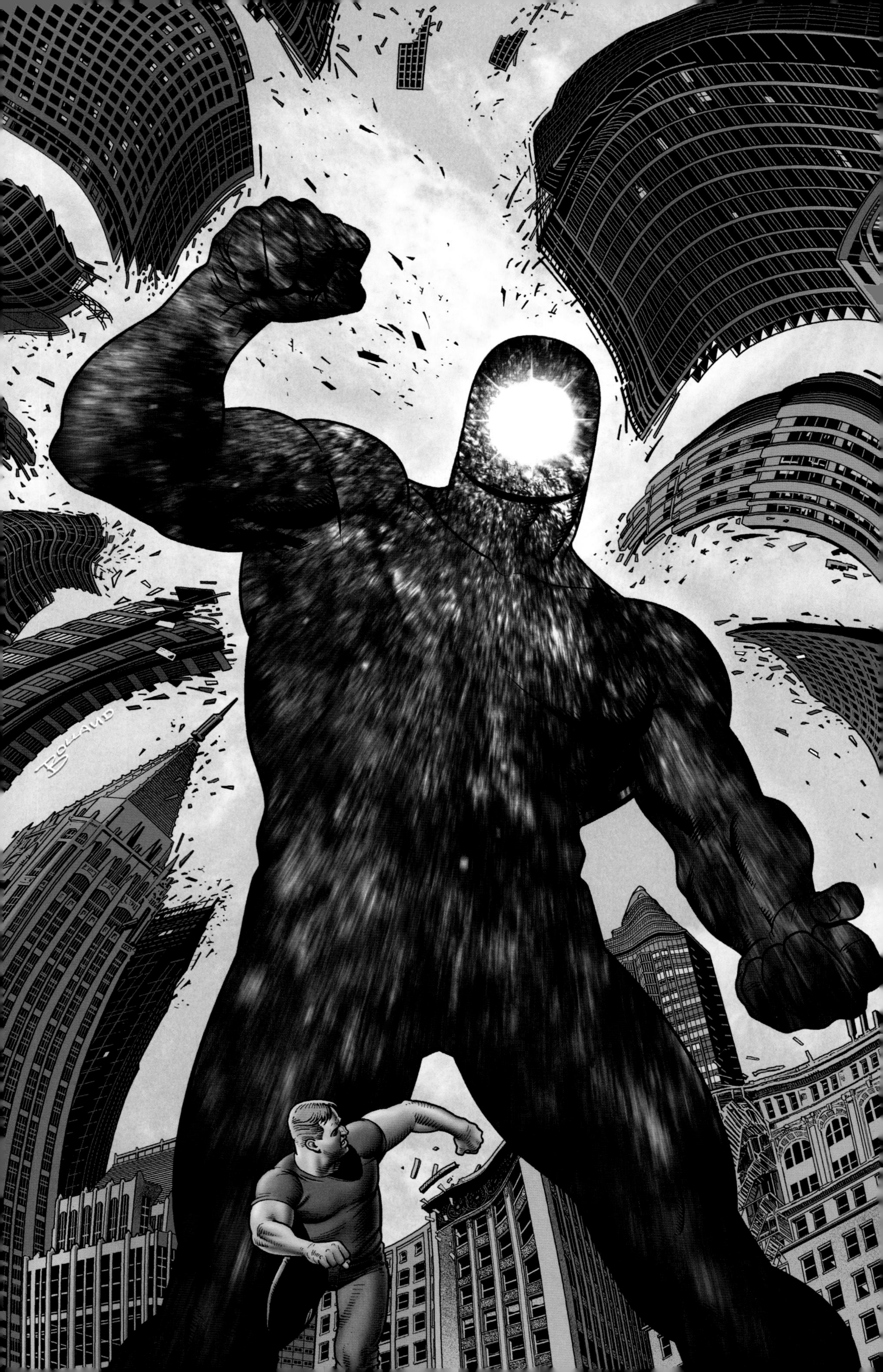
ROLLAND

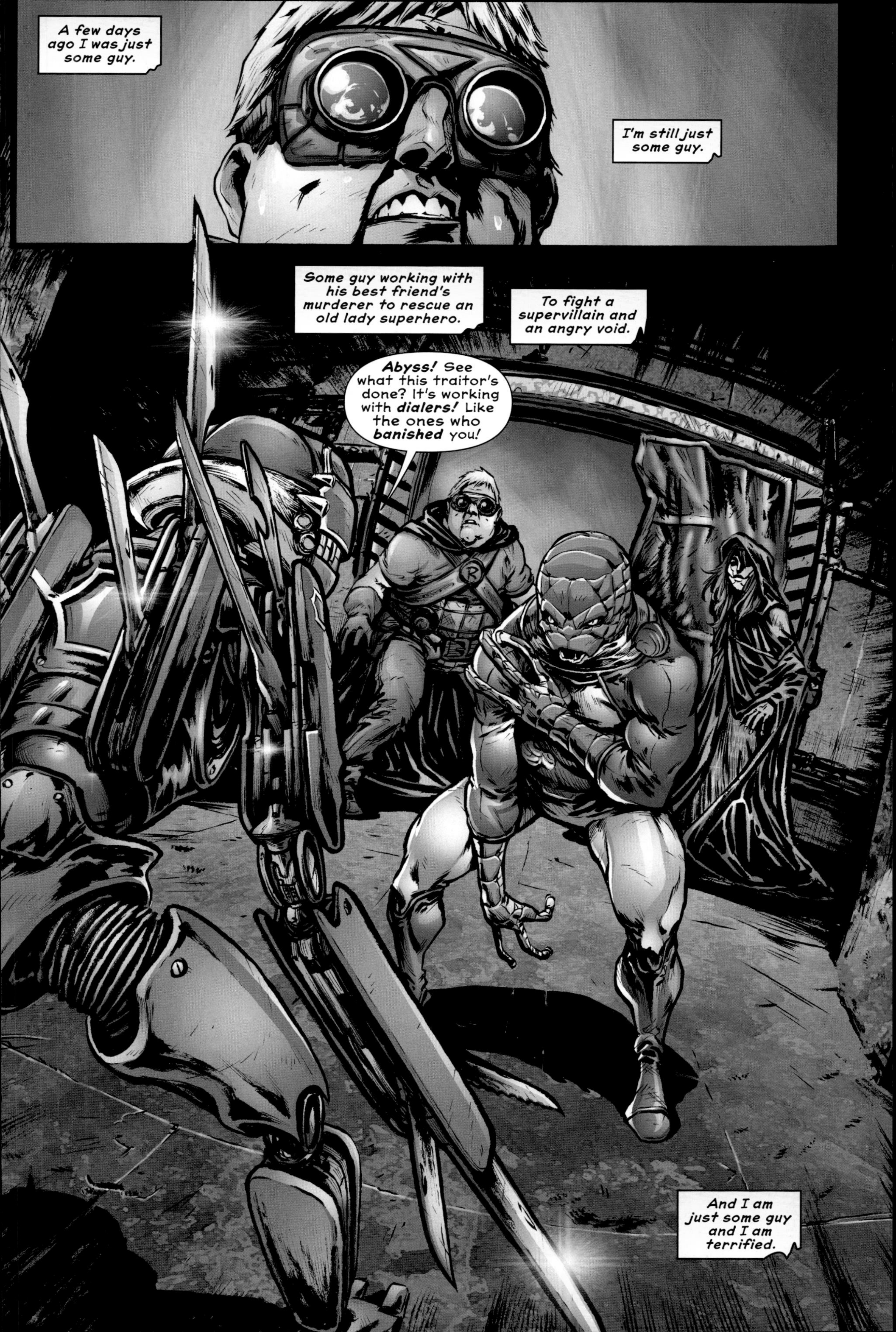
A few days ago I was just some guy.
I'm still just some guy.
Some guy working with his best friend's murderer to rescue an old lady superhero.
To fight a supervillain and an angry void.
Abyss! See what this traitor's done? It's working with dialers! Like the ones who banished you!
And I am just some guy and I am terrified.

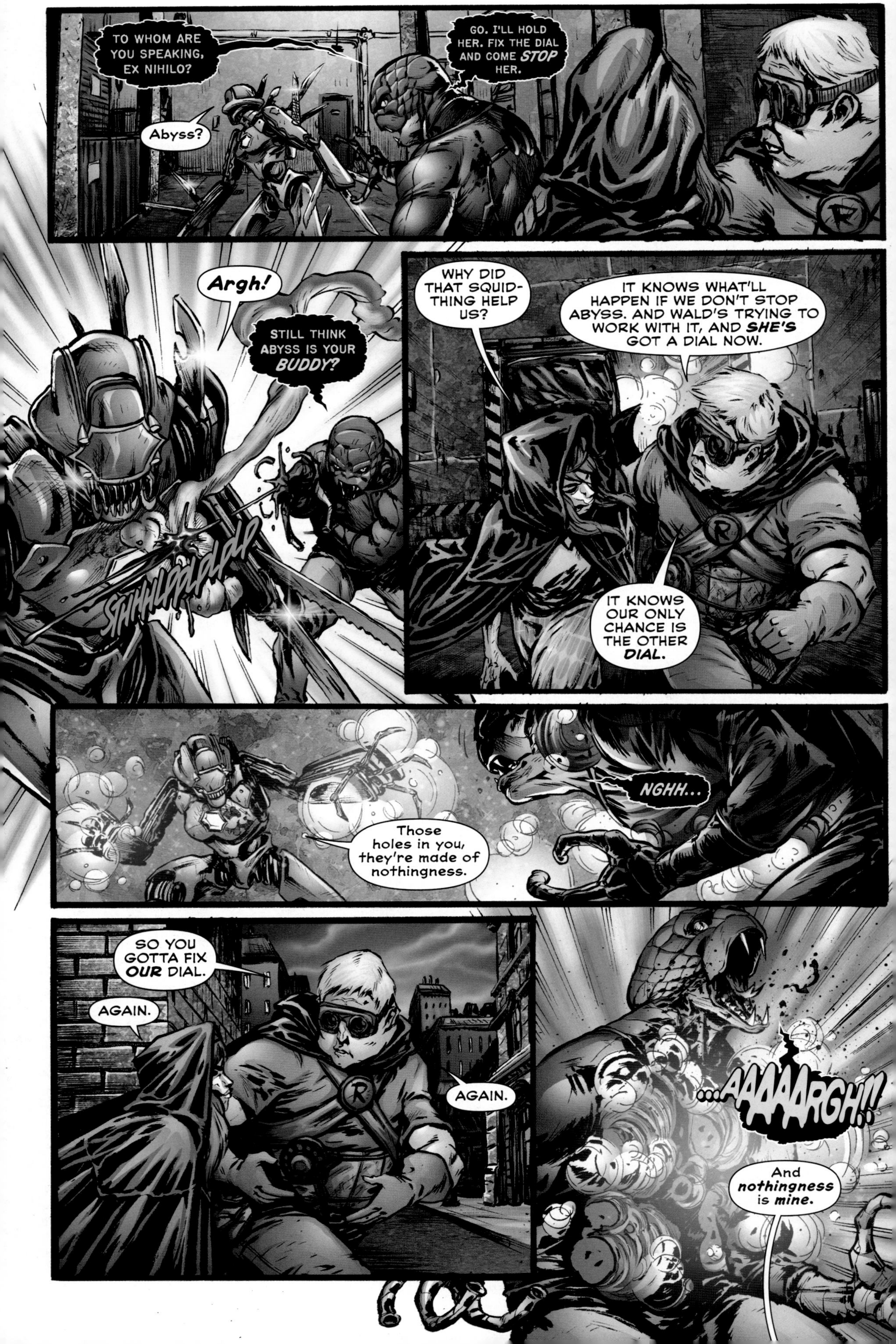
TO WHOM ARE YOU SPEAKING, EX NIHILO?
Abyss?
GO. I'LL HOLD HER. FIX THE DIAL AND COME STOP HER.
Argh!
STILL THINK ABYSS IS YOUR BUDDY?
SHHHLPPLPLPLP
WHY DID THAT SQUID-THING HELP US?
IT KNOWS WHAT'LL HAPPEN IF WE DON'T STOP ABYSS. AND WALD'S TRYING TO WORK WITH IT, AND SHE'S GOT A DIAL NOW.
IT KNOWS OUR ONLY CHANCE IS THE OTHER DIAL.
Those holes in you, they're made of nothingness.
NGHH...
SO YOU GOTTA FIX OUR DIAL.
AGAIN.
AGAIN.
...AAAAARGH!!
And nothingness is mine.

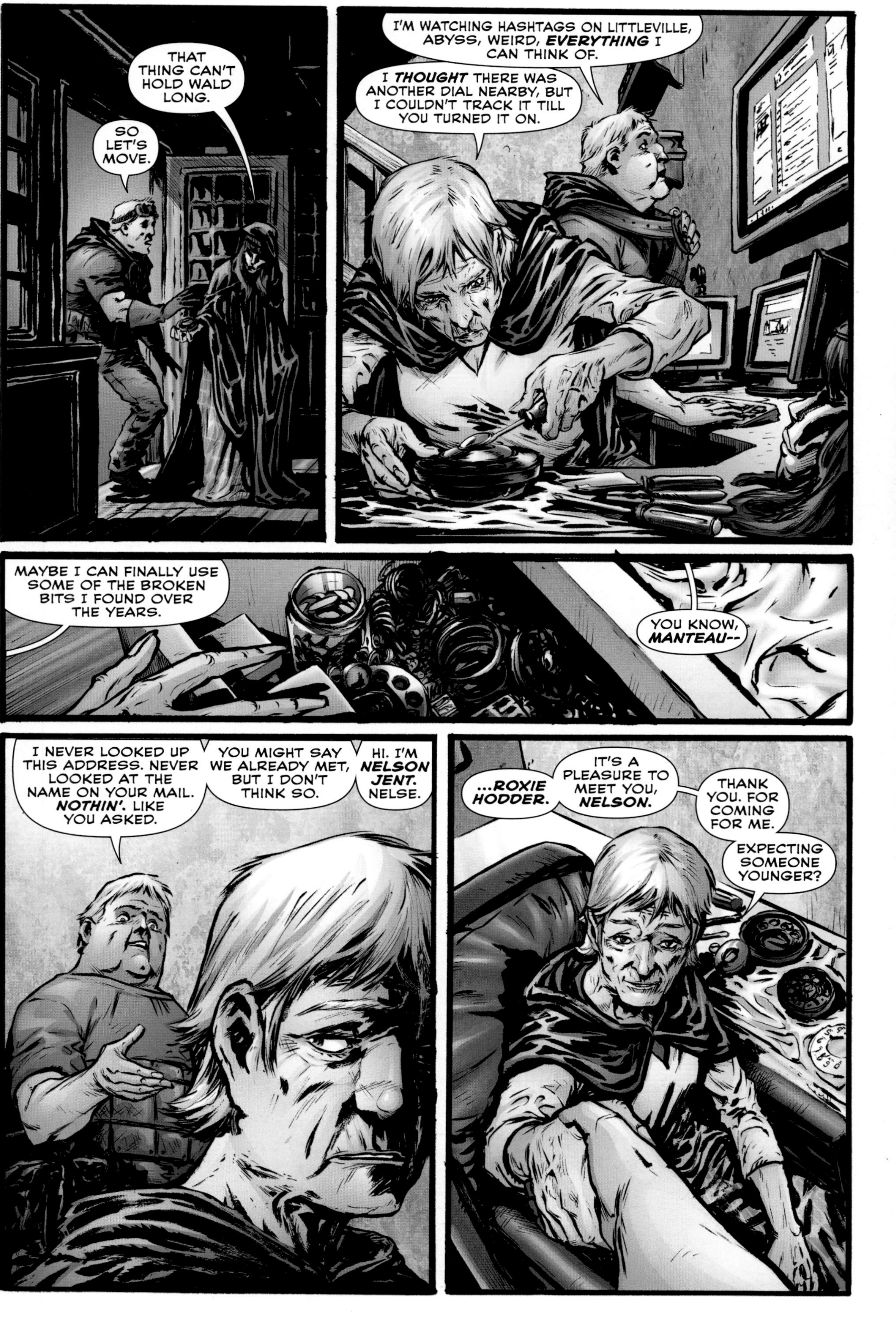
THAT THING CAN'T HOLD WALD LONG.
SO LET'S MOVE.
I'M WATCHING HASHTAGS ON LITTLEVILLE, ABYSS, WEIRD, EVERYTHING I CAN THINK OF.
I THOUGHT THERE WAS ANOTHER DIAL NEARBY, BUT I COULDN'T TRACK IT TILL YOU TURNED IT ON.
MAYBE I CAN FINALLY USE SOME OF THE BROKEN BITS I FOUND OVER THE YEARS.
YOU KNOW, MANTEAU--
I NEVER LOOKED UP THIS ADDRESS. NEVER LOOKED AT THE NAME ON YOUR MAIL. NOTHIN'. LIKE YOU ASKED.
YOU MIGHT SAY WE ALREADY MET, BUT I DON'T THINK SO.
HI. I'M NELSON JENT. NELSE.
...ROXIE HODDER.
IT'S A PLEASURE TO MEET YOU, NELSON.
THANK YOU. FOR COMING FOR ME.
EXPECTING SOMEONE YOUNGER?

"WHEN I WAS YOUR AGE I WAS GOING FOR MY PHD, IN BOULDER. HISTORY OF SCIENCE. TELEPHONY."

"SERIOUSLY?"

"THE 60S ALMOST PASSED ME BY.

"UNTIL THE JOY FESTIVAL. 1967. I FOUND MY WAY TO DROP CITY. THEN TO CRISS CROSS.

...TAKE FULLER'S ZONOHEDRA AS A MODEL FOR SPACE-TIME...

...SO WHAT ABOUT WHERE ITS VECTORS CROSS OVER OTHERS, MAN?

CUT OUT ALL THE THEOSOPHY CRAP, THERE'S STILL STUFF IN BLAVATSKY AND BESANT...

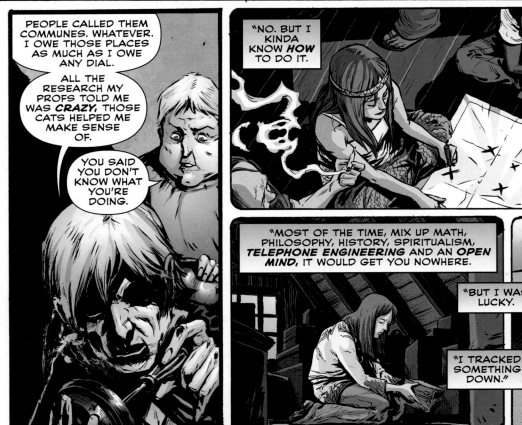

PEOPLE CALLED THEM COMMUNES. WHATEVER. I OWE THOSE PLACES AS MUCH AS I OWE ANY DIAL.

ALL THE RESEARCH MY PROFS TOLD ME WAS *CRAZY,* THOSE CATS HELPED ME MAKE SENSE OF.

YOU SAID YOU DON'T KNOW WHAT YOU'RE DOING.

"NO. BUT I KINDA KNOW *HOW* TO DO IT.

"MOST OF THE TIME, MIX UP MATH, PHILOSOPHY, HISTORY, SPIRITUALISM, *TELEPHONE ENGINEERING* AND AN *OPEN MIND,* IT WOULD GET YOU NOWHERE."

"BUT I WAS LUCKY.

"I TRACKED SOMETHING DOWN."

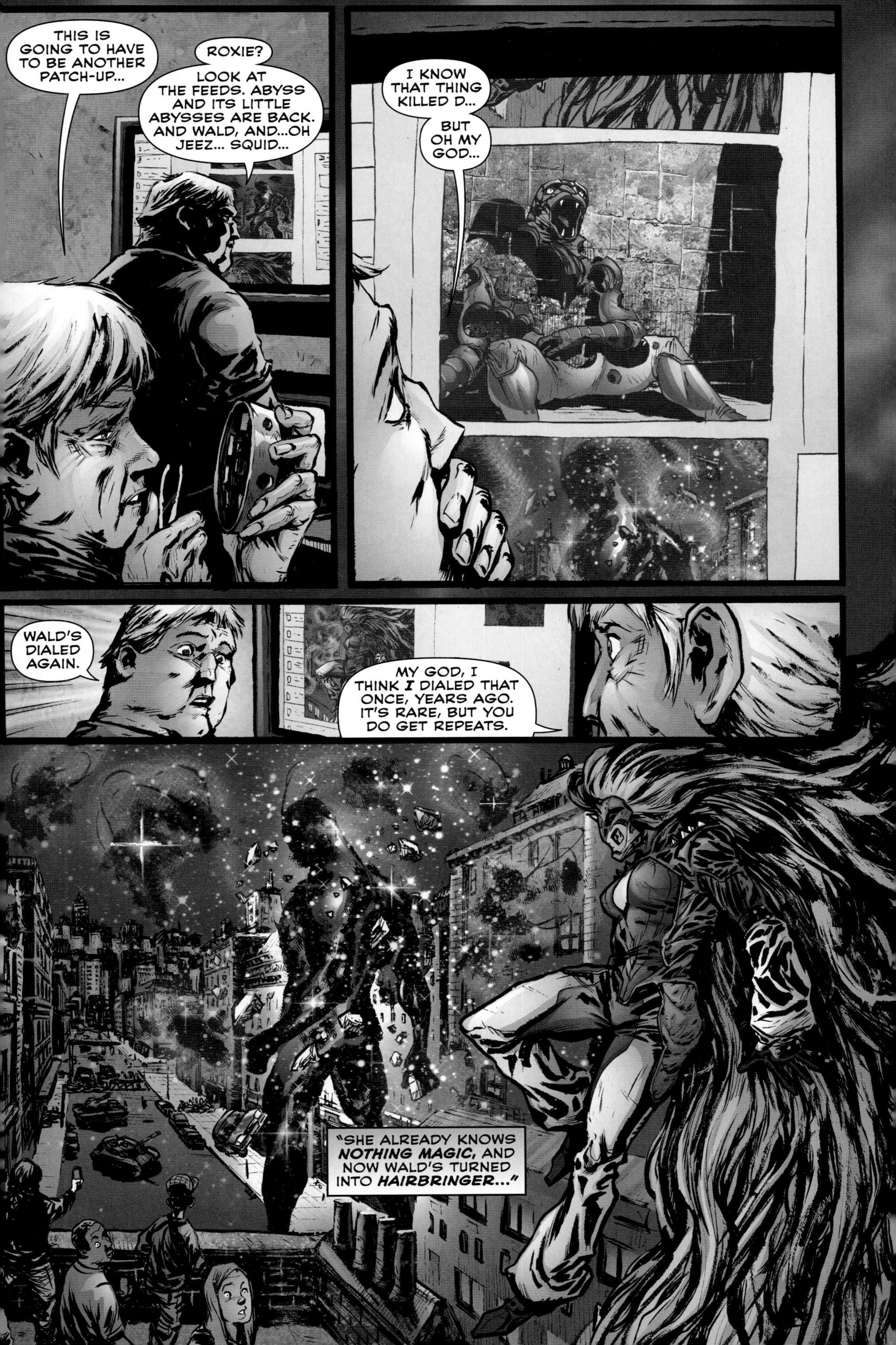

THIS IS GOING TO HAVE TO BE ANOTHER PATCH-UP...
ROXIE?
LOOK AT THE FEEDS. ABYSS AND ITS LITTLE ABYSSES ARE BACK. AND WALD, AND...OH JEEZ... SQUID...
I KNOW THAT THING KILLED D...
BUT OH MY GOD...
WALD'S DIALED AGAIN.
MY GOD, I THINK *I* DIALED THAT ONCE, YEARS AGO. IT'S RARE, BUT YOU DO GET REPEATS.
"SHE ALREADY KNOWS ***NOTHING MAGIC,*** AND NOW WALD'S TURNED INTO ***HAIRBRINGER...***"

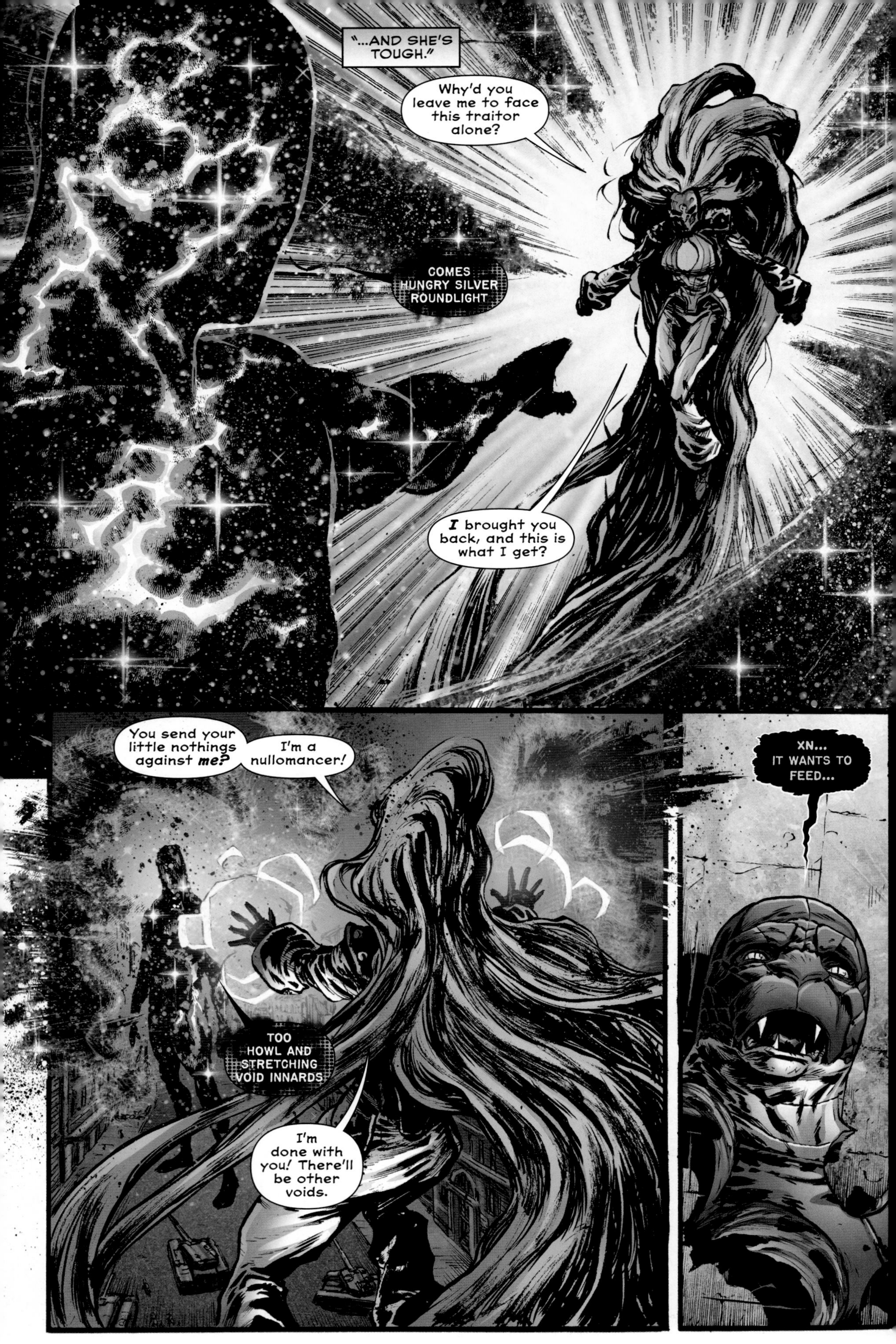
"...AND SHE'S TOUGH."
Why'd you leave me to face this traitor alone?
COMES HUNGRY SILVER ROUNDLIGHT
I brought you back, and this is what I get?
You send your little nothings against ***me?***
I'm a nullomancer!
TOO HOWL AND STRETCHING VOID INNARDS
I'm done with you! There'll be other voids.
XN... IT WANTS TO FEED...

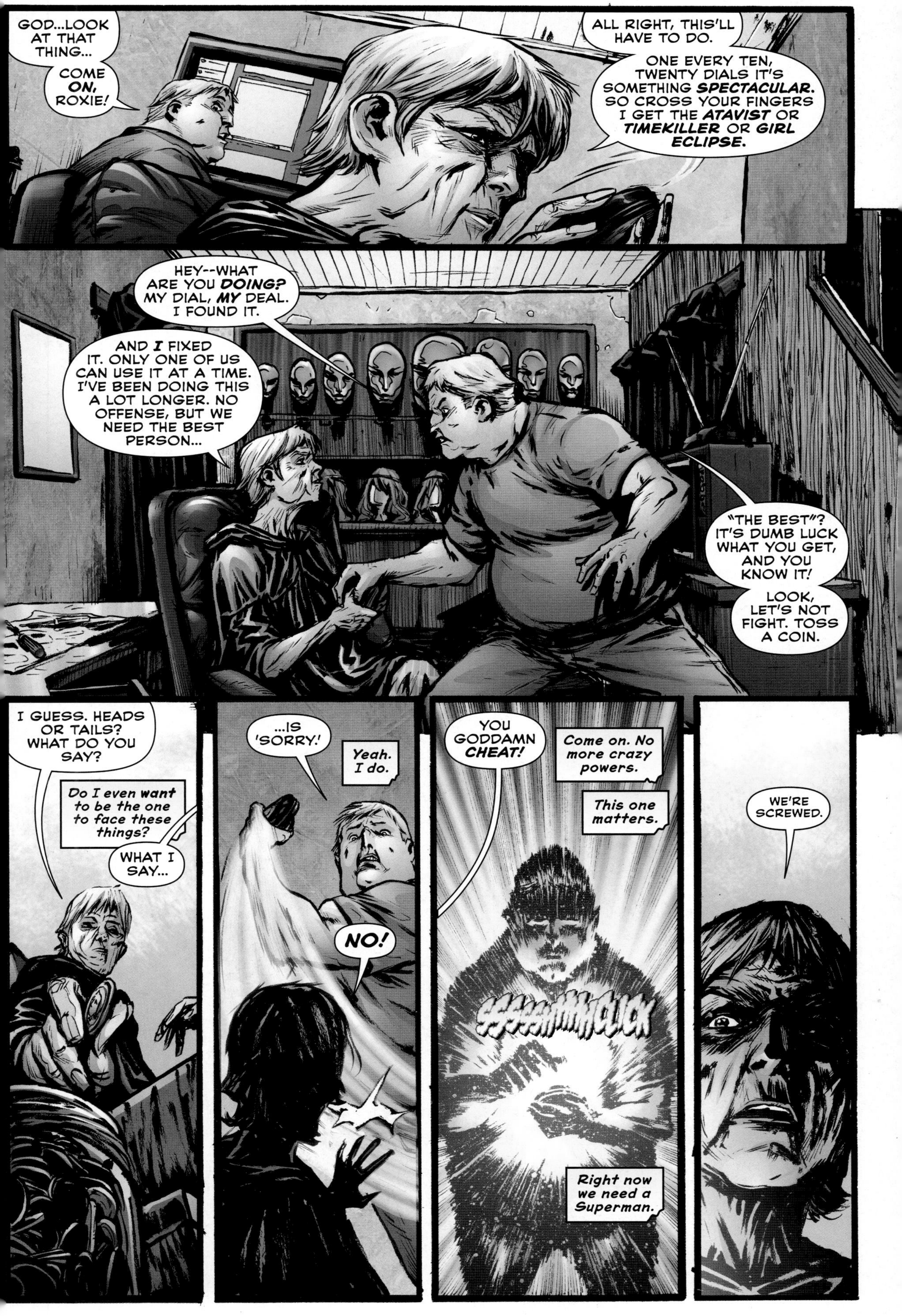
GOD...LOOK AT THAT THING...
COME ON, ROXIE!
ALL RIGHT, THIS'LL HAVE TO DO.
ONE EVERY TEN, TWENTY DIALS IT'S SOMETHING SPECTACULAR. SO CROSS YOUR FINGERS I GET THE ATAVIST OR TIMEKILLER OR GIRL ECLIPSE.
HEY--WHAT ARE YOU DOING? MY DIAL, MY DEAL. I FOUND IT.
AND I FIXED IT. ONLY ONE OF US CAN USE IT AT A TIME. I'VE BEEN DOING THIS A LOT LONGER. NO OFFENSE, BUT WE NEED THE BEST PERSON...
"THE BEST"? IT'S DUMB LUCK WHAT YOU GET, AND YOU KNOW IT!
LOOK, LET'S NOT FIGHT. TOSS A COIN.
I GUESS. HEADS OR TAILS? WHAT DO YOU SAY?
Do I even want to be the one to face these things?
WHAT I SAY...
...IS 'SORRY.'
Yeah. I do.
NO!
YOU GODDAMN CHEAT!
Come on. No more crazy powers.
This one matters.
SSSSSHHHHCLICK
Right now we need a Superman.
WE'RE SCREWED.

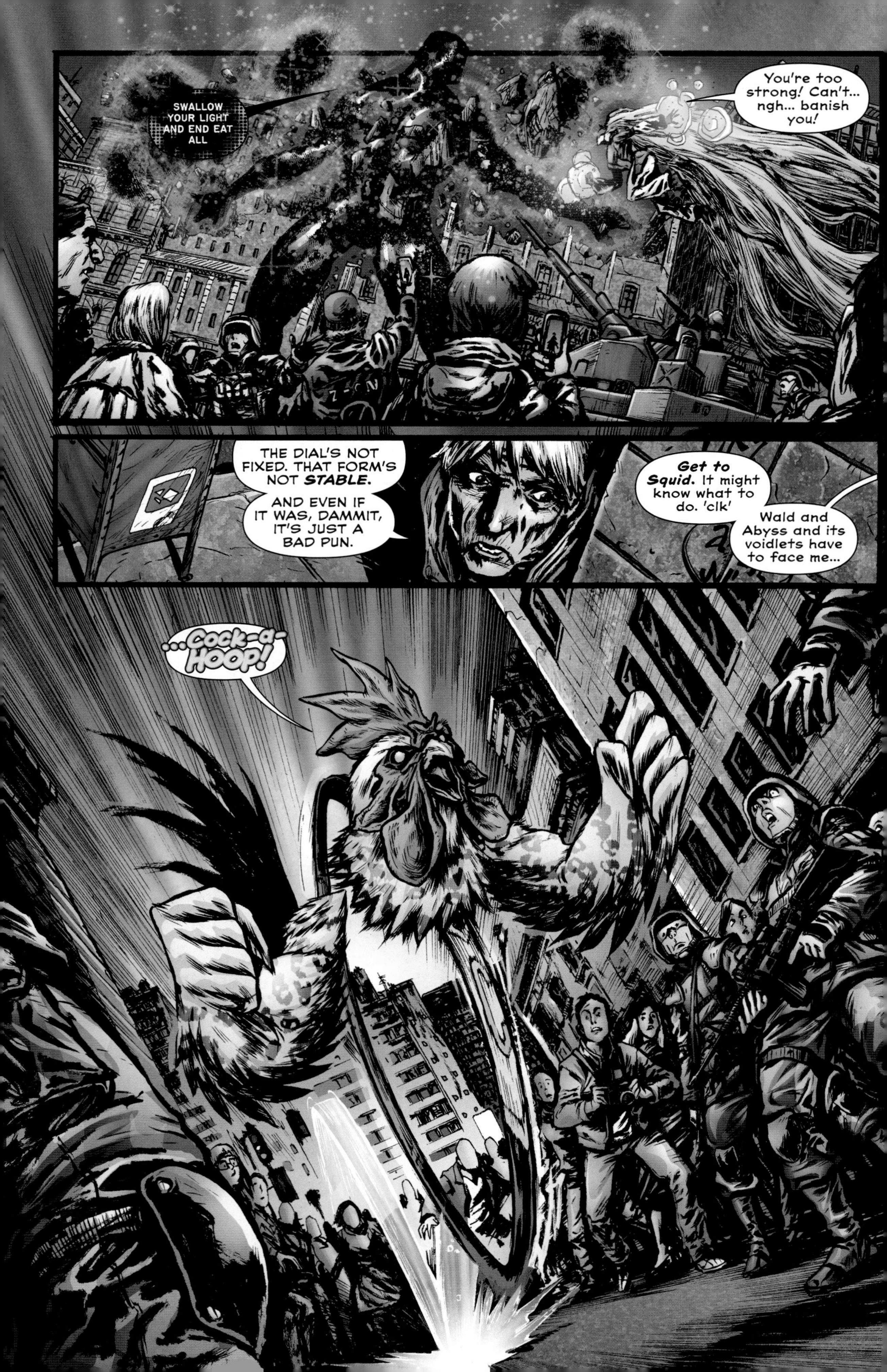
SWALLOW YOUR LIGHT AND END EAT ALL
You're too strong! Can't... ngh... banish you!
THE DIAL'S NOT FIXED. THAT FORM'S NOT *STABLE.*
AND EVEN IF IT WAS, DAMMIT, IT'S JUST A BAD PUN.
Get to Squid. It might know what to do. 'clk'
Wald and Abyss and its voidlets have to face me...
...Cock-a-Hoop!

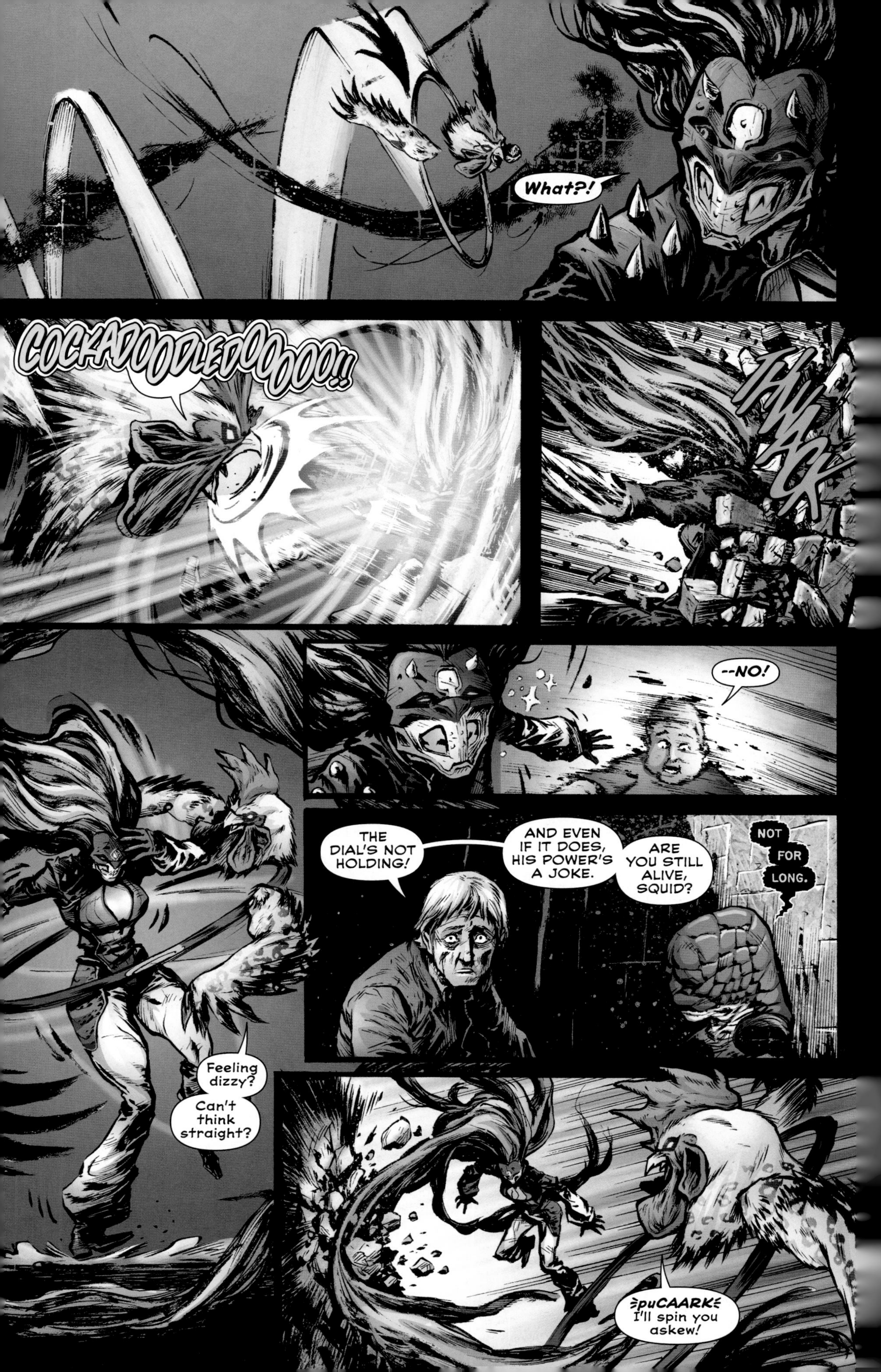
What?!
COCKADOOODLEDOOOOOOO!!
THWACK
--NO!
THE DIAL'S NOT HOLDING!
AND EVEN IF IT DOES, HIS POWER'S A JOKE.
ARE YOU STILL ALIVE, SQUID?
NOT FOR LONG.
Feeling dizzy?
Can't think straight?
puCAARK
I'll spin you askew!

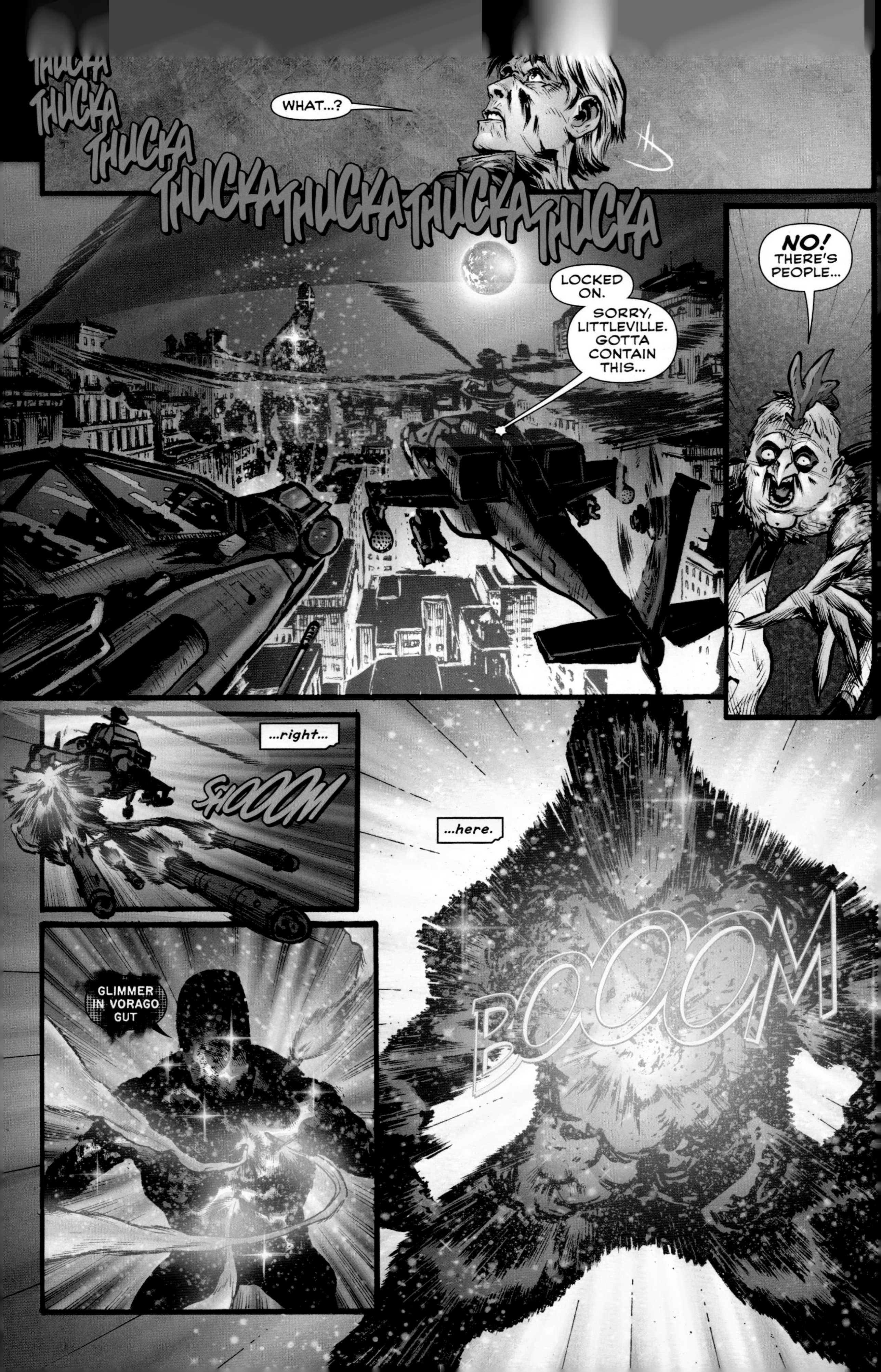
THUCKA
THUCKA
THUCKA
WHAT...?
THUCKA THUCKA THUCKA THUCKA
LOCKED ON.
SORRY, LITTLEVILLE. GOTTA CONTAIN THIS...
NO! THERE'S PEOPLE...
...right...
SHOOOM
...here.
GLIMMER IN VORAGO GUT
BOOOM

LLLLLLLLLL

LLLLLLLLIGHT

AAAAAAGH!

IT'S DARKENING THE MOON!

IT IS EATING THE LIGHT.

You trying to take me, little void?

Mess with me, I'll get you giddy and gone!

NELSON CAN CONFUSE THE YOUNG NOTHINGS.

SEND THEM SPINNING.

WALD CAN'T DEFLECT ABYSS.

BUT MADE DRUNK BY NELSON, ITS CUBS SHE CAN.

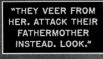

"THEY VEER FROM HER. ATTACK THEIR FATHERMOTHER INSTEAD. LOOK."

SOON THIS TOILET WORLD COLD GUANO ONLY IN SPACE NIGHTSOIL DUNG DROPPINGS OF LIGHT EATEN BY DARK

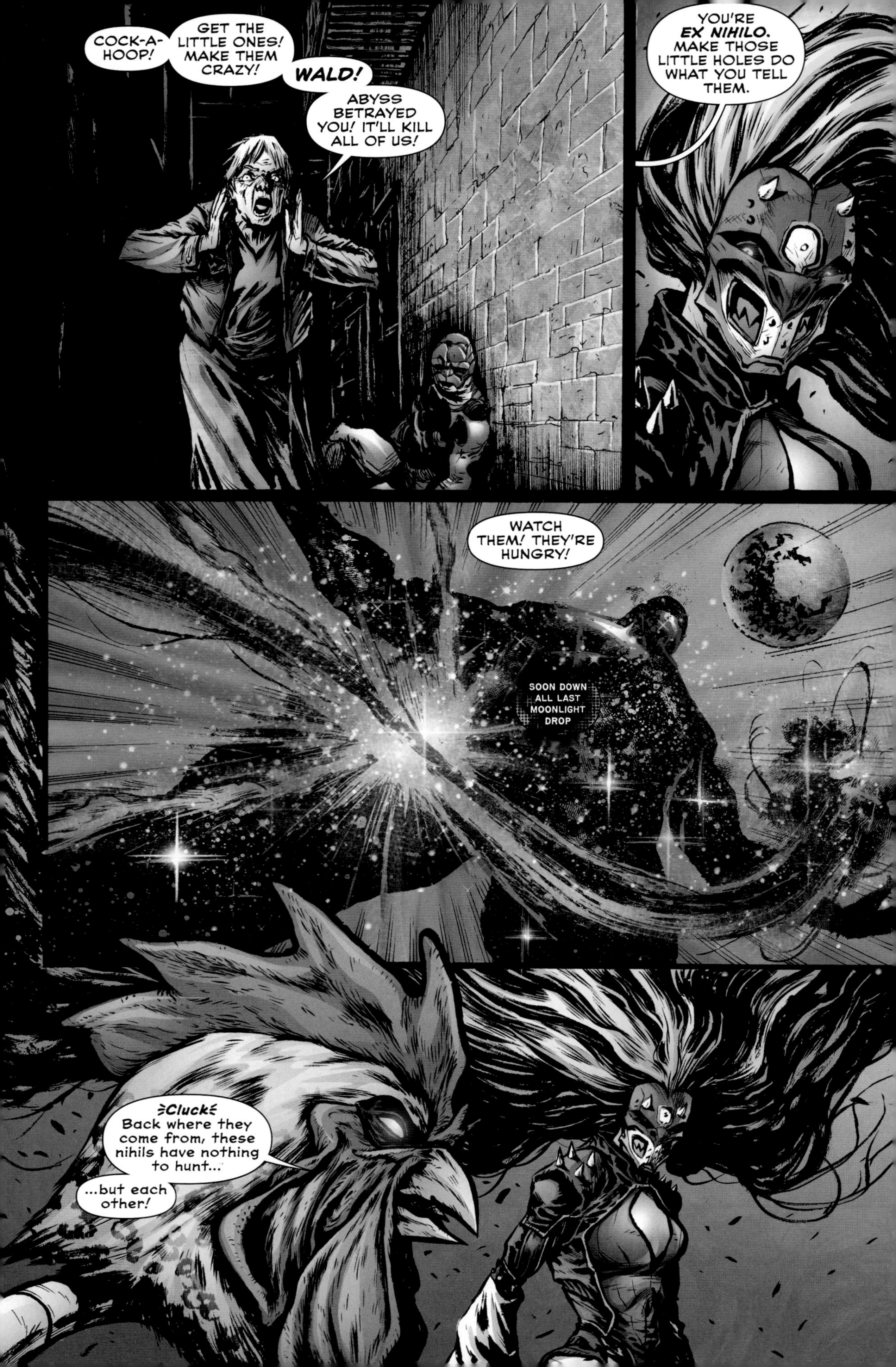
COCK-A-HOOP!
GET THE LITTLE ONES! MAKE THEM CRAZY!
WALD!
ABYSS BETRAYED YOU! IT'LL KILL ALL OF US!
YOU'RE EX NIHILO. MAKE THOSE LITTLE HOLES DO WHAT YOU TELL THEM.
WATCH THEM! THEY'RE HUNGRY!
SOON DOWN ALL LAST MOONLIGHT DROP
Cluck
Back where they come from, these nihils have nothing to hunt...
...but each other!

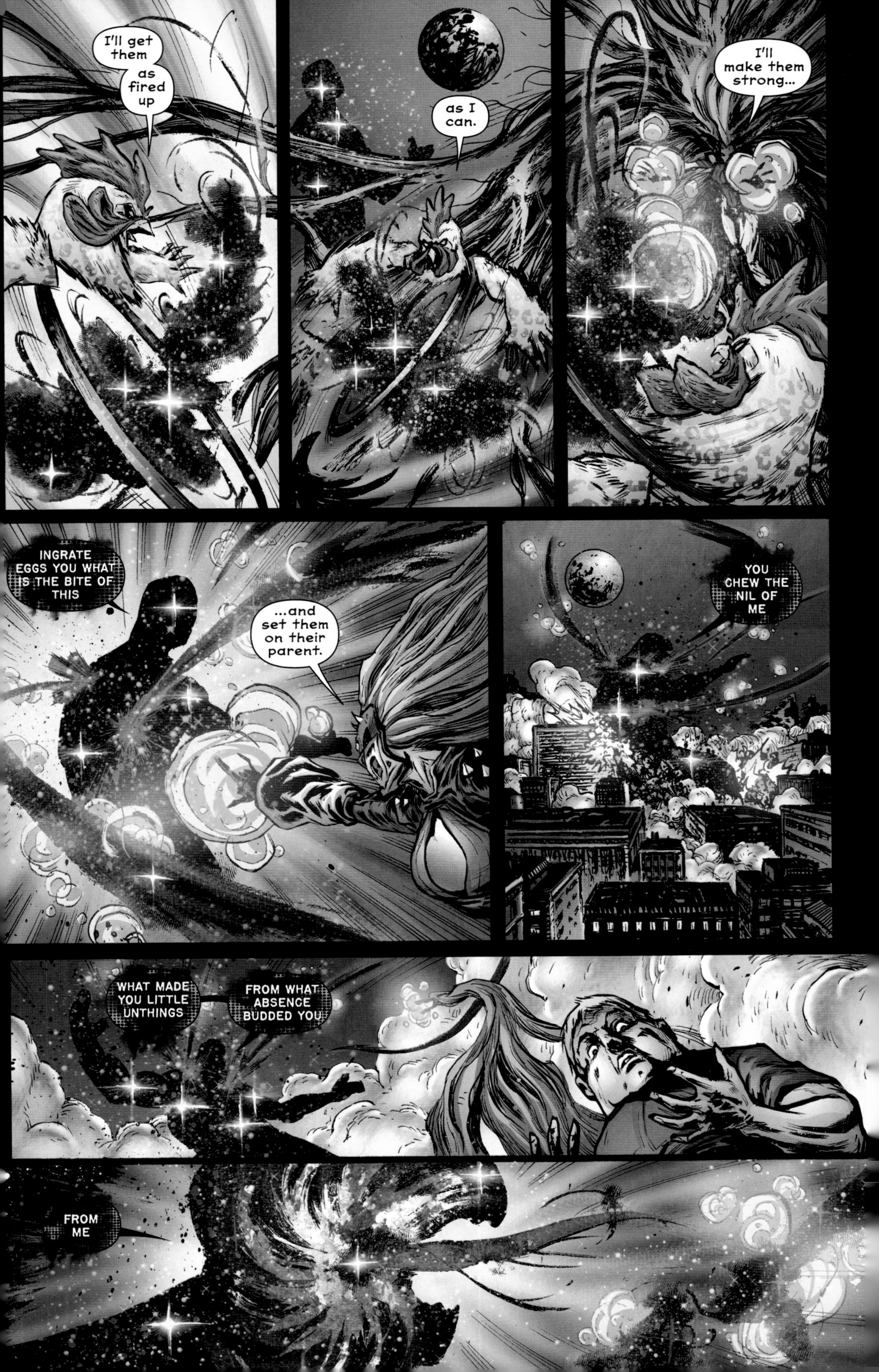
I'll get them as fired up
as I can.
I'll make them strong...
INGRATE EGGS YOU WHAT IS THE BITE OF THIS
...and set them on their parent.
YOU CHEW THE NIL OF ME
WHAT MADE YOU LITTLE UNTHINGS
FROM WHAT ABSENCE BUDDED YOU
FROM ME

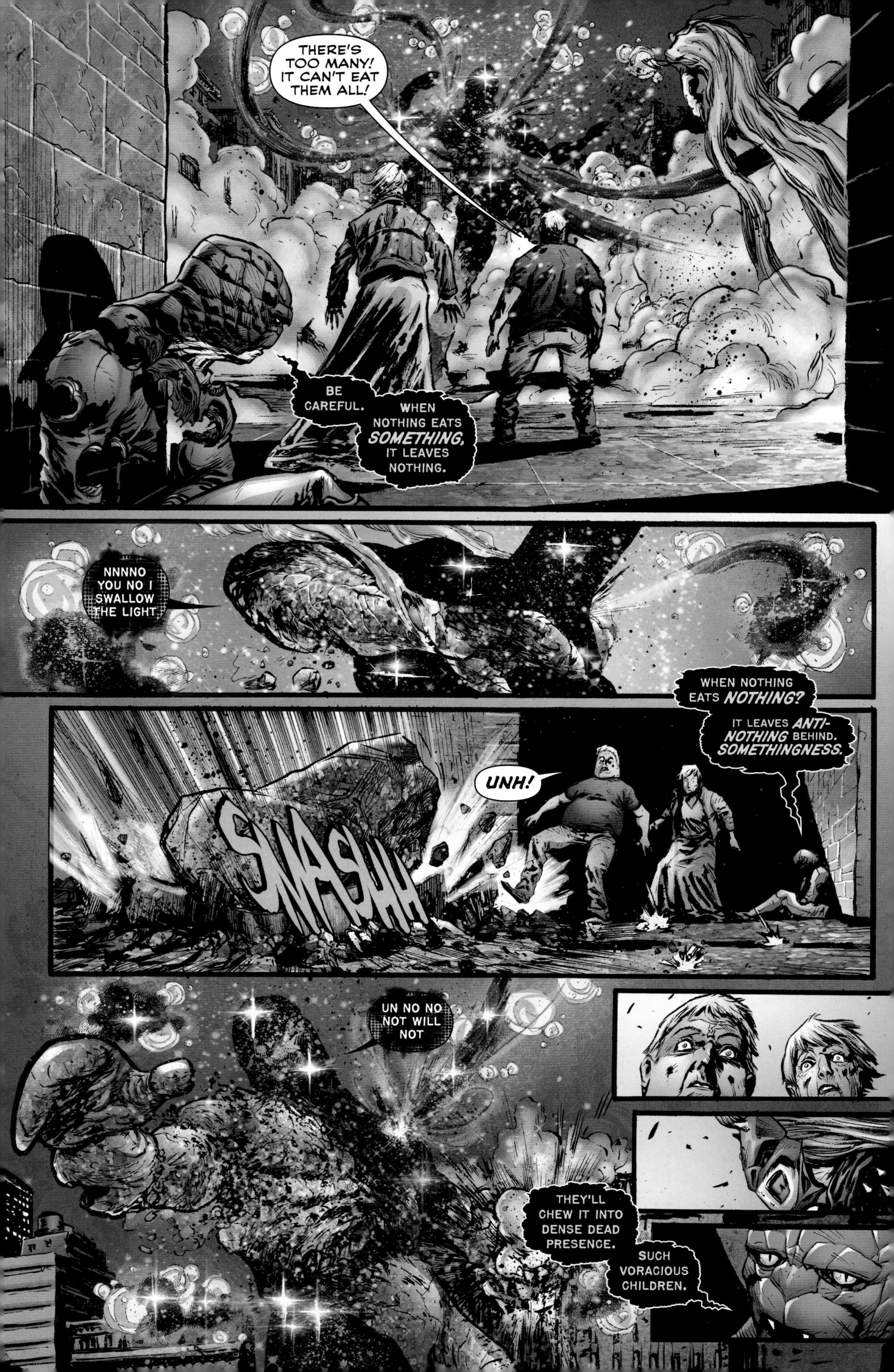
THERE'S TOO MANY! IT CAN'T EAT THEM ALL!
BE CAREFUL.
WHEN NOTHING EATS SOMETHING, IT LEAVES NOTHING.
NNNNO YOU NO I SWALLOW THE LIGHT
WHEN NOTHING EATS NOTHING?
IT LEAVES ANTI-NOTHING BEHIND. SOMETHINGNESS.
UNH!
SMASHH
UN NO NO NOT WILL NOT
THEY'LL CHEW IT INTO DENSE DEAD PRESENCE.
SUCH VORACIOUS CHILDREN.

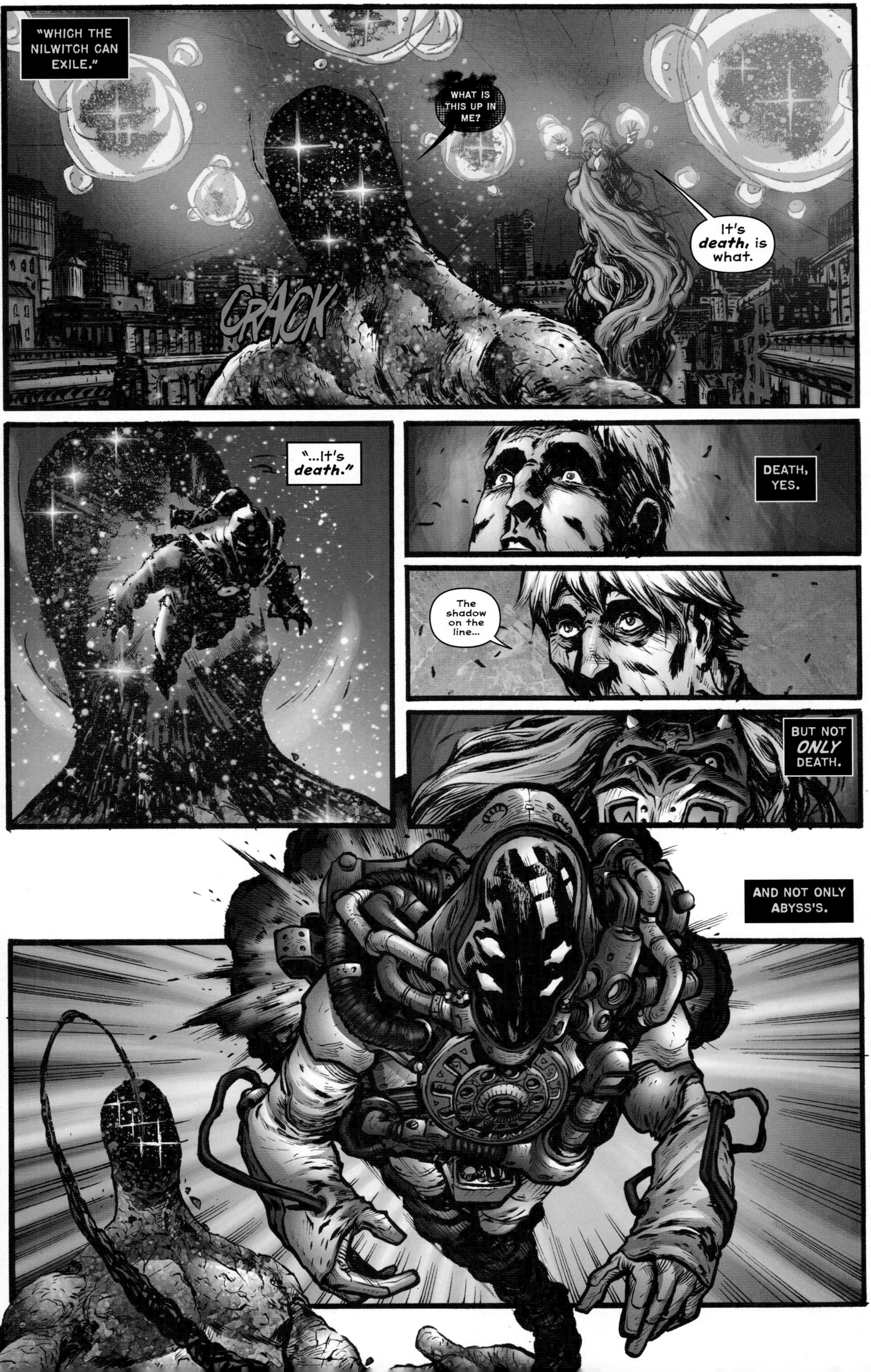
"WHICH THE NILWITCH CAN EXILE."
WHAT IS THIS UP IN ME?
It's death, is what.
CRACK
"...It's death."
DEATH, YES.
The shadow on the line...
BUT NOT ONLY DEATH.
AND NOT ONLY ABYSS'S.

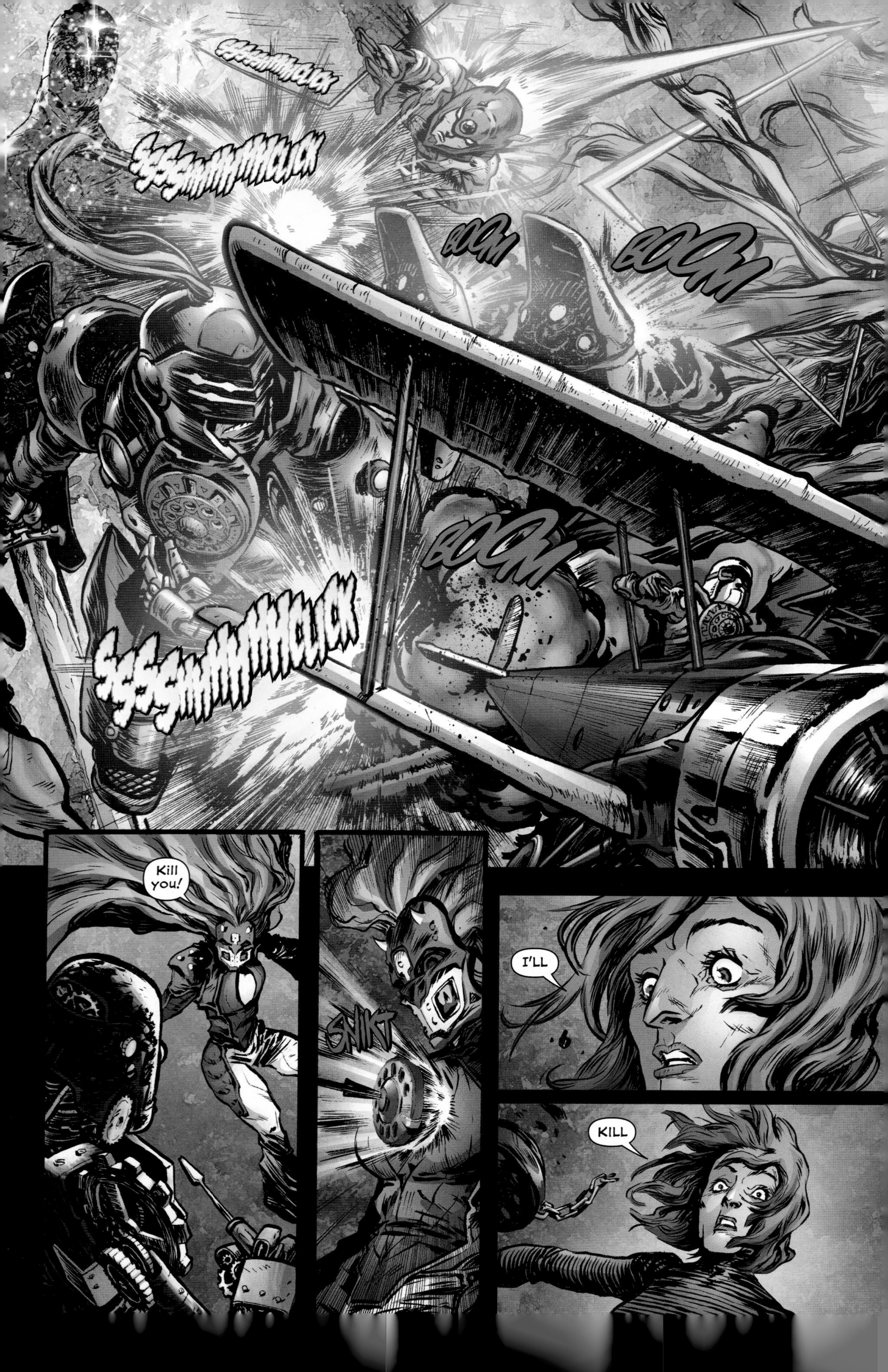
SSSSHHHHHCLICK
SSSSHHHHHCLICK
BOOM
BOOM
BOOM
SSSSHHHHHCLICK
Kill you!
SNIKT
I'LL
KILL

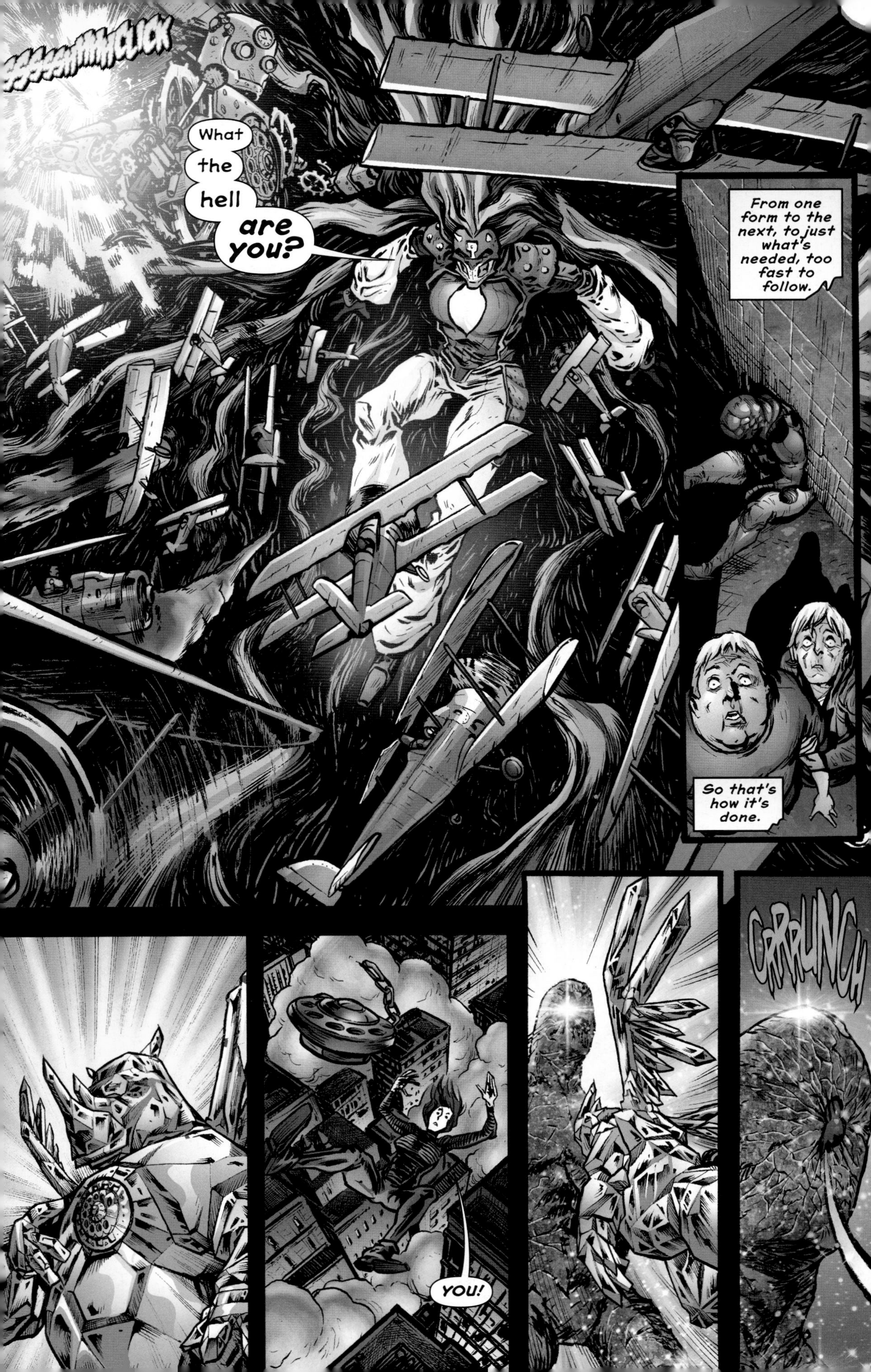
What the hell are you?
From one form to the next, to just what's needed, too fast to follow.
So that's how it's done.
YOU!
CRRUNCH

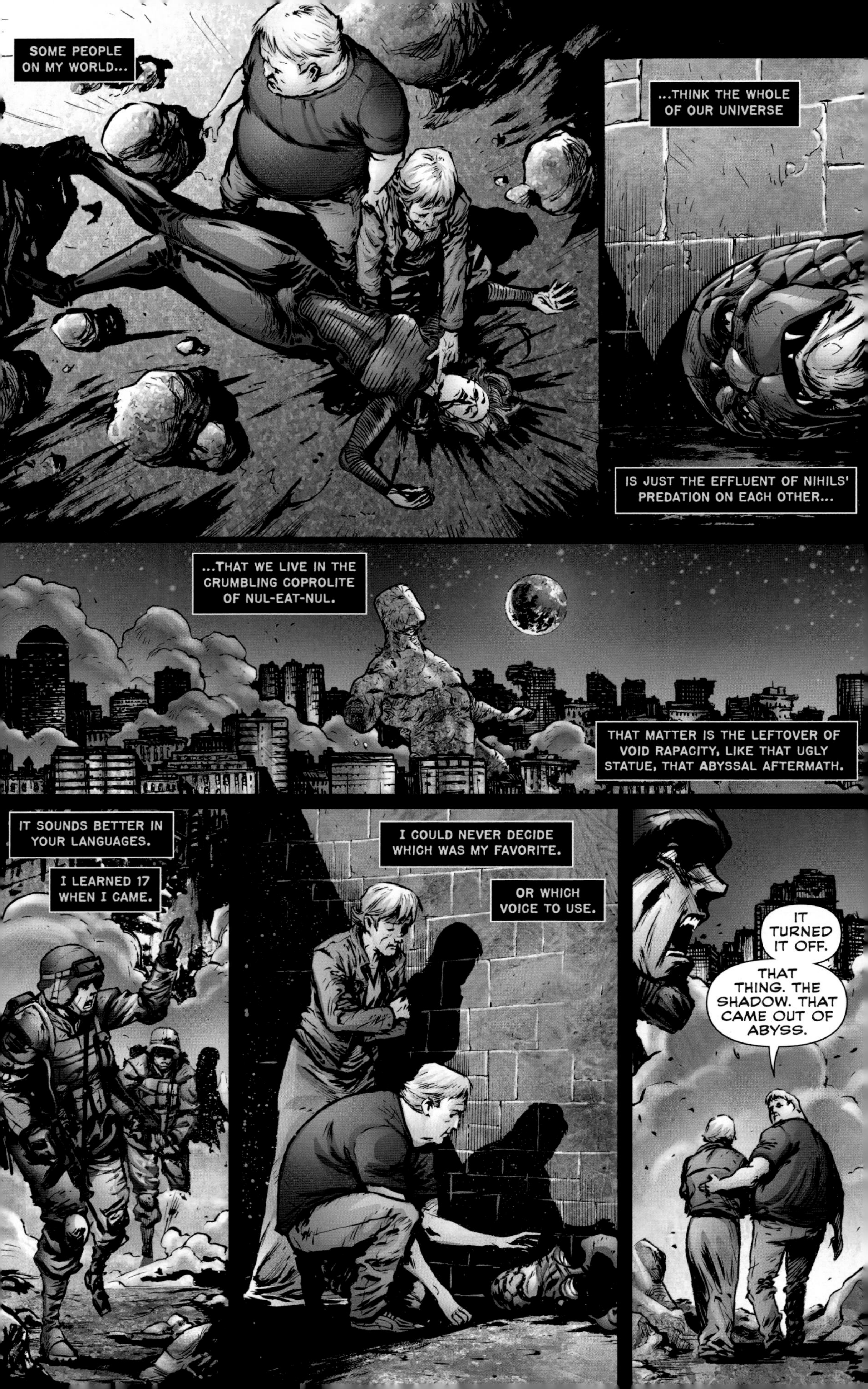
SOME PEOPLE ON MY WORLD...
...THINK THE WHOLE OF OUR UNIVERSE
IS JUST THE EFFLUENT OF NIHILS' PREDATION ON EACH OTHER...
...THAT WE LIVE IN THE CRUMBLING COPROLITE OF NUL-EAT-NUL.
THAT MATTER IS THE LEFTOVER OF VOID RAPACITY, LIKE THAT UGLY STATUE, THAT ABYSSAL AFTERMATH.
IT SOUNDS BETTER IN YOUR LANGUAGES.
I LEARNED 17 WHEN I CAME.
I COULD NEVER DECIDE WHICH WAS MY FAVORITE.
OR WHICH VOICE TO USE.
IT TURNED IT OFF.
THAT THING. THE SHADOW. THAT CAME OUT OF ABYSS.

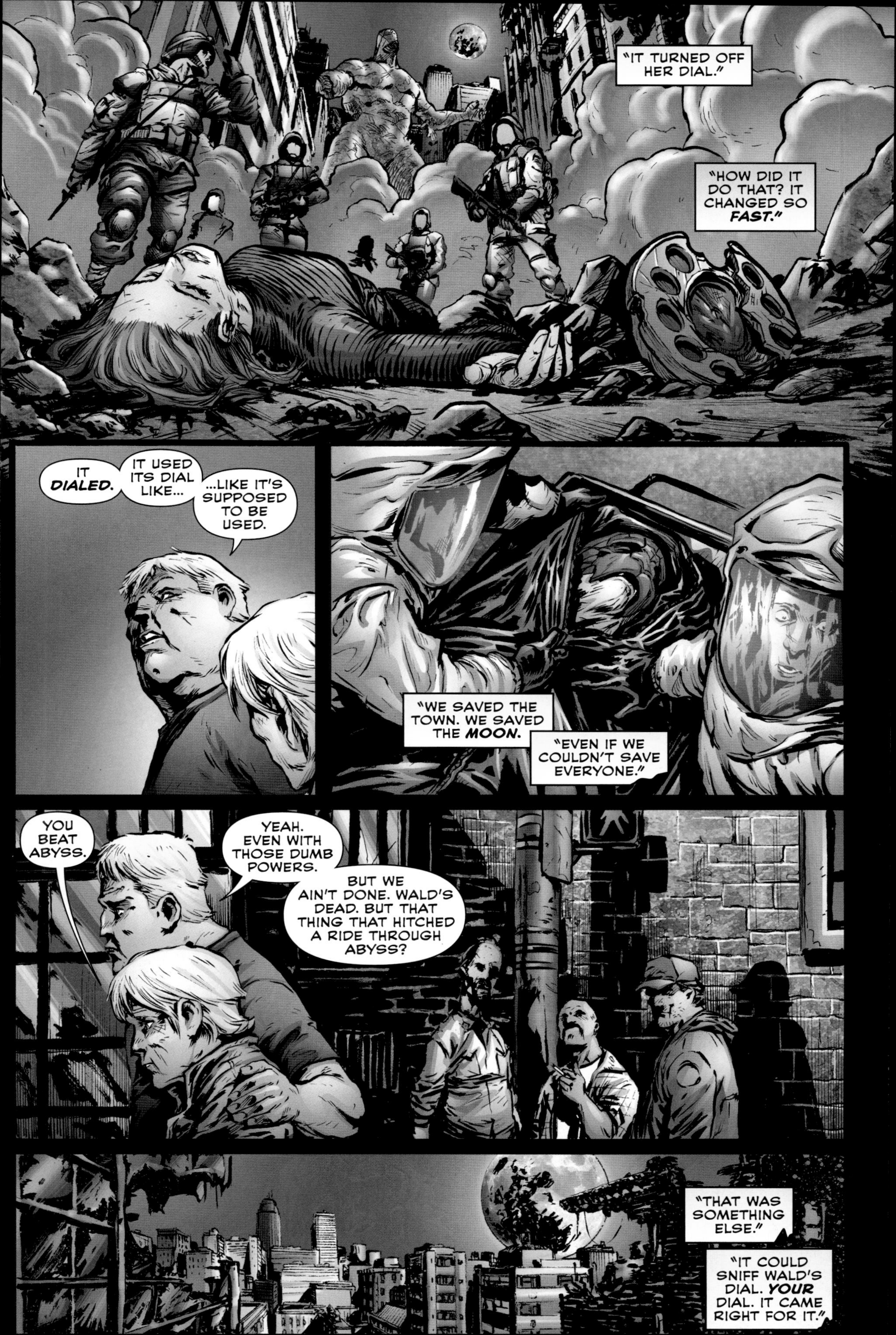
"IT TURNED OFF HER DIAL."
"HOW DID IT DO THAT? IT CHANGED SO FAST."
IT DIALED.
IT USED ITS DIAL LIKE...
...LIKE IT'S SUPPOSED TO BE USED.
"WE SAVED THE TOWN. WE SAVED THE MOON.
"EVEN IF WE COULDN'T SAVE EVERYONE."
YOU BEAT ABYSS.
YEAH. EVEN WITH THOSE DUMB POWERS.
BUT WE AIN'T DONE. WALD'S DEAD. BUT THAT THING THAT HITCHED A RIDE THROUGH ABYSS?
"THAT WAS SOMETHING ELSE."
"IT COULD SNIFF WALD'S DIAL. YOUR DIAL. IT CAME RIGHT FOR IT."

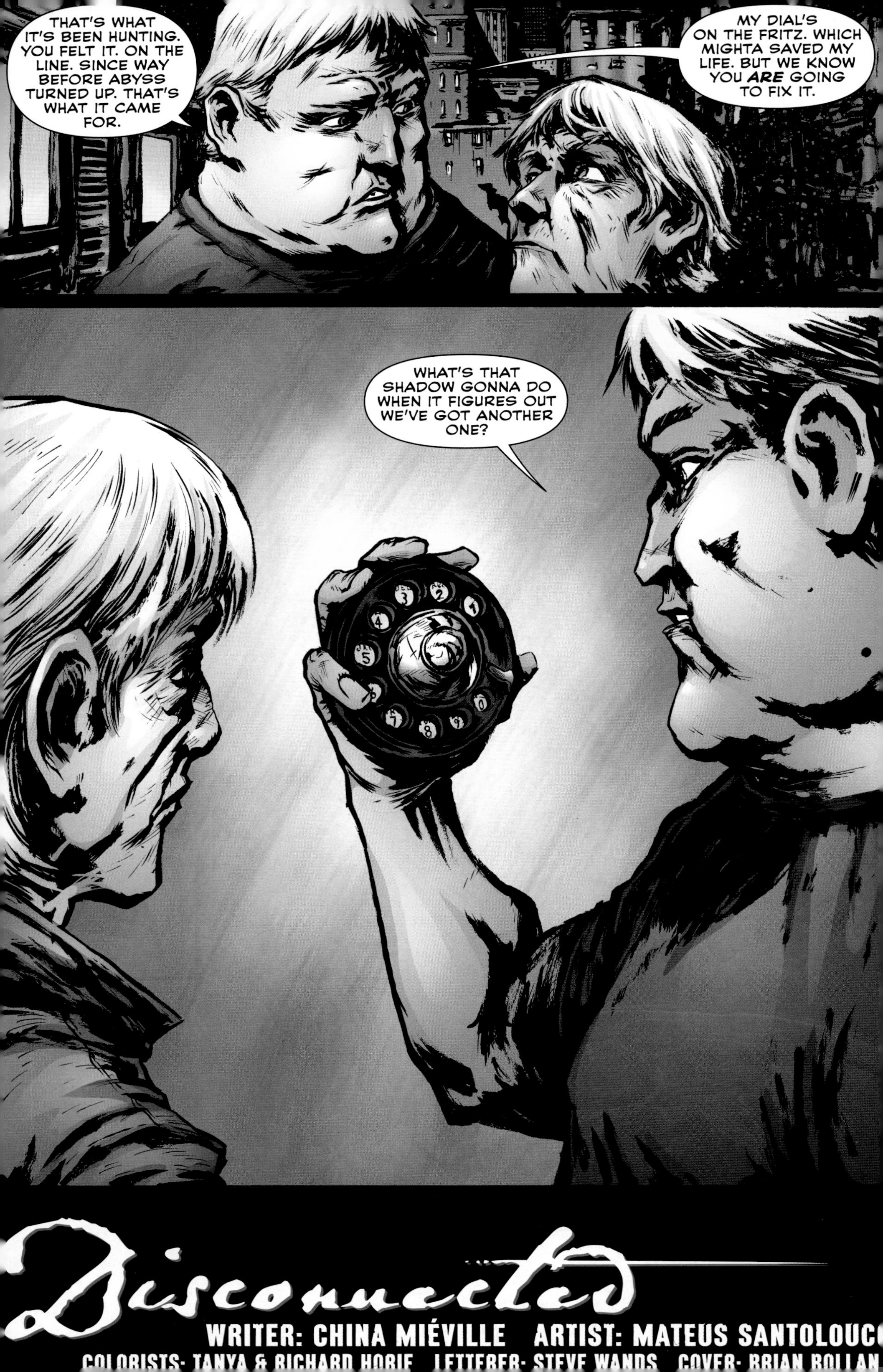
THAT'S WHAT IT'S BEEN HUNTING. YOU FELT IT. ON THE LINE. SINCE WAY BEFORE ABYSS TURNED UP. THAT'S WHAT IT CAME FOR.
MY DIAL'S ON THE FRITZ. WHICH MIGHTA SAVED MY LIFE. BUT WE KNOW YOU ARE GOING TO FIX IT.
WHAT'S THAT SHADOW GONNA DO WHEN IT FIGURES OUT WE'VE GOT ANOTHER ONE?
Disconnected
WRITER: CHINA MIÉVILLE ARTIST: MATEUS SANTOLOUCO
COLORISTS: TANYA & RICHARD HORIE LETTERER: STEVE WANDS COVER: BRIAN BOLLAND

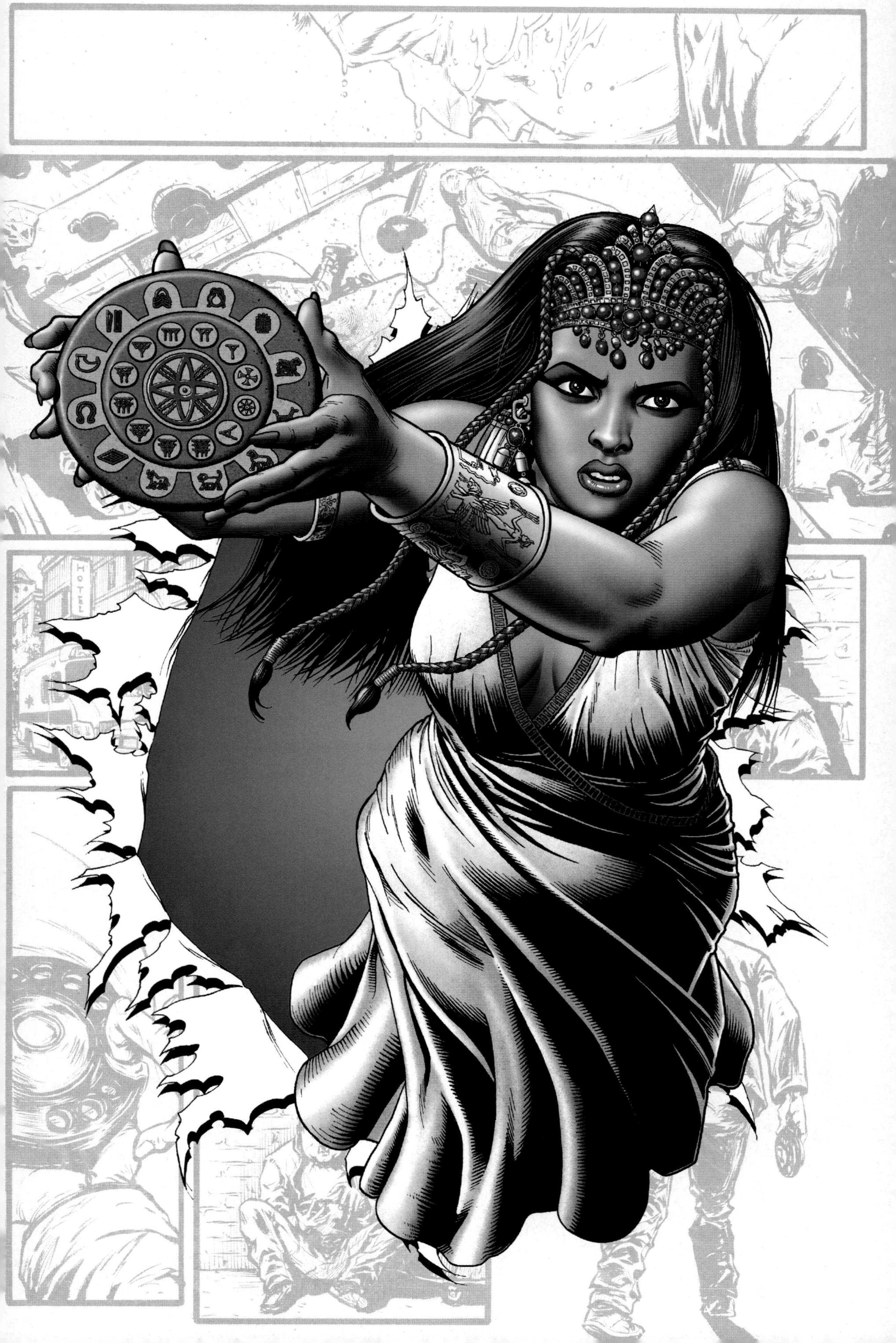
HOTEL

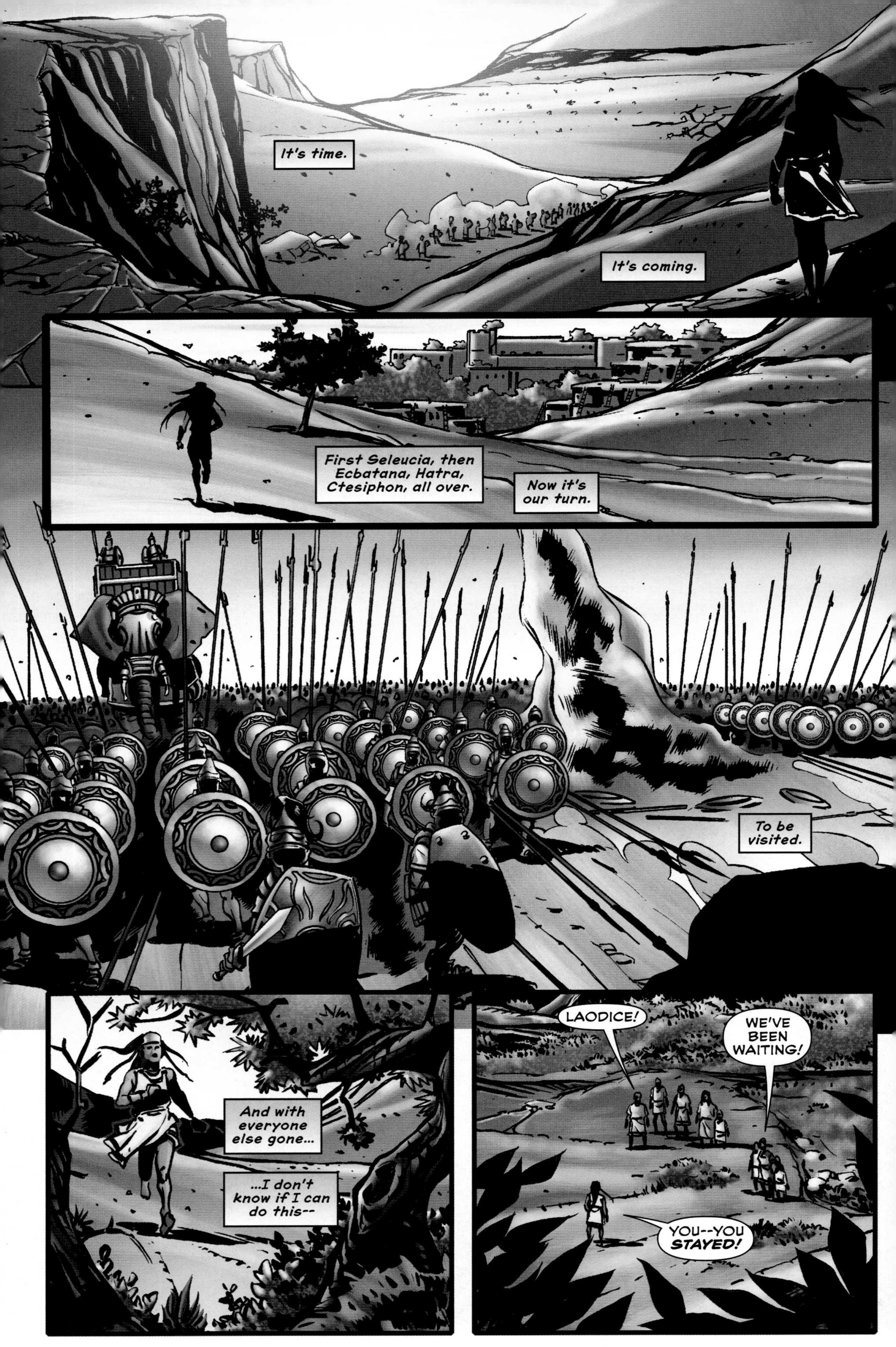

It's time.
It's coming.
First Seleucia, then Ecbatana, Hatra, Ctesiphon, all over.
Now it's our turn.
To be visited.
And with everyone else gone...
...I don't know if I can do this--
LAODICE!
WE'VE BEEN WAITING!
YOU--YOU STAYED!

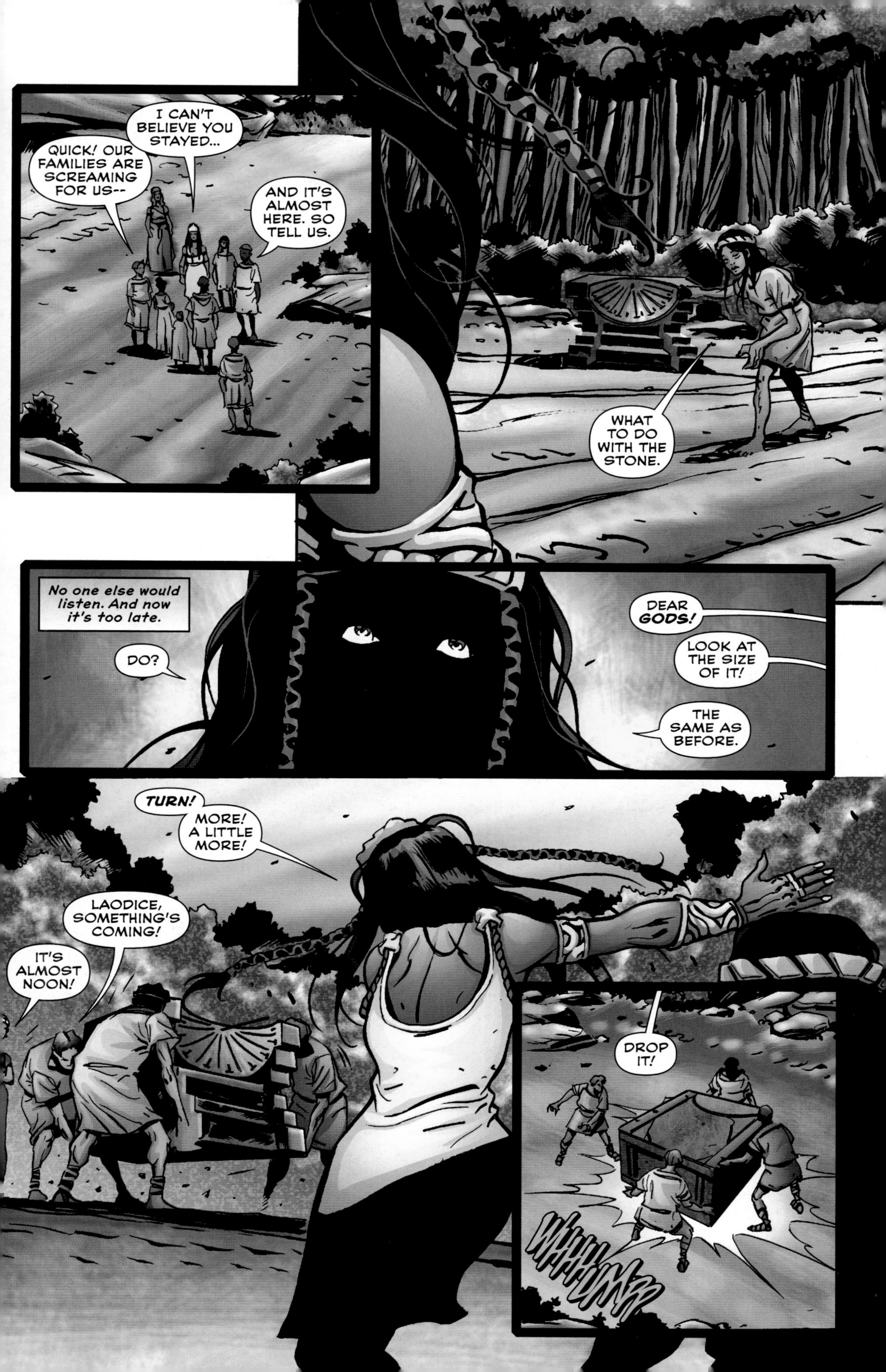
I CAN'T BELIEVE YOU STAYED...
QUICK! OUR FAMILIES ARE SCREAMING FOR US--
AND IT'S ALMOST HERE. SO TELL US.
WHAT TO DO WITH THE STONE.
No one else would listen. And now it's too late.
DO?
DEAR GODS!
LOOK AT THE SIZE OF IT!
THE SAME AS BEFORE.
TURN!
MORE! A LITTLE MORE!
LAODICE, SOMETHING'S COMING!
IT'S ALMOST NOON!
DROP IT!
WHHUMM

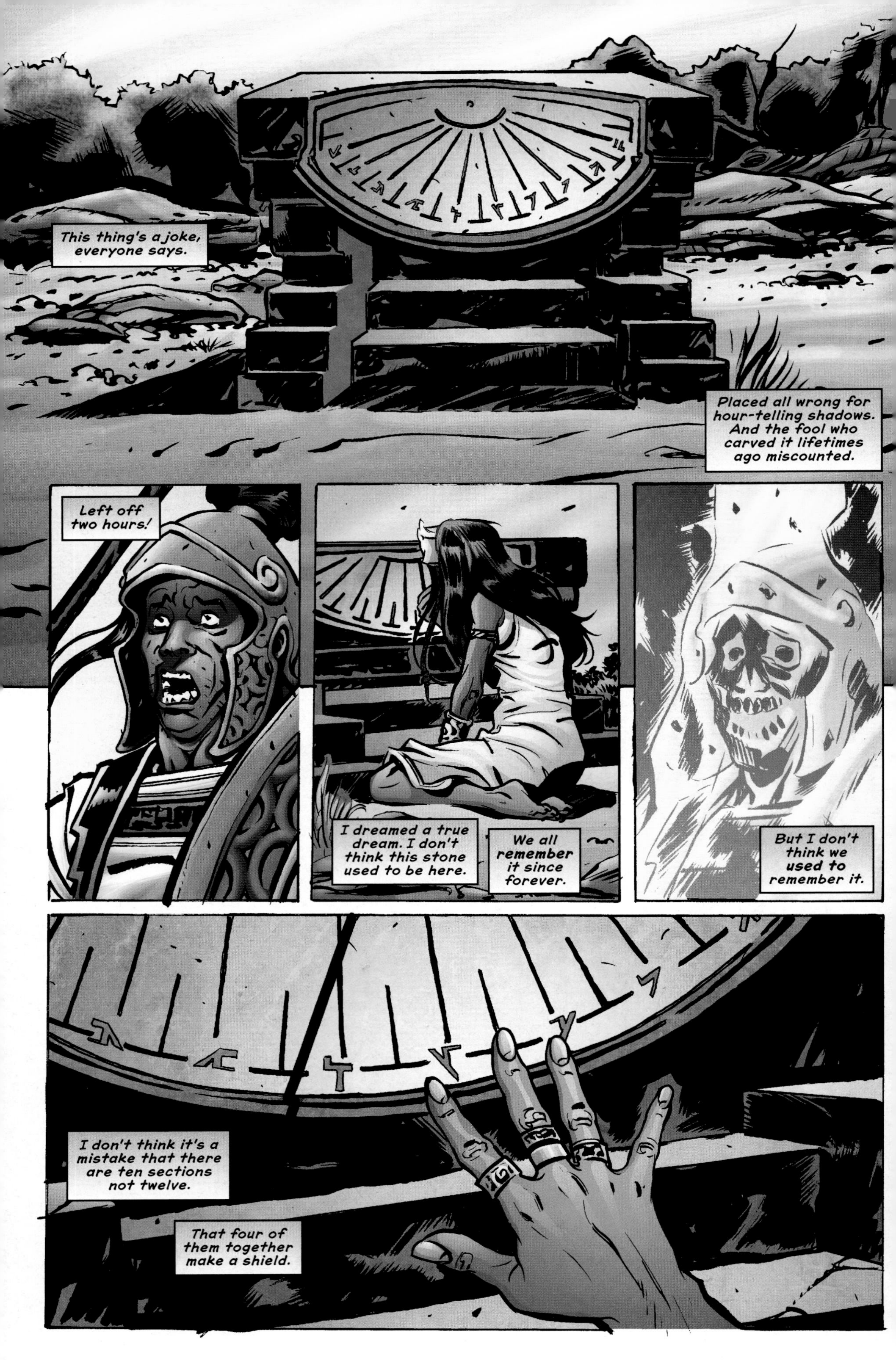
This thing's a joke, everyone says.
Placed all wrong for hour-telling shadows. And the fool who carved it lifetimes ago miscounted.
Left off two hours!
I dreamed a true dream. I don't think this stone used to be here.
We all remember it since forever.
But I don't think we used to remember it.
I don't think it's a mistake that there are ten sections not twelve.
That four of them together make a shield.

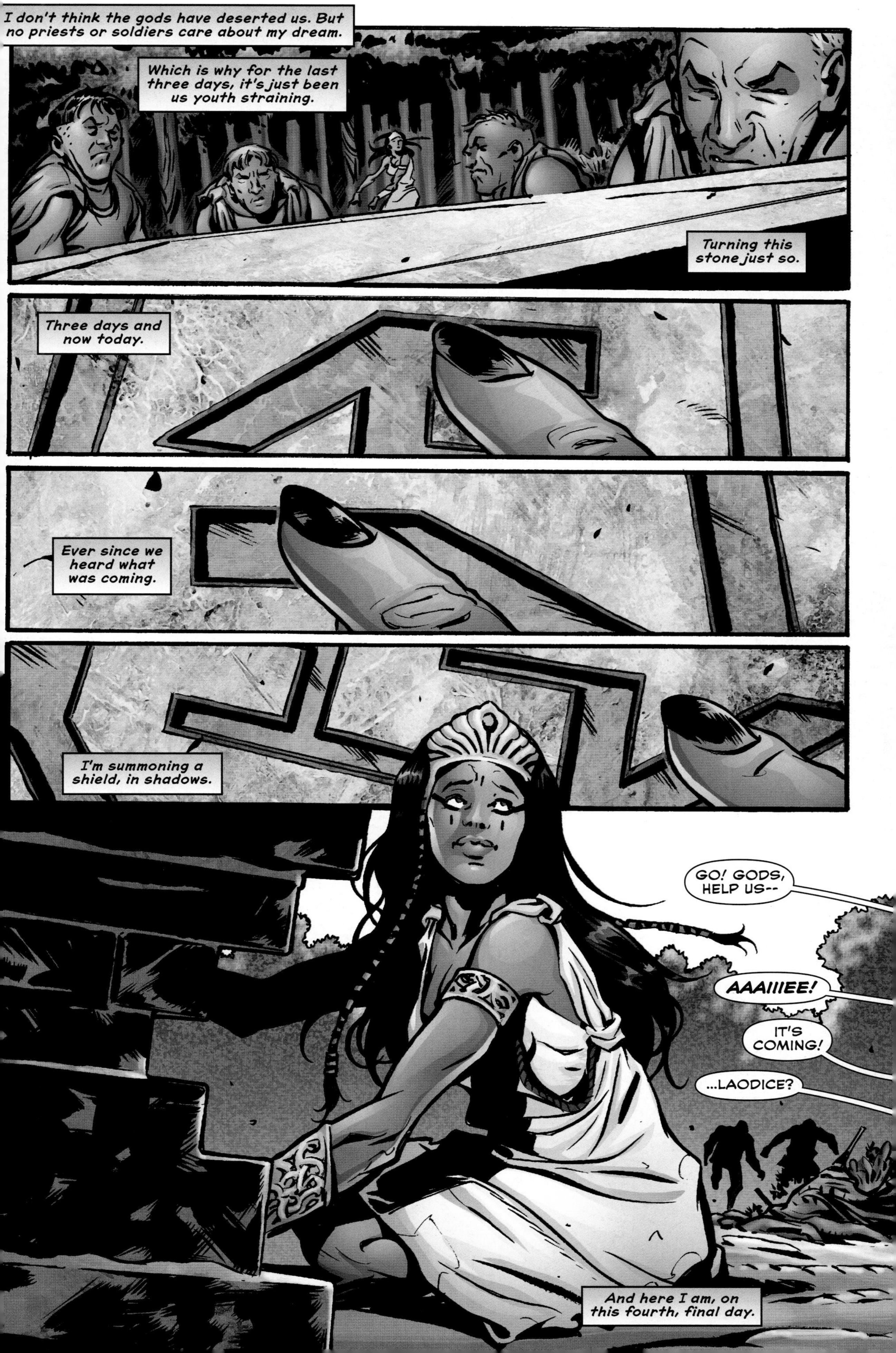
I don't think the gods have deserted us. But no priests or soldiers care about my dream.
Which is why for the last three days, it's just been us youth straining.
Turning this stone just so.
Three days and now today.
Ever since we heard what was coming.
I'm summoning a shield, in shadows.
GO! GODS, HELP US--
AAAIIIEE!
IT'S COMING!
...LAODICE?
And here I am, on this fourth, final day.

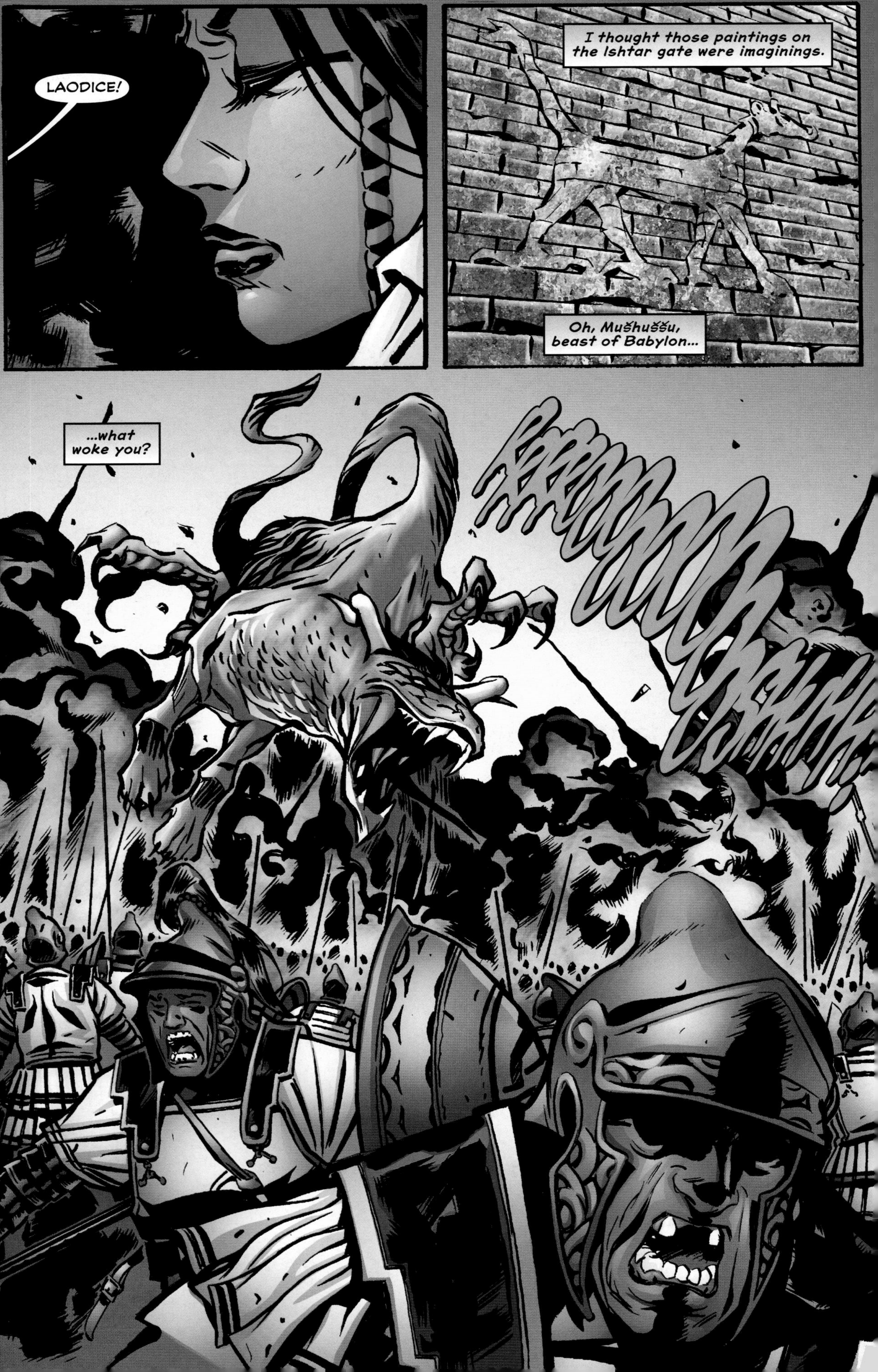
LAODICE!
I thought those paintings on the Ishtar gate were imaginings.
Oh, Mušhuššu, beast of Babylon...
...what woke you?

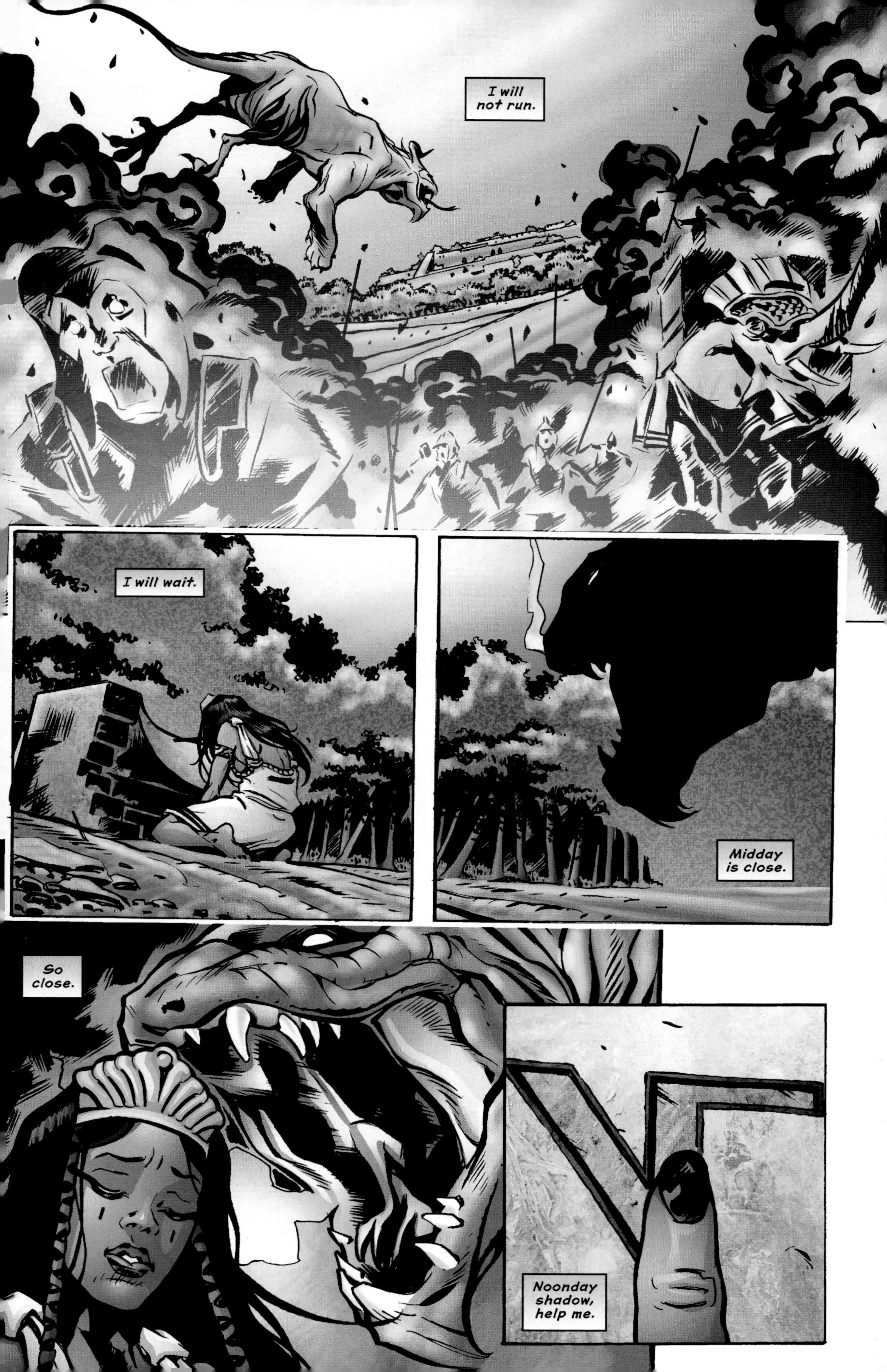
I will not run.
I will wait.
Midday is close.
So close.
Noonday shadow, help me.

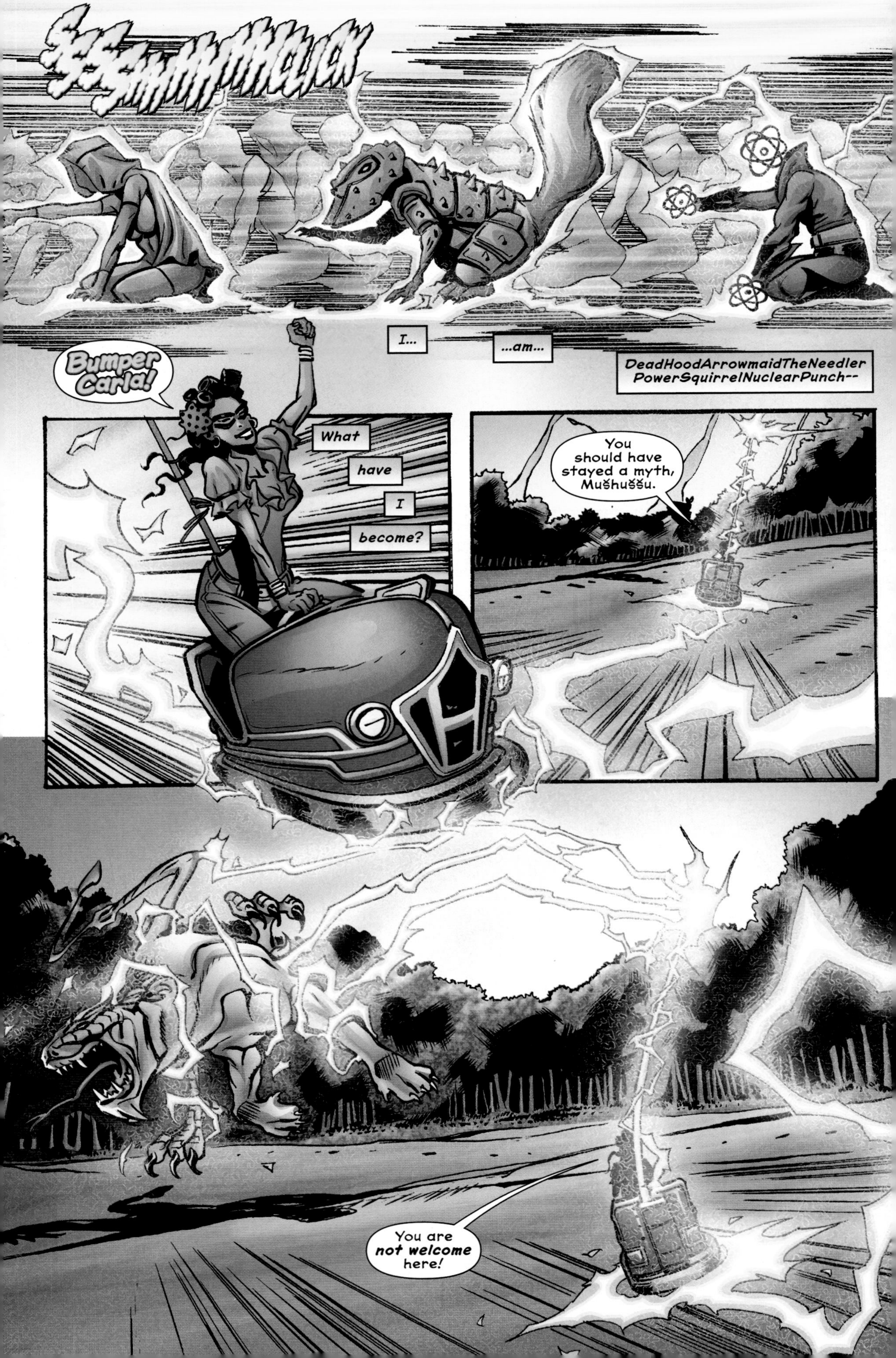
SS-SHHHHHHHCLICK
I...
...am...
DeadHoodArrowmaidTheNeedler PowerSquirrelNuclearPunch--
Bumper Carla!
What
have
I
become?
You should have stayed a myth, Mušhuššu.
You are not welcome here!

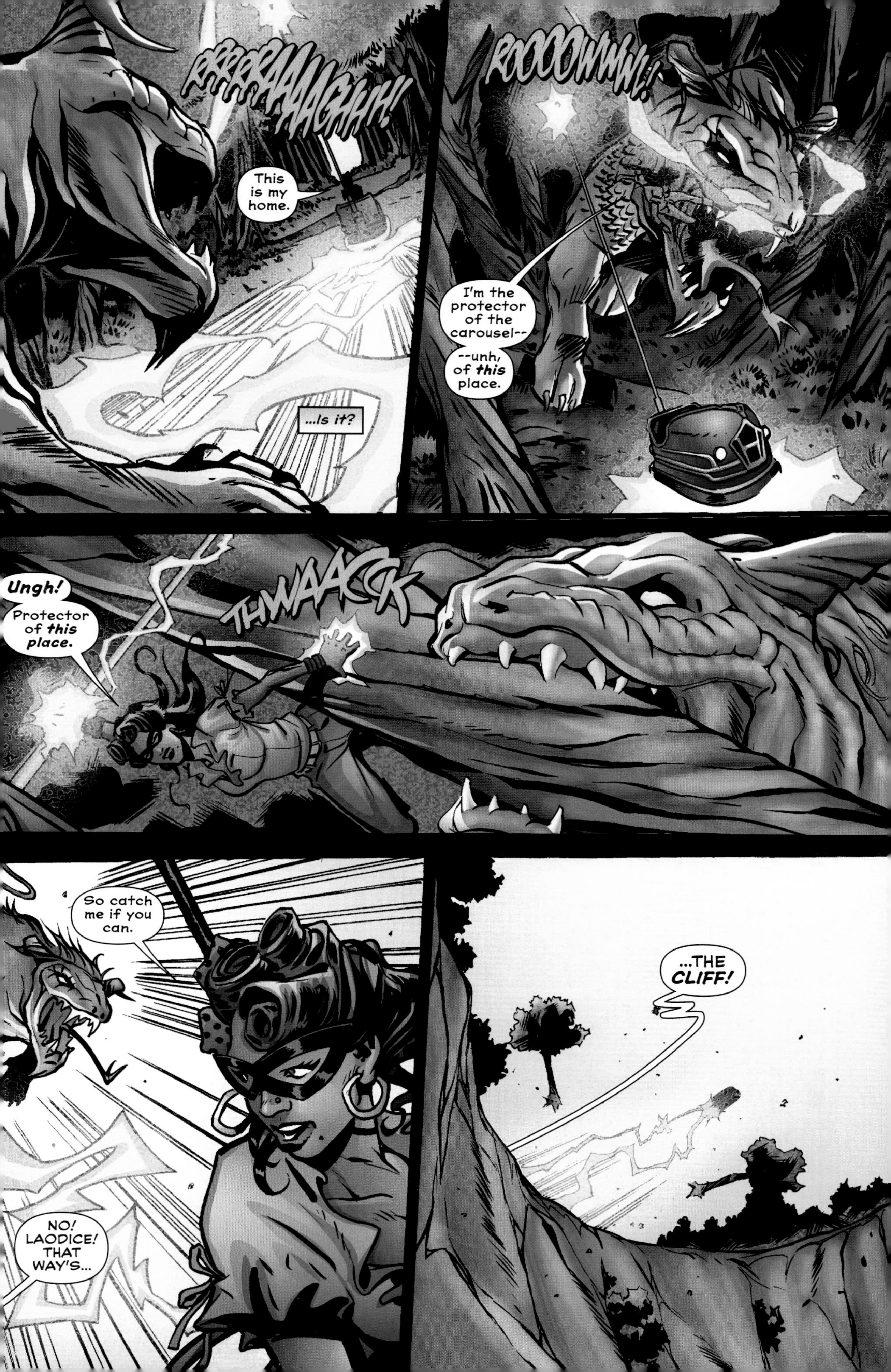
RRRRRAAAAGHHH!
This is my home.
...Is it?
ROOOOWWW!!
I'm the protector of the carousel--
--unh, of *this* place.
THWAACCK
Ungh! Protector of *this place.*
So catch me if you can.
NO! LAODICE! THAT WAY'S...
...THE *CLIFF!*

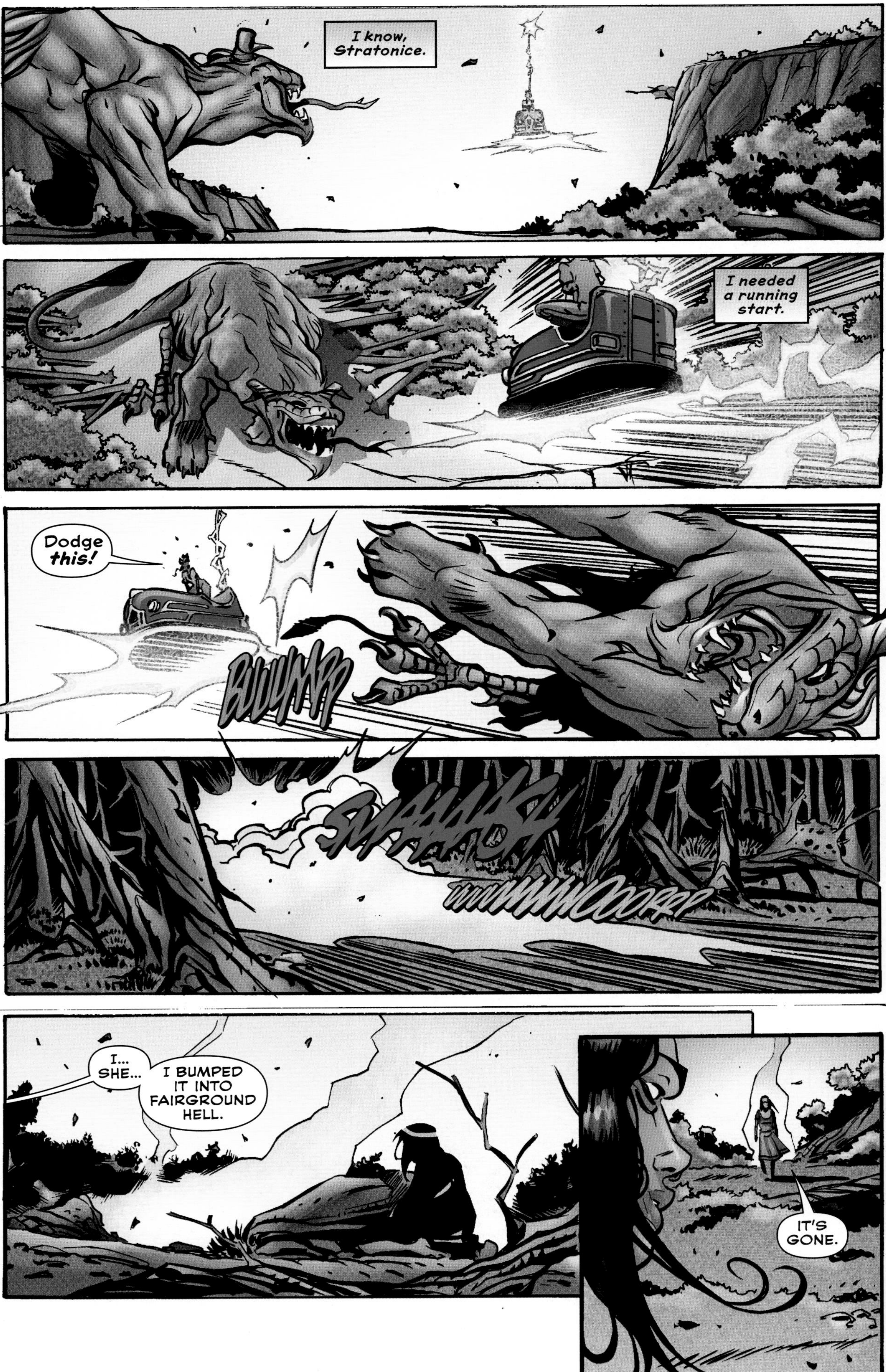
I know, Stratonice.
I needed a running start.
Dodge this!
BUUMP
SWAAAASH
WOOORP
I... SHE...
I BUMPED IT INTO FAIRGROUND HELL.
IT'S GONE.

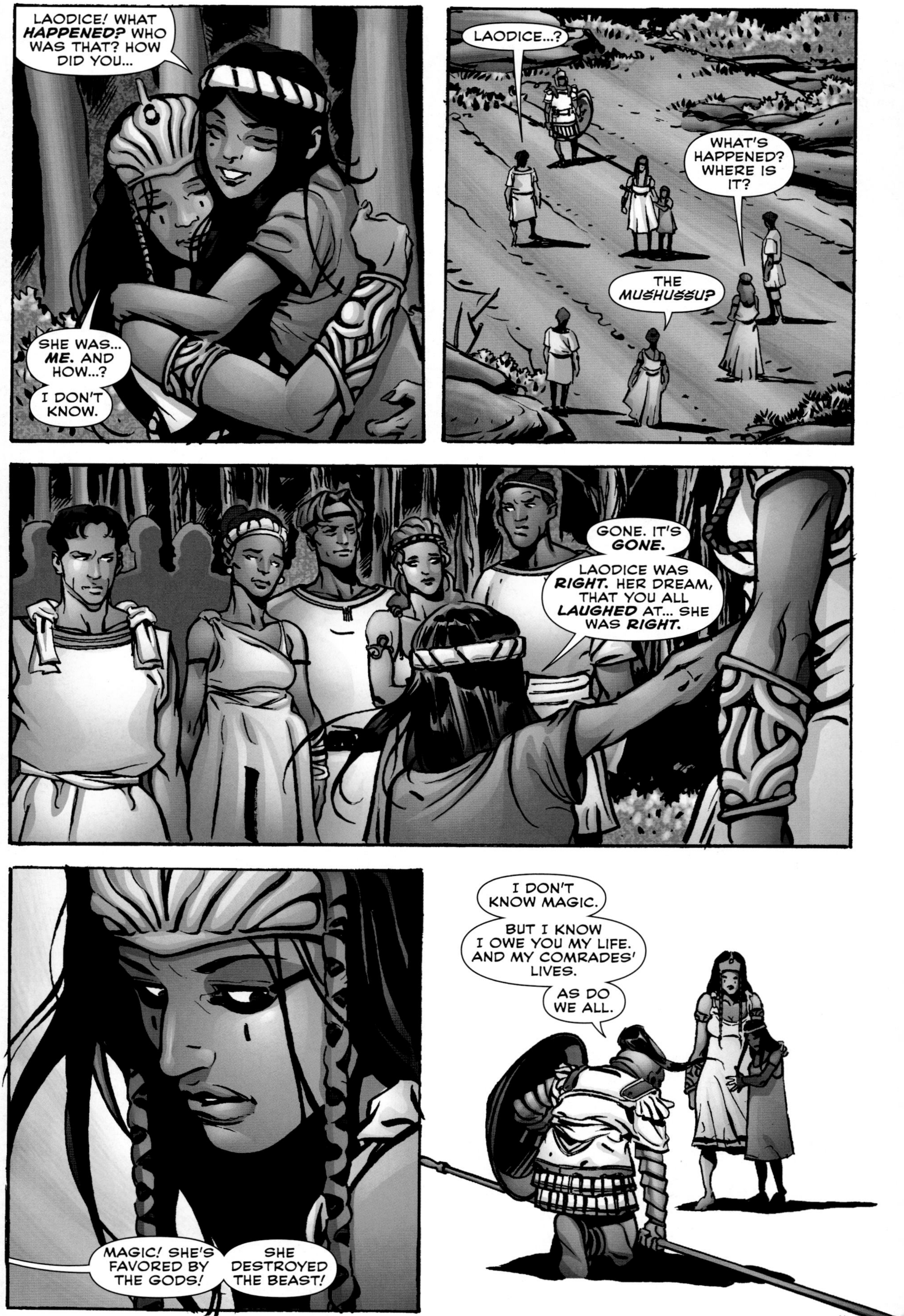
LAODICE! WHAT HAPPENED? WHO WAS THAT? HOW DID YOU...
SHE WAS... ME. AND HOW...?
I DON'T KNOW.
LAODICE...?
WHAT'S HAPPENED? WHERE IS IT?
THE MUSHUSSU?
GONE. IT'S GONE.
LAODICE WAS RIGHT. HER DREAM, THAT YOU ALL LAUGHED AT... SHE WAS RIGHT.
MAGIC! SHE'S FAVORED BY THE GODS!
SHE DESTROYED THE BEAST!
I DON'T KNOW MAGIC.
BUT I KNOW I OWE YOU MY LIFE. AND MY COMRADES' LIVES.
AS DO WE ALL.

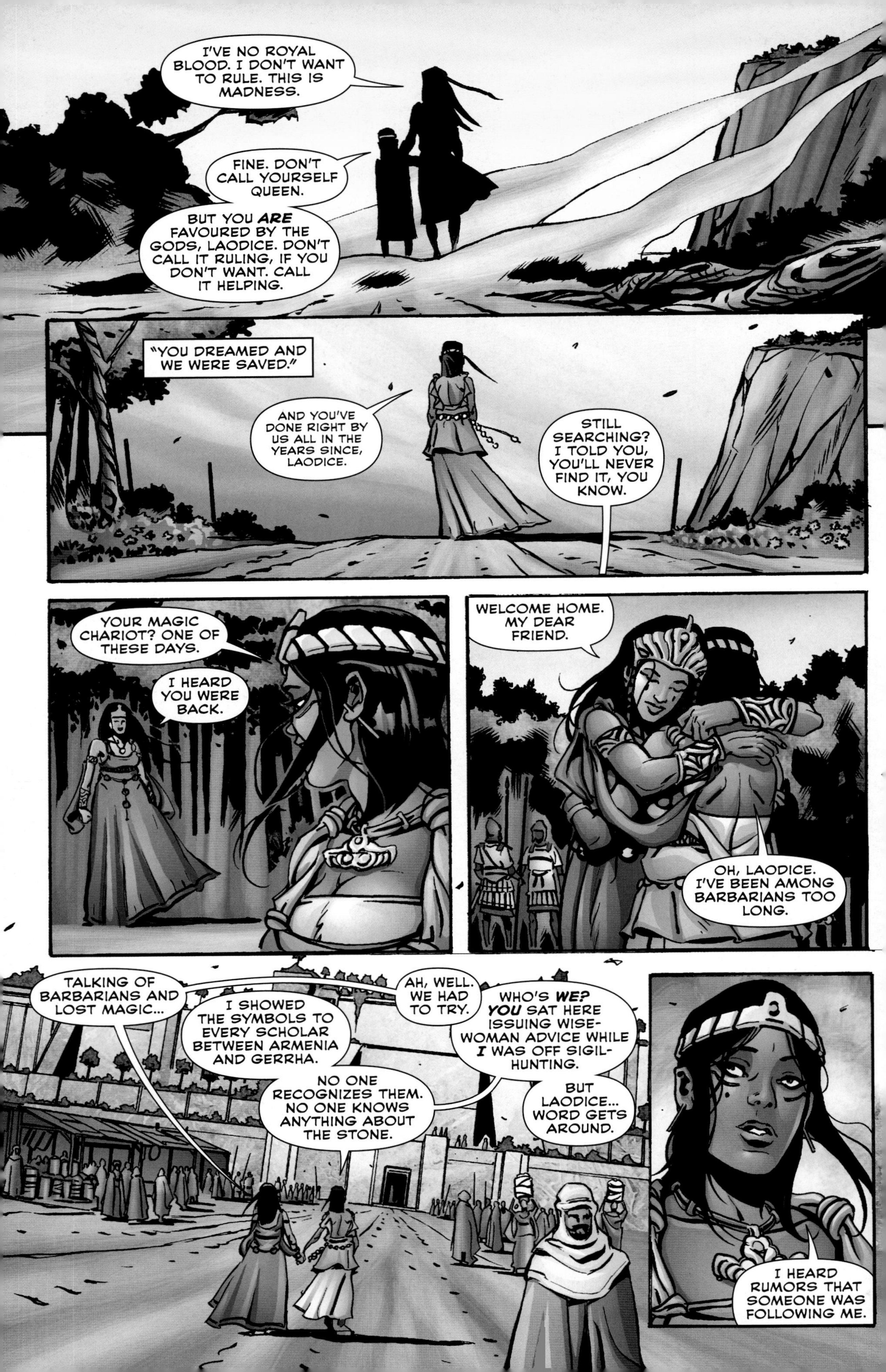
I'VE NO ROYAL BLOOD. I DON'T WANT TO RULE. THIS IS MADNESS.
FINE. DON'T CALL YOURSELF QUEEN.
BUT YOU *ARE* FAVOURED BY THE GODS, LAODICE. DON'T CALL IT RULING, IF YOU DON'T WANT. CALL IT HELPING.
"YOU DREAMED AND WE WERE SAVED."
AND YOU'VE DONE RIGHT BY US ALL IN THE YEARS SINCE, LAODICE.
STILL SEARCHING? I TOLD YOU, YOU'LL NEVER FIND IT, YOU KNOW.
YOUR MAGIC CHARIOT? ONE OF THESE DAYS.
I HEARD YOU WERE BACK.
WELCOME HOME. MY DEAR FRIEND.
OH, LAODICE. I'VE BEEN AMONG BARBARIANS TOO LONG.
TALKING OF BARBARIANS AND LOST MAGIC...
I SHOWED THE SYMBOLS TO EVERY SCHOLAR BETWEEN ARMENIA AND GERRHA.
NO ONE RECOGNIZES THEM. NO ONE KNOWS ANYTHING ABOUT THE STONE.
AH, WELL. WE HAD TO TRY.
WHO'S *WE? YOU* SAT HERE ISSUING WISE-WOMAN ADVICE WHILE *I* WAS OFF SIGIL-HUNTING.
BUT LAODICE... WORD GETS AROUND.
I HEARD RUMORS THAT SOMEONE WAS FOLLOWING ME.

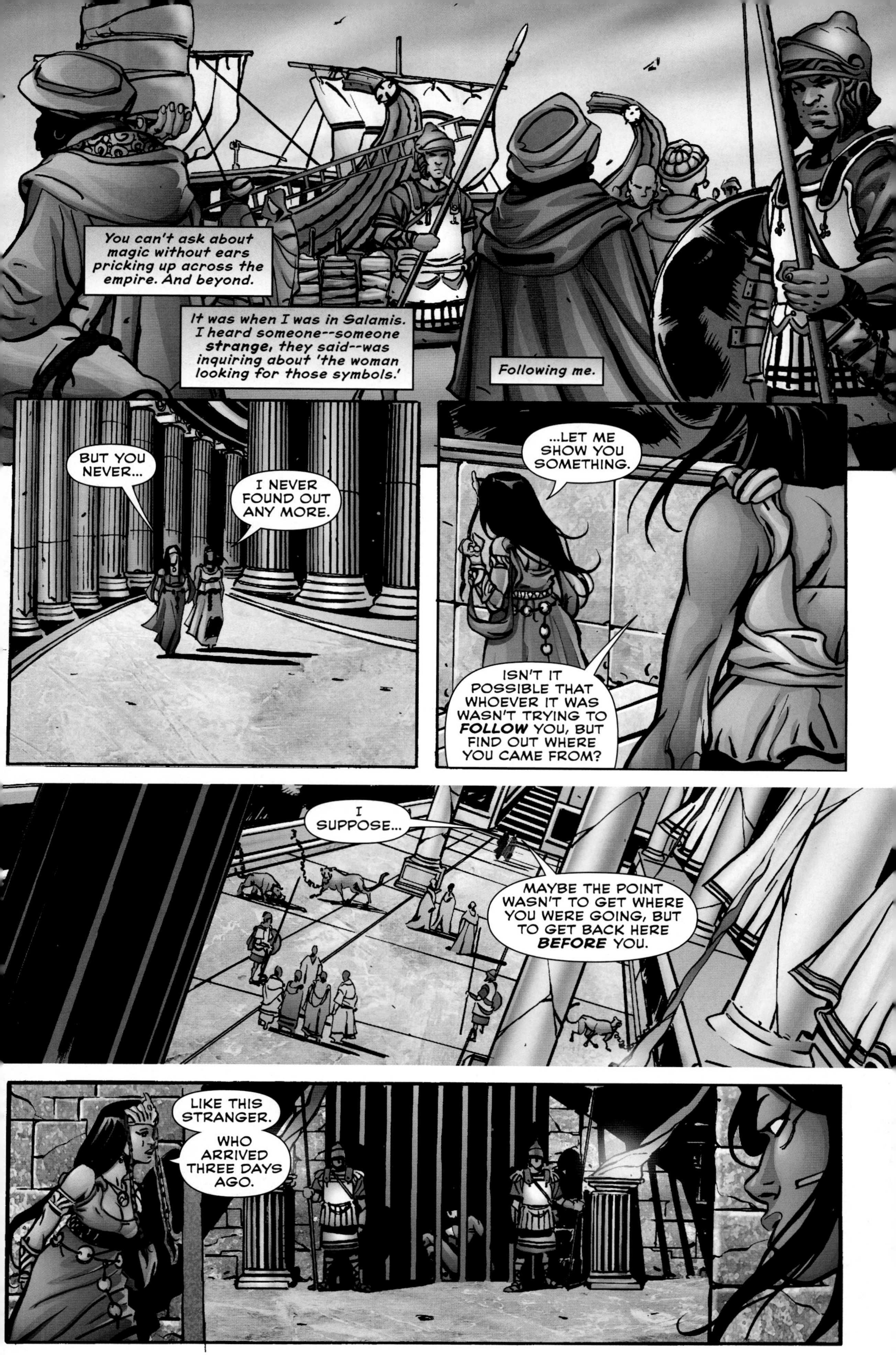
You can't ask about magic without ears pricking up across the empire. And beyond.
It was when I was in Salamis. I heard someone--someone strange, they said--was inquiring about 'the woman looking for those symbols.'
Following me.
BUT YOU NEVER...
I NEVER FOUND OUT ANY MORE.
...LET ME SHOW YOU SOMETHING.
ISN'T IT POSSIBLE THAT WHOEVER IT WAS WASN'T TRYING TO FOLLOW YOU, BUT FIND OUT WHERE YOU CAME FROM?
I SUPPOSE...
MAYBE THE POINT WASN'T TO GET WHERE YOU WERE GOING, BUT TO GET BACK HERE BEFORE YOU.
LIKE THIS STRANGER.
WHO ARRIVED THREE DAYS AGO.

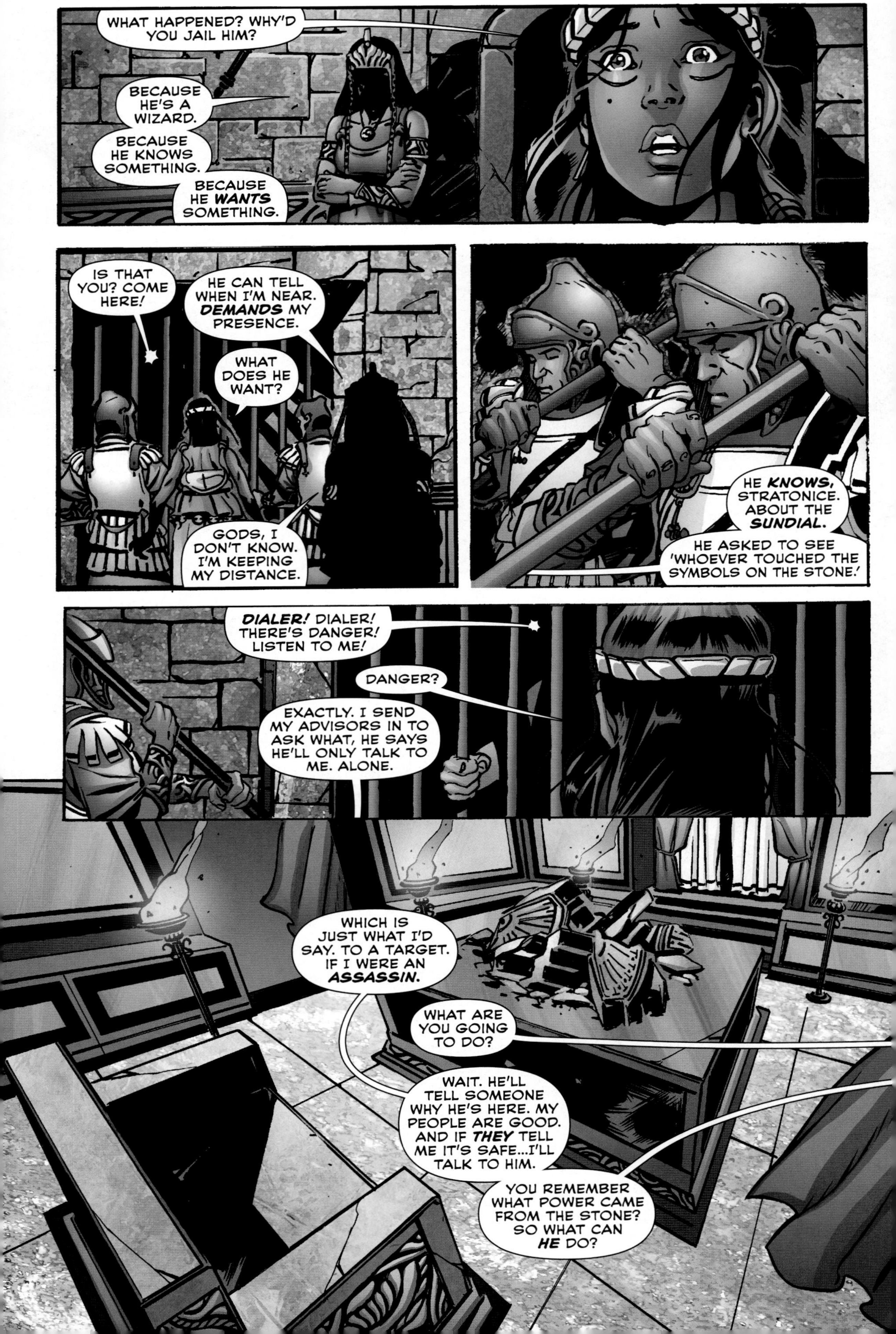
WHAT HAPPENED? WHY'D YOU JAIL HIM?
BECAUSE HE'S A WIZARD.
BECAUSE HE KNOWS SOMETHING.
BECAUSE HE *WANTS* SOMETHING.
IS THAT YOU? COME HERE!
HE CAN TELL WHEN I'M NEAR. *DEMANDS* MY PRESENCE.
WHAT DOES HE WANT?
GODS, I DON'T KNOW. I'M KEEPING MY DISTANCE.
HE *KNOWS*, STRATONICE. ABOUT THE *SUNDIAL.*
HE ASKED TO SEE 'WHOEVER TOUCHED THE SYMBOLS ON THE STONE.'
DIALER! DIALER! THERE'S DANGER! LISTEN TO ME!
DANGER?
EXACTLY. I SEND MY ADVISORS IN TO ASK WHAT, HE SAYS HE'LL ONLY TALK TO ME. ALONE.
WHICH IS JUST WHAT I'D SAY. TO A TARGET. IF I WERE AN *ASSASSIN.*
WHAT ARE YOU GOING TO DO?
WAIT. HE'LL TELL SOMEONE WHY HE'S HERE. MY PEOPLE ARE GOOD. AND IF *THEY* TELL ME IT'S SAFE...I'LL TALK TO HIM.
YOU REMEMBER WHAT POWER CAME FROM THE STONE? SO WHAT CAN *HE* DO?

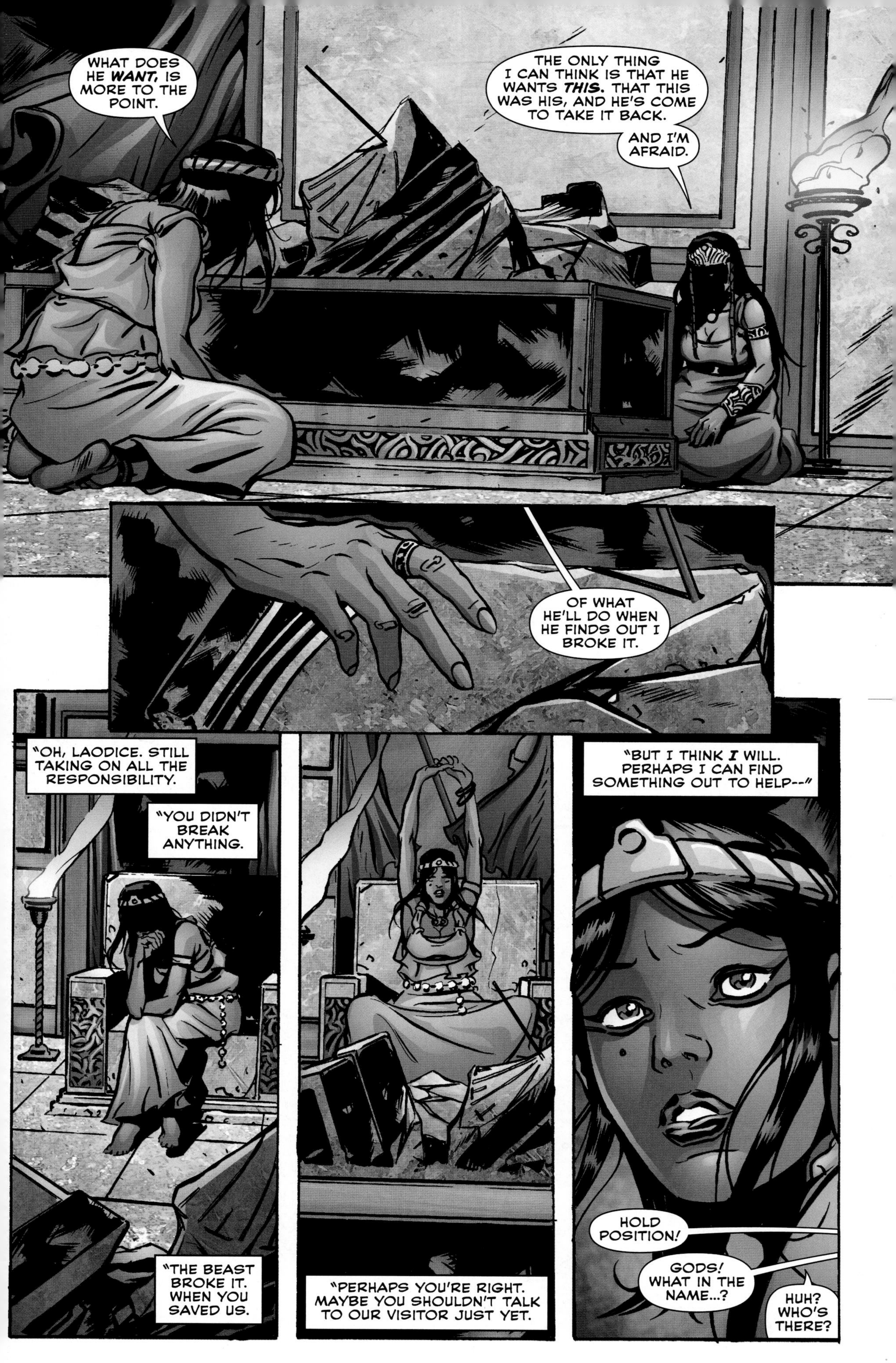
WHAT DOES HE *WANT,* IS MORE TO THE POINT.
THE ONLY THING I CAN THINK IS THAT HE WANTS *THIS.* THAT THIS WAS HIS, AND HE'S COME TO TAKE IT BACK.
AND I'M AFRAID.
OF WHAT HE'LL DO WHEN HE FINDS OUT I BROKE IT.
"OH, LAODICE. STILL TAKING ON ALL THE RESPONSIBILITY.
"YOU DIDN'T BREAK ANYTHING.
"THE BEAST BROKE IT. WHEN YOU SAVED US.
"PERHAPS YOU'RE RIGHT. MAYBE YOU SHOULDN'T TALK TO OUR VISITOR JUST YET.
"BUT I THINK *I* WILL. PERHAPS I CAN FIND SOMETHING OUT TO HELP--"
HOLD POSITION!
GODS! WHAT IN THE NAME...?
HUH? WHO'S THERE?

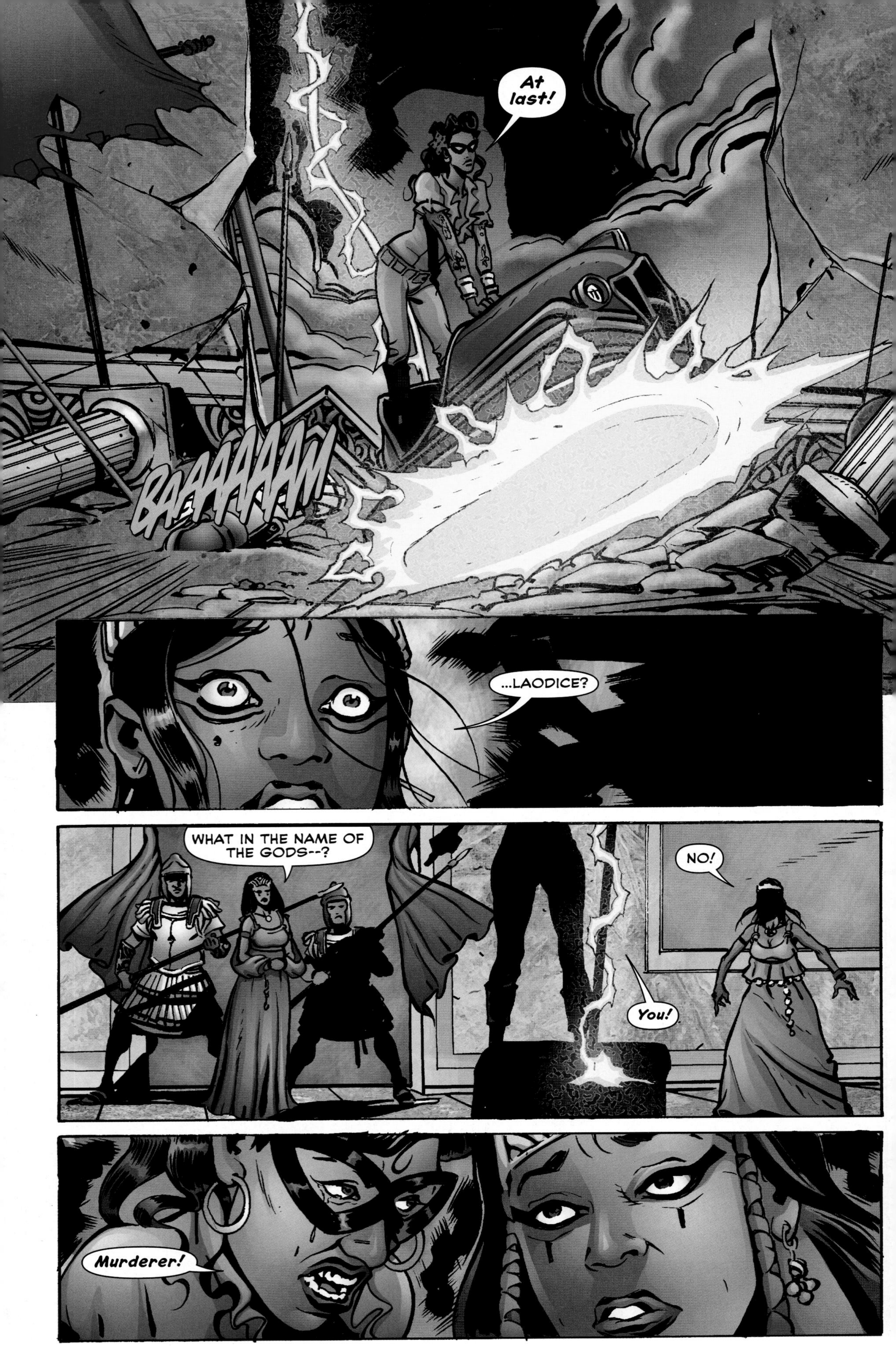
At last!
BAAAAAAM
...LAODICE?
WHAT IN THE NAME OF THE GODS--?
NO!
You!
Murderer!

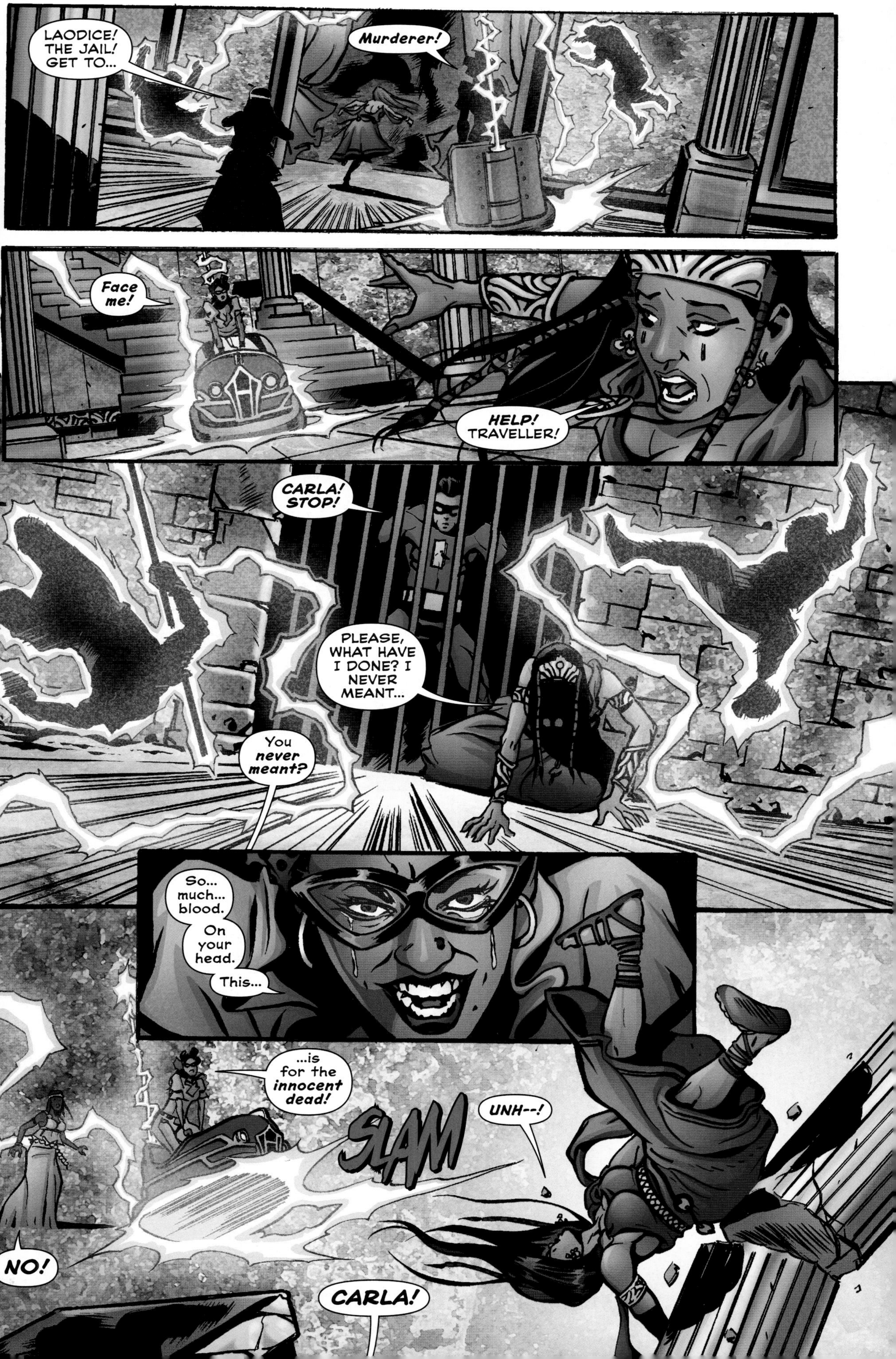

LAODICE! THE JAIL! GET TO...
Murderer!
Face me!
HELP! TRAVELLER!
CARLA! STOP!
PLEASE, WHAT HAVE I DONE? I NEVER MEANT...
You ***never meant?***
So... much... blood.
On your head.
This...
...is for the ***innocent dead!***
SLAM
UNH--!
NO!
CARLA!

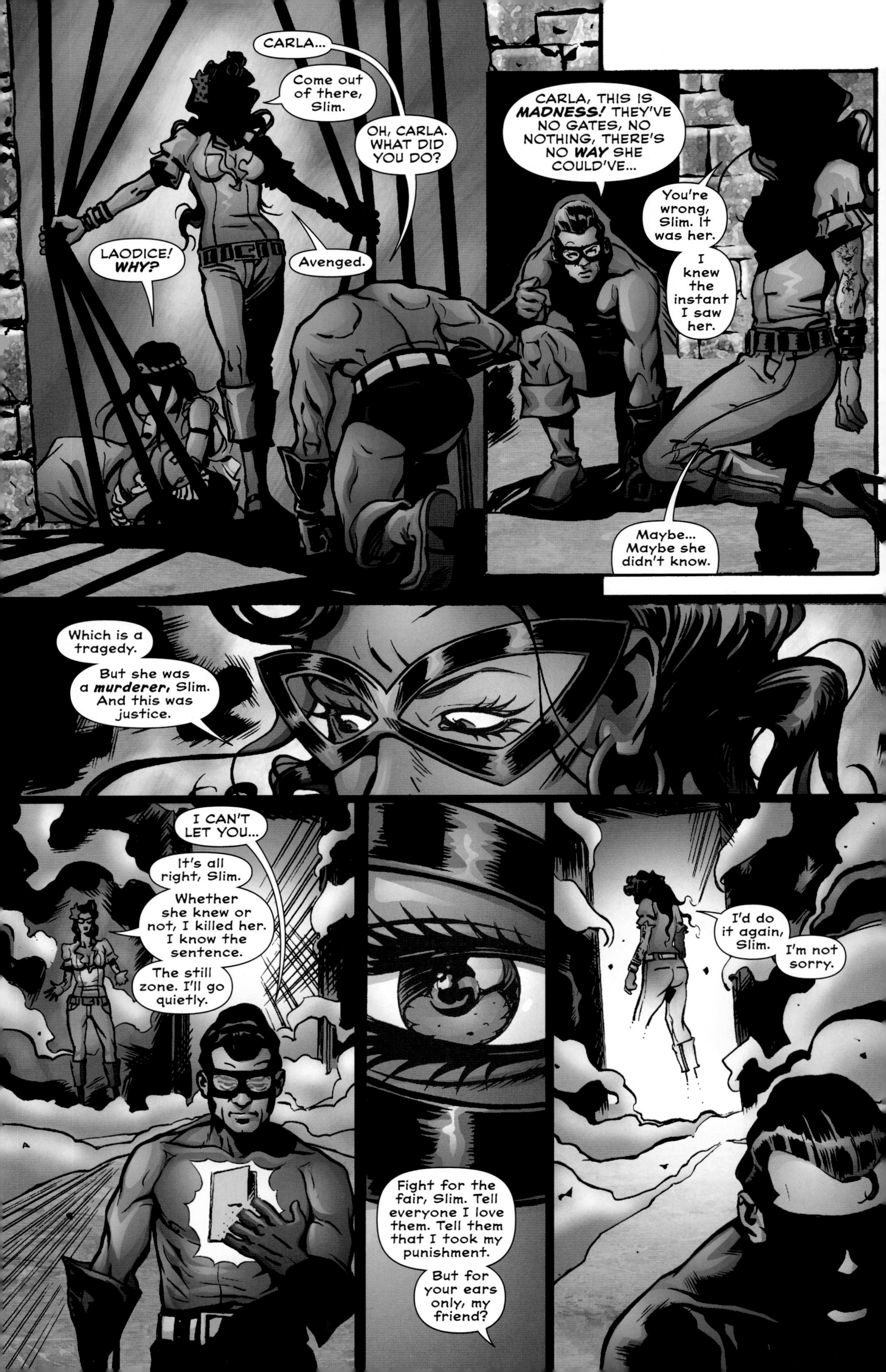
CARLA...
Come out of there, Slim.
OH, CARLA. WHAT DID YOU DO?
LAODICE! WHY?
Avenged.
CARLA, THIS IS MADNESS! THEY'VE NO GATES, NO NOTHING, THERE'S NO WAY SHE COULD'VE...
You're wrong, Slim. It was her.
I knew the instant I saw her.
Maybe... Maybe she didn't know.
Which is a tragedy.
But she was a murderer, Slim. And this was justice.
I CAN'T LET YOU...
It's all right, Slim.
Whether she knew or not, I killed her. I know the sentence.
The still zone. I'll go quietly.
Fight for the fair, Slim. Tell everyone I love them. Tell them that I took my punishment.
But for your ears only, my friend?
I'd do it again, Slim.
I'm not sorry.

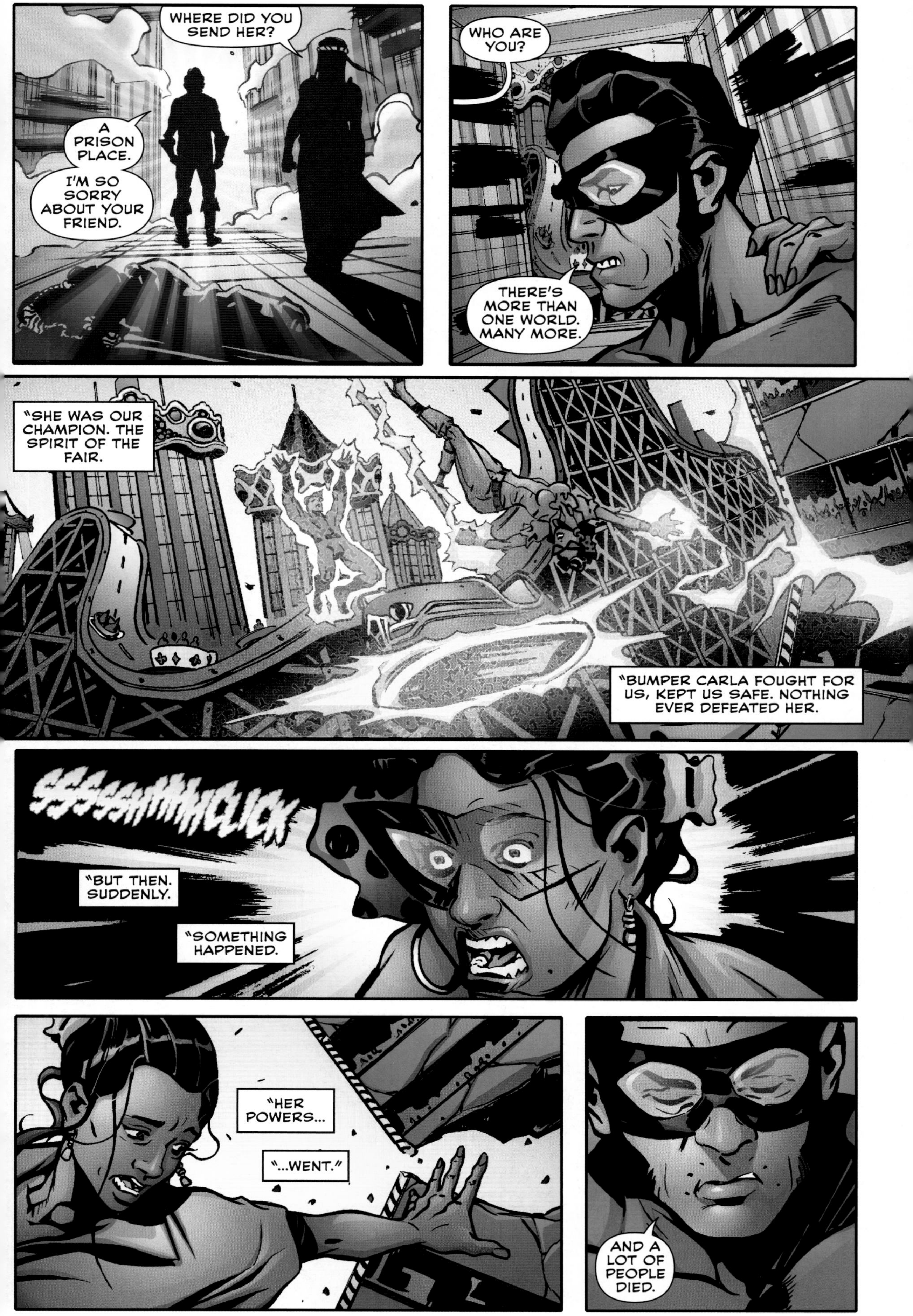
WHERE DID YOU SEND HER?
A PRISON PLACE.
I'M SO SORRY ABOUT YOUR FRIEND.
WHO ARE YOU?
THERE'S MORE THAN ONE WORLD. MANY MORE.
"SHE WAS OUR CHAMPION. THE SPIRIT OF THE FAIR.
"BUMPER CARLA FOUGHT FOR US, KEPT US SAFE. NOTHING EVER DEFEATED HER.
SSSSSHHHHCLICK
"BUT THEN. SUDDENLY.
"SOMETHING HAPPENED.
"HER POWERS...
"...WENT."
AND A LOT OF PEOPLE DIED.

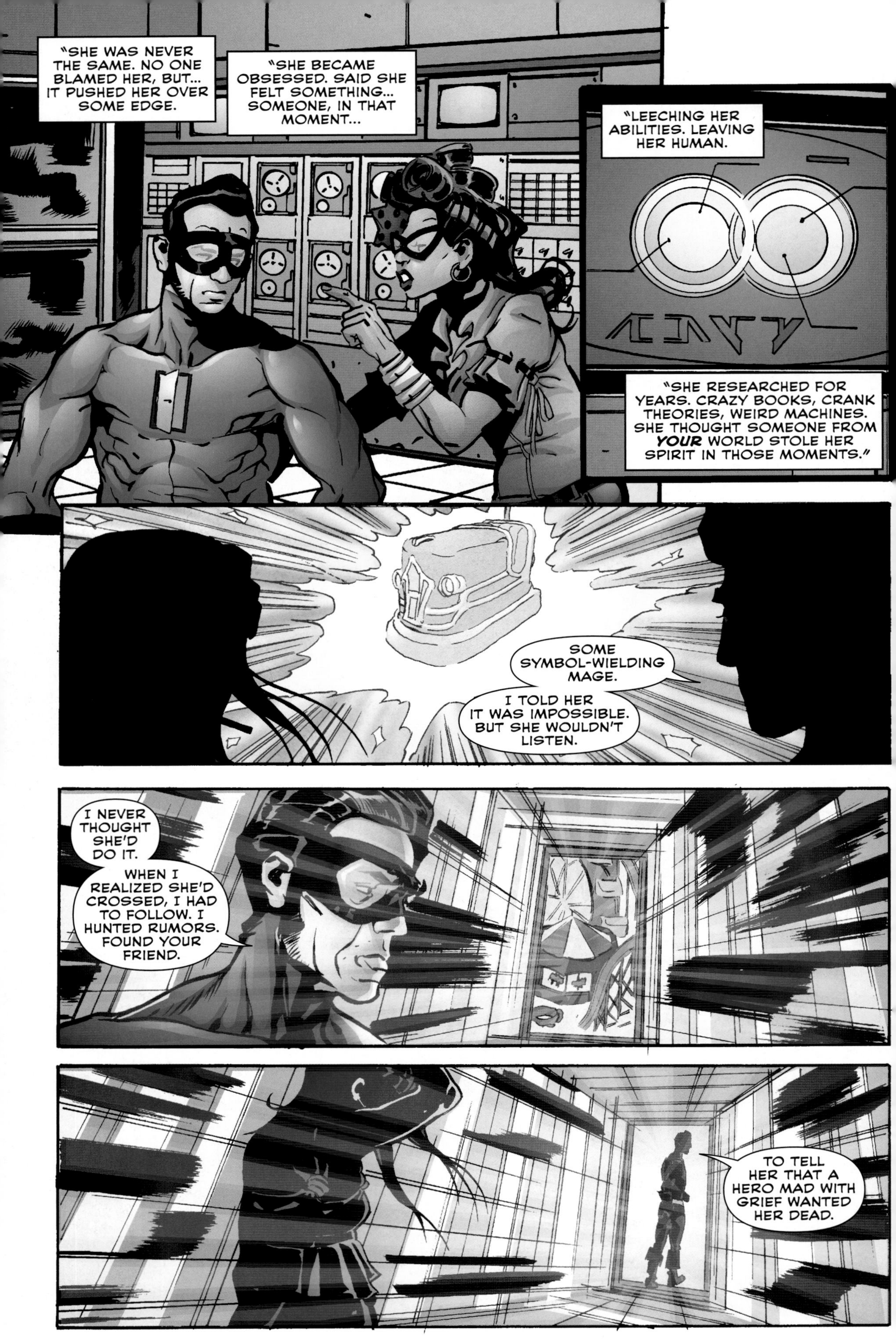
"SHE WAS NEVER THE SAME. NO ONE BLAMED HER, BUT... IT PUSHED HER OVER SOME EDGE.
"SHE BECAME OBSESSED. SAID SHE FELT SOMETHING... SOMEONE, IN THAT MOMENT...
"LEECHING HER ABILITIES. LEAVING HER HUMAN.
"SHE RESEARCHED FOR YEARS. CRAZY BOOKS, CRANK THEORIES, WEIRD MACHINES. SHE THOUGHT SOMEONE FROM *YOUR* WORLD STOLE HER SPIRIT IN THOSE MOMENTS."
SOME SYMBOL-WIELDING MAGE.
I TOLD HER IT WAS IMPOSSIBLE. BUT SHE WOULDN'T LISTEN.
I NEVER THOUGHT SHE'D DO IT.
WHEN I REALIZED SHE'D CROSSED, I HAD TO FOLLOW. I HUNTED RUMORS. FOUND YOUR FRIEND.
TO TELL HER THAT A HERO MAD WITH GRIEF WANTED HER DEAD.

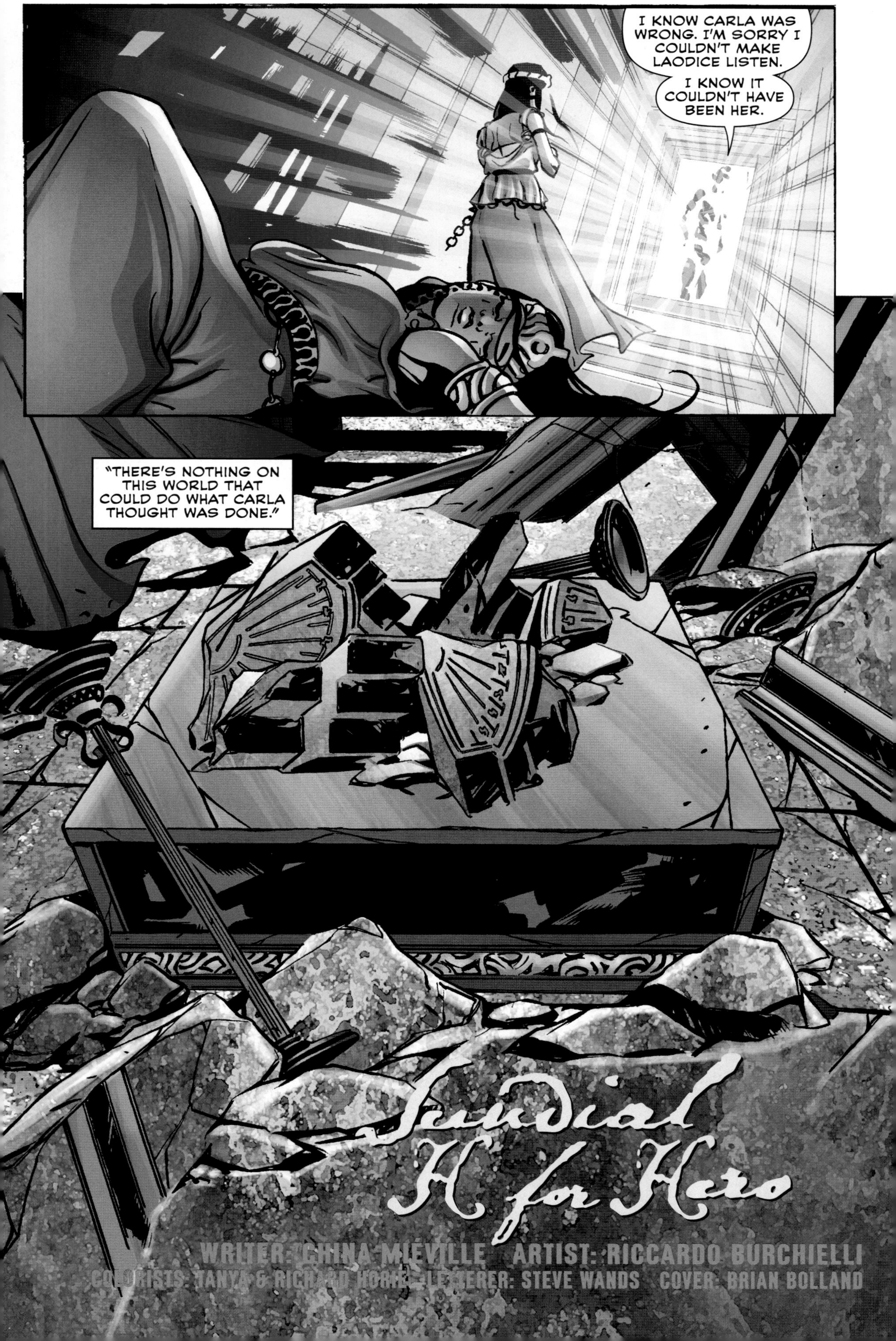
I KNOW CARLA WAS WRONG. I'M SORRY I COULDN'T MAKE LAODICE LISTEN.
I KNOW IT COULDN'T HAVE BEEN HER.
"THERE'S NOTHING ON THIS WORLD THAT COULD DO WHAT CARLA THOUGHT WAS DONE."
Sundial
H for Hero
WRITER: CHINA MIÉVILLE ARTIST: RICCARDO BURCHIELLI
COLORISTS: TANYA & RICHARD HORIE LETTERER: STEVE WANDS COVER: BRIAN BOLLAND

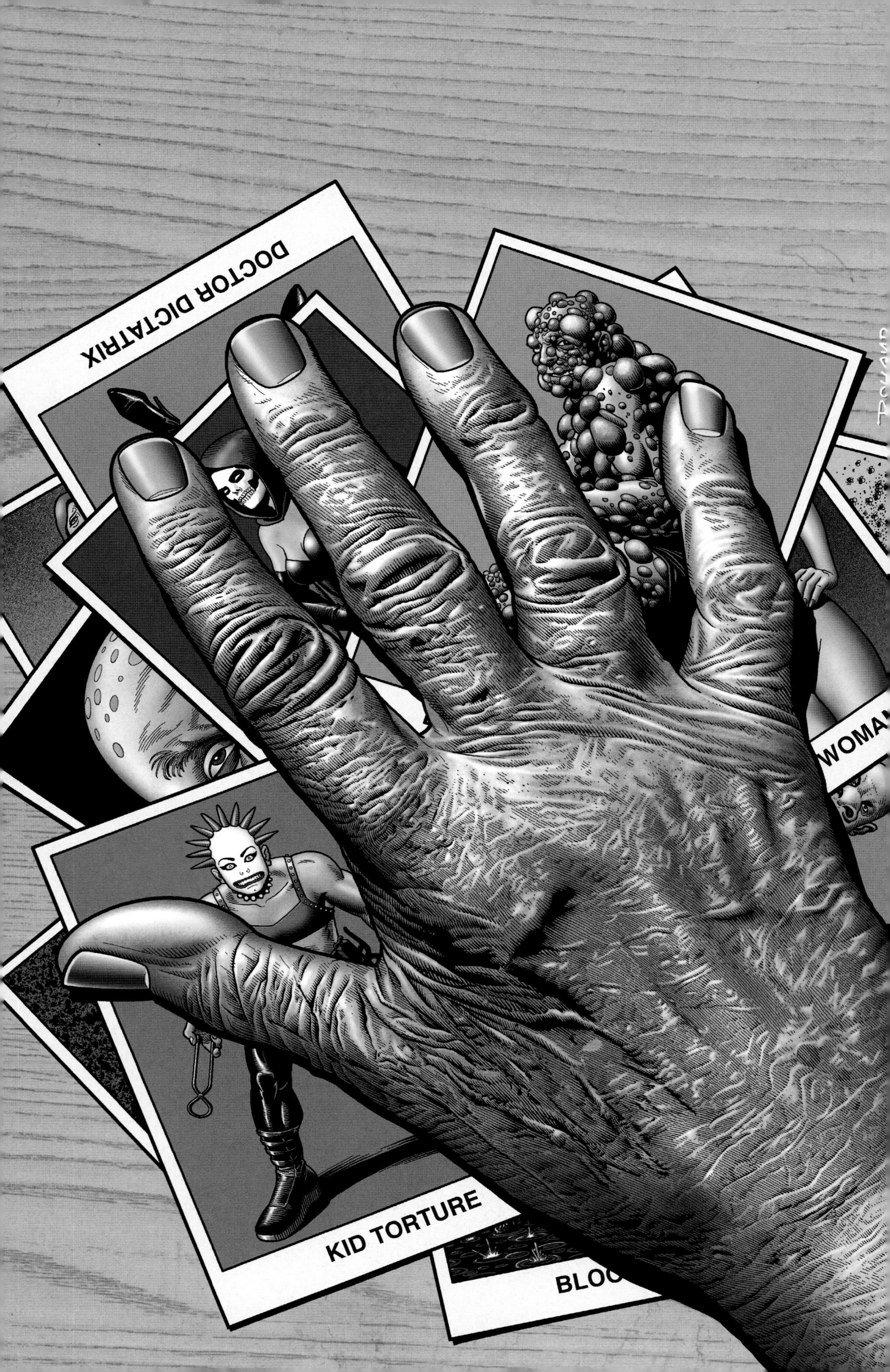
DOCTOR DICTATRIX
WOMAN
KID TORTURE
BLOO

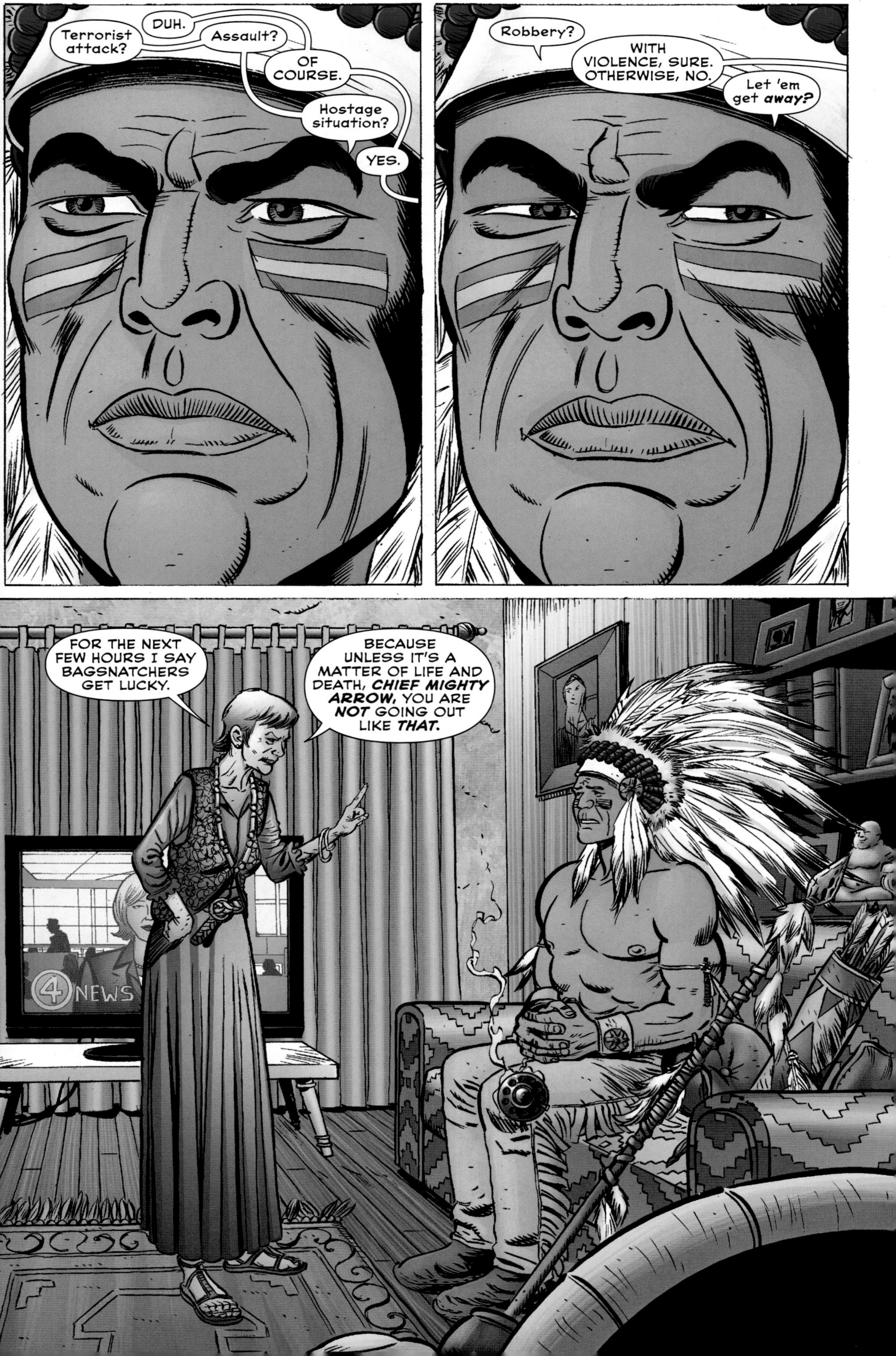
Terrorist attack?
DUH.
Assault?
OF COURSE.
Hostage situation?
YES.
Robbery?
WITH VIOLENCE, SURE. OTHERWISE, NO.
Let 'em get *away?*
FOR THE NEXT FEW HOURS I SAY BAGSNATCHERS GET LUCKY.
BECAUSE UNLESS IT'S A MATTER OF LIFE AND DEATH, ***CHIEF MIGHTY ARROW,*** YOU ARE ***NOT*** GOING OUT LIKE ***THAT.***
4 NEWS

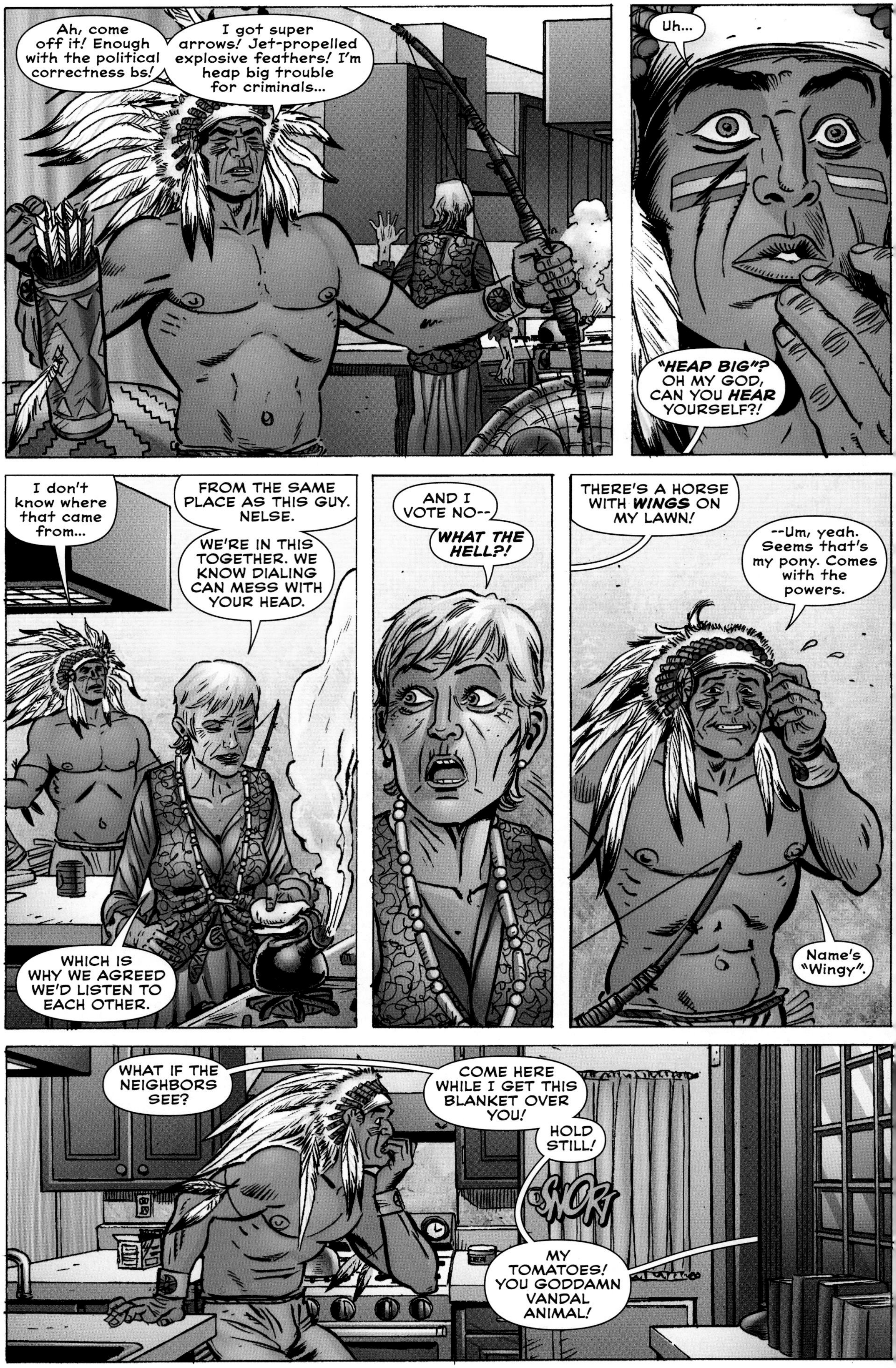

Ah, come off it! Enough with the political correctness bs!
I got super arrows! Jet-propelled explosive feathers! I'm heap big trouble for criminals...
Uh...
"HEAP BIG"? OH MY GOD, CAN YOU HEAR YOURSELF?!
I don't know where that came from...
FROM THE SAME PLACE AS THIS GUY. NELSE.
WE'RE IN THIS TOGETHER. WE KNOW DIALING CAN MESS WITH YOUR HEAD.
WHICH IS WHY WE AGREED WE'D LISTEN TO EACH OTHER.
AND I VOTE NO--
WHAT THE HELL?!
THERE'S A HORSE WITH WINGS ON MY LAWN!
--Um, yeah. Seems that's my pony. Comes with the powers.
Name's "Wingy".
WHAT IF THE NEIGHBORS SEE?
COME HERE WHILE I GET THIS BLANKET OVER YOU!
HOLD STILL!
SNORT
MY TOMATOES! YOU GODDAMN VANDAL ANIMAL!

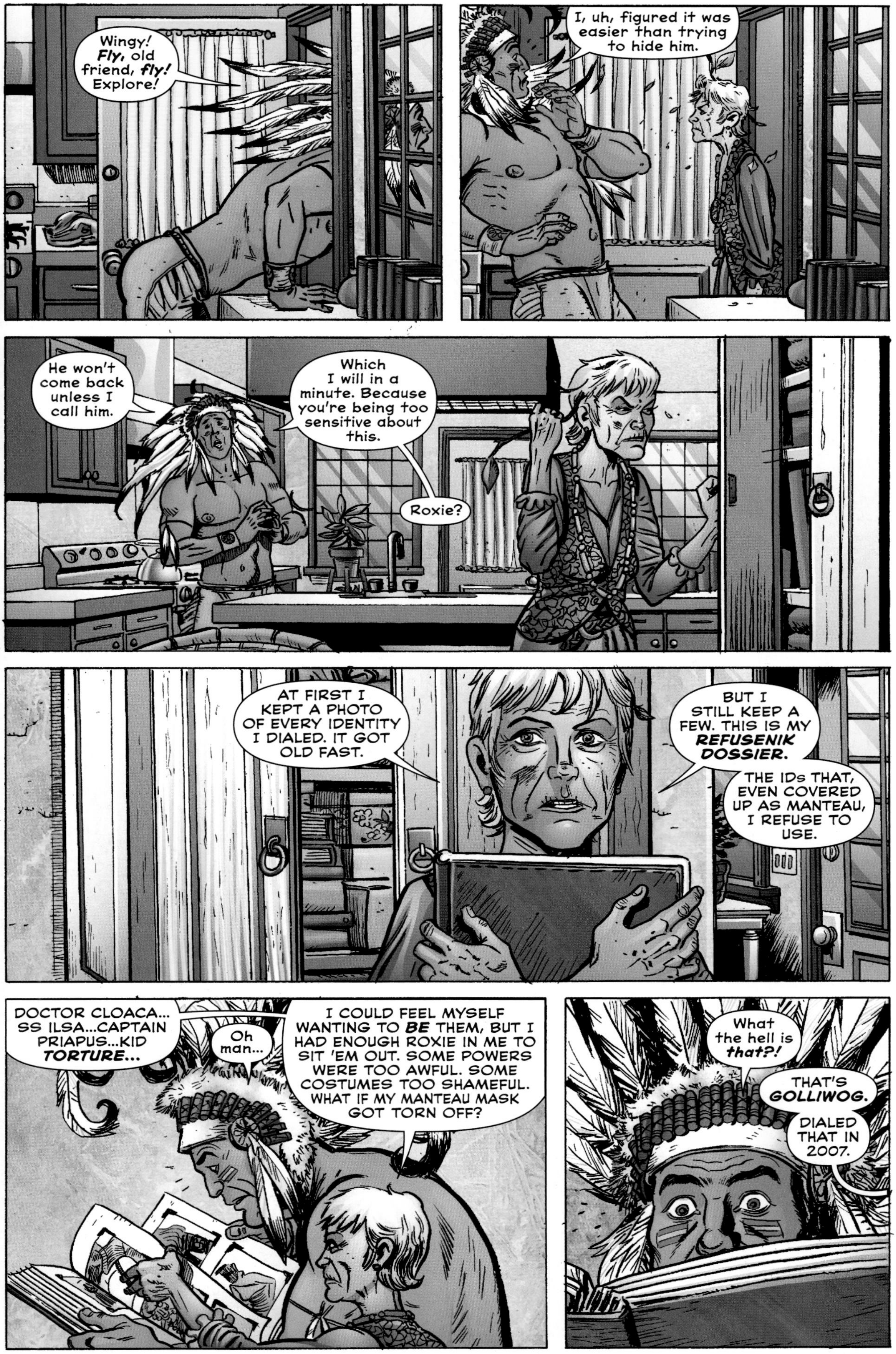
Wingy! Fly, old friend, fly! Explore!
I, uh, figured it was easier than trying to hide him.
He won't come back unless I call him.
Which I will in a minute. Because you're being too sensitive about this.
Roxie?
AT FIRST I KEPT A PHOTO OF EVERY IDENTITY I DIALED. IT GOT OLD FAST.
BUT I STILL KEEP A FEW. THIS IS MY REFUSENIK DOSSIER.
THE IDs THAT, EVEN COVERED UP AS MANTEAU, I REFUSE TO USE.
DOCTOR CLOACA... SS ILSA...CAPTAIN PRIAPUS...KID TORTURE...
Oh man...
I COULD FEEL MYSELF WANTING TO BE THEM, BUT I HAD ENOUGH ROXIE IN ME TO SIT 'EM OUT. SOME POWERS WERE TOO AWFUL. SOME COSTUMES TOO SHAMEFUL. WHAT IF MY MANTEAU MASK GOT TORN OFF?
What the hell is that?!
THAT'S GOLLIWOG.
DIALED THAT IN 2007.

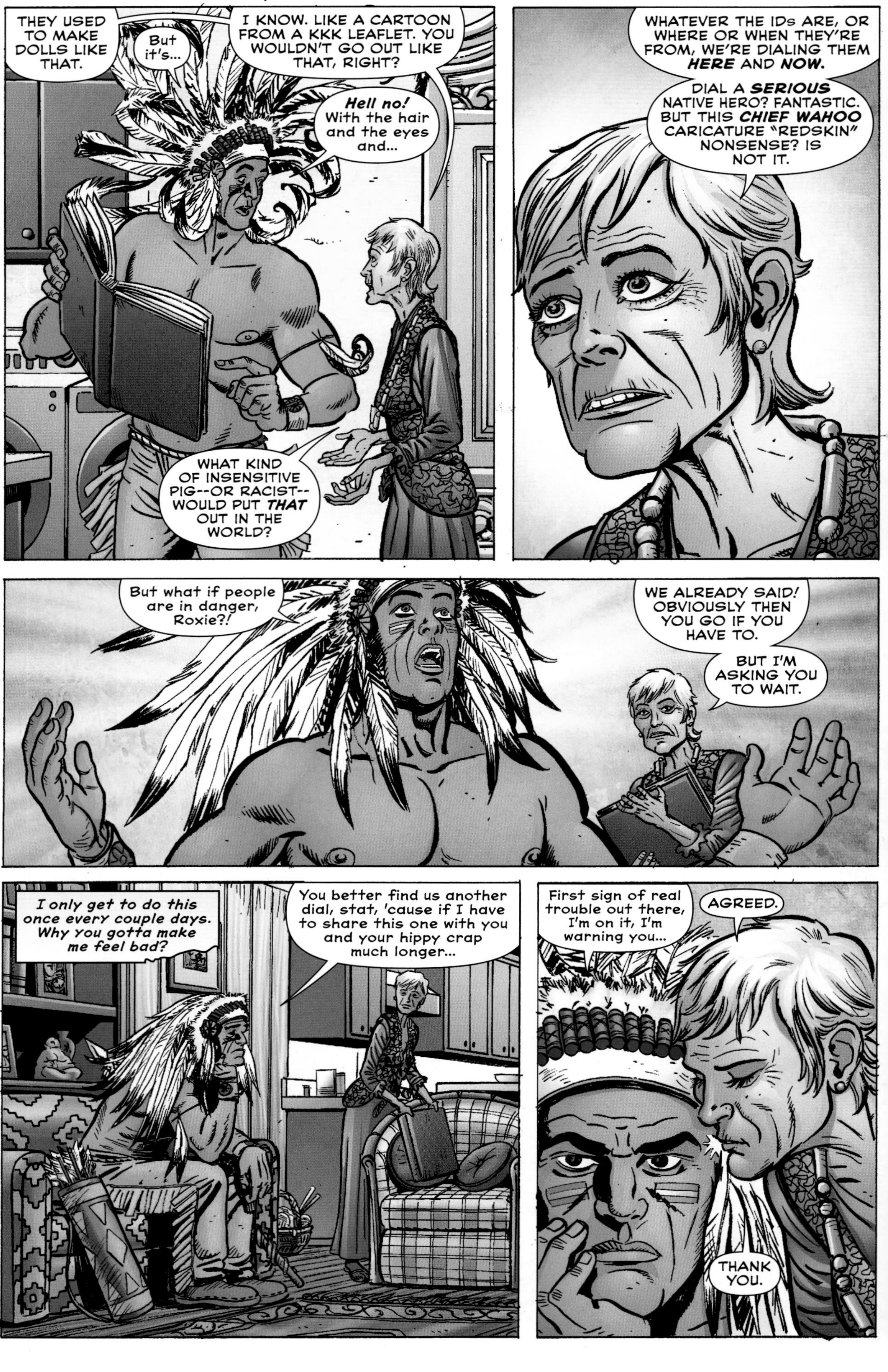
THEY USED TO MAKE DOLLS LIKE THAT.
But it's...
I KNOW. LIKE A CARTOON FROM A KKK LEAFLET. YOU WOULDN'T GO OUT LIKE THAT, RIGHT?
Hell no! With the hair and the eyes and...
WHAT KIND OF INSENSITIVE PIG--OR RACIST--WOULD PUT THAT OUT IN THE WORLD?
WHATEVER THE IDs ARE, OR WHERE OR WHEN THEY'RE FROM, WE'RE DIALING THEM HERE AND NOW.
DIAL A SERIOUS NATIVE HERO? FANTASTIC. BUT THIS CHIEF WAHOO CARICATURE "REDSKIN" NONSENSE? IS NOT IT.
But what if people are in danger, Roxie?!
WE ALREADY SAID! OBVIOUSLY THEN YOU GO IF YOU HAVE TO.
BUT I'M ASKING YOU TO WAIT.
I only get to do this once every couple days. Why you gotta make me feel bad?
You better find us another dial, stat, 'cause if I have to share this one with you and your hippy crap much longer...
First sign of real trouble out there, I'm on it, I'm warning you...
AGREED.
THANK YOU.

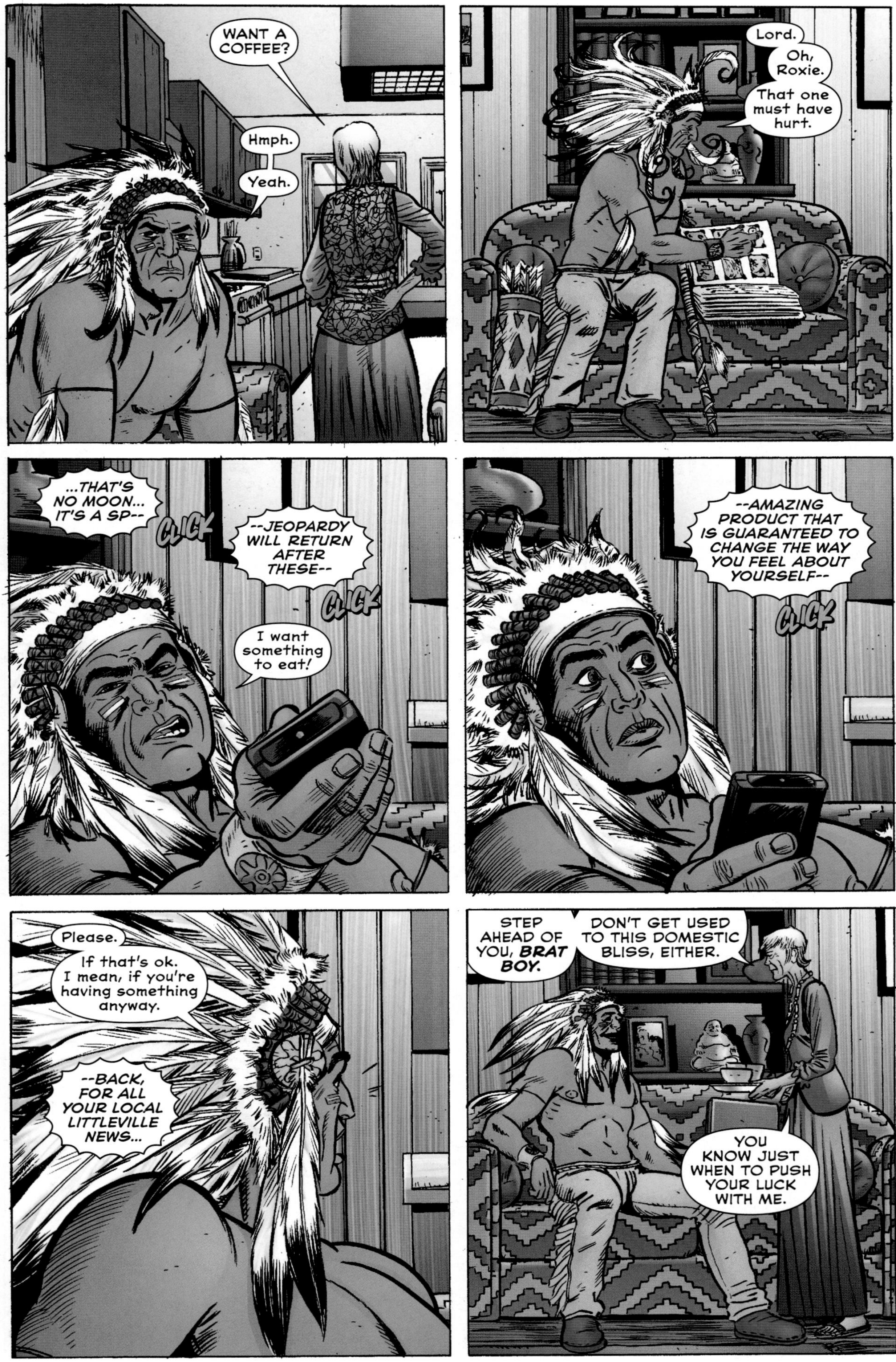
WANT A COFFEE?
Hmph.
Yeah.
Lord.
Oh, Roxie.
That one must have hurt.
...THAT'S NO MOON... IT'S A SP--
CLICK
--JEOPARDY WILL RETURN AFTER THESE--
CLICK
I want something to eat!
--AMAZING PRODUCT THAT IS GUARANTEED TO CHANGE THE WAY YOU FEEL ABOUT YOURSELF--
CLICK
Please.
If that's ok. I mean, if you're having something anyway.
--BACK, FOR ALL YOUR LOCAL LITTLEVILLE NEWS...
STEP AHEAD OF YOU, BRAT BOY.
DON'T GET USED TO THIS DOMESTIC BLISS, EITHER.
YOU KNOW JUST WHEN TO PUSH YOUR LUCK WITH ME.

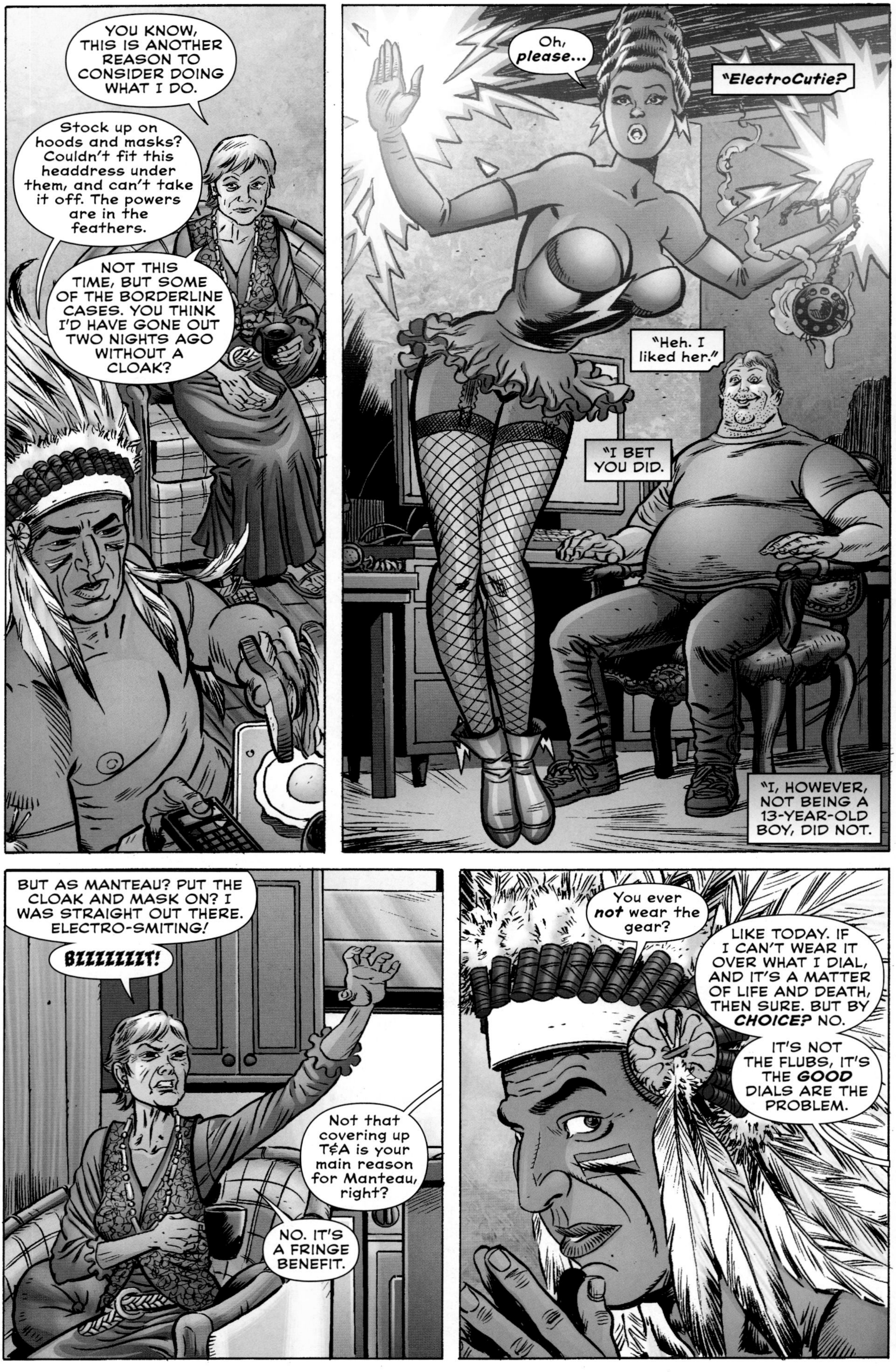

YOU KNOW, THIS IS ANOTHER REASON TO CONSIDER DOING WHAT I DO.
Stock up on hoods and masks? Couldn't fit this headdress under them, and can't take it off. The powers are in the feathers.
NOT THIS TIME, BUT SOME OF THE BORDERLINE CASES. YOU THINK I'D HAVE GONE OUT TWO NIGHTS AGO WITHOUT A CLOAK?
Oh, *please...*
"*ElectroCutie?*
"Heh. I liked her."
"I BET YOU DID.
"I, HOWEVER, NOT BEING A 13-YEAR-OLD BOY, DID NOT.
BUT AS MANTEAU? PUT THE CLOAK AND MASK ON? I WAS STRAIGHT OUT THERE. ELECTRO-SMITING!
BZZZZZZZT!
Not that covering up T&A is your main reason for Manteau, right?
NO. IT'S A FRINGE BENEFIT.
You ever *not* wear the gear?
LIKE TODAY. IF I CAN'T WEAR IT OVER WHAT I DIAL, AND IT'S A MATTER OF LIFE AND DEATH, THEN SURE. BUT BY *CHOICE?* NO.
IT'S NOT THE FLUBS, IT'S THE *GOOD* DIALS ARE THE PROBLEM.

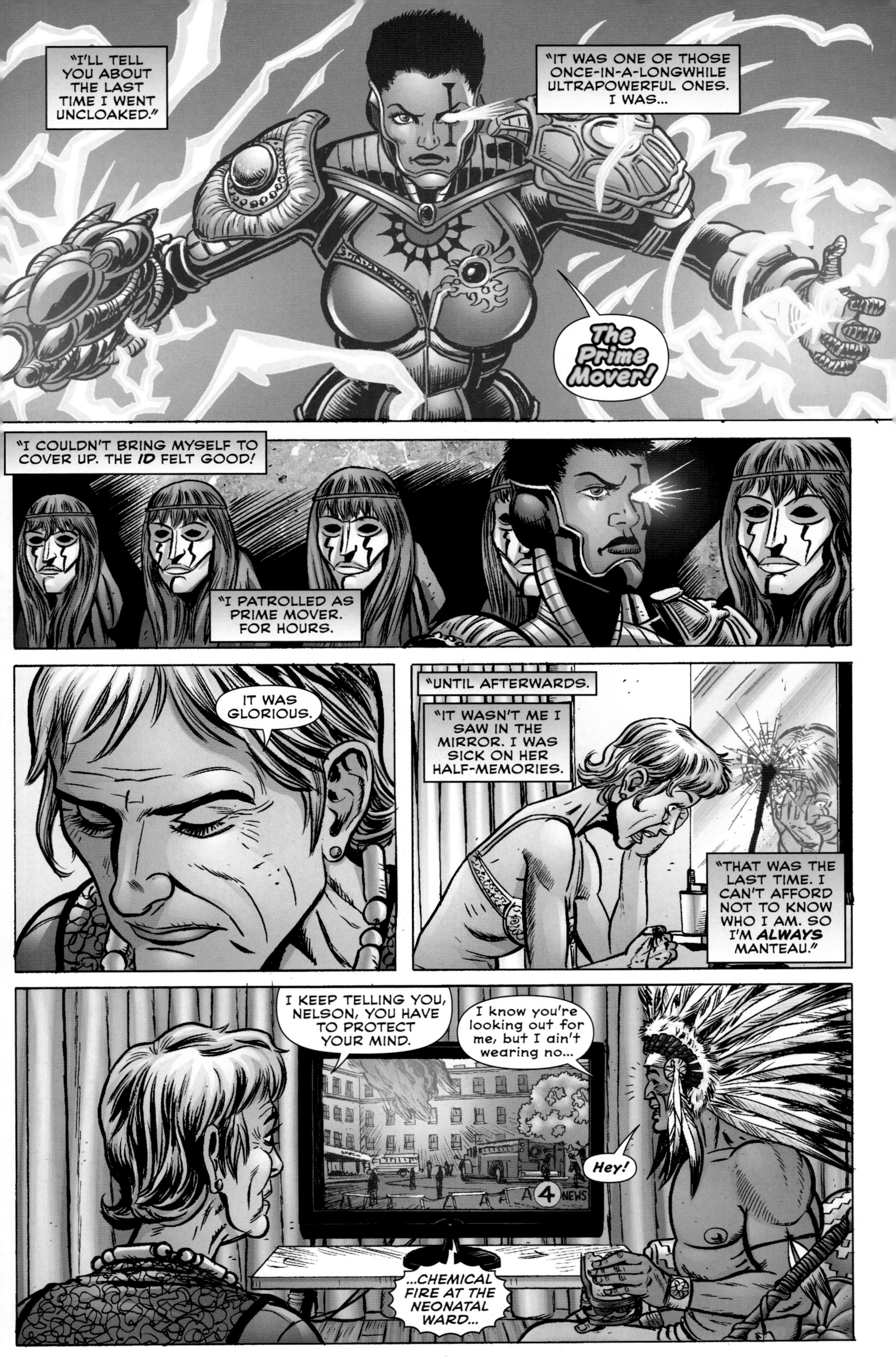
"I'LL TELL YOU ABOUT THE LAST TIME I WENT UNCLOAKED."
"IT WAS ONE OF THOSE ONCE-IN-A-LONGWHILE ULTRAPOWERFUL ONES. I WAS...
The Prime Mover!
"I COULDN'T BRING MYSELF TO COVER UP. THE ID FELT GOOD!
"I PATROLLED AS PRIME MOVER. FOR HOURS.
IT WAS GLORIOUS.
"UNTIL AFTERWARDS.
"IT WASN'T ME I SAW IN THE MIRROR. I WAS SICK ON HER HALF-MEMORIES.
"THAT WAS THE LAST TIME. I CAN'T AFFORD NOT TO KNOW WHO I AM. SO I'M ALWAYS MANTEAU."
I KEEP TELLING YOU, NELSON, YOU HAVE TO PROTECT YOUR MIND.
I know you're looking out for me, but I ain't wearing no...
Hey!
4 NEWS
...CHEMICAL FIRE AT THE NEONATAL WARD...

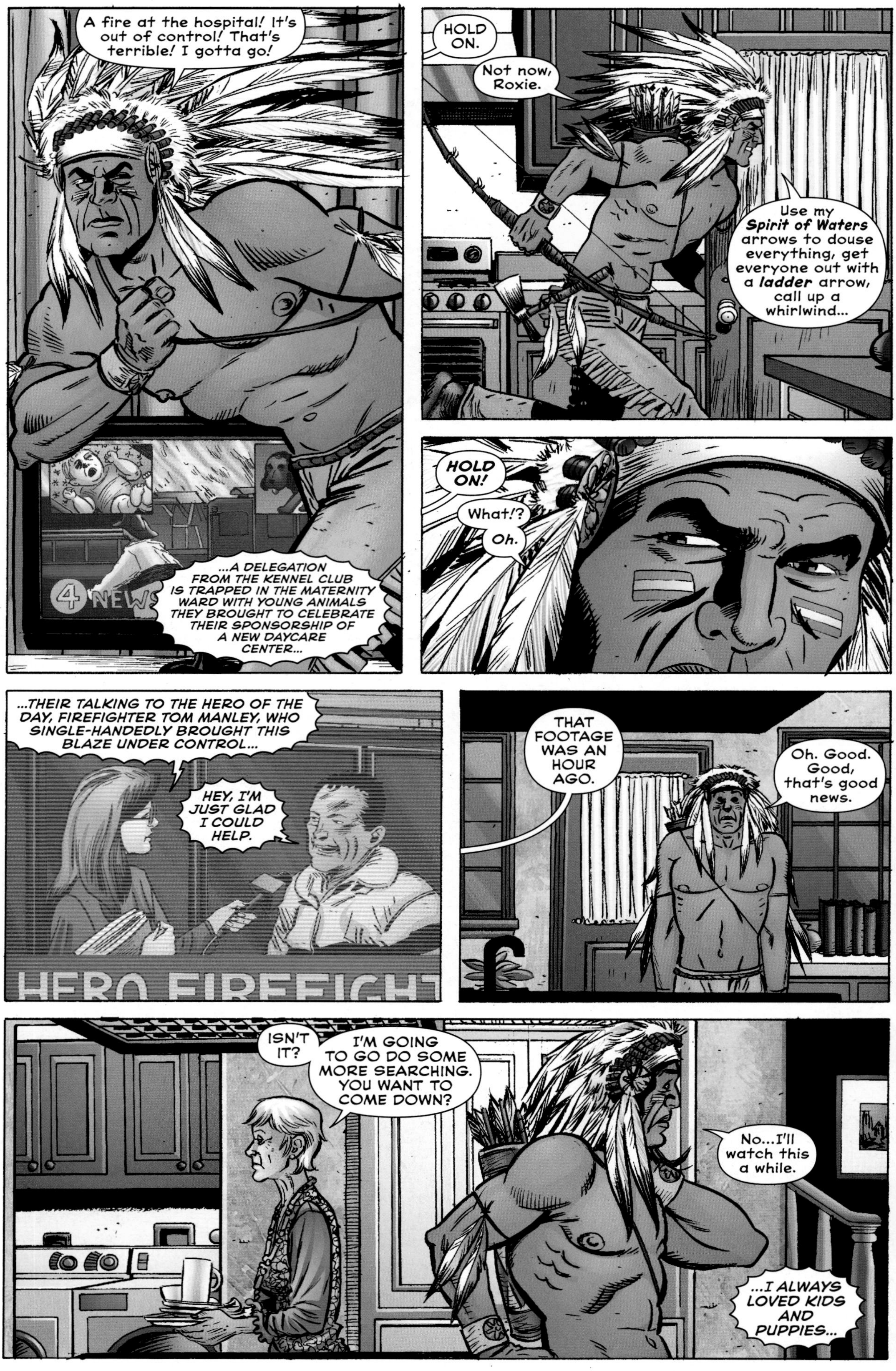
A fire at the hospital! It's out of control! That's terrible! I gotta go!
...A DELEGATION FROM THE KENNEL CLUB IS TRAPPED IN THE MATERNITY WARD WITH YOUNG ANIMALS THEY BROUGHT TO CELEBRATE THEIR SPONSORSHIP OF A NEW DAYCARE CENTER...
4 NEWS
HOLD ON.
Not now, Roxie.
Use my Spirit of Waters arrows to douse everything, get everyone out with a ladder arrow, call up a whirlwind...
HOLD ON!
What!?
Oh.
...THEIR TALKING TO THE HERO OF THE DAY, FIREFIGHTER TOM MANLEY, WHO SINGLE-HANDEDLY BROUGHT THIS BLAZE UNDER CONTROL...
HEY, I'M JUST GLAD I COULD HELP.
HERO FIREFIGHT
THAT FOOTAGE WAS AN HOUR AGO.
Oh. Good. Good, that's good news.
ISN'T IT?
I'M GOING TO GO DO SOME MORE SEARCHING. YOU WANT TO COME DOWN?
No...I'll watch this a while.
...I ALWAYS LOVED KIDS AND PUPPIES...

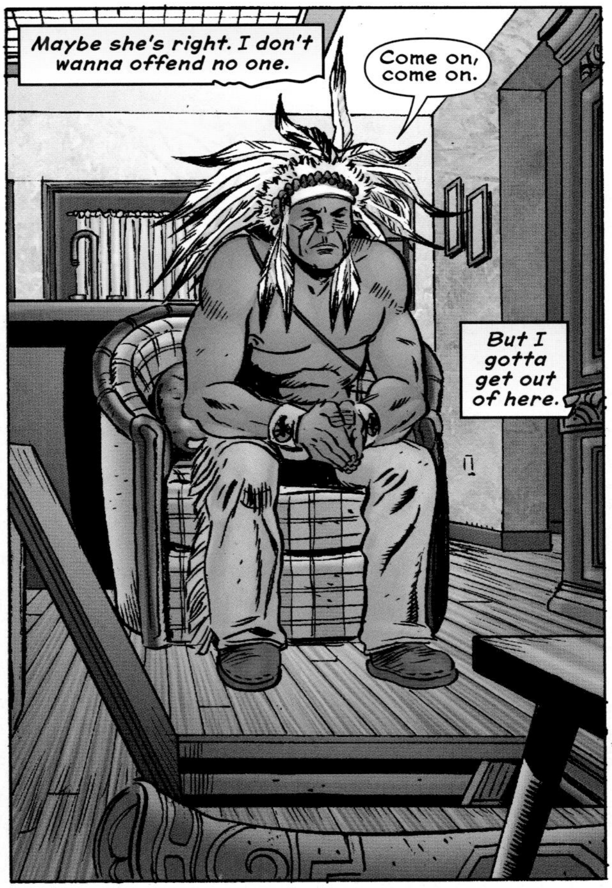

Maybe she's right. I don't wanna offend no one.
Come on, come on.
But I gotta get out of here.

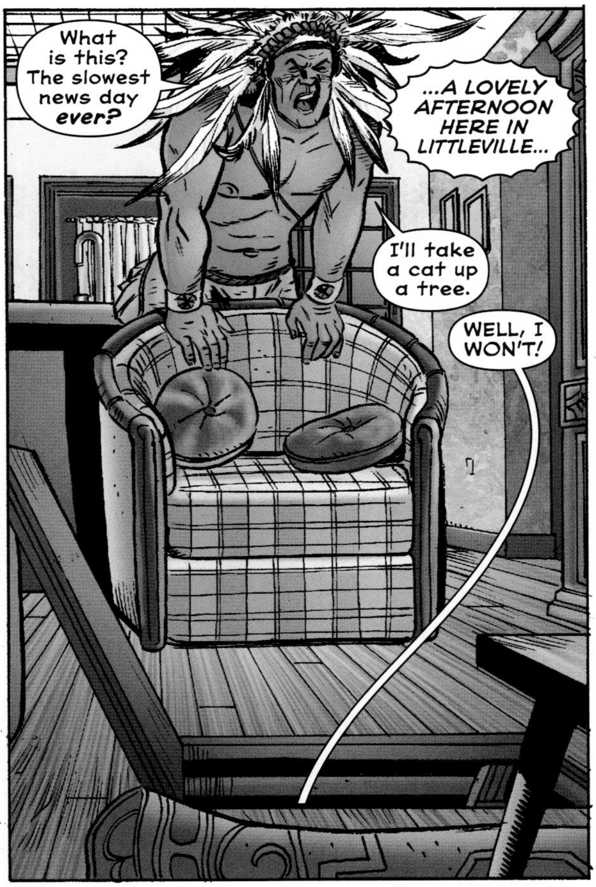

What is this? The slowest news day *ever?*
...A LOVELY AFTERNOON HERE IN LITTLEVILLE...
I'll take a cat up a tree.
WELL, I WON'T!

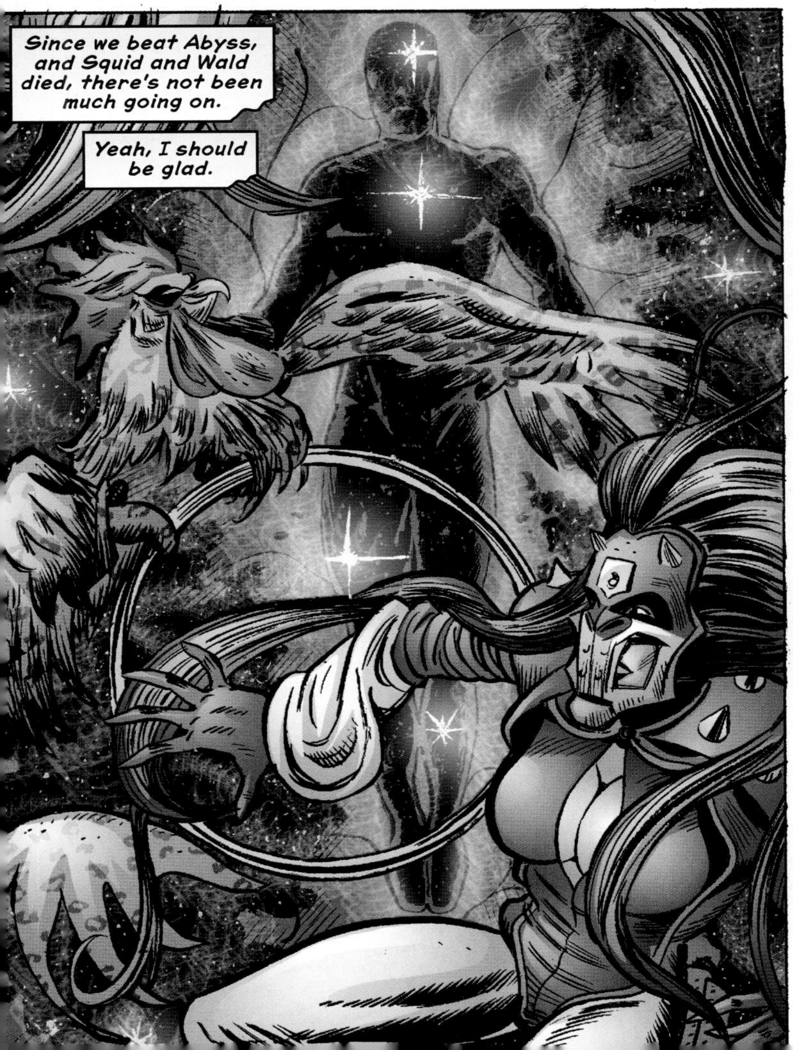

Since we beat Abyss, and Squid and Wald died, there's not been much going on.
Yeah, I should be glad.

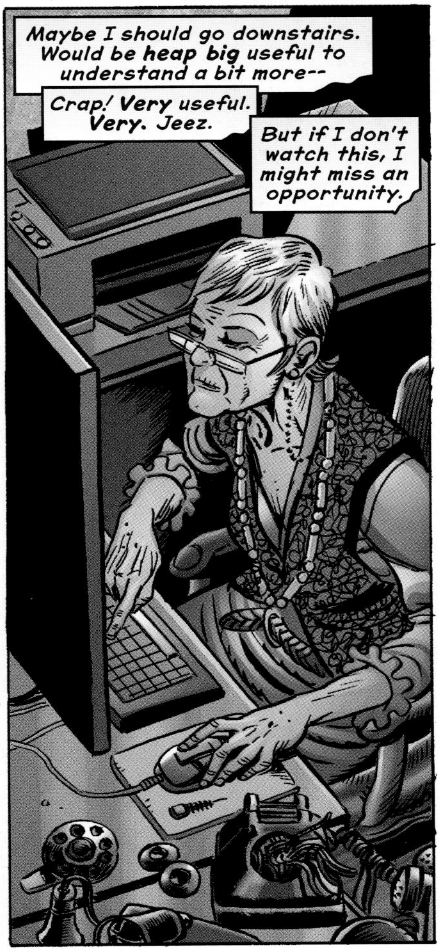

Maybe I should go downstairs. Would be **heap big** useful to understand a bit more--
Crap! **Very** useful. **Very**. Jeez.
But if I don't watch this, I might miss an opportunity.

Roxie knows more about dials than anyone.

And she don't know *much*.

She's a historian, as well as an engineer.

The dial we have works as well as it ever did, now, since she finally fixed it.

But at first even she didn't know there was a dial sitting there in that booth. On her doorstep.

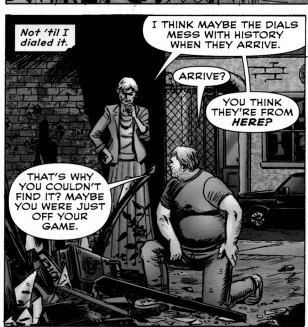

Not 'til I dialed it.

I THINK MAYBE THE DIALS MESS WITH HISTORY WHEN THEY ARRIVE.

ARRIVE?

YOU THINK THEY'RE FROM *HERE*?

THAT'S WHY YOU COULDN'T FIND IT? MAYBE YOU WERE JUST OFF YOUR GAME.

I shouldn't give her a hard time. Like I said, she knows more about this stuff than anyone ever.

'Cept maybe that guy "O" she told me about.

Whoever he was.

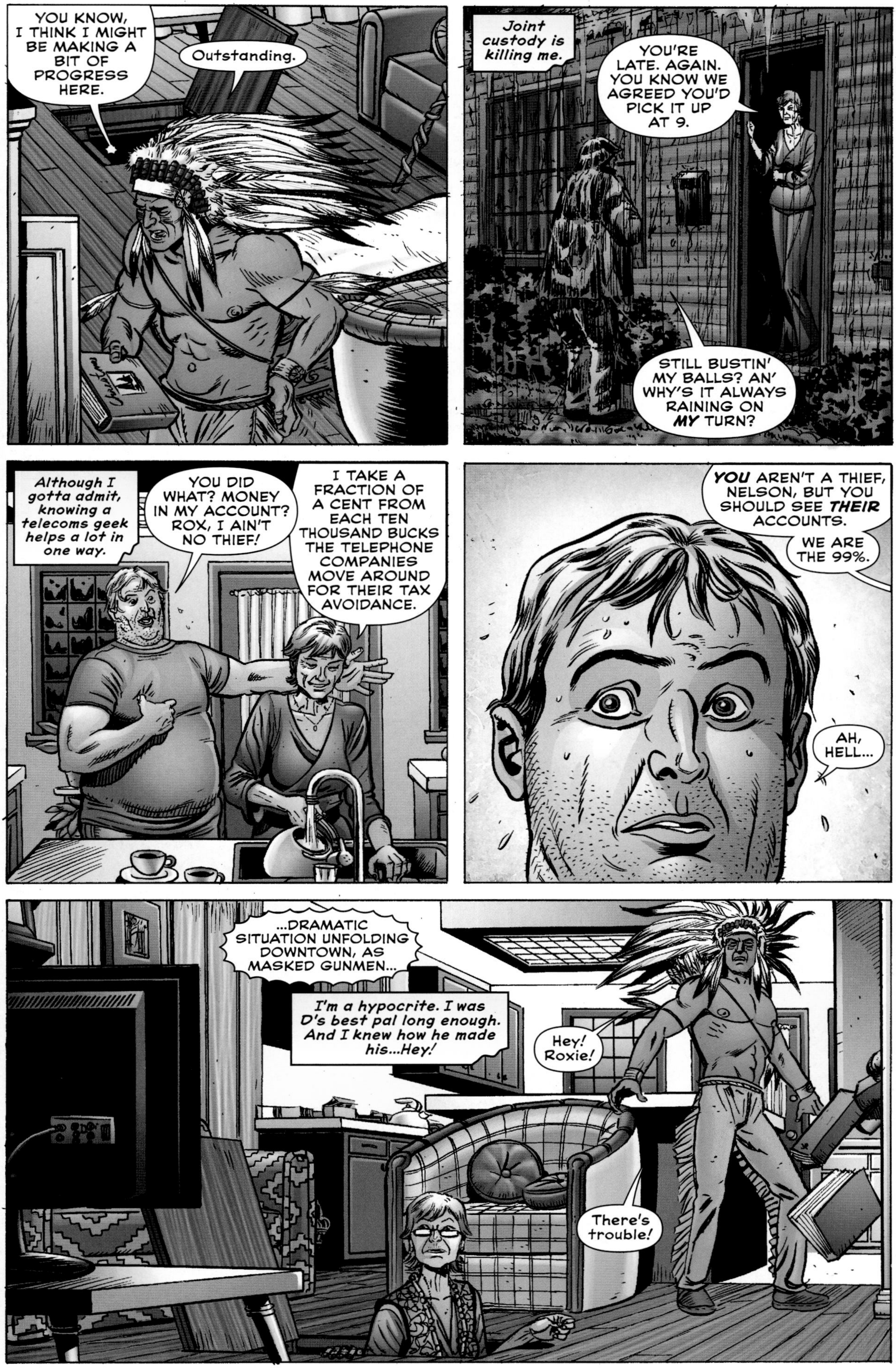
YOU KNOW, I THINK I MIGHT BE MAKING A BIT OF PROGRESS HERE.
Outstanding.
Joint custody is killing me.
YOU'RE LATE. AGAIN. YOU KNOW WE AGREED YOU'D PICK IT UP AT 9.
STILL BUSTIN' MY BALLS? AN' WHY'S IT ALWAYS RAINING ON MY TURN?
Although I gotta admit, knowing a telecoms geek helps a lot in one way.
YOU DID WHAT? MONEY IN MY ACCOUNT? ROX, I AIN'T NO THIEF!
I TAKE A FRACTION OF A CENT FROM EACH TEN THOUSAND BUCKS THE TELEPHONE COMPANIES MOVE AROUND FOR THEIR TAX AVOIDANCE.
YOU AREN'T A THIEF, NELSON, BUT YOU SHOULD SEE THEIR ACCOUNTS.
WE ARE THE 99%.
AH, HELL...
...DRAMATIC SITUATION UNFOLDING DOWNTOWN, AS MASKED GUNMEN...
I'm a hypocrite. I was D's best pal long enough. And I knew how he made his...Hey!
Hey! Roxie!
There's trouble!

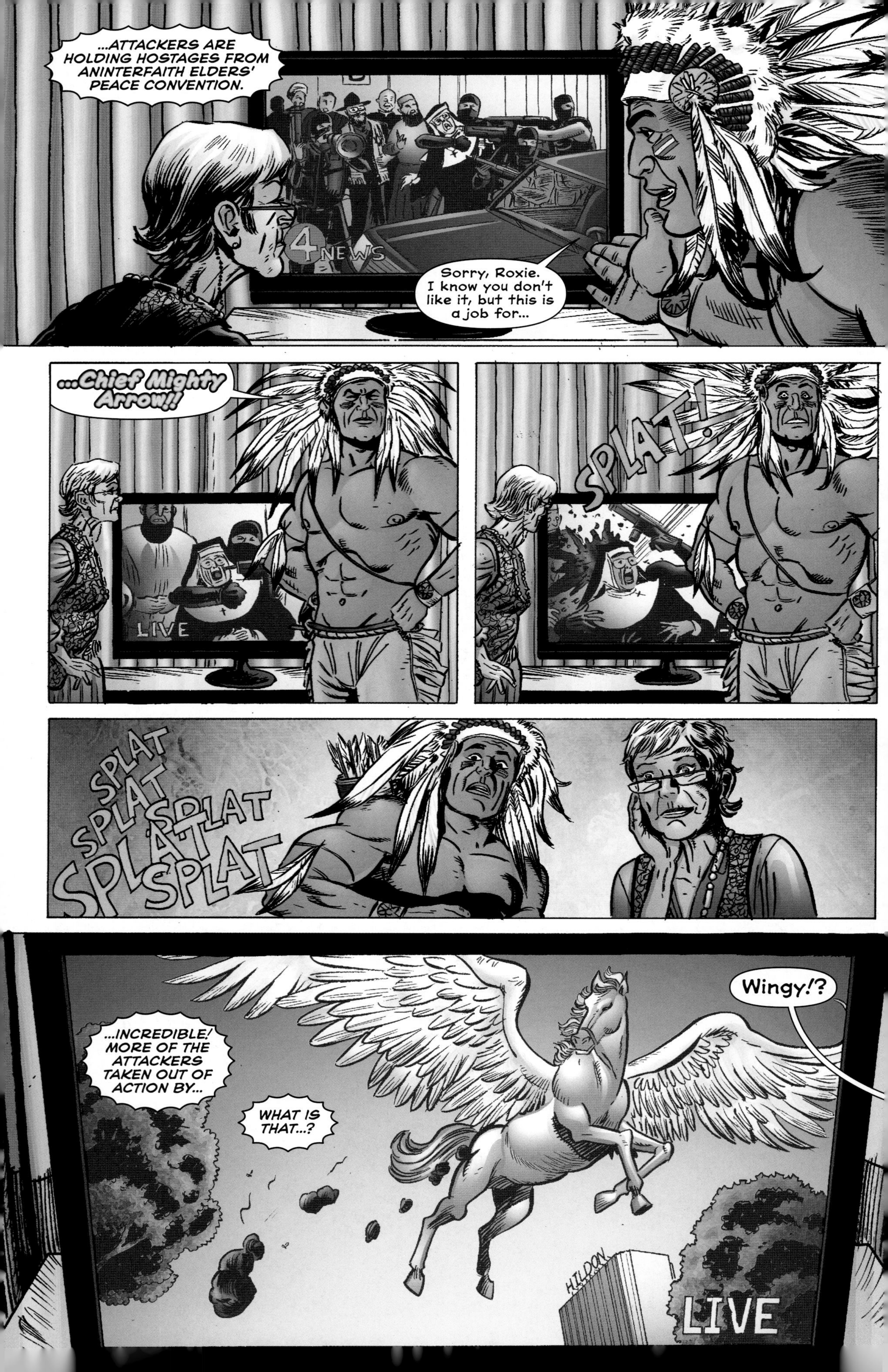
...ATTACKERS ARE HOLDING HOSTAGES FROM ANINTERFAITH ELDERS' PEACE CONVENTION.
4 NEWS
Sorry, Roxie. I know you don't like it, but this is a job for...
...Chief Mighty Arrow!!
LIVE
SPLAT!
SPLAT SPLAT SPLAT SPLAT SPLAT SPLAT
Wingy!?
...INCREDIBLE! MORE OF THE ATTACKERS TAKEN OUT OF ACTION BY...
WHAT IS THAT...?
HILDON
LIVE

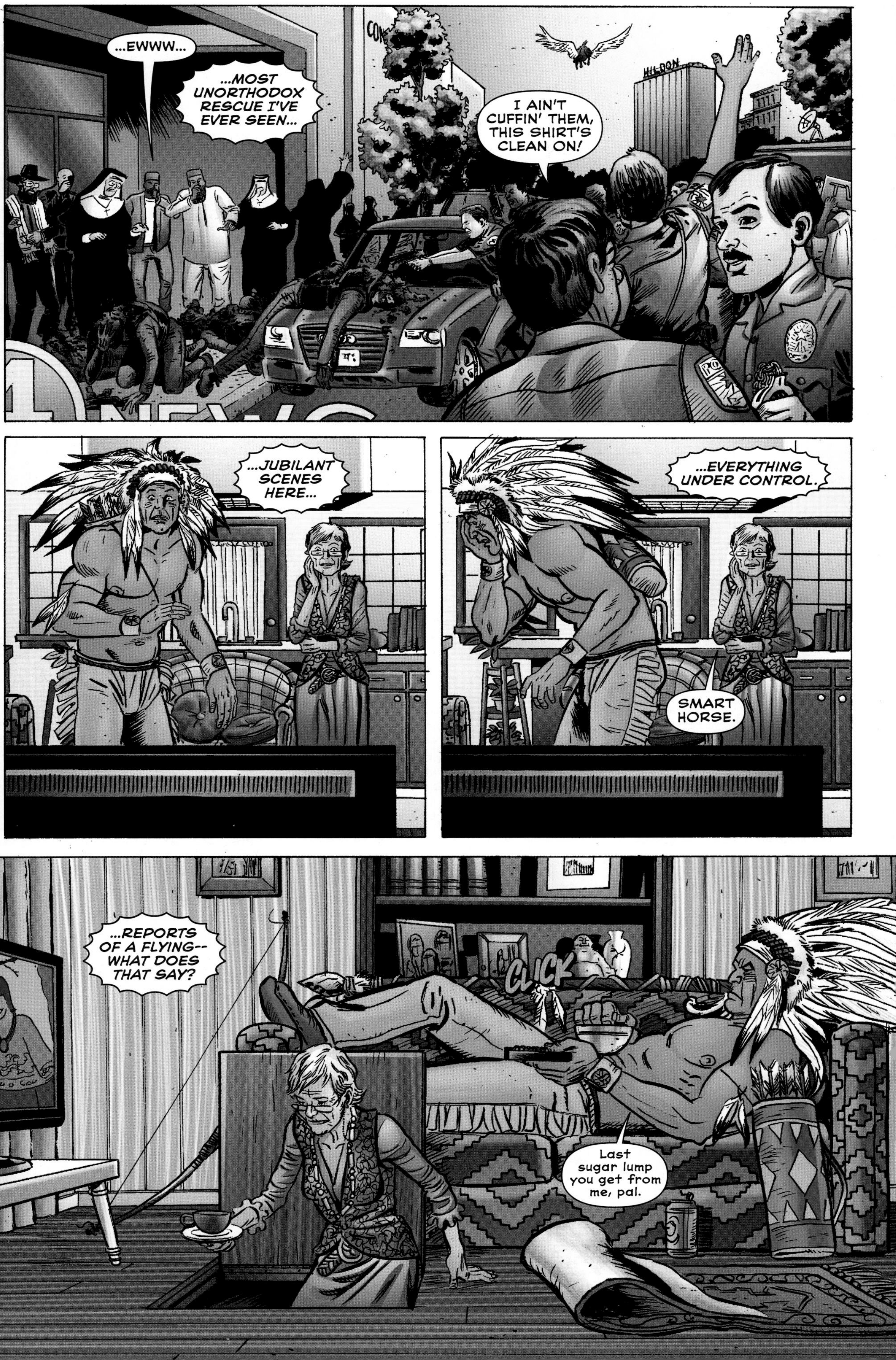
...EWWW...
...MOST UNORTHODOX RESCUE I'VE EVER SEEN...
I AIN'T CUFFIN' THEM, THIS SHIRT'S CLEAN ON!
...JUBILANT SCENES HERE...
...EVERYTHING UNDER CONTROL.
SMART HORSE.
...REPORTS OF A FLYING-- WHAT DOES THAT SAY?
CLICK
Last sugar lump you get from me, pal.

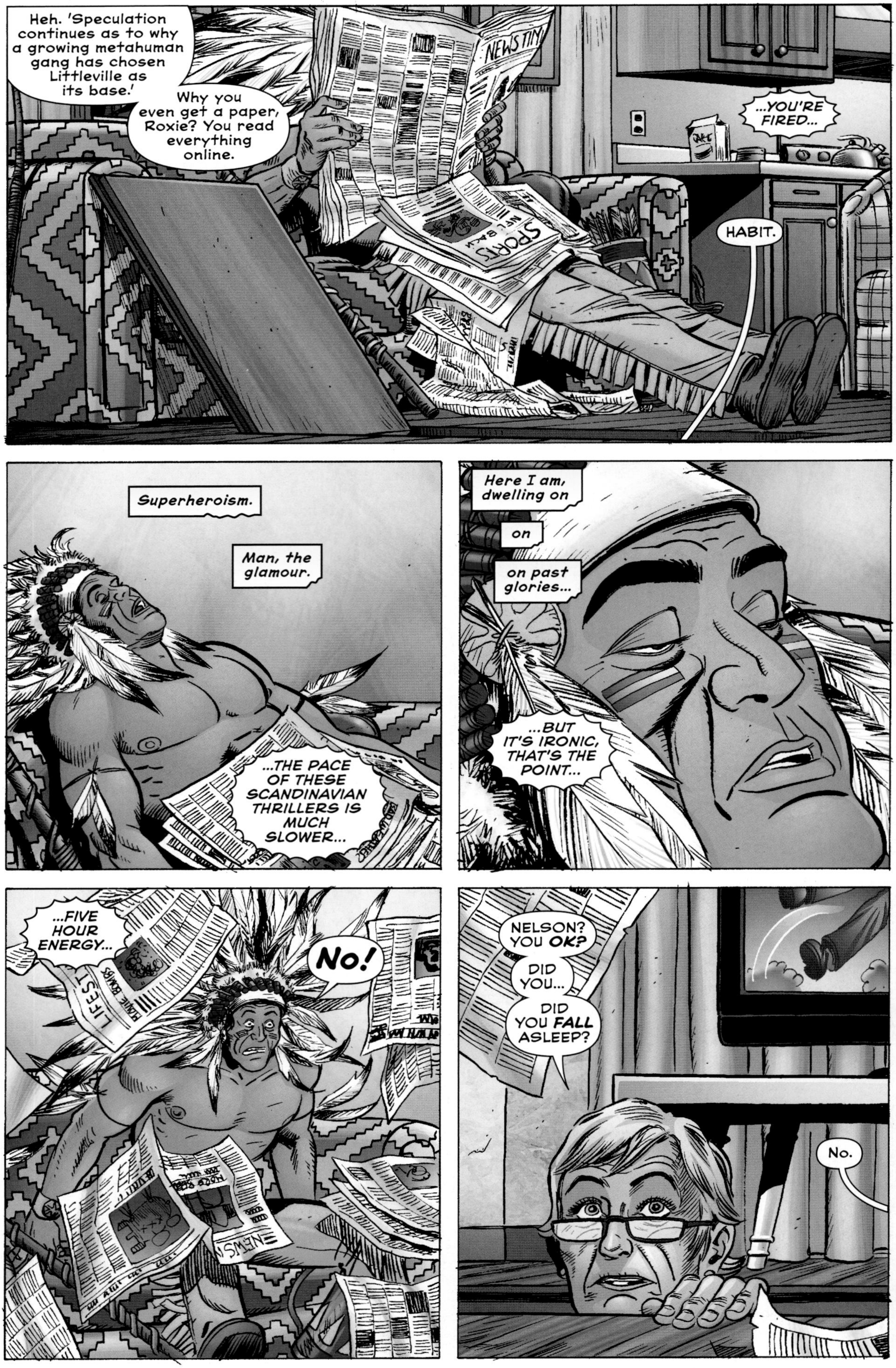
Heh. 'Speculation continues as to why a growing metahuman gang has chosen Littleville as its base.'
Why you even get a paper, Roxie? You read everything online.
...YOU'RE FIRED...
HABIT.
Superheroism.
Man, the glamour.
...THE PACE OF THESE SCANDINAVIAN THRILLERS IS MUCH SLOWER...
Here I am, dwelling on
on
on past glories...
...BUT IT'S IRONIC, THAT'S THE POINT...
...FIVE HOUR ENERGY...
No!
NELSON? YOU OK?
DID YOU...
DID YOU FALL ASLEEP?
No.

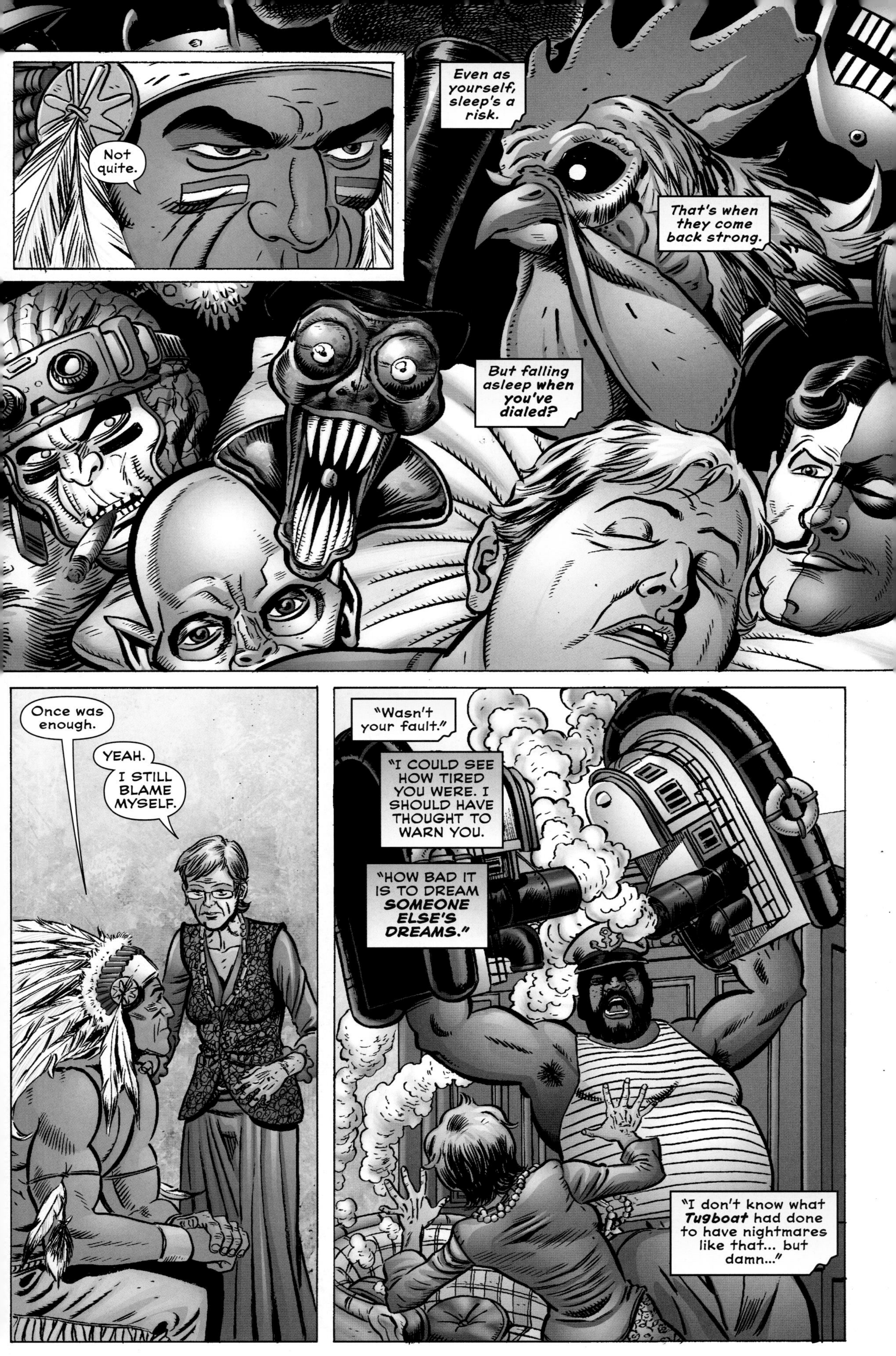
Not quite.
Even as yourself, sleep's a risk.
That's when they come back strong.
But falling asleep when you've dialed?
Once was enough.
YEAH. I STILL BLAME MYSELF.
"Wasn't your fault."
"I COULD SEE HOW TIRED YOU WERE. I SHOULD HAVE THOUGHT TO WARN YOU.
"HOW BAD IT IS TO DREAM SOMEONE ELSE'S DREAMS."
"I don't know what Tugboat had done to have nightmares like that... but damn..."

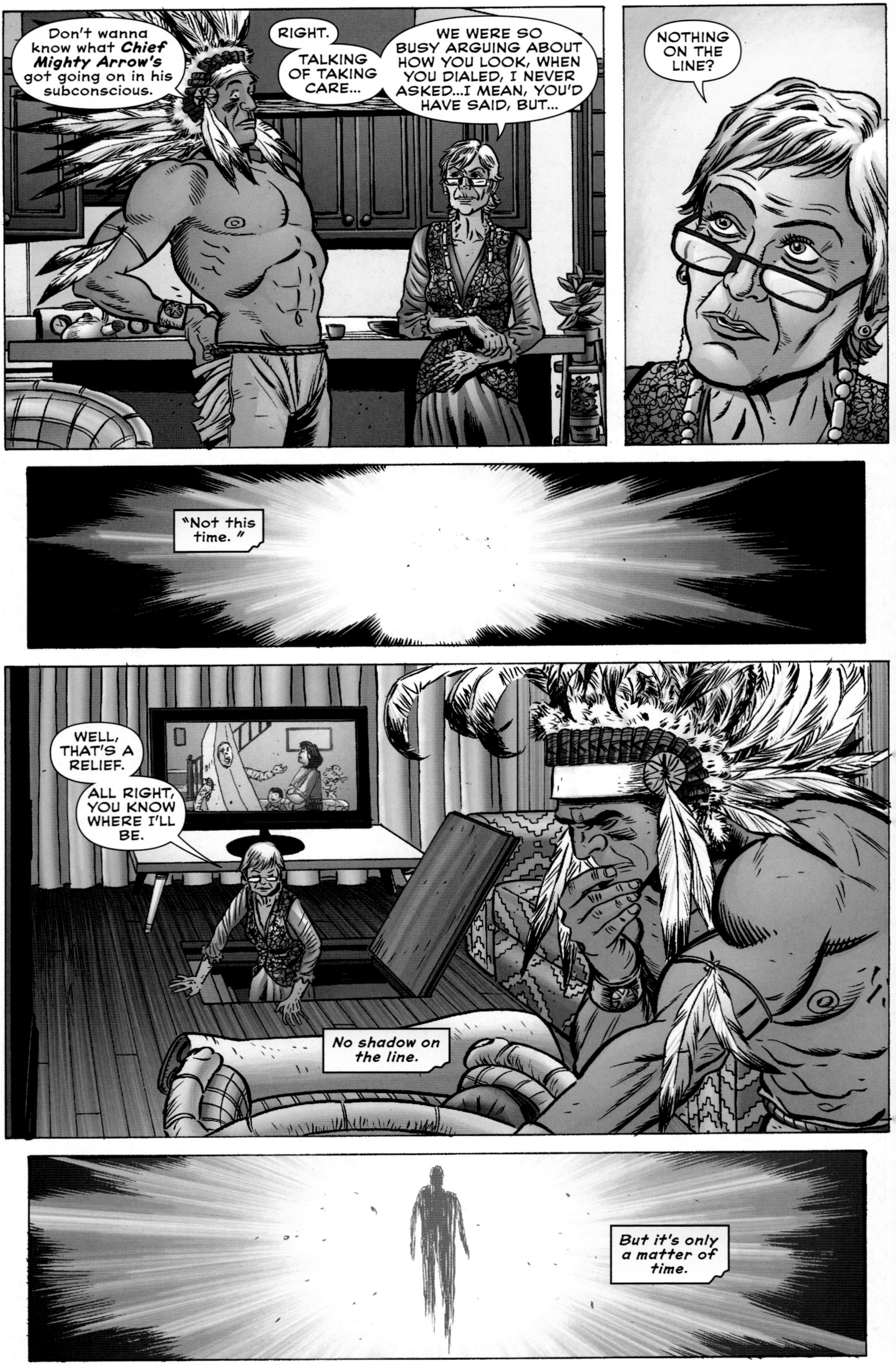
Don't wanna know what *Chief Mighty Arrow's* got going on in his subconscious.
RIGHT.
TALKING OF TAKING CARE...
WE WERE SO BUSY ARGUING ABOUT HOW YOU LOOK, WHEN YOU DIALED, I NEVER ASKED...I MEAN, YOU'D HAVE SAID, BUT...
NOTHING ON THE LINE?
"Not this time."
WELL, THAT'S A RELIEF.
ALL RIGHT, YOU KNOW WHERE I'LL BE.
No shadow on the line.
But it's only a matter of time.

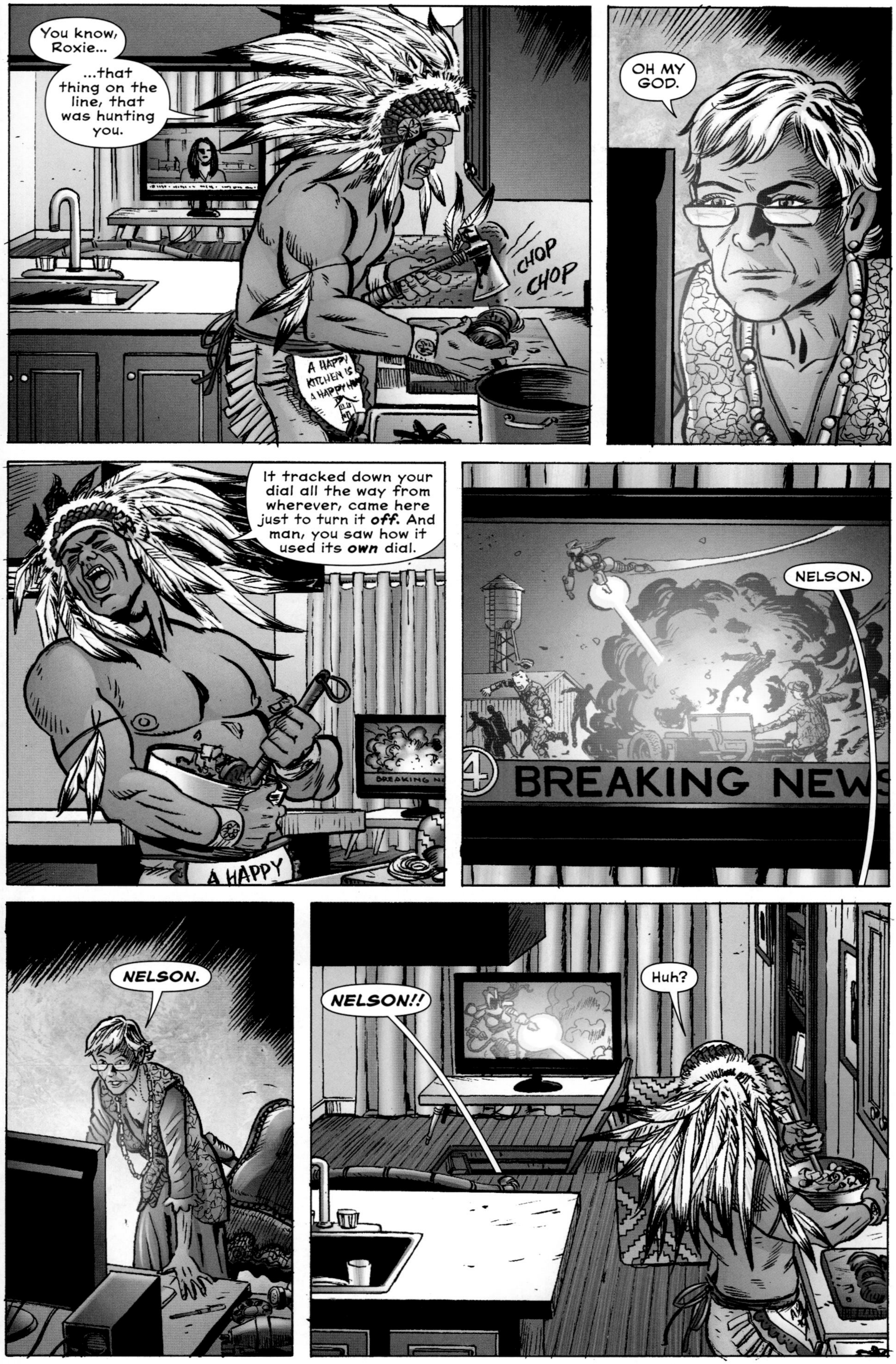
You know, Roxie...
...that thing on the line, that was hunting you.
CHOP CHOP
A HAPPY KITCHEN IS A HAPPY
OH MY GOD.
It tracked down your dial all the way from wherever, came here just to turn it off. And man, you saw how it used its own dial.
A HAPPY
BREAKING NEWS
NELSON.
NELSON.
NELSON!!
Huh?

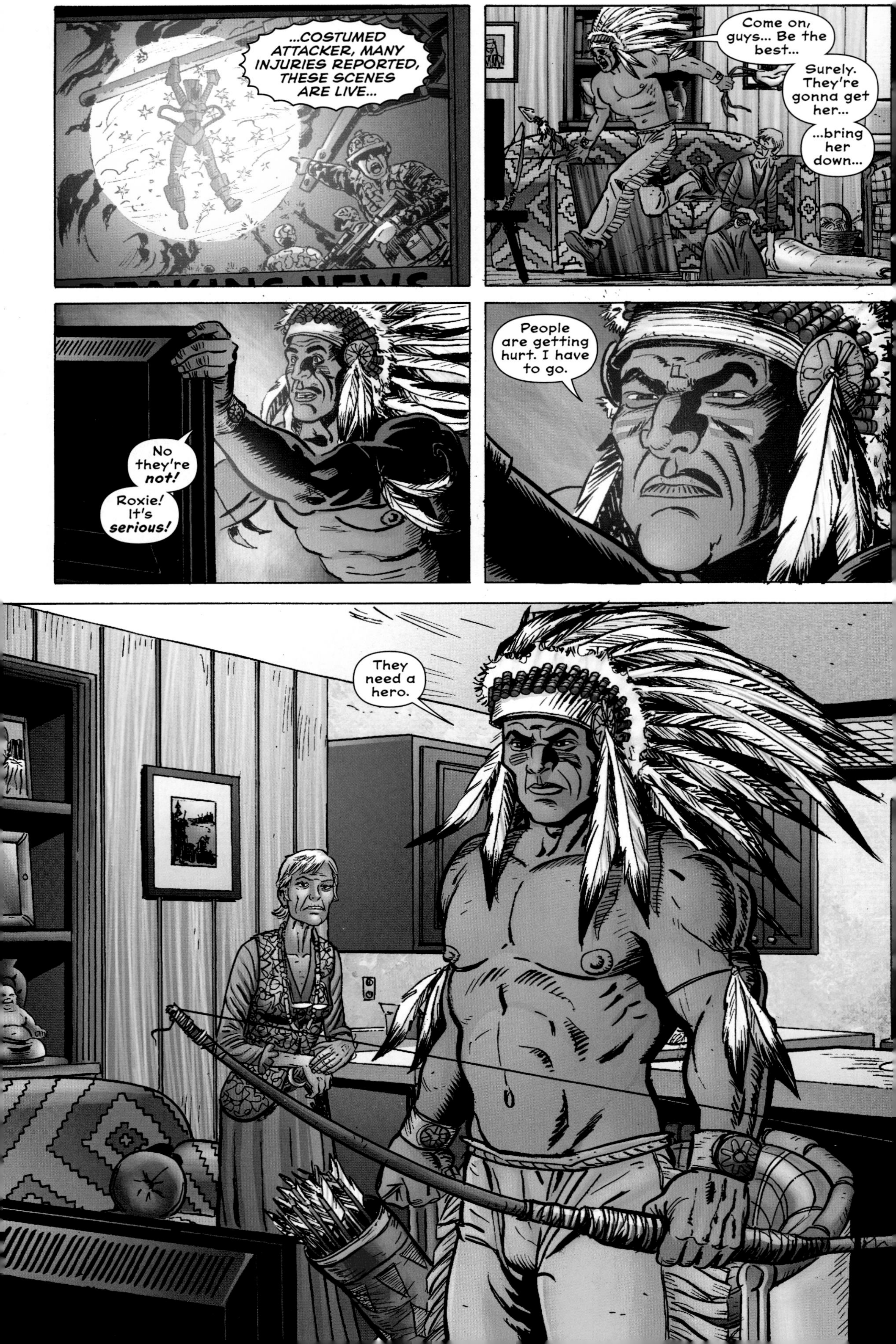
...COSTUMED ATTACKER, MANY INJURIES REPORTED, THESE SCENES ARE LIVE...
Come on, guys... Be the best...
Surely. They're gonna get her...
...bring her down...
No they're not!
Roxie! It's serious!
People are getting hurt. I have to go.
They need a hero.

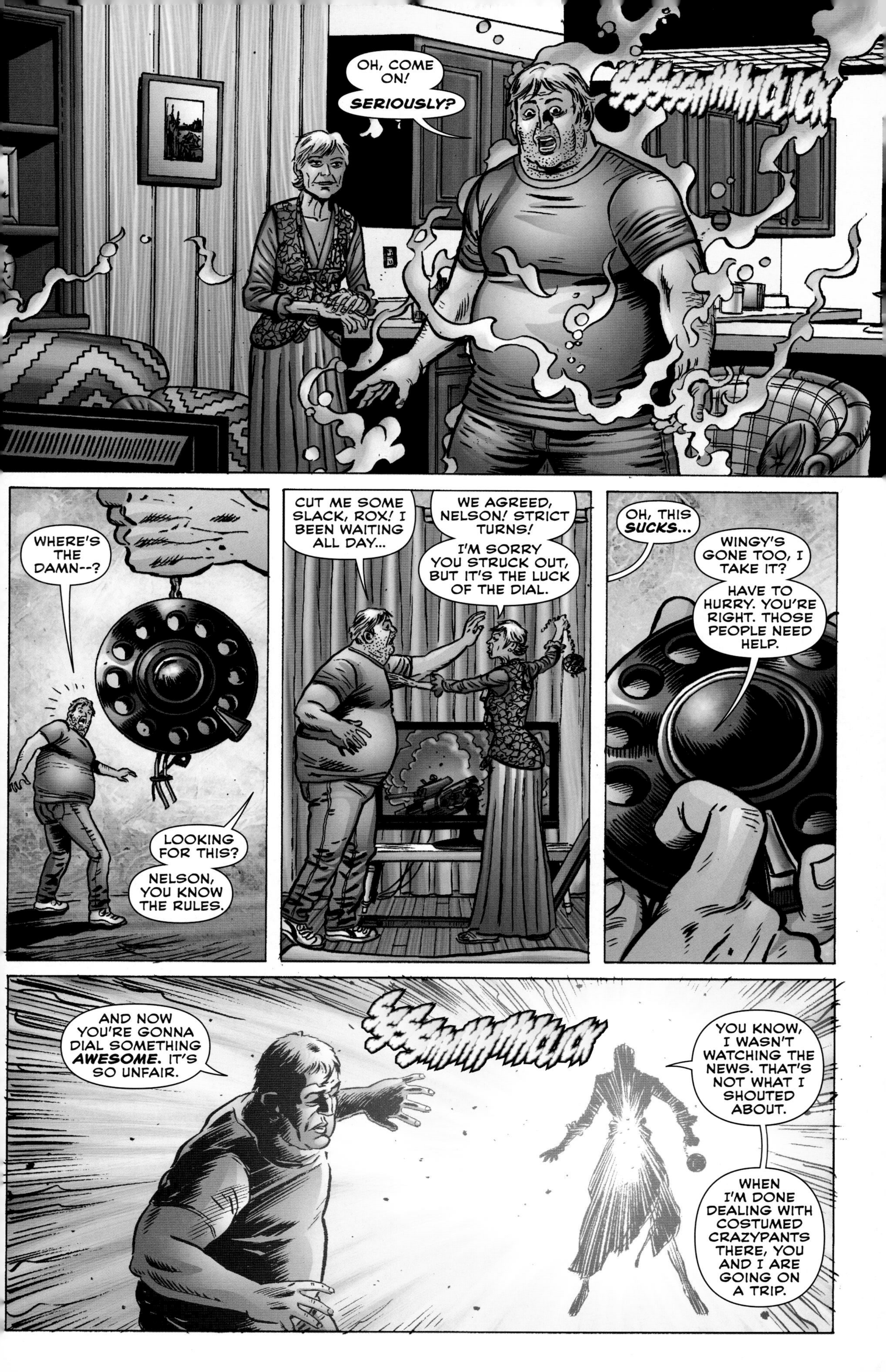

OH, COME ON! SERIOUSLY?
SSSSSHHHHCLICK
WHERE'S THE DAMN--?
LOOKING FOR THIS?
NELSON, YOU KNOW THE RULES.
CUT ME SOME SLACK, ROX! I BEEN WAITING ALL DAY...
WE AGREED, NELSON! STRICT TURNS!
I'M SORRY YOU STRUCK OUT, BUT IT'S THE LUCK OF THE DIAL.
OH, THIS SUCKS...
WINGY'S GONE TOO, I TAKE IT?
HAVE TO HURRY. YOU'RE RIGHT. THOSE PEOPLE NEED HELP.
AND NOW YOU'RE GONNA DIAL SOMETHING AWESOME. IT'S SO UNFAIR.
SSSSHHHHHHCLICK
YOU KNOW, I WASN'T WATCHING THE NEWS. THAT'S NOT WHAT I SHOUTED ABOUT.
WHEN I'M DONE DEALING WITH COSTUMED CRAZYPANTS THERE, YOU AND I ARE GOING ON A TRIP.

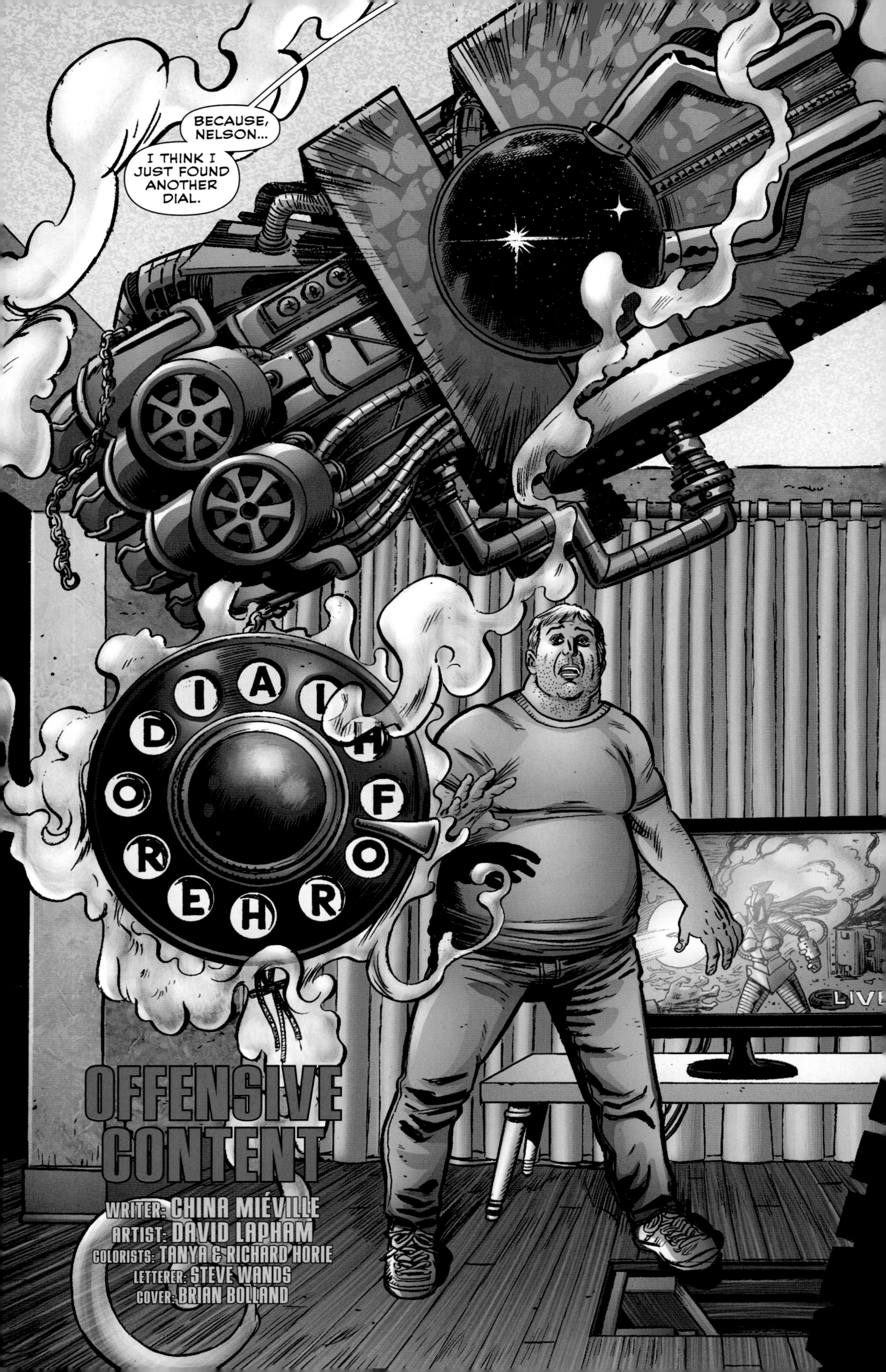
BECAUSE, NELSON...
I THINK I JUST FOUND ANOTHER DIAL.
DIAL H FOR HERO
LIVE
OFFENSIVE CONTENT
WRITER: CHINA MIÉVILLE
ARTIST: DAVID LAPHAM
COLORISTS: TANYA & RICHARD HORIE
LETTERER: STEVE WANDS
COVER: BRIAN BOLLAND

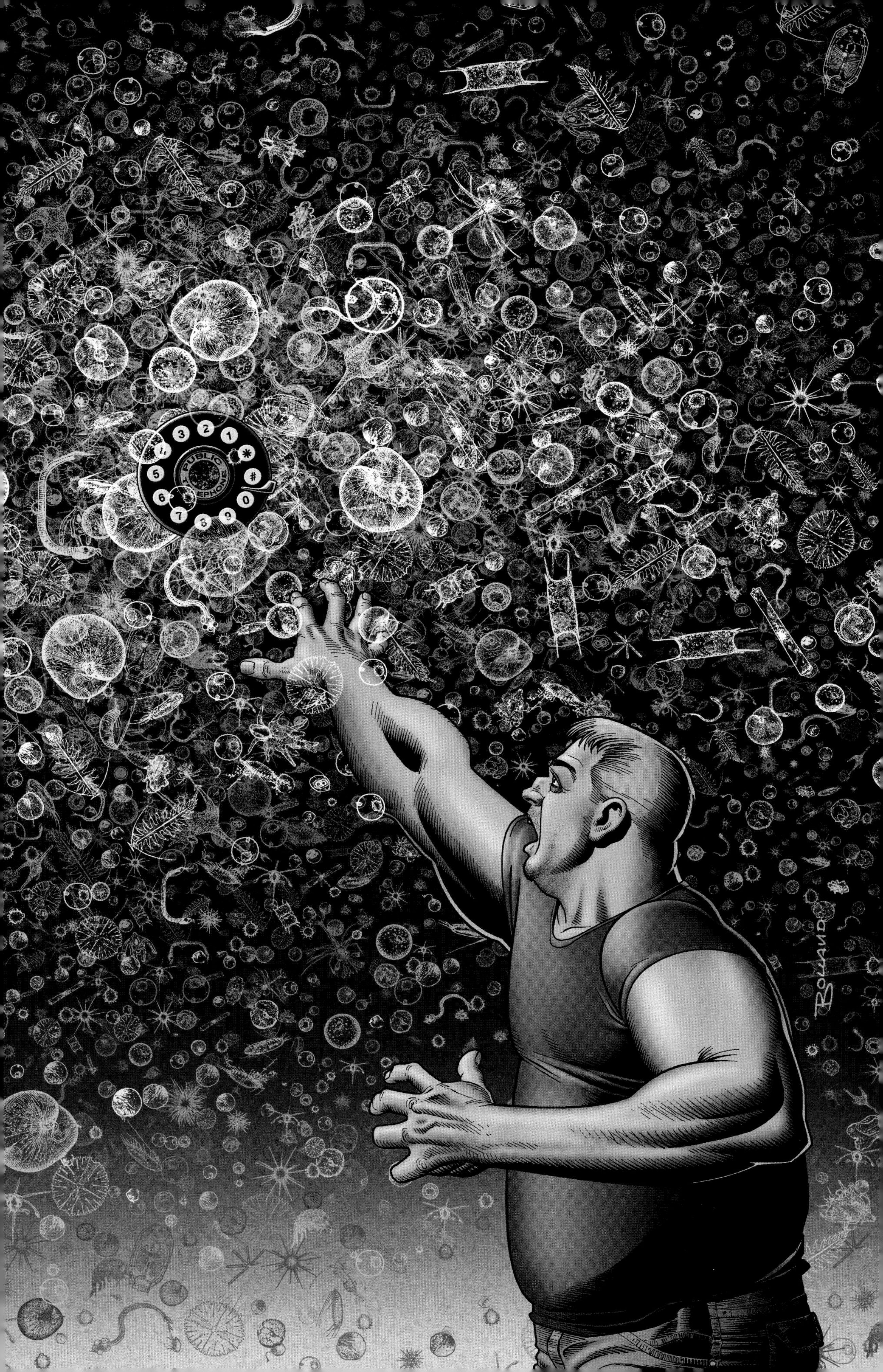
PUBLIC TELEPHONE
BOLLAND

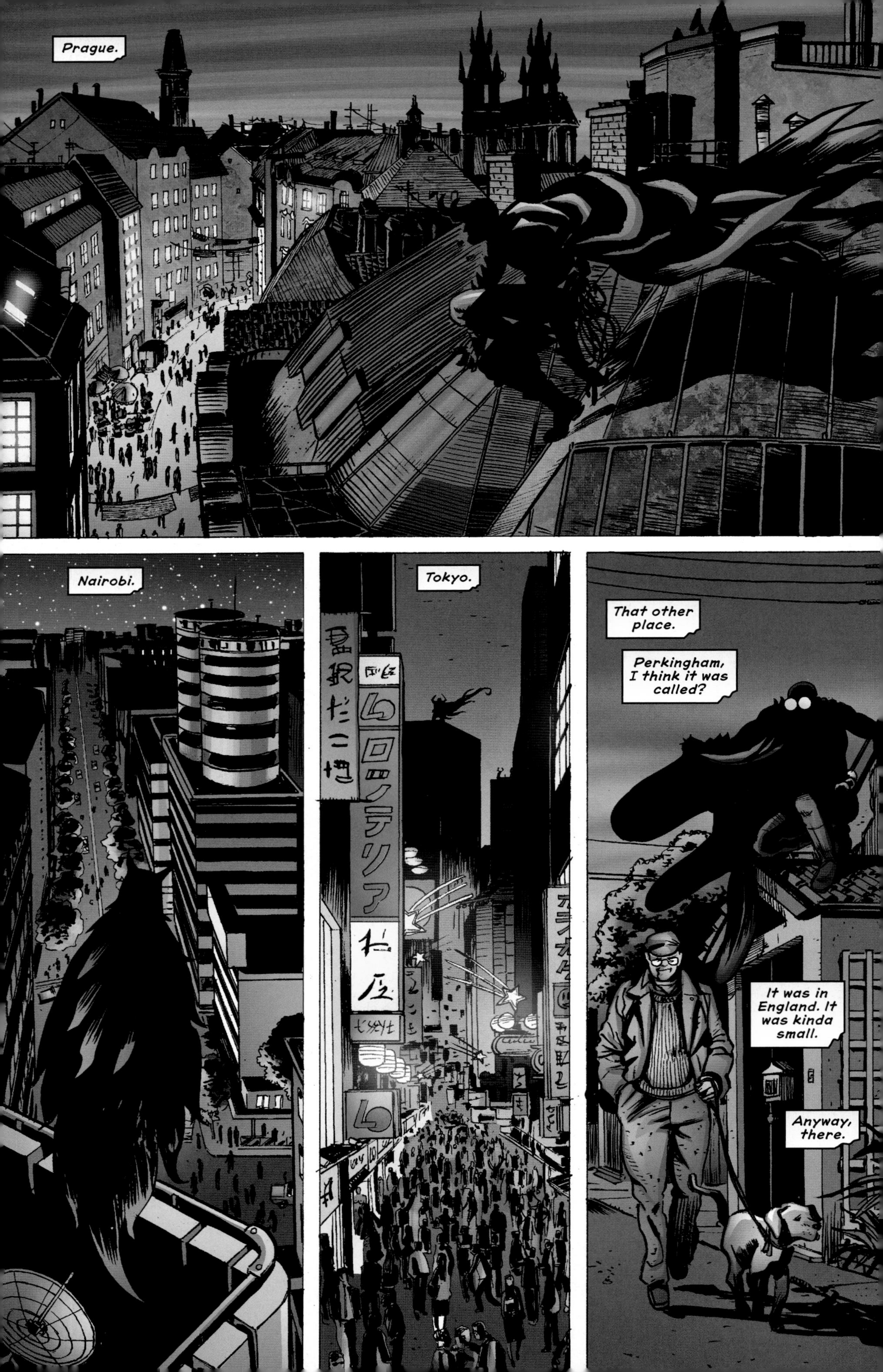
Prague.
Nairobi.
Tokyo.
That other place.
Perkingham, I think it was called?
It was in England. It was kinda small.
Anyway, there.

Wherever we go, I'm a champion.

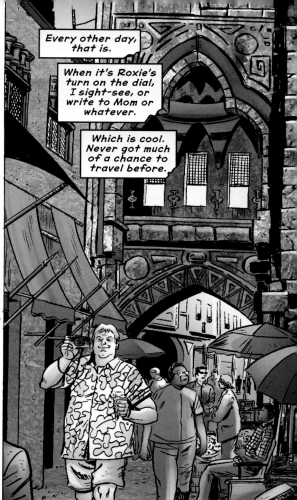

Every other day, that is.

When it's Roxie's turn on the dial, I sight-see, or write to Mom or whatever.

Which is cool. Never got much of a chance to travel before.

But I ain't gonna pretend dial days ain't my favorite.

NELSON, GET BACK HERE ASAP.

Who be-eth Nelson, milady? I am **Tree Knight!**

BE-ETH? REALLY?

JUST COME BACK.

I'VE GOT ANOTHER LEAD.

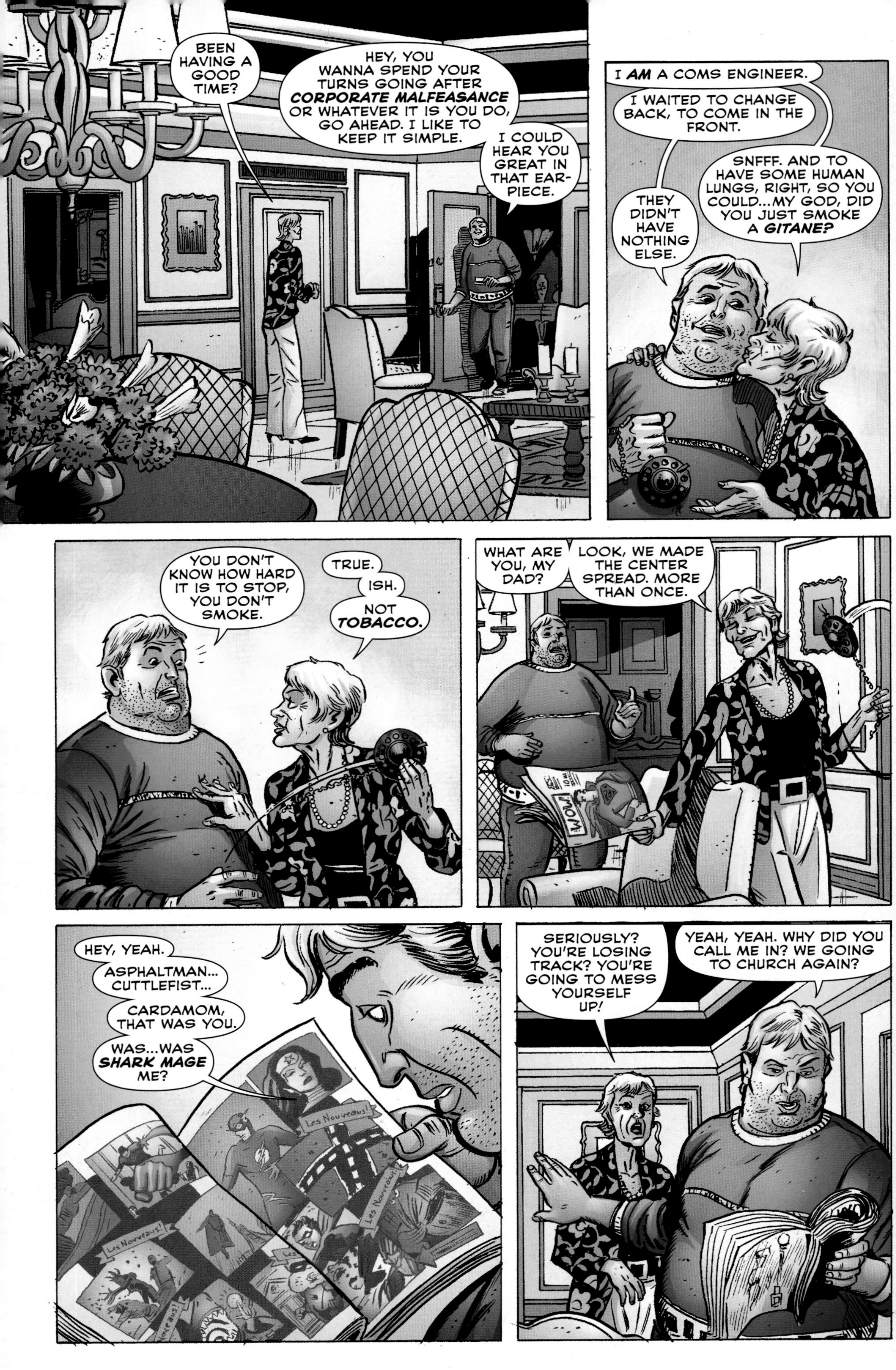
BEEN HAVING A GOOD TIME?
HEY, YOU WANNA SPEND YOUR TURNS GOING AFTER ***CORPORATE MALFEASANCE*** OR WHATEVER IT IS YOU DO, GO AHEAD. I LIKE TO KEEP IT SIMPLE.
I COULD HEAR YOU GREAT IN THAT EAR-PIECE.
I ***AM*** A COMS ENGINEER.
I WAITED TO CHANGE BACK, TO COME IN THE FRONT.
SNFFF. AND TO HAVE SOME HUMAN LUNGS, RIGHT, SO YOU COULD...MY GOD, DID YOU JUST SMOKE A ***GITANE?***
THEY DIDN'T HAVE NOTHING ELSE.
YOU DON'T KNOW HOW HARD IT IS TO STOP, YOU DON'T SMOKE.
TRUE.
ISH.
NOT ***TOBACCO.***
WHAT ARE YOU, MY DAD?
LOOK, WE MADE THE CENTER SPREAD. MORE THAN ONCE.
HEY, YEAH.
ASPHALTMAN... CUTTLEFIST...
CARDAMOM, THAT WAS YOU.
WAS...WAS ***SHARK MAGE*** ME?
SERIOUSLY? YOU'RE LOSING TRACK? YOU'RE GOING TO MESS YOURSELF UP!
YEAH, YEAH. WHY DID YOU CALL ME IN? WE GOING TO CHURCH AGAIN?

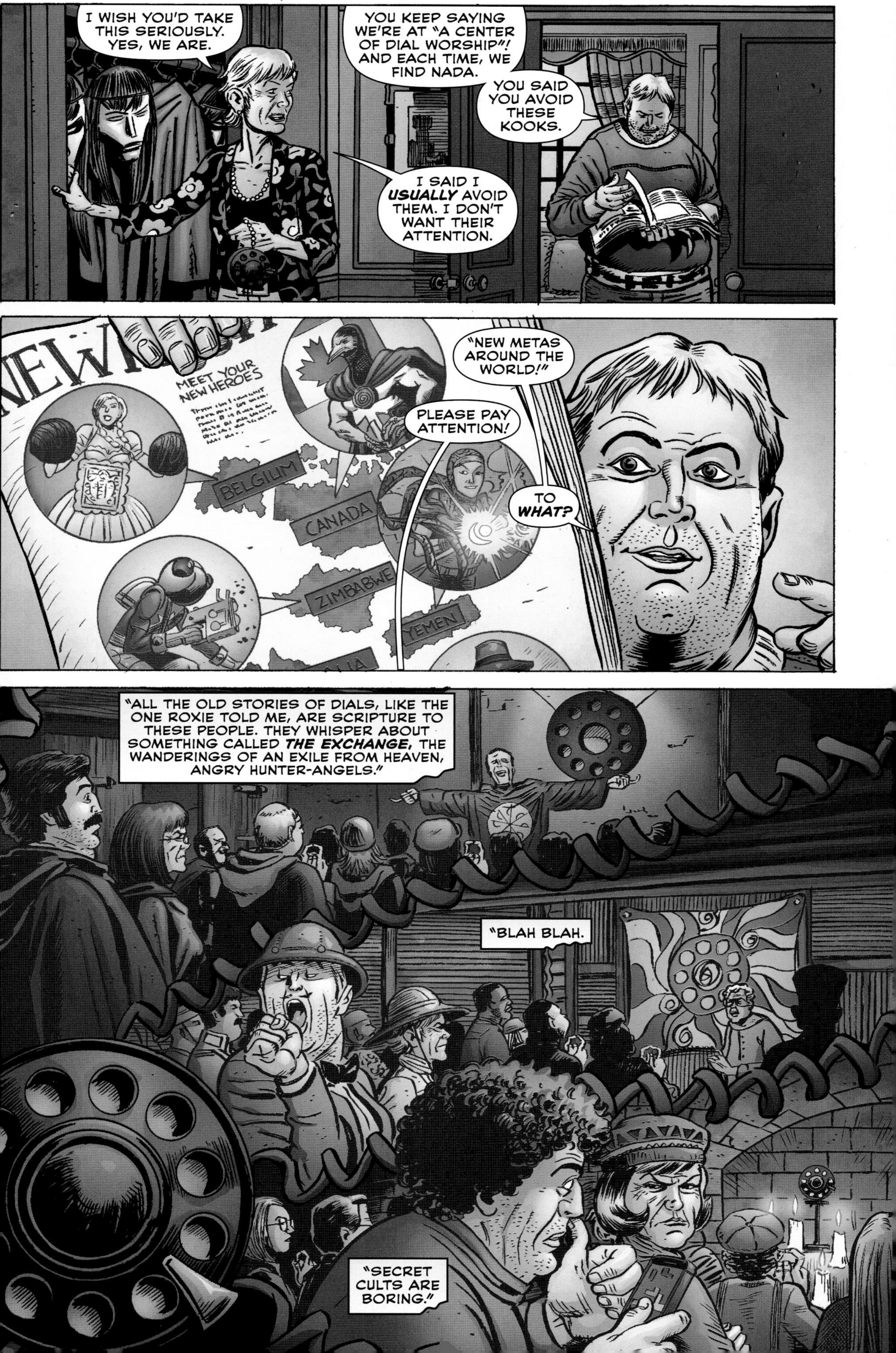
I WISH YOU'D TAKE THIS SERIOUSLY. YES, WE ARE.
YOU KEEP SAYING WE'RE AT "A CENTER OF DIAL WORSHIP"! AND EACH TIME, WE FIND NADA.
YOU SAID YOU AVOID THESE KOOKS.
I SAID I USUALLY AVOID THEM. I DON'T WANT THEIR ATTENTION.
MEET YOUR NEW HEROES
BELGIUM
CANADA
ZIMBABWE
YEMEN
"NEW METAS AROUND THE WORLD!"
PLEASE PAY ATTENTION!
TO WHAT?
"ALL THE OLD STORIES OF DIALS, LIKE THE ONE ROXIE TOLD ME, ARE SCRIPTURE TO THESE PEOPLE. THEY WHISPER ABOUT SOMETHING CALLED THE EXCHANGE, THE WANDERINGS OF AN EXILE FROM HEAVEN, ANGRY HUNTER-ANGELS."
"BLAH BLAH.
"SECRET CULTS ARE BORING."

I KNOW THIS TRIP'S BEEN A BIT MORE ROUNDABOUT THAN I'D HOPED.

A BIT?! I DIDN'T EVEN HAVE A PASSPORT A COUPLE WEEKS AGO, NOW IT'S ALMOST FULL.

NOT THAT I'M COMPLAINING ABOUT GOING ON THE ROAD.

I'VE GOT GOOD AT FILTERING OUT THESE FOLKS' CRAZY. THIS IS DIFFERENT. ALL THESE RUMORS THAT A RELIC'S BEEN FOUND... I BELIEVE THEM.

SO WHY CAN'T WE FIND IT?

WE'VE BEEN TRYING TO KEEP A LOW PROFILE. POSE AS NEW CONVERTS. TEMPT HINTS AND HOLY SECRETS OUT OF PRIESTS IN THE KNOW, RIGHT?

RIGHT.

WELL *SCREW THAT.*

UH...

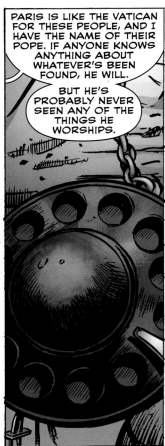

PARIS IS LIKE THE VATICAN FOR THESE PEOPLE, AND I HAVE THE NAME OF THEIR POPE. IF ANYONE KNOWS ANYTHING ABOUT WHATEVER'S BEEN FOUND, HE WILL.

BUT HE'S PROBABLY NEVER SEEN ANY OF THE THINGS HE WORSHIPS.

"HE'S WAITING FOR A MIRACLE.

"LET'S GIVE IT TO HIM."

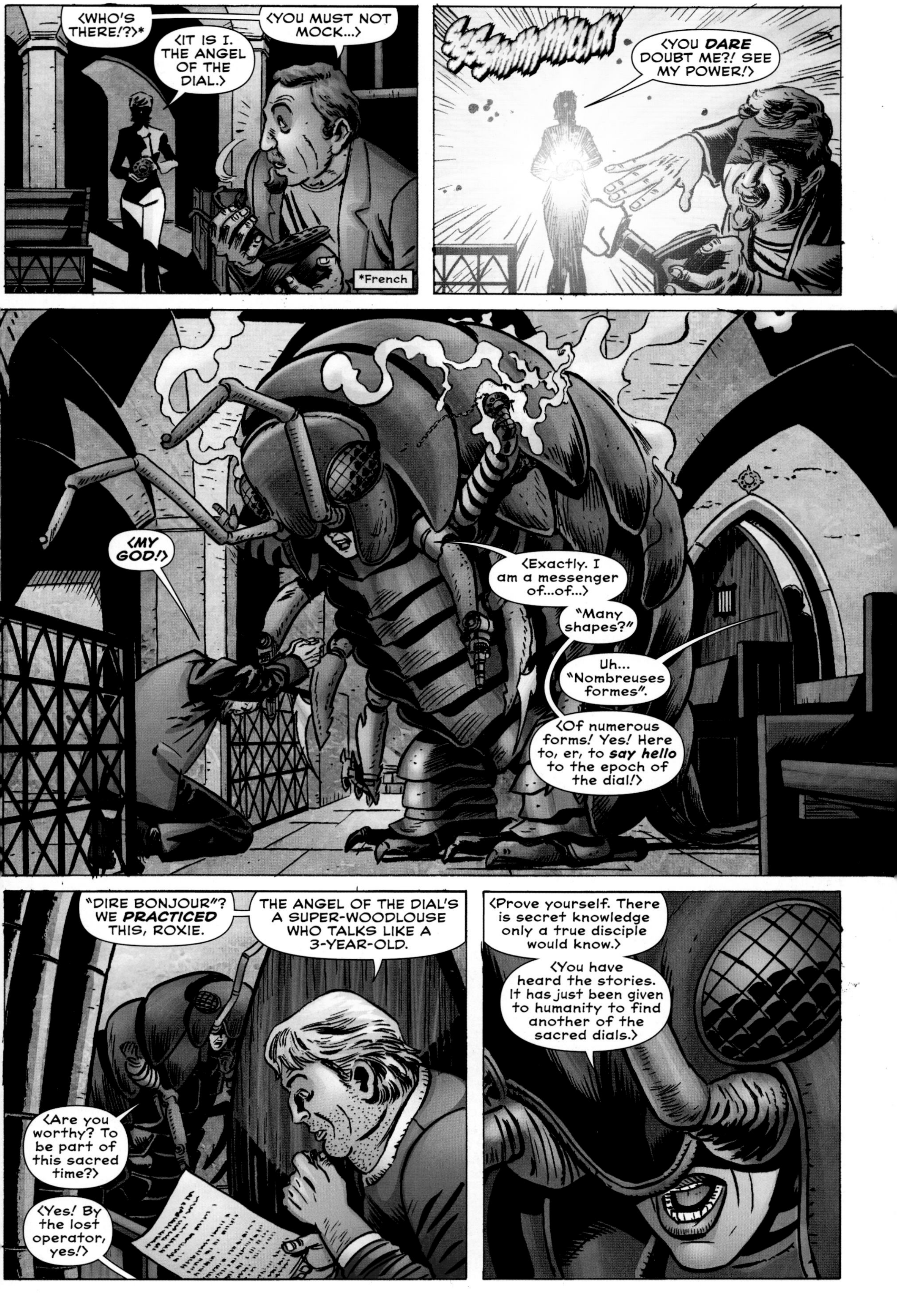

<WHO'S THERE!?>*
<YOU MUST NOT MOCK...>
<IT IS I. THE ANGEL OF THE DIAL.>
*French
<YOU DARE DOUBT ME?! SEE MY POWER!>
<MY GOD!>
<Exactly. I am a messenger of...of...>
"Many shapes?"
Uh... "Nombreuses formes".
<Of numerous forms! Yes! Here to, er, to say hello to the epoch of the dial!>
"DIRE BONJOUR"? WE PRACTICED THIS, ROXIE.
THE ANGEL OF THE DIAL'S A SUPER-WOODLOUSE WHO TALKS LIKE A 3-YEAR-OLD.
<Are you worthy? To be part of this sacred time?>
<Yes! By the lost operator, yes!>
<Prove yourself. There is secret knowledge only a true disciple would know.>
<You have heard the stories. It has just been given to humanity to find another of the sacred dials.>

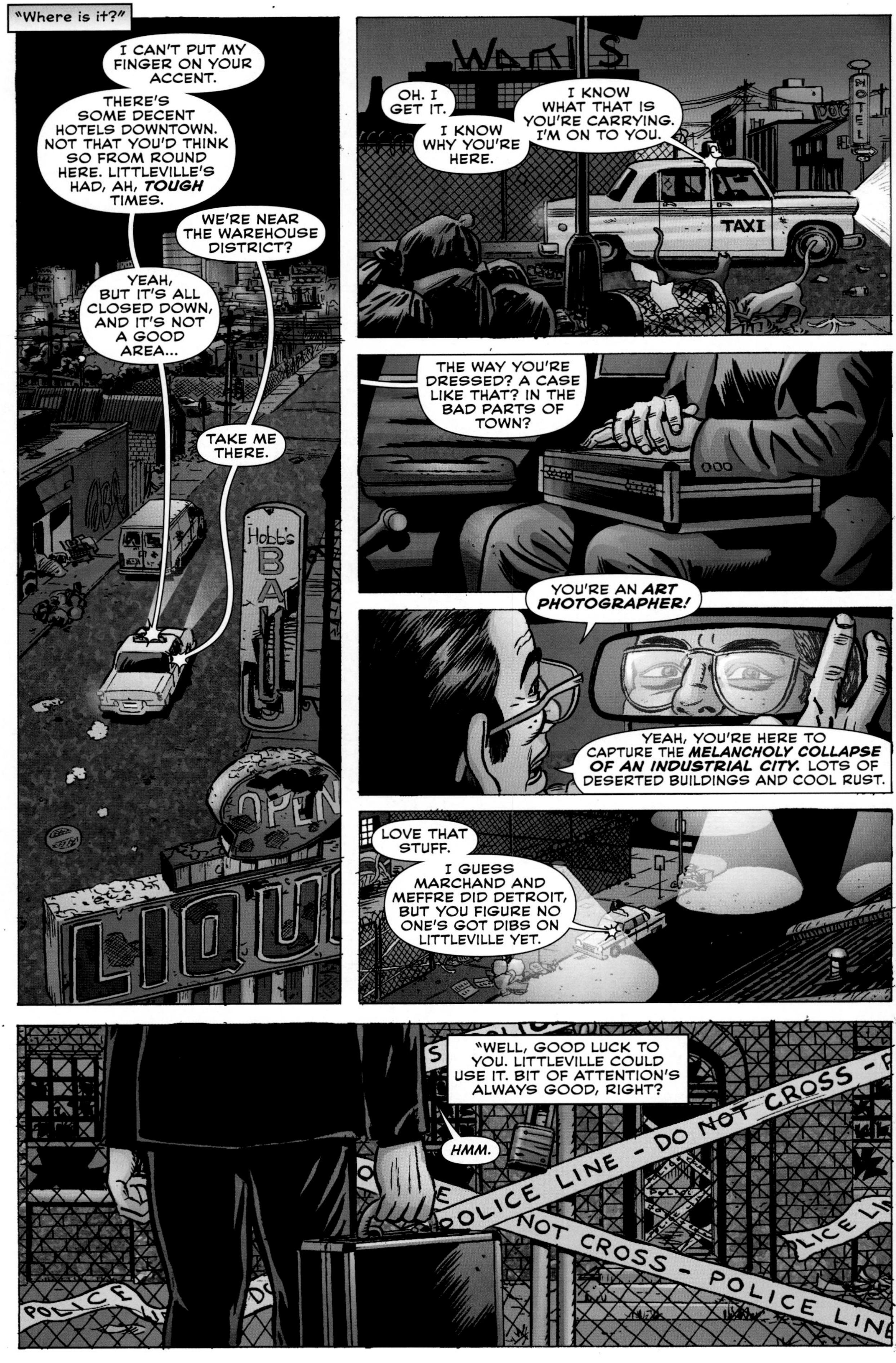
"Where is it?"
I CAN'T PUT MY FINGER ON YOUR ACCENT.
THERE'S SOME DECENT HOTELS DOWNTOWN. NOT THAT YOU'D THINK SO FROM ROUND HERE. LITTLEVILLE'S HAD, AH, TOUGH TIMES.
WE'RE NEAR THE WAREHOUSE DISTRICT?
YEAH, BUT IT'S ALL CLOSED DOWN, AND IT'S NOT A GOOD AREA...
TAKE ME THERE.
Hobb's
OPEN
LIQU
OH. I GET IT.
I KNOW WHY YOU'RE HERE.
I KNOW WHAT THAT IS YOU'RE CARRYING. I'M ON TO YOU.
MOTEL
TAXI
THE WAY YOU'RE DRESSED? A CASE LIKE THAT? IN THE BAD PARTS OF TOWN?
YOU'RE AN ART PHOTOGRAPHER!
YEAH, YOU'RE HERE TO CAPTURE THE MELANCHOLY COLLAPSE OF AN INDUSTRIAL CITY. LOTS OF DESERTED BUILDINGS AND COOL RUST.
LOVE THAT STUFF.
I GUESS MARCHAND AND MEFFRE DID DETROIT, BUT YOU FIGURE NO ONE'S GOT DIBS ON LITTLEVILLE YET.
"WELL, GOOD LUCK TO YOU. LITTLEVILLE COULD USE IT. BIT OF ATTENTION'S ALWAYS GOOD, RIGHT?
HMM.
POLICE LINE - DO NOT CROSS
NOT CROSS - POLICE LINE

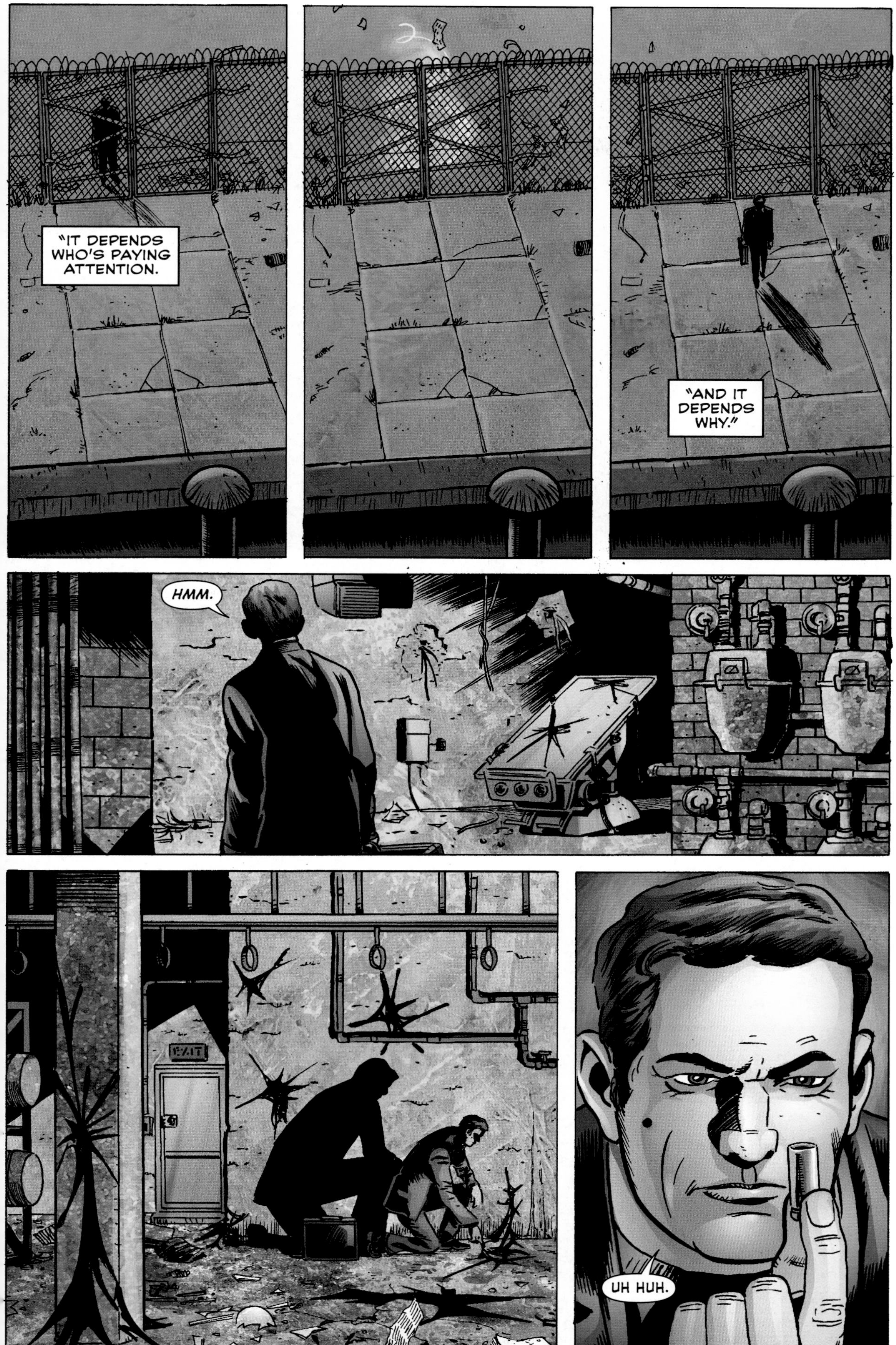
"IT DEPENDS WHO'S PAYING ATTENTION.
"AND IT DEPENDS WHY."
HMM.
UH HUH.

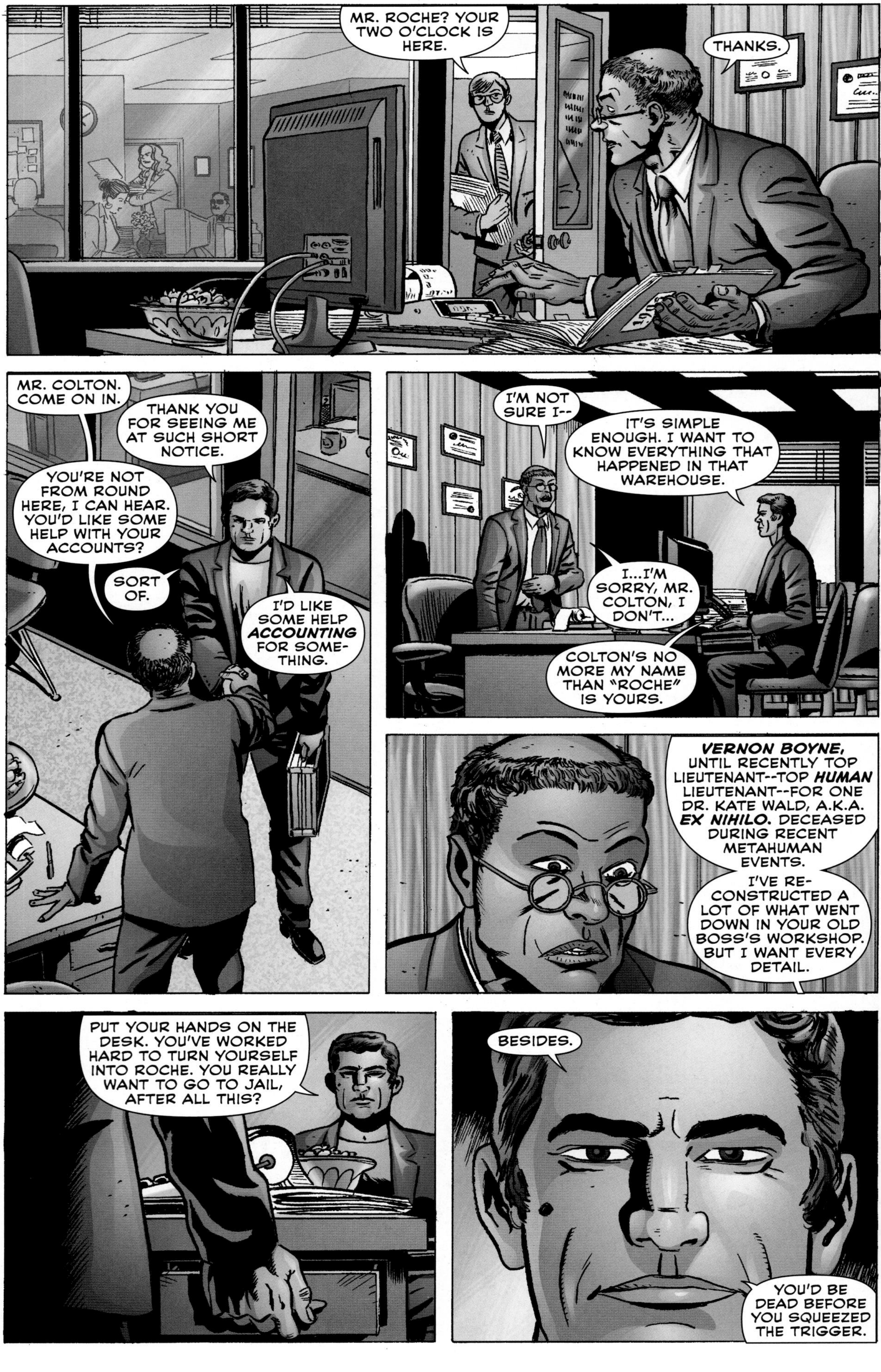

MR. ROCHE? YOUR TWO O'CLOCK IS HERE.
THANKS.
MR. COLTON. COME ON IN.
THANK YOU FOR SEEING ME AT SUCH SHORT NOTICE.
YOU'RE NOT FROM ROUND HERE, I CAN HEAR. YOU'D LIKE SOME HELP WITH YOUR ACCOUNTS?
SORT OF.
I'D LIKE SOME HELP ***ACCOUNTING*** FOR SOMETHING.
I'M NOT SURE I--
IT'S SIMPLE ENOUGH. I WANT TO KNOW EVERYTHING THAT HAPPENED IN THAT WAREHOUSE.
I...I'M SORRY, MR. COLTON, I DON'T...
COLTON'S NO MORE MY NAME THAN "ROCHE" IS YOURS.
VERNON BOYNE, UNTIL RECENTLY TOP LIEUTENANT--TOP ***HUMAN*** LIEUTENANT--FOR ONE DR. KATE WALD, A.K.A. ***EX NIHILO.*** DECEASED DURING RECENT METAHUMAN EVENTS.
I'VE RE-CONSTRUCTED A LOT OF WHAT WENT DOWN IN YOUR OLD BOSS'S WORKSHOP. BUT I WANT EVERY DETAIL.
PUT YOUR HANDS ON THE DESK. YOU'VE WORKED HARD TO TURN YOURSELF INTO ROCHE. YOU REALLY WANT TO GO TO JAIL, AFTER ALL THIS?
BESIDES.
YOU'D BE DEAD BEFORE YOU SQUEEZED THE TRIGGER.

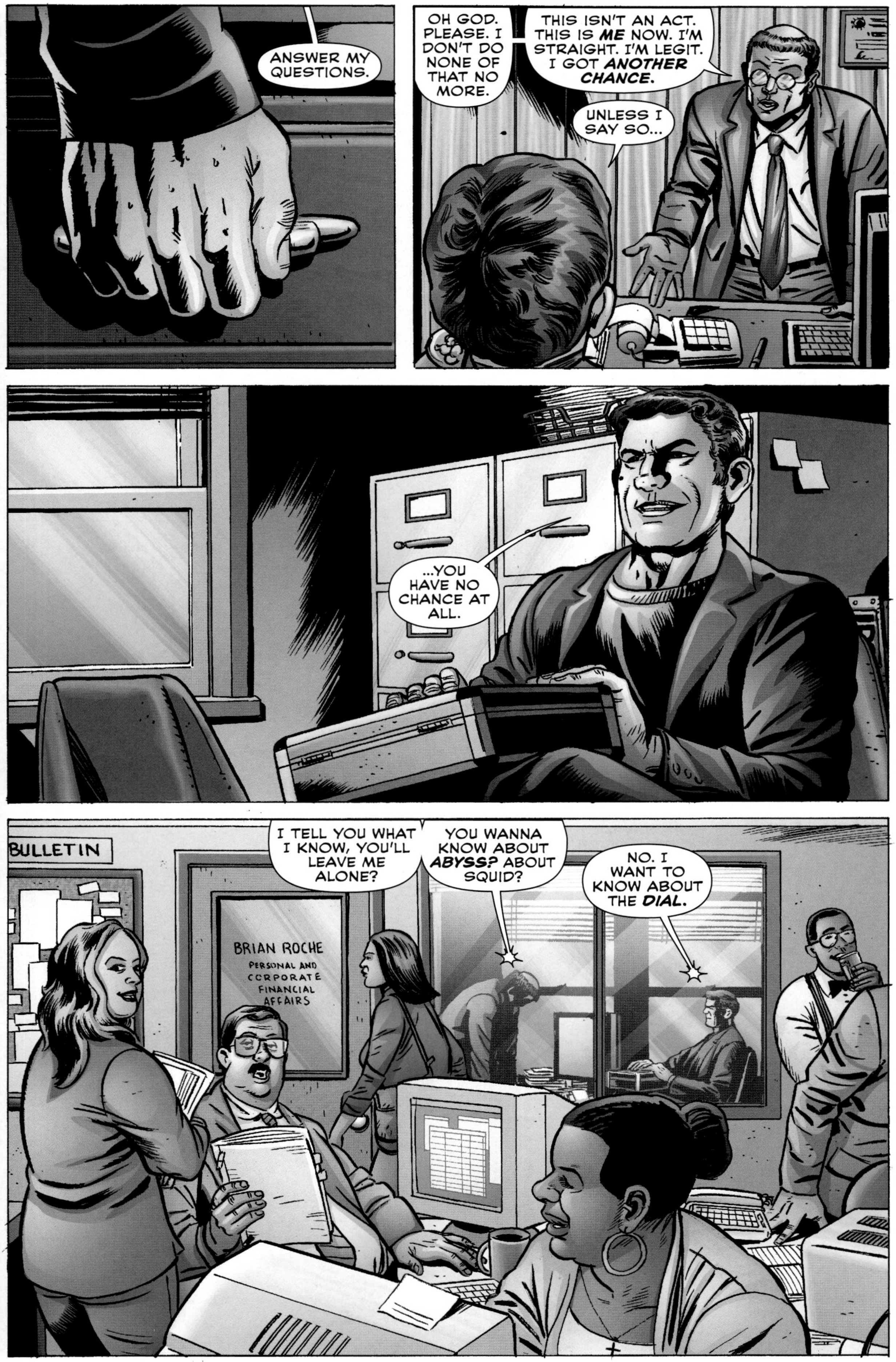
ANSWER MY QUESTIONS.
OH GOD. PLEASE. I DON'T DO NONE OF THAT NO MORE.
THIS ISN'T AN ACT. THIS IS ME NOW. I'M STRAIGHT. I'M LEGIT. I GOT ANOTHER CHANCE.
UNLESS I SAY SO...
...YOU HAVE NO CHANCE AT ALL.
BULLETIN
I TELL YOU WHAT I KNOW, YOU'LL LEAVE ME ALONE?
YOU WANNA KNOW ABOUT ABYSS? ABOUT SQUID?
NO. I WANT TO KNOW ABOUT THE DIAL.
BRIAN ROCHE
PERSONAL AND CORPORATE FINANCIAL AFFAIRS

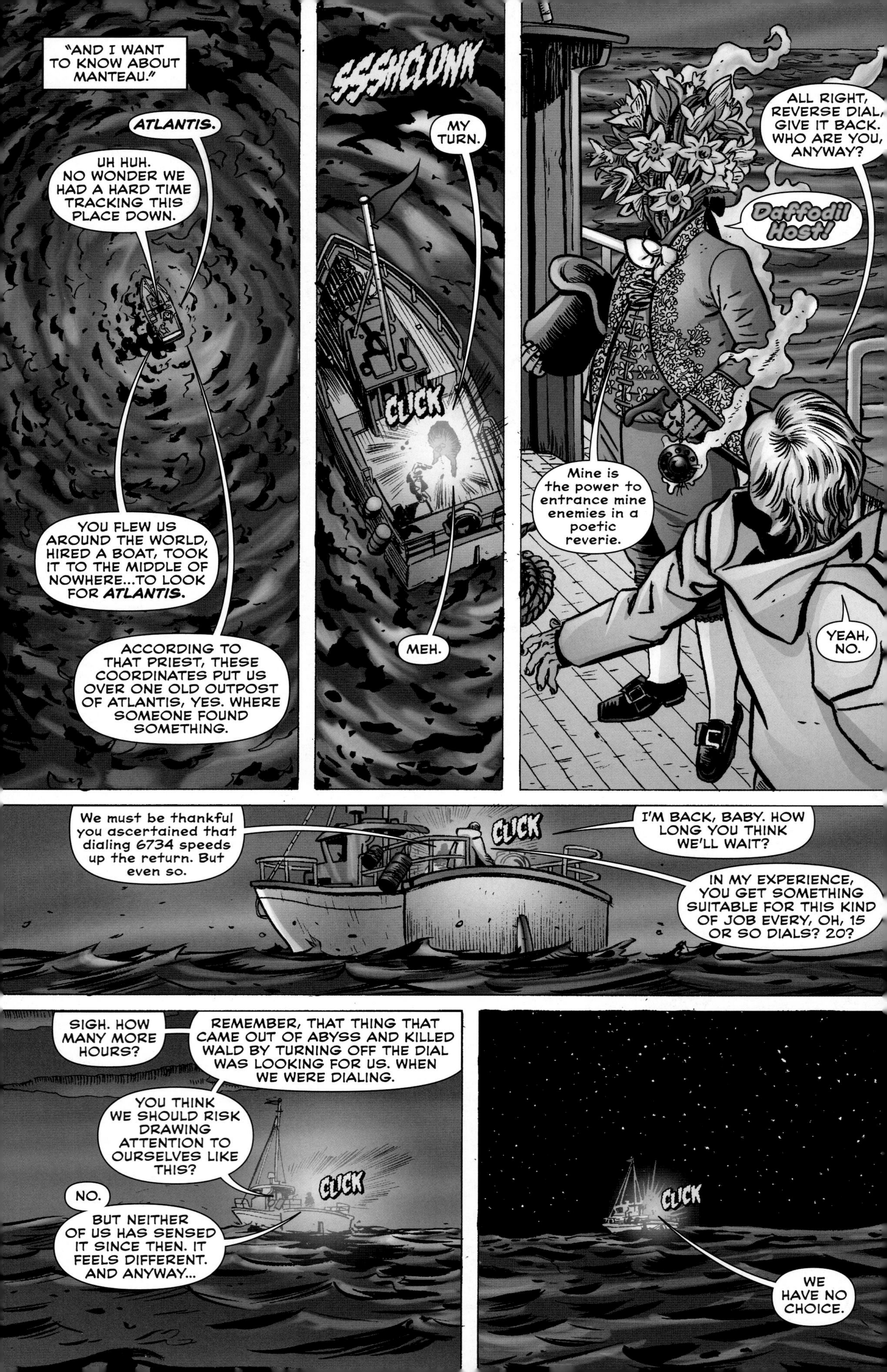
"AND I WANT TO KNOW ABOUT MANTEAU."
ATLANTIS.
UH HUH. NO WONDER WE HAD A HARD TIME TRACKING THIS PLACE DOWN.
YOU FLEW US AROUND THE WORLD, HIRED A BOAT, TOOK IT TO THE MIDDLE OF NOWHERE...TO LOOK FOR ATLANTIS.
ACCORDING TO THAT PRIEST, THESE COORDINATES PUT US OVER ONE OLD OUTPOST OF ATLANTIS, YES. WHERE SOMEONE FOUND SOMETHING.
SSSHCLUNK
MY TURN.
CLICK
MEH.
ALL RIGHT, REVERSE DIAL, GIVE IT BACK. WHO ARE YOU, ANYWAY?
Daffodil Host!
Mine is the power to entrance mine enemies in a poetic reverie.
YEAH, NO.
We must be thankful you ascertained that dialing 6734 speeds up the return. But even so.
CLICK
I'M BACK, BABY. HOW LONG YOU THINK WE'LL WAIT?
IN MY EXPERIENCE, YOU GET SOMETHING SUITABLE FOR THIS KIND OF JOB EVERY, OH, 15 OR SO DIALS? 20?
SIGH. HOW MANY MORE HOURS?
REMEMBER, THAT THING THAT CAME OUT OF ABYSS AND KILLED WALD BY TURNING OFF THE DIAL WAS LOOKING FOR US. WHEN WE WERE DIALING.
YOU THINK WE SHOULD RISK DRAWING ATTENTION TO OURSELVES LIKE THIS?
CLICK
NO.
BUT NEITHER OF US HAS SENSED IT SINCE THEN. IT FEELS DIFFERENT. AND ANYWAY...
CLICK
WE HAVE NO CHOICE.

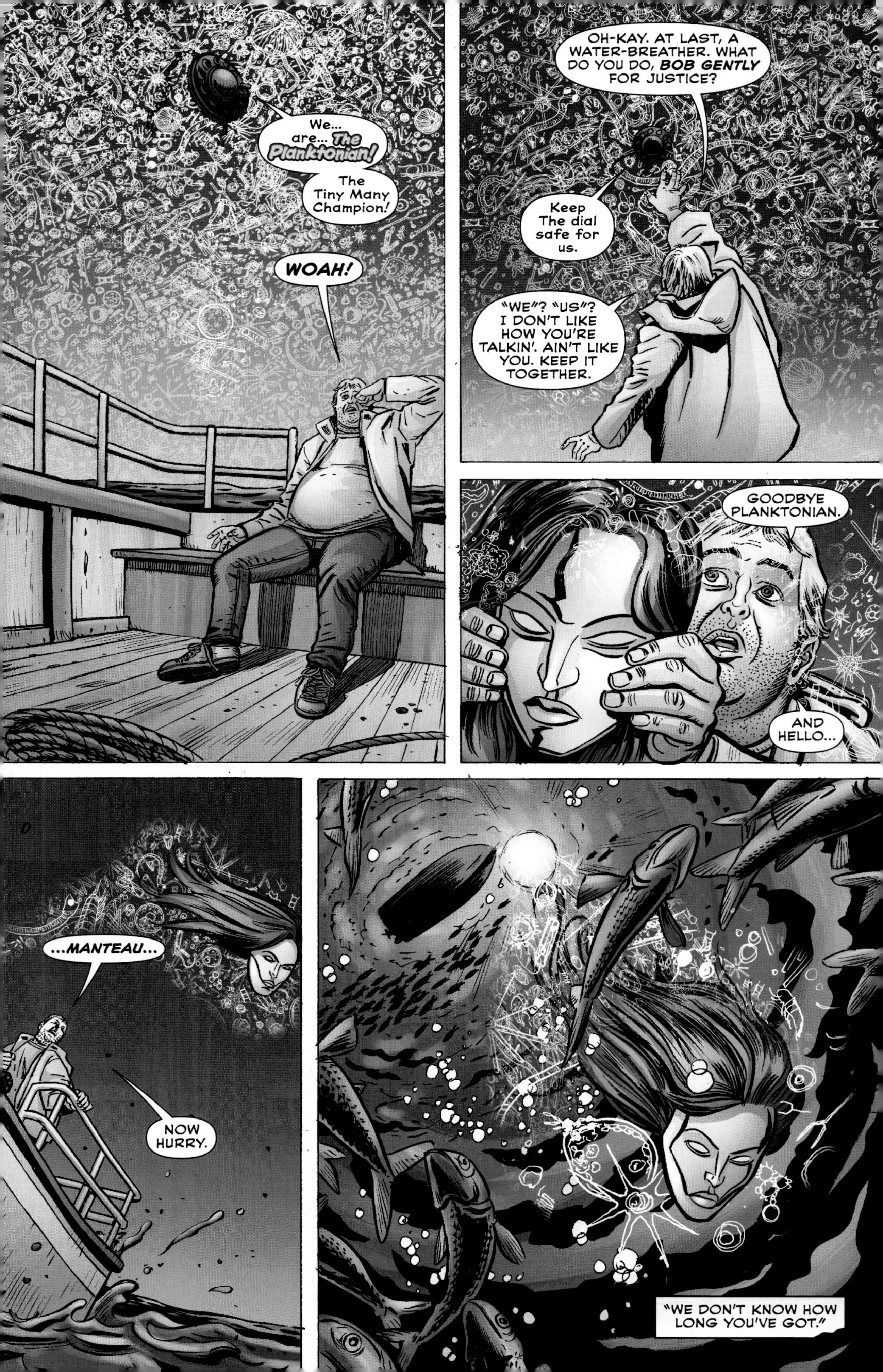

We... are... The Planktonian!
The Tiny Many Champion!
WOAH!
OH-KAY. AT LAST, A WATER-BREATHER. WHAT DO YOU DO, BOB GENTLY FOR JUSTICE?
Keep The dial safe for us.
"WE"? "US"? I DON'T LIKE HOW YOU'RE TALKIN'. AIN'T LIKE YOU. KEEP IT TOGETHER.
GOODBYE PLANKTONIAN.
AND HELLO...
...MANTEAU...
NOW HURRY.
"WE DON'T KNOW HOW LONG YOU'VE GOT."

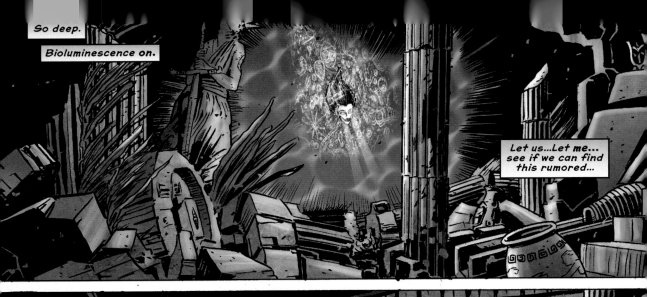

So deep.

Bioluminescence on.

Let us...Let me... see if we can find this rumored...

...ruin.

Something was here.

Someone took it.

Was interrupted.

This tomb's a beacon.

Power like this would never rest unguarded.

But these sharks aren't interested in meat like mine--

EEEEOOOOOOEEEEE

IRRRRUMBLE RUMBLE RUMBLE

What--?

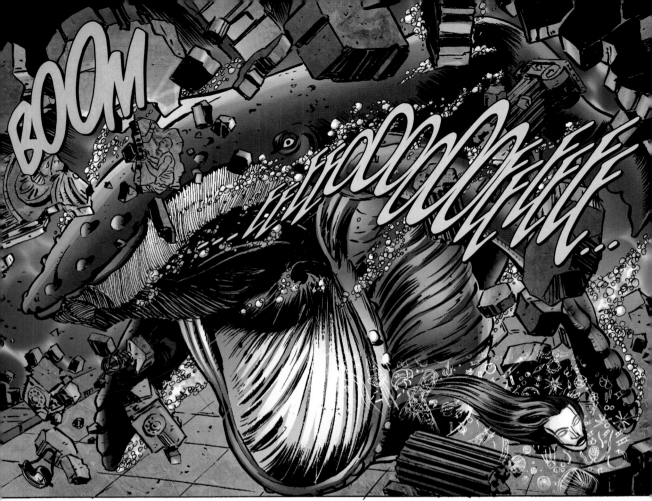

BOOM

Old nemesis.

Great maw.

I...we... must focus.

Need all my...our... strength.

we

we

we

we

We are the rage of amphipods.

Krillstorm.

The vengeance of fry.

Our strategy is multitude.

No more masks.

We are

we

we

we

The Pelagic Paladin.

The Planktonian.

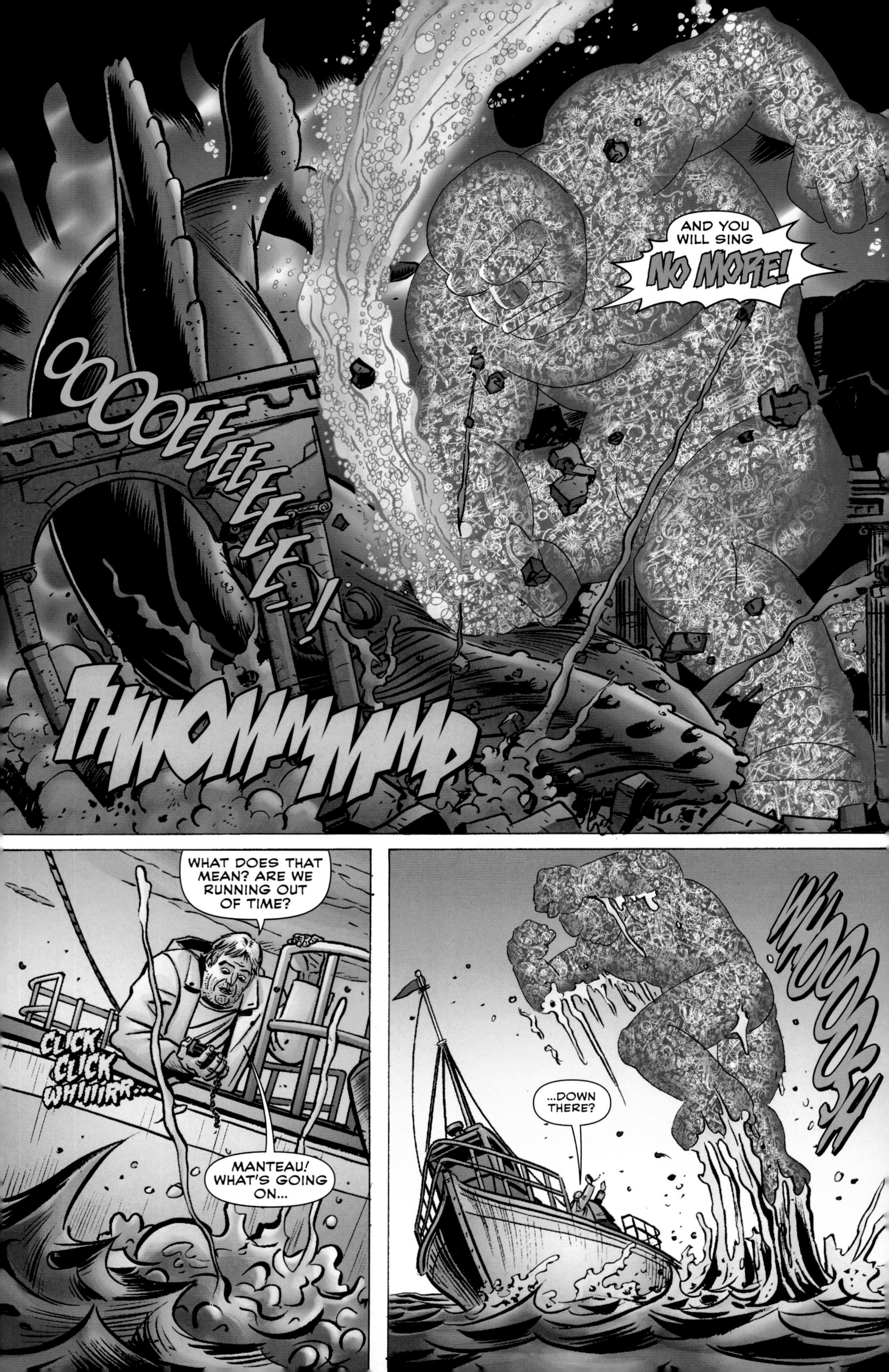
AND YOU WILL SING NO MORE!
OOOOEEEEEEEEE--!
THWOMMMMMP
WHAT DOES THAT MEAN? ARE WE RUNNING OUT OF TIME?
CLICK CLICK WHIIIIRR...
MANTEAU! WHAT'S GOING ON...
...DOWN THERE?
WHOOOOOSH

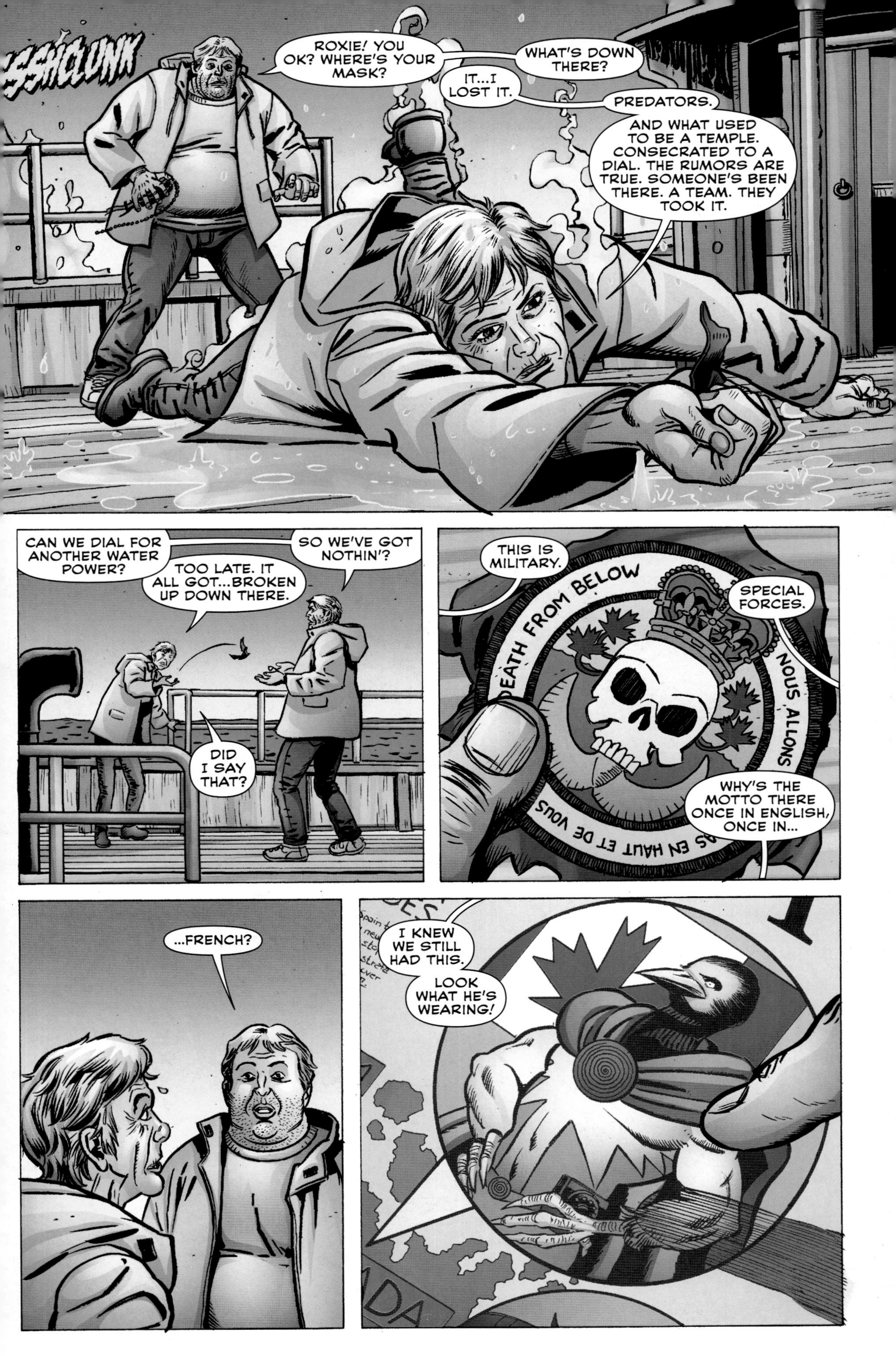
SSHCLUNK
ROXIE! YOU OK? WHERE'S YOUR MASK?
IT...I LOST IT.
WHAT'S DOWN THERE?
PREDATORS.
AND WHAT USED TO BE A TEMPLE. CONSECRATED TO A DIAL. THE RUMORS ARE TRUE. SOMEONE'S BEEN THERE. A TEAM. THEY TOOK IT.
CAN WE DIAL FOR ANOTHER WATER POWER?
TOO LATE. IT ALL GOT...BROKEN UP DOWN THERE.
SO WE'VE GOT NOTHIN'?
DID I SAY THAT?
THIS IS MILITARY.
DEATH FROM BELOW
NOUS ALLONS
AS EN HAUT ET DE VOUS
SPECIAL FORCES.
WHY'S THE MOTTO THERE ONCE IN ENGLISH, ONCE IN...
...FRENCH?
I KNEW WE STILL HAD THIS.
LOOK WHAT HE'S WEARING!

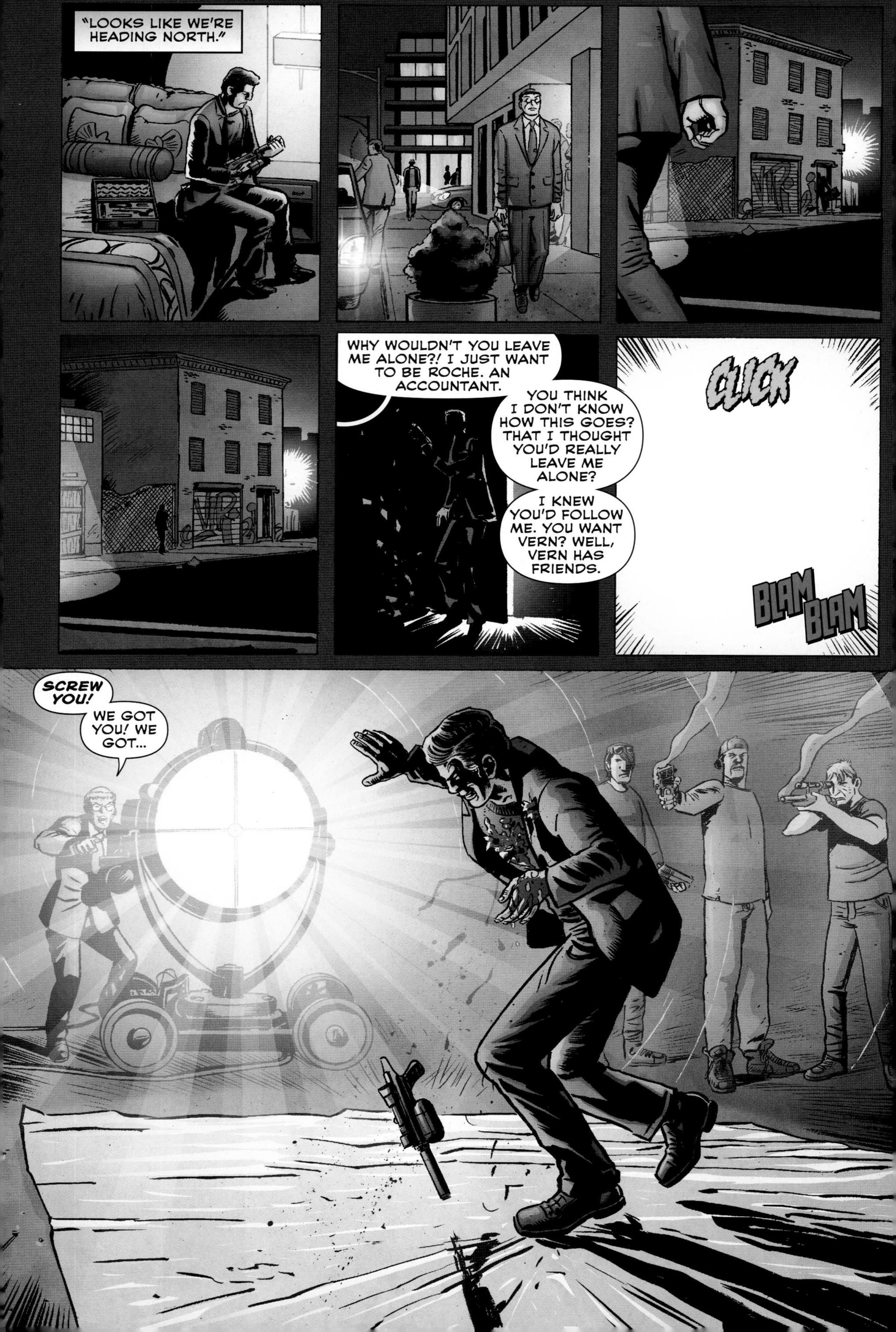
"LOOKS LIKE WE'RE HEADING NORTH."
WHY WOULDN'T YOU LEAVE ME ALONE?! I JUST WANT TO BE ROCHE. AN ACCOUNTANT.
YOU THINK I DON'T KNOW HOW THIS GOES? THAT I THOUGHT YOU'D REALLY LEAVE ME ALONE?
I KNEW YOU'D FOLLOW ME. YOU WANT VERN? WELL, VERN HAS FRIENDS.
CLICK
BLAM BLAM
SCREW YOU!
WE GOT YOU! WE GOT...

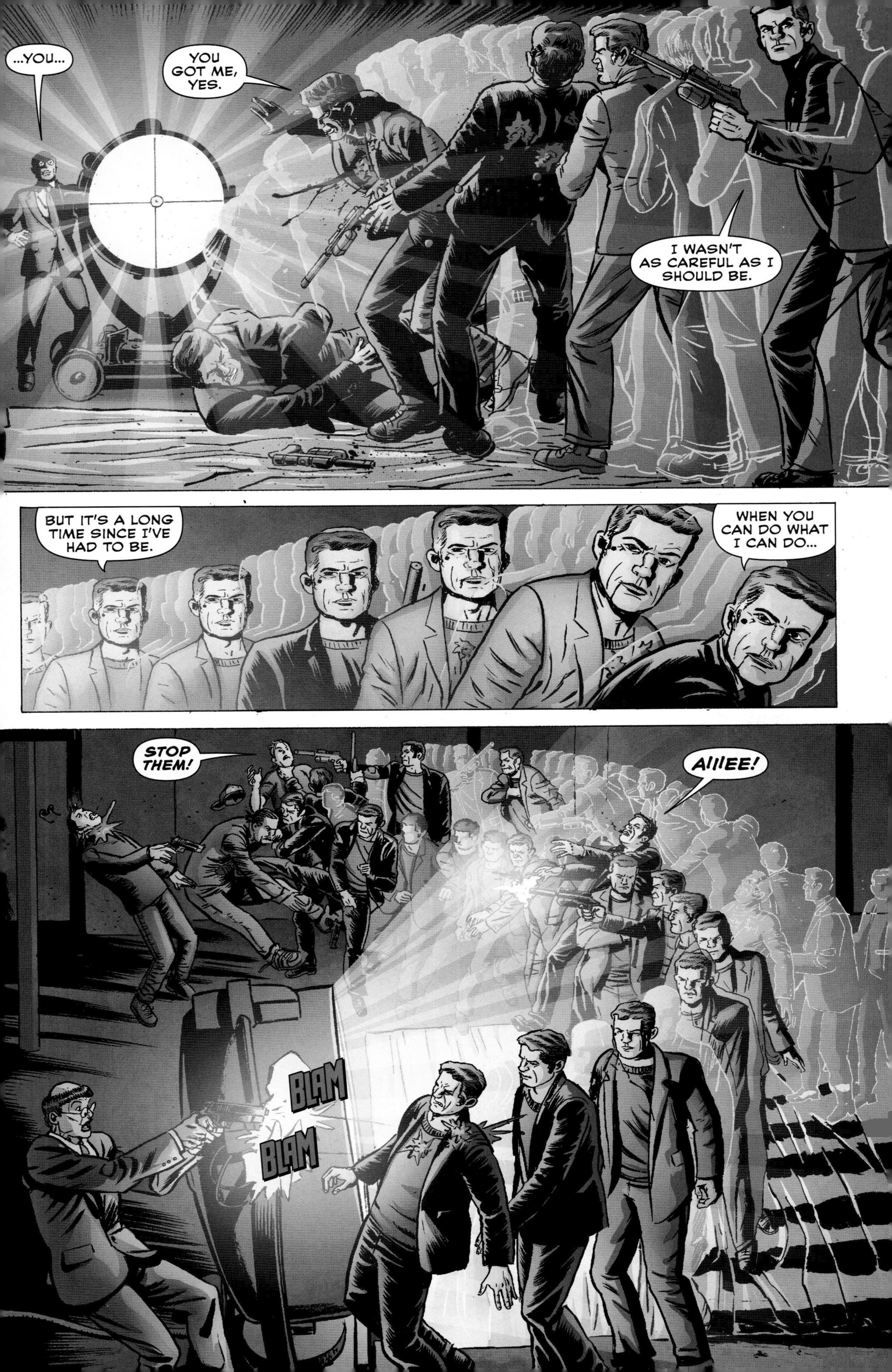
...YOU...
YOU GOT ME, YES.
I WASN'T AS CAREFUL AS I SHOULD BE.
BUT IT'S A LONG TIME SINCE I'VE HAD TO BE.
WHEN YOU CAN DO WHAT I CAN DO...
STOP THEM!
AIIIEE!
BLAM
BLAM

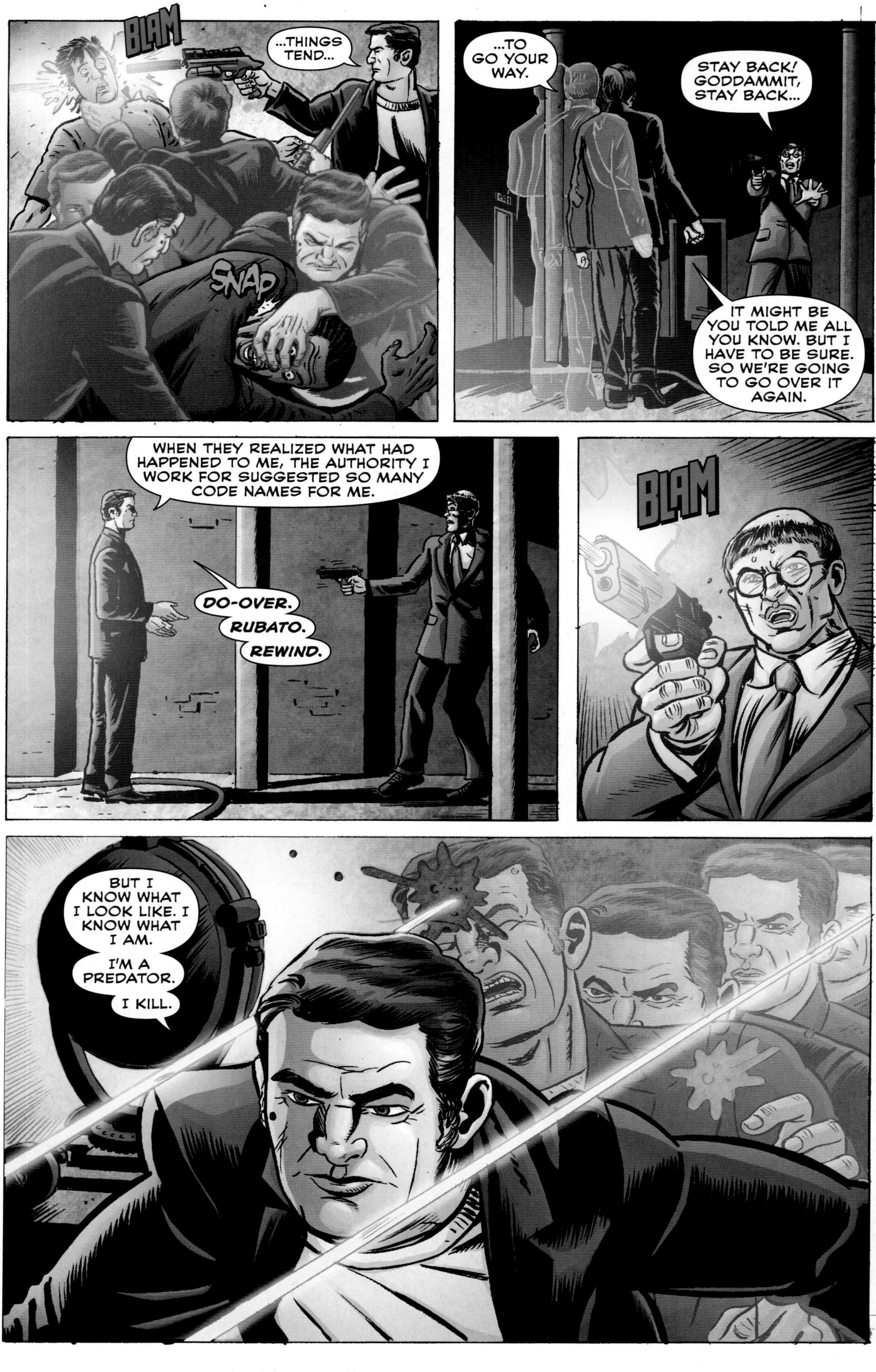
BLAM
...THINGS TEND...
SNAP
...TO GO YOUR WAY.
STAY BACK! GODDAMMIT, STAY BACK...
IT MIGHT BE YOU TOLD ME ALL YOU KNOW. BUT I HAVE TO BE SURE. SO WE'RE GOING TO GO OVER IT AGAIN.
WHEN THEY REALIZED WHAT HAD HAPPENED TO ME, THE AUTHORITY I WORK FOR SUGGESTED SO MANY CODE NAMES FOR ME.
DO-OVER.
RUBATO.
REWIND.
BLAM
BUT I KNOW WHAT I LOOK LIKE. I KNOW WHAT I AM.
I'M A PREDATOR.
I KILL.

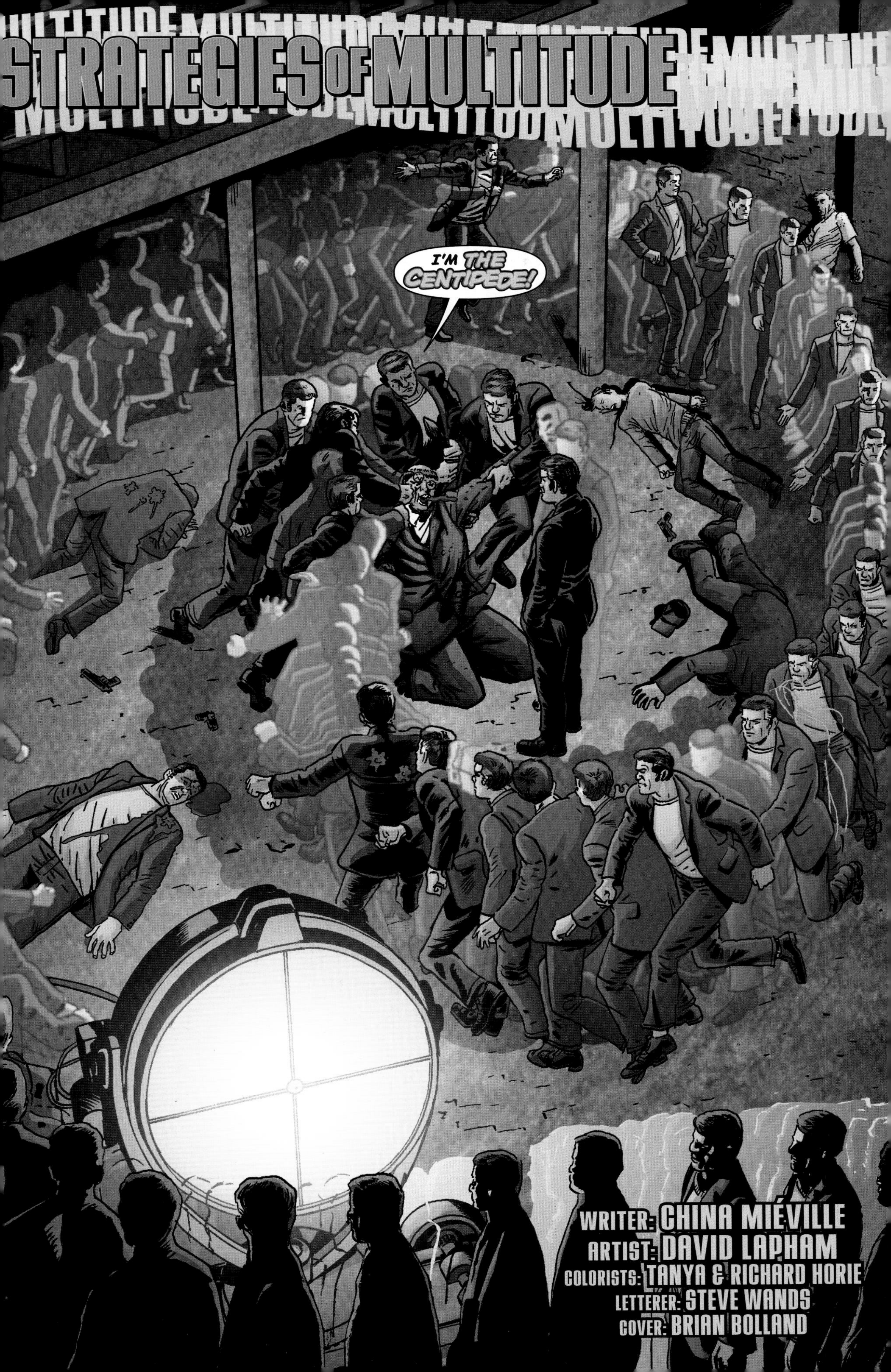
STRATEGIES OF MULTITUDE
I'M THE CENTIPEDE!
WRITER: CHINA MIÉVILLE
ARTIST: DAVID LAPHAM
COLORISTS: TANYA & RICHARD HORIE
LETTERER: STEVE WANDS
COVER: BRIAN BOLLAND

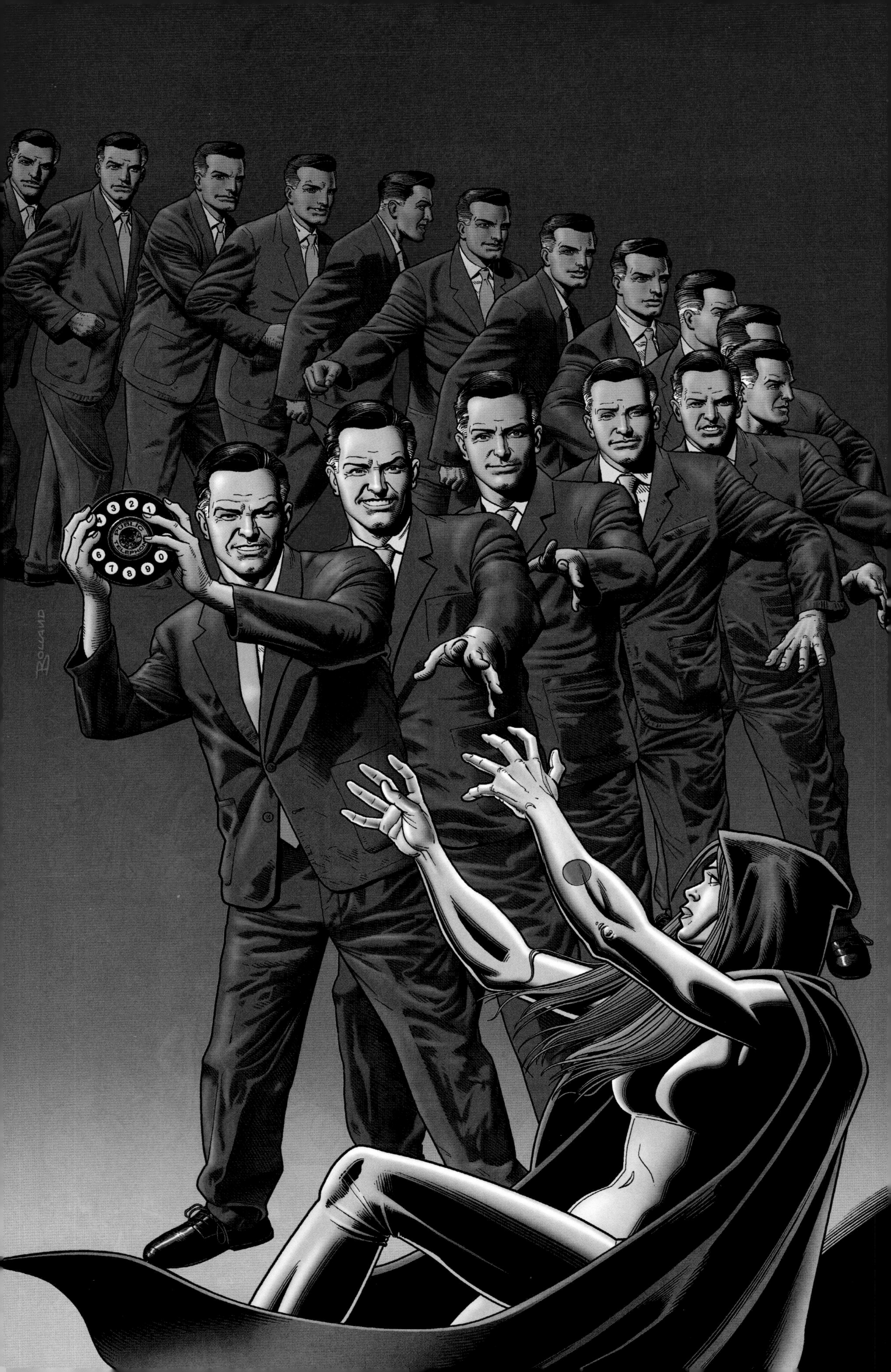
PUBLIC
BOLLAND

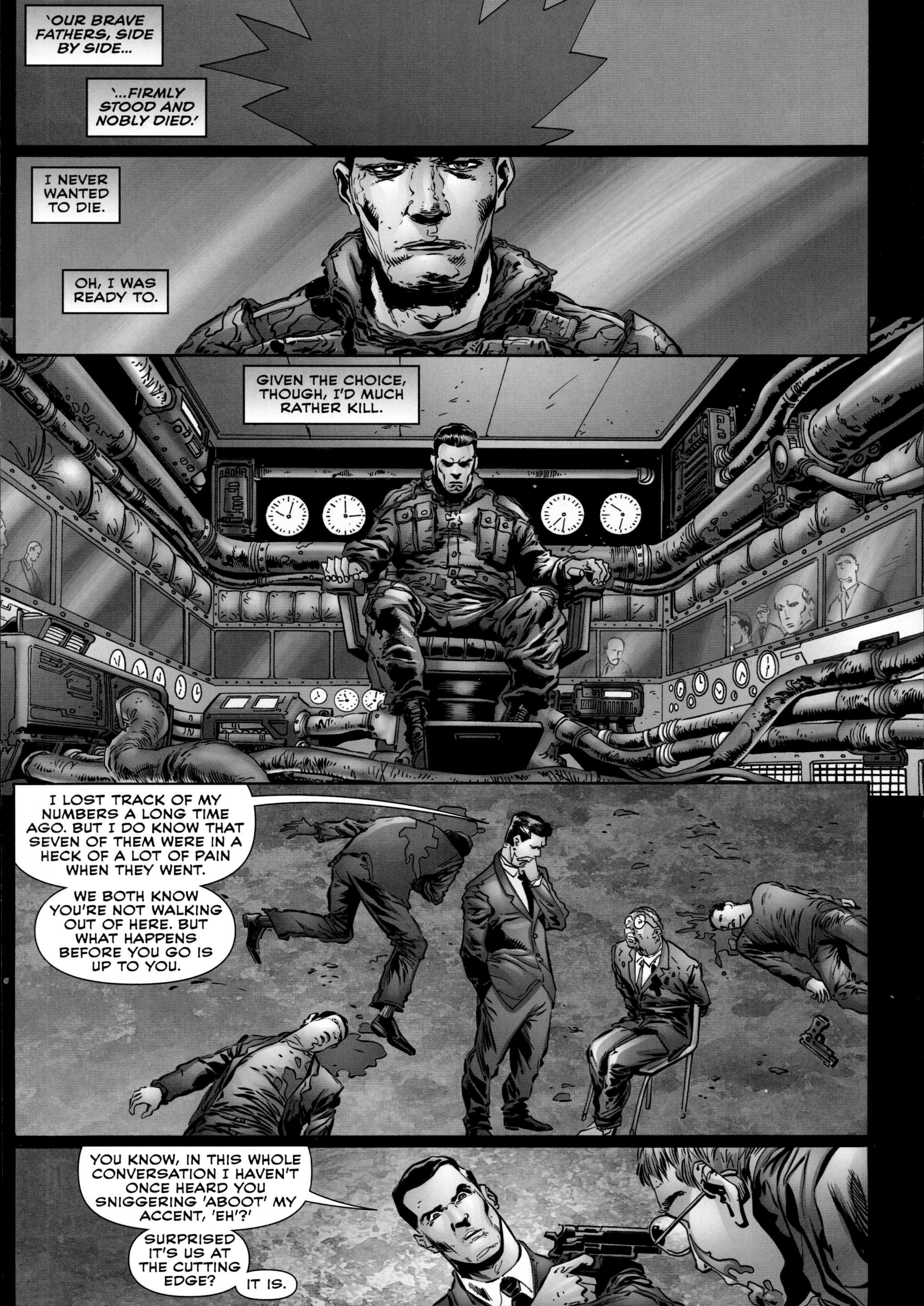
'OUR BRAVE FATHERS, SIDE BY SIDE...
'...FIRMLY STOOD AND NOBLY DIED.'
I NEVER WANTED TO DIE.
OH, I WAS READY TO.
GIVEN THE CHOICE, THOUGH, I'D MUCH RATHER KILL.
I LOST TRACK OF MY NUMBERS A LONG TIME AGO. BUT I DO KNOW THAT SEVEN OF THEM WERE IN A HECK OF A LOT OF PAIN WHEN THEY WENT.
WE BOTH KNOW YOU'RE NOT WALKING OUT OF HERE. BUT WHAT HAPPENS BEFORE YOU GO IS UP TO YOU.
YOU KNOW, IN THIS WHOLE CONVERSATION I HAVEN'T ONCE HEARD YOU SNIGGERING 'ABOOT' MY ACCENT, 'EH'?'
SURPRISED IT'S US AT THE CUTTING EDGE?
IT IS.

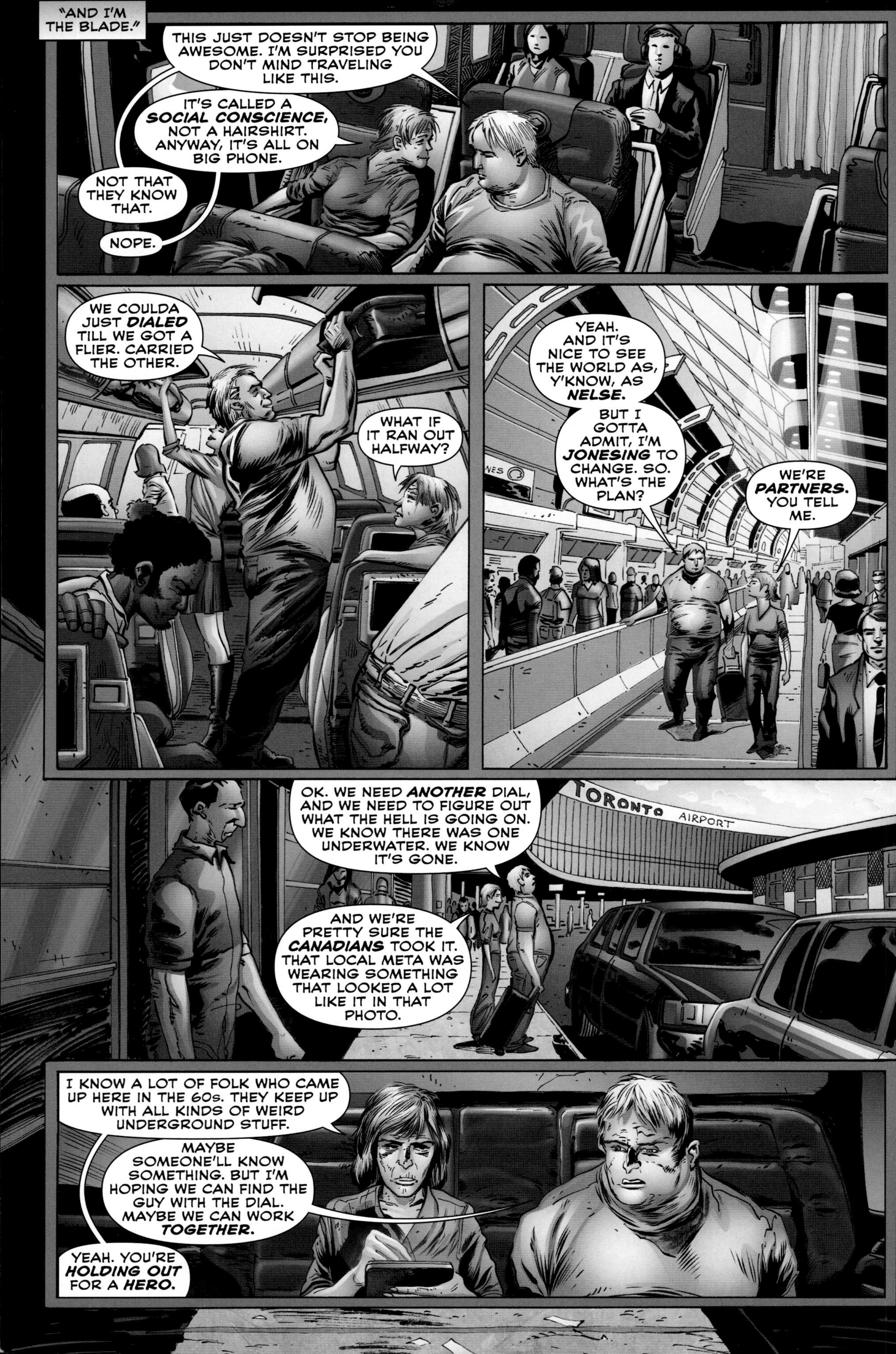
"AND I'M THE BLADE."
THIS JUST DOESN'T STOP BEING AWESOME. I'M SURPRISED YOU DON'T MIND TRAVELING LIKE THIS.
IT'S CALLED A **SOCIAL CONSCIENCE,** NOT A HAIRSHIRT. ANYWAY, IT'S ALL ON BIG PHONE.
NOT THAT THEY KNOW THAT.
NOPE.
WE COULDA JUST **DIALED** TILL WE GOT A FLIER. CARRIED THE OTHER.
WHAT IF IT RAN OUT HALFWAY?
YEAH. AND IT'S NICE TO SEE THE WORLD AS, Y'KNOW, AS **NELSE.**
BUT I GOTTA ADMIT, I'M **JONESING** TO CHANGE. SO. WHAT'S THE PLAN?
WE'RE **PARTNERS.** YOU TELL ME.
TORONTO AIRPORT
OK. WE NEED **ANOTHER** DIAL, AND WE NEED TO FIGURE OUT WHAT THE HELL IS GOING ON. WE KNOW THERE WAS ONE UNDERWATER. WE KNOW IT'S GONE.
AND WE'RE PRETTY SURE THE **CANADIANS** TOOK IT. THAT LOCAL META WAS WEARING SOMETHING THAT LOOKED A LOT LIKE IT IN THAT PHOTO.
I KNOW A LOT OF FOLK WHO CAME UP HERE IN THE 60s. THEY KEEP UP WITH ALL KINDS OF WEIRD UNDERGROUND STUFF.
MAYBE SOMEONE'LL KNOW SOMETHING. BUT I'M HOPING WE CAN FIND THE GUY WITH THE DIAL. MAYBE WE CAN WORK **TOGETHER.**
YEAH. YOU'RE **HOLDING OUT** FOR A **HERO.**

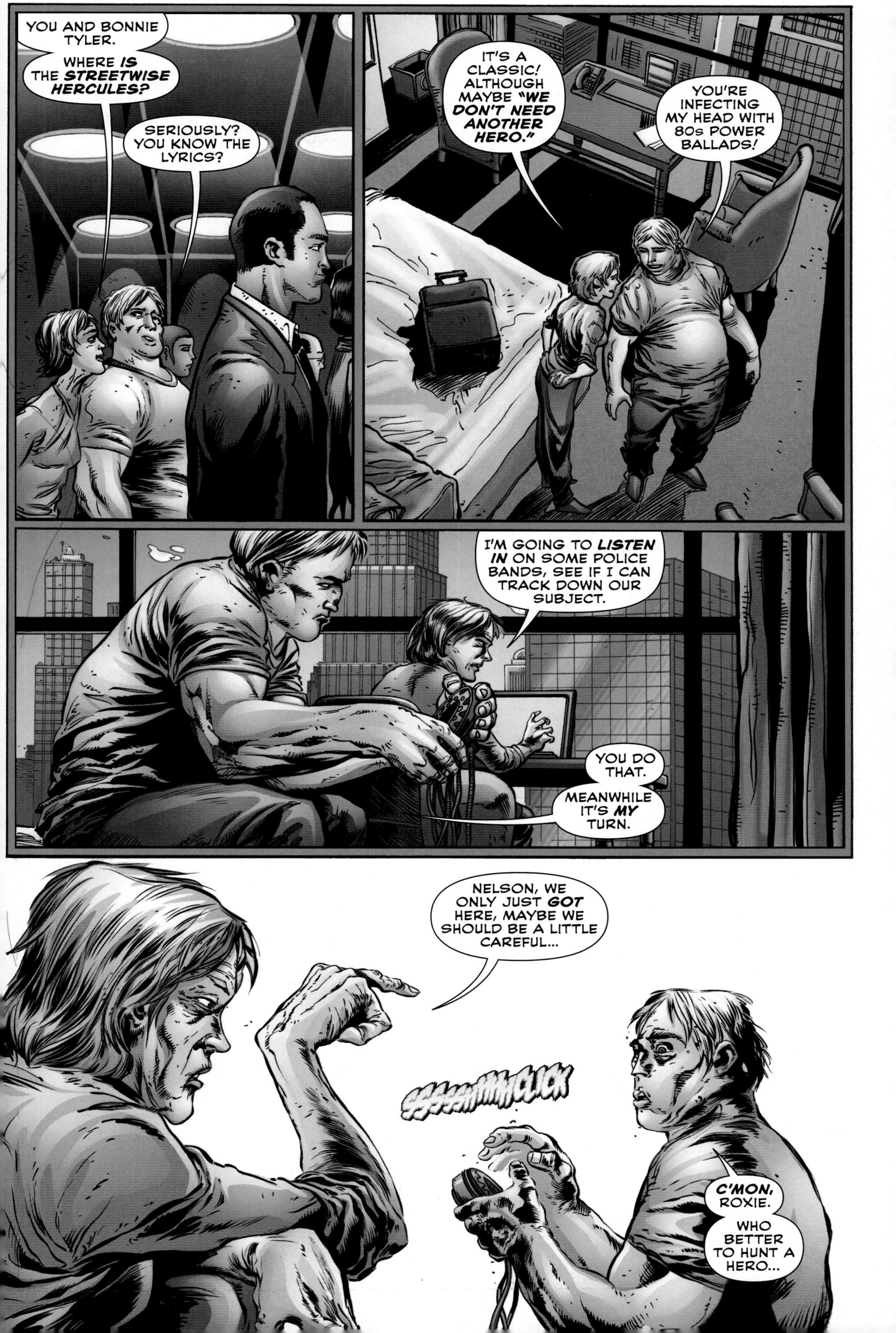

YOU AND BONNIE TYLER.
WHERE IS THE STREETWISE HERCULES?
SERIOUSLY? YOU KNOW THE LYRICS?
IT'S A CLASSIC! ALTHOUGH MAYBE "WE DON'T NEED ANOTHER HERO."
YOU'RE INFECTING MY HEAD WITH 80s POWER BALLADS!
I'M GOING TO LISTEN IN ON SOME POLICE BANDS, SEE IF I CAN TRACK DOWN OUR SUBJECT.
YOU DO THAT.
MEANWHILE IT'S MY TURN.
NELSON, WE ONLY JUST GOT HERE, MAYBE WE SHOULD BE A LITTLE CAREFUL...
SSSSSHHHHCLICK
C'MON, ROXIE.
WHO BETTER TO HUNT A HERO...

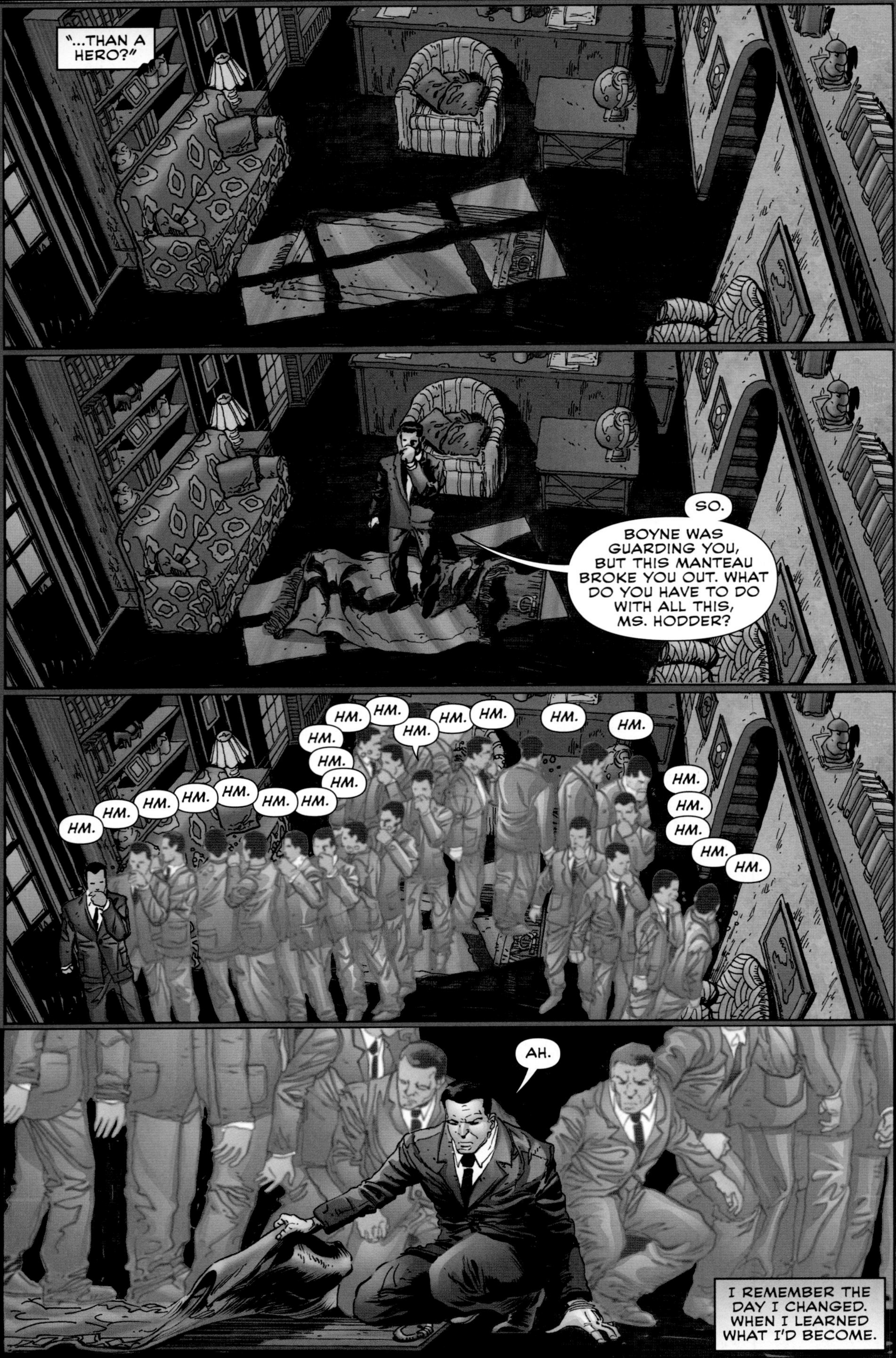

"...THAN A HERO?"
SO.
BOYNE WAS GUARDING YOU, BUT THIS MANTEAU BROKE YOU OUT. WHAT DO YOU HAVE TO DO WITH ALL THIS, MS. HODDER?
HM.
HM.
HM.
HM.
HM.
HM.
HM.
HM.
HM.
HM.
HM.
HM.
HM.
HM.
HM.
HM.
HM.
HM.
HM.
HM.
HM.
HM.
AH.
I REMEMBER THE DAY I CHANGED. WHEN I LEARNED WHAT I'D BECOME.

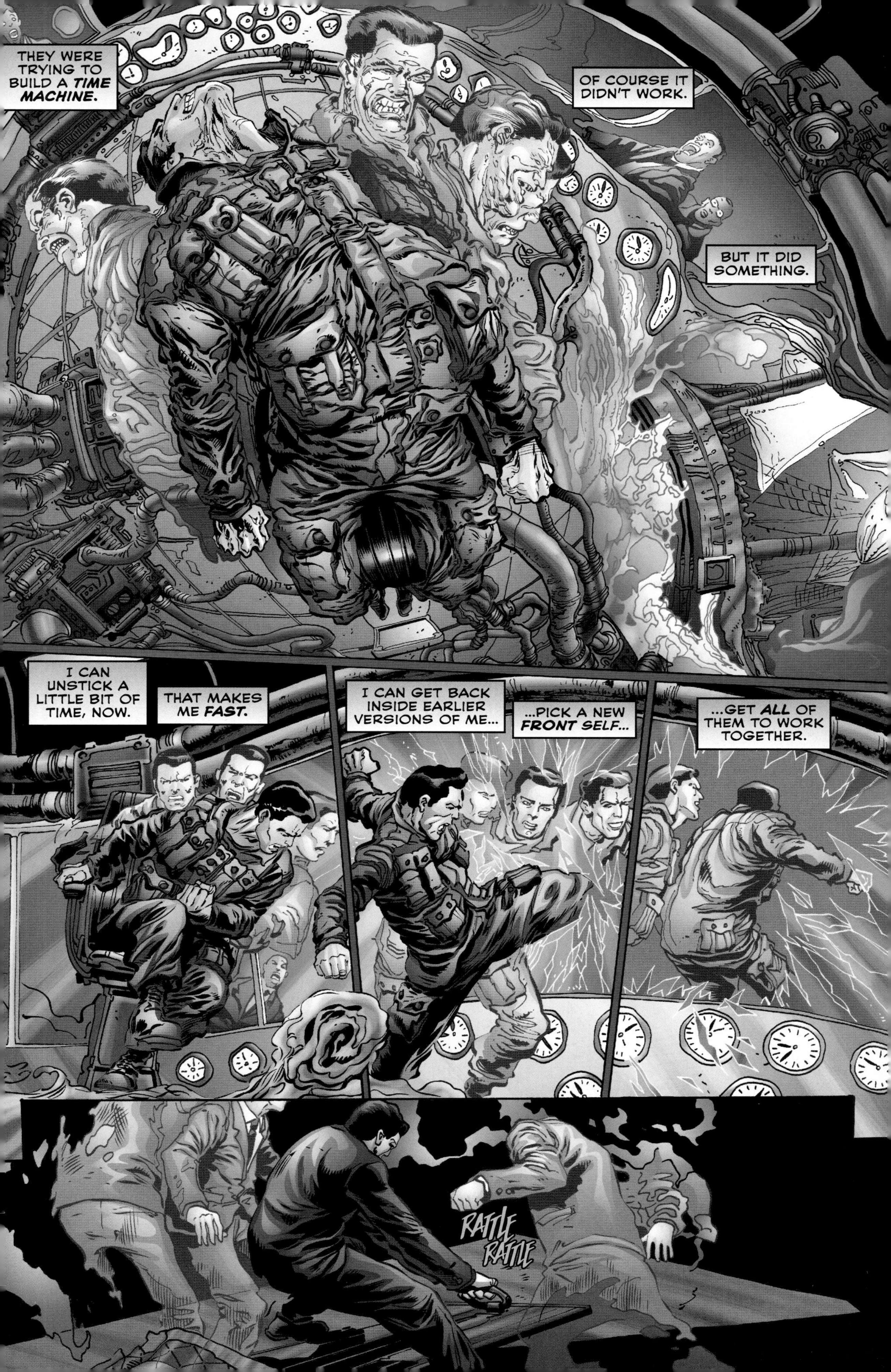
THEY WERE TRYING TO BUILD A *TIME MACHINE*.
OF COURSE IT DIDN'T WORK.
BUT IT DID SOMETHING.
I CAN UNSTICK A LITTLE BIT OF TIME, NOW.
THAT MAKES ME *FAST*.
I CAN GET BACK INSIDE EARLIER VERSIONS OF ME...
...PICK A NEW *FRONT SELF*...
...GET *ALL* OF THEM TO WORK TOGETHER.
RATTLE RATTLE

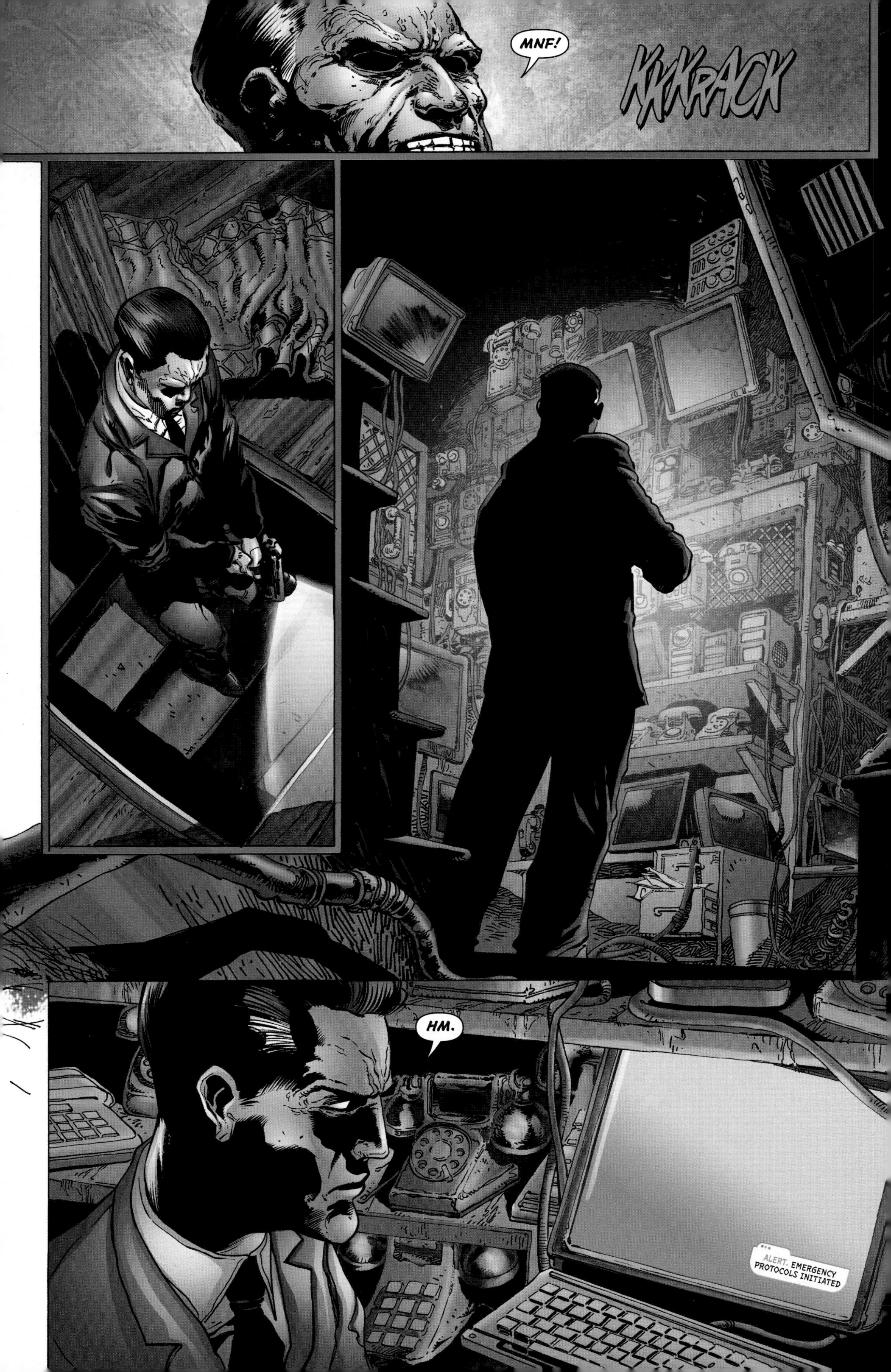
MNF!
KKKRACK
HM.
ALERT. EMERGENCY PROTOCOLS INITIATED

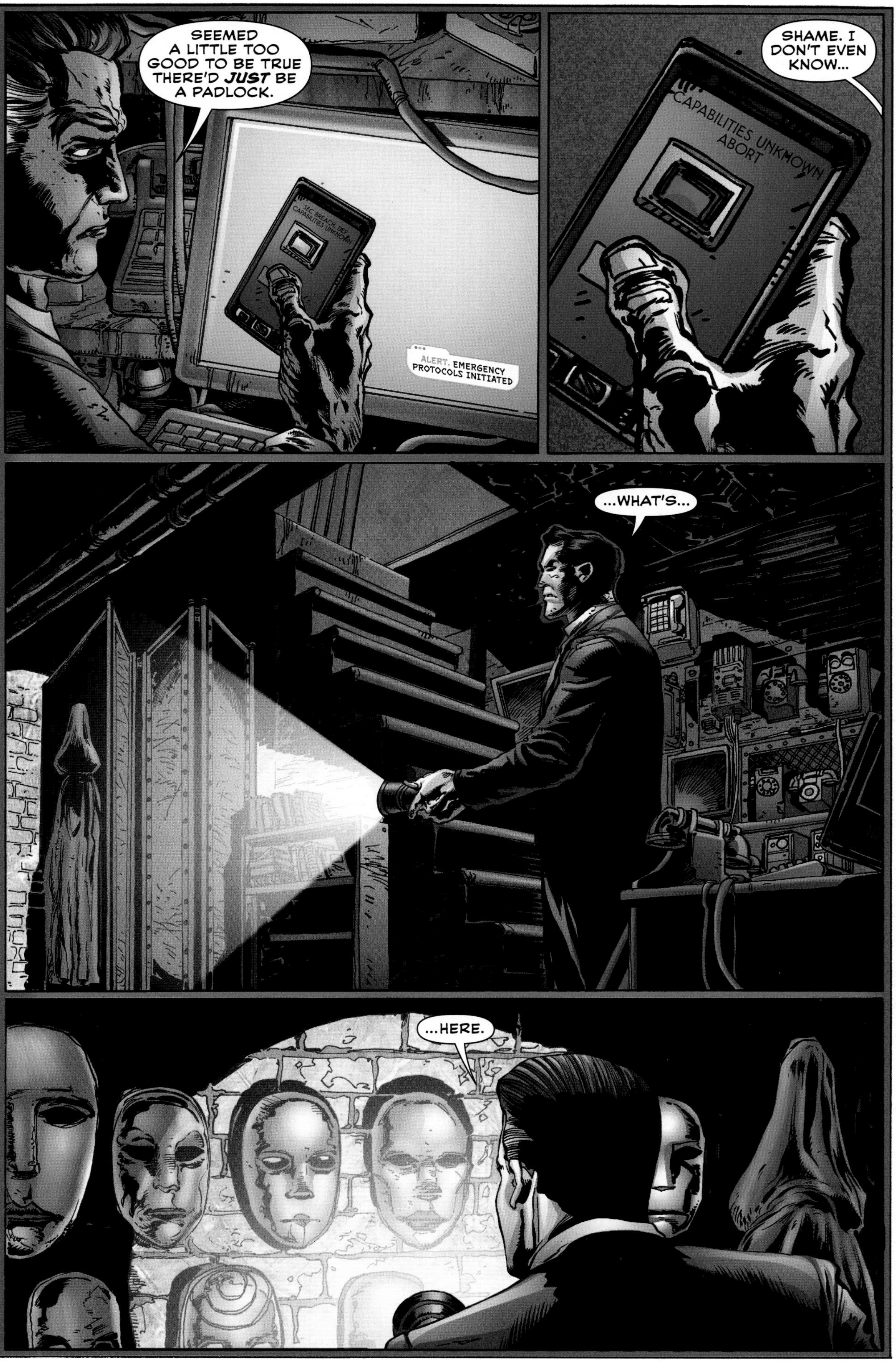
SEEMED A LITTLE TOO GOOD TO BE TRUE THERE'D ***JUST*** BE A PADLOCK.
SEC BREACH. DEF. CAPABILITIES UNKNOWN
ALERT. EMERGENCY PROTOCOLS INITIATED
SHAME. I DON'T EVEN KNOW...
CAPABILITIES UNKNOWN
ABORT
...WHAT'S...
...HERE.

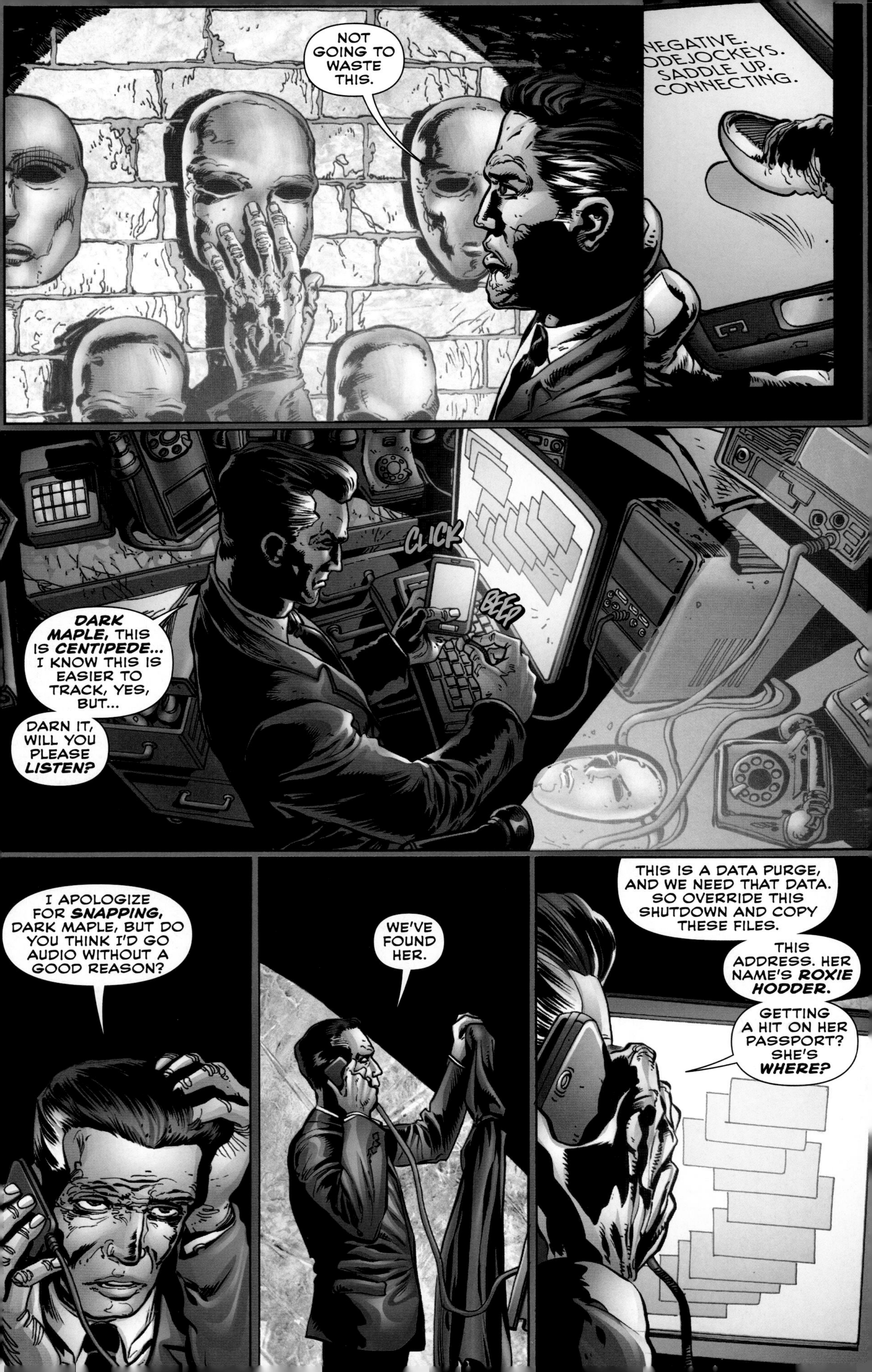
NOT GOING TO WASTE THIS.
NEGATIVE. ODEJOCKEYS. SADDLE UP. CONNECTING.
CLICK
BEEP
DARK MAPLE, THIS IS CENTIPEDE... I KNOW THIS IS EASIER TO TRACK, YES, BUT...
DARN IT, WILL YOU PLEASE LISTEN?
I APOLOGIZE FOR SNAPPING, DARK MAPLE, BUT DO YOU THINK I'D GO AUDIO WITHOUT A GOOD REASON?
WE'VE FOUND HER.
THIS IS A DATA PURGE, AND WE NEED THAT DATA. SO OVERRIDE THIS SHUTDOWN AND COPY THESE FILES.
THIS ADDRESS. HER NAME'S ROXIE HODDER.
GETTING A HIT ON HER PASSPORT? SHE'S WHERE?

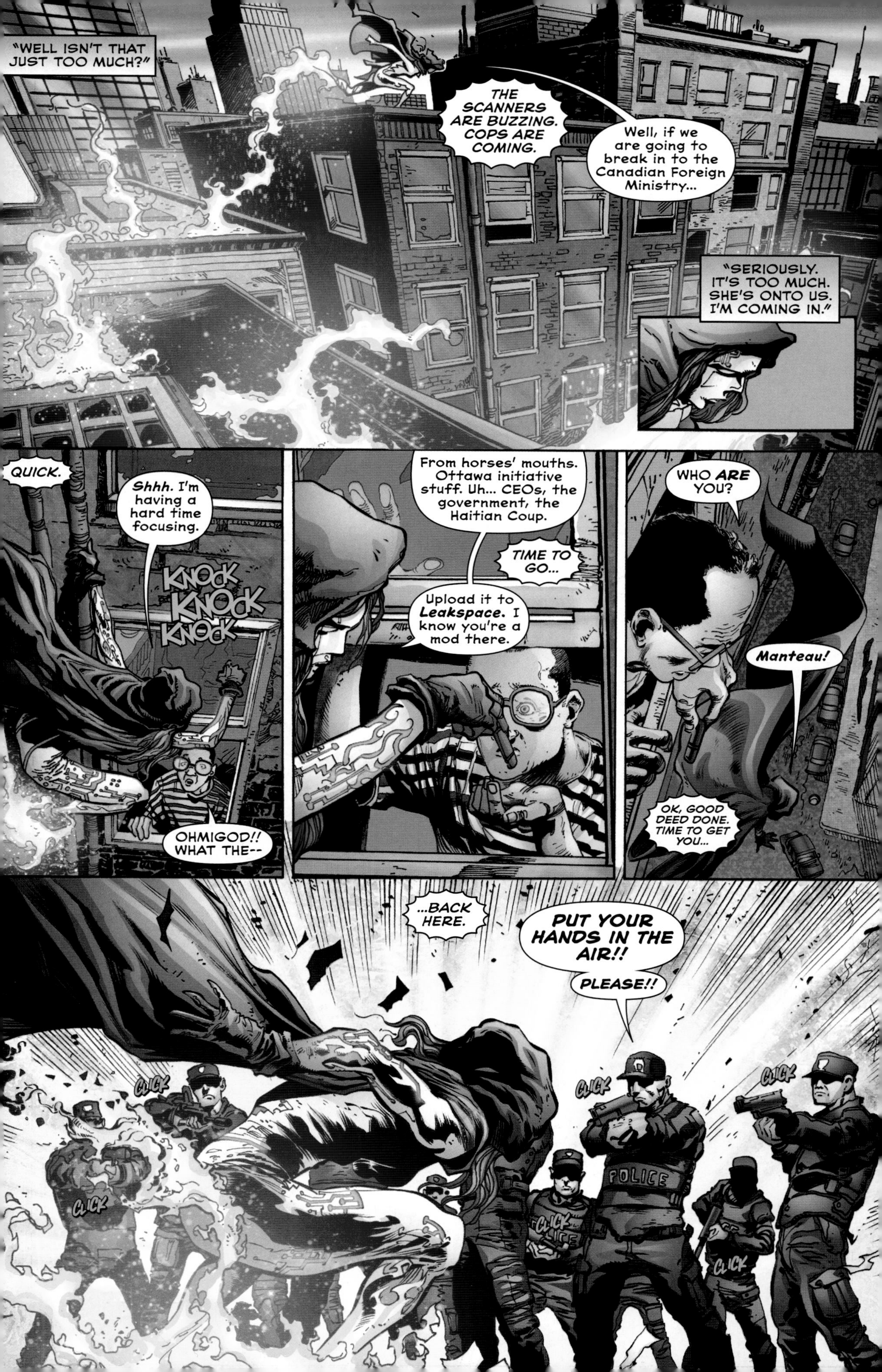
"WELL ISN'T THAT JUST TOO MUCH?"
THE SCANNERS ARE BUZZING. COPS ARE COMING.
Well, if we are going to break in to the Canadian Foreign Ministry...
"SERIOUSLY. IT'S TOO MUCH. SHE'S ONTO US. I'M COMING IN."
QUICK.
Shhh. I'm having a hard time focusing.
KNOCK KNOCK KNOCK
OHMIGOD!! WHAT THE--
From horses' mouths. Ottawa initiative stuff. Uh... CEOs, the government, the Haitian Coup.
TIME TO GO...
Upload it to Leakspace. I know you're a mod there.
WHO ARE YOU?
Manteau!
OK, GOOD DEED DONE. TIME TO GET YOU...
...BACK HERE.
PUT YOUR HANDS IN THE AIR!!
PLEASE!!
CLICK
CLICK
CLICK
CLICK
CLICK
POLICE

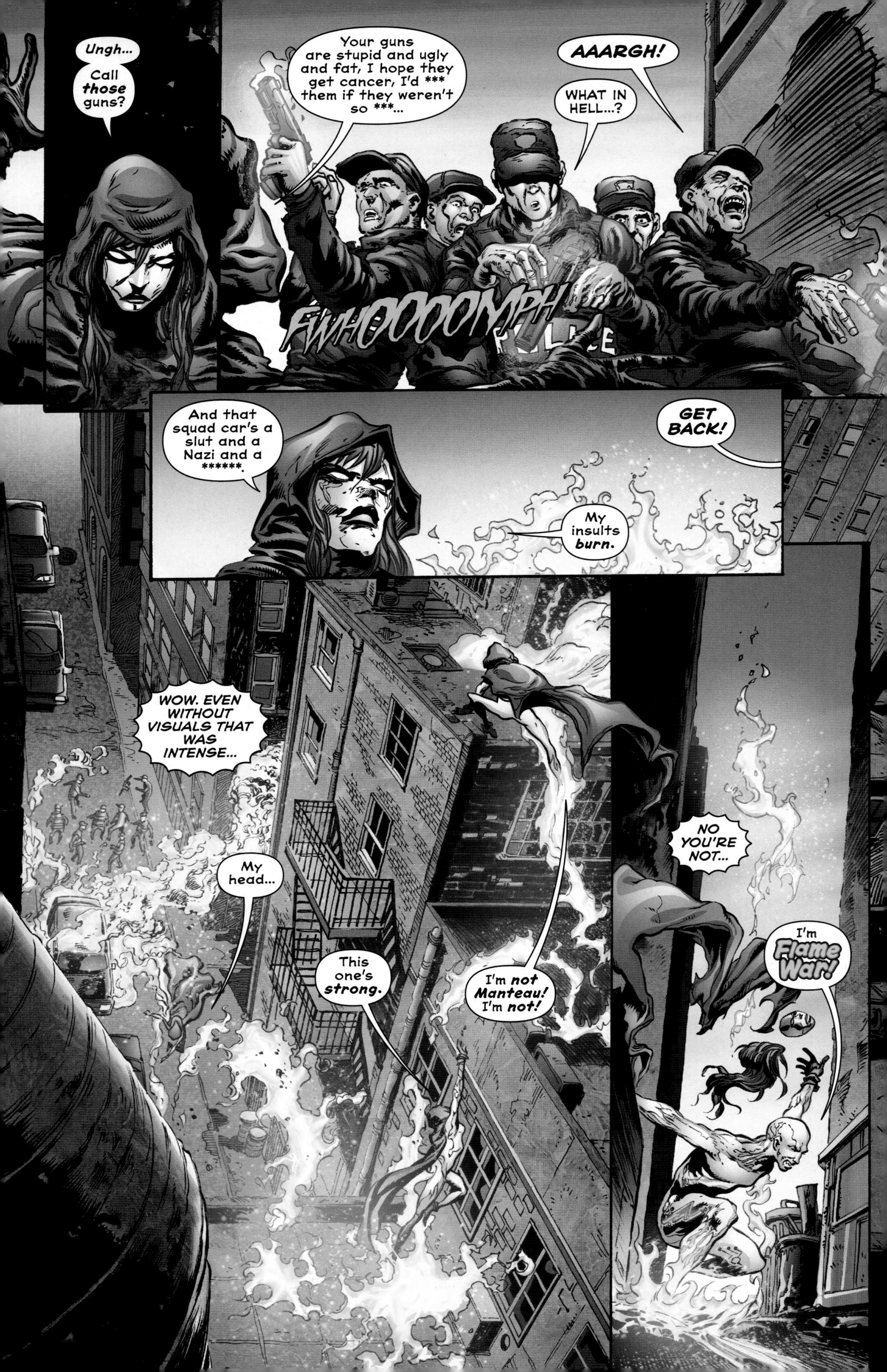
Ungh...
Call those guns?
Your guns are stupid and ugly and fat, I hope they get cancer, I'd *** them if they weren't so ***...
AAARGH!
WHAT IN HELL...?
FWHOOOOOMPH
And that squad car's a slut and a Nazi and a ******.
GET BACK!
My insults burn.
WOW. EVEN WITHOUT VISUALS THAT WAS INTENSE...
My head...
This one's strong.
I'm not Manteau! I'm not!
NO YOU'RE NOT...
I'm Flame War!

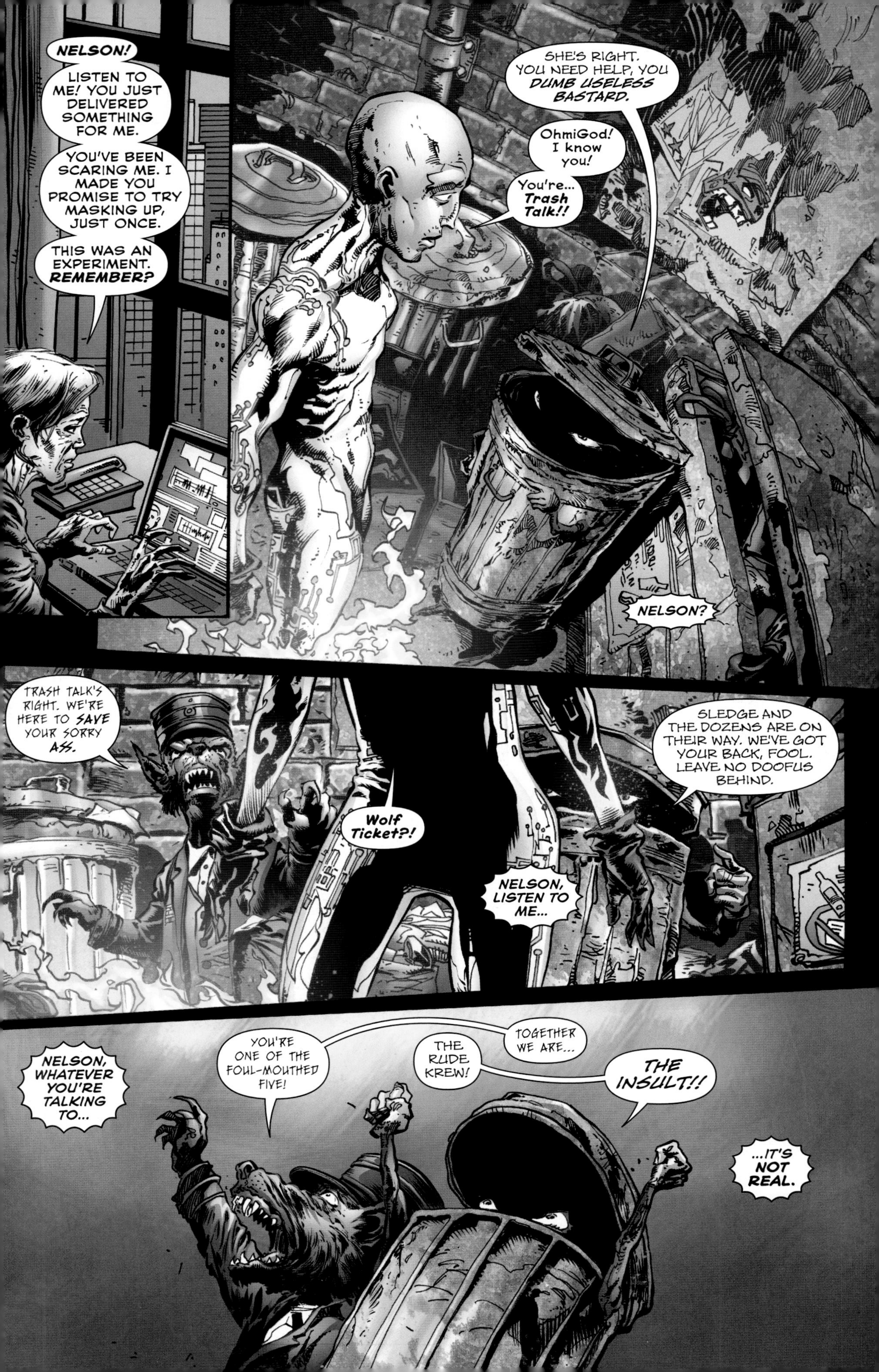
NELSON!
LISTEN TO ME! YOU JUST DELIVERED SOMETHING FOR ME.
YOU'VE BEEN SCARING ME. I MADE YOU PROMISE TO TRY MASKING UP, JUST ONCE.
THIS WAS AN EXPERIMENT. REMEMBER?
SHE'S RIGHT. YOU NEED HELP, YOU DUMB USELESS BASTARD.
OhmiGod! I know you!
You're... Trash Talk!!
NELSON?
TRASH TALK'S RIGHT. WE'RE HERE TO SAVE YOUR SORRY ASS.
Wolf Ticket?!
SLEDGE AND THE DOZENS ARE ON THEIR WAY. WE'VE GOT YOUR BACK, FOOL. LEAVE NO DOOFUS BEHIND.
NELSON, LISTEN TO ME...
NELSON, WHATEVER YOU'RE TALKING TO...
YOU'RE ONE OF THE FOUL-MOUTHED FIVE!
THE RUDE KREW!
TOGETHER WE ARE...
THE INSULT!!
...IT'S NOT REAL.

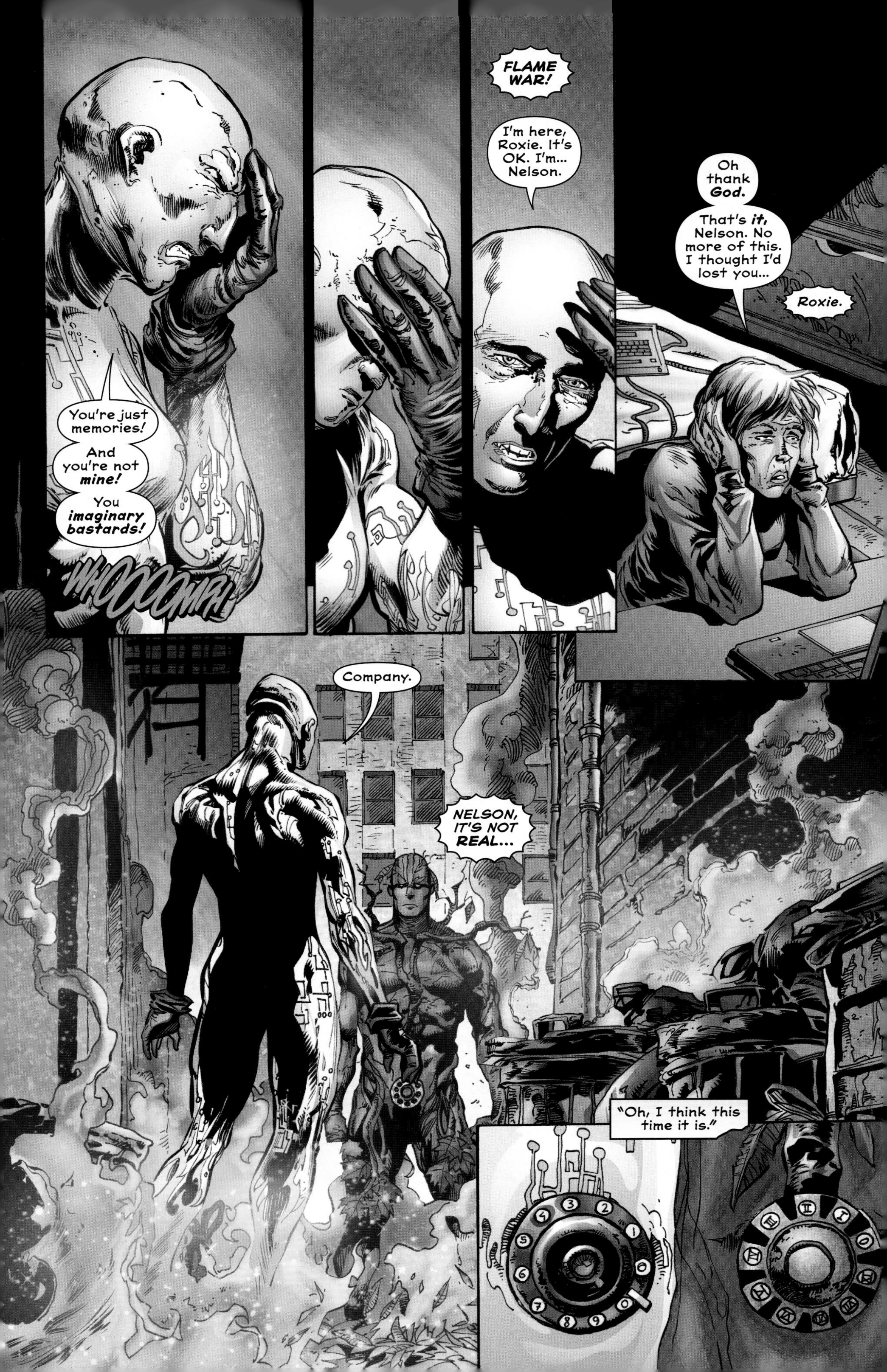
You're just memories!
And you're not mine!
You imaginary bastards!
WHOOOOOMPH!
FLAME WAR!
I'm here, Roxie. It's OK. I'm... Nelson.
Oh thank God.
That's it, Nelson. No more of this. I thought I'd lost you...
Roxie.
Company.
NELSON, IT'S NOT REAL...
"Oh, I think this time it is."

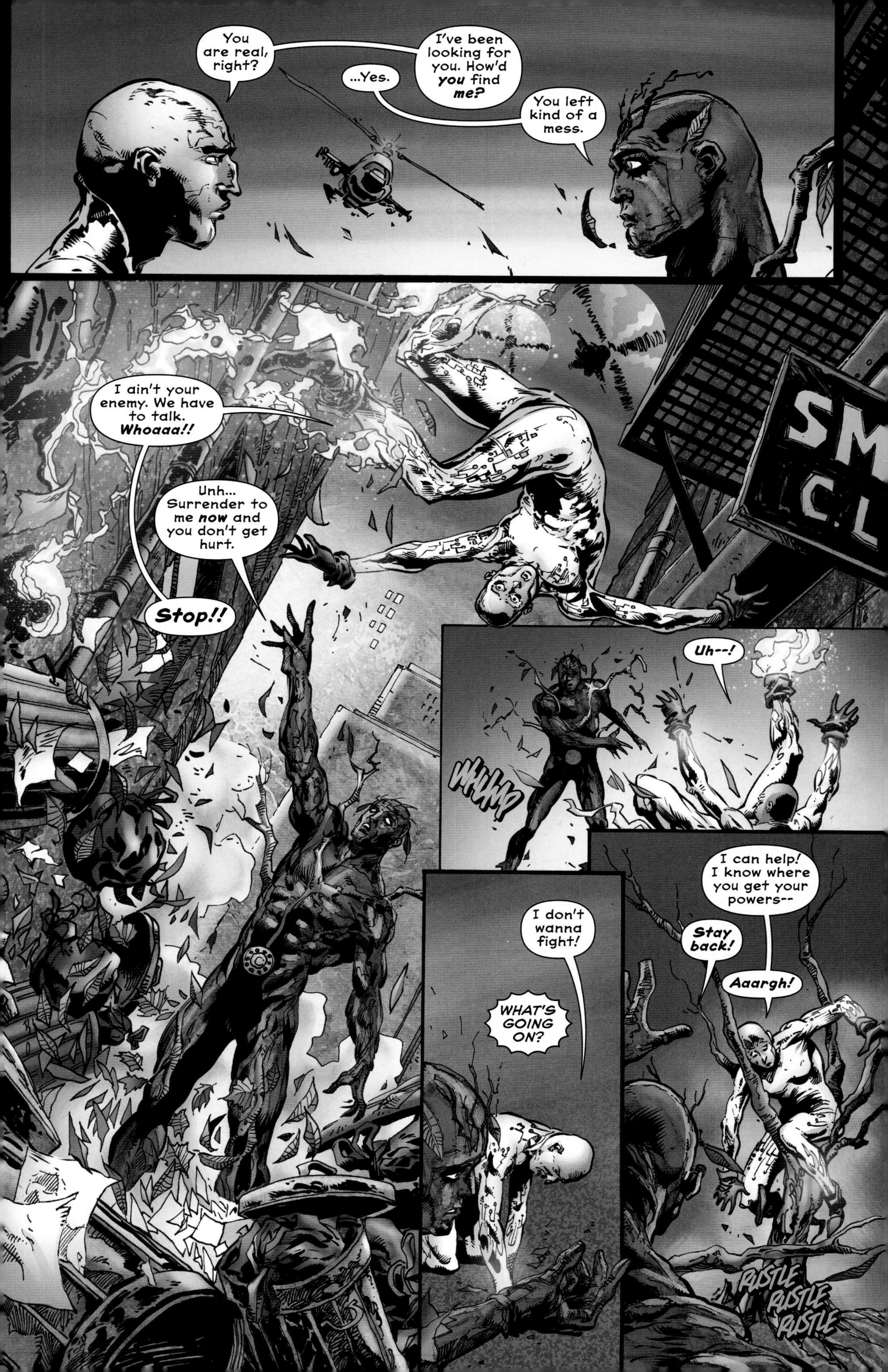

You are real, right?
I've been looking for you. How'd *you* find *me?*
...Yes.
You left kind of a mess.
I ain't your enemy. We have to talk. *Whoaaa!!*
Unh... Surrender to me *now* and you don't get hurt.
Stop!!
Uh--!
WHUMP
I can help! I know where you get your powers--
I don't wanna fight!
Stay back!
Aaargh!
WHAT'S GOING ON?
RUSTLE RUSTLE RUSTLE

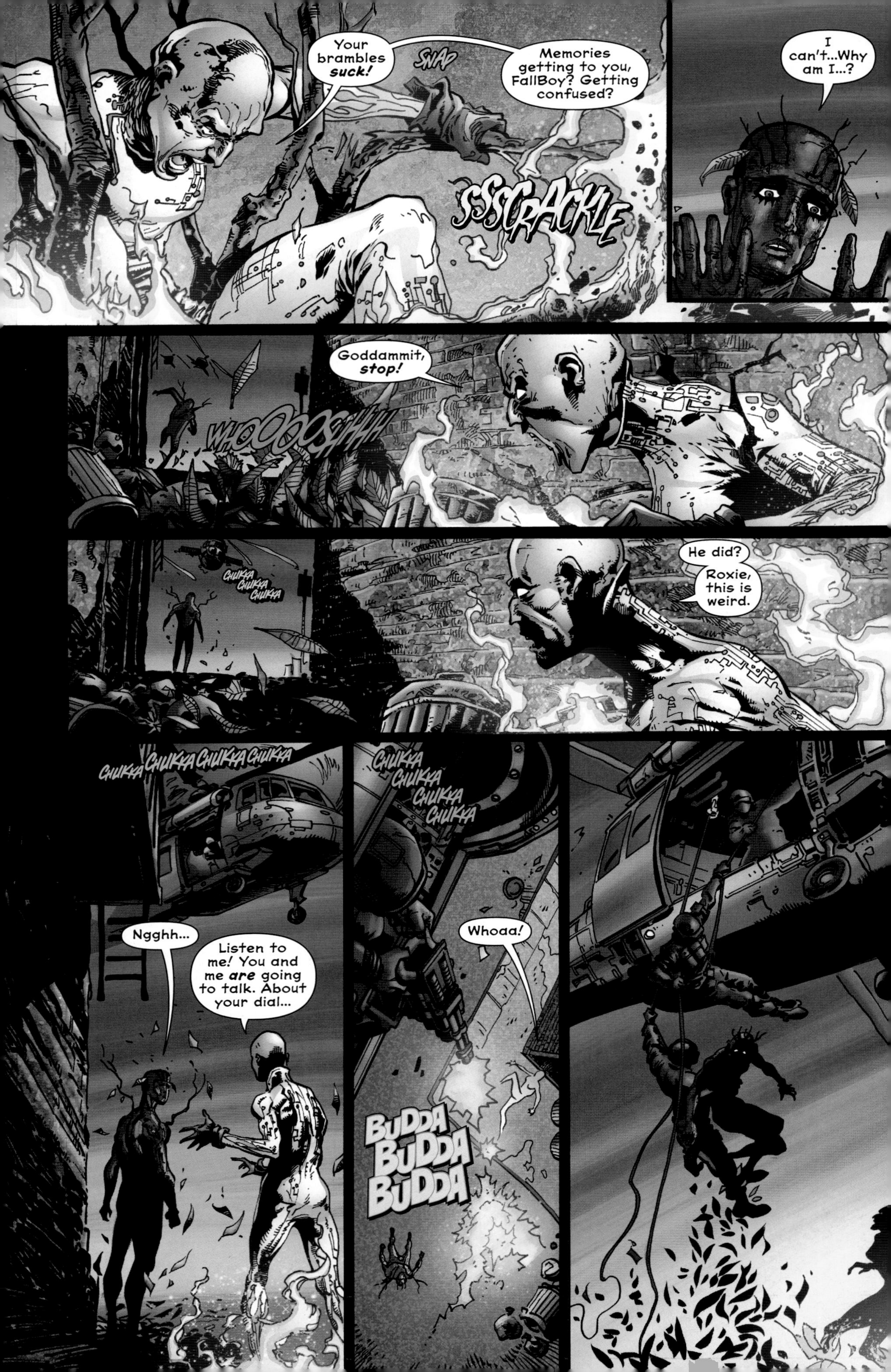
Your brambles *suck!*
SNAP
Memories getting to you, FallBoy? Getting confused?
SSSCRACKLE
I can't...Why am I...?
Goddammit, *stop!*
WHOOOOOSHHH
CHUKKA CHUKKA CHUKKA
He did?
Roxie, this is weird.
CHUKKA CHUKKA CHUKKA CHUKKA
Ngghh...
Listen to me! You and me *are* going to talk. About your dial...
CHUKKA CHUKKA CHUKKA CHUKKA
Whoaa!
BUDDA BUDDA BUDDA

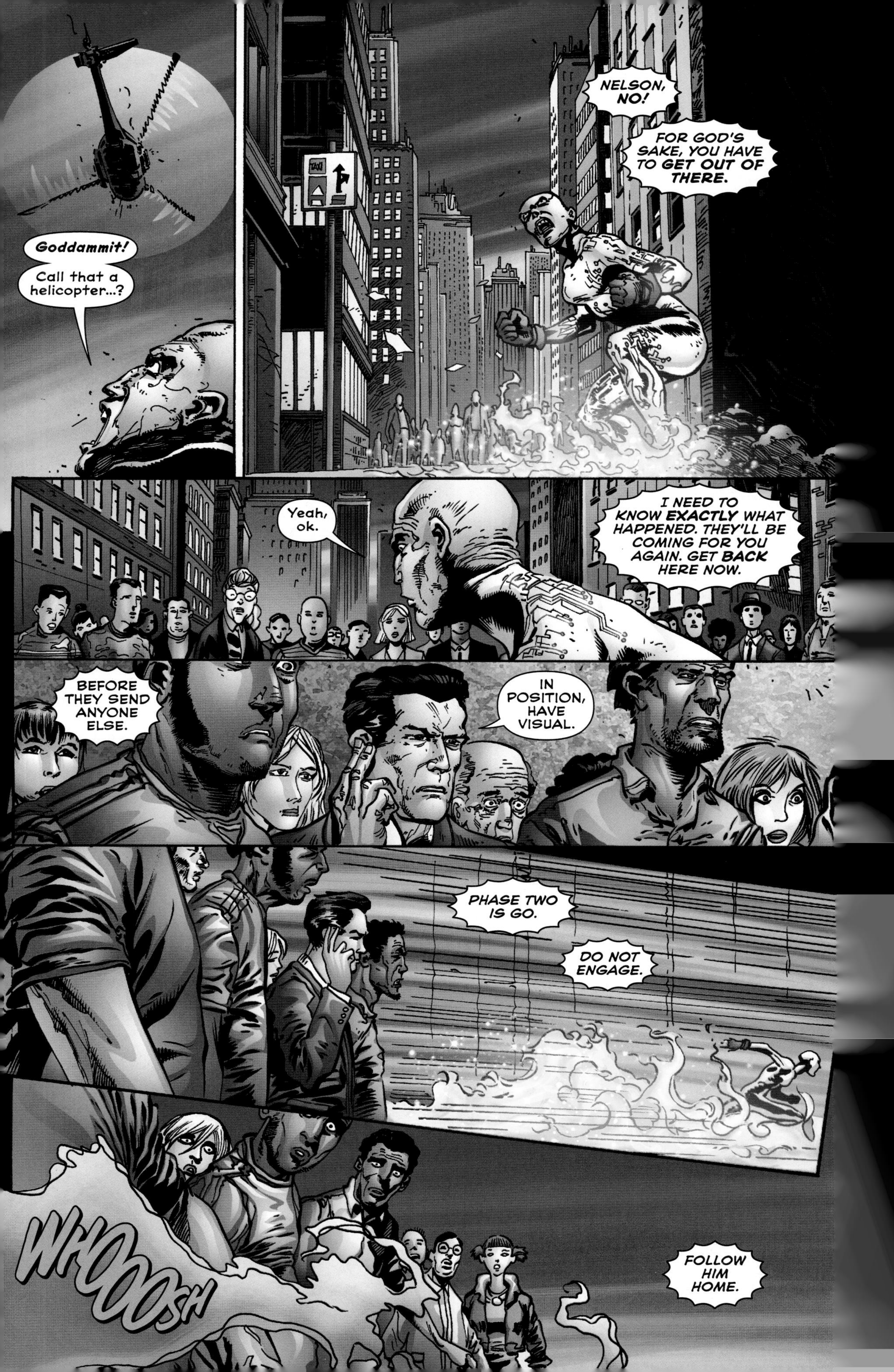
Goddammit!
Call that a helicopter...?
NELSON, NO!
FOR GOD'S SAKE, YOU HAVE TO GET OUT OF THERE.
Yeah, ok.
I NEED TO KNOW EXACTLY WHAT HAPPENED. THEY'LL BE COMING FOR YOU AGAIN. GET BACK HERE NOW.
BEFORE THEY SEND ANYONE ELSE.
IN POSITION, HAVE VISUAL.
PHASE TWO IS GO.
DO NOT ENGAGE.
WHOOOSH
FOLLOW HIM HOME.

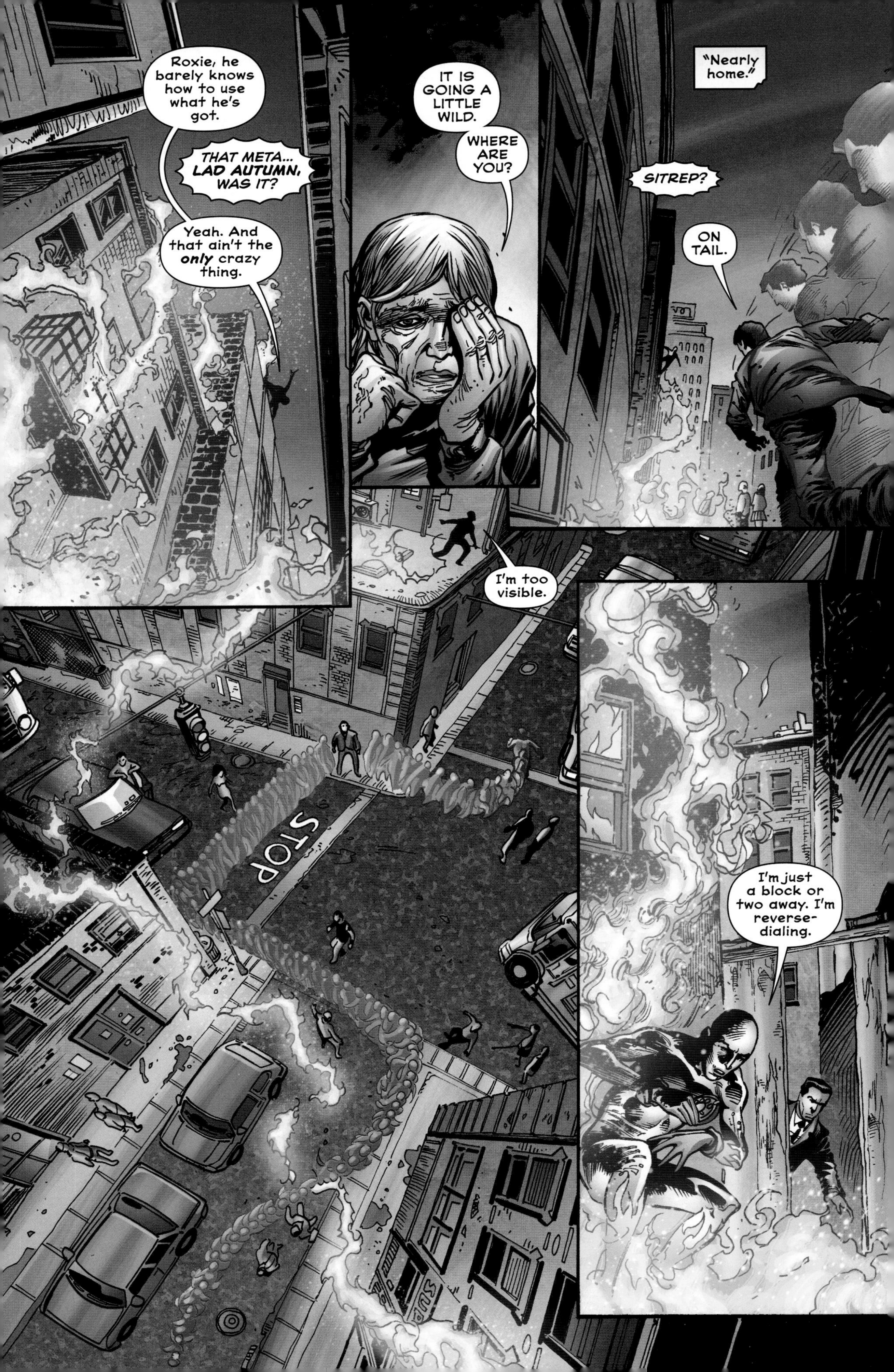

Roxie, he barely knows how to use what he's got.
THAT META... LAD AUTUMN, WAS IT?
Yeah. And that ain't the only crazy thing.
IT IS GOING A LITTLE WILD.
WHERE ARE YOU?
"Nearly home."
SITREP?
ON TAIL.
I'm too visible.
STOP
I'm just a block or two away. I'm reverse-dialing.

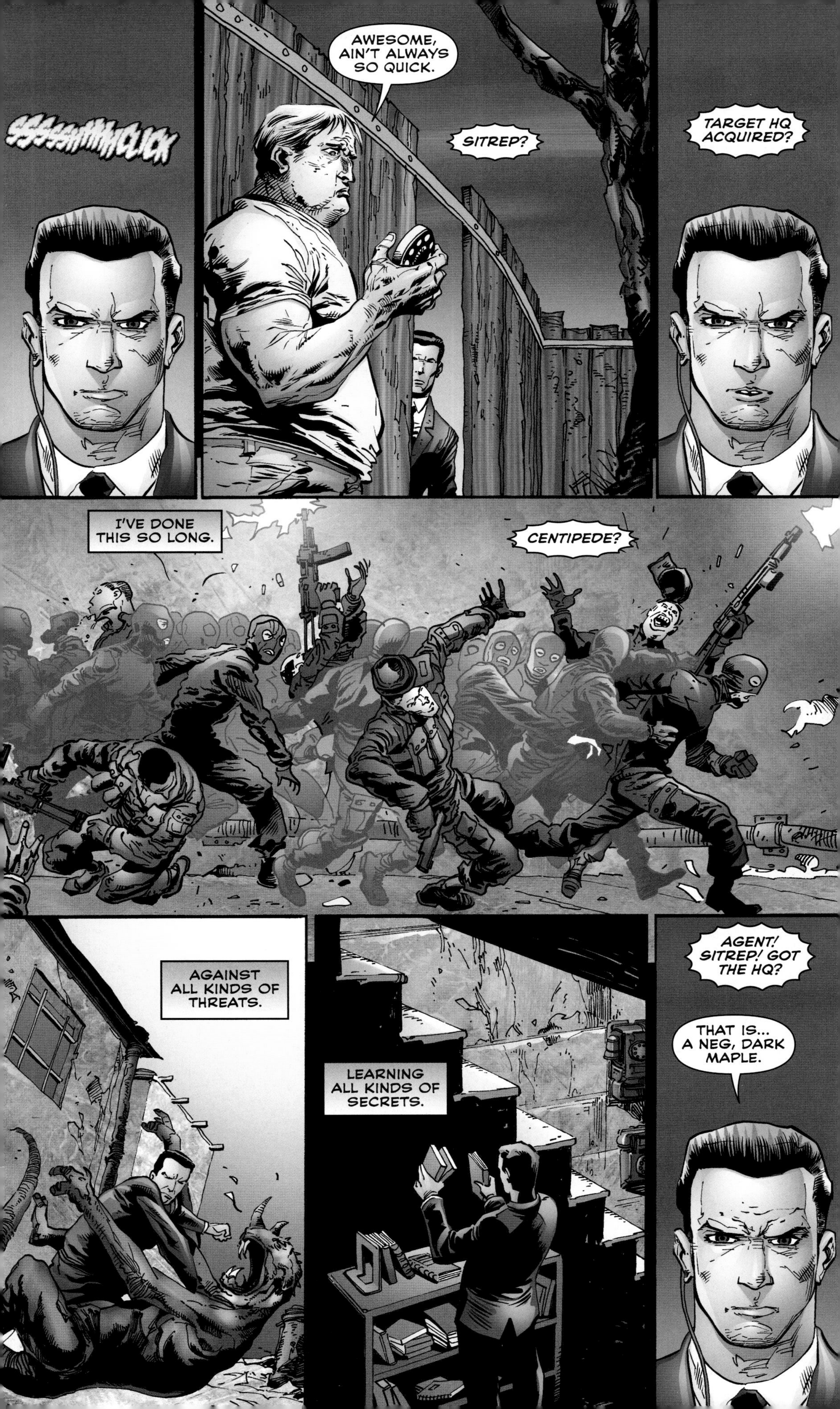
SSSSSHHHHCLICK
AWESOME, AIN'T ALWAYS SO QUICK.
SITREP?
TARGET HQ ACQUIRED?
I'VE DONE THIS SO LONG.
CENTIPEDE?
AGAINST ALL KINDS OF THREATS.
LEARNING ALL KINDS OF SECRETS.
AGENT! SITREP! GOT THE HQ?
THAT IS... A NEG, DARK MAPLE.

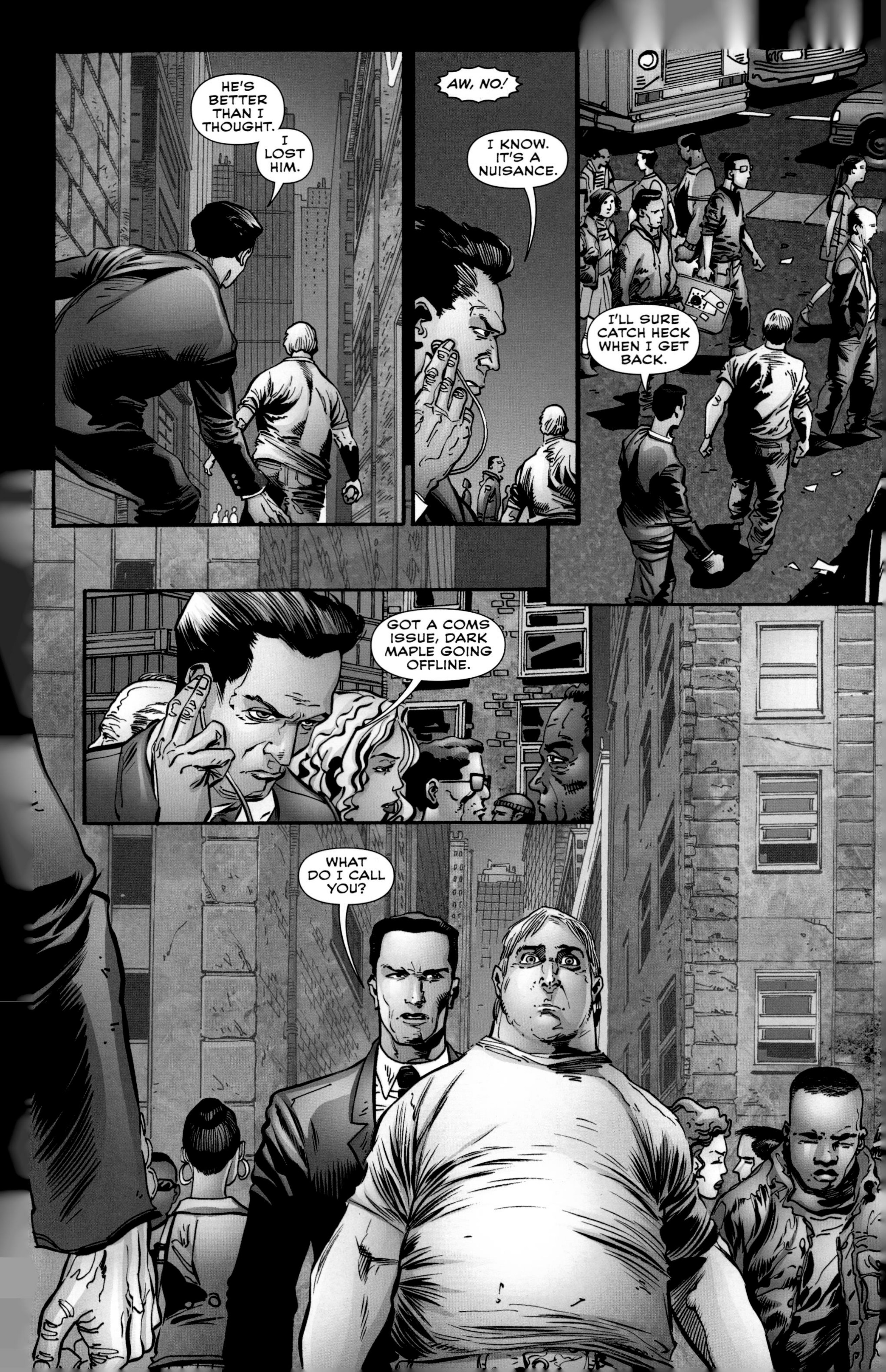
HE'S BETTER THAN I THOUGHT.
I LOST HIM.
AW, NO!
I KNOW. IT'S A NUISANCE.
I'LL SURE CATCH HECK WHEN I GET BACK.
GOT A COMS ISSUE, DARK MAPLE GOING OFFLINE.
WHAT DO I CALL YOU?

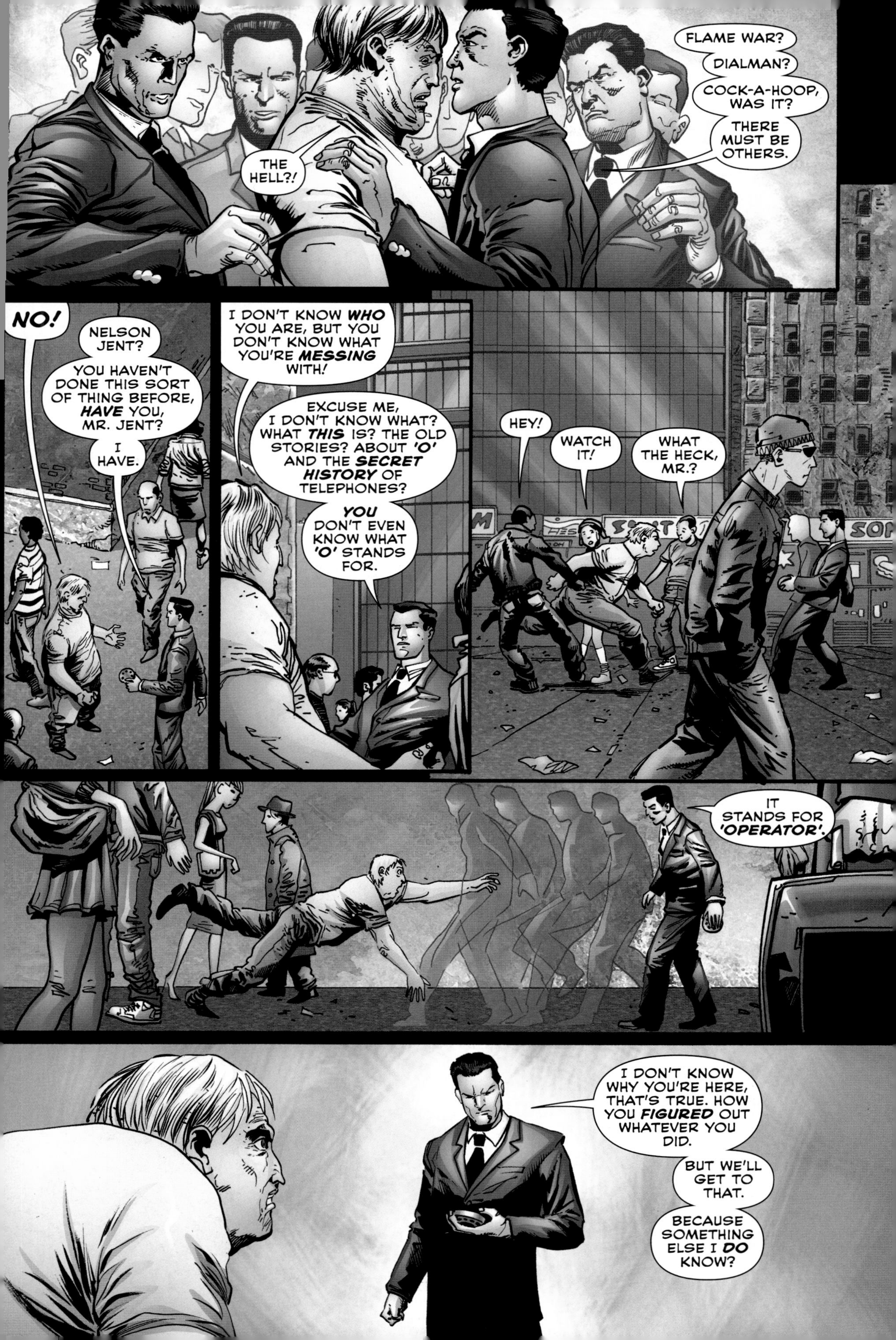
FLAME WAR?
DIALMAN?
COCK-A-HOOP, WAS IT?
THERE MUST BE OTHERS.
THE HELL?!
NO!
NELSON JENT?
YOU HAVEN'T DONE THIS SORT OF THING BEFORE, HAVE YOU, MR. JENT?
I HAVE.
I DON'T KNOW WHO YOU ARE, BUT YOU DON'T KNOW WHAT YOU'RE MESSING WITH!
EXCUSE ME, I DON'T KNOW WHAT? WHAT THIS IS? THE OLD STORIES? ABOUT 'O' AND THE SECRET HISTORY OF TELEPHONES?
YOU DON'T EVEN KNOW WHAT 'O' STANDS FOR.
HEY!
WATCH IT!
WHAT THE HECK, MR.?
IT STANDS FOR 'OPERATOR'.
I DON'T KNOW WHY YOU'RE HERE, THAT'S TRUE. HOW YOU FIGURED OUT WHATEVER YOU DID.
BUT WE'LL GET TO THAT.
BECAUSE SOMETHING ELSE I DO KNOW?

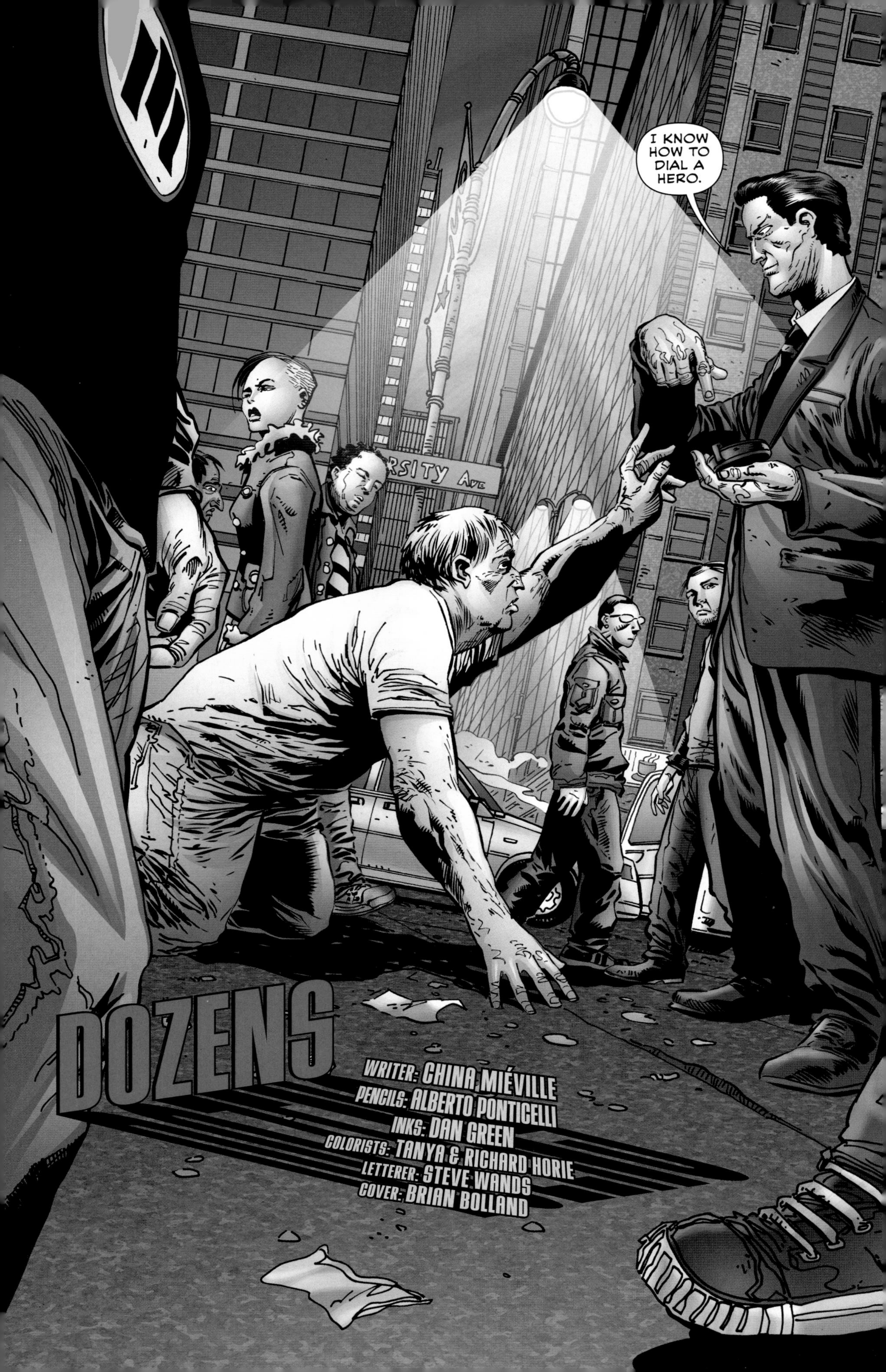
I KNOW HOW TO DIAL A HERO.
RSITY AVE
DOZENS
WRITER: CHINA MIÉVILLE
PENCILS: ALBERTO PONTICELLI
INKS: DAN GREEN
COLORISTS: TANYA & RICHARD HORIE
LETTERER: STEVE WANDS
COVER: BRIAN BOLLAND

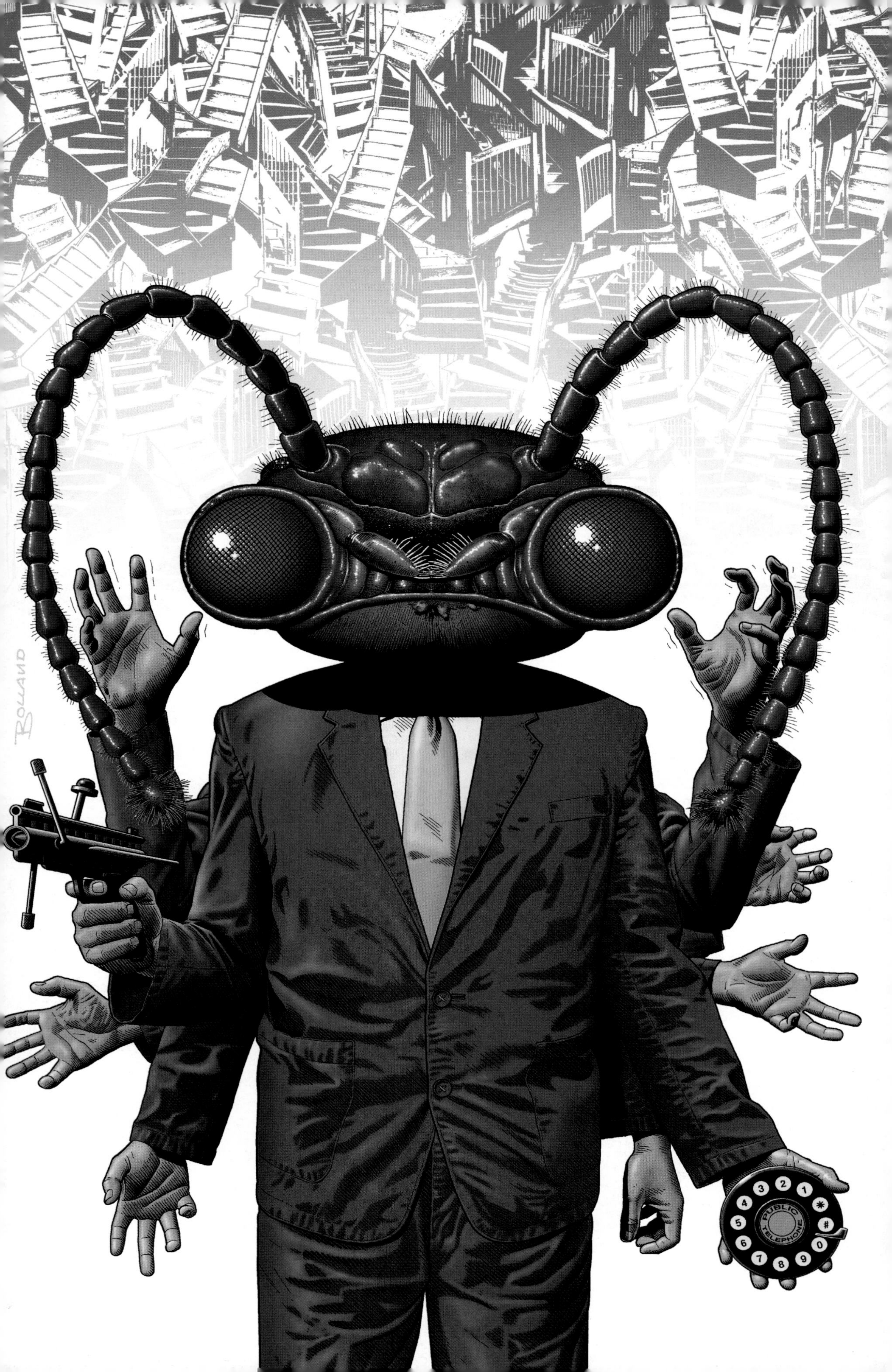
BOLLAND
PUBLIC TELEPHONE

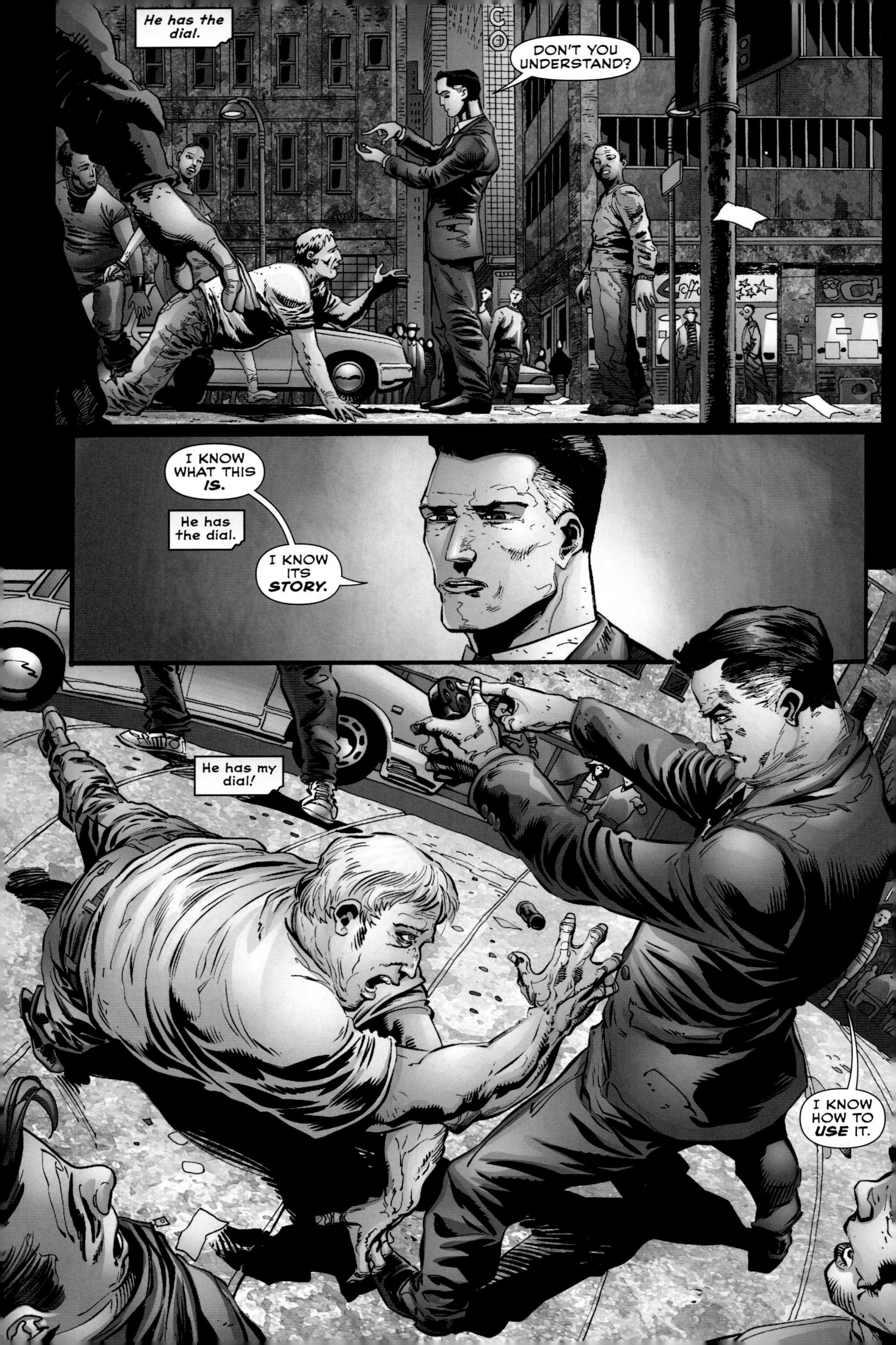
He has the dial.
DON'T YOU UNDERSTAND?
I KNOW WHAT THIS IS.
He has the dial.
I KNOW ITS STORY.
He has my dial!
I KNOW HOW TO USE IT.

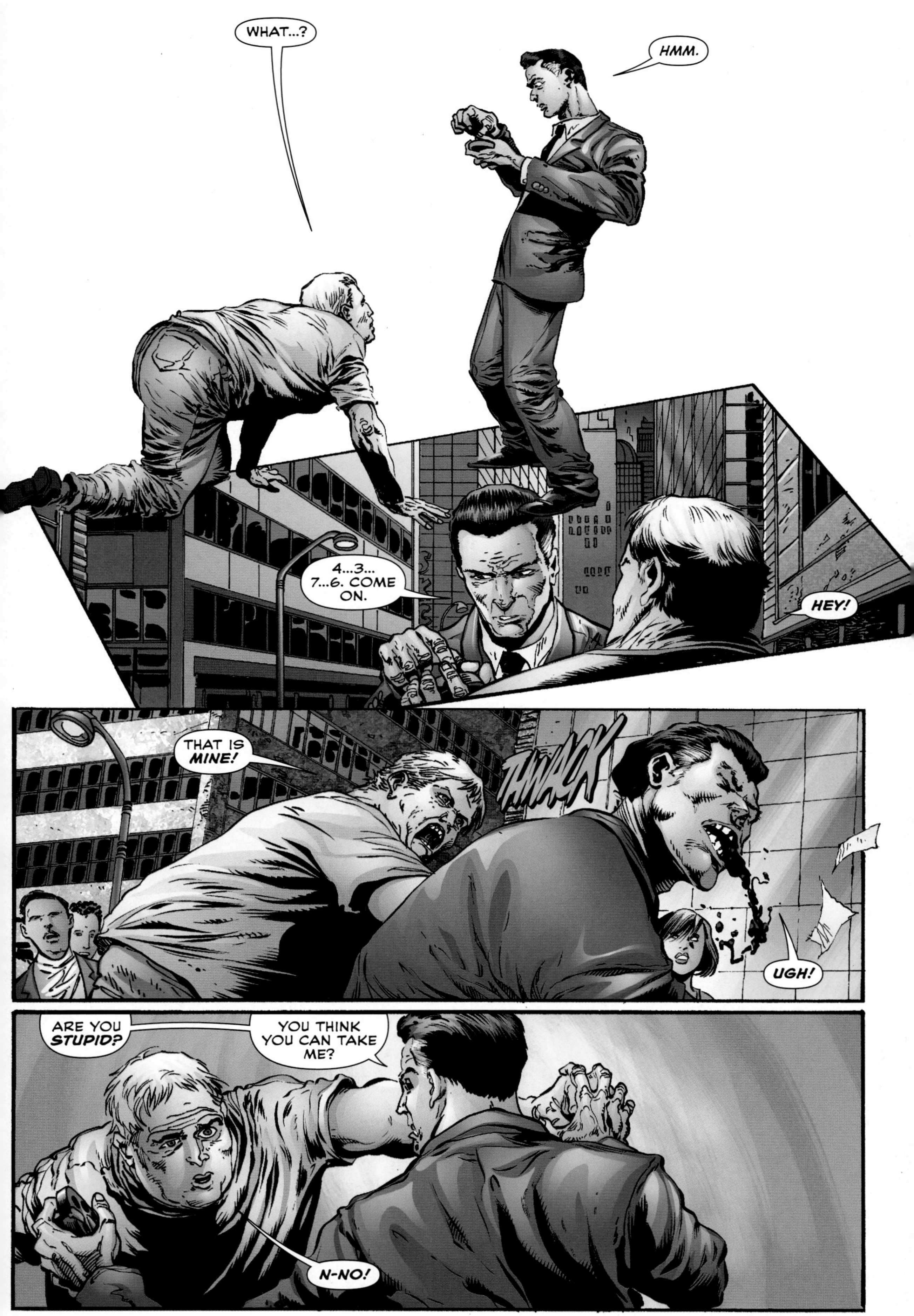
WHAT...?
HMM.
4...3...
7...6. COME ON.
HEY!
THAT IS MINE!
THWACK
UGH!
ARE YOU STUPID?
YOU THINK YOU CAN TAKE ME?
N-NO!

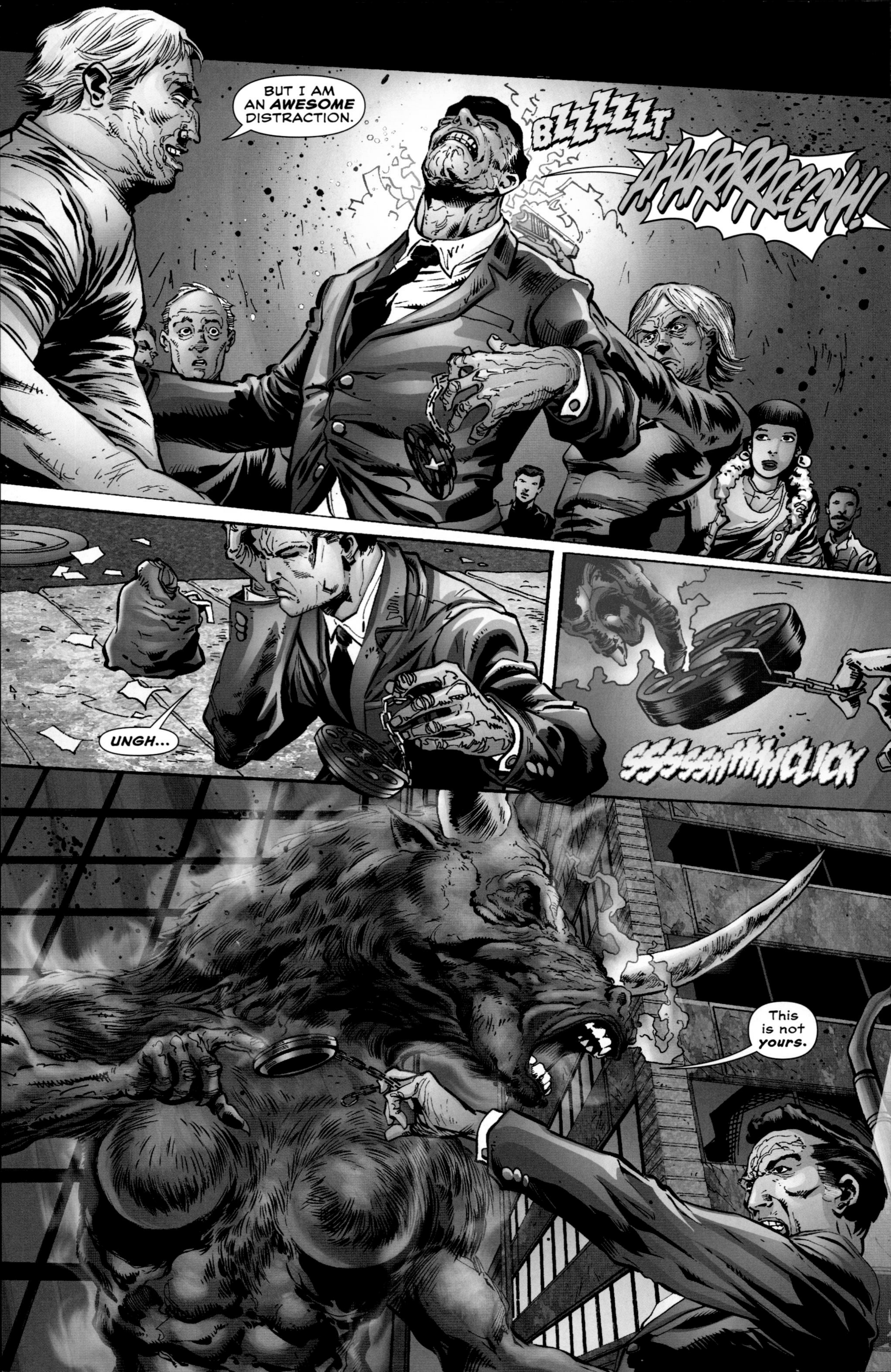
BUT I AM AN AWESOME DISTRACTION.
BZZZZZT
AAARRRRGGHH!
UNGH...
SSSSSHHHHCLICK
This is not yours.

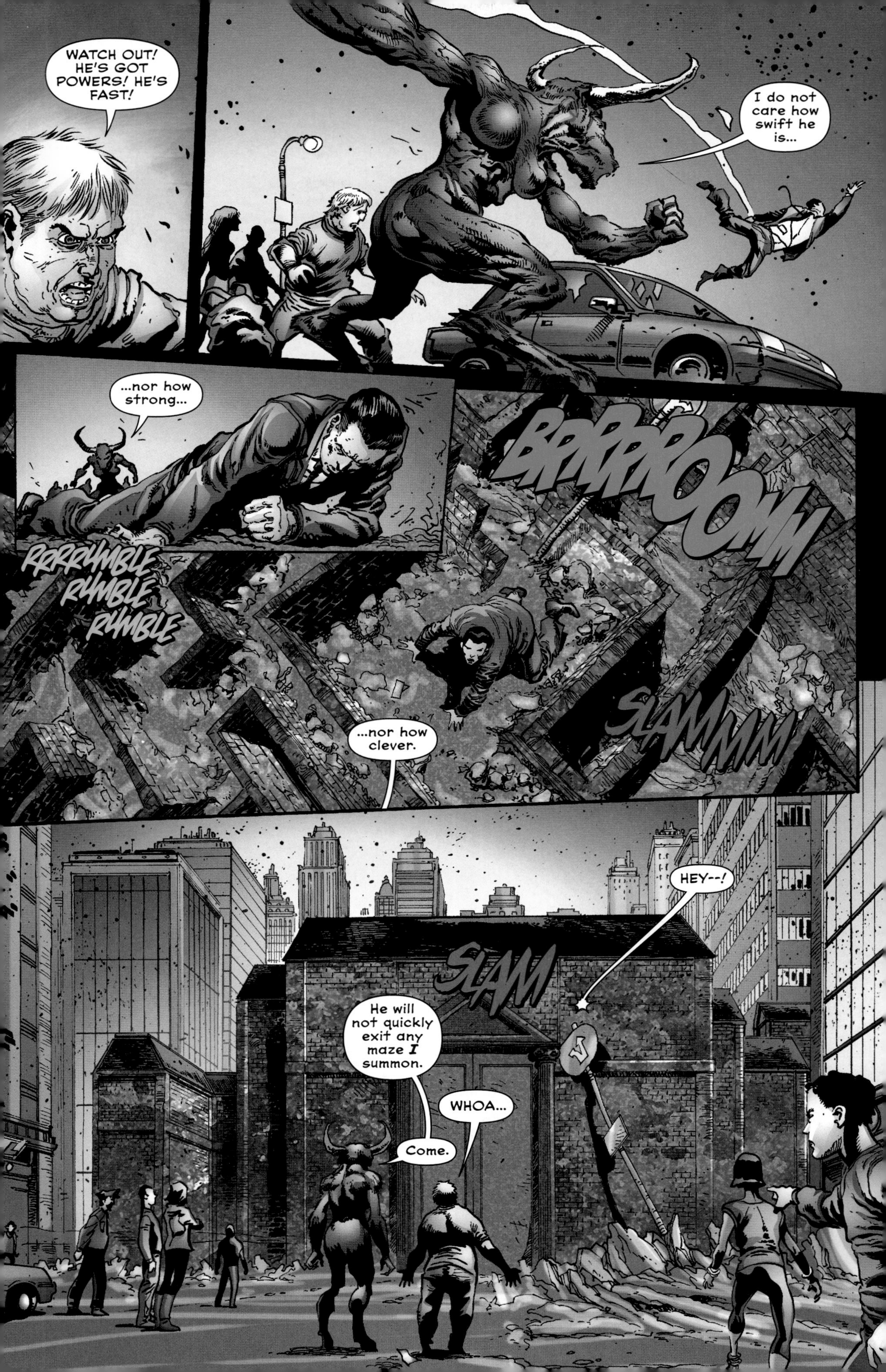
WATCH OUT! HE'S GOT POWERS! HE'S FAST!
I do not care how swift he is...
...nor how strong...
BRRRROOOMM
RRRRUMBLE RUMBLE RUMBLE
SLAMMMM
...nor how clever.
HEY--!
SLAM
He will not quickly exit any maze *I* summon.
WHOA...
Come.

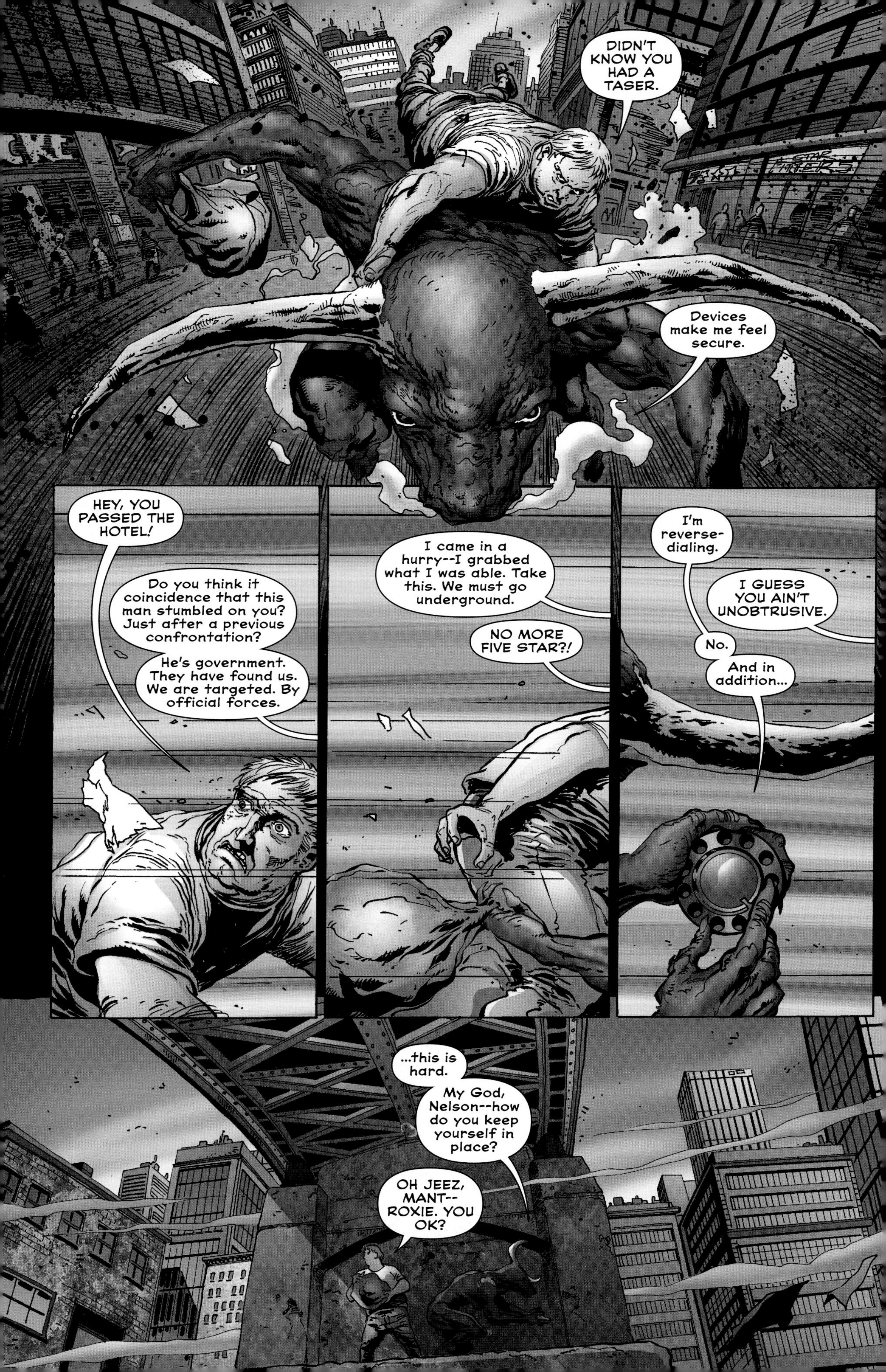
DIDN'T KNOW YOU HAD A TASER.
Devices make me feel secure.
HEY, YOU PASSED THE HOTEL!
Do you think it coincidence that this man stumbled on you? Just after a previous confrontation?
He's government. They have found us. We are targeted. By official forces.
I came in a hurry--I grabbed what I was able. Take this. We must go underground.
NO MORE FIVE STAR?!
I'm reverse-dialing.
I GUESS YOU AIN'T UNOBTRUSIVE.
No.
And in addition...
...this is hard.
My God, Nelson--how do you keep yourself in place?
OH JEEZ, MANT--ROXIE. YOU OK?

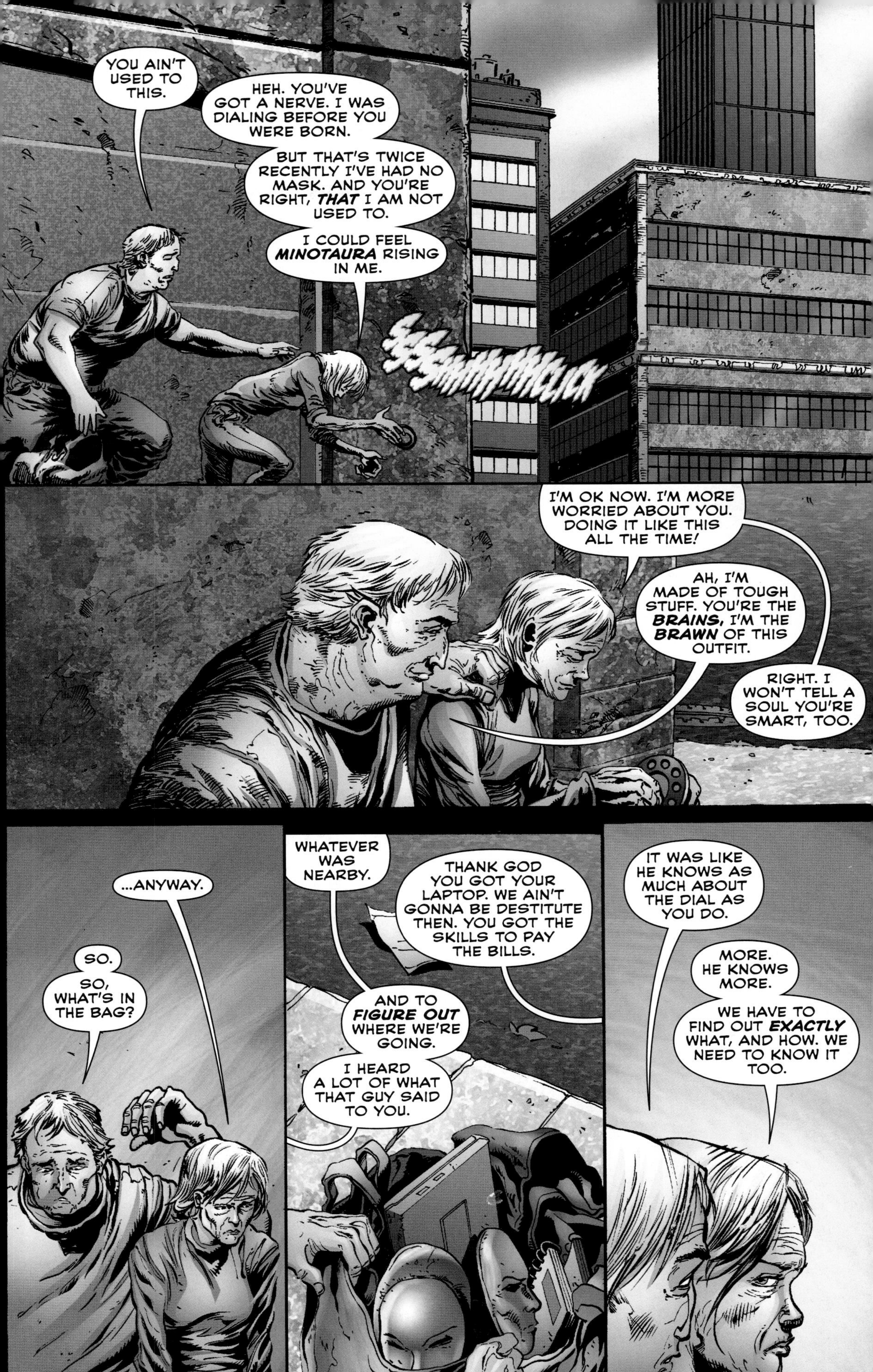
YOU AIN'T USED TO THIS.
HEH. YOU'VE GOT A NERVE. I WAS DIALING BEFORE YOU WERE BORN.
BUT THAT'S TWICE RECENTLY I'VE HAD NO MASK. AND YOU'RE RIGHT, *THAT* I AM NOT USED TO.
I COULD FEEL *MINOTAURA* RISING IN ME.
SSSHHHHHHCLICK
I'M OK NOW. I'M MORE WORRIED ABOUT YOU. DOING IT LIKE THIS ALL THE TIME!
AH, I'M MADE OF TOUGH STUFF. YOU'RE THE *BRAINS,* I'M THE *BRAWN* OF THIS OUTFIT.
RIGHT. I WON'T TELL A SOUL YOU'RE SMART, TOO.
...ANYWAY.
SO.
SO, WHAT'S IN THE BAG?
WHATEVER WAS NEARBY.
THANK GOD YOU GOT YOUR LAPTOP. WE AIN'T GONNA BE DESTITUTE THEN. YOU GOT THE SKILLS TO PAY THE BILLS.
AND TO *FIGURE OUT* WHERE WE'RE GOING.
I HEARD A LOT OF WHAT THAT GUY SAID TO YOU.
IT WAS LIKE HE KNOWS AS MUCH ABOUT THE DIAL AS YOU DO.
MORE. HE KNOWS MORE.
WE HAVE TO FIND OUT *EXACTLY* WHAT, AND HOW. WE NEED TO KNOW IT TOO.

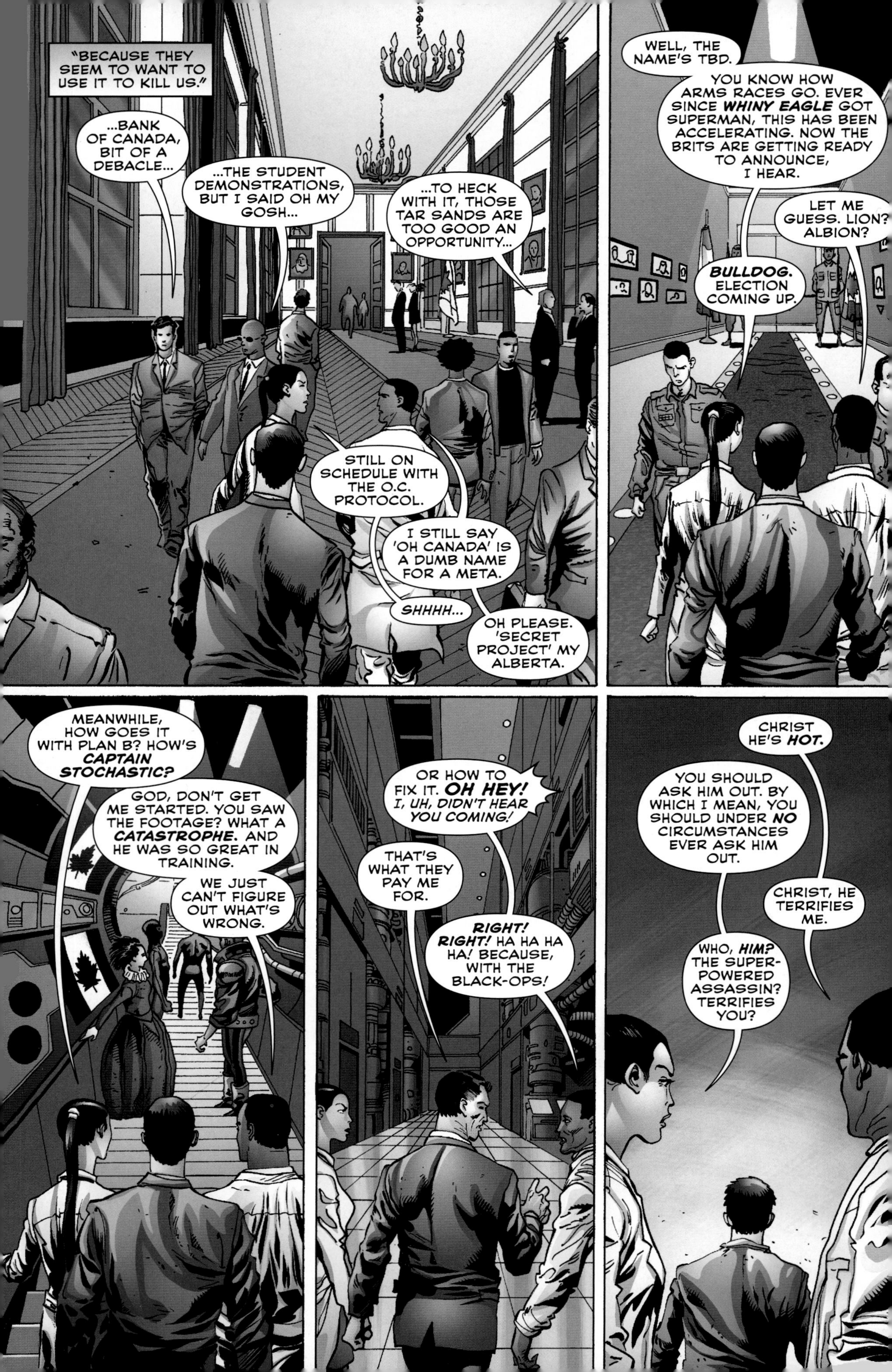
"BECAUSE THEY SEEM TO WANT TO USE IT TO KILL US."
...BANK OF CANADA, BIT OF A DEBACLE...
...THE STUDENT DEMONSTRATIONS, BUT I SAID OH MY GOSH...
...TO HECK WITH IT, THOSE TAR SANDS ARE TOO GOOD AN OPPORTUNITY...
STILL ON SCHEDULE WITH THE O.C. PROTOCOL.
I STILL SAY 'OH CANADA' IS A DUMB NAME FOR A META.
SHHHH...
OH PLEASE. 'SECRET PROJECT' MY ALBERTA.
WELL, THE NAME'S TBD.
YOU KNOW HOW ARMS RACES GO. EVER SINCE WHINY EAGLE GOT SUPERMAN, THIS HAS BEEN ACCELERATING. NOW THE BRITS ARE GETTING READY TO ANNOUNCE, I HEAR.
LET ME GUESS. LION? ALBION?
BULLDOG. ELECTION COMING UP.
MEANWHILE, HOW GOES IT WITH PLAN B? HOW'S CAPTAIN STOCHASTIC?
GOD, DON'T GET ME STARTED. YOU SAW THE FOOTAGE? WHAT A CATASTROPHE. AND HE WAS SO GREAT IN TRAINING.
WE JUST CAN'T FIGURE OUT WHAT'S WRONG.
OR HOW TO FIX IT. OH HEY! I, UH, DIDN'T HEAR YOU COMING!
THAT'S WHAT THEY PAY ME FOR.
RIGHT! RIGHT! HA HA HA HA! BECAUSE, WITH THE BLACK-OPS!
CHRIST HE'S HOT.
YOU SHOULD ASK HIM OUT. BY WHICH I MEAN, YOU SHOULD UNDER NO CIRCUMSTANCES EVER ASK HIM OUT.
CHRIST, HE TERRIFIES ME.
WHO, HIM? THE SUPER-POWERED ASSASSIN? TERRIFIES YOU?

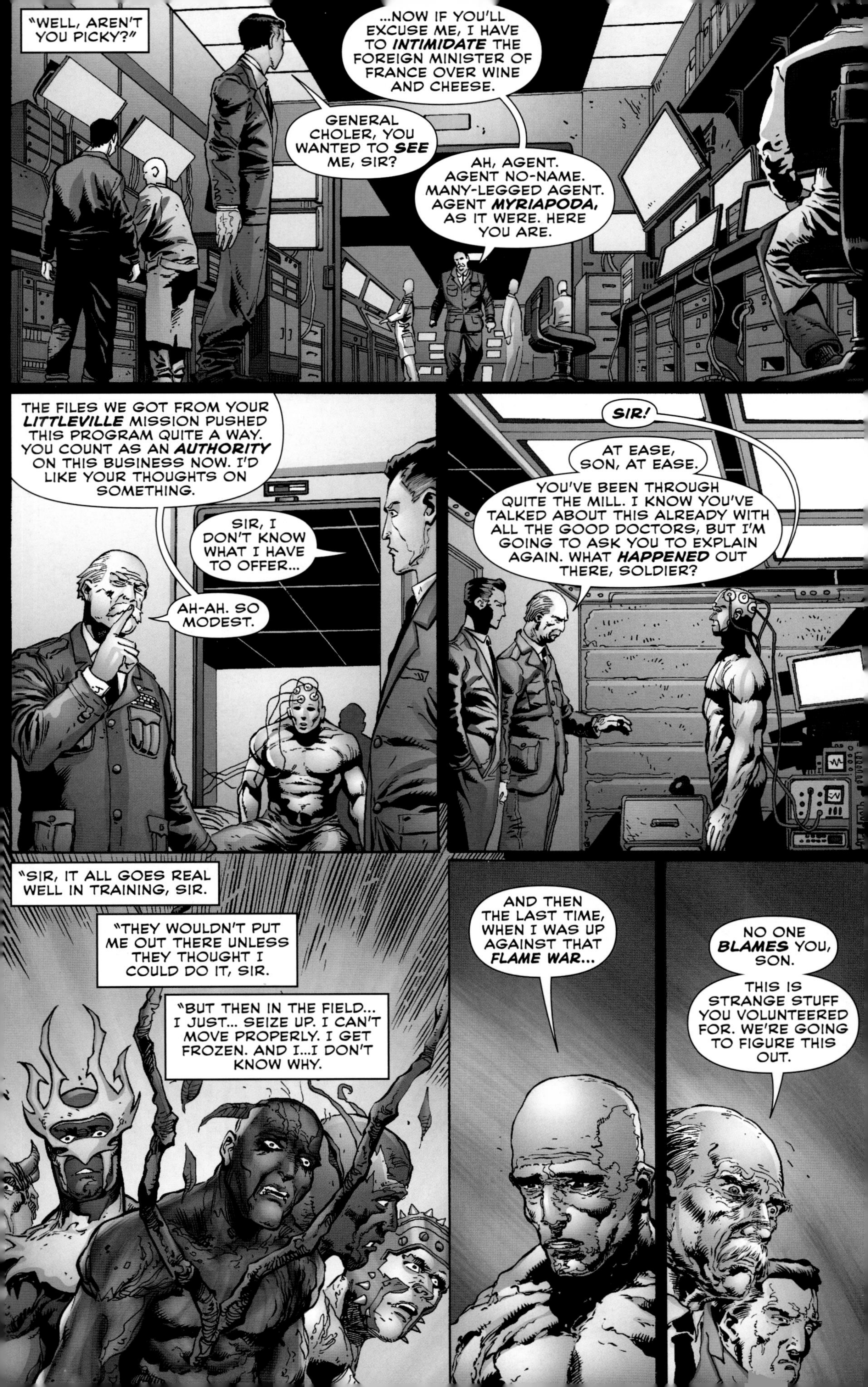
"WELL, AREN'T YOU PICKY?"
...NOW IF YOU'LL EXCUSE ME, I HAVE TO INTIMIDATE THE FOREIGN MINISTER OF FRANCE OVER WINE AND CHEESE.
GENERAL CHOLER, YOU WANTED TO SEE ME, SIR?
AH, AGENT. AGENT NO-NAME. MANY-LEGGED AGENT. AGENT MYRIAPODA, AS IT WERE. HERE YOU ARE.
THE FILES WE GOT FROM YOUR LITTLEVILLE MISSION PUSHED THIS PROGRAM QUITE A WAY. YOU COUNT AS AN AUTHORITY ON THIS BUSINESS NOW. I'D LIKE YOUR THOUGHTS ON SOMETHING.
SIR, I DON'T KNOW WHAT I HAVE TO OFFER...
AH-AH. SO MODEST.
SIR!
AT EASE, SON, AT EASE.
YOU'VE BEEN THROUGH QUITE THE MILL. I KNOW YOU'VE TALKED ABOUT THIS ALREADY WITH ALL THE GOOD DOCTORS, BUT I'M GOING TO ASK YOU TO EXPLAIN AGAIN. WHAT HAPPENED OUT THERE, SOLDIER?
"SIR, IT ALL GOES REAL WELL IN TRAINING, SIR.
"THEY WOULDN'T PUT ME OUT THERE UNLESS THEY THOUGHT I COULD DO IT, SIR.
"BUT THEN IN THE FIELD... I JUST... SEIZE UP. I CAN'T MOVE PROPERLY. I GET FROZEN. AND I...I DON'T KNOW WHY.
AND THEN THE LAST TIME, WHEN I WAS UP AGAINST THAT FLAME WAR...
NO ONE BLAMES YOU, SON.
THIS IS STRANGE STUFF YOU VOLUNTEERED FOR. WE'RE GOING TO FIGURE THIS OUT.

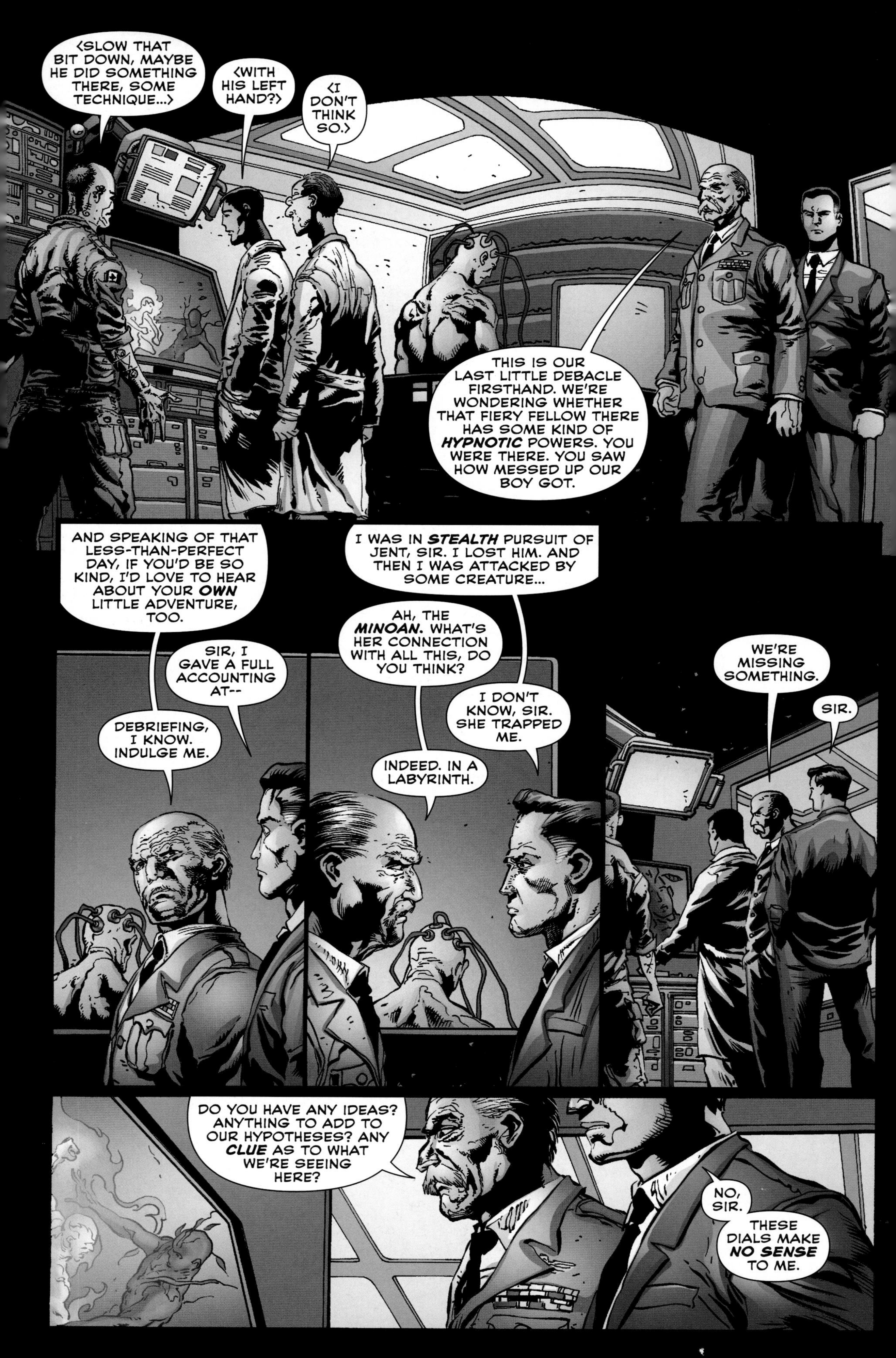
<SLOW THAT BIT DOWN, MAYBE HE DID SOMETHING THERE, SOME TECHNIQUE...>
<WITH HIS LEFT HAND?>
<I DON'T THINK SO.>
THIS IS OUR LAST LITTLE DEBACLE FIRSTHAND. WE'RE WONDERING WHETHER THAT FIERY FELLOW THERE HAS SOME KIND OF HYPNOTIC POWERS. YOU WERE THERE. YOU SAW HOW MESSED UP OUR BOY GOT.
AND SPEAKING OF THAT LESS-THAN-PERFECT DAY, IF YOU'D BE SO KIND, I'D LOVE TO HEAR ABOUT YOUR OWN LITTLE ADVENTURE, TOO.
SIR, I GAVE A FULL ACCOUNTING AT--
DEBRIEFING, I KNOW. INDULGE ME.
I WAS IN STEALTH PURSUIT OF JENT, SIR. I LOST HIM. AND THEN I WAS ATTACKED BY SOME CREATURE...
AH, THE MINOAN. WHAT'S HER CONNECTION WITH ALL THIS, DO YOU THINK?
I DON'T KNOW, SIR. SHE TRAPPED ME.
INDEED. IN A LABYRINTH.
WE'RE MISSING SOMETHING.
SIR.
DO YOU HAVE ANY IDEAS? ANYTHING TO ADD TO OUR HYPOTHESES? ANY CLUE AS TO WHAT WE'RE SEEING HERE?
NO, SIR.
THESE DIALS MAKE NO SENSE TO ME.

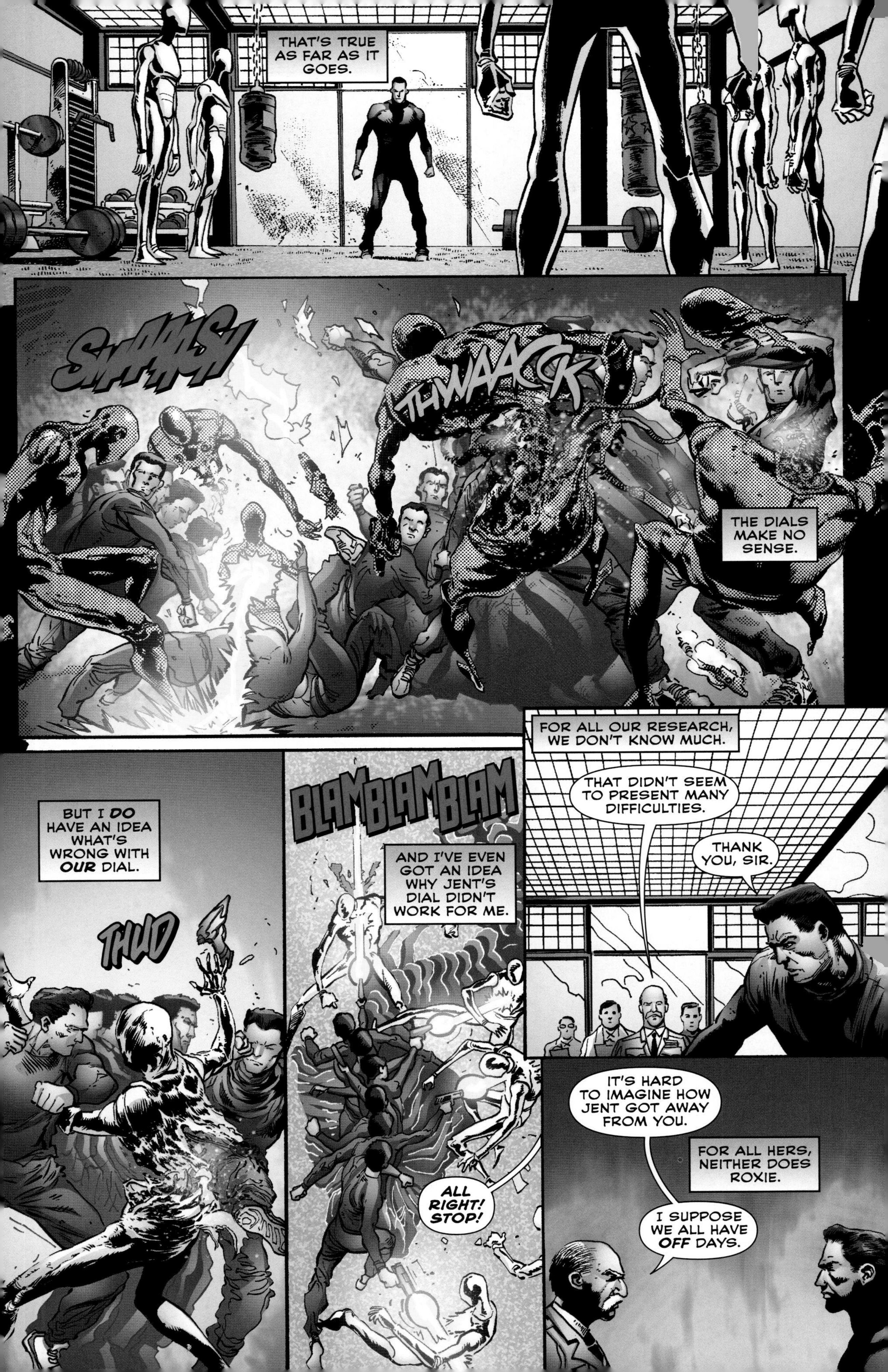

THAT'S TRUE AS FAR AS IT GOES.
SMAAASH
THWAACCK
THE DIALS MAKE NO SENSE.
FOR ALL OUR RESEARCH, WE DON'T KNOW MUCH.
THAT DIDN'T SEEM TO PRESENT MANY DIFFICULTIES.
THANK YOU, SIR.
BUT I **DO** HAVE AN IDEA WHAT'S WRONG WITH **OUR** DIAL.
THUD
BLAMBLAMBLAM
AND I'VE EVEN GOT AN IDEA WHY JENT'S DIAL DIDN'T WORK FOR ME.
ALL RIGHT! STOP!
IT'S HARD TO IMAGINE HOW JENT GOT AWAY FROM YOU.
FOR ALL HERS, NEITHER DOES ROXIE.
I SUPPOSE WE ALL HAVE **OFF** DAYS.

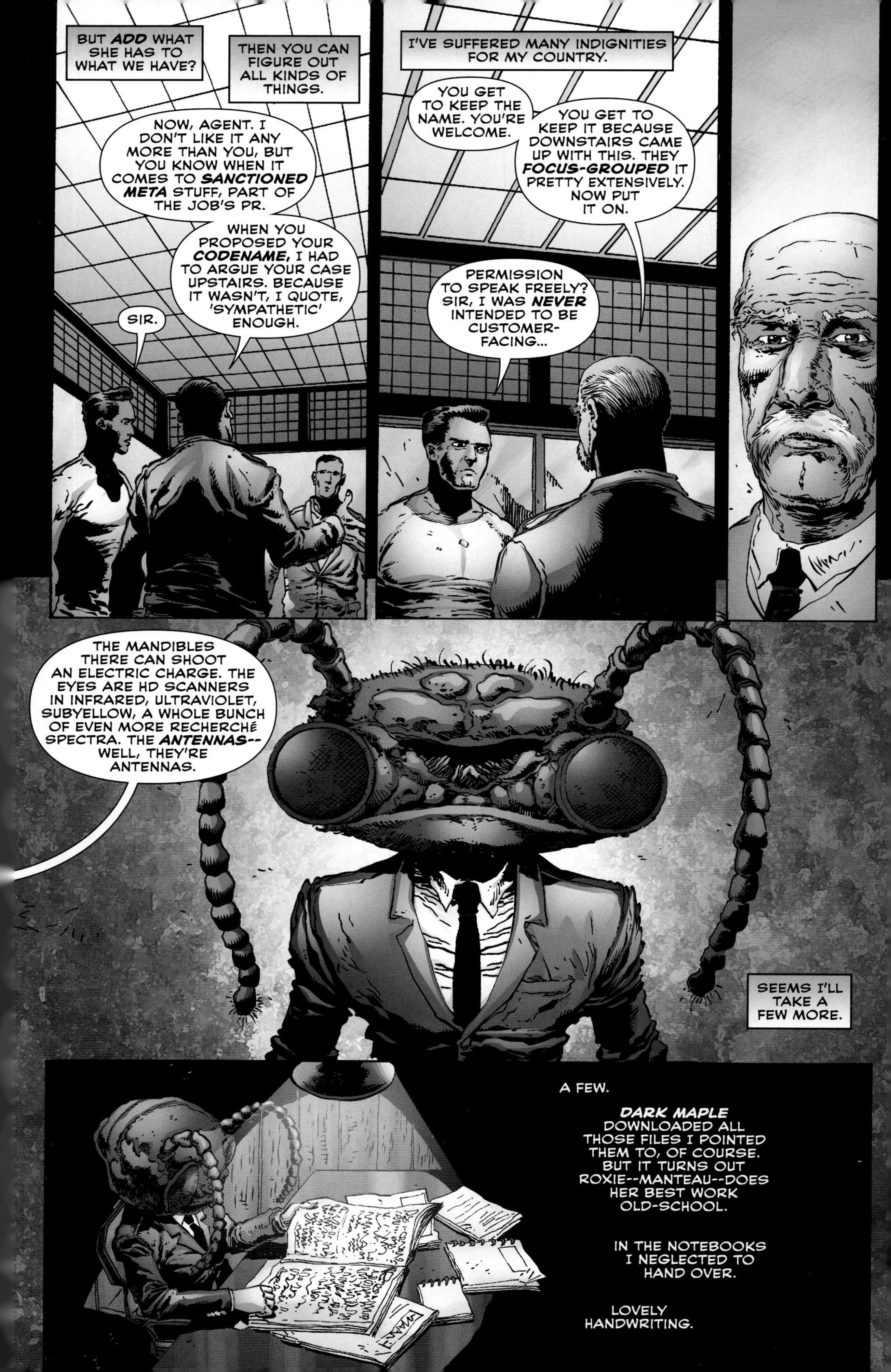
BUT ADD WHAT SHE HAS TO WHAT WE HAVE?
THEN YOU CAN FIGURE OUT ALL KINDS OF THINGS.
NOW, AGENT. I DON'T LIKE IT ANY MORE THAN YOU, BUT YOU KNOW WHEN IT COMES TO SANCTIONED META STUFF, PART OF THE JOB'S PR.
WHEN YOU PROPOSED YOUR CODENAME, I HAD TO ARGUE YOUR CASE UPSTAIRS. BECAUSE IT WASN'T, I QUOTE, 'SYMPATHETIC' ENOUGH.
SIR.
I'VE SUFFERED MANY INDIGNITIES FOR MY COUNTRY.
YOU GET TO KEEP THE NAME. YOU'RE WELCOME.
YOU GET TO KEEP IT BECAUSE DOWNSTAIRS CAME UP WITH THIS. THEY FOCUS-GROUPED IT PRETTY EXTENSIVELY. NOW PUT IT ON.
PERMISSION TO SPEAK FREELY? SIR, I WAS NEVER INTENDED TO BE CUSTOMER-FACING...
THE MANDIBLES THERE CAN SHOOT AN ELECTRIC CHARGE. THE EYES ARE HD SCANNERS IN INFRARED, ULTRAVIOLET, SUBYELLOW, A WHOLE BUNCH OF EVEN MORE RECHERCHÉ SPECTRA. THE ANTENNAS--WELL, THEY'RE ANTENNAS.
SEEMS I'LL TAKE A FEW MORE.
A FEW.
DARK MAPLE DOWNLOADED ALL THOSE FILES I POINTED THEM TO, OF COURSE. BUT IT TURNS OUT ROXIE--MANTEAU--DOES HER BEST WORK OLD-SCHOOL.
IN THE NOTEBOOKS I NEGLECTED TO HAND OVER.
LOVELY HANDWRITING.

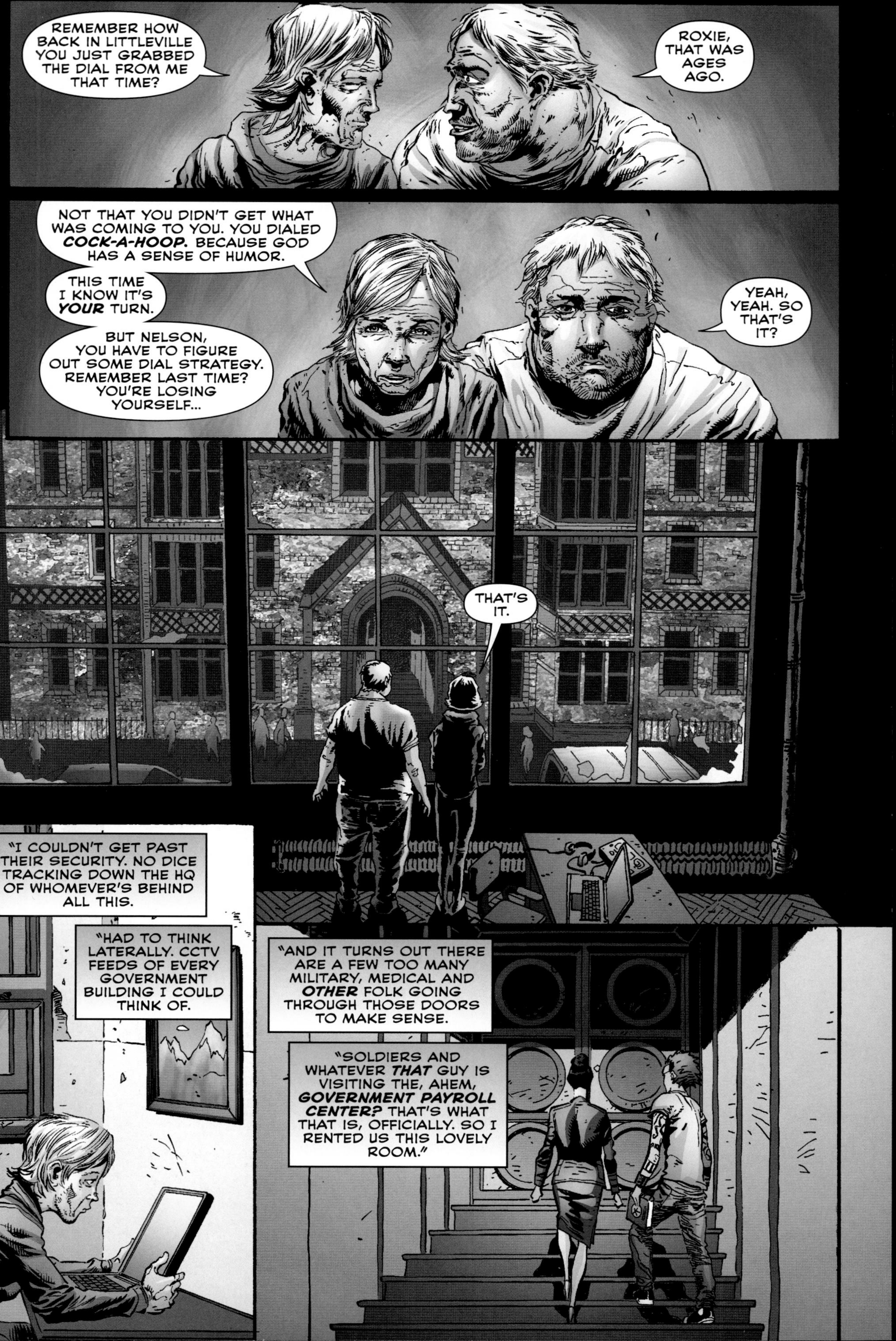
REMEMBER HOW BACK IN LITTLEVILLE YOU JUST GRABBED THE DIAL FROM ME THAT TIME?
ROXIE, THAT WAS AGES AGO.
NOT THAT YOU DIDN'T GET WHAT WAS COMING TO YOU. YOU DIALED COCK-A-HOOP. BECAUSE GOD HAS A SENSE OF HUMOR.
THIS TIME I KNOW IT'S YOUR TURN.
BUT NELSON, YOU HAVE TO FIGURE OUT SOME DIAL STRATEGY. REMEMBER LAST TIME? YOU'RE LOSING YOURSELF...
YEAH, YEAH. SO THAT'S IT?
THAT'S IT.
"I COULDN'T GET PAST THEIR SECURITY. NO DICE TRACKING DOWN THE HQ OF WHOMEVER'S BEHIND ALL THIS.
"HAD TO THINK LATERALLY. CCTV FEEDS OF EVERY GOVERNMENT BUILDING I COULD THINK OF.
"AND IT TURNS OUT THERE ARE A FEW TOO MANY MILITARY, MEDICAL AND OTHER FOLK GOING THROUGH THOSE DOORS TO MAKE SENSE.
"SOLDIERS AND WHATEVER THAT GUY IS VISITING THE, AHEM, GOVERNMENT PAYROLL CENTER? THAT'S WHAT THAT IS, OFFICIALLY. SO I RENTED US THIS LOVELY ROOM."

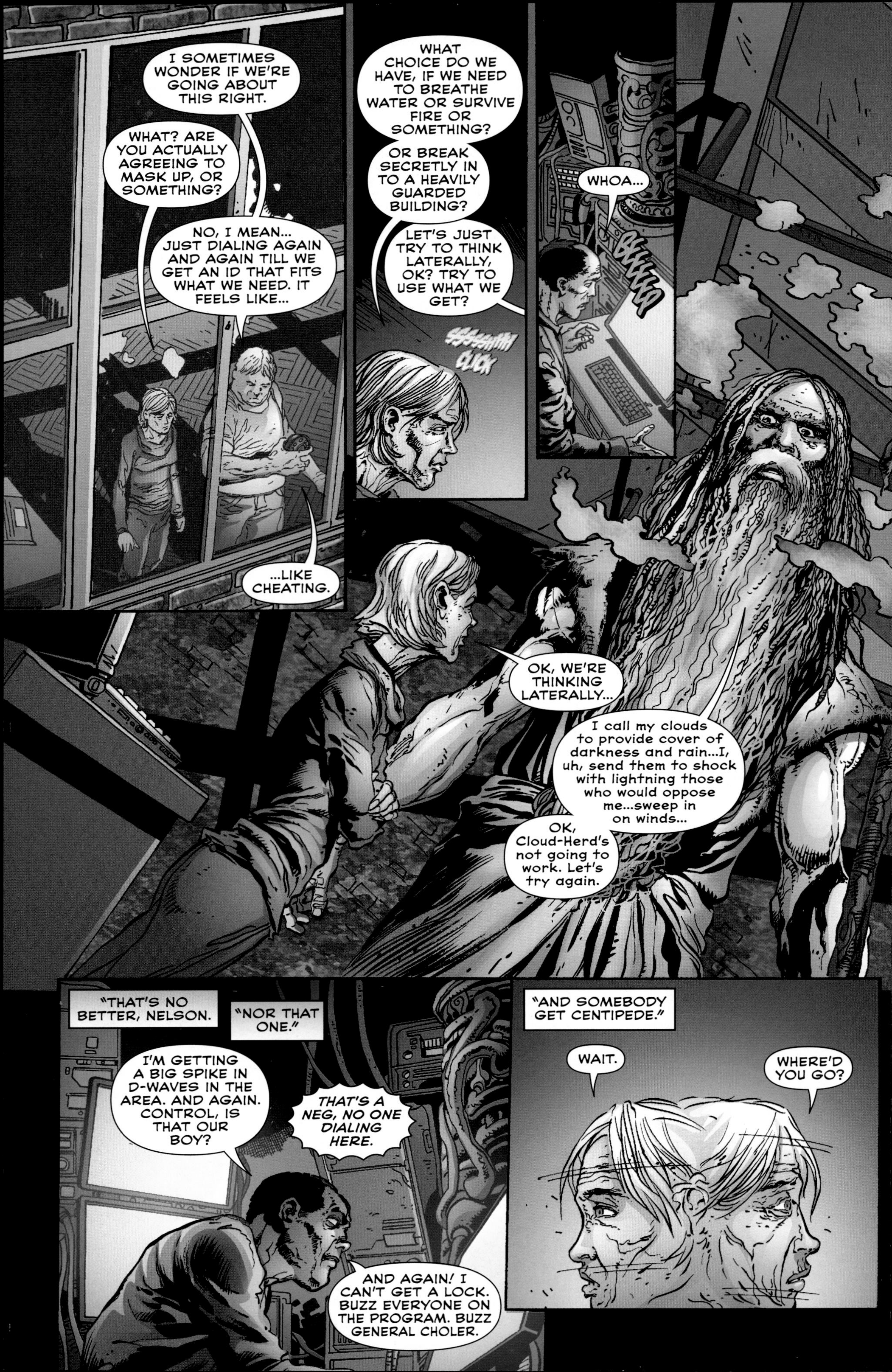
I SOMETIMES WONDER IF WE'RE GOING ABOUT THIS RIGHT.
WHAT? ARE YOU ACTUALLY AGREEING TO MASK UP, OR SOMETHING?
NO, I MEAN... JUST DIALING AGAIN AND AGAIN TILL WE GET AN ID THAT FITS WHAT WE NEED. IT FEELS LIKE...
...LIKE CHEATING.
WHAT CHOICE DO WE HAVE, IF WE NEED TO BREATHE WATER OR SURVIVE FIRE OR SOMETHING?
OR BREAK SECRETLY IN TO A HEAVILY GUARDED BUILDING?
LET'S JUST TRY TO THINK LATERALLY, OK? TRY TO USE WHAT WE GET?
SSSSHHH CLICK
WHOA...
OK, WE'RE THINKING LATERALLY...
I call my clouds to provide cover of darkness and rain...I, uh, send them to shock with lightning those who would oppose me...sweep in on winds...
OK, Cloud-Herd's not going to work. Let's try again.
"THAT'S NO BETTER, NELSON.
"NOR THAT ONE."
I'M GETTING A BIG SPIKE IN D-WAVES IN THE AREA. AND AGAIN. CONTROL, IS THAT OUR BOY?
THAT'S A NEG, NO ONE DIALING HERE.
AND AGAIN! I CAN'T GET A LOCK. BUZZ EVERYONE ON THE PROGRAM. BUZZ GENERAL CHOLER.
"AND SOMEBODY GET CENTIPEDE."
WAIT.
WHERE'D YOU GO?

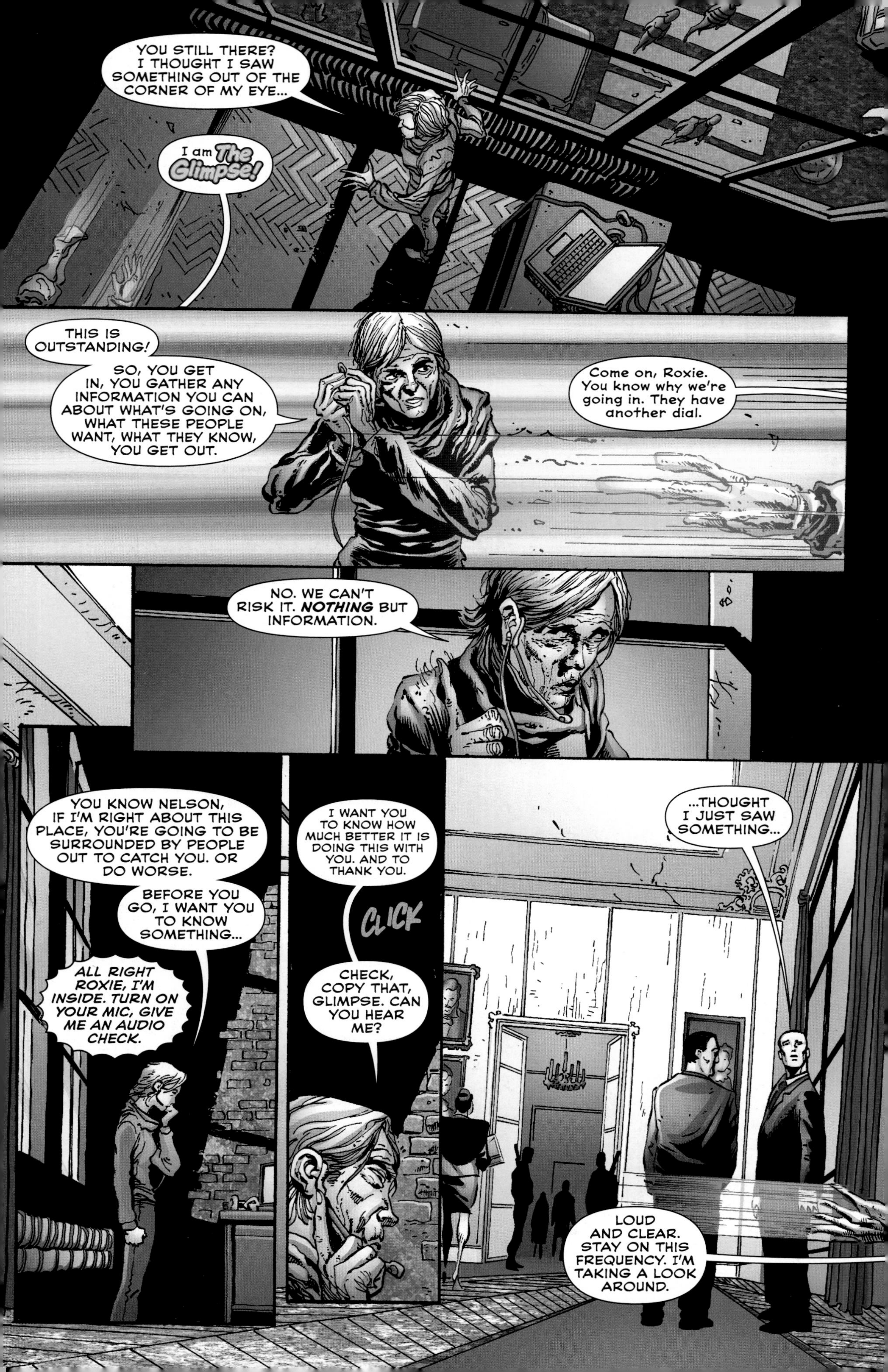
YOU STILL THERE? I THOUGHT I SAW SOMETHING OUT OF THE CORNER OF MY EYE...
I am The Glimpse!
THIS IS OUTSTANDING!
SO, YOU GET IN, YOU GATHER ANY INFORMATION YOU CAN ABOUT WHAT'S GOING ON, WHAT THESE PEOPLE WANT, WHAT THEY KNOW, YOU GET OUT.
Come on, Roxie. You know why we're going in. They have another dial.
NO. WE CAN'T RISK IT. NOTHING BUT INFORMATION.
YOU KNOW NELSON, IF I'M RIGHT ABOUT THIS PLACE, YOU'RE GOING TO BE SURROUNDED BY PEOPLE OUT TO CATCH YOU. OR DO WORSE.
BEFORE YOU GO, I WANT YOU TO KNOW SOMETHING...
I WANT YOU TO KNOW HOW MUCH BETTER IT IS DOING THIS WITH YOU. AND TO THANK YOU.
CLICK
ALL RIGHT ROXIE, I'M INSIDE. TURN ON YOUR MIC, GIVE ME AN AUDIO CHECK.
CHECK, COPY THAT, GLIMPSE. CAN YOU HEAR ME?
...THOUGHT I JUST SAW SOMETHING...
LOUD AND CLEAR. STAY ON THIS FREQUENCY. I'M TAKING A LOOK AROUND.

HMMM.

THEY'RE TRYING TO KEEP IT CALM, BUT IF YOU KNOW WHERE TO LOOK...

SOMETHING'S GOING ON.

YEAH, OUTSIDE TOO.

BE CAREFUL.

DID YOU SAY SOMETHING?

MAYBE *YOU'RE* WHAT'S GOING ON.

THESE GUYS ARE LIKE A TRAIL OF BREADCRUMBS. I'M FOLLOWING THEM BACK.

BUUUMPP

OH, EXCUSE ME!

I DIDN'T...

...SEE YOU...

...IS SOMEONE THERE?

SHHHHH.

I'M LOSING MY MIND...

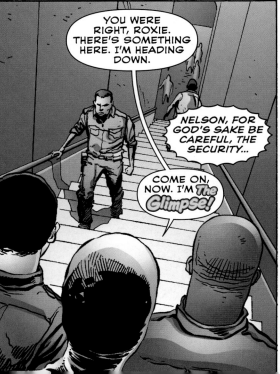

YOU WERE RIGHT, ROXIE. THERE'S SOMETHING HERE. I'M HEADING DOWN.

NELSON, FOR GOD'S SAKE BE CAREFUL, THE SECURITY...

COME ON, NOW. I'M *The Glimpse!*

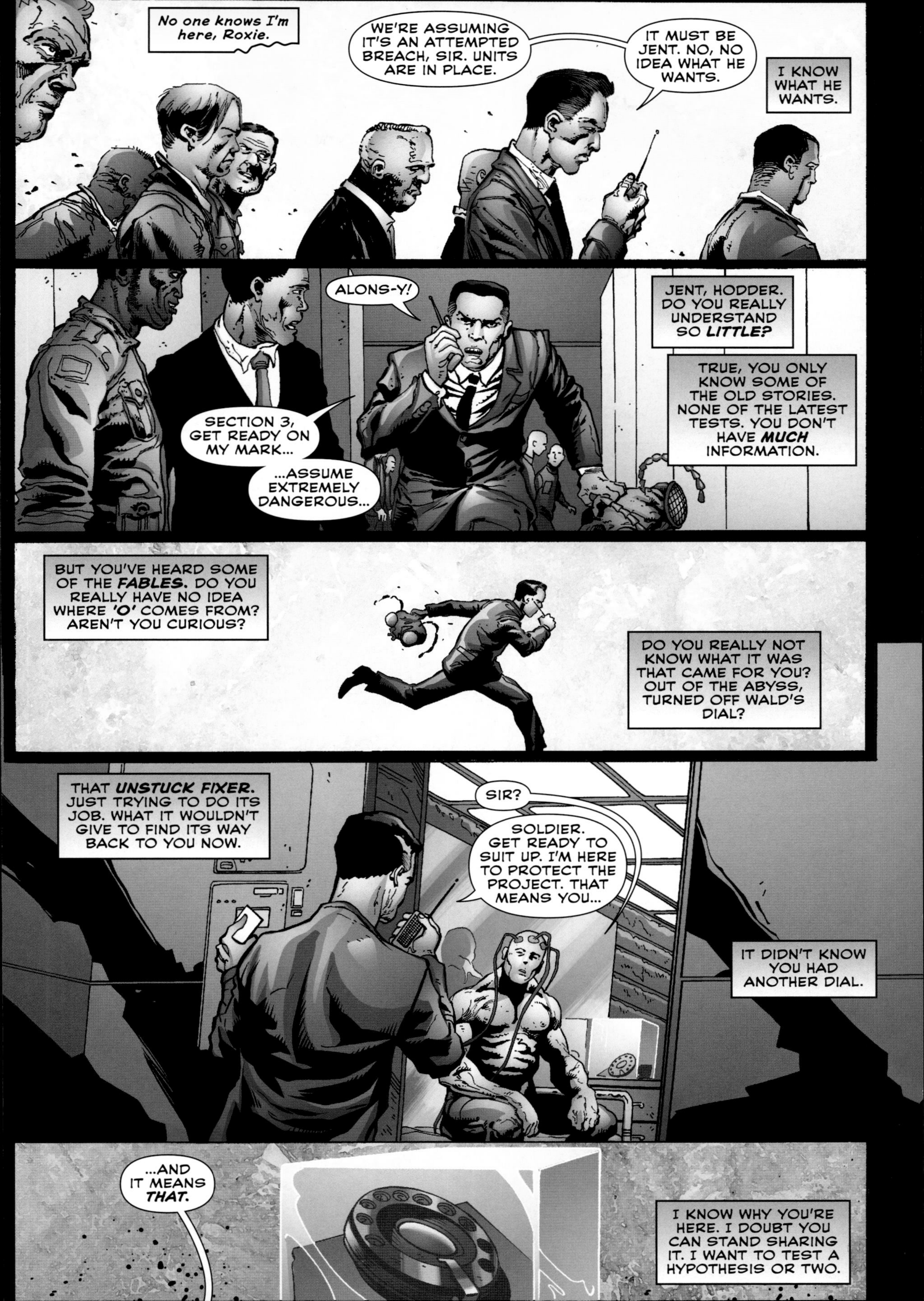
No one knows I'm here, Roxie.
WE'RE ASSUMING IT'S AN ATTEMPTED BREACH, SIR. UNITS ARE IN PLACE.
IT MUST BE JENT. NO, NO IDEA WHAT HE WANTS.
I KNOW WHAT HE WANTS.
ALONS-Y!
JENT, HODDER. DO YOU REALLY UNDERSTAND SO LITTLE?
TRUE, YOU ONLY KNOW SOME OF THE OLD STORIES. NONE OF THE LATEST TESTS. YOU DON'T HAVE MUCH INFORMATION.
SECTION 3, GET READY ON MY MARK...
...ASSUME EXTREMELY DANGEROUS...
BUT YOU'VE HEARD SOME OF THE FABLES. DO YOU REALLY HAVE NO IDEA WHERE 'O' COMES FROM? AREN'T YOU CURIOUS?
DO YOU REALLY NOT KNOW WHAT IT WAS THAT CAME FOR YOU? OUT OF THE ABYSS, TURNED OFF WALD'S DIAL?
THAT UNSTUCK FIXER. JUST TRYING TO DO ITS JOB. WHAT IT WOULDN'T GIVE TO FIND ITS WAY BACK TO YOU NOW.
SIR?
SOLDIER. GET READY TO SUIT UP. I'M HERE TO PROTECT THE PROJECT. THAT MEANS YOU...
IT DIDN'T KNOW YOU HAD ANOTHER DIAL.
...AND IT MEANS THAT.
I KNOW WHY YOU'RE HERE. I DOUBT YOU CAN STAND SHARING IT. I WANT TO TEST A HYPOTHESIS OR TWO.

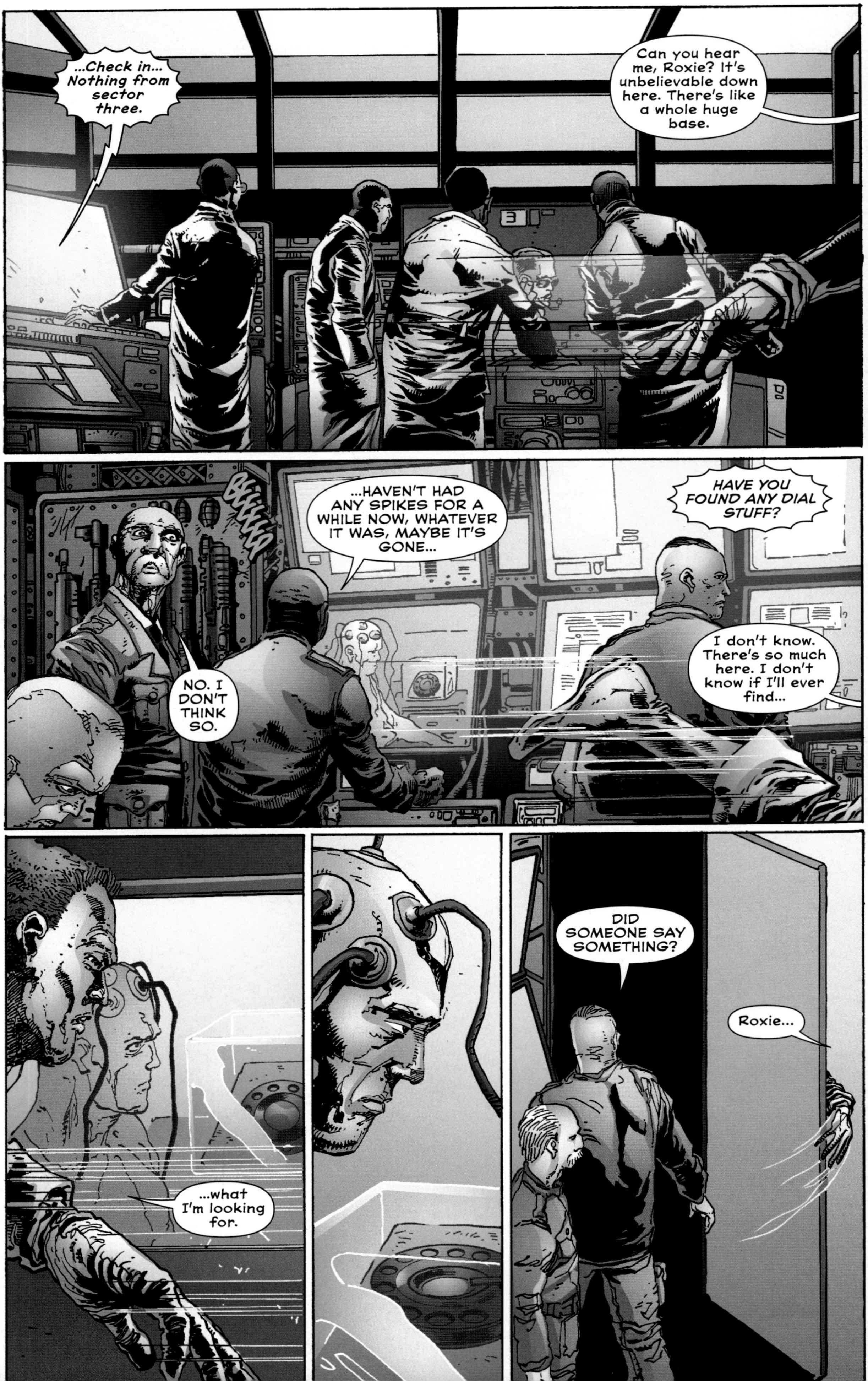
...Check in... Nothing from sector three.
Can you hear me, Roxie? It's unbelievable down here. There's like a whole huge base.
...HAVEN'T HAD ANY SPIKES FOR A WHILE NOW, WHATEVER IT WAS, MAYBE IT'S GONE...
HAVE YOU FOUND ANY DIAL STUFF?
NO. I DON'T THINK SO.
I don't know. There's so much here. I don't know if I'll ever find...
...what I'm looking for.
DID SOMEONE SAY SOMETHING?
Roxie...

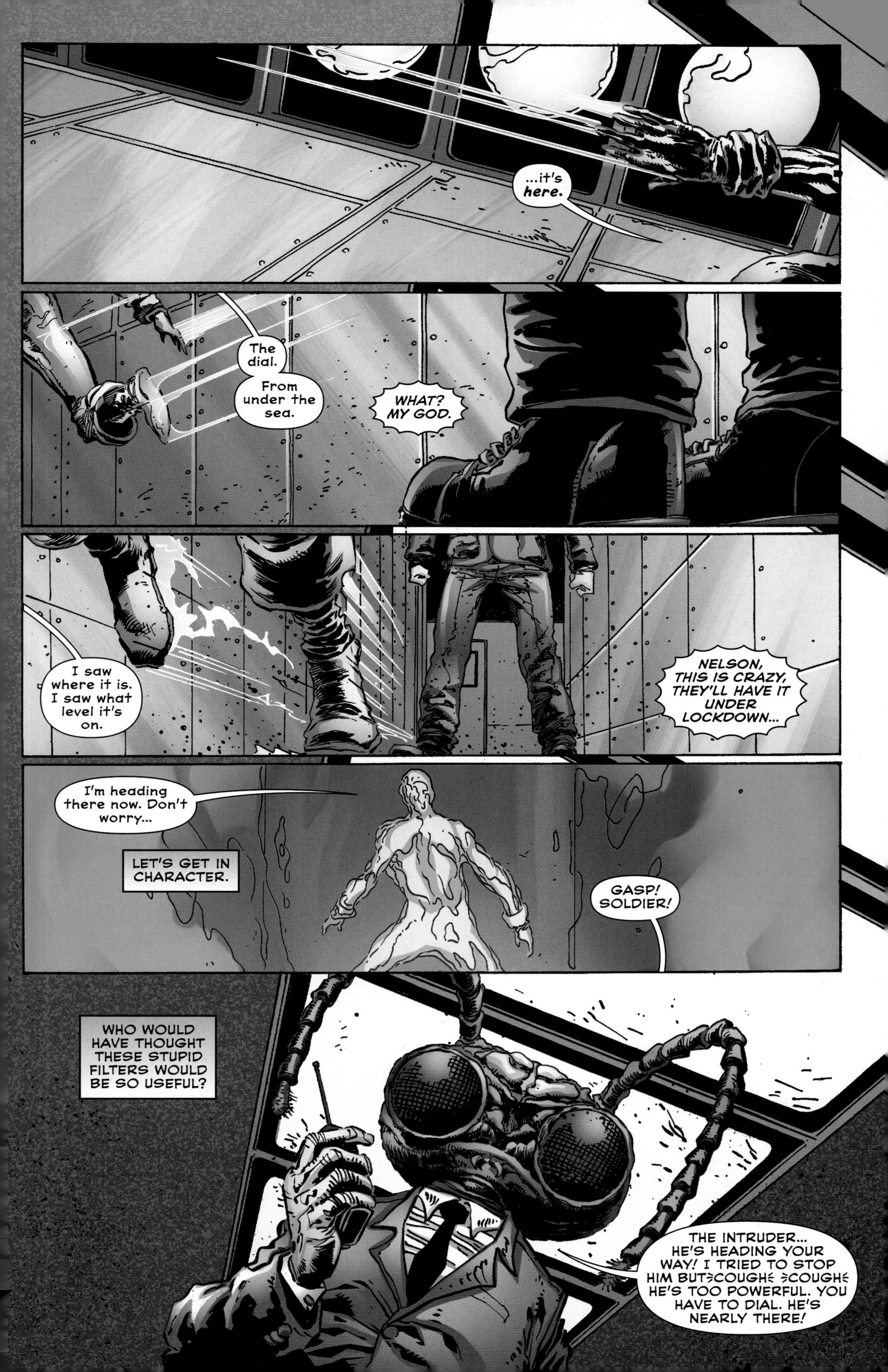
...it's here.
The dial.
From under the sea.
WHAT? MY GOD.
I saw where it is. I saw what level it's on.
NELSON, THIS IS CRAZY, THEY'LL HAVE IT UNDER LOCKDOWN...
I'm heading there now. Don't worry...
LET'S GET IN CHARACTER.
GASP! SOLDIER!
WHO WOULD HAVE THOUGHT THESE STUPID FILTERS WOULD BE SO USEFUL?
THE INTRUDER... HE'S HEADING YOUR WAY! I TRIED TO STOP HIM BUT *COUGH* *COUGH* HE'S TOO POWERFUL. YOU HAVE TO DIAL. HE'S NEARLY THERE!

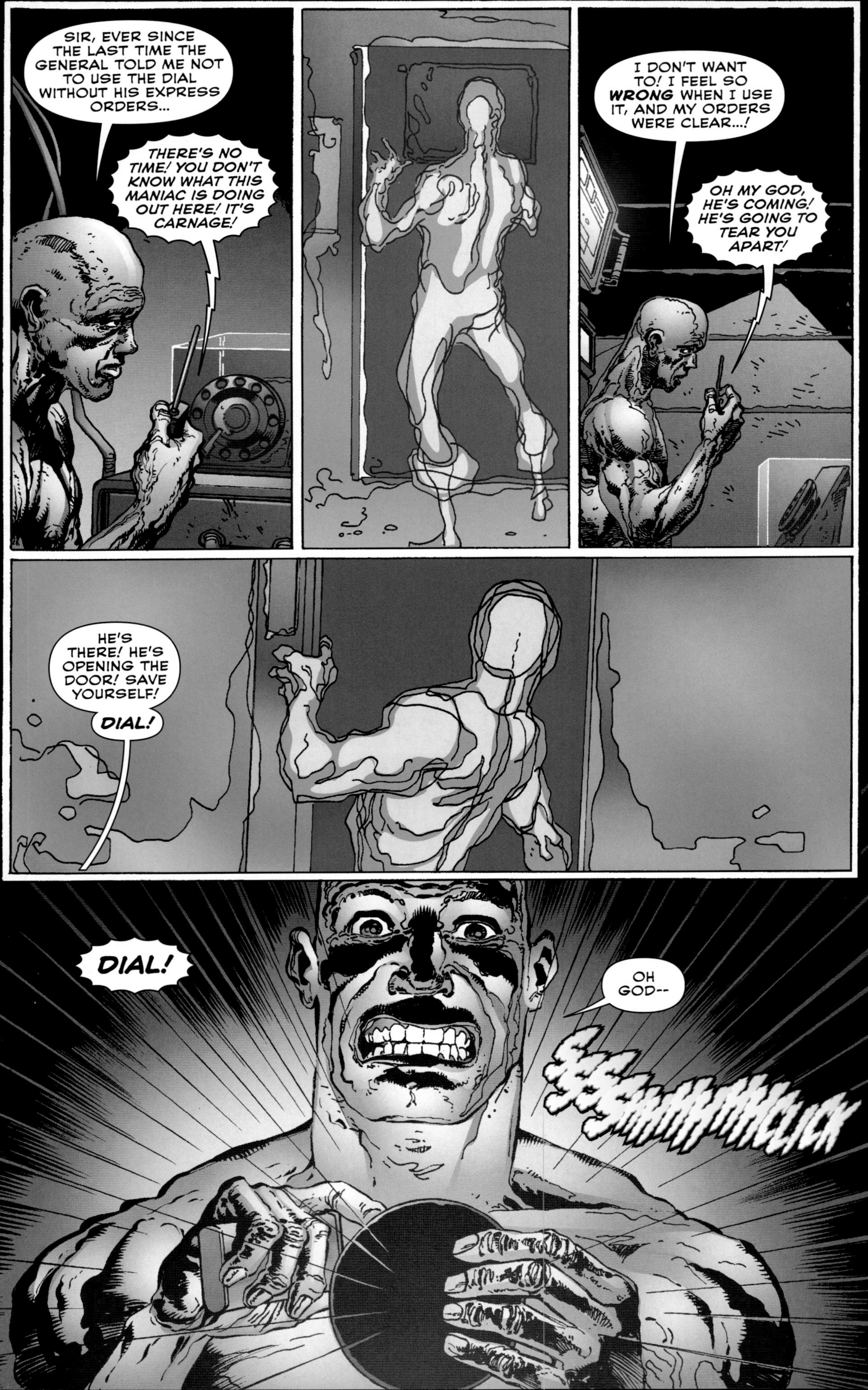
SIR, EVER SINCE THE LAST TIME THE GENERAL TOLD ME NOT TO USE THE DIAL WITHOUT HIS EXPRESS ORDERS...
THERE'S NO TIME! YOU DON'T KNOW WHAT THIS MANIAC IS DOING OUT HERE! IT'S CARNAGE!
I DON'T WANT TO! I FEEL SO **WRONG** WHEN I USE IT, AND MY ORDERS WERE CLEAR...!
OH MY GOD, HE'S COMING! HE'S GOING TO TEAR YOU APART!
HE'S THERE! HE'S OPENING THE DOOR! SAVE YOURSELF!
DIAL!
DIAL!
OH GOD--
SKRRRRRRRCLICK

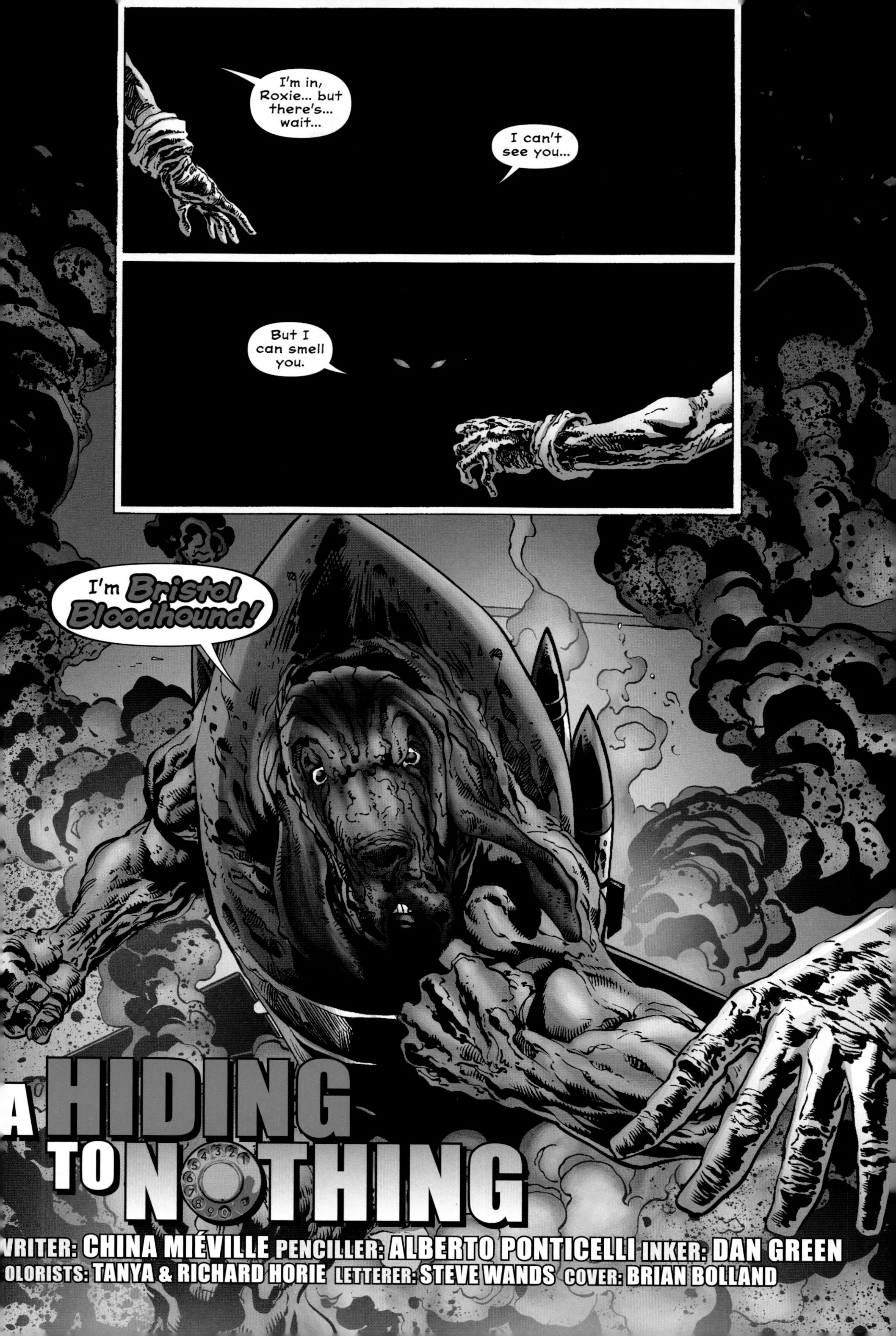

I'm in, Roxie... but there's... wait...
I can't see you...
But I can smell you.
I'm Bristol Bloodhound!
A HIDING TO NOTHING
WRITER: CHINA MIÉVILLE PENCILLER: ALBERTO PONTICELLI INKER: DAN GREEN
COLORISTS: TANYA & RICHARD HORIE LETTERER: STEVE WANDS COVER: BRIAN BOLLAND

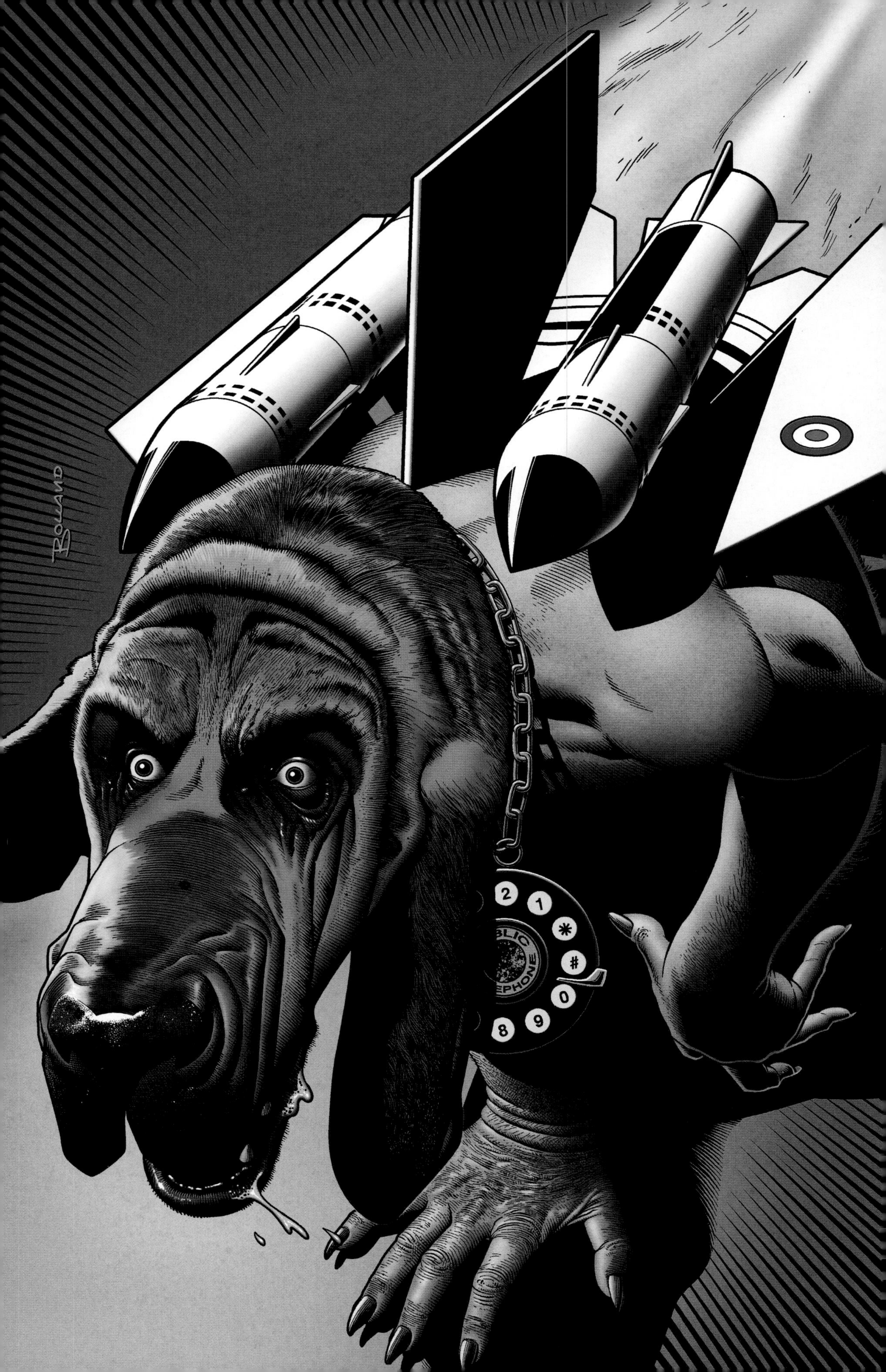
BOLLAND
BLIC
EPHONE

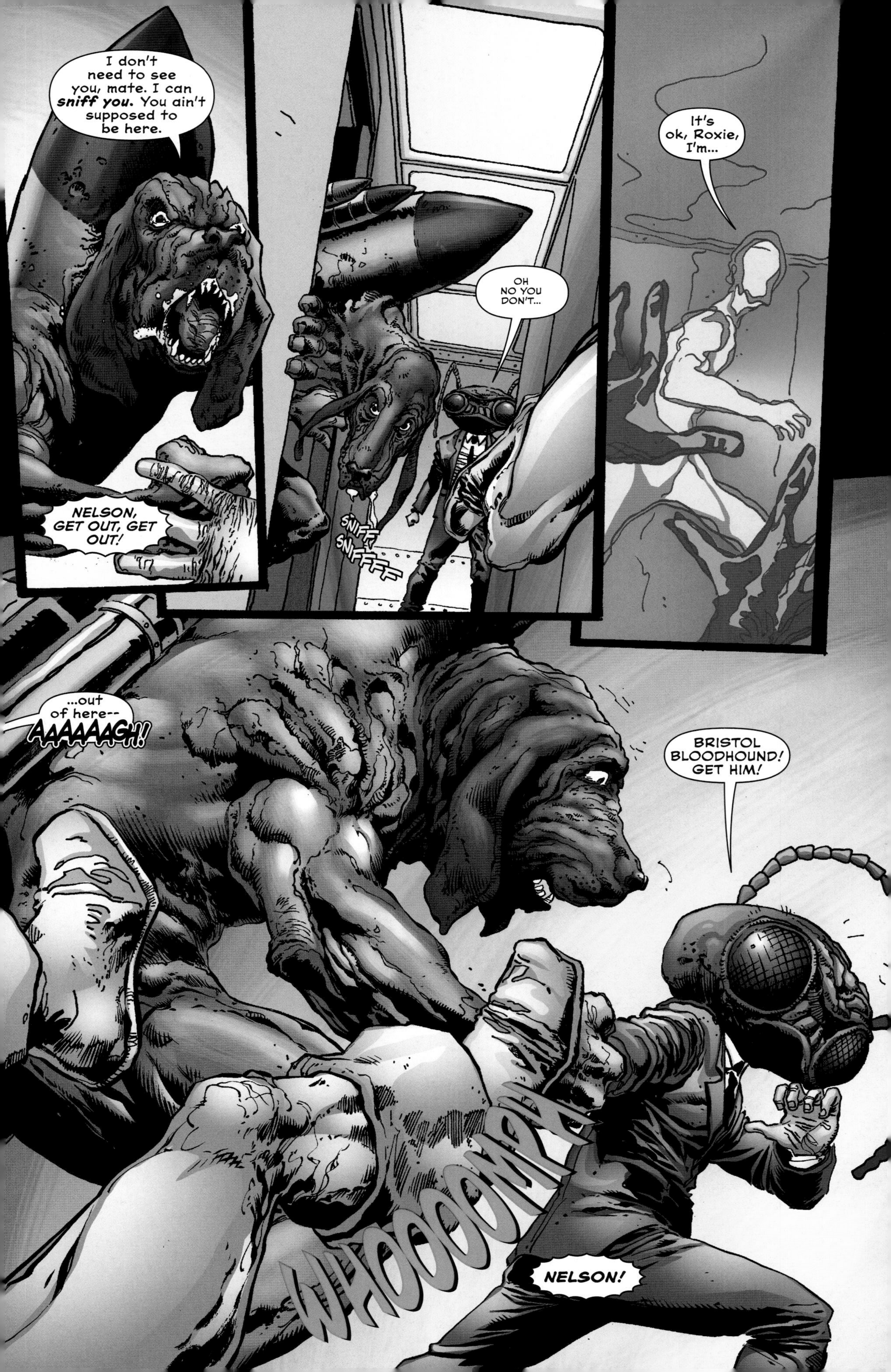
I don't need to see you, mate. I can **sniff you.** You ain't supposed to be here.
NELSON, GET OUT, GET OUT!
OH NO YOU DON'T...
SNIFF
SNIFFFFF
It's ok, Roxie, I'm...
...out of here--
AAAAAAGH!
BRISTOL BLOODHOUND! GET HIM!
WHOOOOMPH
NELSON!

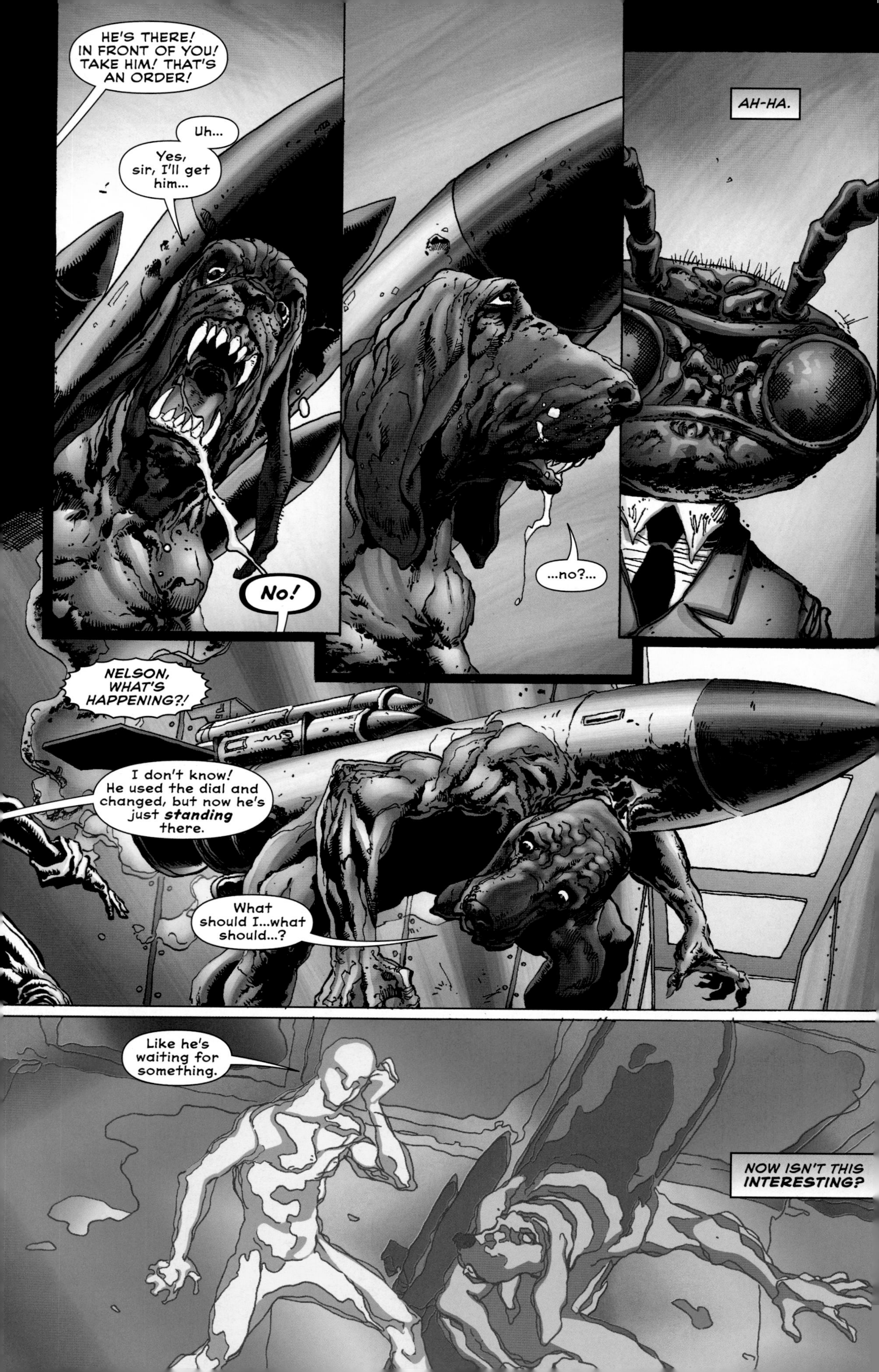
HE'S THERE! IN FRONT OF YOU! TAKE HIM! THAT'S AN ORDER!
Uh...
Yes, sir, I'll get him...
No!
...no?...
AH-HA.
NELSON, WHAT'S HAPPENING?!
I don't know! He used the dial and changed, but now he's just standing there.
What should I...what should...?
Like he's waiting for something.
NOW ISN'T THIS INTERESTING?

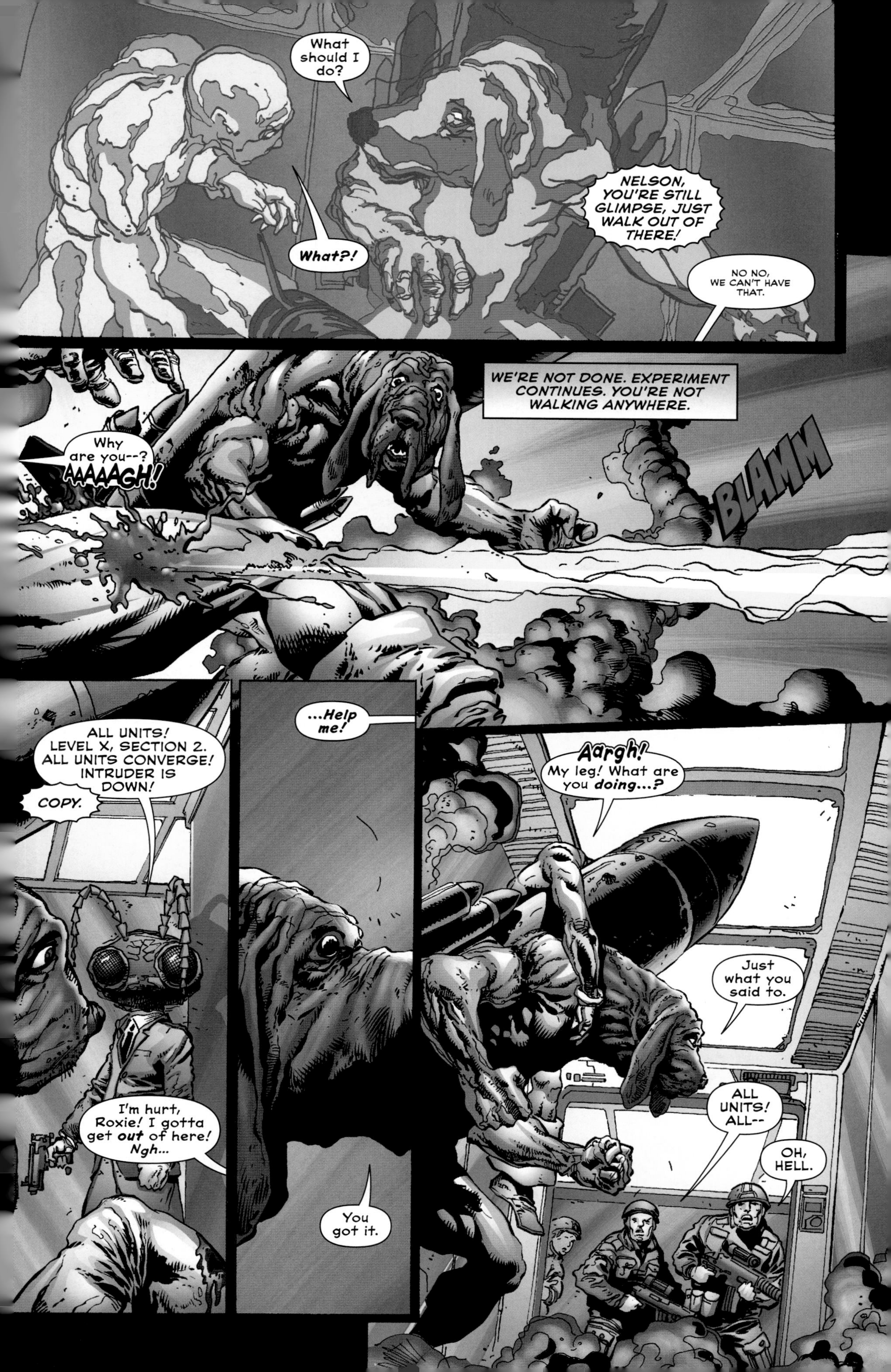
What should I do?
NELSON, YOU'RE STILL GLIMPSE, JUST WALK OUT OF THERE!
What?!
NO NO, WE CAN'T HAVE THAT.
WE'RE NOT DONE. EXPERIMENT CONTINUES. YOU'RE NOT WALKING ANYWHERE.
Why are you--? AAAAAGH!
BLAMM
ALL UNITS! LEVEL X, SECTION 2. ALL UNITS CONVERGE! INTRUDER IS DOWN!
COPY.
...Help me!
Aargh! My leg! What are you doing...?
Just what you said to.
I'm hurt, Roxie! I gotta get out of here! Ngh...
You got it.
ALL UNITS! ALL--
OH, HELL.

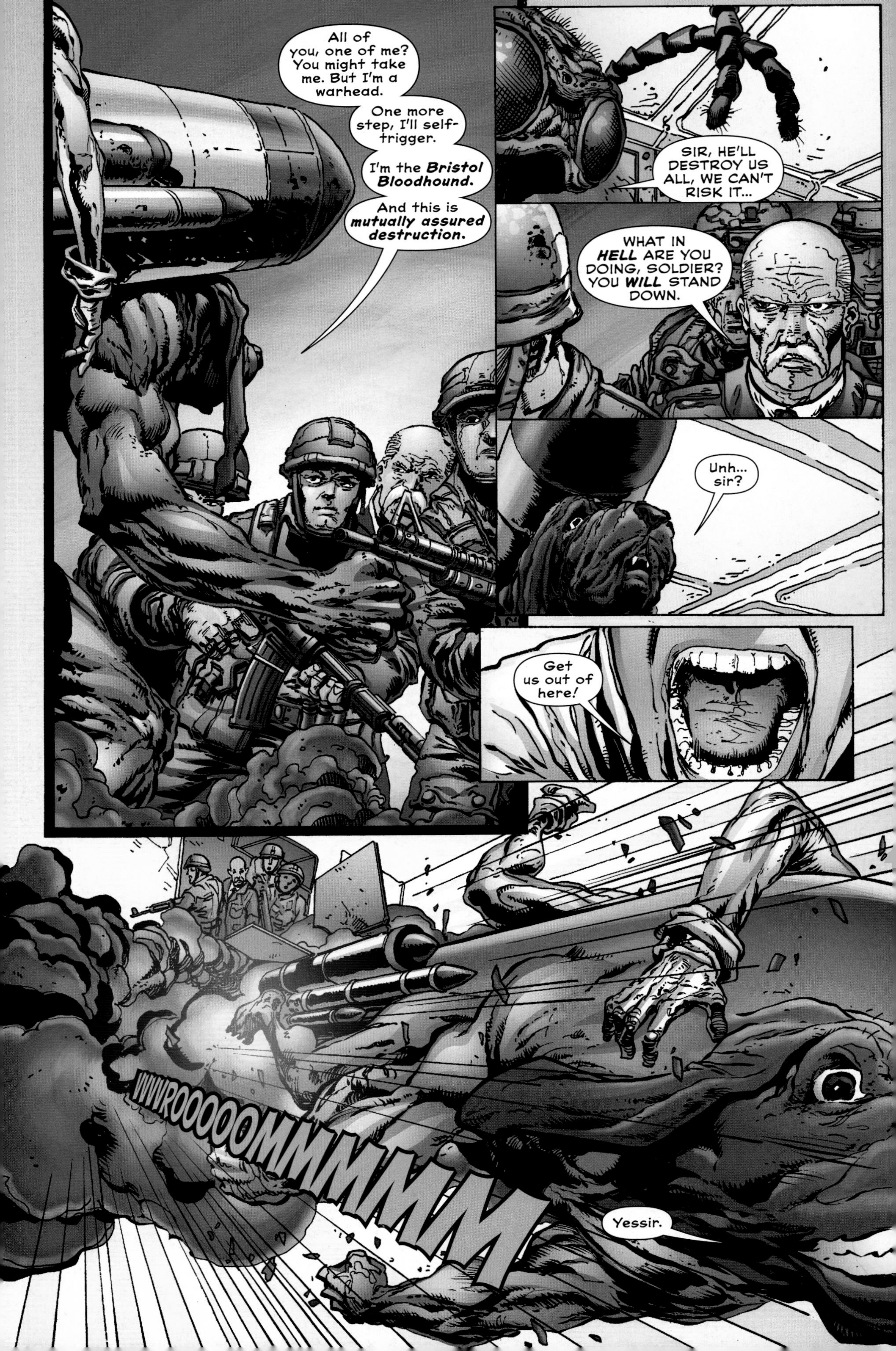
All of you, one of me? You might take me. But I'm a warhead.
One more step, I'll self-trigger.
I'm the Bristol Bloodhound.
And this is mutually assured destruction.
SIR, HE'LL DESTROY US ALL, WE CAN'T RISK IT...
WHAT IN HELL ARE YOU DOING, SOLDIER? YOU WILL STAND DOWN.
Unh... sir?
Get us out of here!
VVVVROOOOOOMMMMMMMM
Yessir.

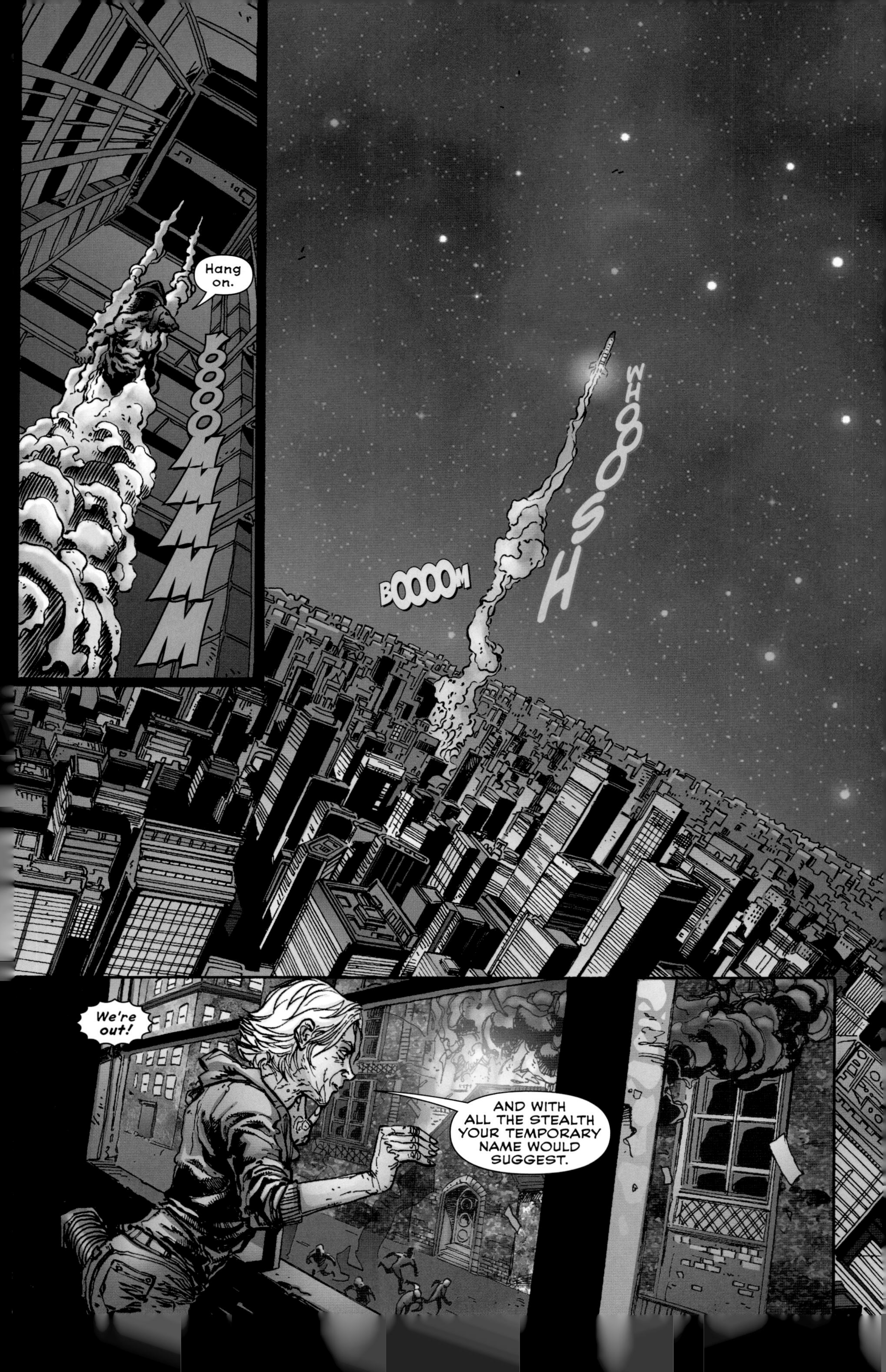
Hang on.
VOOOOMMMMMMM
WHOOOOSH
BOOOOM
We're out!
AND WITH ALL THE STEALTH YOUR TEMPORARY NAME WOULD SUGGEST.

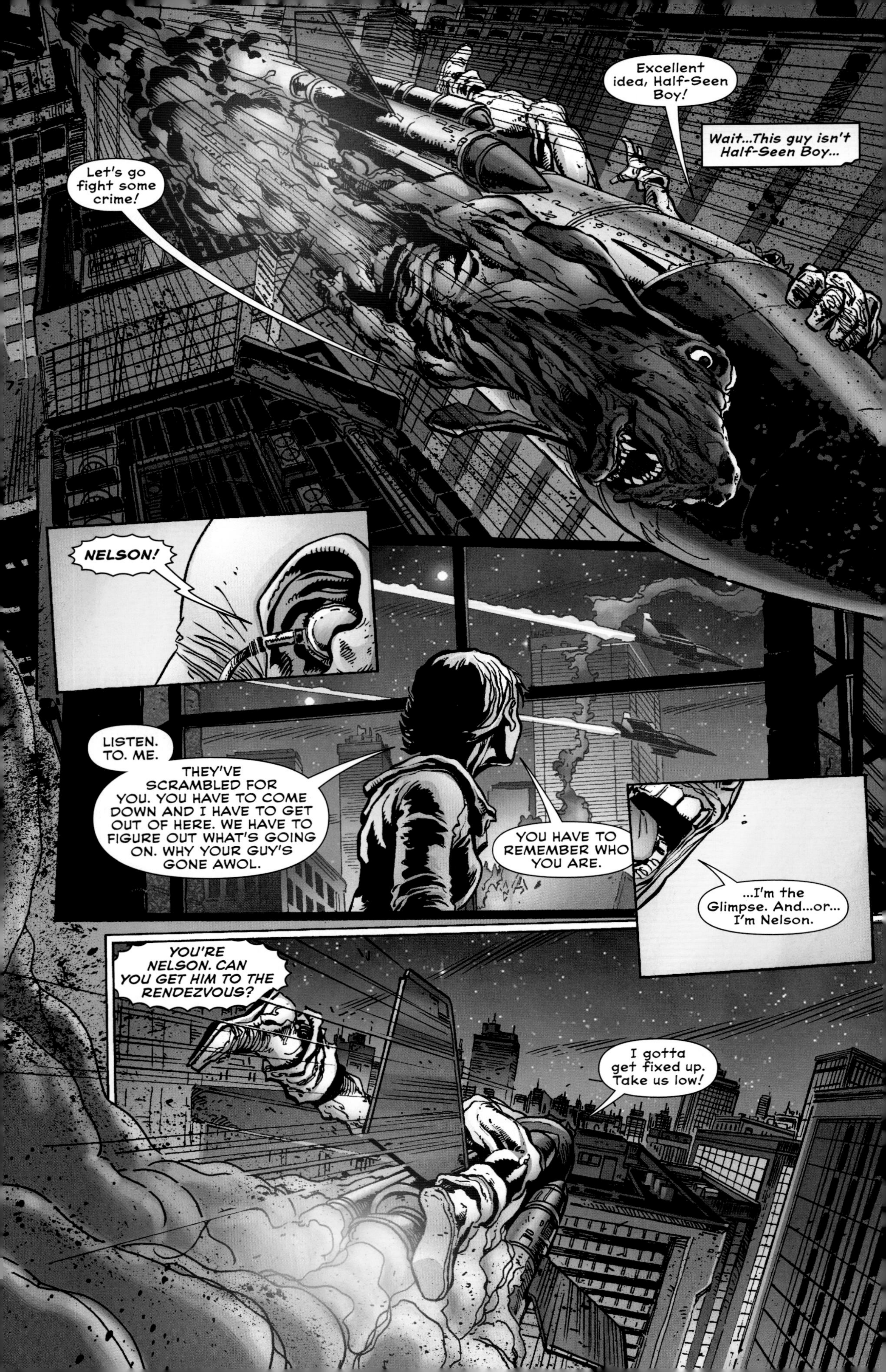

Excellent idea, Half-Seen Boy!
Wait...This guy isn't Half-Seen Boy...
Let's go fight some crime!
NELSON!
LISTEN. TO. ME.
THEY'VE SCRAMBLED FOR YOU. YOU HAVE TO COME DOWN AND I HAVE TO GET OUT OF HERE. WE HAVE TO FIGURE OUT WHAT'S GOING ON. WHY YOUR GUY'S GONE AWOL.
YOU HAVE TO REMEMBER WHO YOU ARE.
...I'm the Glimpse. And...or... I'm Nelson.
YOU'RE NELSON. CAN YOU GET HIM TO THE RENDEZVOUS?
I gotta get fixed up. Take us low!

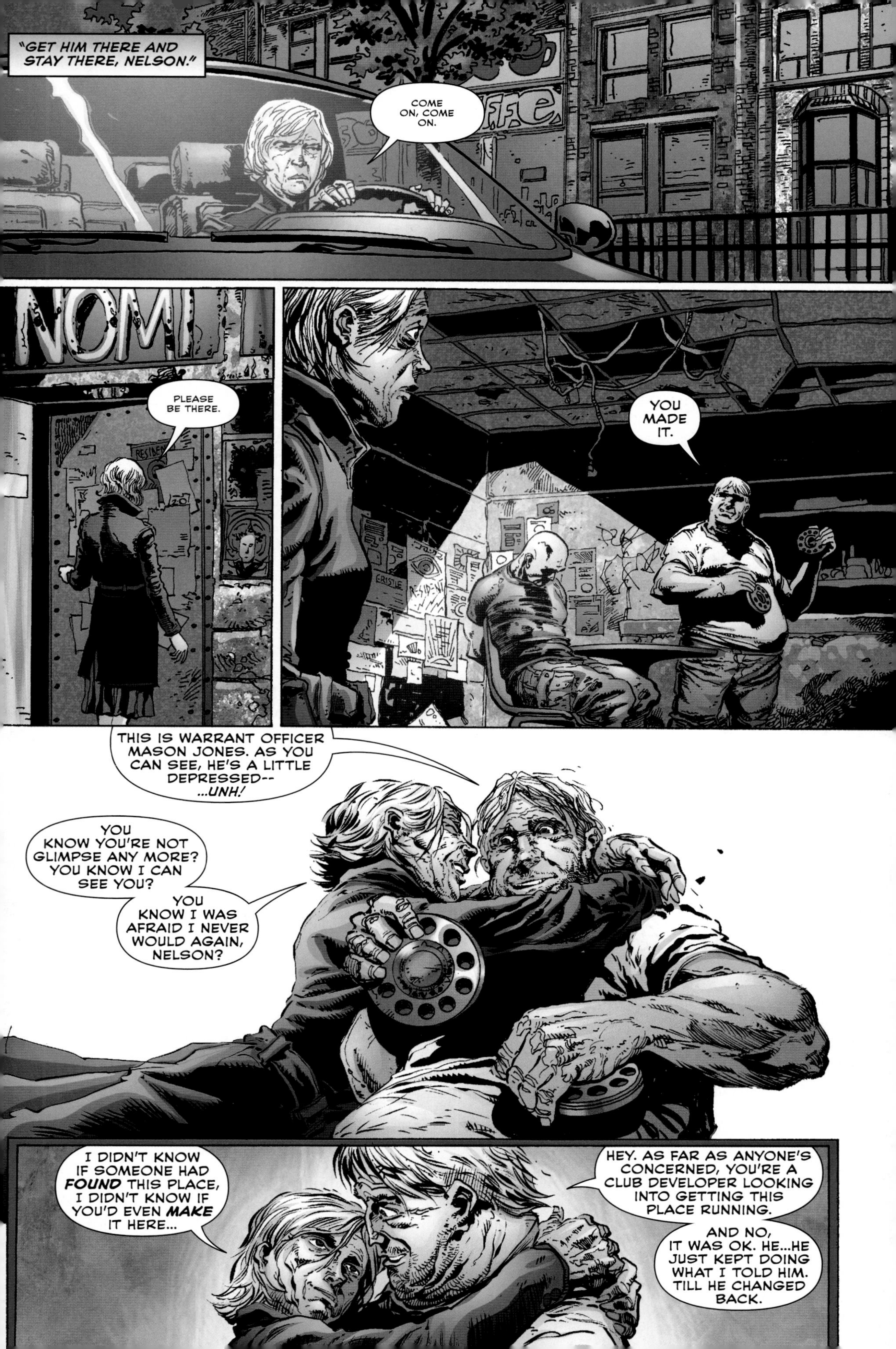
"GET HIM THERE AND STAY THERE, NELSON."
COME ON, COME ON.
PLEASE BE THERE.
YOU MADE IT.
THIS IS WARRANT OFFICER MASON JONES. AS YOU CAN SEE, HE'S A LITTLE DEPRESSED-- ...UNH!
YOU KNOW YOU'RE NOT GLIMPSE ANY MORE? YOU KNOW I CAN SEE YOU?
YOU KNOW I WAS AFRAID I NEVER WOULD AGAIN, NELSON?
I DIDN'T KNOW IF SOMEONE HAD **FOUND** THIS PLACE, I DIDN'T KNOW IF YOU'D EVEN **MAKE** IT HERE...
HEY. AS FAR AS ANYONE'S CONCERNED, YOU'RE A CLUB DEVELOPER LOOKING INTO GETTING THIS PLACE RUNNING.
AND NO, IT WAS OK. HE...HE JUST KEPT DOING WHAT I TOLD HIM. TILL HE CHANGED BACK.

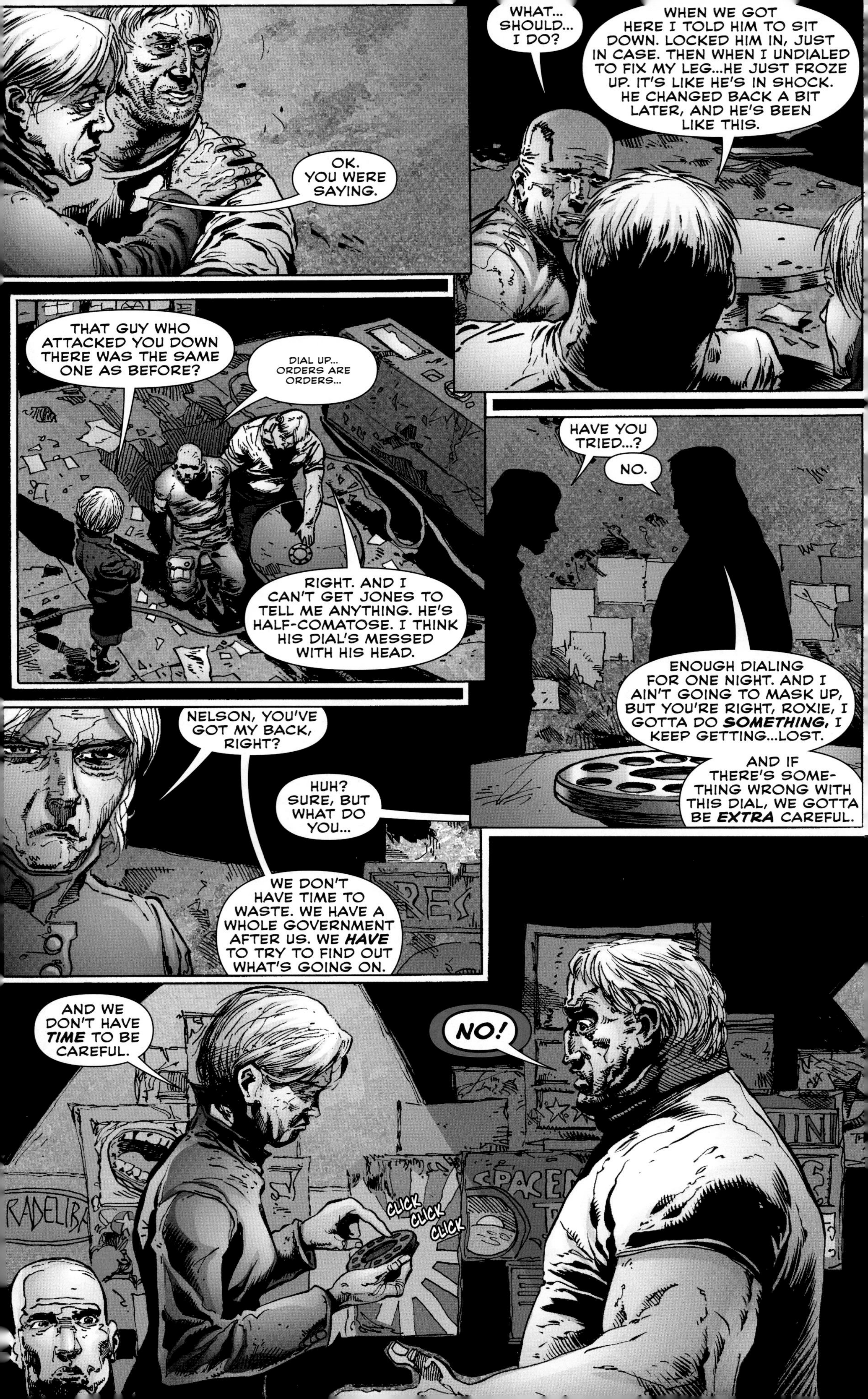
OK. YOU WERE SAYING.
WHAT... SHOULD... I DO?
WHEN WE GOT HERE I TOLD HIM TO SIT DOWN. LOCKED HIM IN, JUST IN CASE. THEN WHEN I UNDIALED TO FIX MY LEG...HE JUST FROZE UP. IT'S LIKE HE'S IN SHOCK. HE CHANGED BACK A BIT LATER, AND HE'S BEEN LIKE THIS.
THAT GUY WHO ATTACKED YOU DOWN THERE WAS THE SAME ONE AS BEFORE?
DIAL UP... ORDERS ARE ORDERS...
RIGHT. AND I CAN'T GET JONES TO TELL ME ANYTHING. HE'S HALF-COMATOSE. I THINK HIS DIAL'S MESSED WITH HIS HEAD.
HAVE YOU TRIED...?
NO.
ENOUGH DIALING FOR ONE NIGHT. AND I AIN'T GOING TO MASK UP, BUT YOU'RE RIGHT, ROXIE, I GOTTA DO ***SOMETHING,*** I KEEP GETTING...LOST.
AND IF THERE'S SOMETHING WRONG WITH THIS DIAL, WE GOTTA BE ***EXTRA*** CAREFUL.
NELSON, YOU'VE GOT MY BACK, RIGHT?
HUH? SURE, BUT WHAT DO YOU...
WE DON'T HAVE TIME TO WASTE. WE HAVE A WHOLE GOVERNMENT AFTER US. WE ***HAVE*** TO TRY TO FIND OUT WHAT'S GOING ON.
AND WE DON'T HAVE ***TIME*** TO BE CAREFUL.
NO!
CLICK CLICK CLICK

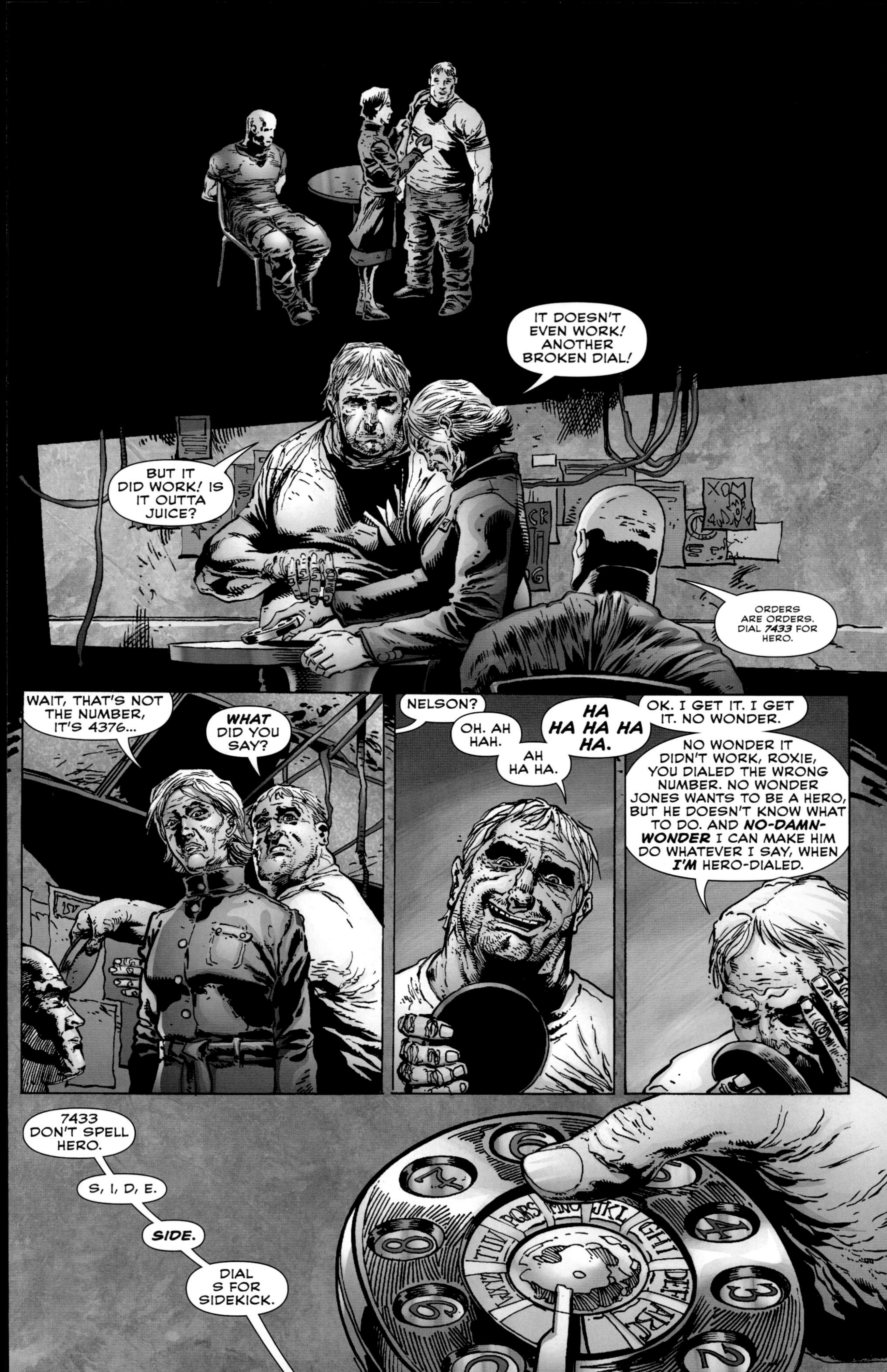
IT DOESN'T EVEN WORK! ANOTHER BROKEN DIAL!
BUT IT DID WORK! IS IT OUTTA JUICE?
ORDERS ARE ORDERS. DIAL 7433 FOR HERO.
WAIT, THAT'S NOT THE NUMBER, IT'S 4376...
WHAT DID YOU SAY?
NELSON?
OH. AH HAH.
AH HA HA.
HA HA HA HA HA.
OK. I GET IT. I GET IT. NO WONDER.
NO WONDER IT DIDN'T WORK, ROXIE, YOU DIALED THE WRONG NUMBER. NO WONDER JONES WANTS TO BE A HERO, BUT HE DOESN'T KNOW WHAT TO DO. AND NO-DAMN-WONDER I CAN MAKE HIM DO WHATEVER I SAY, WHEN I'M HERO-DIALED.
7433 DON'T SPELL HERO.
S, I, D, E.
SIDE.
DIAL S FOR SIDEKICK.

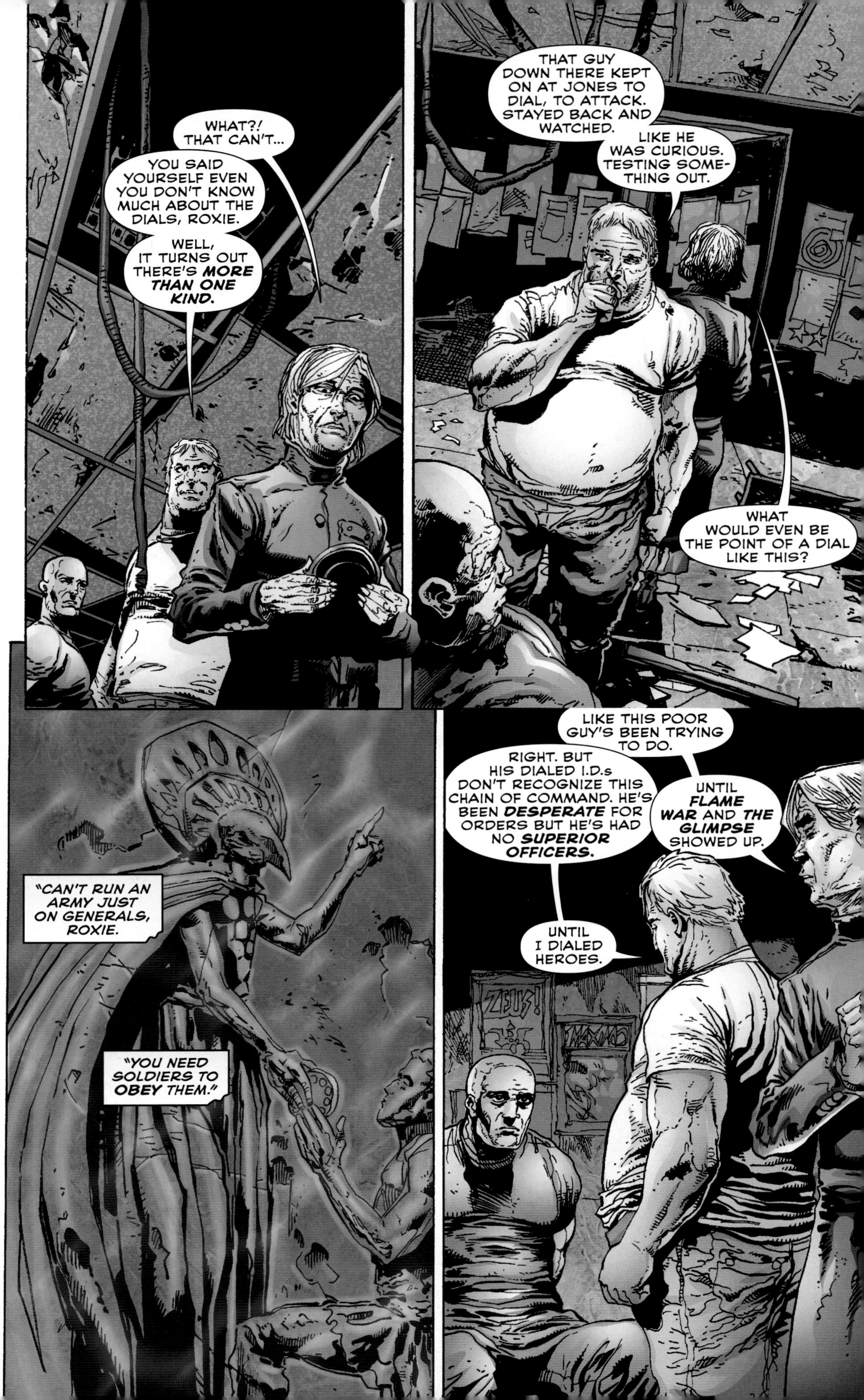

WHAT?! THAT CAN'T...
YOU SAID YOURSELF EVEN YOU DON'T KNOW MUCH ABOUT THE DIALS, ROXIE.
WELL, IT TURNS OUT THERE'S MORE THAN ONE KIND.
THAT GUY DOWN THERE KEPT ON AT JONES TO DIAL, TO ATTACK. STAYED BACK AND WATCHED.
LIKE HE WAS CURIOUS. TESTING SOME-THING OUT.
WHAT WOULD EVEN BE THE POINT OF A DIAL LIKE THIS?
"CAN'T RUN AN ARMY JUST ON GENERALS, ROXIE.
"YOU NEED SOLDIERS TO OBEY THEM."
LIKE THIS POOR GUY'S BEEN TRYING TO DO.
RIGHT. BUT HIS DIALED I.D.s DON'T RECOGNIZE THIS CHAIN OF COMMAND. HE'S BEEN DESPERATE FOR ORDERS BUT HE'S HAD NO SUPERIOR OFFICERS.
UNTIL FLAME WAR AND THE GLIMPSE SHOWED UP.
UNTIL I DIALED HEROES.
ZEUS!
MAXIMO

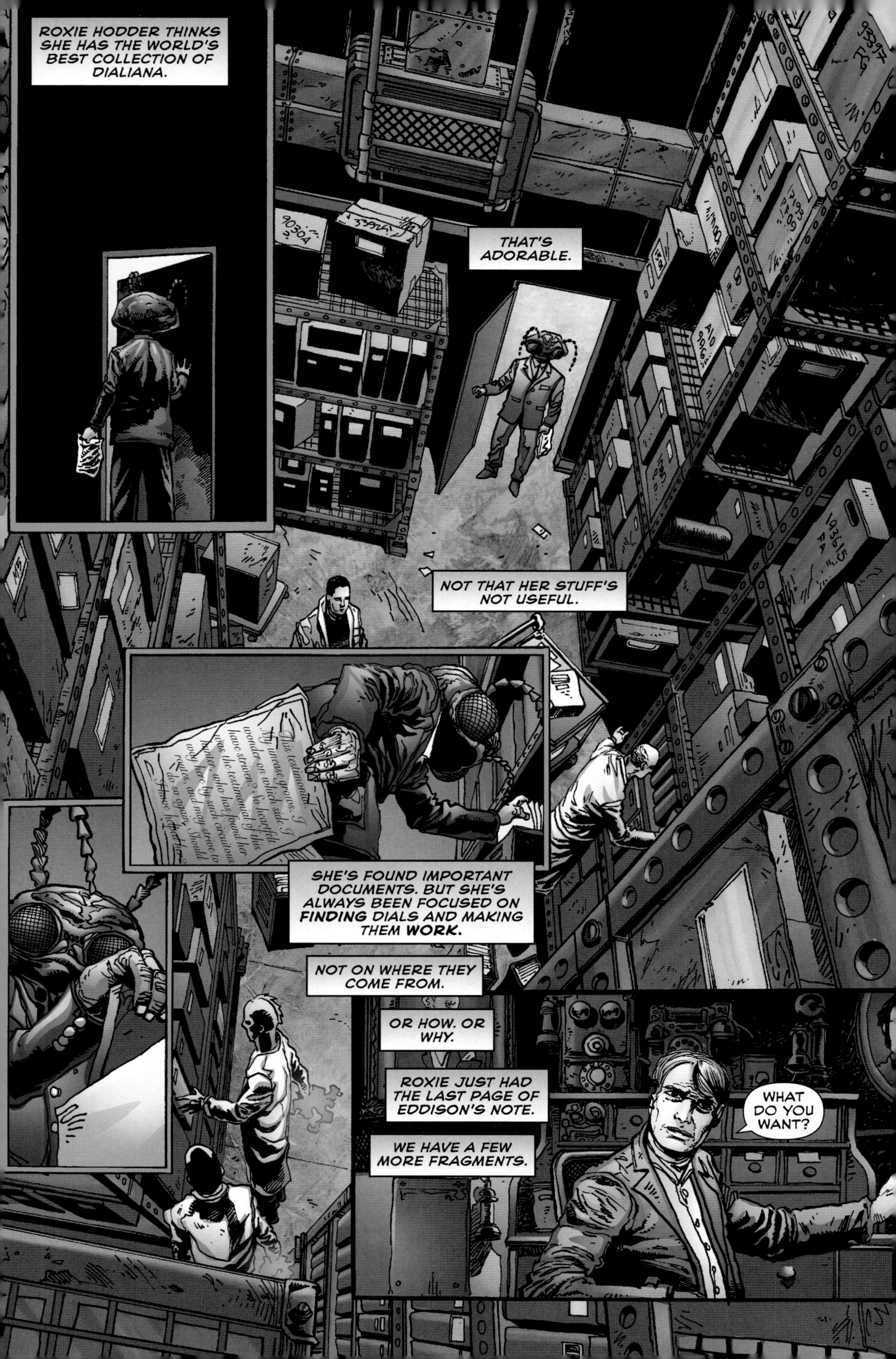
ROXIE HODDER THINKS SHE HAS THE WORLD'S BEST COLLECTION OF DIALIANA.
THAT'S ADORABLE.
NOT THAT HER STUFF'S NOT USEFUL.
SHE'S FOUND IMPORTANT DOCUMENTS. BUT SHE'S ALWAYS BEEN FOCUSED ON FINDING DIALS AND MAKING THEM WORK.
NOT ON WHERE THEY COME FROM.
OR HOW. OR WHY.
ROXIE JUST HAD THE LAST PAGE OF EDDISON'S NOTE.
WE HAVE A FEW MORE FRAGMENTS.
WHAT DO YOU WANT?

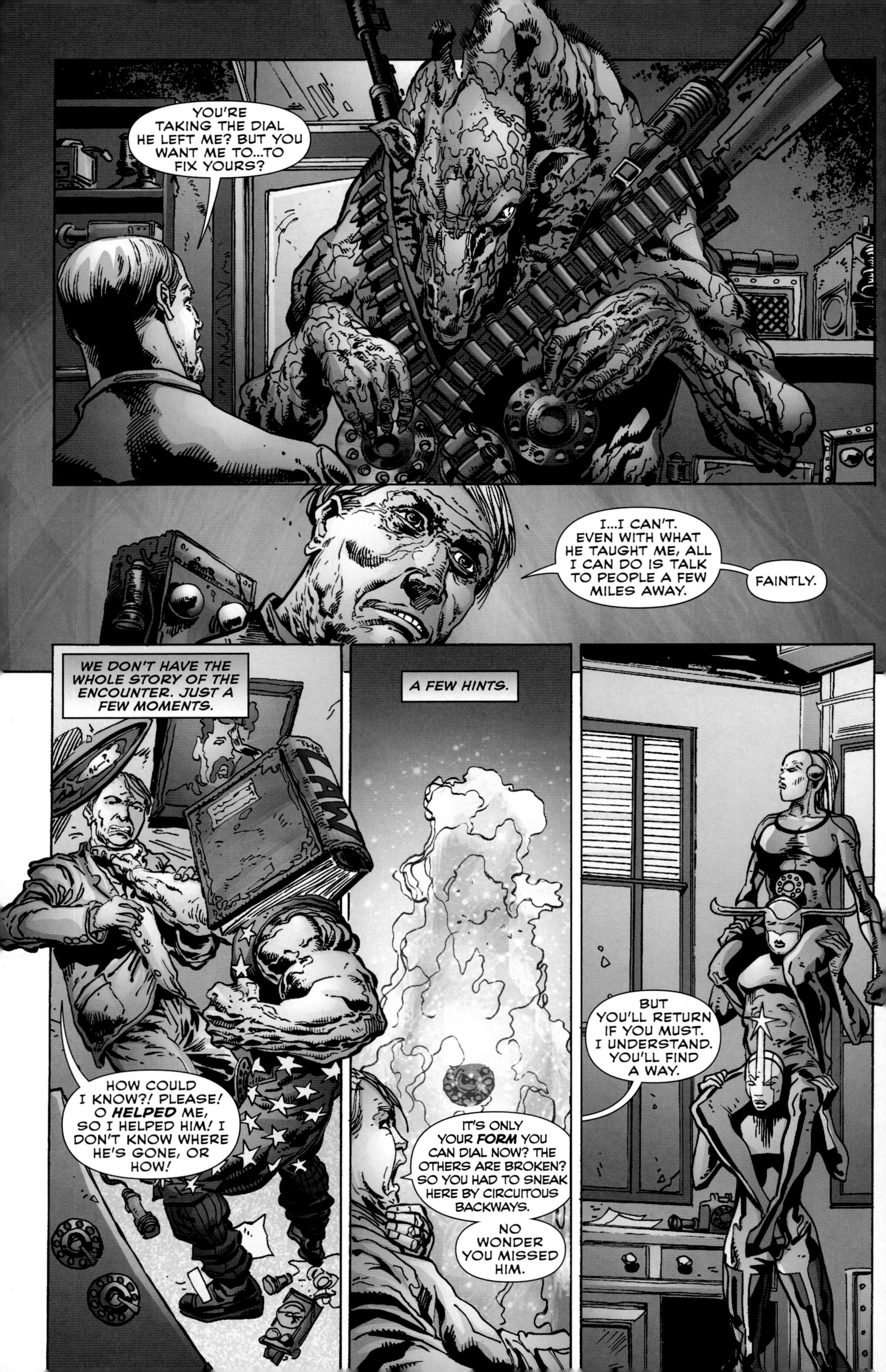
YOU'RE TAKING THE DIAL HE LEFT ME? BUT YOU WANT ME TO...TO FIX YOURS?
I...I CAN'T. EVEN WITH WHAT HE TAUGHT ME, ALL I CAN DO IS TALK TO PEOPLE A FEW MILES AWAY.
FAINTLY.
WE DON'T HAVE THE WHOLE STORY OF THE ENCOUNTER. JUST A FEW MOMENTS.
HOW COULD I KNOW?! PLEASE! O HELPED ME, SO I HELPED HIM! I DON'T KNOW WHERE HE'S GONE, OR HOW!
A FEW HINTS.
IT'S ONLY YOUR FORM YOU CAN DIAL NOW? THE OTHERS ARE BROKEN? SO YOU HAD TO SNEAK HERE BY CIRCUITOUS BACKWAYS.
NO WONDER YOU MISSED HIM.
BUT YOU'LL RETURN IF YOU MUST. I UNDERSTAND. YOU'LL FIND A WAY.

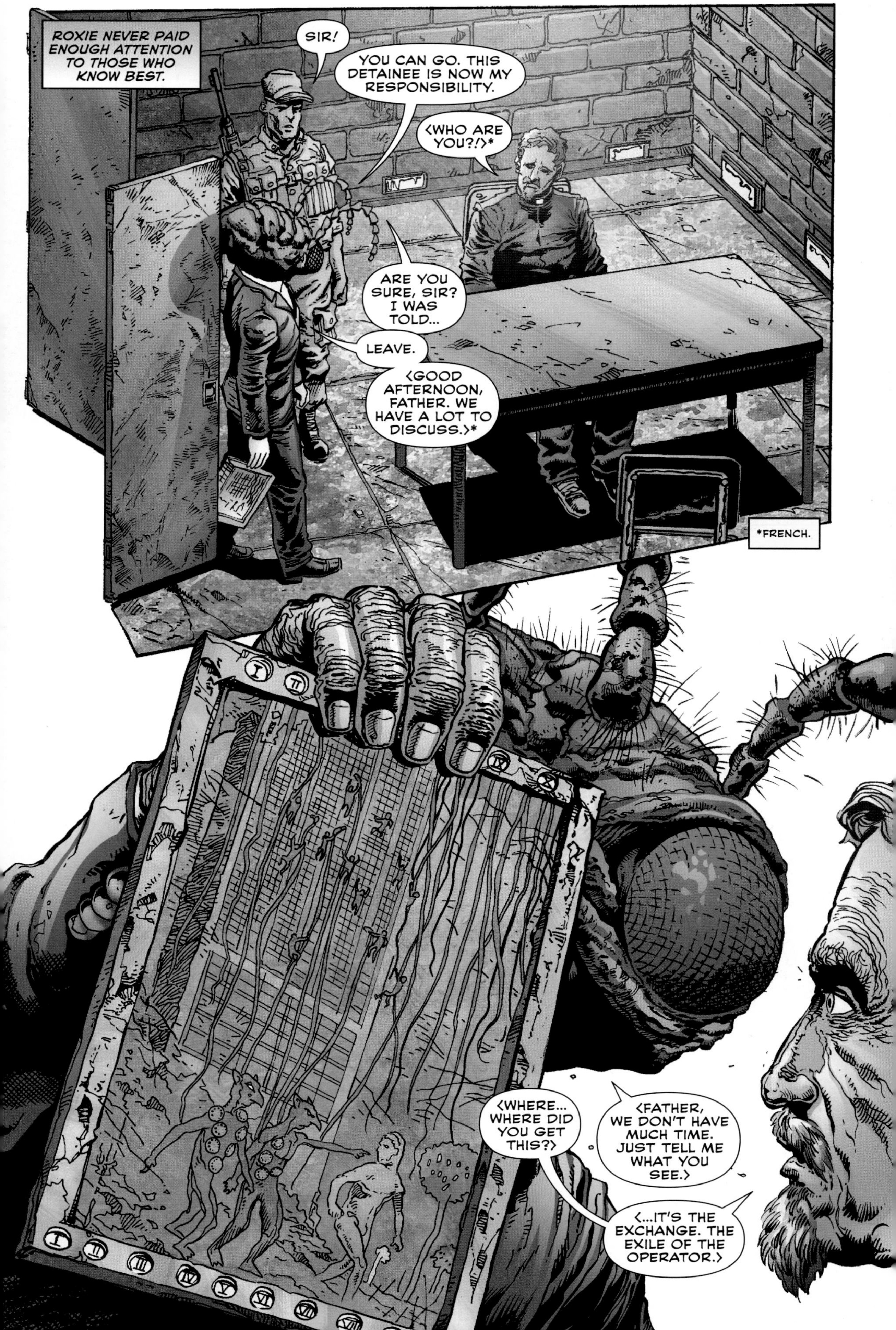
ROXIE NEVER PAID ENOUGH ATTENTION TO THOSE WHO KNOW BEST.
SIR!
YOU CAN GO. THIS DETAINEE IS NOW MY RESPONSIBILITY.
<WHO ARE YOU?!>*
ARE YOU SURE, SIR? I WAS TOLD...
LEAVE.
<GOOD AFTERNOON, FATHER. WE HAVE A LOT TO DISCUSS.>*
*FRENCH.
<WHERE... WHERE DID YOU GET THIS?>
<FATHER, WE DON'T HAVE MUCH TIME. JUST TELL ME WHAT YOU SEE.>
<...IT'S THE EXCHANGE. THE EXILE OF THE OPERATOR.>

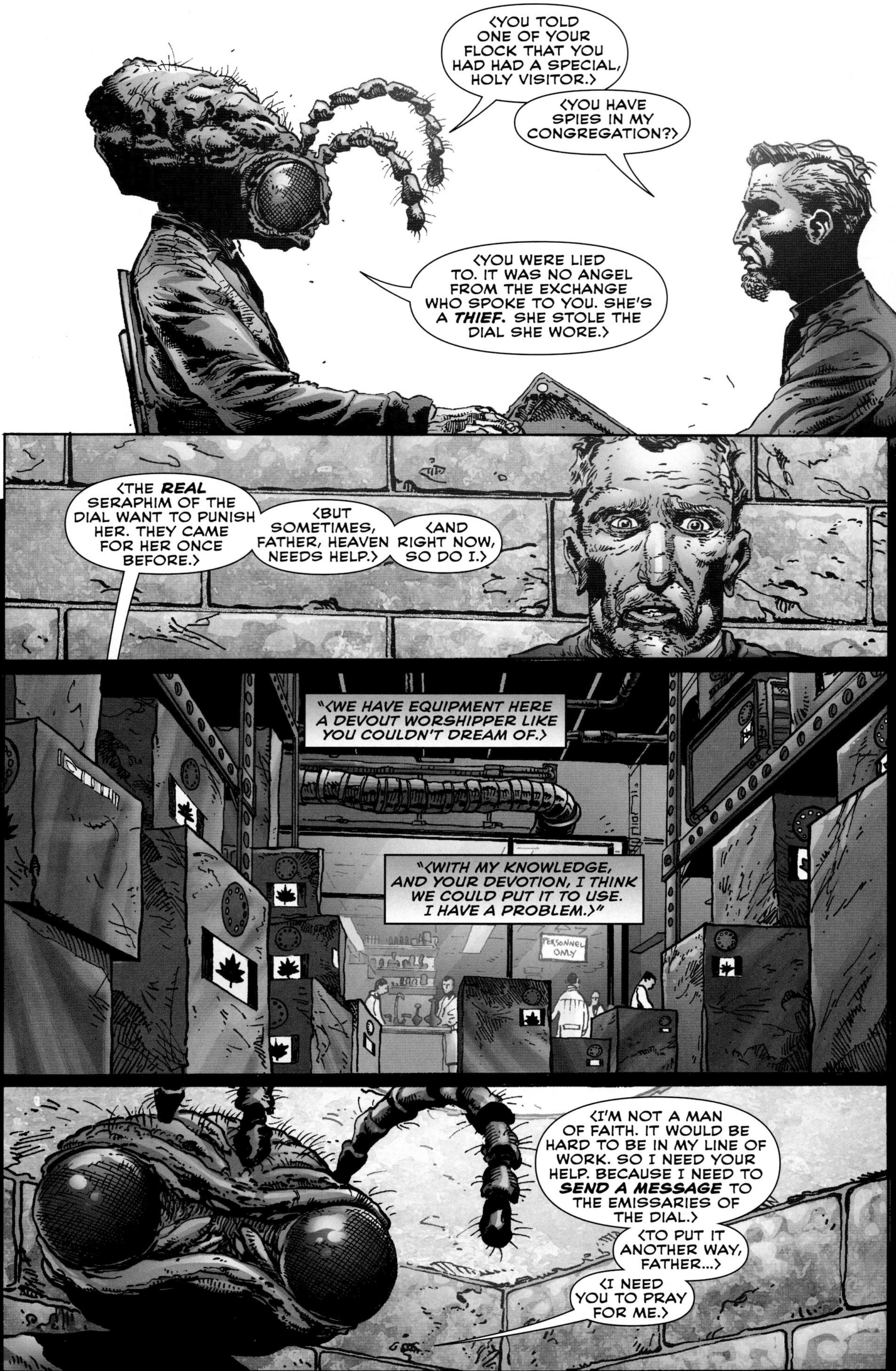

<YOU TOLD ONE OF YOUR FLOCK THAT YOU HAD HAD A SPECIAL, HOLY VISITOR.>
<YOU HAVE SPIES IN MY CONGREGATION?>
<YOU WERE LIED TO. IT WAS NO ANGEL FROM THE EXCHANGE WHO SPOKE TO YOU. SHE'S A *THIEF.* SHE STOLE THE DIAL SHE WORE.>
<THE *REAL* SERAPHIM OF THE DIAL WANT TO PUNISH HER. THEY CAME FOR HER ONCE BEFORE.>
<BUT SOMETIMES, FATHER, HEAVEN NEEDS HELP.>
<AND RIGHT NOW, SO DO I.>
"<WE HAVE EQUIPMENT HERE A DEVOUT WORSHIPPER LIKE YOU COULDN'T DREAM OF.>
"<WITH MY KNOWLEDGE, AND YOUR DEVOTION, I THINK WE COULD PUT IT TO USE. I HAVE A PROBLEM.>"
PERSONNEL ONLY
<I'M NOT A MAN OF FAITH. IT WOULD BE HARD TO BE IN MY LINE OF WORK. SO I NEED YOUR HELP. BECAUSE I NEED TO *SEND A MESSAGE* TO THE EMISSARIES OF THE DIAL.>
<TO PUT IT ANOTHER WAY, FATHER...>
<I NEED YOU TO PRAY FOR ME.>

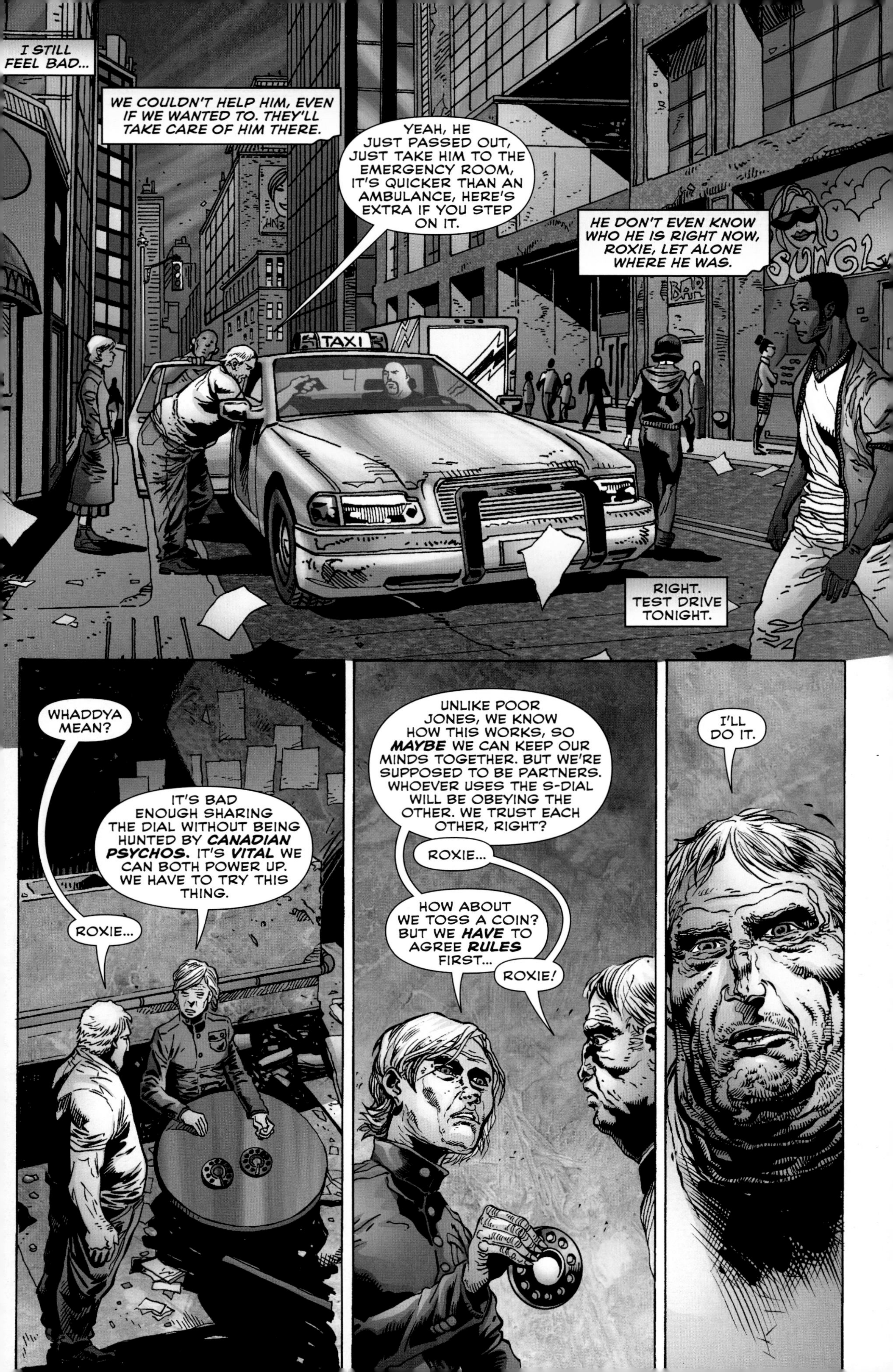
I STILL FEEL BAD...
WE COULDN'T HELP HIM, EVEN IF WE WANTED TO. THEY'LL TAKE CARE OF HIM THERE.
YEAH, HE JUST PASSED OUT, JUST TAKE HIM TO THE EMERGENCY ROOM, IT'S QUICKER THAN AN AMBULANCE, HERE'S EXTRA IF YOU STEP ON IT.
HE DON'T EVEN KNOW WHO HE IS RIGHT NOW, ROXIE, LET ALONE WHERE HE WAS.
RIGHT. TEST DRIVE TONIGHT.
TAXI
WHADDYA MEAN?
IT'S BAD ENOUGH SHARING THE DIAL WITHOUT BEING HUNTED BY ***CANADIAN PSYCHOS.*** IT'S ***VITAL*** WE CAN BOTH POWER UP. WE HAVE TO TRY THIS THING.
ROXIE...
UNLIKE POOR JONES, WE KNOW HOW THIS WORKS, SO ***MAYBE*** WE CAN KEEP OUR MINDS TOGETHER. BUT WE'RE SUPPOSED TO BE PARTNERS. WHOEVER USES THE S-DIAL WILL BE OBEYING THE OTHER. WE TRUST EACH OTHER, RIGHT?
ROXIE...
HOW ABOUT WE TOSS A COIN? BUT WE ***HAVE*** TO AGREE ***RULES*** FIRST...
ROXIE!
I'LL DO IT.

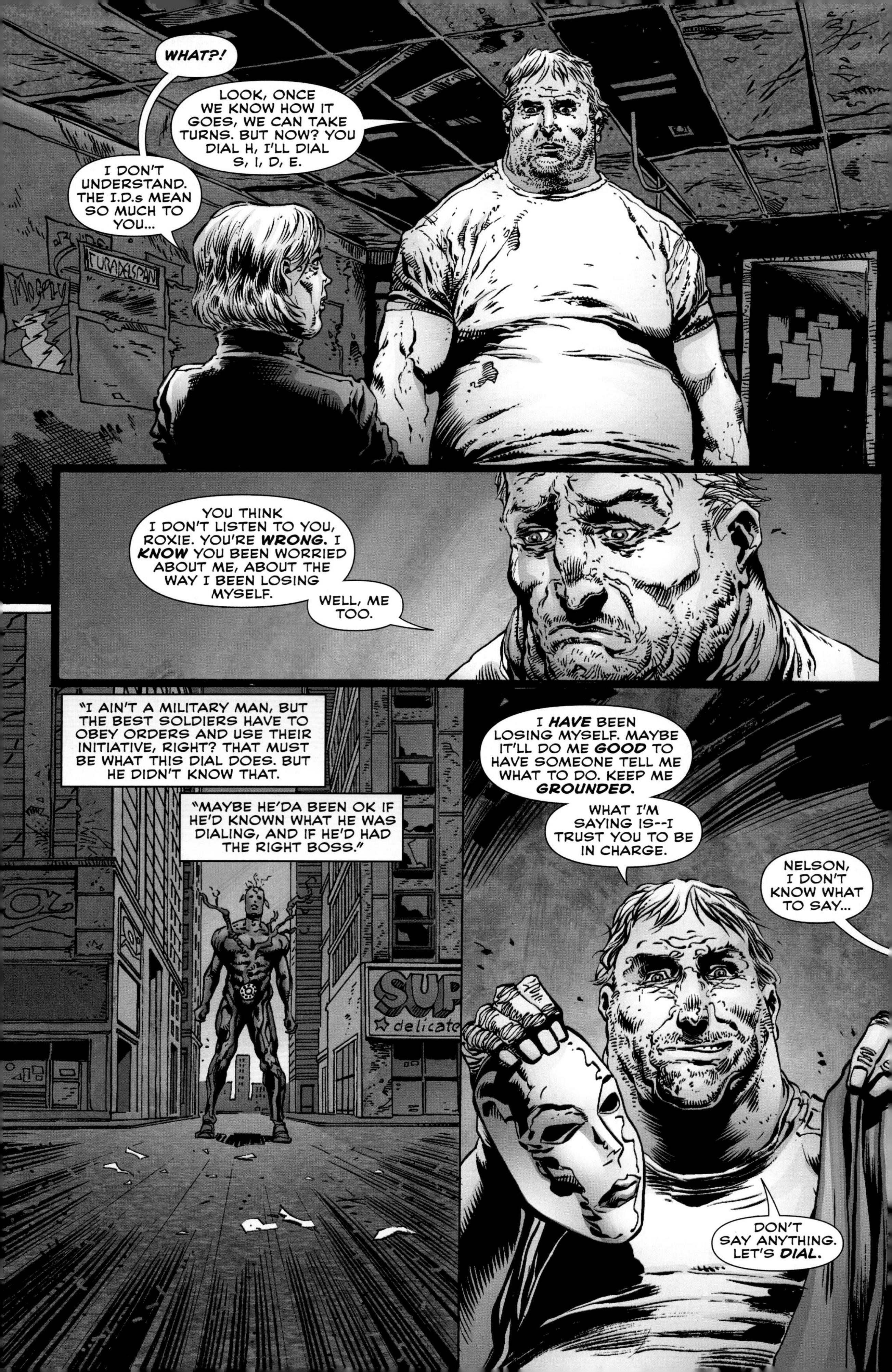
WHAT?!
LOOK, ONCE WE KNOW HOW IT GOES, WE CAN TAKE TURNS. BUT NOW? YOU DIAL H, I'LL DIAL S, I, D, E.
I DON'T UNDERSTAND. THE I.D.s MEAN SO MUCH TO YOU...
YOU THINK I DON'T LISTEN TO YOU, ROXIE. YOU'RE **WRONG.** I **KNOW** YOU BEEN WORRIED ABOUT ME, ABOUT THE WAY I BEEN LOSING MYSELF.
WELL, ME TOO.
"I AIN'T A MILITARY MAN, BUT THE BEST SOLDIERS HAVE TO OBEY ORDERS AND USE THEIR INITIATIVE, RIGHT? THAT MUST BE WHAT THIS DIAL DOES. BUT HE DIDN'T KNOW THAT.
"MAYBE HE'DA BEEN OK IF HE'D KNOWN WHAT HE WAS DIALING, AND IF HE'D HAD THE RIGHT BOSS."
I **HAVE** BEEN LOSING MYSELF. MAYBE IT'LL DO ME **GOOD** TO HAVE SOMEONE TELL ME WHAT TO DO. KEEP ME **GROUNDED.**
WHAT I'M SAYING IS--I TRUST YOU TO BE IN CHARGE.
NELSON, I DON'T KNOW WHAT TO SAY...
DON'T SAY ANYTHING. LET'S **DIAL.**

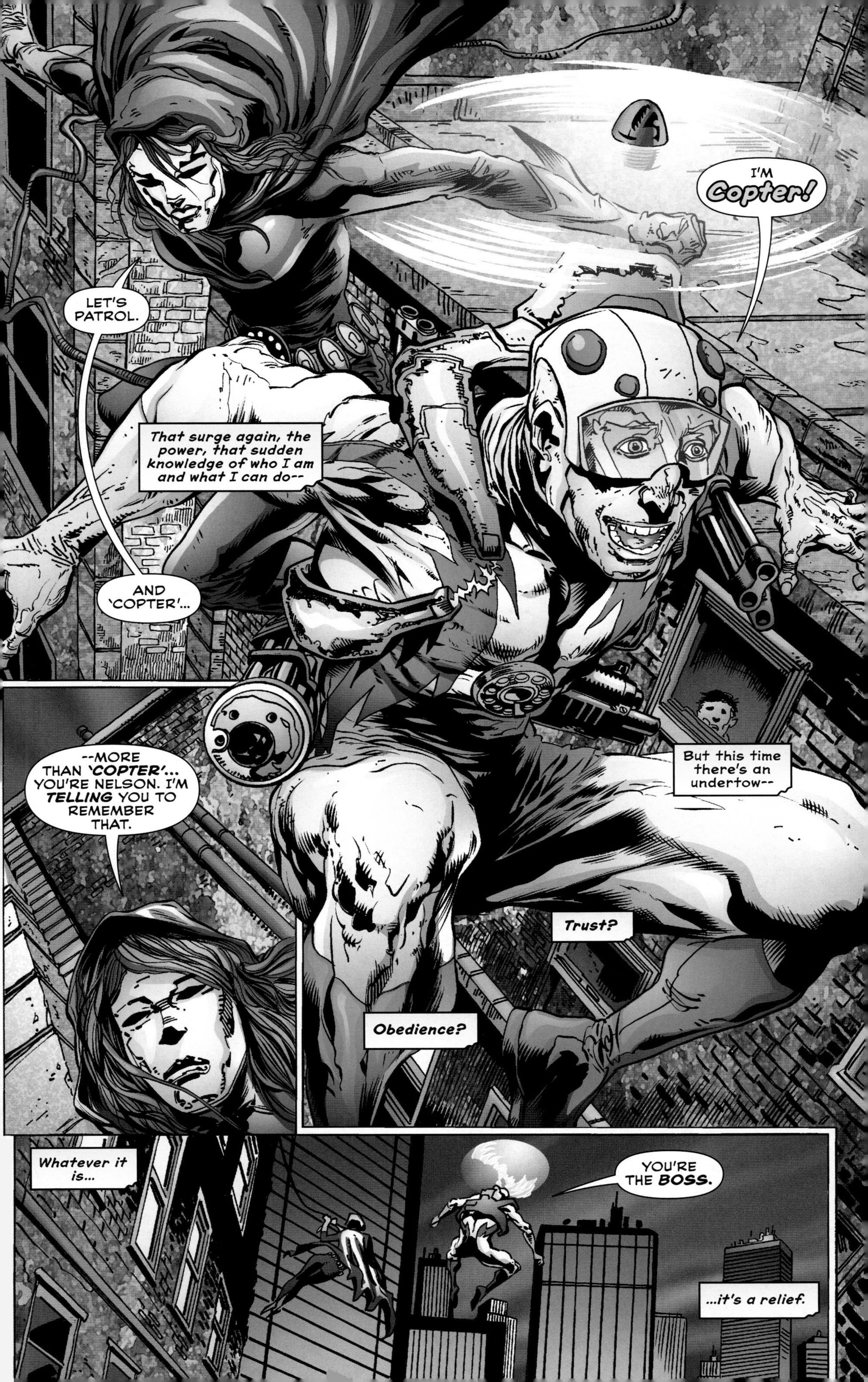
I'M Copter!
LET'S PATROL.
That surge again, the power, that sudden knowledge of who I am and what I can do--
AND 'COPTER'...
--MORE THAN 'COPTER'... YOU'RE NELSON. I'M TELLING YOU TO REMEMBER THAT.
But this time there's an undertow--
Trust?
Obedience?
Whatever it is...
YOU'RE THE BOSS.
...it's a relief.

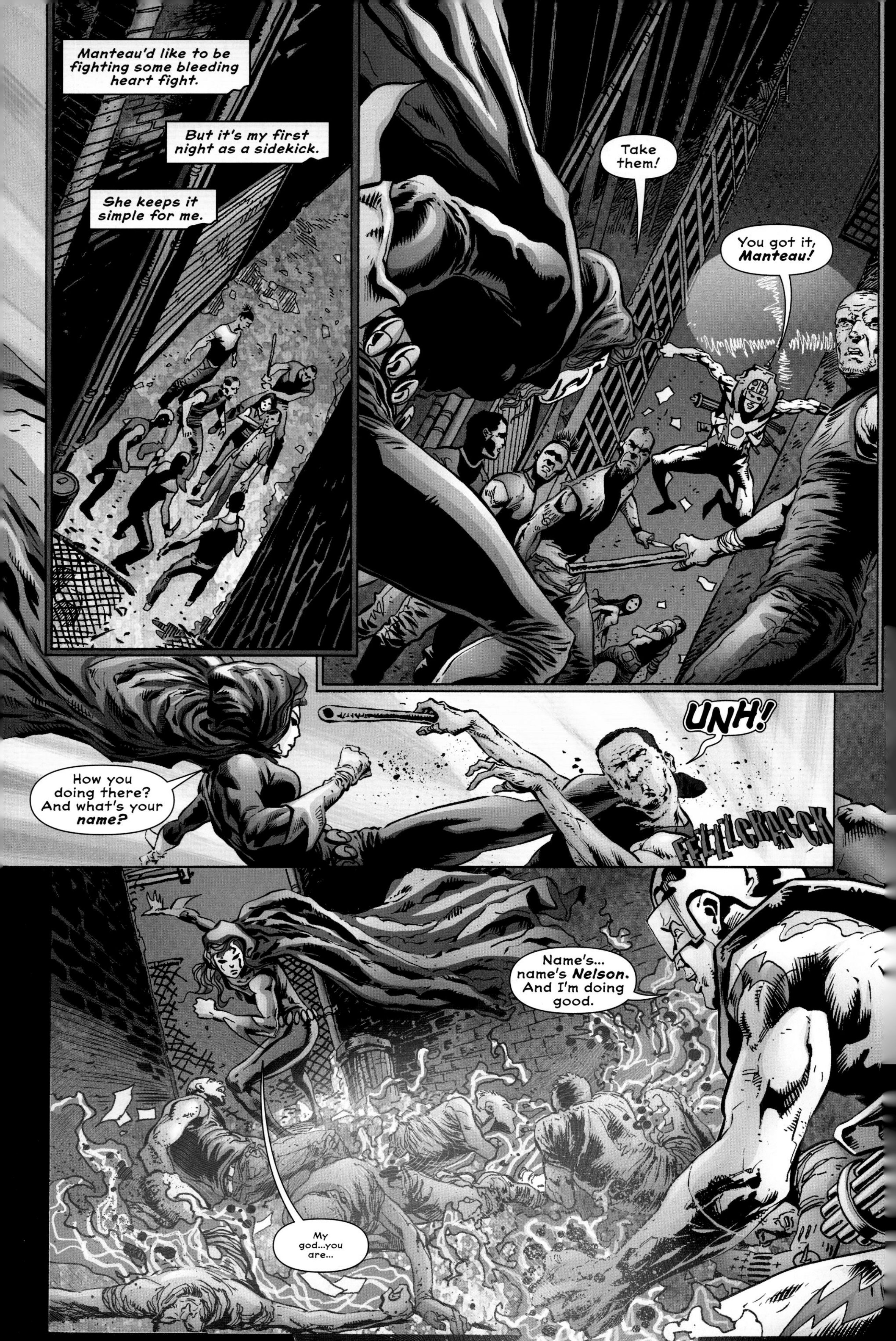
Manteau'd like to be fighting some bleeding heart fight.
But it's my first night as a sidekick.
She keeps it simple for me.
Take them!
You got it, Manteau!
UNH!
How you doing there? And what's your name?
FEZLCRACCK
Name's... name's Nelson. And I'm doing good.
My god...you are...

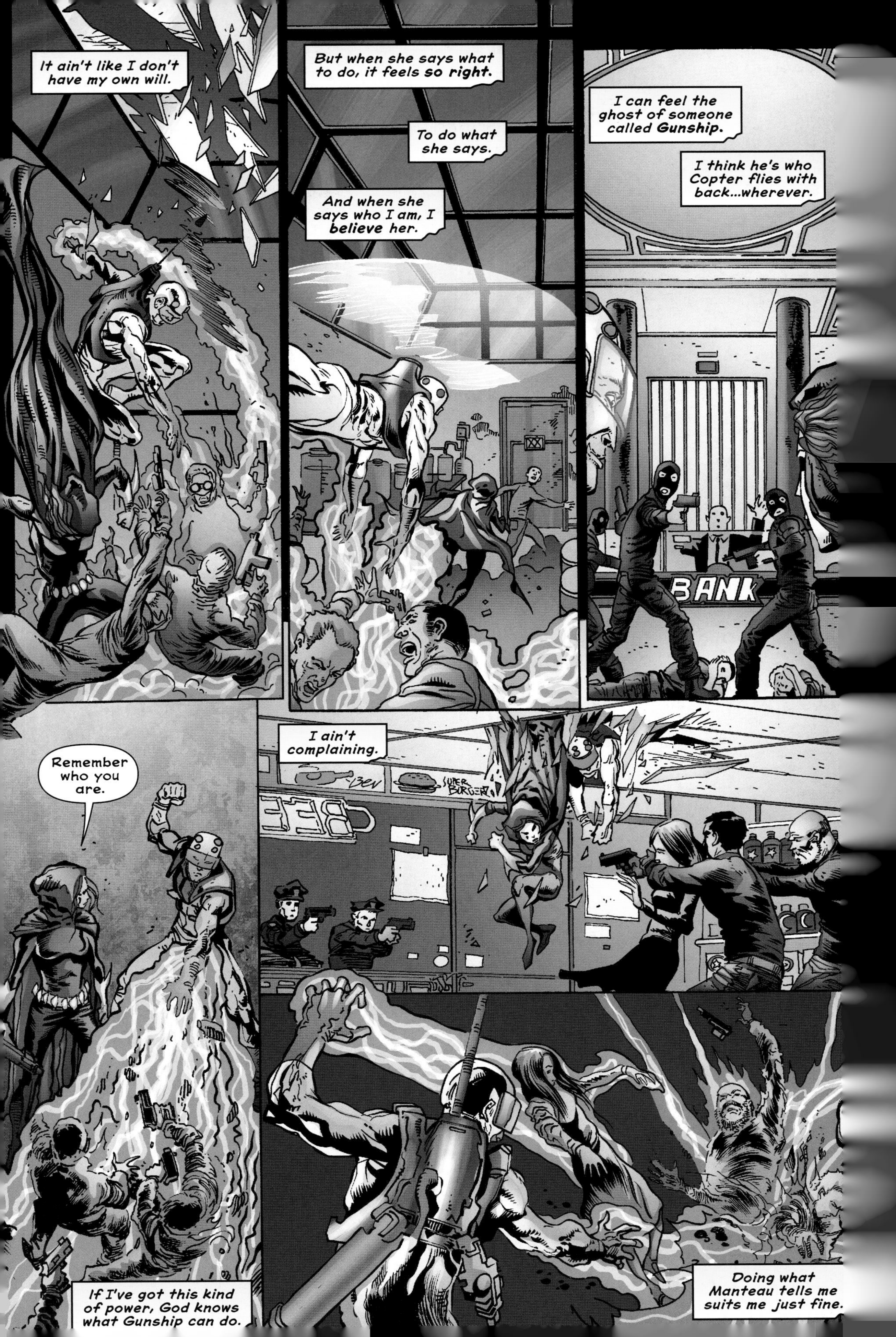
It ain't like I don't have my own will.
But when she says what to do, it feels so right.
To do what she says.
And when she says who I am, I believe her.
I can feel the ghost of someone called Gunship.
I think he's who Copter flies with back...wherever.
BANK
Remember who you are.
If I've got this kind of power, God knows what Gunship can do.
I ain't complaining.
SUPER BURGER
Doing what Manteau tells me suits me just fine.

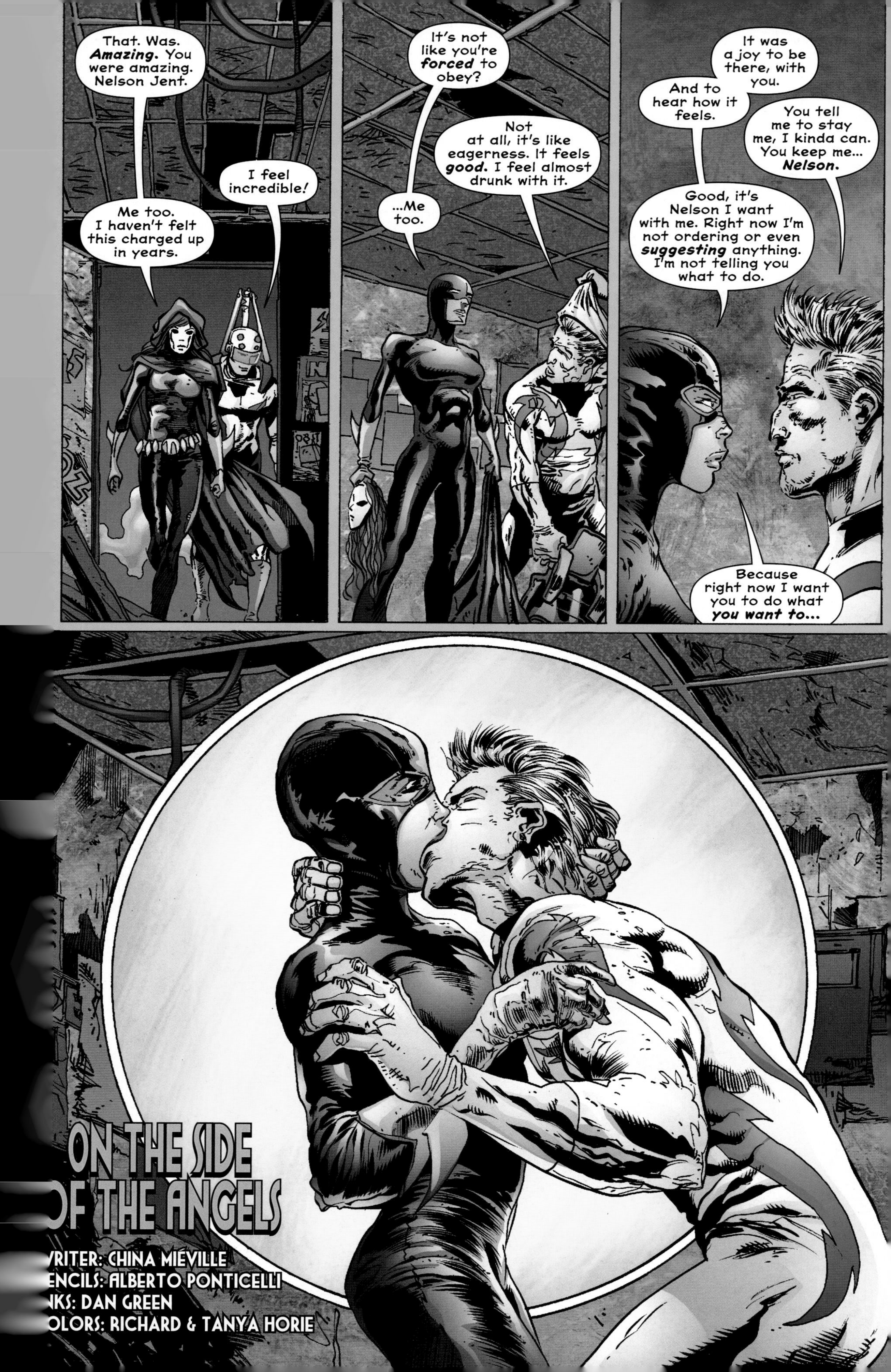

That. Was. Amazing. You were amazing. Nelson Jent.
I feel incredible!
Me too. I haven't felt this charged up in years.
It's not like you're forced to obey?
Not at all, it's like eagerness. It feels good. I feel almost drunk with it.
...Me too.
It was a joy to be there, with you.
And to hear how it feels.
You tell me to stay me, I kinda can. You keep me... Nelson.
Good, it's Nelson I want with me. Right now I'm not ordering or even suggesting anything. I'm not telling you what to do.
Because right now I want you to do what you want to...
ON THE SIDE
OF THE ANGELS
RITER: CHINA MIEVILLE
ENCILS: ALBERTO PONTICELLI
NKS: DAN GREEN
OLORS: RICHARD & TANYA HORIE

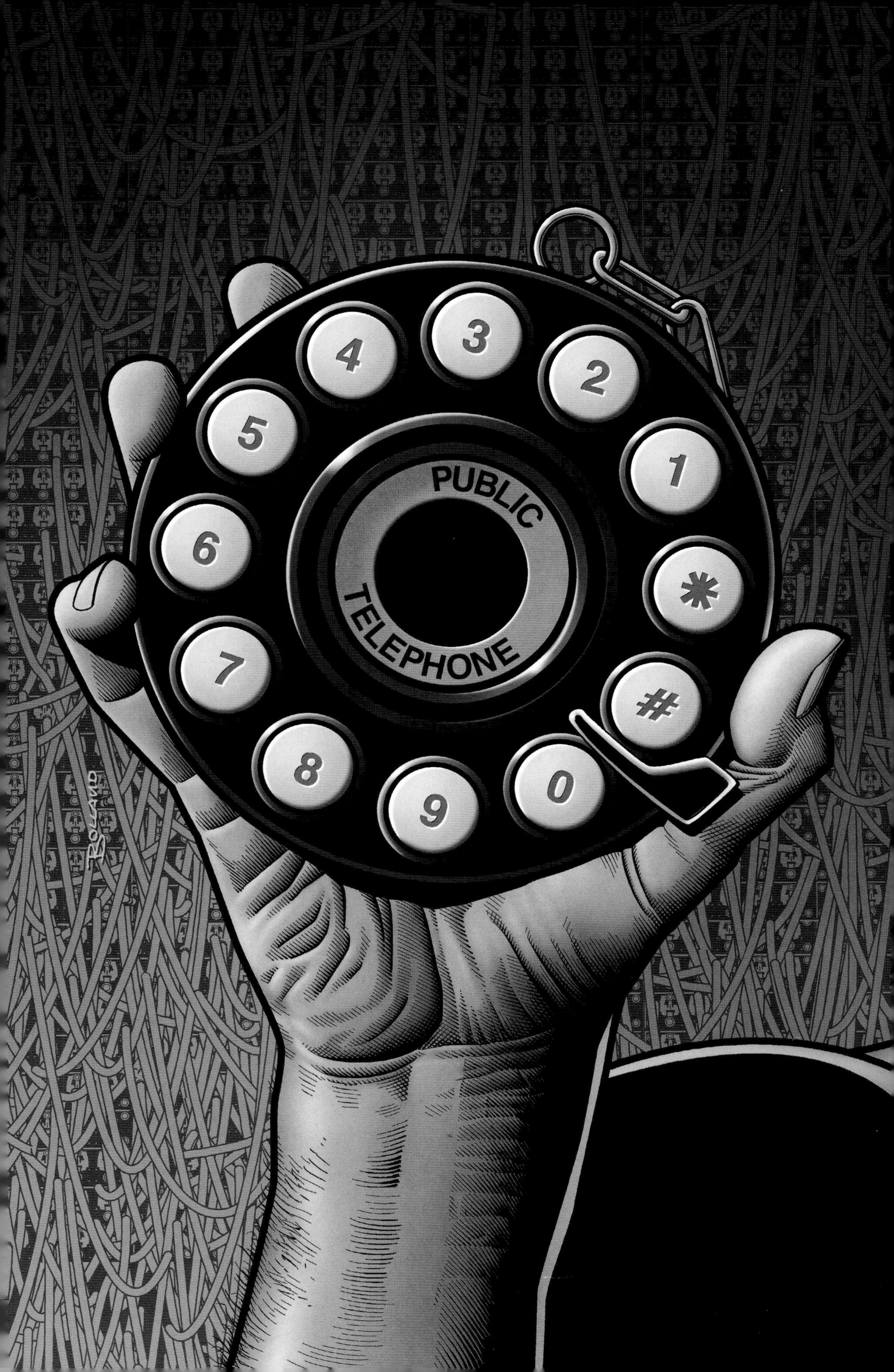
PUBLIC TELEPHONE
1
2
3
4
5
6
7
8
9
0
*
#
BOLLAND

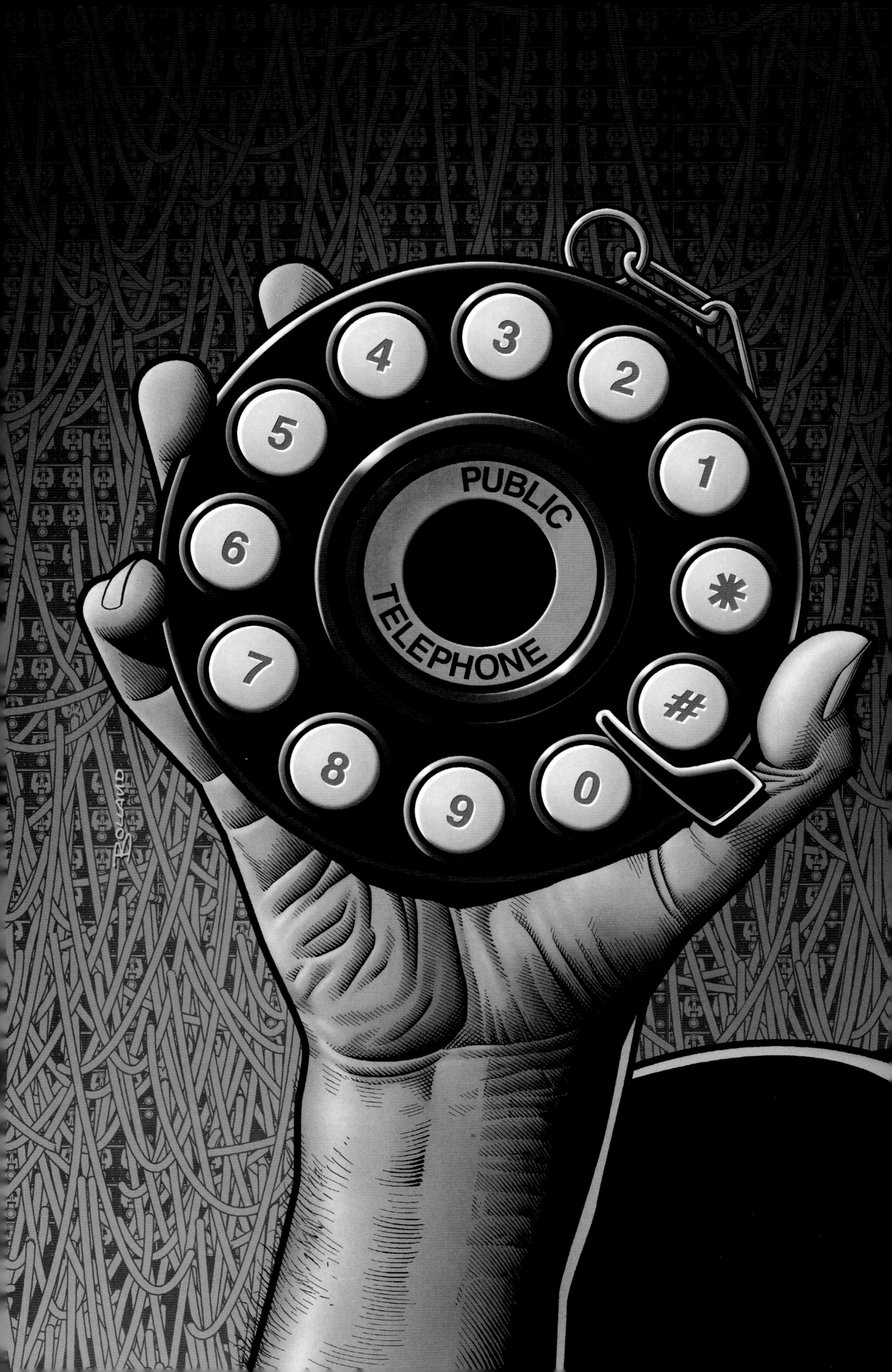
PUBLIC
TELEPHONE
ROLAND

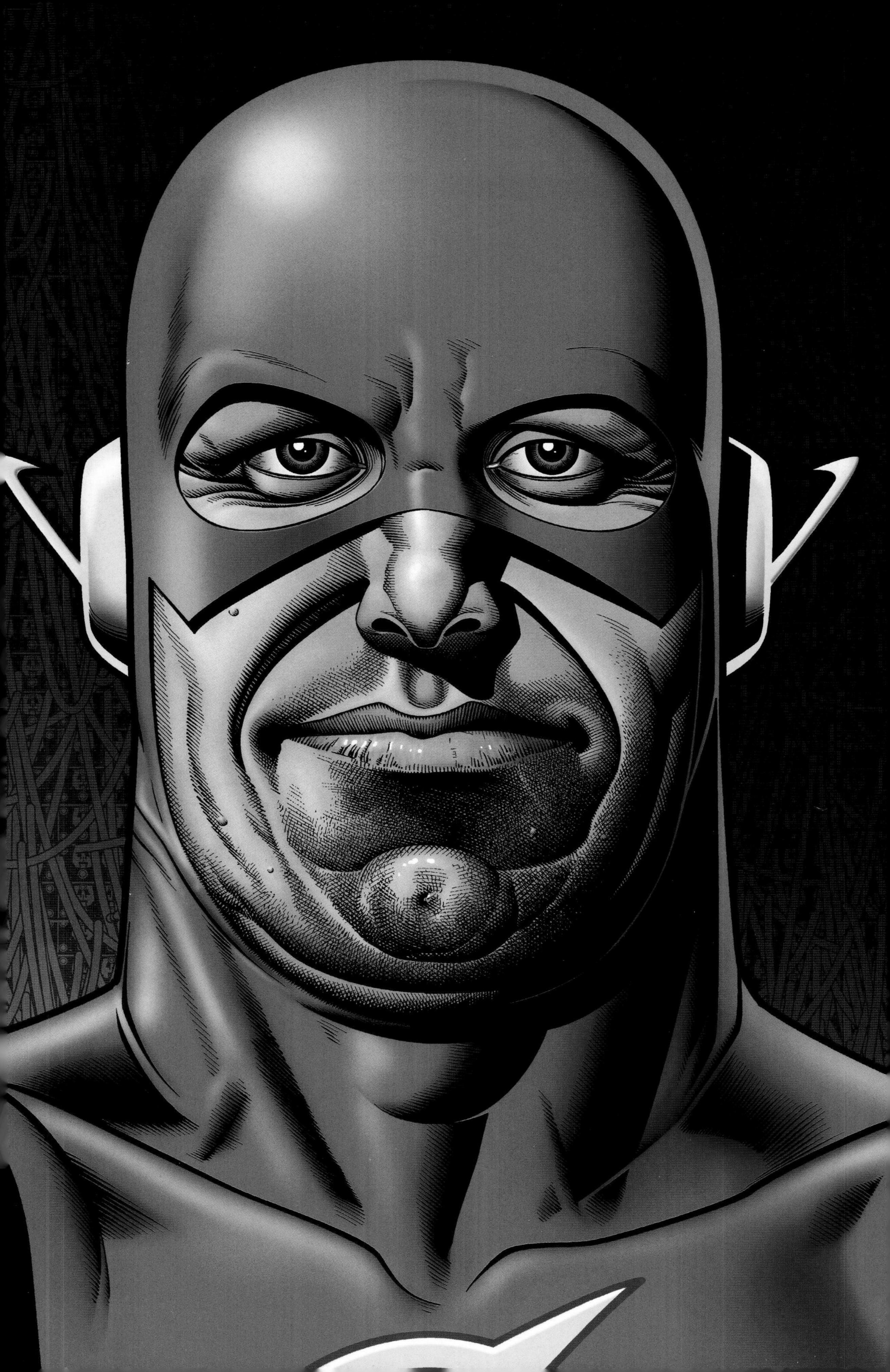

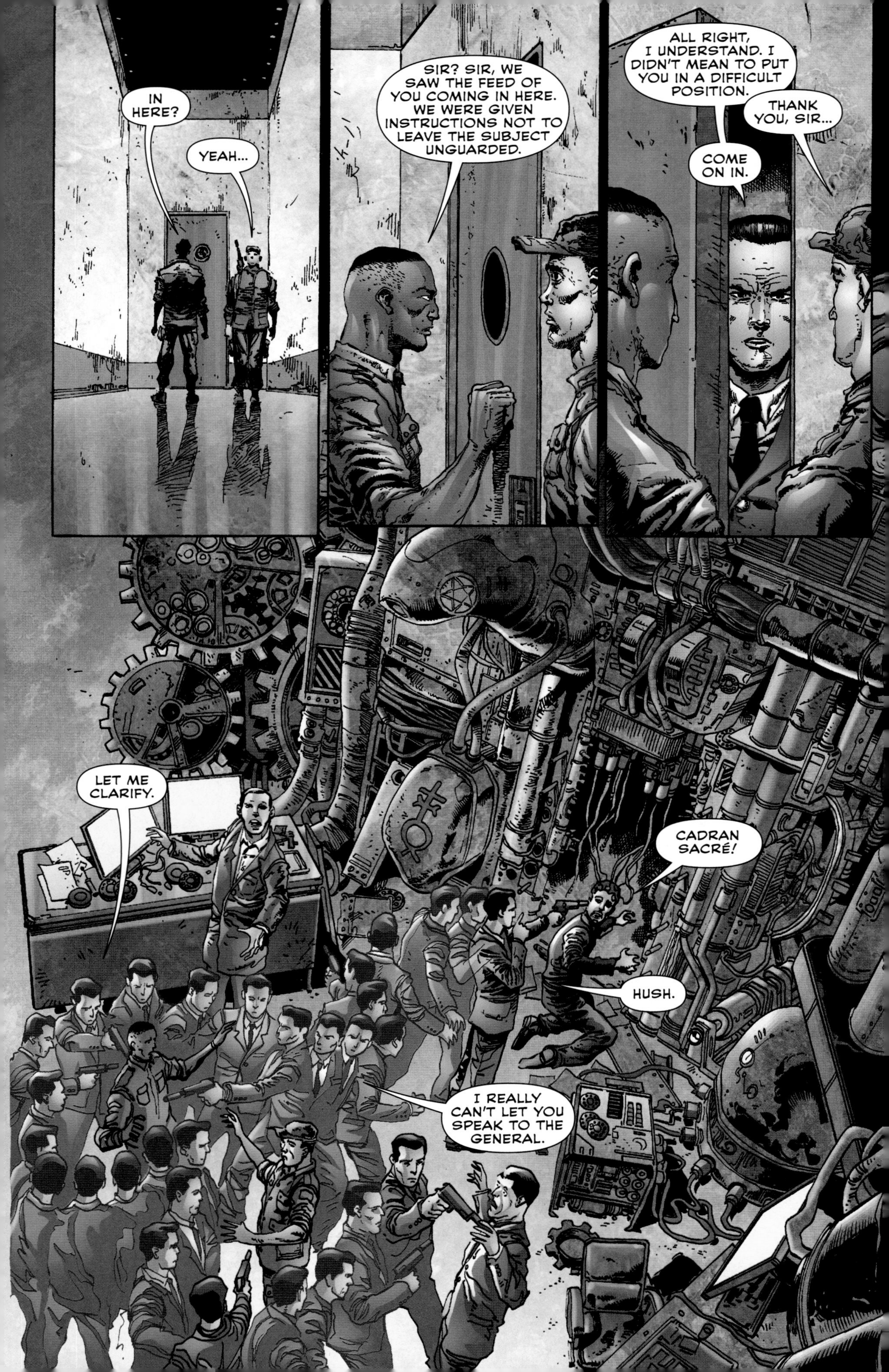
IN HERE?
YEAH...
SIR? SIR, WE SAW THE FEED OF YOU COMING IN HERE. WE WERE GIVEN INSTRUCTIONS NOT TO LEAVE THE SUBJECT UNGUARDED.
ALL RIGHT, I UNDERSTAND. I DIDN'T MEAN TO PUT YOU IN A DIFFICULT POSITION.
COME ON IN.
THANK YOU, SIR...
LET ME CLARIFY.
CADRAN SACRÉ!
HUSH.
I REALLY CAN'T LET YOU SPEAK TO THE GENERAL.

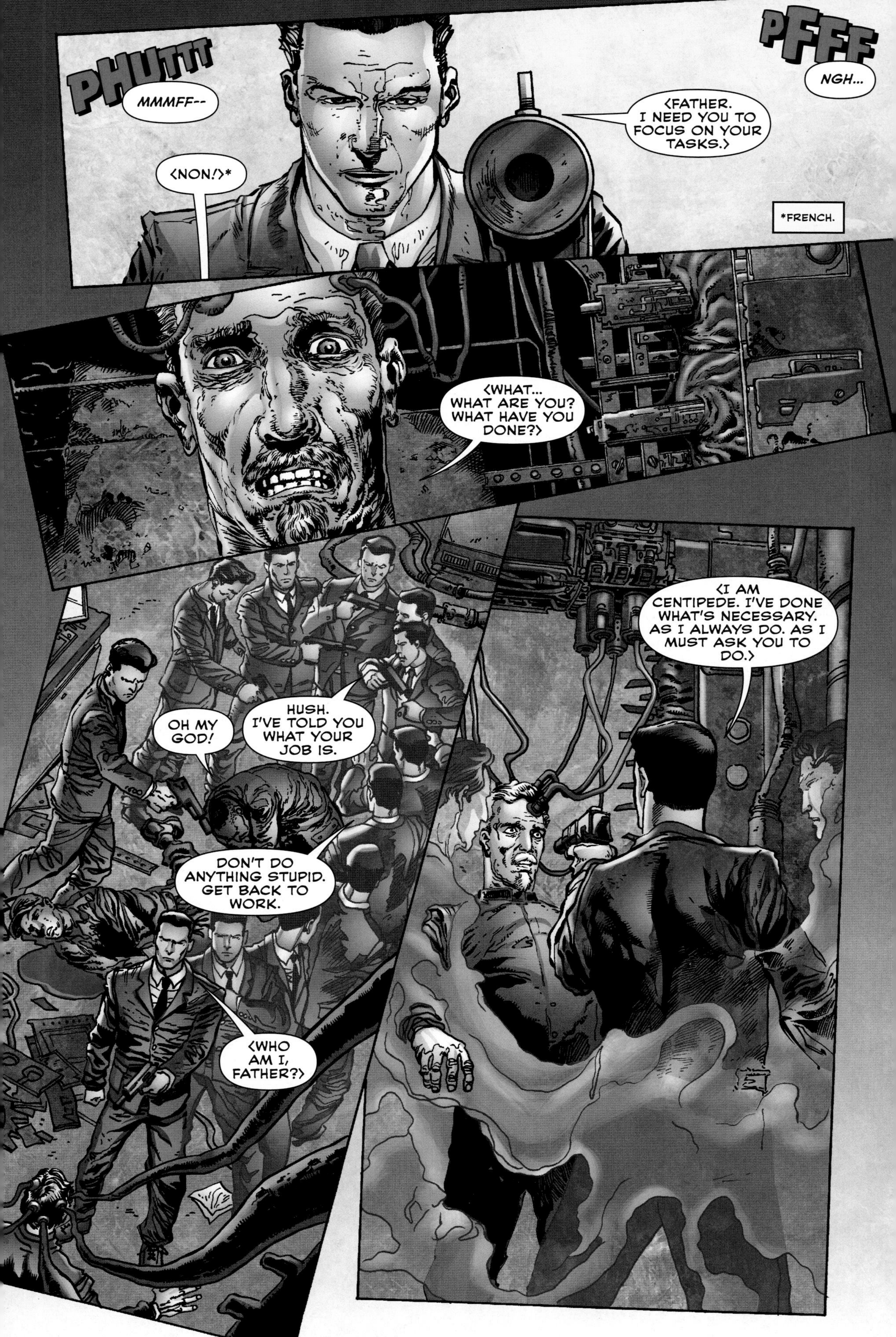
PHUTTT
MMMFF--
<NON!>*
<FATHER. I NEED YOU TO FOCUS ON YOUR TASKS.>
PFFF
NGH...
*FRENCH.
<WHAT... WHAT ARE YOU? WHAT HAVE YOU DONE?>
OH MY GOD!
HUSH. I'VE TOLD YOU WHAT YOUR JOB IS.
DON'T DO ANYTHING STUPID. GET BACK TO WORK.
<WHO AM I, FATHER?>
<I AM CENTIPEDE. I'VE DONE WHAT'S NECESSARY. AS I ALWAYS DO. AS I MUST ASK YOU TO DO.>

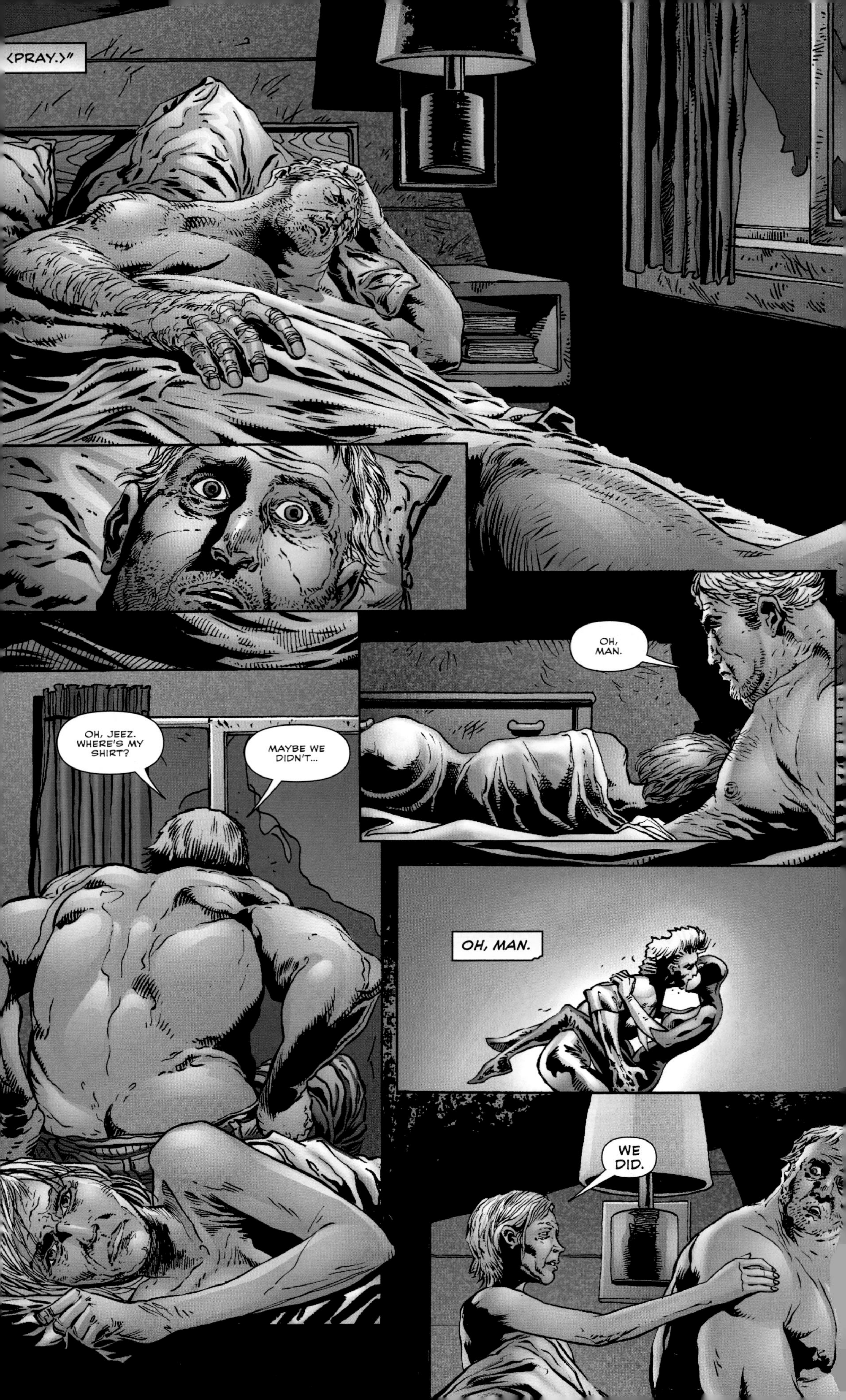
<PRAY.>"
OH, MAN.
OH, JEEZ. WHERE'S MY SHIRT?
MAYBE WE DIDN'T...
OH, MAN.
WE DID.

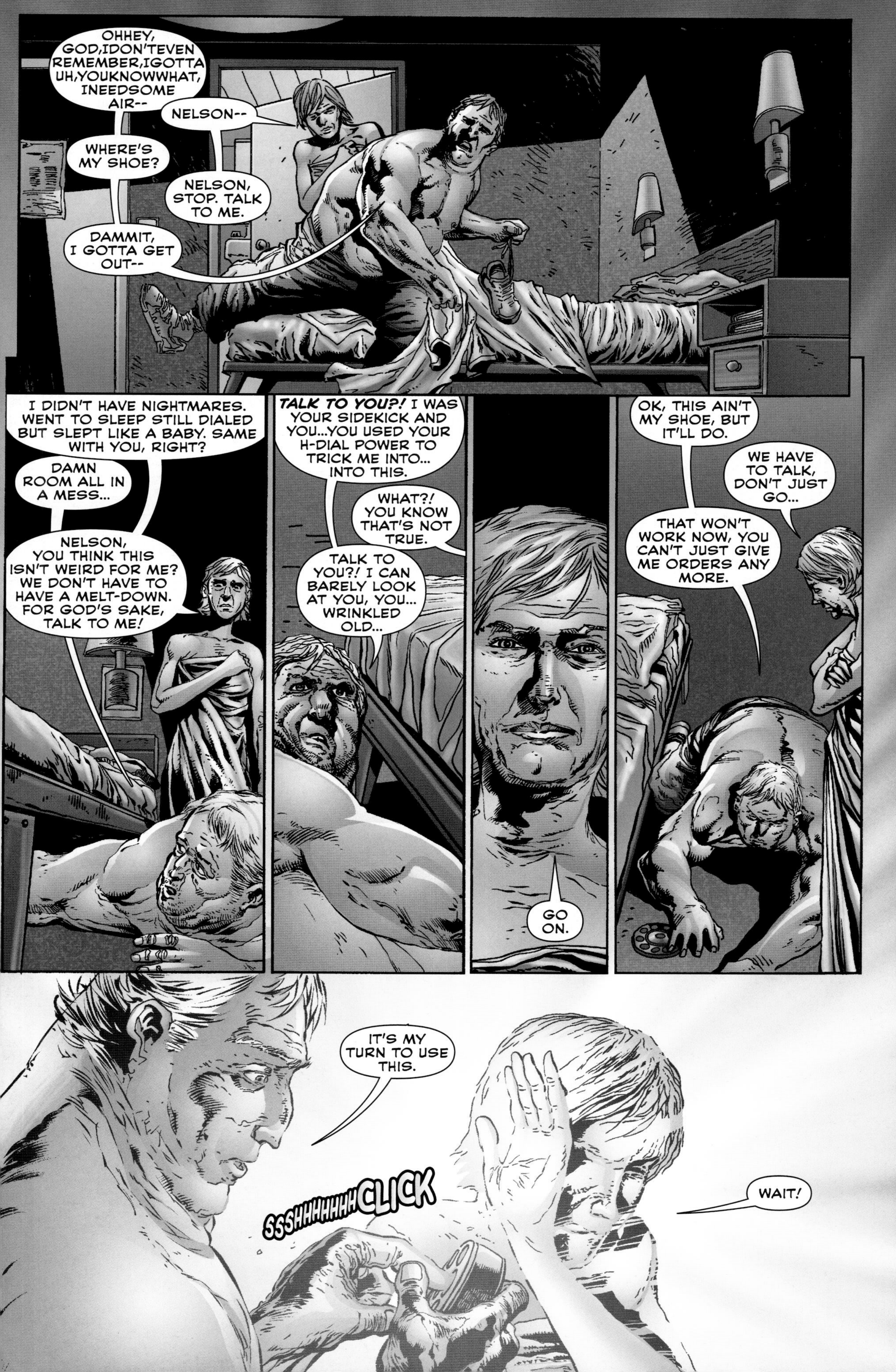
OHHEY, GOD,IDON'TEVEN REMEMBER,IGOTTA UH,YOUKNOWWHAT, INEEDSOME AIR--
NELSON--
WHERE'S MY SHOE?
NELSON, STOP. TALK TO ME.
DAMMIT, I GOTTA GET OUT--
I DIDN'T HAVE NIGHTMARES. WENT TO SLEEP STILL DIALED BUT SLEPT LIKE A BABY. SAME WITH YOU, RIGHT?
DAMN ROOM ALL IN A MESS...
NELSON, YOU THINK THIS ISN'T WEIRD FOR ME? WE DON'T HAVE TO HAVE A MELT-DOWN. FOR GOD'S SAKE, TALK TO ME!
TALK TO YOU?! I WAS YOUR SIDEKICK AND YOU...YOU USED YOUR H-DIAL POWER TO TRICK ME INTO... INTO THIS.
WHAT?! YOU KNOW THAT'S NOT TRUE.
TALK TO YOU?! I CAN BARELY LOOK AT YOU, YOU... WRINKLED OLD...
GO ON.
OK, THIS AIN'T MY SHOE, BUT IT'LL DO.
WE HAVE TO TALK, DON'T JUST GO...
THAT WON'T WORK NOW, YOU CAN'T JUST GIVE ME ORDERS ANY MORE.
IT'S MY TURN TO USE THIS.
SSSHHHHHHHCLICK
WAIT!

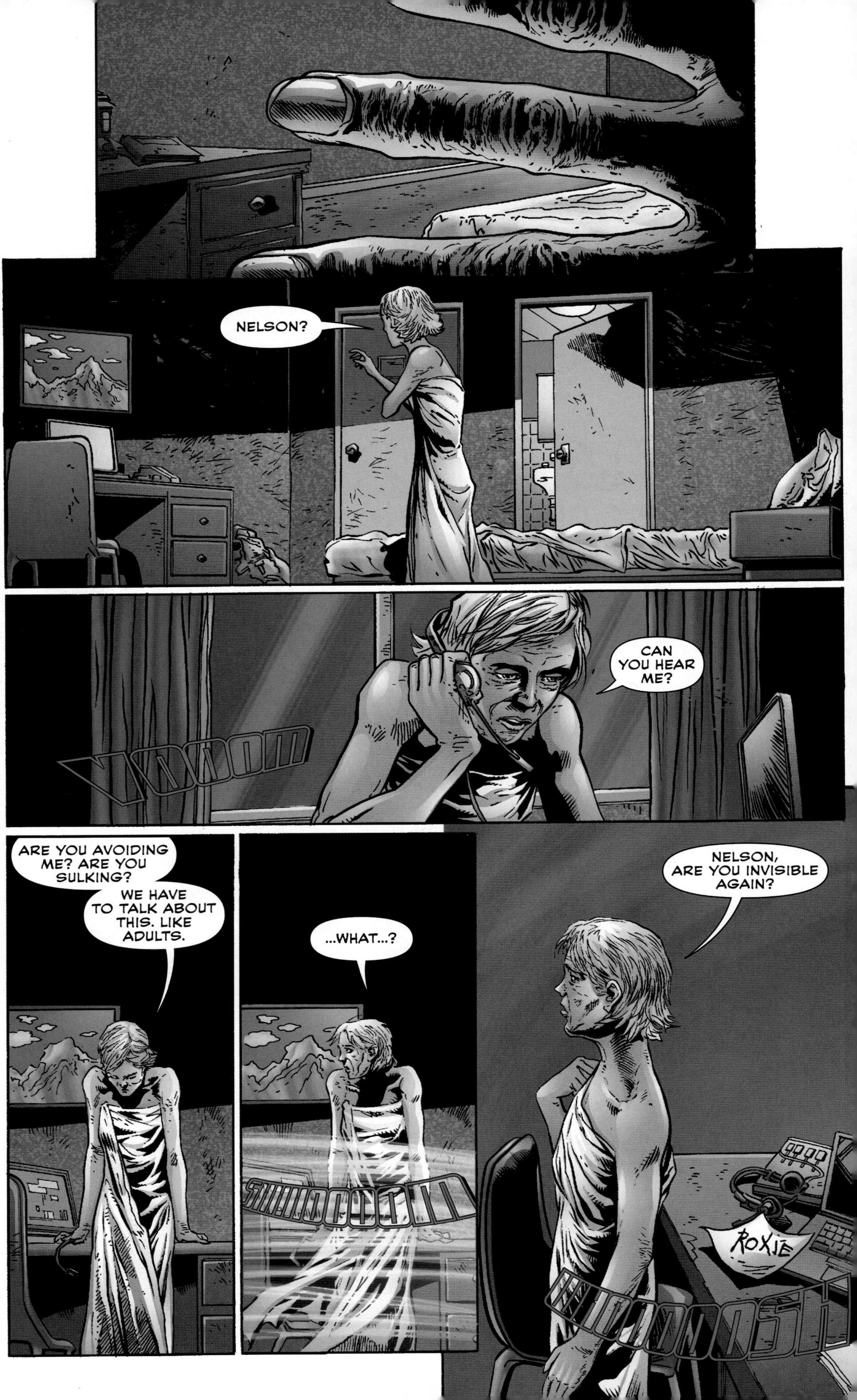
NELSON?
CAN YOU HEAR ME?
VOOOOM
ARE YOU AVOIDING ME? ARE YOU SULKING?
WE HAVE TO TALK ABOUT THIS. LIKE ADULTS.
...WHAT...?
SHHOOOOOM
NELSON, ARE YOU INVISIBLE AGAIN?
ROXIE
WHOOOOOSH

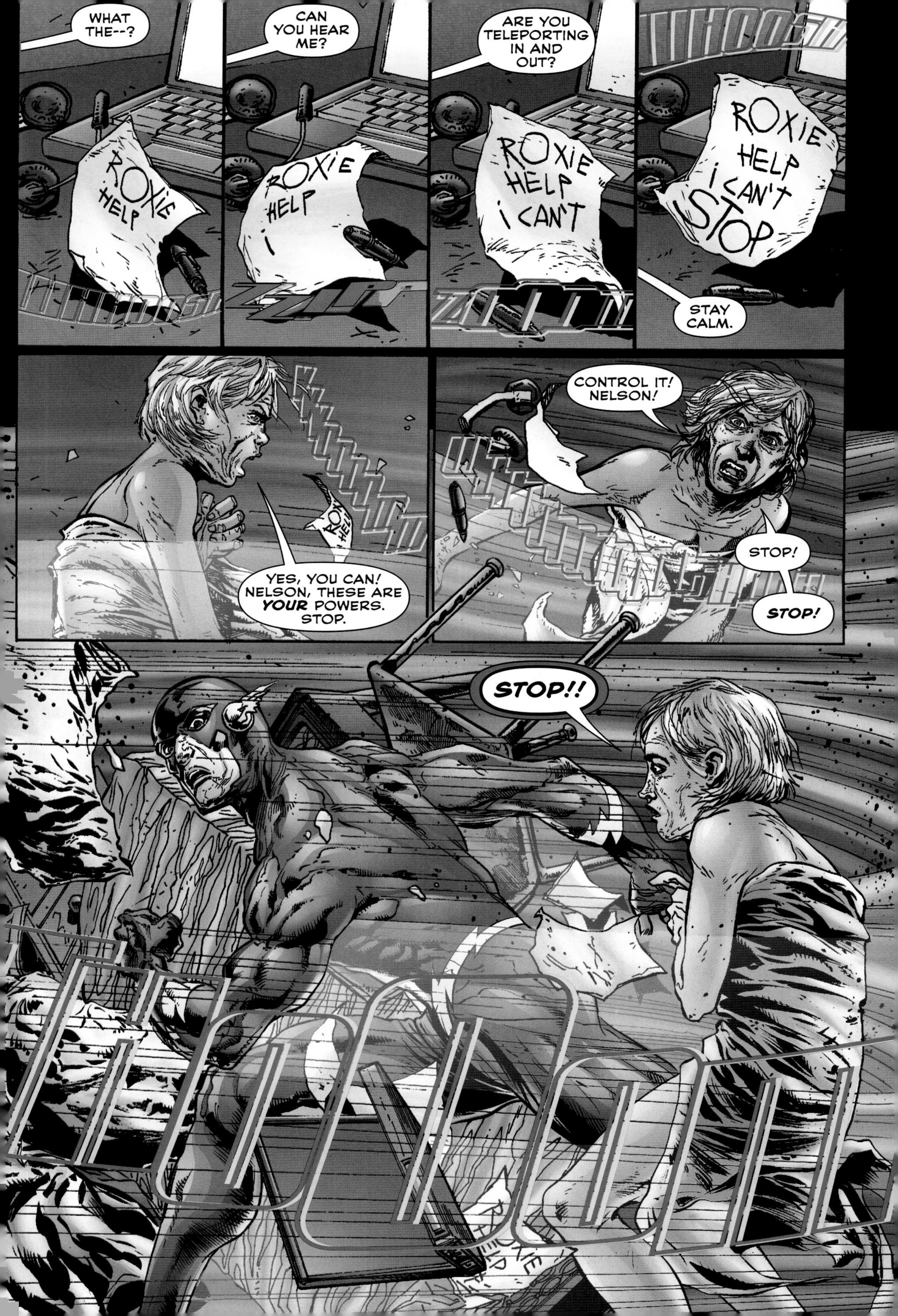
WHAT THE--?
ROXIE HELP
CAN YOU HEAR ME?
ROXIE HELP I
ARE YOU TELEPORTING IN AND OUT?
ROXIE HELP I CAN'T
ROXIE HELP I CAN'T STOP
STAY CALM.
YES, YOU CAN! NELSON, THESE ARE ***YOUR*** POWERS. STOP.
CONTROL IT! NELSON!
STOP!
STOP!
STOP!!

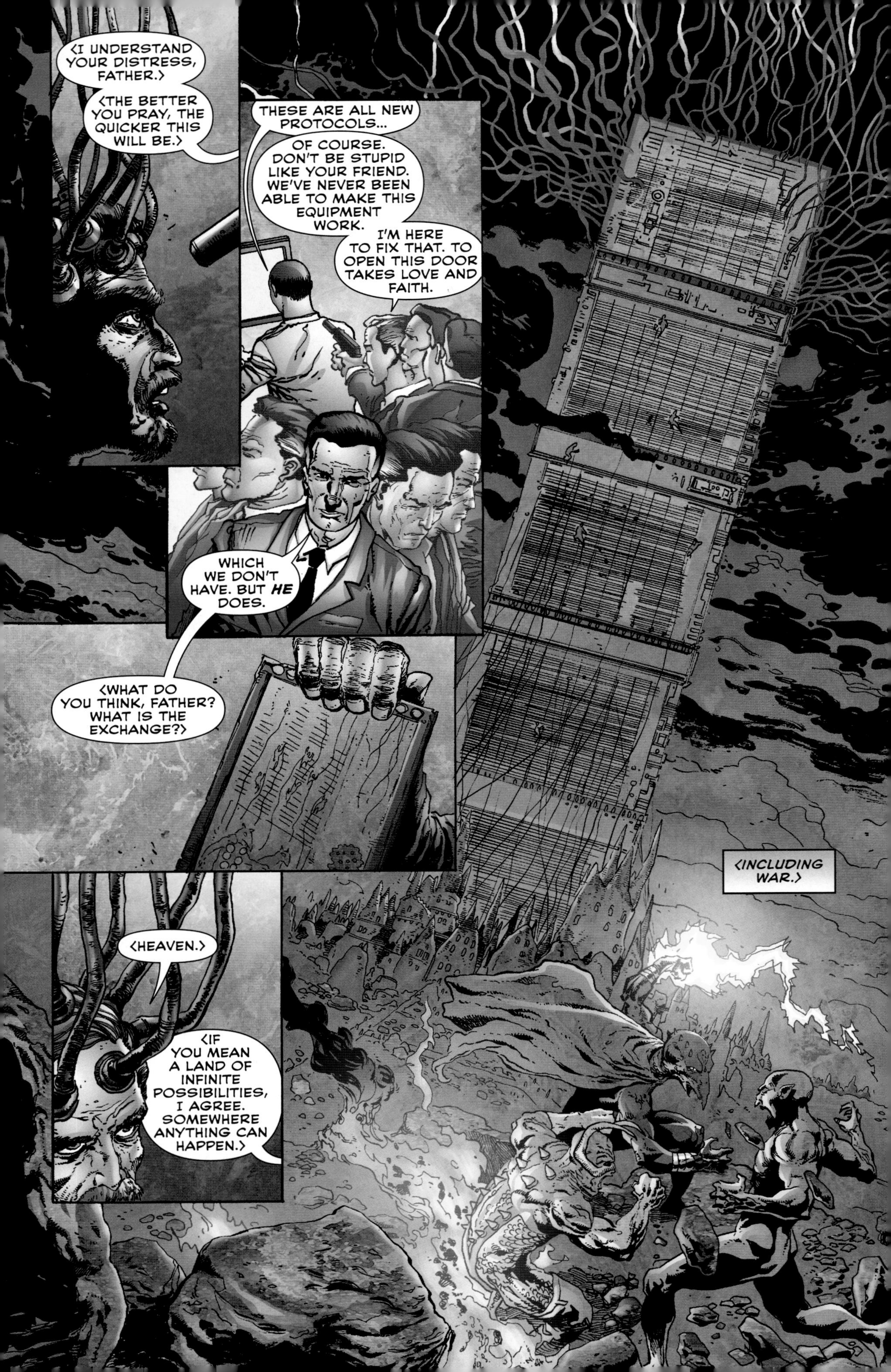
<I UNDERSTAND YOUR DISTRESS, FATHER.>
<THE BETTER YOU PRAY, THE QUICKER THIS WILL BE.>
THESE ARE ALL NEW PROTOCOLS...
OF COURSE. DON'T BE STUPID LIKE YOUR FRIEND. WE'VE NEVER BEEN ABLE TO MAKE THIS EQUIPMENT WORK.
I'M HERE TO FIX THAT. TO OPEN THIS DOOR TAKES LOVE AND FAITH.
WHICH WE DON'T HAVE. BUT ***HE*** DOES.
<WHAT DO YOU THINK, FATHER? WHAT IS THE EXCHANGE?>
<HEAVEN.>
<IF YOU MEAN A LAND OF INFINITE POSSIBILITIES, I AGREE. SOMEWHERE ANYTHING CAN HAPPEN.>
<INCLUDING WAR.>

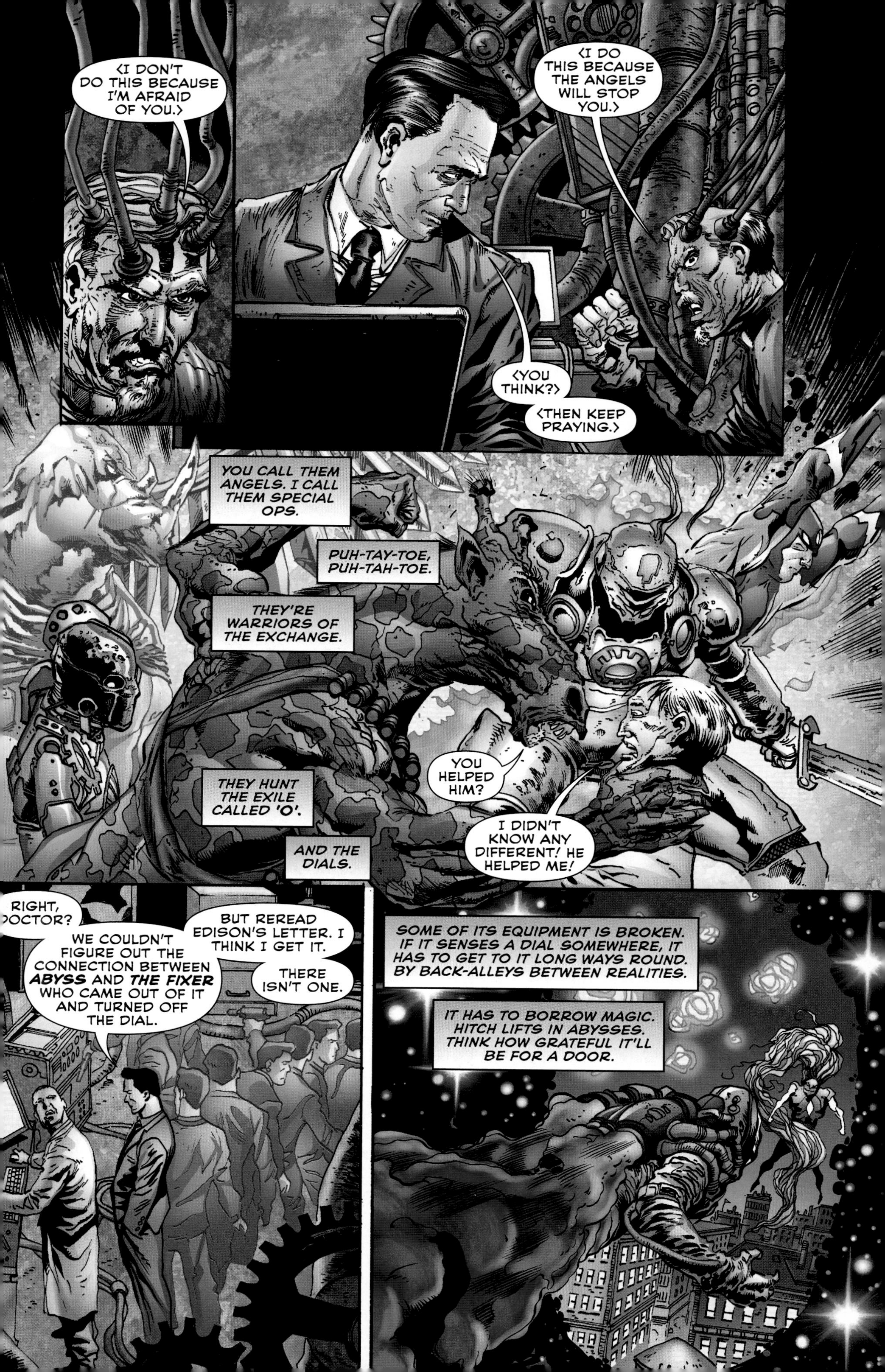

<I DON'T DO THIS BECAUSE I'M AFRAID OF YOU.>
<I DO THIS BECAUSE THE ANGELS WILL STOP YOU.>
<YOU THINK?>
<THEN KEEP PRAYING.>
YOU CALL THEM ANGELS. I CALL THEM SPECIAL OPS.
PUH-TAY-TOE, PUH-TAH-TOE.
THEY'RE WARRIORS OF THE EXCHANGE.
THEY HUNT THE EXILE CALLED 'O'.
AND THE DIALS.
YOU HELPED HIM?
I DIDN'T KNOW ANY DIFFERENT! HE HELPED ME!
RIGHT, DOCTOR?
WE COULDN'T FIGURE OUT THE CONNECTION BETWEEN ABYSS AND THE FIXER WHO CAME OUT OF IT AND TURNED OFF THE DIAL.
BUT REREAD EDISON'S LETTER. I THINK I GET IT.
THERE ISN'T ONE.
SOME OF ITS EQUIPMENT IS BROKEN. IF IT SENSES A DIAL SOMEWHERE, IT HAS TO GET TO IT LONG WAYS ROUND. BY BACK-ALLEYS BETWEEN REALITIES.
IT HAS TO BORROW MAGIC. HITCH LIFTS IN ABYSSES. THINK HOW GRATEFUL IT'LL BE FOR A DOOR.

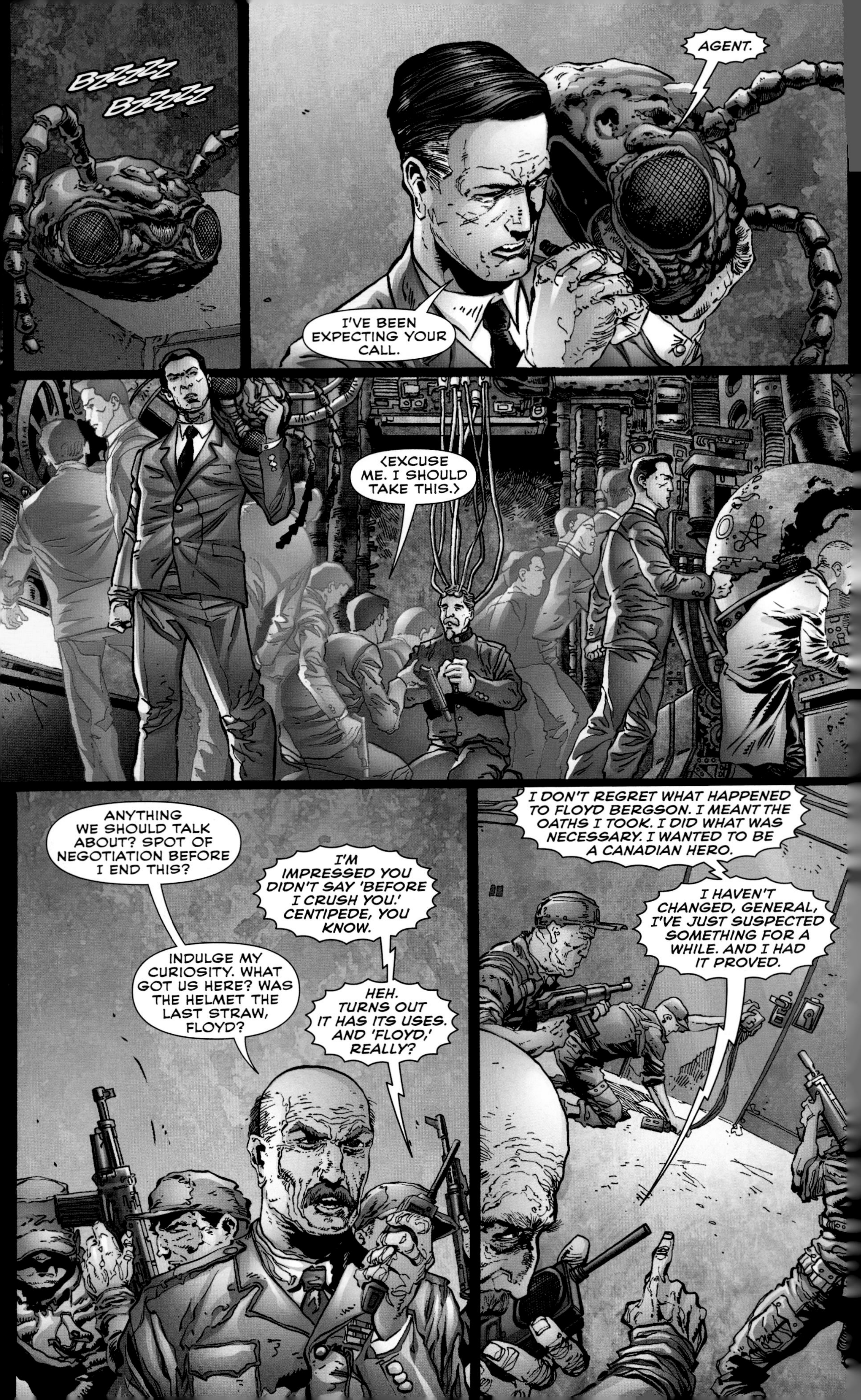
BZZZZZ BZZZZZ
AGENT.
I'VE BEEN EXPECTING YOUR CALL.
<EXCUSE ME. I SHOULD TAKE THIS.>
ANYTHING WE SHOULD TALK ABOUT? SPOT OF NEGOTIATION BEFORE I END THIS?
I'M IMPRESSED YOU DIDN'T SAY 'BEFORE I CRUSH YOU.' CENTIPEDE, YOU KNOW.
INDULGE MY CURIOSITY. WHAT GOT US HERE? WAS THE HELMET THE LAST STRAW, FLOYD?
HEH. TURNS OUT IT HAS ITS USES. AND 'FLOYD,' REALLY?
I DON'T REGRET WHAT HAPPENED TO FLOYD BERGSON. I MEANT THE OATHS I TOOK. I DID WHAT WAS NECESSARY. I WANTED TO BE A CANADIAN HERO.
I HAVEN'T CHANGED, GENERAL, I'VE JUST SUSPECTED SOMETHING FOR A WHILE. AND I HAD IT PROVED.

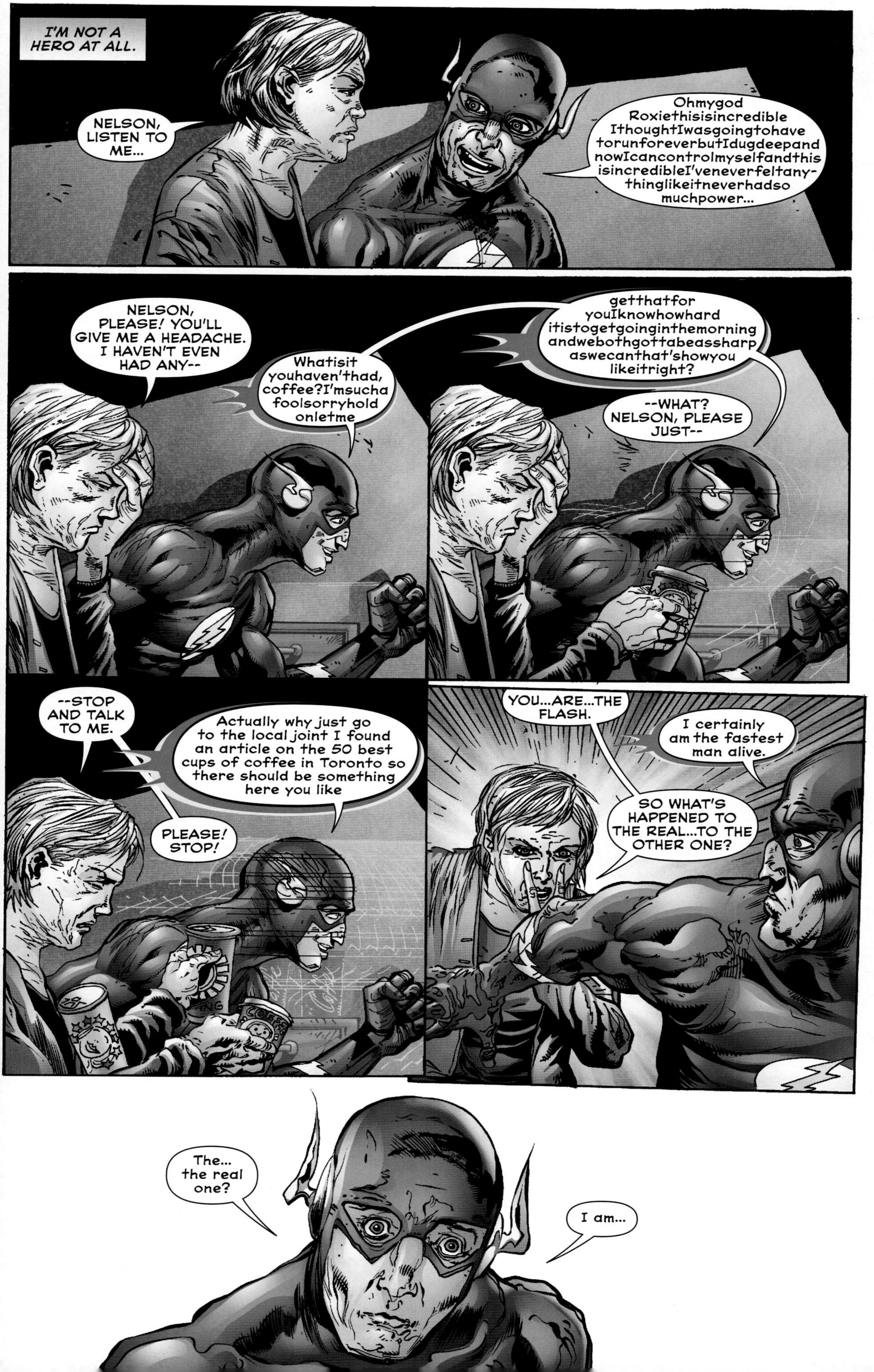

I'M NOT A HERO AT ALL.
NELSON, LISTEN TO ME...
Ohmygod Roxiethisisincredible IthoughtIwasgoingtohave torunforeverbutIdugdeepand nowIcancontrolmyselfandthis isincredibleI'veneverfeltany-thinglikeitneverhadso muchpower...
NELSON, PLEASE! YOU'LL GIVE ME A HEADACHE. I HAVEN'T EVEN HAD ANY--
Whatisit youhaven'thad, coffee?I'msucha foolsorryhold onletme
getthatfor youIknowhowhard itistogetgoinginthemorning andwebothgottabeassharp aswecanthat'showyou likeitright?
--WHAT? NELSON, PLEASE JUST--
--STOP AND TALK TO ME.
Actually why just go to the local joint I found an article on the 50 best cups of coffee in Toronto so there should be something here you like
PLEASE! STOP!
YOU...ARE...THE FLASH.
I certainly am the fastest man alive.
SO WHAT'S HAPPENED TO THE REAL...TO THE OTHER ONE?
The... the real one?
I am...

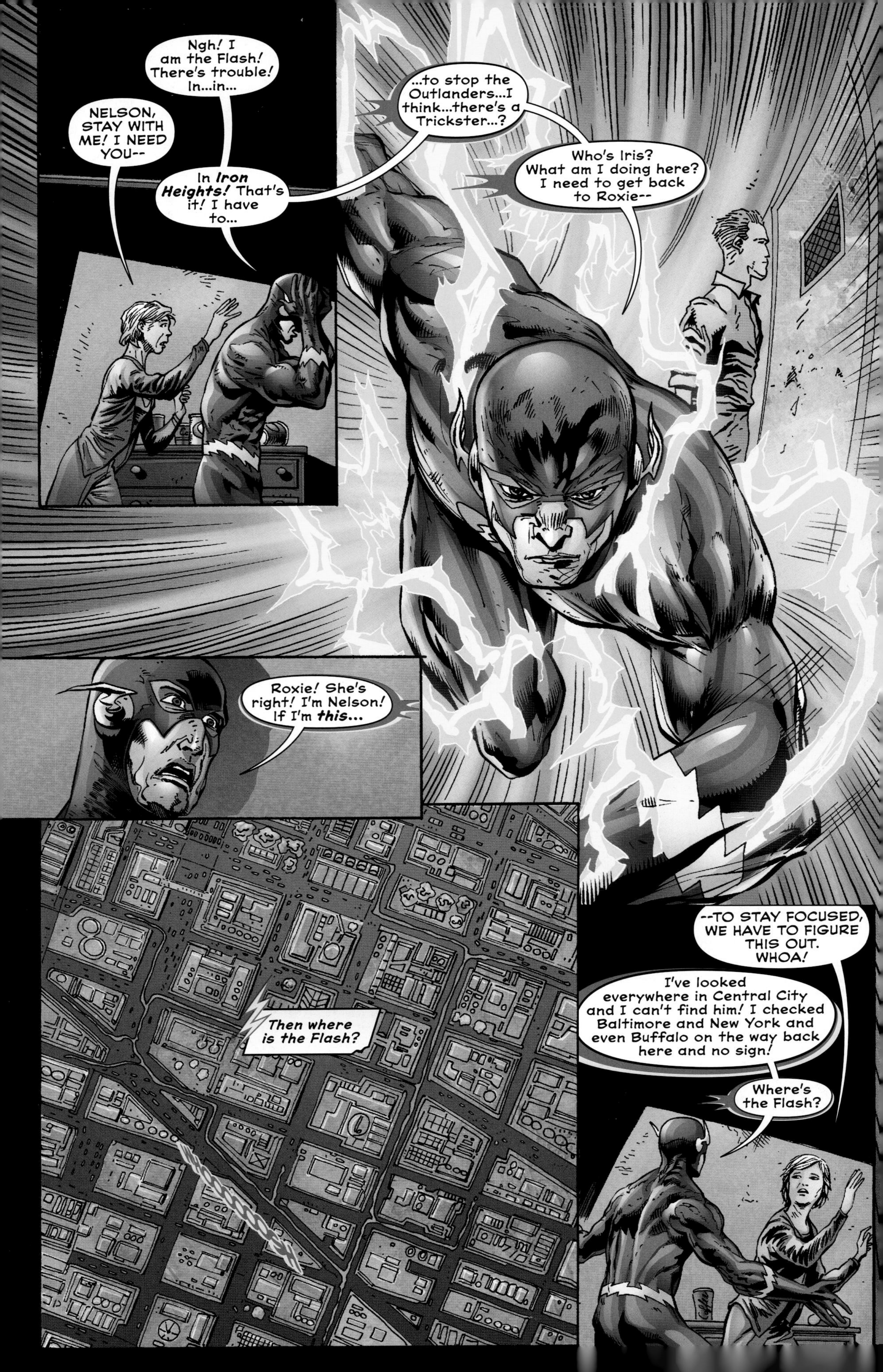
Ngh! I am the Flash! There's trouble! In...in...
NELSON, STAY WITH ME! I NEED YOU--
In *Iron Heights!* That's it! I have to...
...to stop the Outlanders...I think...there's a Trickster...?
Who's Iris? What am I doing here? I need to get back to Roxie--
Roxie! She's right! I'm Nelson! If I'm *this...*
Then where is the Flash?
--TO STAY FOCUSED, WE HAVE TO FIGURE THIS OUT. WHOA!
I've looked everywhere in Central City and I can't find him! I checked Baltimore and New York and even Buffalo on the way back here and no sign!
Where's the Flash?

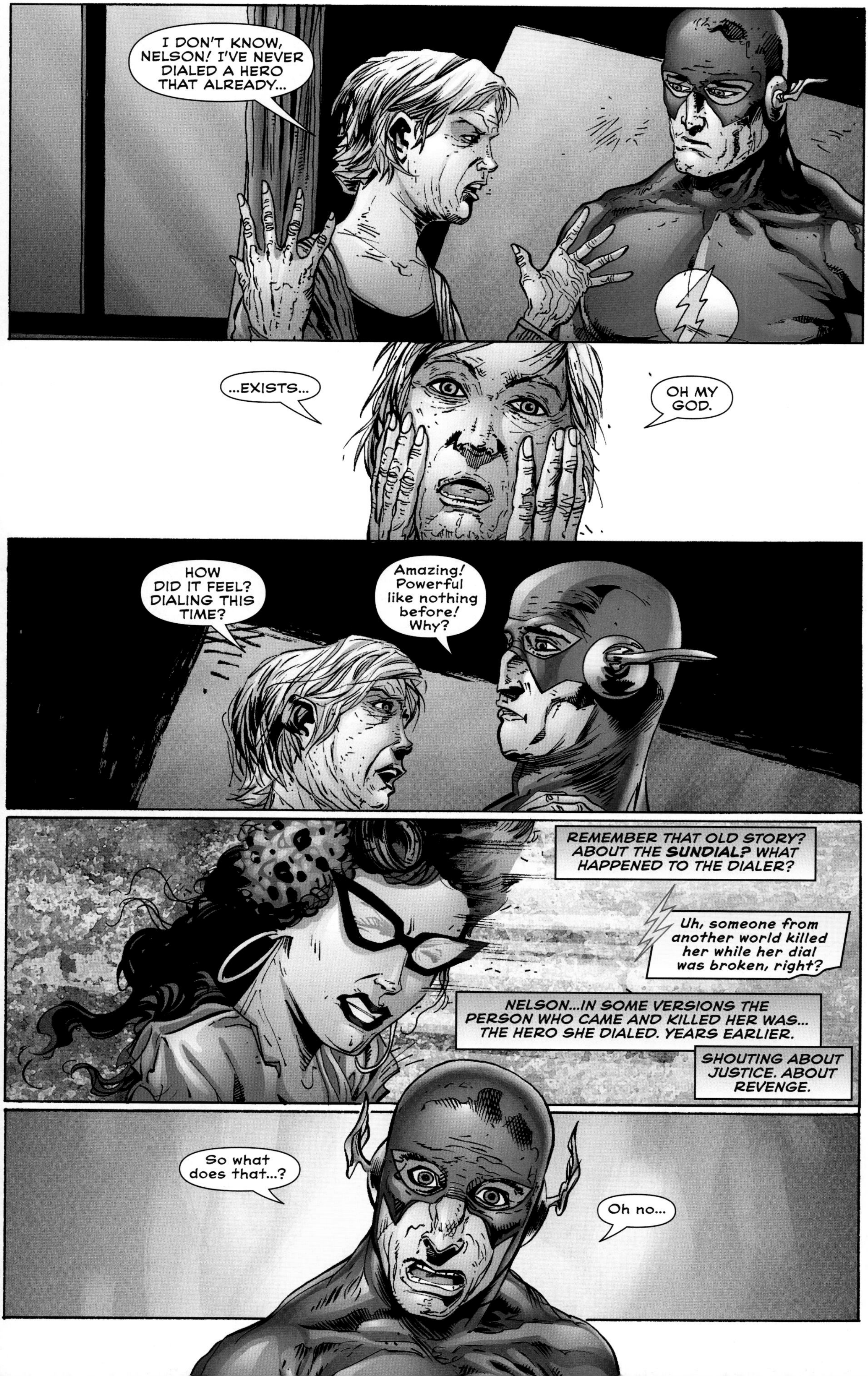
I DON'T KNOW, NELSON! I'VE NEVER DIALED A HERO THAT ALREADY...
...EXISTS...
OH MY GOD.
HOW DID IT FEEL? DIALING THIS TIME?
Amazing! Powerful like nothing before! Why?
REMEMBER THAT OLD STORY? ABOUT THE SUNDIAL? WHAT HAPPENED TO THE DIALER?
Uh, someone from another world killed her while her dial was broken, right?
NELSON...IN SOME VERSIONS THE PERSON WHO CAME AND KILLED HER WAS... THE HERO SHE DIALED. YEARS EARLIER.
SHOUTING ABOUT JUSTICE. ABOUT REVENGE.
So what does that...?
Oh no...

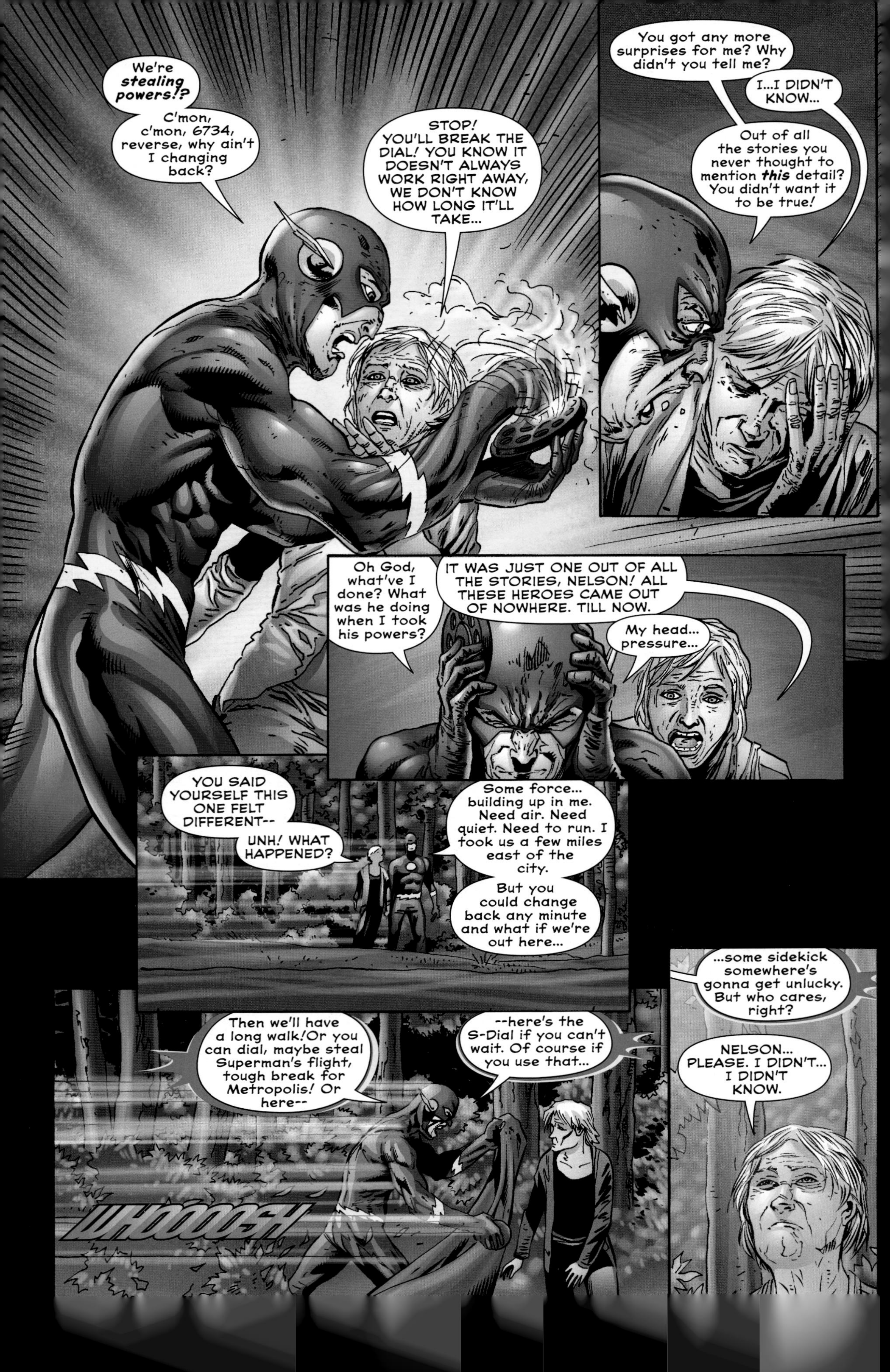
We're stealing powers!?
C'mon, c'mon, 6734, reverse, why ain't I changing back?
STOP! YOU'LL BREAK THE DIAL! YOU KNOW IT DOESN'T ALWAYS WORK RIGHT AWAY, WE DON'T KNOW HOW LONG IT'LL TAKE...
You got any more surprises for me? Why didn't you tell me?
I...I DIDN'T KNOW...
Out of all the stories you never thought to mention this detail? You didn't want it to be true!
Oh God, what've I done? What was he doing when I took his powers?
IT WAS JUST ONE OUT OF ALL THE STORIES, NELSON! ALL THESE HEROES CAME OUT OF NOWHERE. TILL NOW.
My head... pressure...
YOU SAID YOURSELF THIS ONE FELT DIFFERENT--
UNH! WHAT HAPPENED?
Some force... building up in me. Need air. Need quiet. Need to run. I took us a few miles east of the city.
But you could change back any minute and what if we're out here...
Then we'll have a long walk! Or you can dial, maybe steal Superman's flight, tough break for Metropolis! Or here--
--here's the S-Dial if you can't wait. Of course if you use that...
WHOOOOOSH
...some sidekick somewhere's gonna get unlucky. But who cares, right?
NELSON... PLEASE. I DIDN'T... I DIDN'T KNOW.

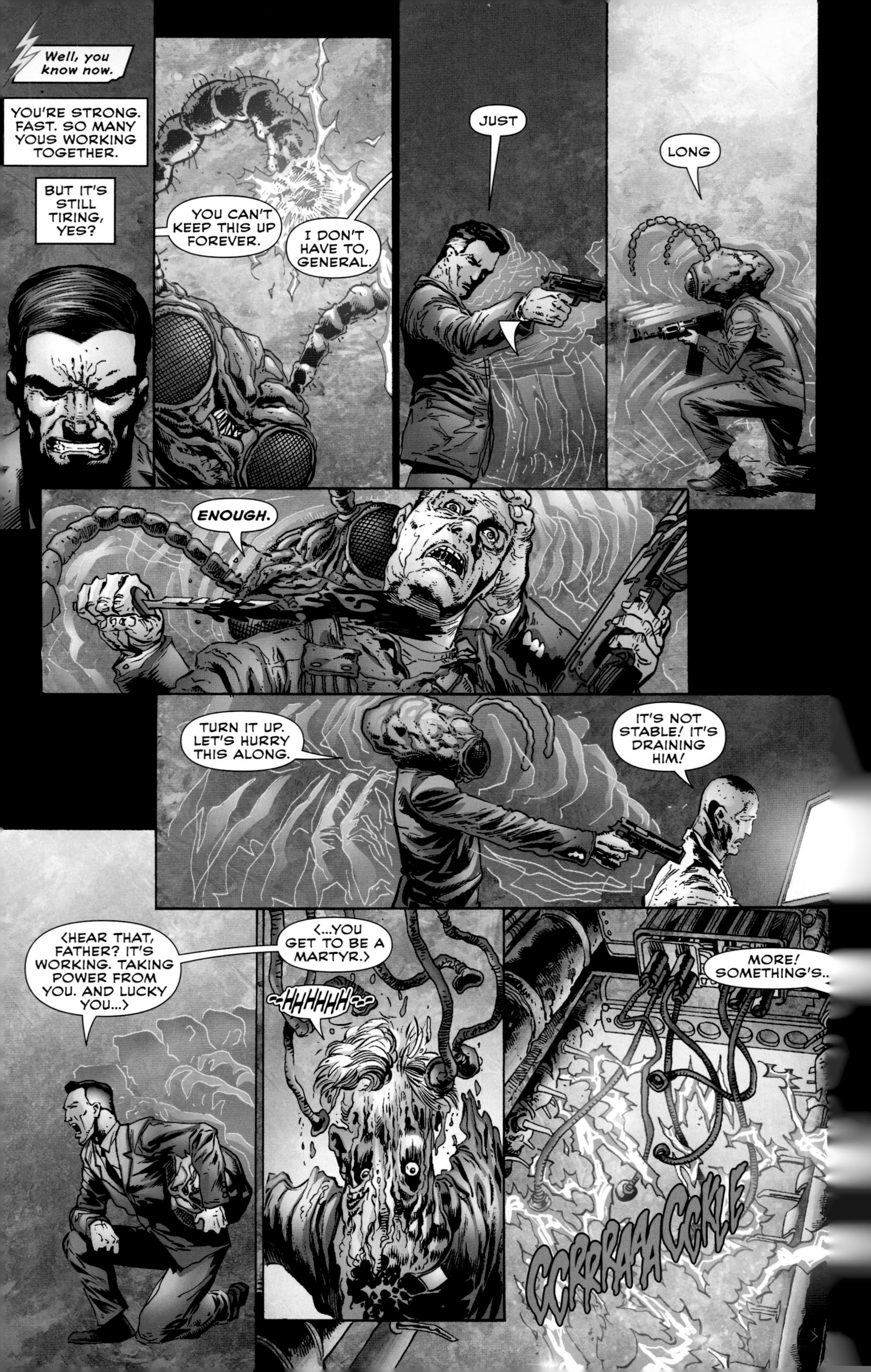
Well, you know now.
YOU'RE STRONG. FAST. SO MANY YOUS WORKING TOGETHER.
BUT IT'S STILL TIRING, YES?
YOU CAN'T KEEP THIS UP FOREVER.
I DON'T HAVE TO, GENERAL.
JUST
LONG
ENOUGH.
TURN IT UP. LET'S HURRY THIS ALONG.
IT'S NOT STABLE! IT'S DRAINING HIM!
<HEAR THAT, FATHER? IT'S WORKING. TAKING POWER FROM YOU. AND LUCKY YOU...>
<...YOU GET TO BE A MARTYR.>
-HHHHHH-
MORE! SOMETHING'S..
CCRRRAAACCKLE

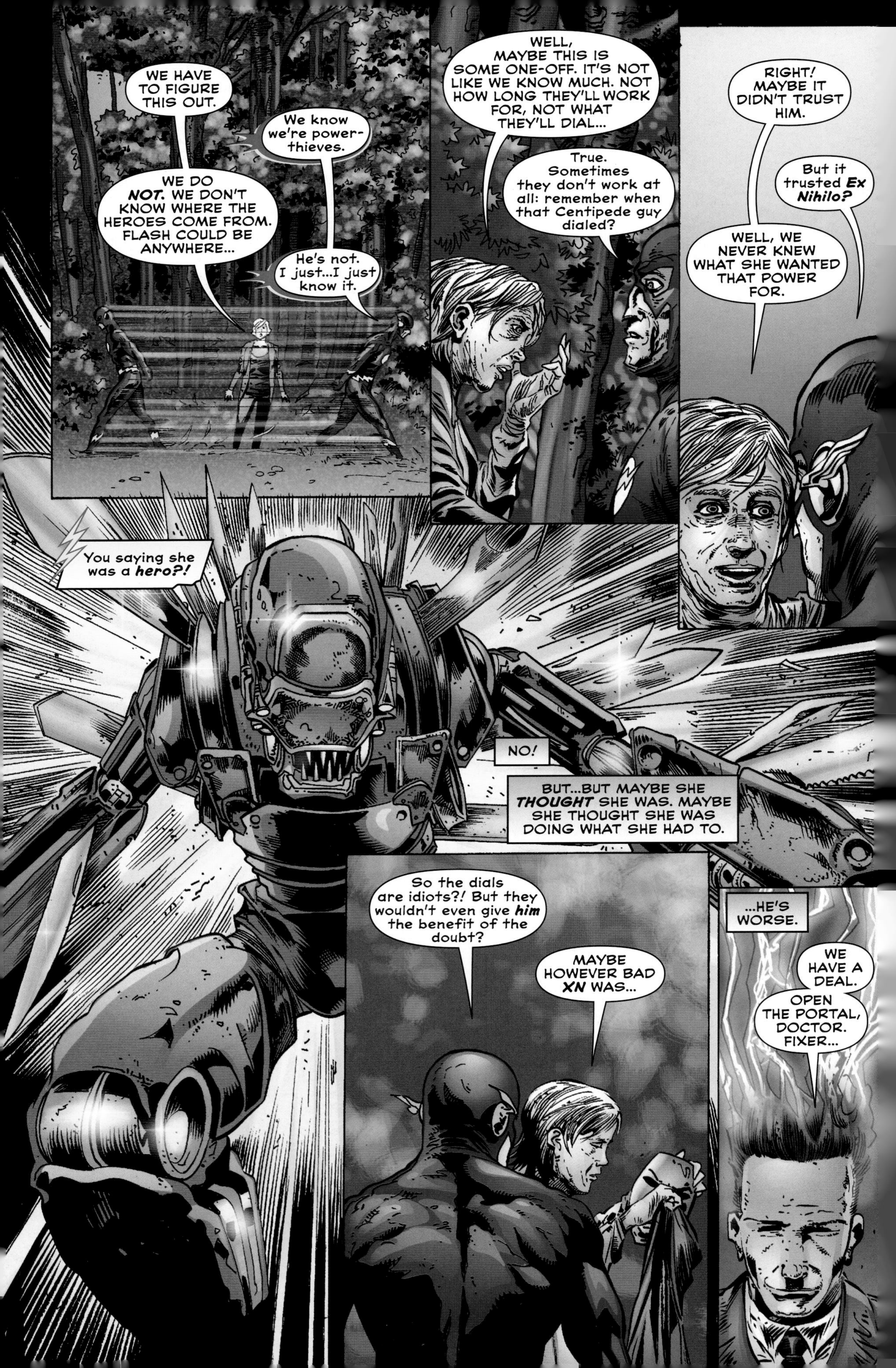
WE HAVE TO FIGURE THIS OUT.
We know we're power-thieves.
WE DO *NOT.* WE DON'T KNOW WHERE THE HEROES COME FROM. FLASH COULD BE ANYWHERE...
He's not. I just...I just know it.
WELL, MAYBE THIS IS SOME ONE-OFF. IT'S NOT LIKE WE KNOW MUCH. NOT HOW LONG THEY'LL WORK FOR, NOT WHAT THEY'LL DIAL...
True. Sometimes they don't work at all: remember when that Centipede guy dialed?
RIGHT! MAYBE IT DIDN'T TRUST HIM.
But it trusted *Ex Nihilo?*
WELL, WE NEVER KNEW WHAT SHE WANTED THAT POWER FOR.
You saying she was a *hero?!*
NO!
BUT...BUT MAYBE SHE *THOUGHT* SHE WAS. MAYBE SHE THOUGHT SHE WAS DOING WHAT SHE HAD TO.
So the dials are idiots?! But they wouldn't even give *him* the benefit of the doubt?
MAYBE HOWEVER BAD *XN* WAS...
...HE'S WORSE.
WE HAVE A DEAL.
OPEN THE PORTAL, DOCTOR. FIXER...

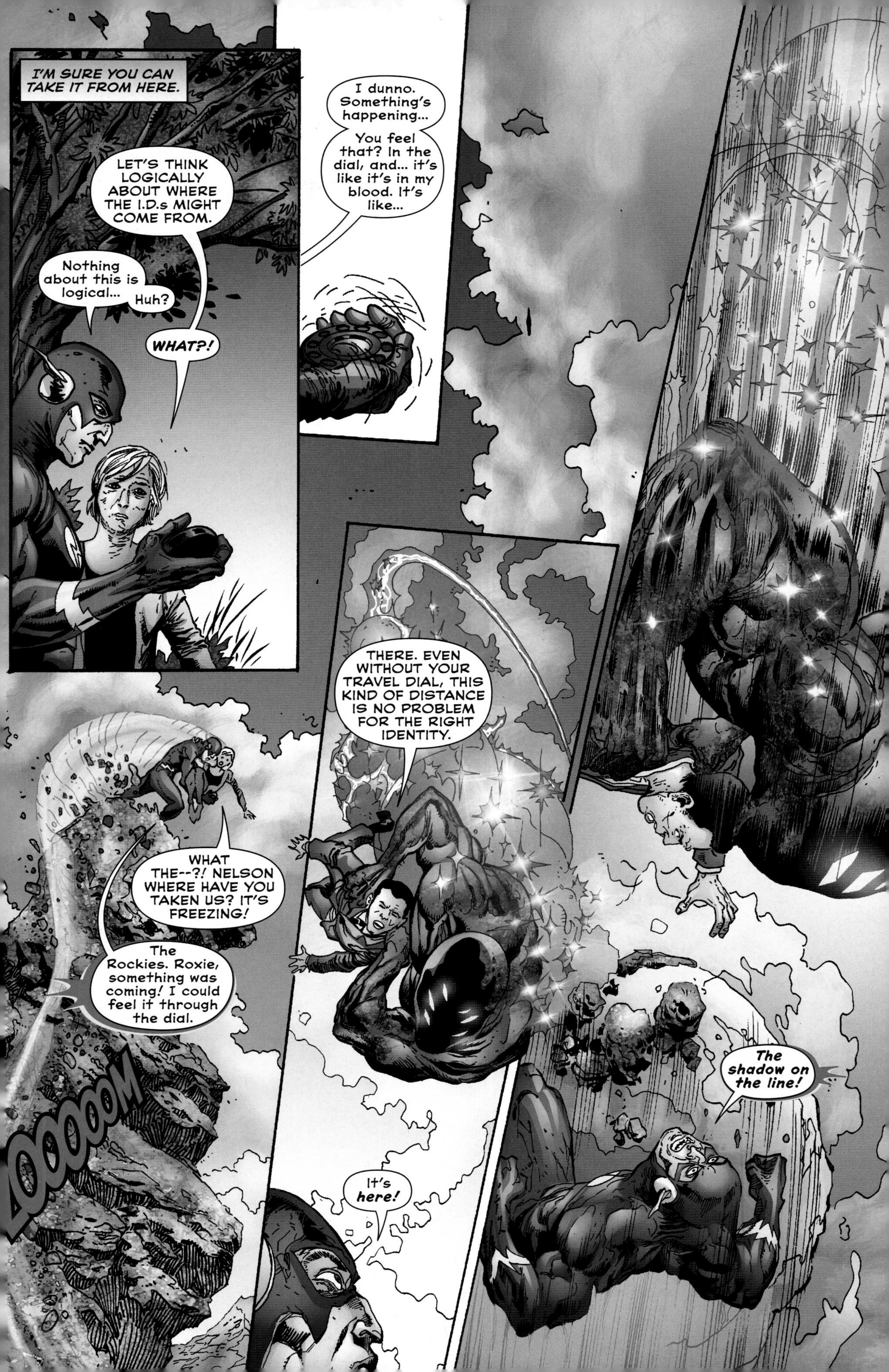
I'M SURE YOU CAN TAKE IT FROM HERE.
LET'S THINK LOGICALLY ABOUT WHERE THE I.D.s MIGHT COME FROM.
Nothing about this is logical...
Huh?
WHAT?!
I dunno. Something's happening...
You feel that? In the dial, and... it's like it's in my blood. It's like...
...
THERE. EVEN WITHOUT YOUR TRAVEL DIAL, THIS KIND OF DISTANCE IS NO PROBLEM FOR THE RIGHT IDENTITY.
WHAT THE--?! NELSON WHERE HAVE YOU TAKEN US? IT'S FREEZING!
The Rockies. Roxie, something was coming! I could feel it through the dial.
ZOOOOOM
It's here!
The shadow on the line!

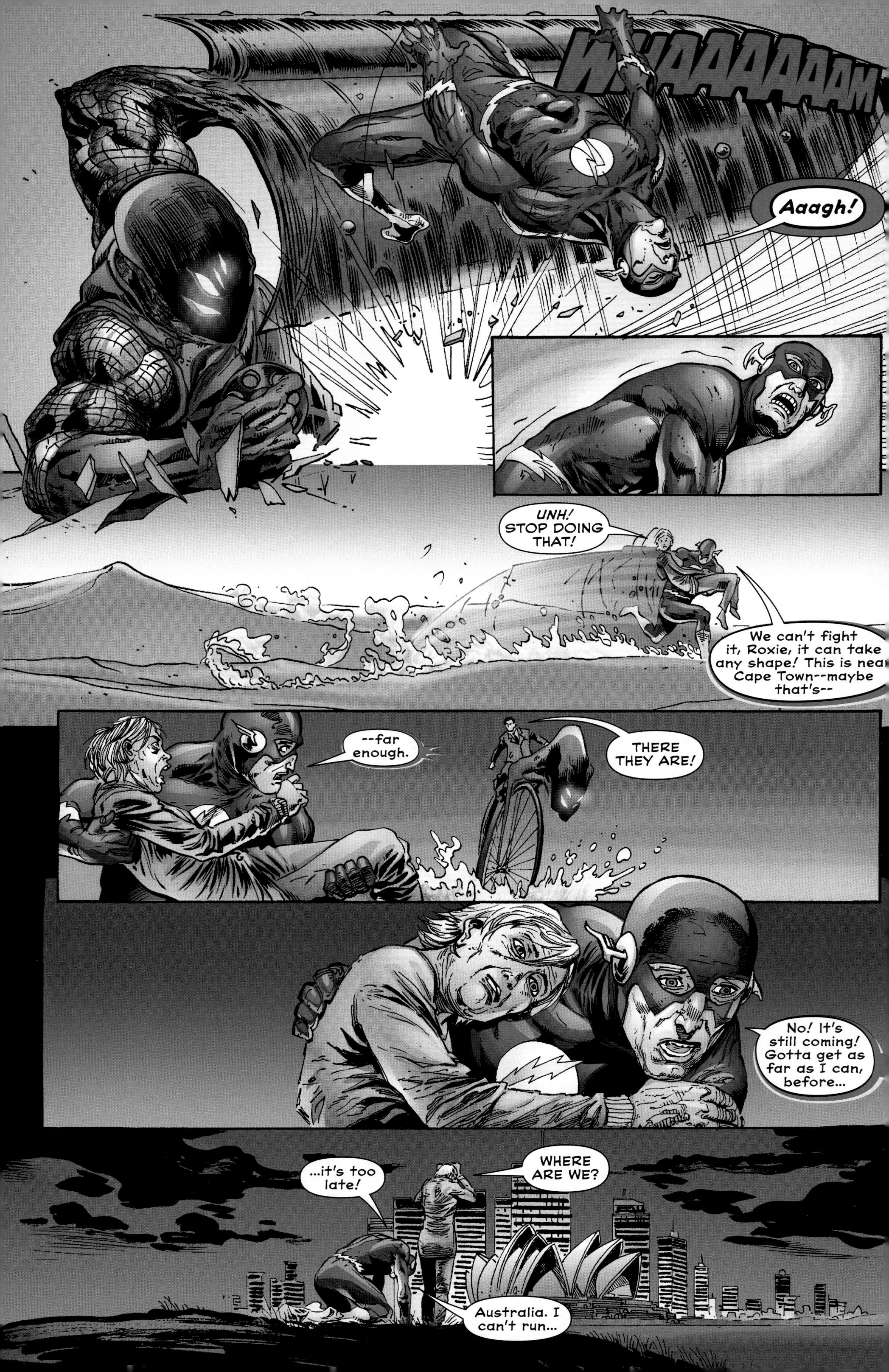
WHAAAAAAAM
Aaagh!
UNH! STOP DOING THAT!
We can't fight it, Roxie, it can take any shape! This is near Cape Town--maybe that's--
--far enough.
THERE THEY ARE!
No! It's still coming! Gotta get as far as I can, before...
...it's too late!
WHERE ARE WE?
Australia. I can't run...

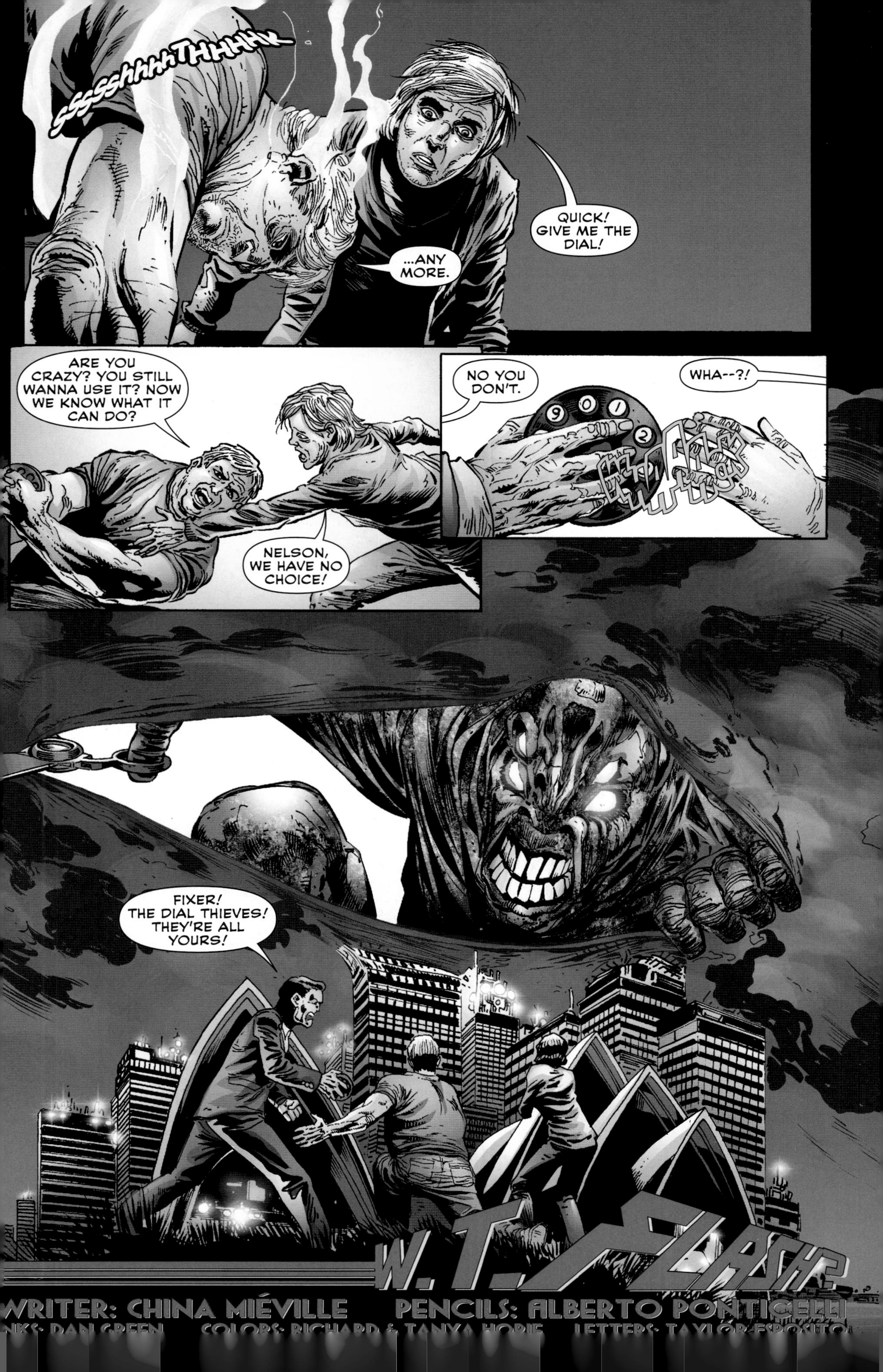
SSSSSHHHHTHHHHK
...ANY MORE.
QUICK! GIVE ME THE DIAL!
ARE YOU CRAZY? YOU STILL WANNA USE IT? NOW WE KNOW WHAT IT CAN DO?
NELSON, WE HAVE NO CHOICE!
NO YOU DON'T.
WHA--?!
FIXER! THE DIAL THIEVES! THEY'RE ALL YOURS!
W.T.FLASH?
WRITER: CHINA MIÉVILLE PENCILS: ALBERTO PONTICELLI
NKS: DAN GREEN COLORS: RICHARD & TANYA HORIE LETTERS: TAYLOR ESPOSITO

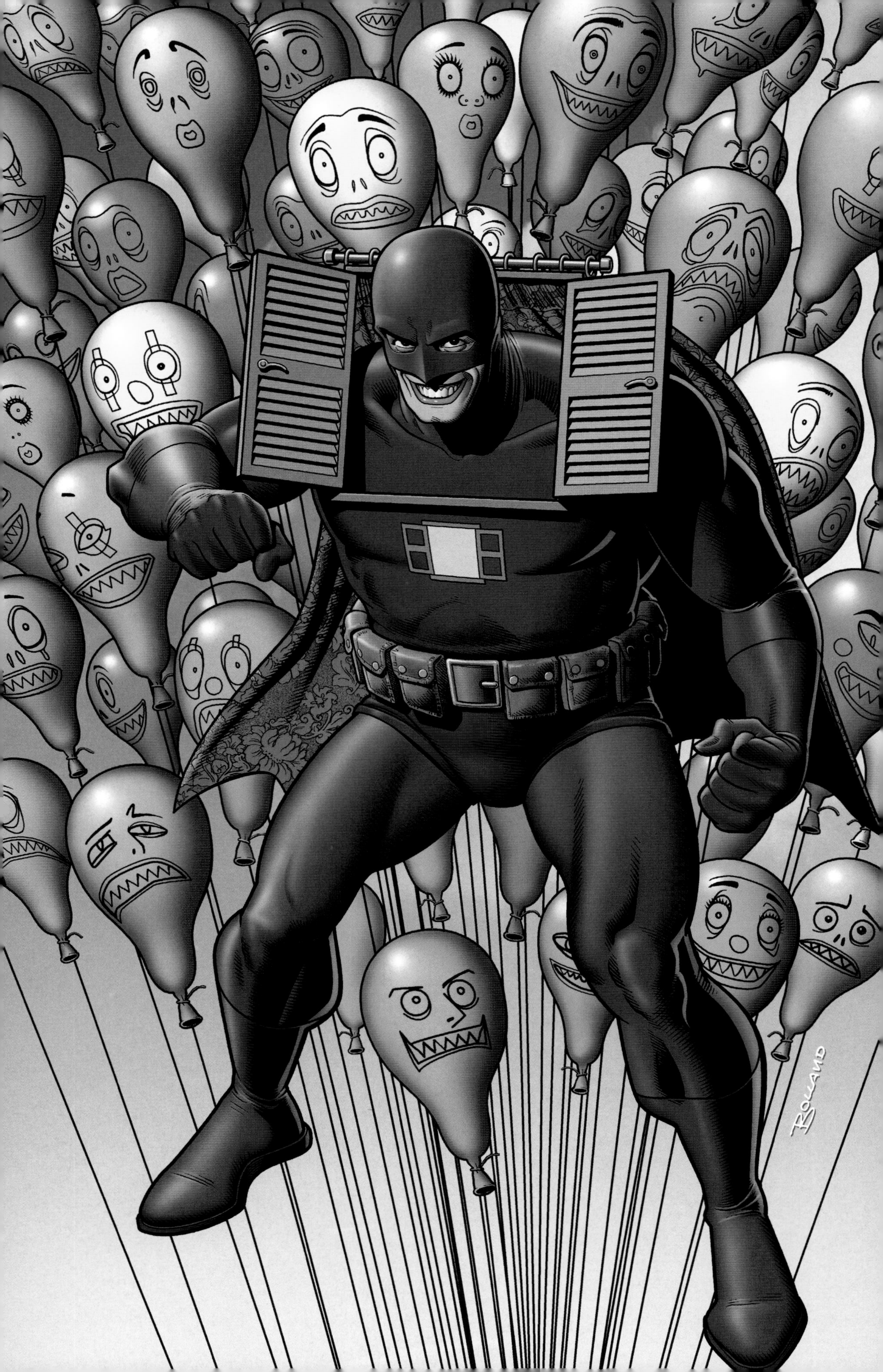

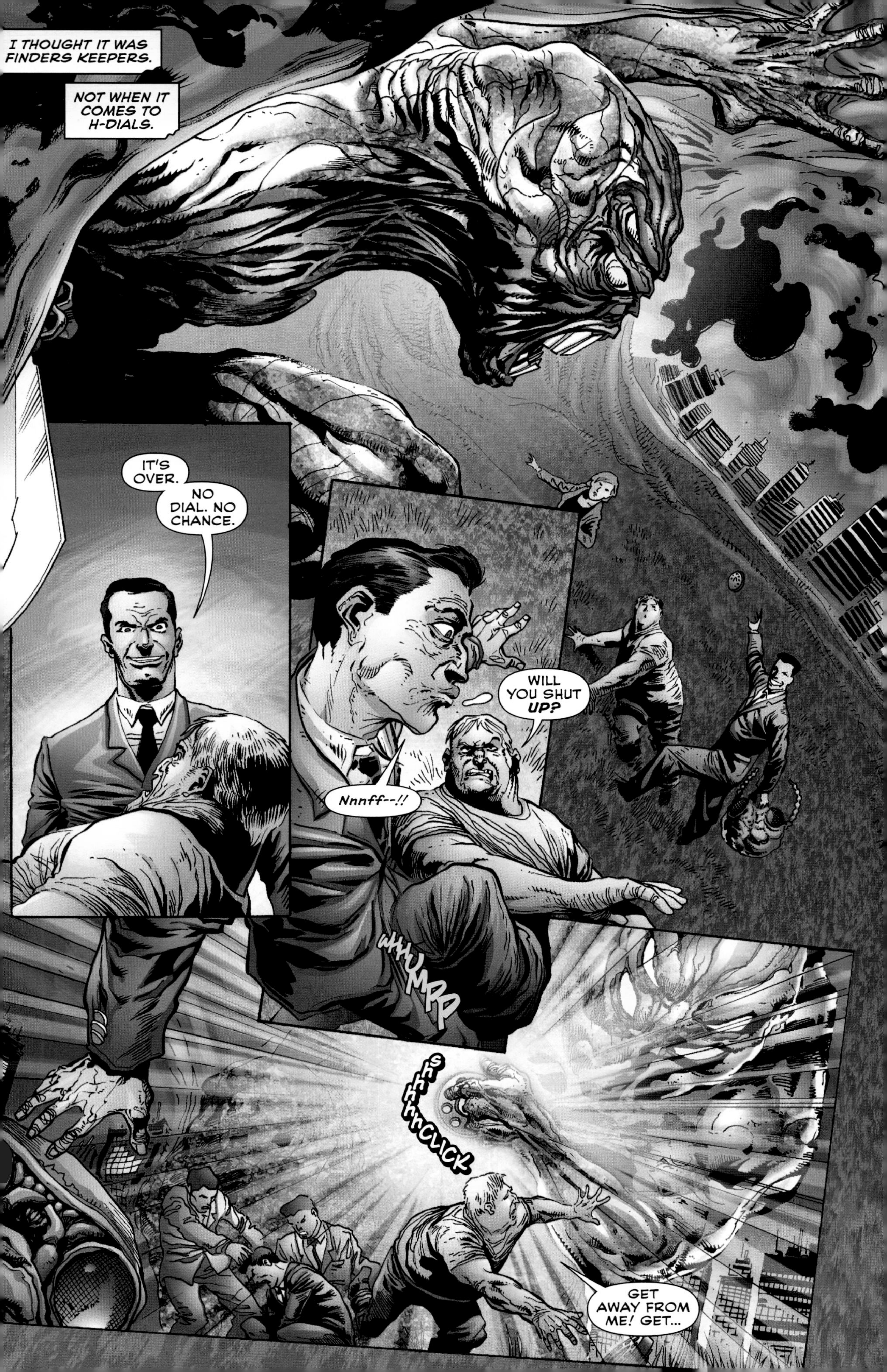
I THOUGHT IT WAS FINDERS KEEPERS.
NOT WHEN IT COMES TO H-DIALS.
IT'S OVER.
NO DIAL. NO CHANCE.
WILL YOU SHUT *UP?*
Nnnff--!!
WHHUMPP
SHHHKCLICK
GET AWAY FROM ME! GET...

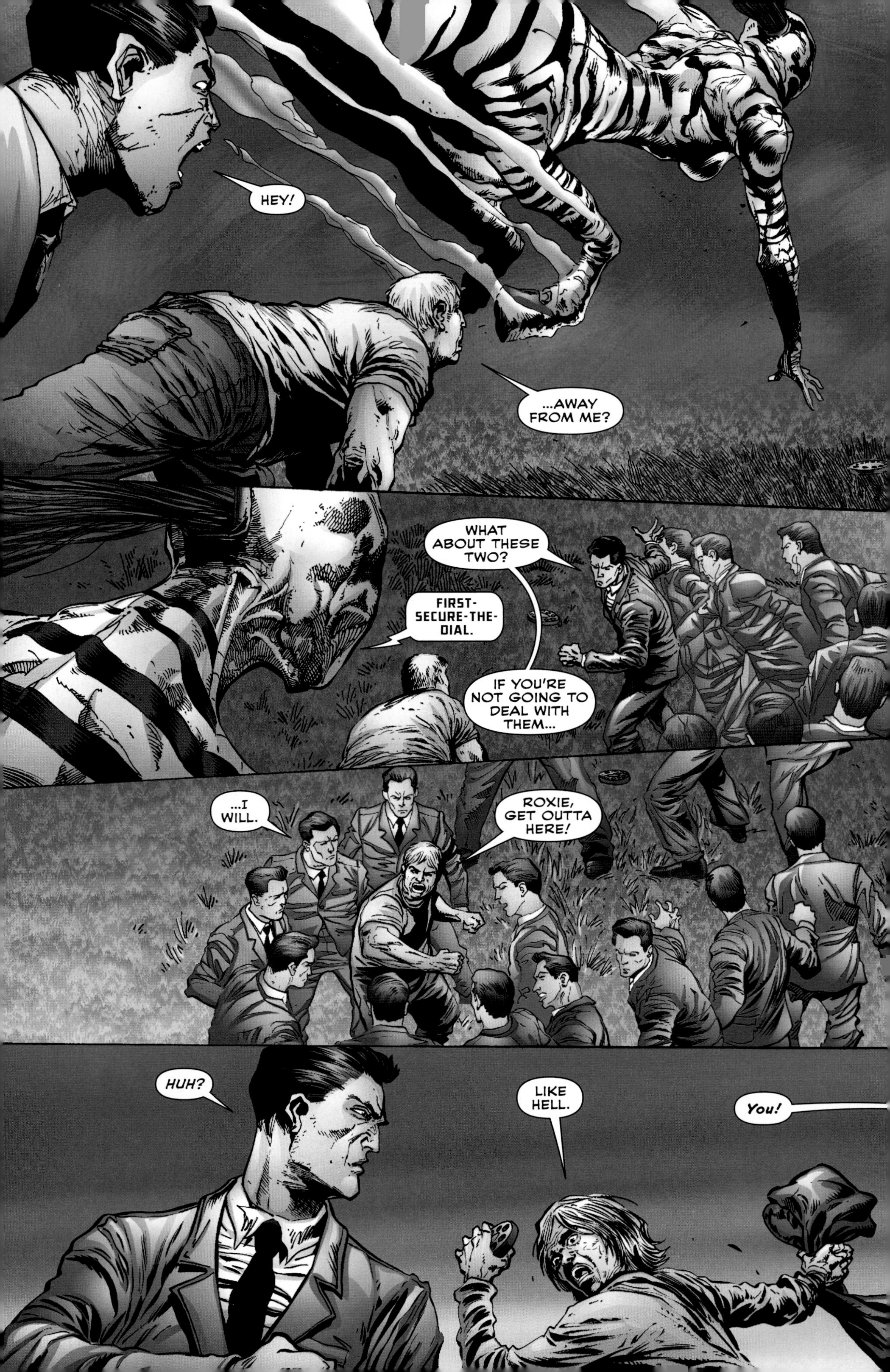
HEY!
...AWAY FROM ME?
WHAT ABOUT THESE TWO?
FIRST-SECURE-THE-DIAL.
IF YOU'RE NOT GOING TO DEAL WITH THEM...
...I WILL.
ROXIE, GET OUTTA HERE!
HUH?
LIKE HELL.
You!

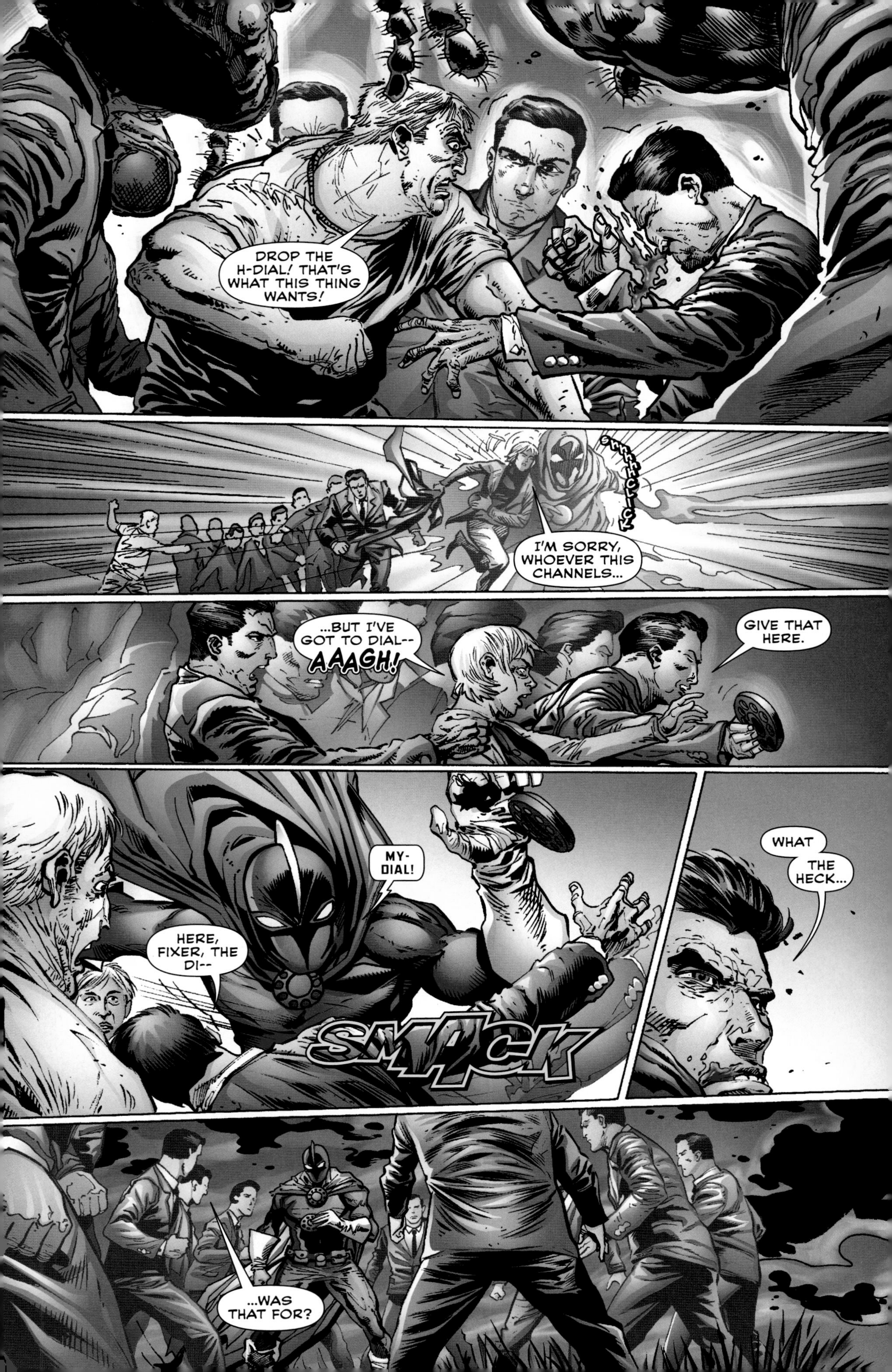
DROP THE H-DIAL! THAT'S WHAT THIS THING WANTS!
shhhhCLICK
I'M SORRY, WHOEVER THIS CHANNELS...
...BUT I'VE GOT TO DIAL-- AAAGH!
GIVE THAT HERE.
MY-DIAL!
HERE, FIXER, THE DI--
SMACK
WHAT THE HECK...
...WAS THAT FOR?

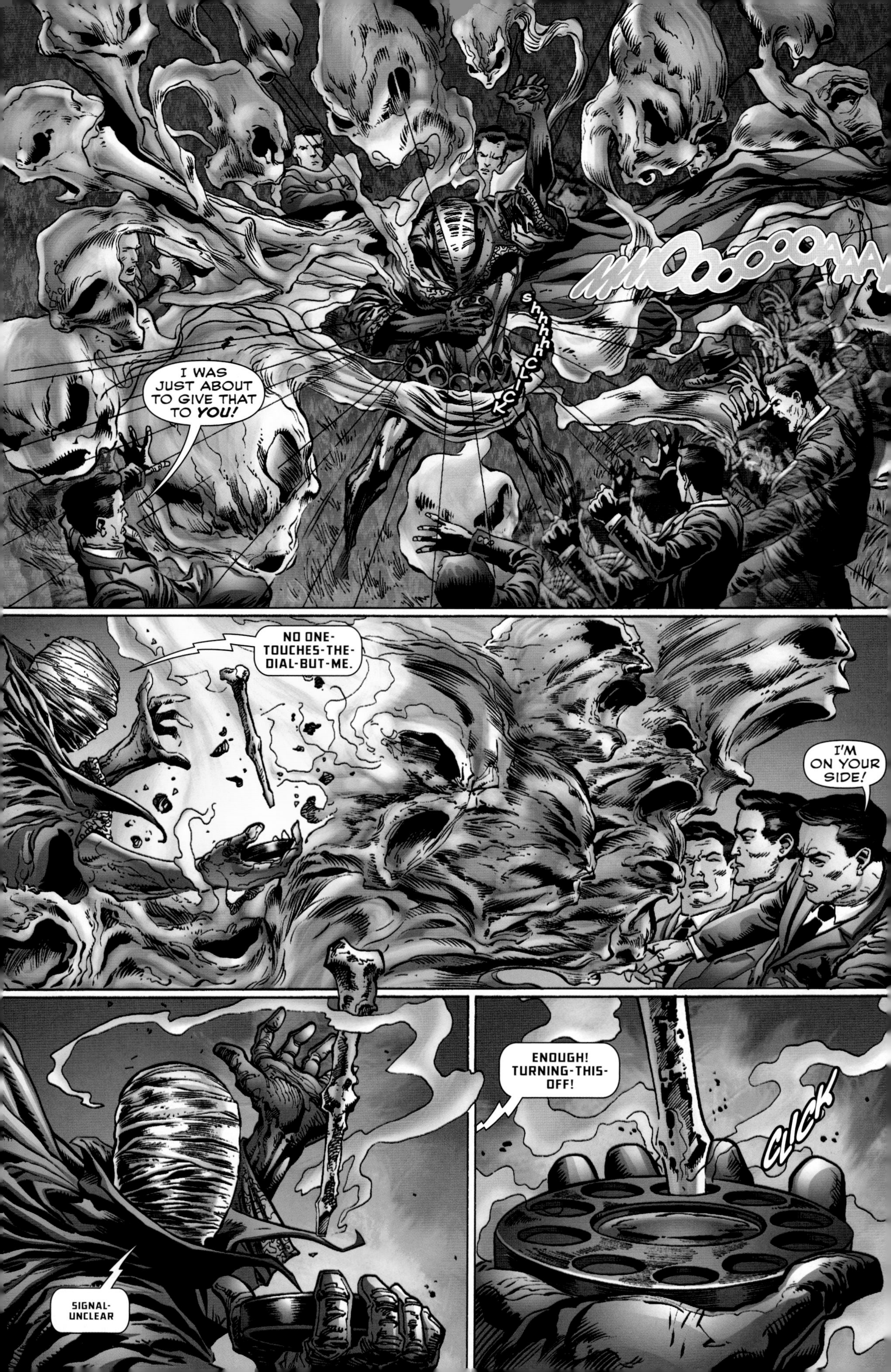
MMMOOoooOOOAAAA
SHHHHCLICK
I WAS JUST ABOUT TO GIVE THAT TO *YOU!*
NO ONE-TOUCHES-THE-DIAL-BUT-ME.
I'M ON YOUR SIDE!
SIGNAL-UNCLEAR
ENOUGH! TURNING-THIS-OFF!
CLICK

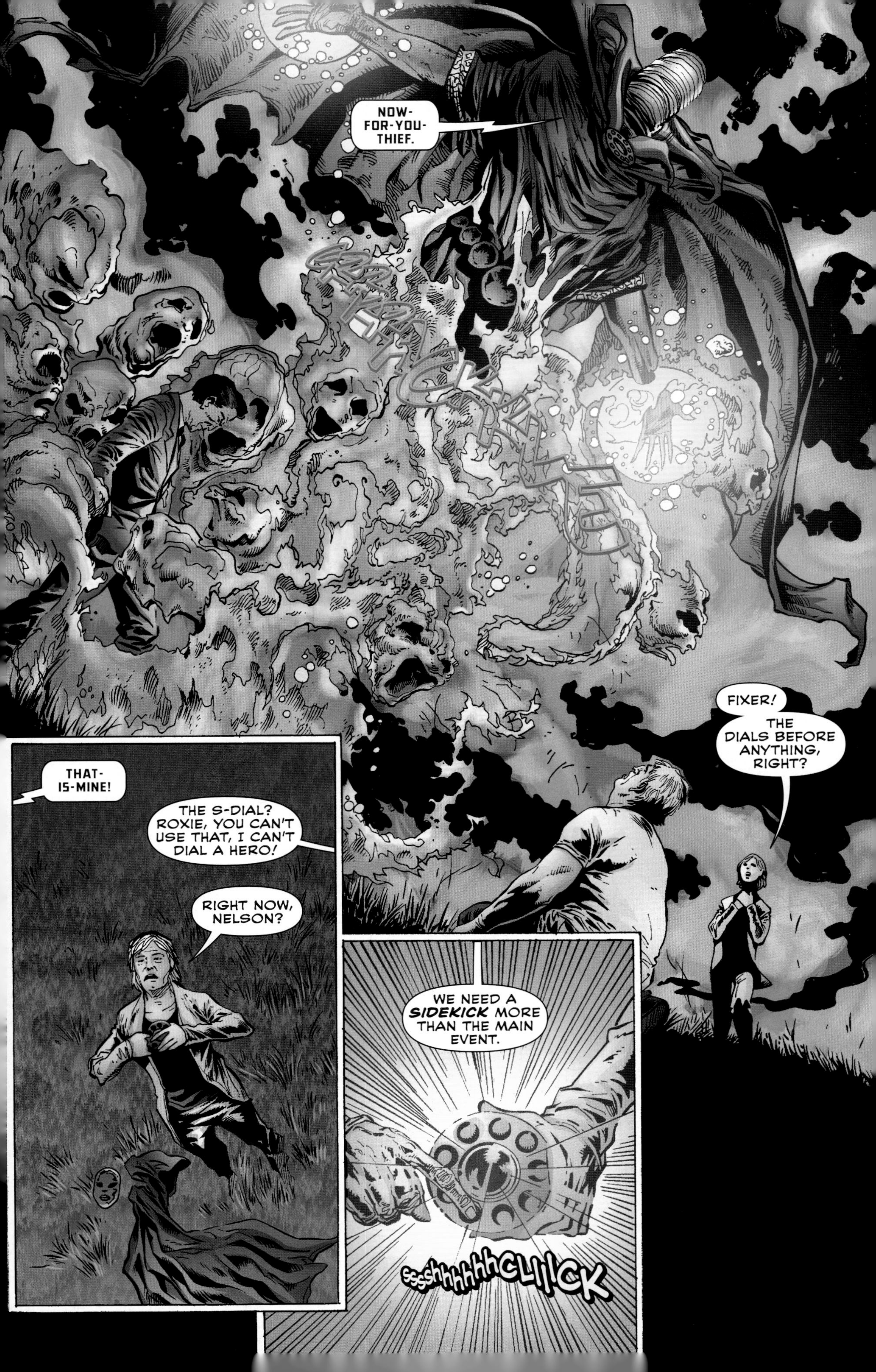
NOW-FOR-YOU-THIEF.
FIXER!
THE DIALS BEFORE ANYTHING, RIGHT?
THAT-IS-MINE!
THE S-DIAL? ROXIE, YOU CAN'T USE THAT, I CAN'T DIAL A HERO!
RIGHT NOW, NELSON?
WE NEED A *SIDEKICK* MORE THAN THE MAIN EVENT.
SSSSHHHHHHCLIIICK

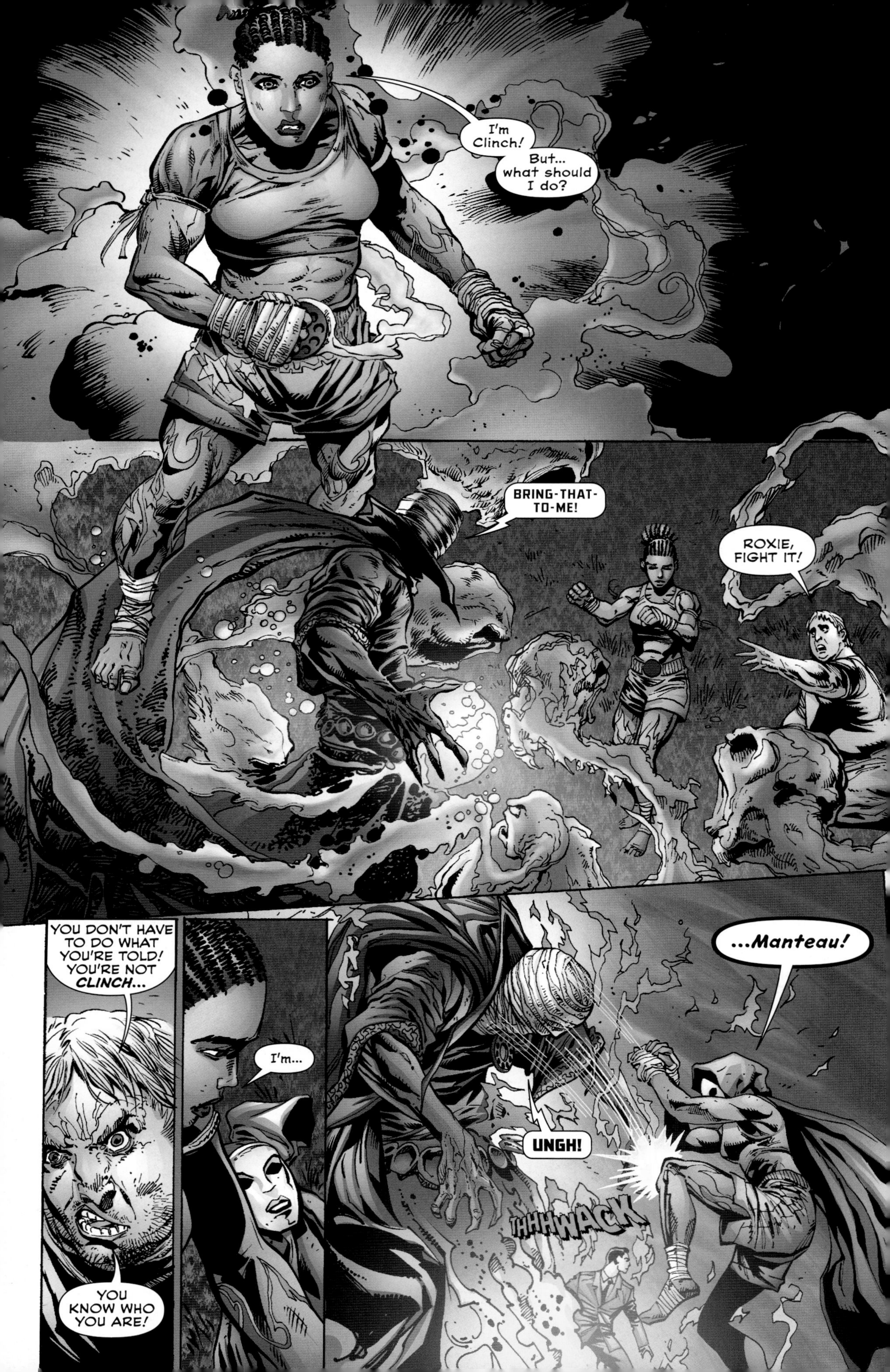
I'm Clinch!
But... what should I do?
BRING-THAT-TO-ME!
ROXIE, FIGHT IT!
YOU DON'T HAVE TO DO WHAT YOU'RE TOLD! YOU'RE NOT CLINCH...
YOU KNOW WHO YOU ARE!
I'm...
...Manteau!
UNGH!
THHHWACK

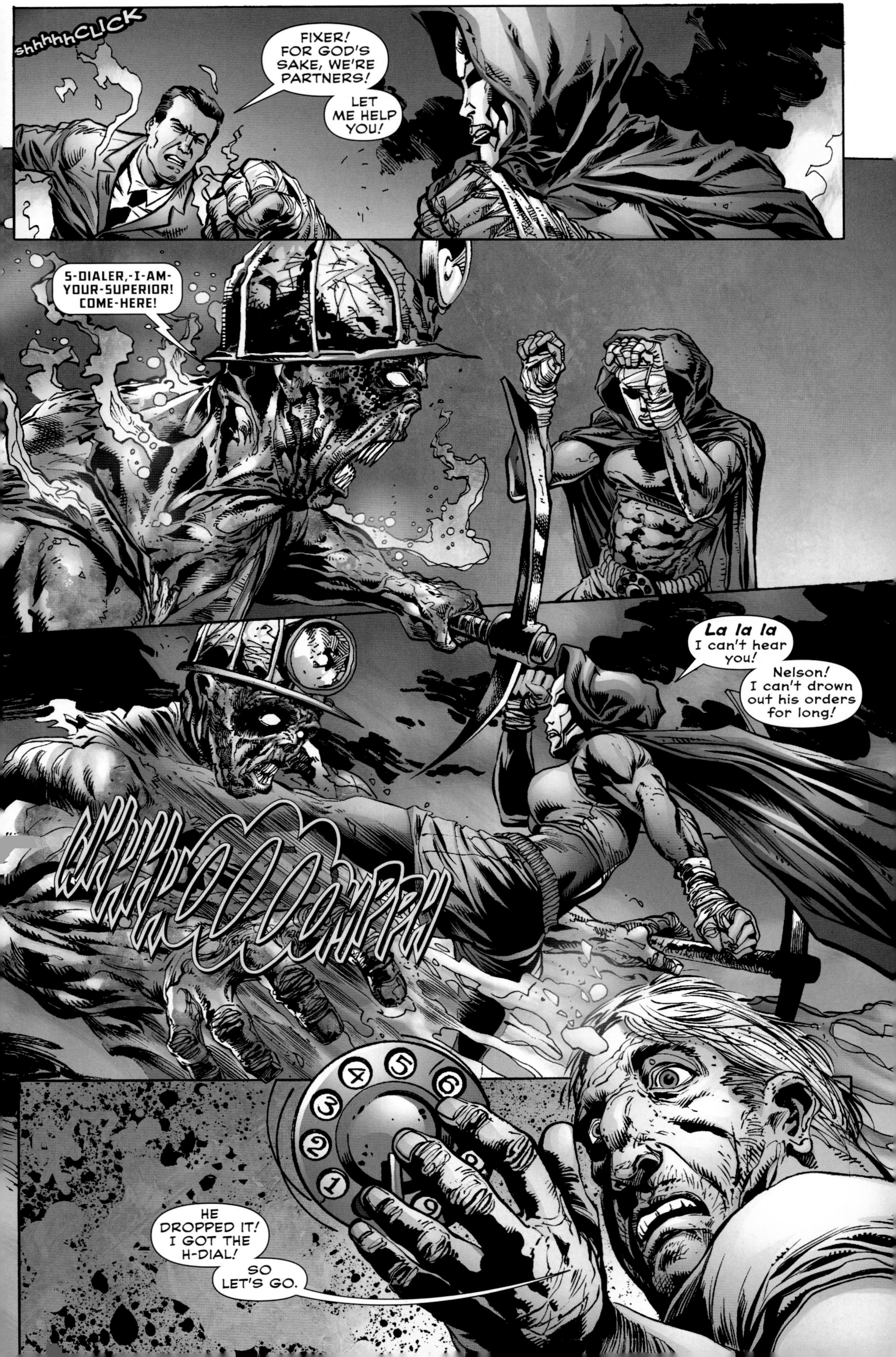
shhhhhCLICK
FIXER! FOR GOD'S SAKE, WE'RE PARTNERS!
LET ME HELP YOU!
S-DIALER,-I-AM-YOUR-SUPERIOR! COME-HERE!
La la la I can't hear you!
Nelson! I can't drown out his orders for long!
HE DROPPED IT! I GOT THE H-DIAL!
SO LET'S GO.

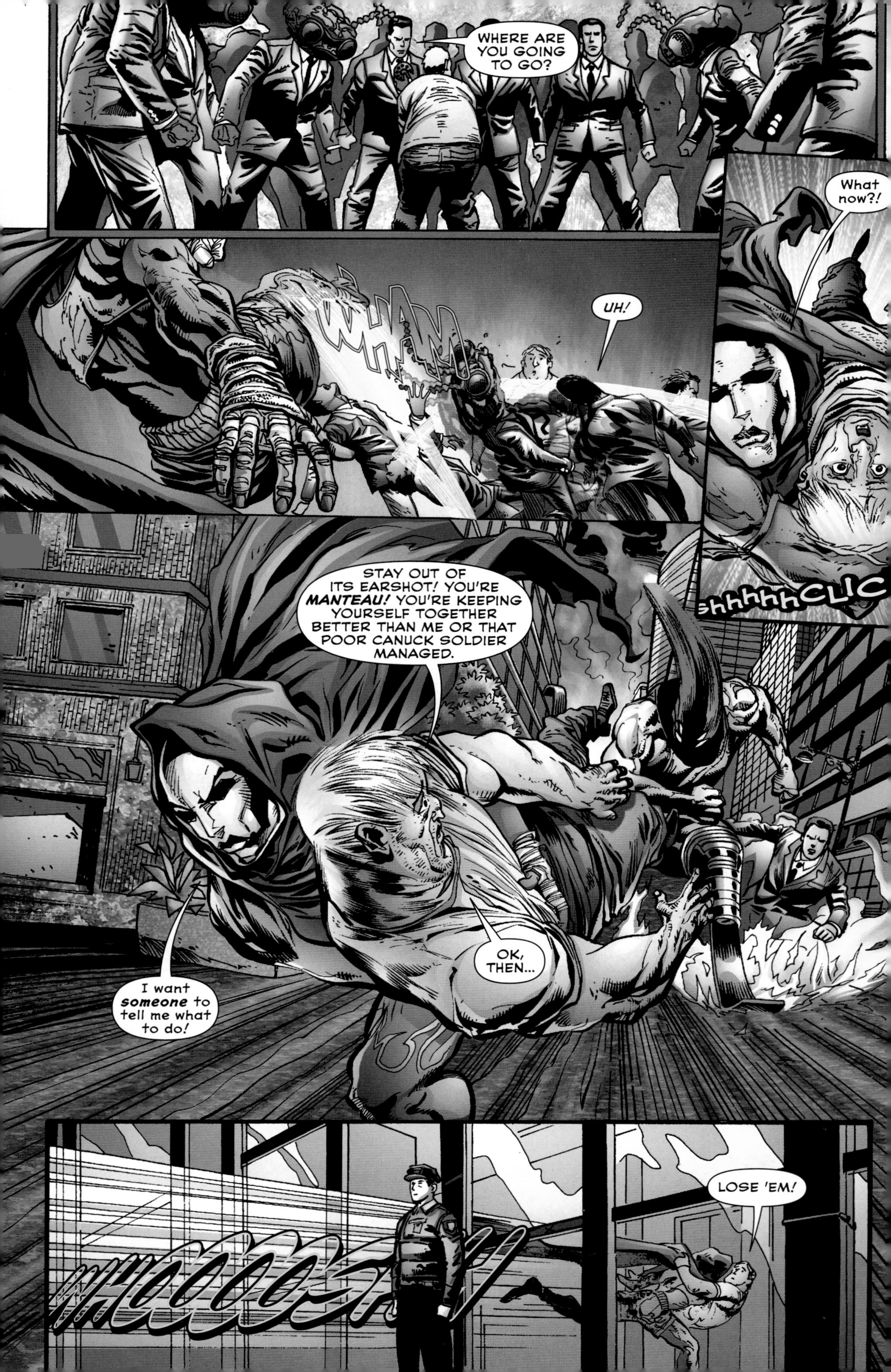
WHERE ARE YOU GOING TO GO?
What now?!
UH!
ShhhhhCLIC
STAY OUT OF ITS EARSHOT! YOU'RE MANTEAU! YOU'RE KEEPING YOURSELF TOGETHER BETTER THAN ME OR THAT POOR CANUCK SOLDIER MANAGED.
OK, THEN...
I want someone to tell me what to do!
LOSE 'EM!

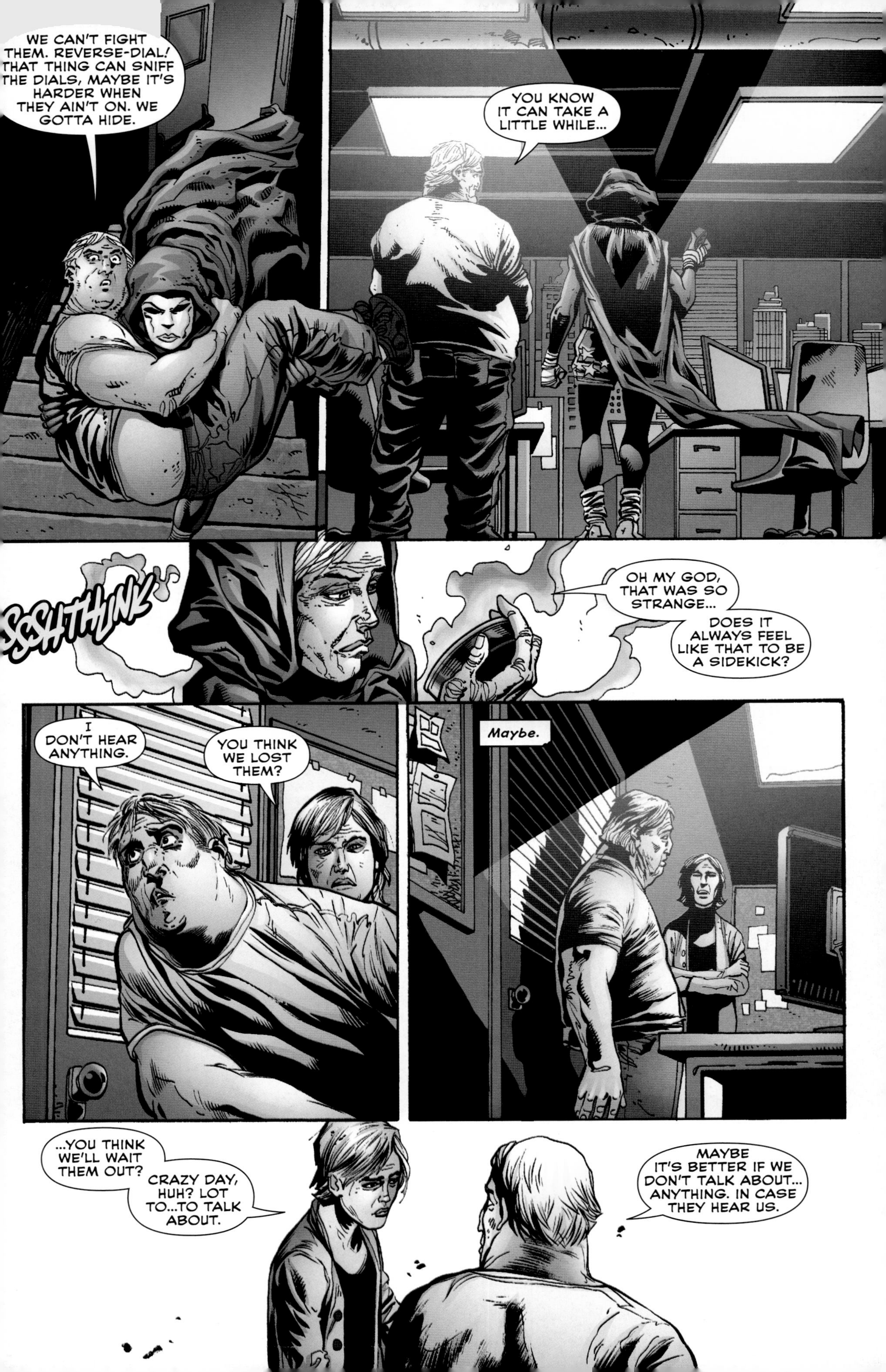
WE CAN'T FIGHT THEM. REVERSE-DIAL! THAT THING CAN SNIFF THE DIALS, MAYBE IT'S HARDER WHEN THEY AIN'T ON. WE GOTTA HIDE.
YOU KNOW IT CAN TAKE A LITTLE WHILE...
SSHTHUNK
OH MY GOD, THAT WAS SO STRANGE...
DOES IT ALWAYS FEEL LIKE THAT TO BE A SIDEKICK?
I DON'T HEAR ANYTHING.
YOU THINK WE LOST THEM?
Maybe.
...YOU THINK WE'LL WAIT THEM OUT?
CRAZY DAY, HUH? LOT TO...TO TALK ABOUT.
MAYBE IT'S BETTER IF WE DON'T TALK ABOUT... ANYTHING. IN CASE THEY HEAR US.

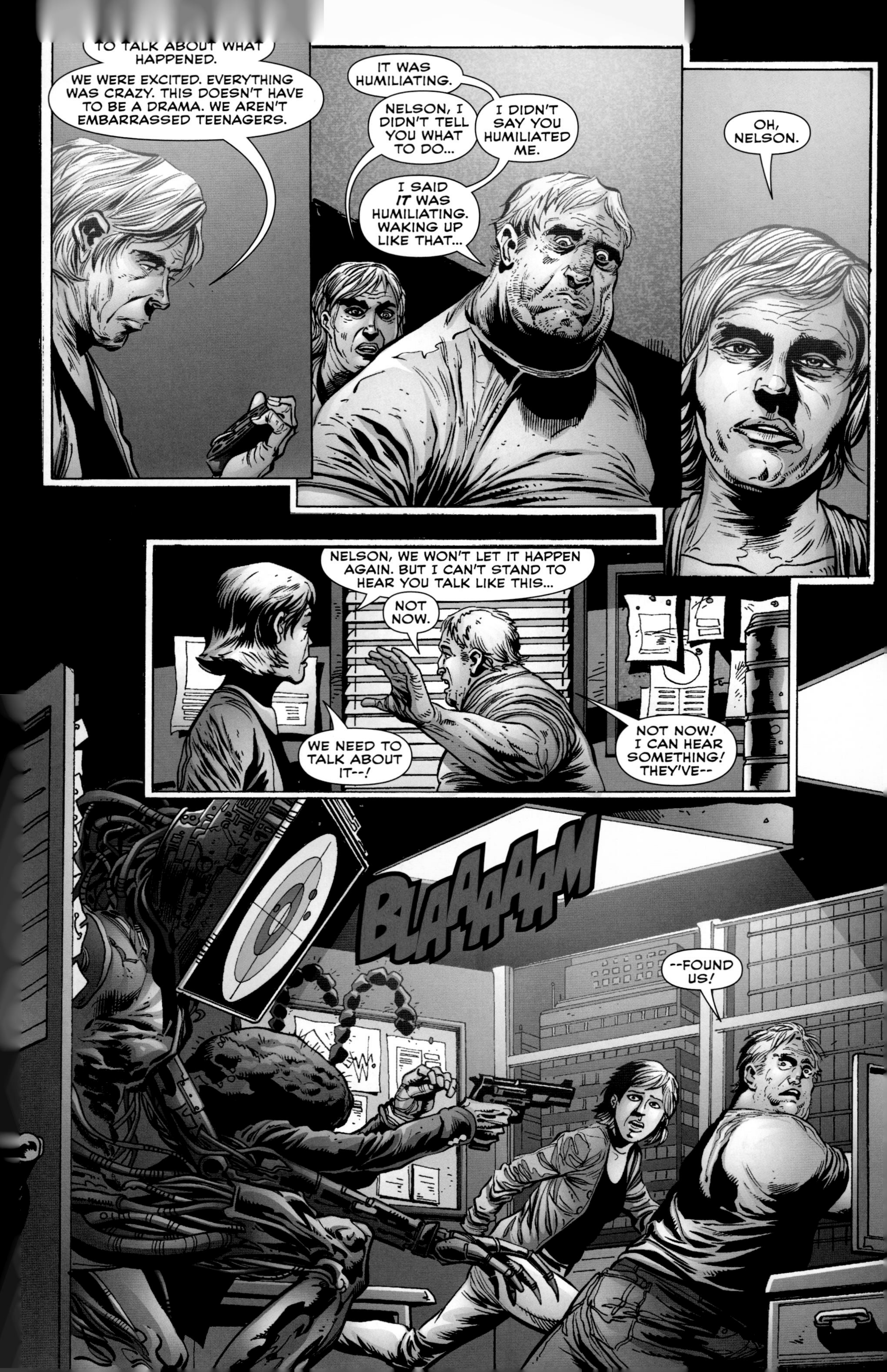

TO TALK ABOUT WHAT HAPPENED.
WE WERE EXCITED. EVERYTHING WAS CRAZY. THIS DOESN'T HAVE TO BE A DRAMA. WE AREN'T EMBARRASSED TEENAGERS.
IT WAS HUMILIATING.
NELSON, I DIDN'T TELL YOU WHAT TO DO...
I DIDN'T SAY YOU HUMILIATED ME.
I SAID *IT* WAS HUMILIATING. WAKING UP LIKE THAT...
OH, NELSON.
NELSON, WE WON'T LET IT HAPPEN AGAIN. BUT I CAN'T STAND TO HEAR YOU TALK LIKE THIS...
NOT NOW.
WE NEED TO TALK ABOUT IT--!
NOT NOW! I CAN HEAR SOMETHING! THEY'VE--
BLAAAAAM
--FOUND US!

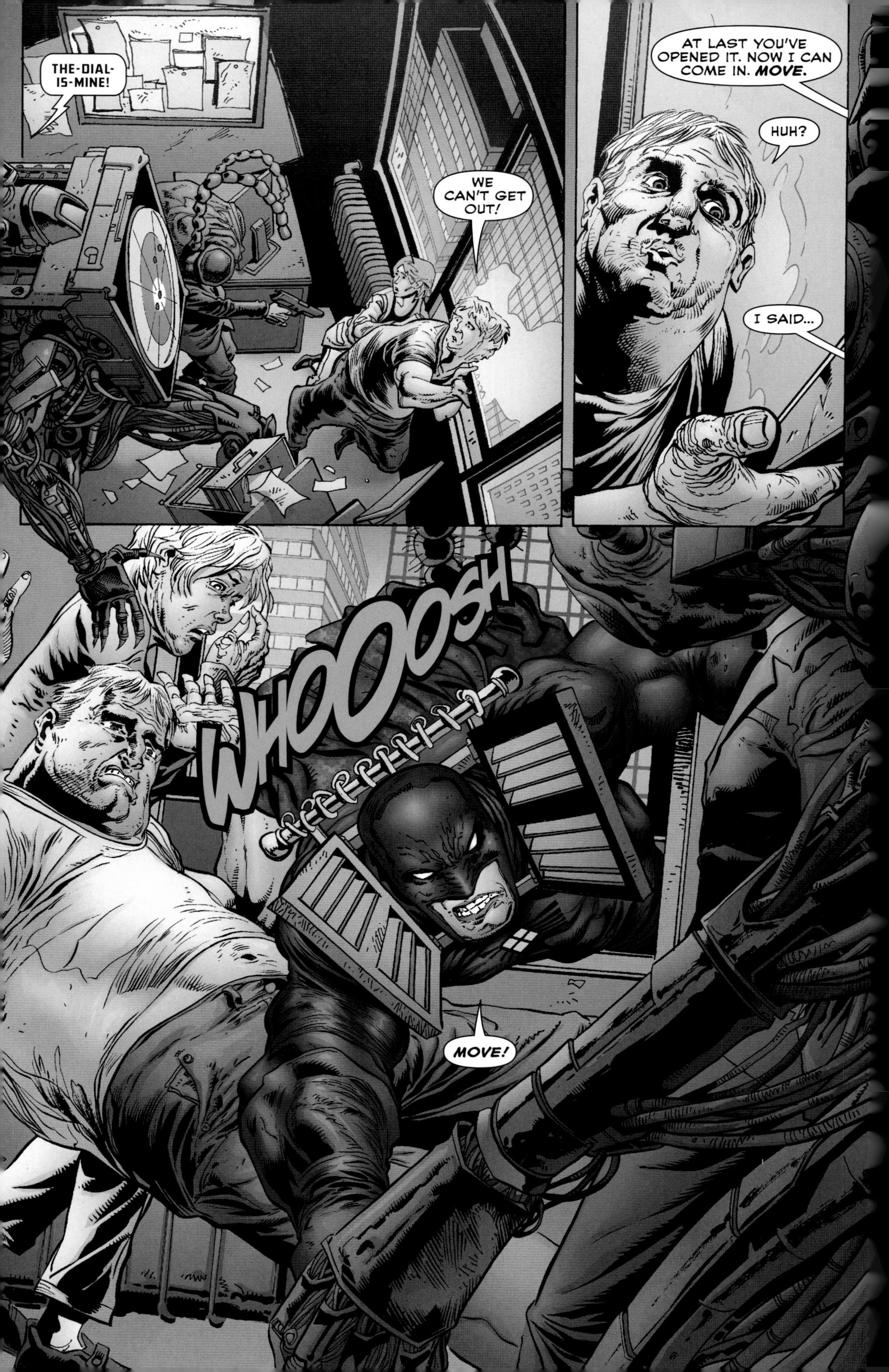
THE-DIAL-IS-MINE!
WE CAN'T GET OUT!
AT LAST YOU'VE OPENED IT. NOW I CAN COME IN. ***MOVE.***
HUH?
I SAID...
WHOOOOSH
MOVE!

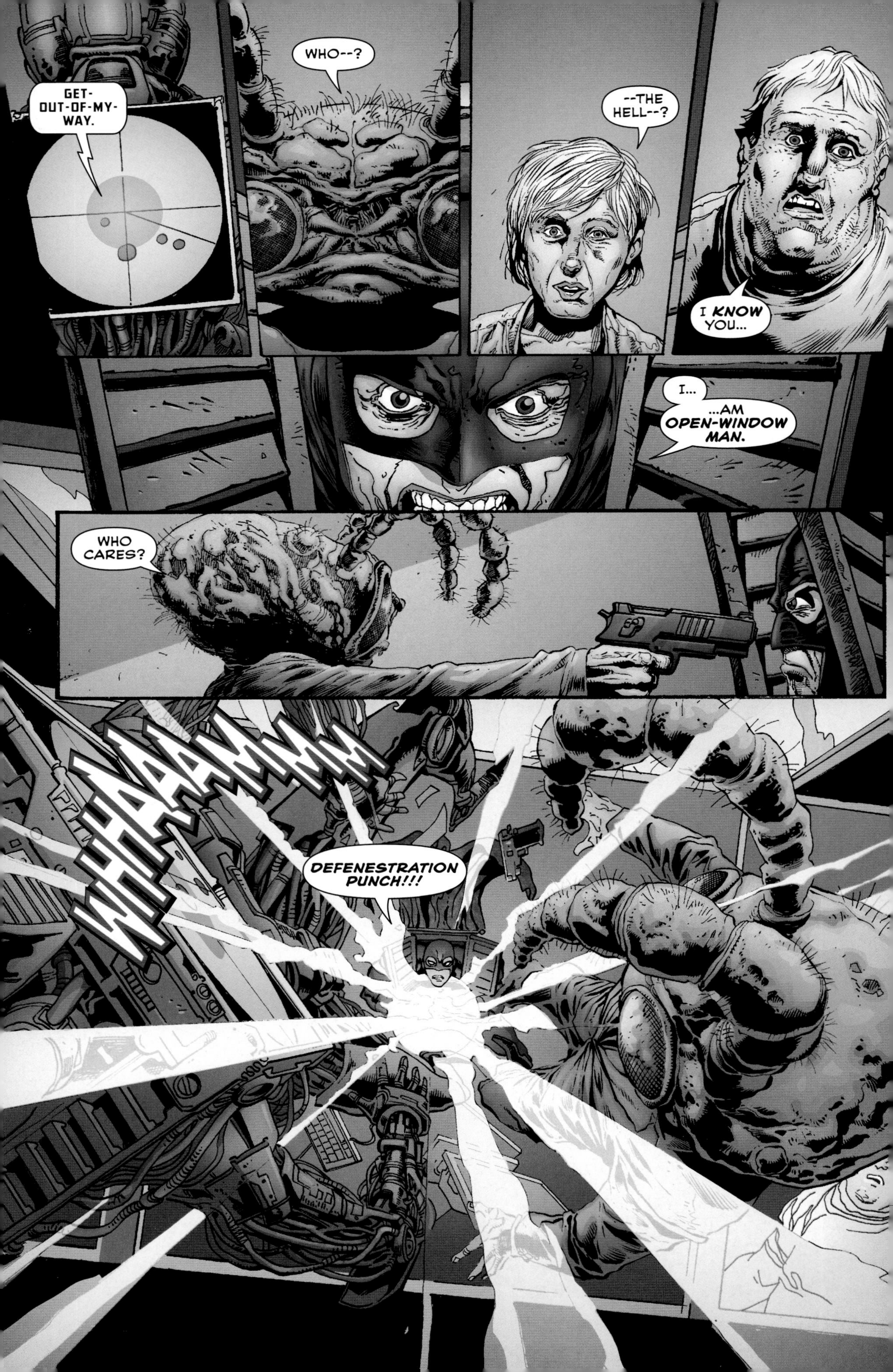
GET-
OUT-OF-MY-
WAY.
WHO--?
--THE
HELL--?
I KNOW
YOU...
I...
...AM
OPEN-WINDOW
MAN.
WHO
CARES?
WHHAAMMM
DEFENESTRATION
PUNCH!!!

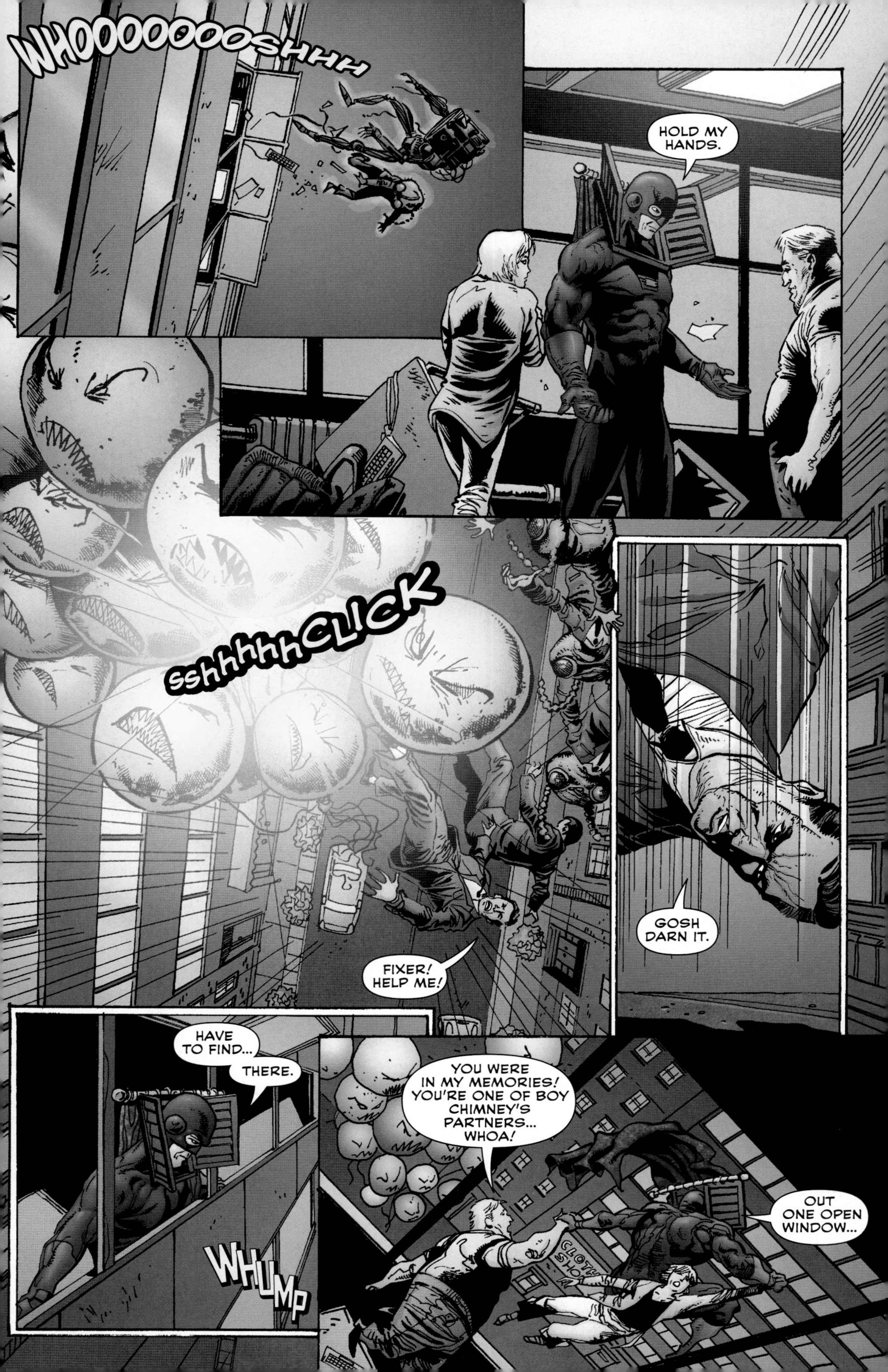
WHOOOOOOOOSHHH
HOLD MY HANDS.
sshhhhhCLICK
GOSH DARN IT.
FIXER! HELP ME!
HAVE TO FIND...
THERE.
WHUMP
YOU WERE IN MY MEMORIES! YOU'RE ONE OF BOY CHIMNEY'S PARTNERS... WHOA!
OUT ONE OPEN WINDOW...

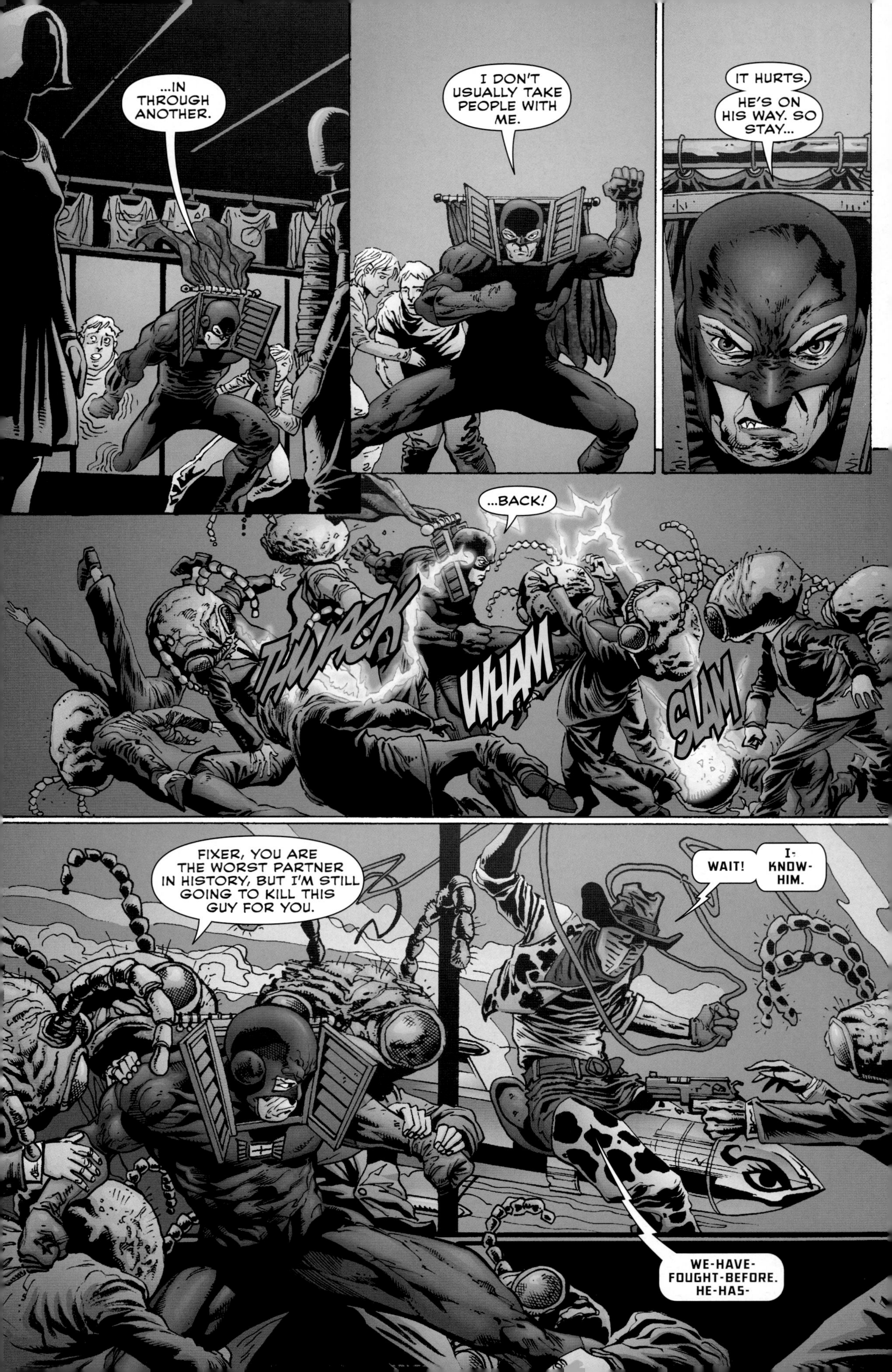
...IN THROUGH ANOTHER.
I DON'T USUALLY TAKE PEOPLE WITH ME.
IT HURTS. HE'S ON HIS WAY. SO STAY...
...BACK!
THWACK
WHAM
SLAM
FIXER, YOU ARE THE WORST PARTNER IN HISTORY, BUT I'M STILL GOING TO KILL THIS GUY FOR YOU.
WAIT!
I- KNOW- HIM.
WE-HAVE- FOUGHT-BEFORE. HE-HAS-

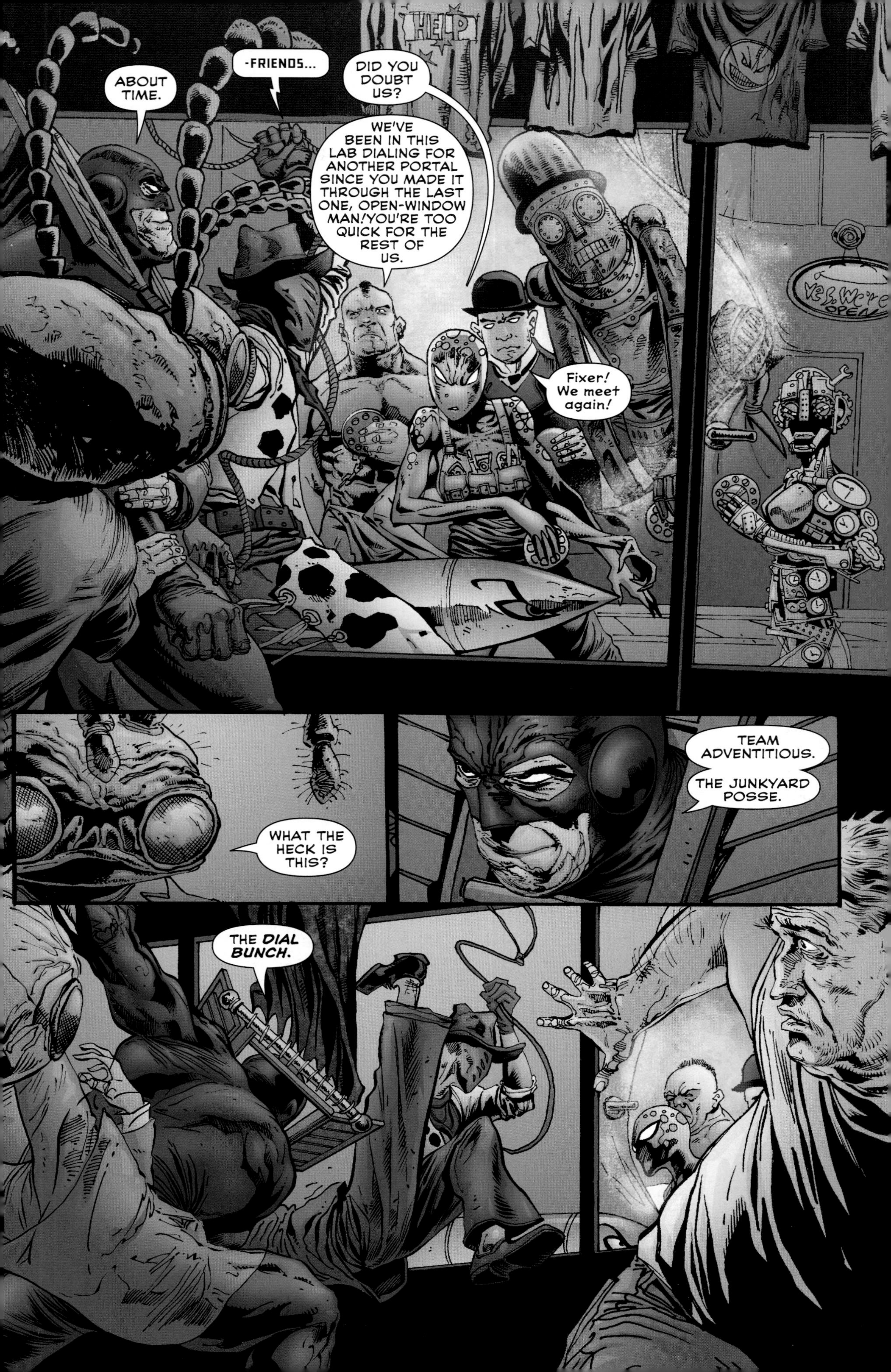

HELP
ABOUT TIME.
-FRIENDS...
DID YOU DOUBT US?
WE'VE BEEN IN THIS LAB DIALING FOR ANOTHER PORTAL SINCE YOU MADE IT THROUGH THE LAST ONE, OPEN-WINDOW MAN! YOU'RE TOO QUICK FOR THE REST OF US.
Fixer! We meet again!
Yes, We're OPEN
WHAT THE HECK IS THIS?
TEAM ADVENTITIOUS.
THE JUNKYARD POSSE.
THE *DIAL BUNCH*.

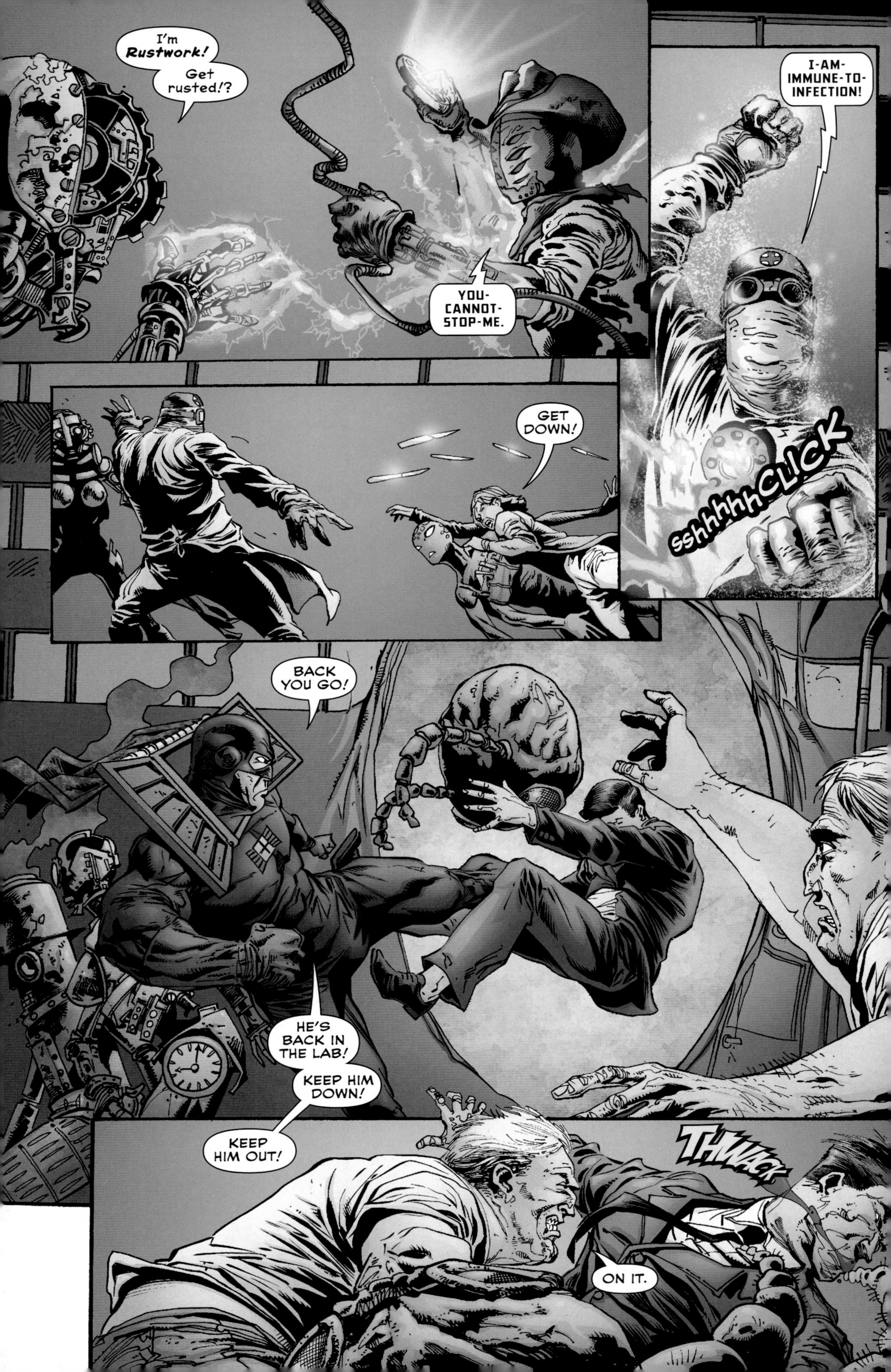
I'm Rustwork! Get rusted!?
YOU-CANNOT-STOP-ME.
I-AM-IMMUNE-TO-INFECTION!
sshhhhCLICK
GET DOWN!
BACK YOU GO!
HE'S BACK IN THE LAB!
KEEP HIM DOWN!
KEEP HIM OUT!
THWACK
ON IT.

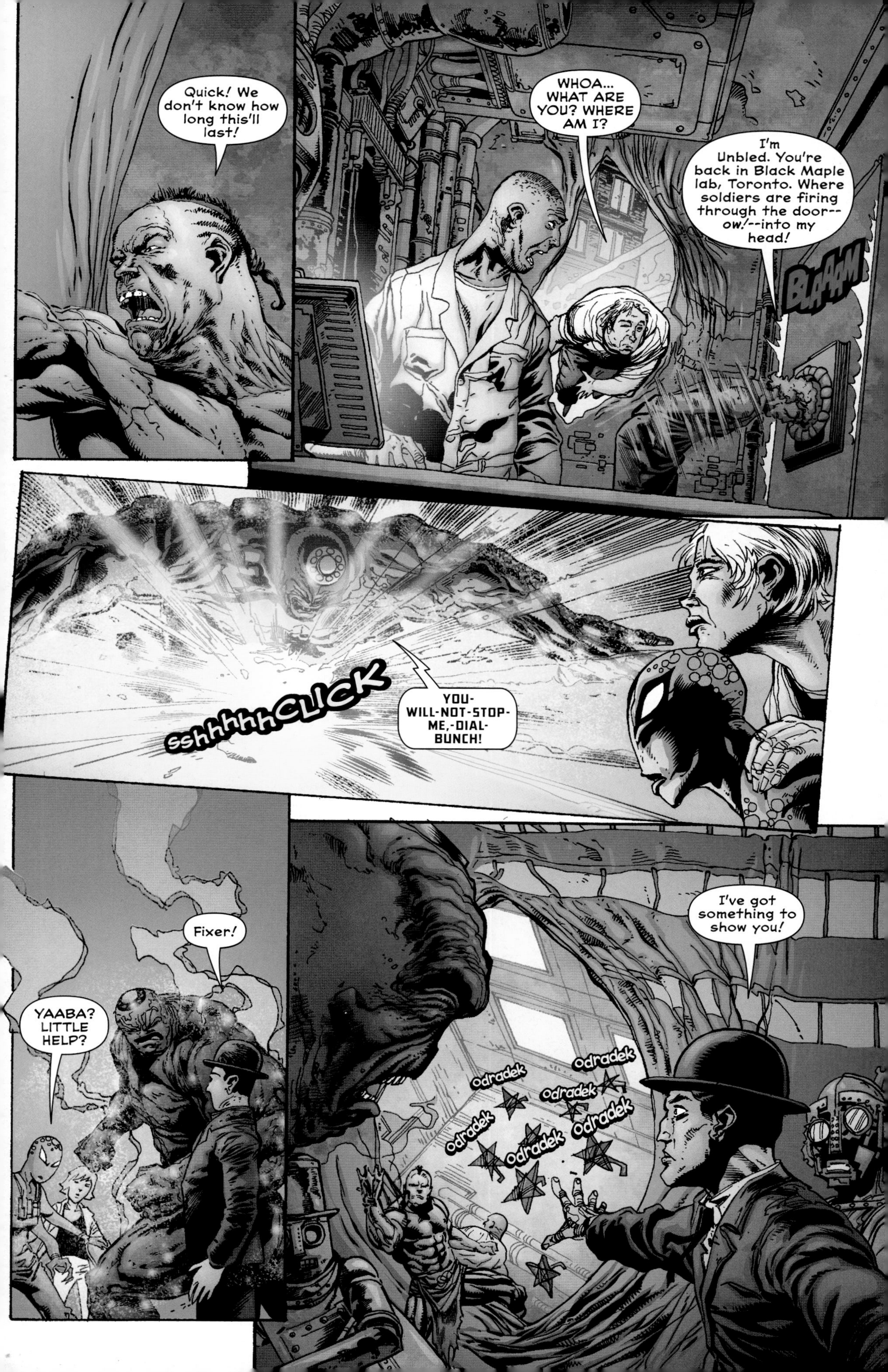
Quick! We don't know how long this'll last!
WHOA... WHAT ARE YOU? WHERE AM I?
I'm Unbled. You're back in Black Maple lab, Toronto. Where soldiers are firing through the door--ow!--into my head!
BLAAAM
SSHHHHHCLICK
YOU-WILL-NOT-STOP-ME,-DIAL-BUNCH!
Fixer!
YAABA? LITTLE HELP?
I've got something to show you!
odradek
odradek
odradek
odradek
odradek
odradek
odradek

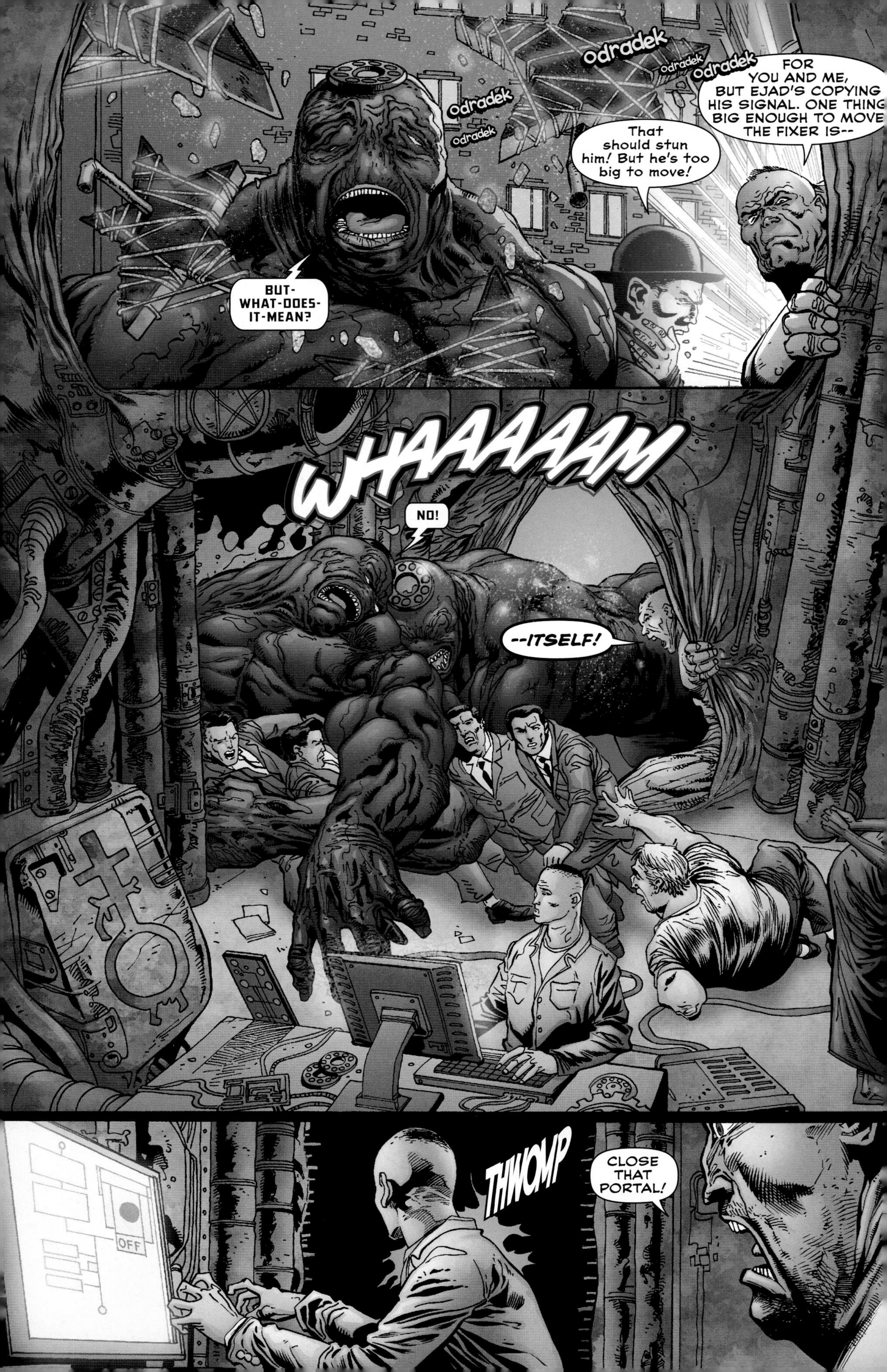
odradek
odradek
odradek
odradek
odradek
BUT-WHAT-DOES-IT-MEAN?
That should stun him! But he's too big to move!
FOR YOU AND ME, BUT EJAD'S COPYING HIS SIGNAL. ONE THING BIG ENOUGH TO MOVE THE FIXER IS--
WHAAAAAAM
NO!
--ITSELF!
OFF
THWOMP
CLOSE THAT PORTAL!

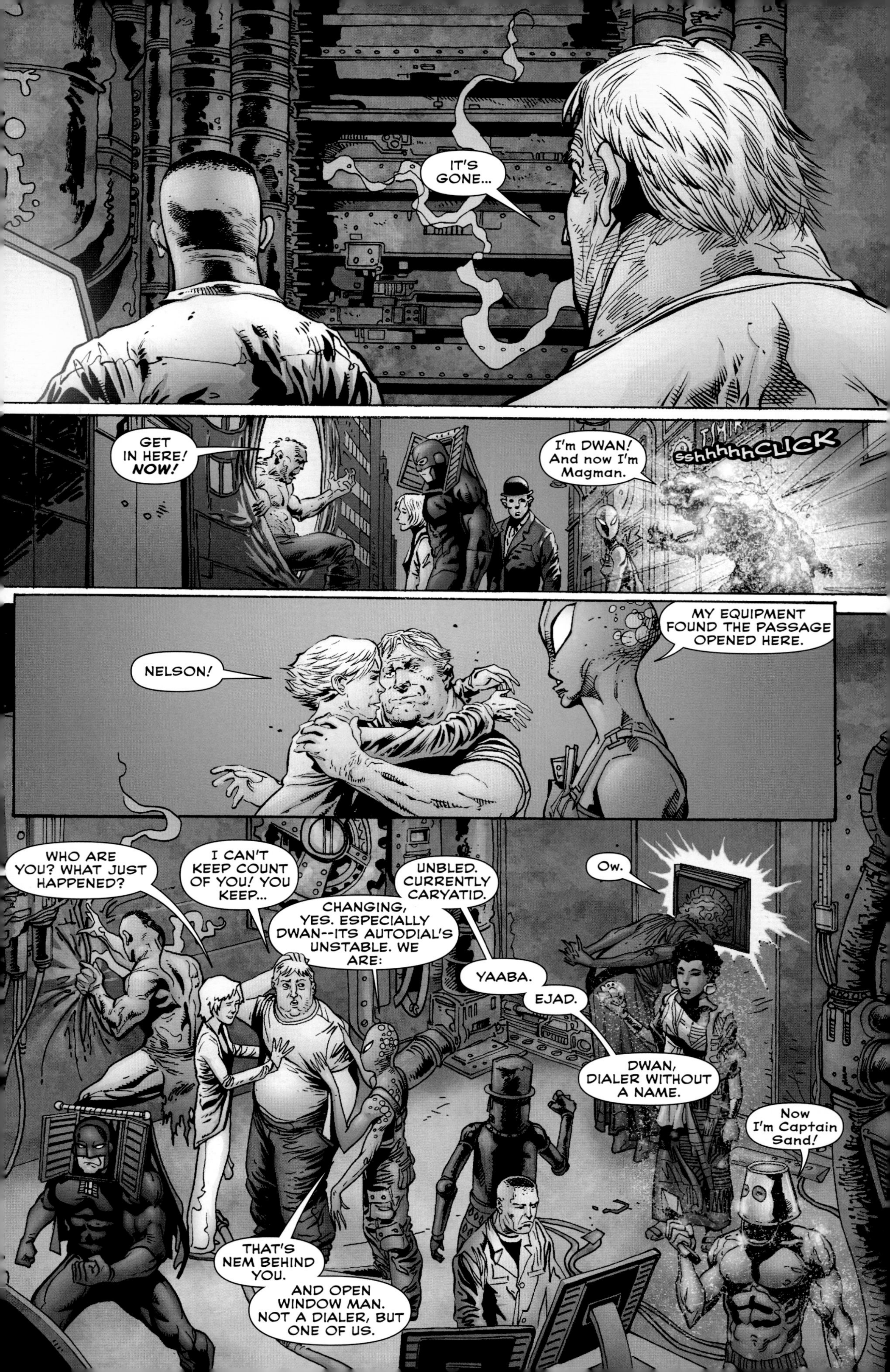
IT'S GONE...
GET IN HERE! NOW!
I'm DWAN! And now I'm Magman.
sshhhhhCLICK
MY EQUIPMENT FOUND THE PASSAGE OPENED HERE.
NELSON!
WHO ARE YOU? WHAT JUST HAPPENED?
I CAN'T KEEP COUNT OF YOU! YOU KEEP...
CHANGING, YES. ESPECIALLY DWAN--ITS AUTODIAL'S UNSTABLE. WE ARE:
UNBLED. CURRENTLY CARYATID.
YAABA.
EJAD.
DWAN, DIALER WITHOUT A NAME.
Ow.
Now I'm Captain Sand!
THAT'S NEM BEHIND YOU.
AND OPEN WINDOW MAN. NOT A DIALER, BUT ONE OF US.

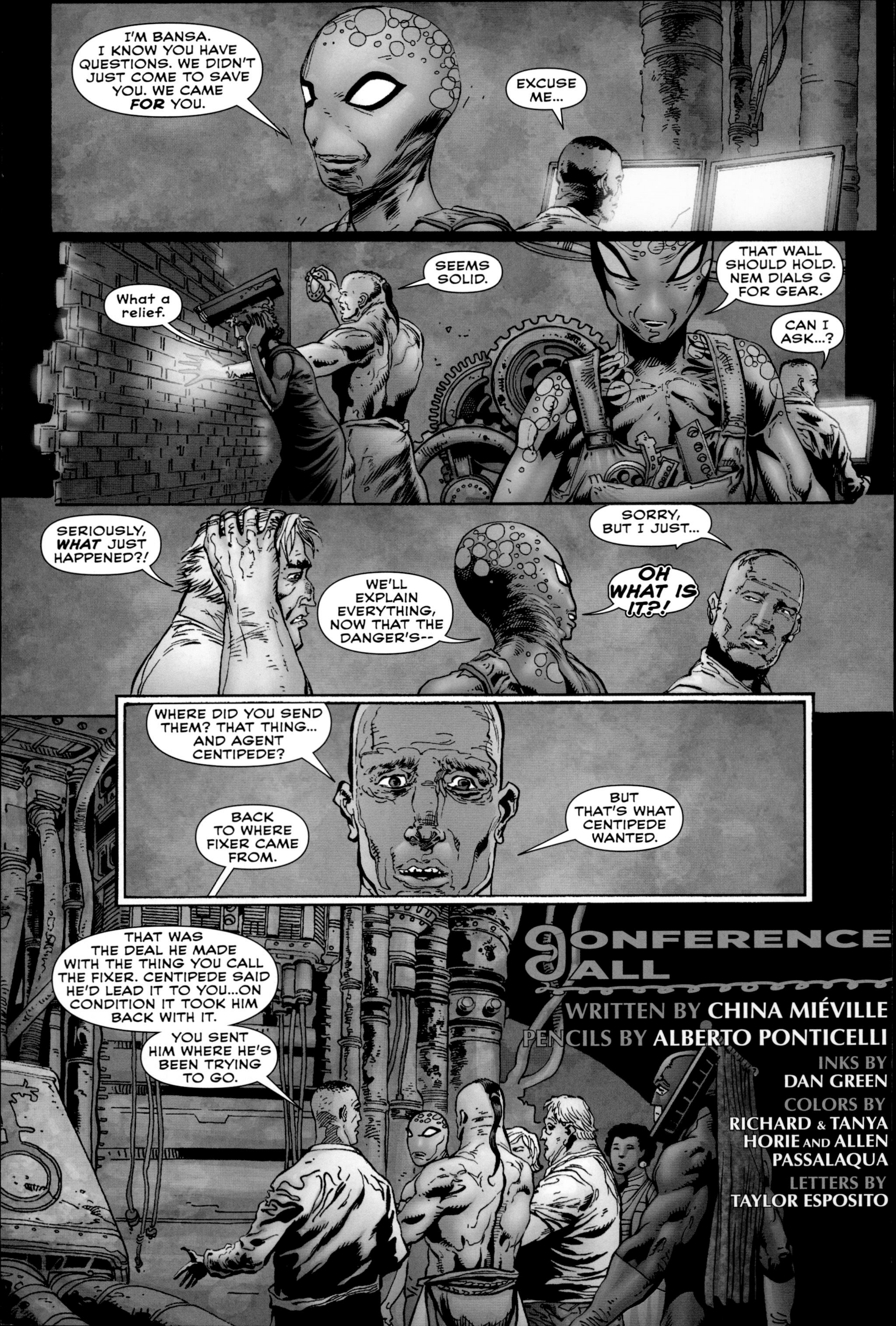

I'M BANSA. I KNOW YOU HAVE QUESTIONS. WE DIDN'T JUST COME TO SAVE YOU. WE CAME FOR YOU.
EXCUSE ME...
What a relief.
SEEMS SOLID.
THAT WALL SHOULD HOLD. NEM DIALS G FOR GEAR.
CAN I ASK...?
SERIOUSLY, WHAT JUST HAPPENED?!
WE'LL EXPLAIN EVERYTHING, NOW THAT THE DANGER'S--
SORRY, BUT I JUST...
OH WHAT IS IT?!
WHERE DID YOU SEND THEM? THAT THING... AND AGENT CENTIPEDE?
BACK TO WHERE FIXER CAME FROM.
BUT THAT'S WHAT CENTIPEDE WANTED.
THAT WAS THE DEAL HE MADE WITH THE THING YOU CALL THE FIXER. CENTIPEDE SAID HE'D LEAD IT TO YOU...ON CONDITION IT TOOK HIM BACK WITH IT.
YOU SENT HIM WHERE HE'S BEEN TRYING TO GO.
CONFERENCE CALL
WRITTEN BY CHINA MIÉVILLE
PENCILS BY ALBERTO PONTICELLI
INKS BY DAN GREEN
COLORS BY RICHARD & TANYA HORIE AND ALLEN PASSALAQUA
LETTERS BY TAYLOR ESPOSITO

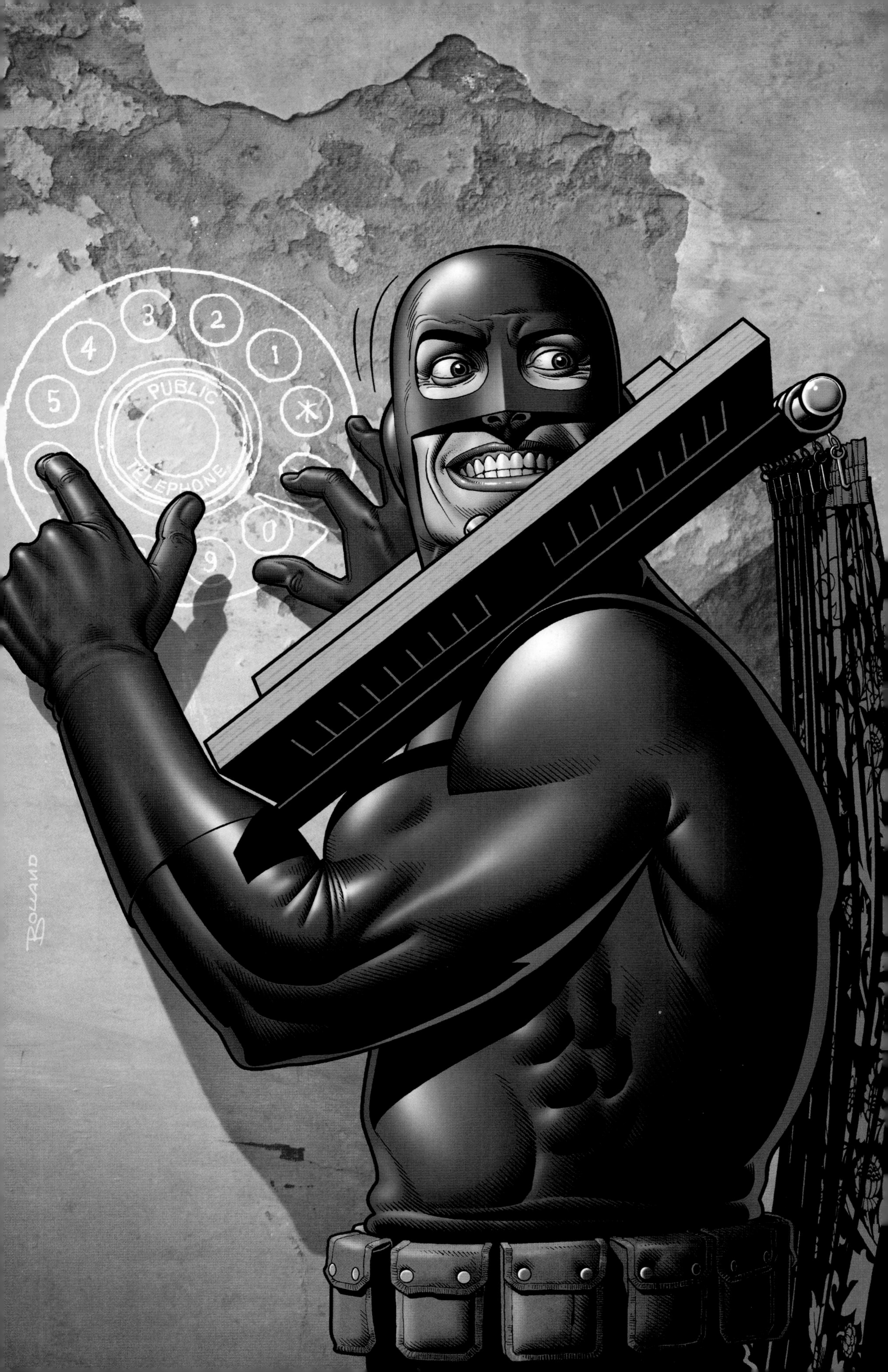
PUBLIC
TELEPHONE
1
2
3
4
5
9
0
BOLLAND

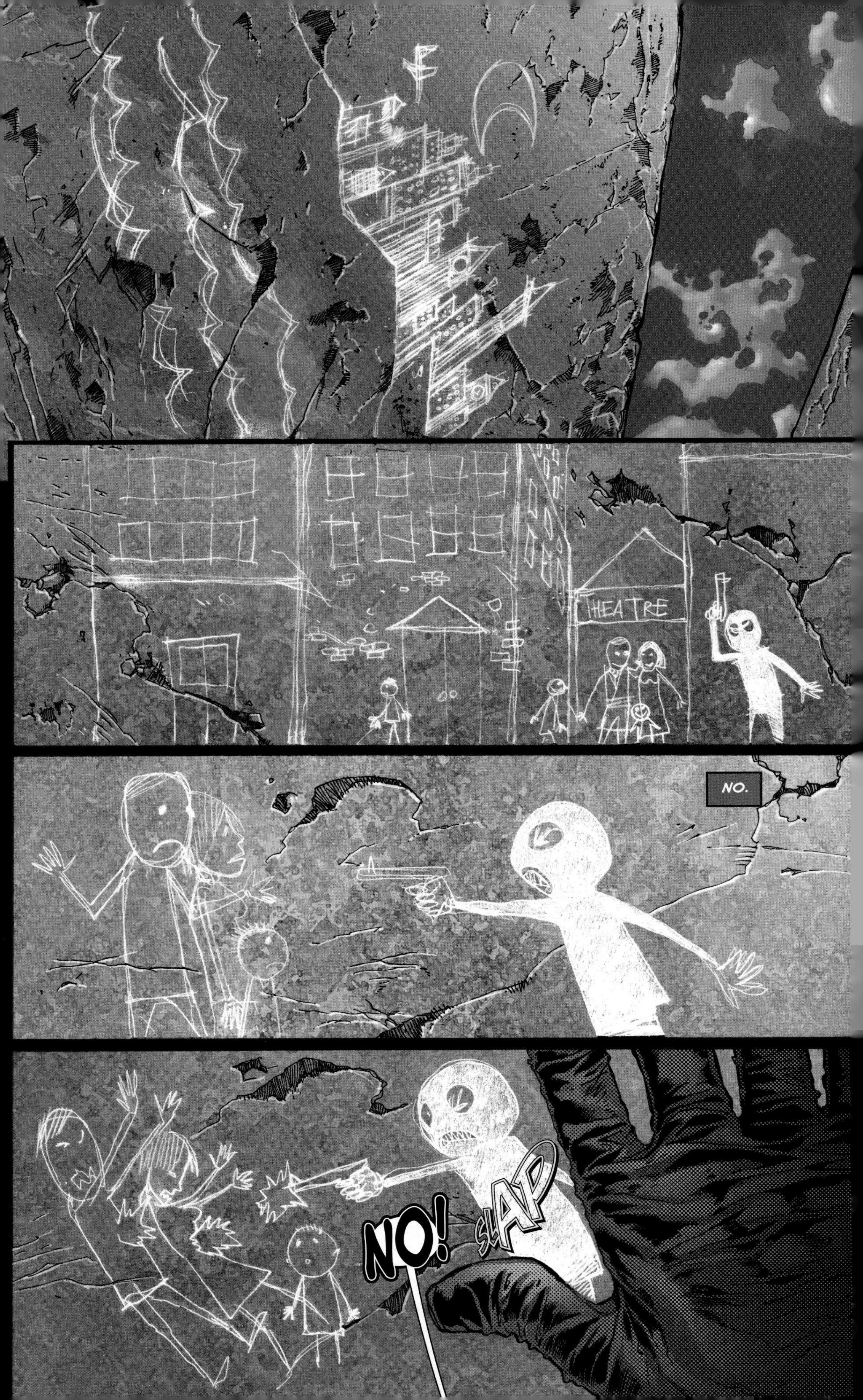
THEATRE
NO.
NO!
SLAP

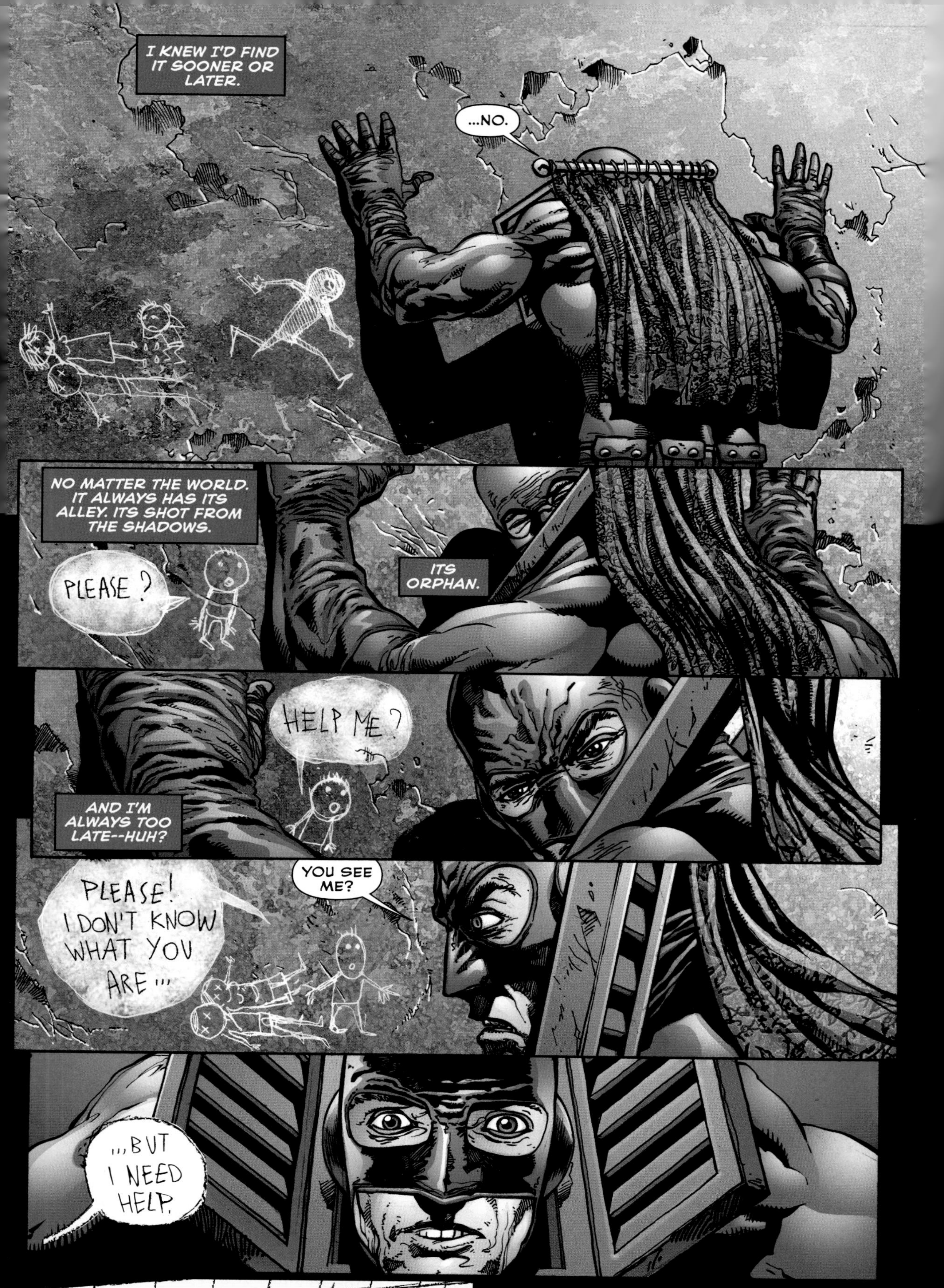
I KNEW I'D FIND IT SOONER OR LATER.
...NO.
NO MATTER THE WORLD. IT ALWAYS HAS ITS ALLEY. ITS SHOT FROM THE SHADOWS.
PLEASE?
ITS ORPHAN.
HELP ME?
AND I'M ALWAYS TOO LATE--HUH?
PLEASE! I DON'T KNOW WHAT YOU ARE...
YOU SEE ME?
...BUT I NEED HELP.

TEKEL UPHARSIN

WRITER – CHINA MIEVILLE
PENCILS – ALBERTO PONTICELL
INKS – DAN GREEN
COLORS– TANYA & RICHARD HORIE
LETTERS – TAYLOR ESPOSITO

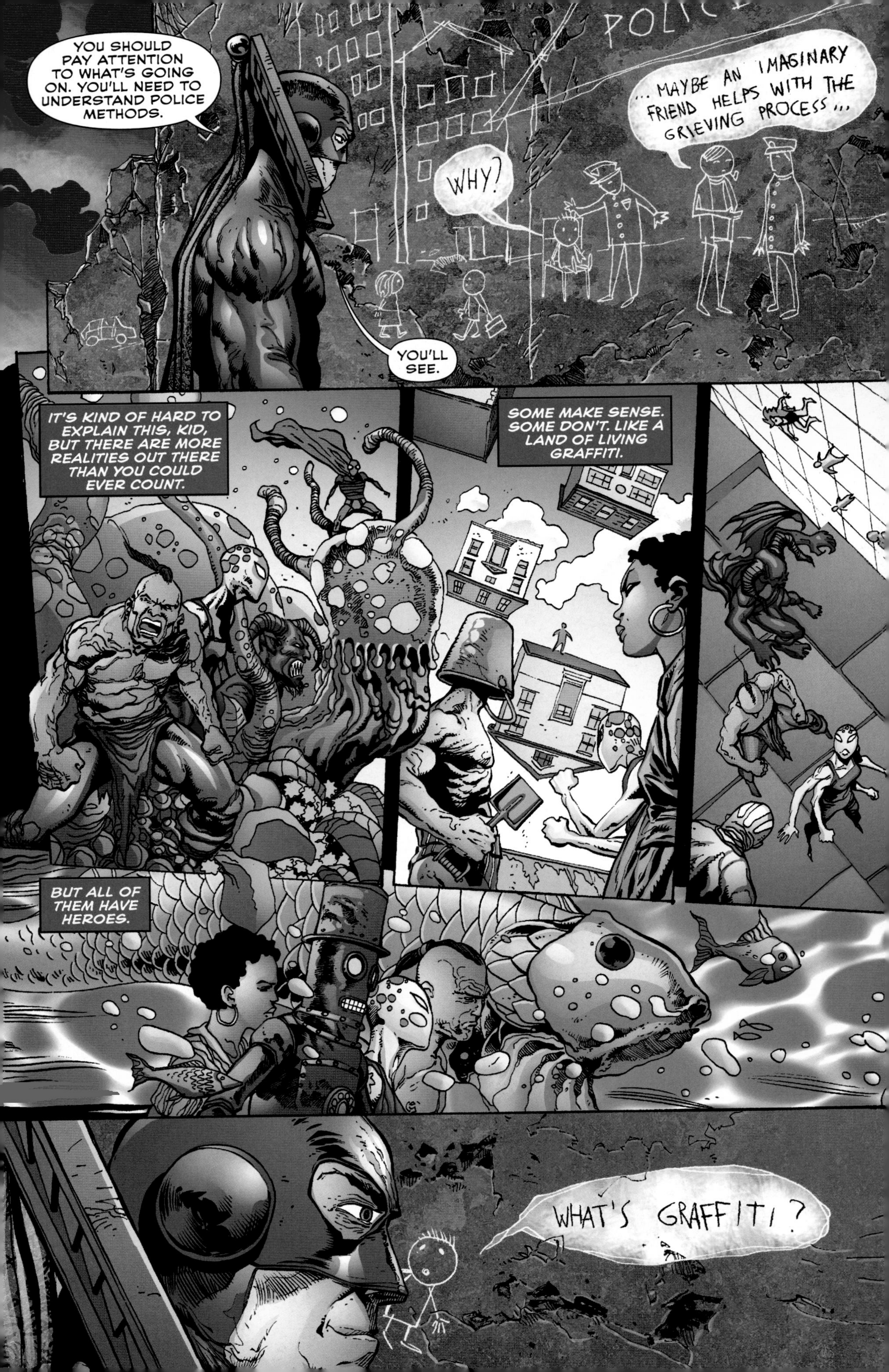
YOU SHOULD PAY ATTENTION TO WHAT'S GOING ON. YOU'LL NEED TO UNDERSTAND POLICE METHODS.
POLICE
WHY?
...MAYBE AN IMAGINARY FRIEND HELPS WITH THE GRIEVING PROCESS...
YOU'LL SEE.
IT'S KIND OF HARD TO EXPLAIN THIS, KID, BUT THERE ARE MORE REALITIES OUT THERE THAN YOU COULD EVER COUNT.
SOME MAKE SENSE. SOME DON'T. LIKE A LAND OF LIVING GRAFFITI.
BUT ALL OF THEM HAVE HEROES.
WHAT'S GRAFFITI?

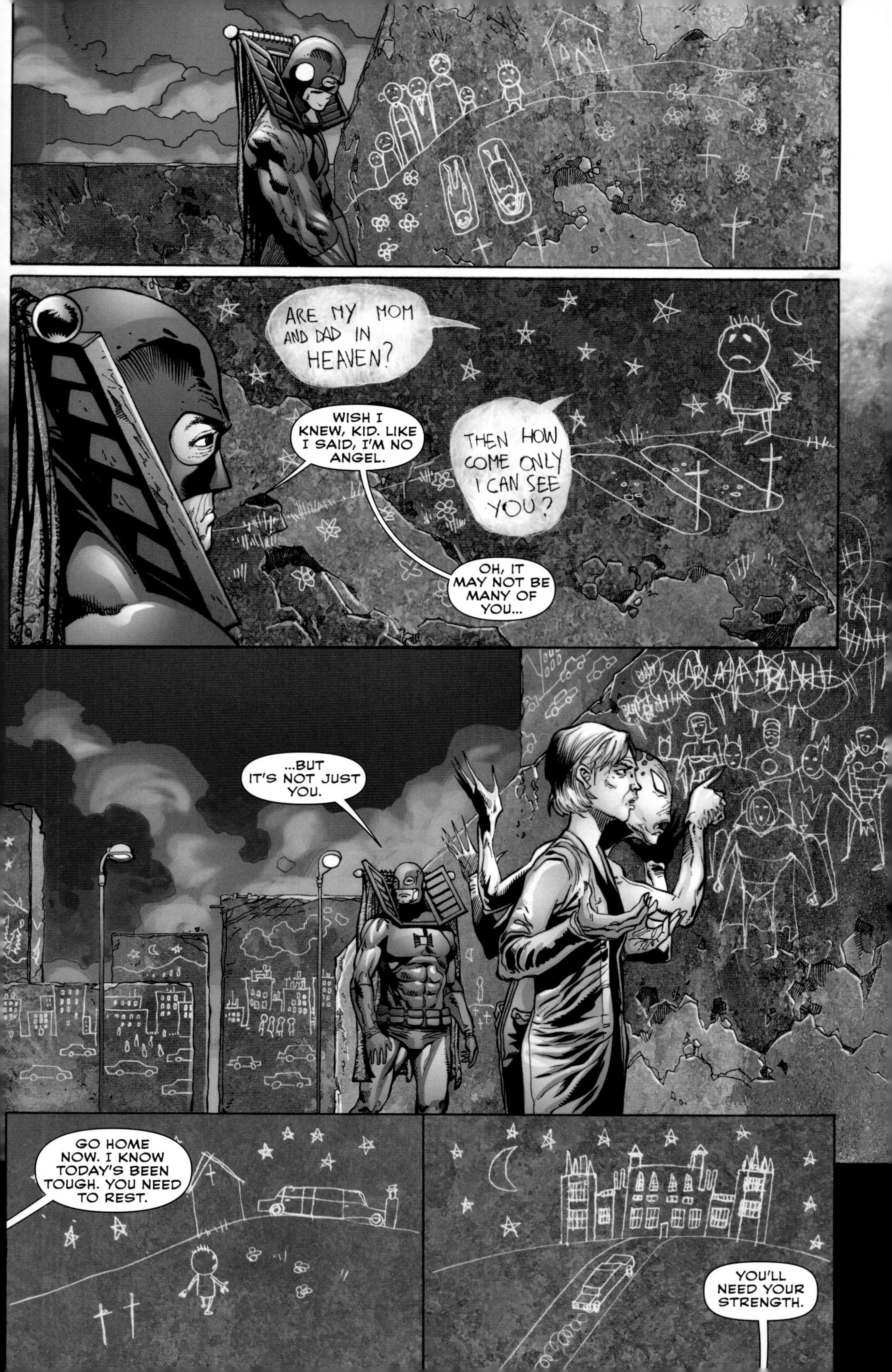
ARE MY MOM AND DAD IN HEAVEN?
WISH I KNEW, KID. LIKE I SAID, I'M NO ANGEL.
THEN HOW COME ONLY I CAN SEE YOU?
OH, IT MAY NOT BE MANY OF YOU...
...BUT IT'S NOT JUST YOU.
GO HOME NOW. I KNOW TODAY'S BEEN TOUGH. YOU NEED TO REST.
YOU'LL NEED YOUR STRENGTH.

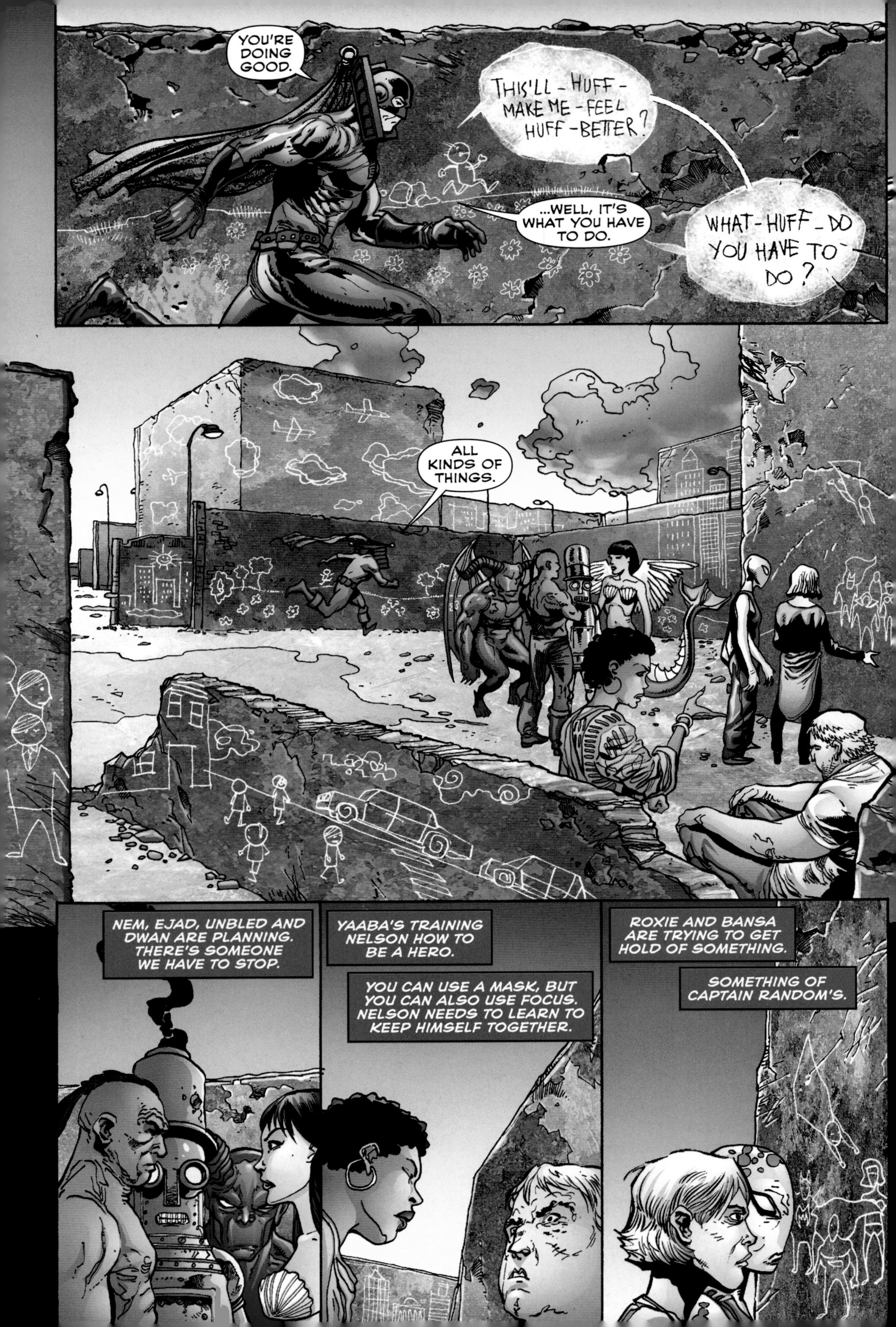
YOU'RE DOING GOOD.
THIS'LL - HUFF - MAKE ME - FEEL HUFF - BETTER?
...WELL, IT'S WHAT YOU HAVE TO DO.
WHAT - HUFF - DO YOU HAVE TO DO?
ALL KINDS OF THINGS.
NEM, EJAD, UNBLED AND DWAN ARE PLANNING. THERE'S SOMEONE WE HAVE TO STOP.
YAABA'S TRAINING NELSON HOW TO BE A HERO.
YOU CAN USE A MASK, BUT YOU CAN ALSO USE FOCUS. NELSON NEEDS TO LEARN TO KEEP HIMSELF TOGETHER.
ROXIE AND BANSA ARE TRYING TO GET HOLD OF SOMETHING.
SOMETHING OF CAPTAIN RANDOM'S.

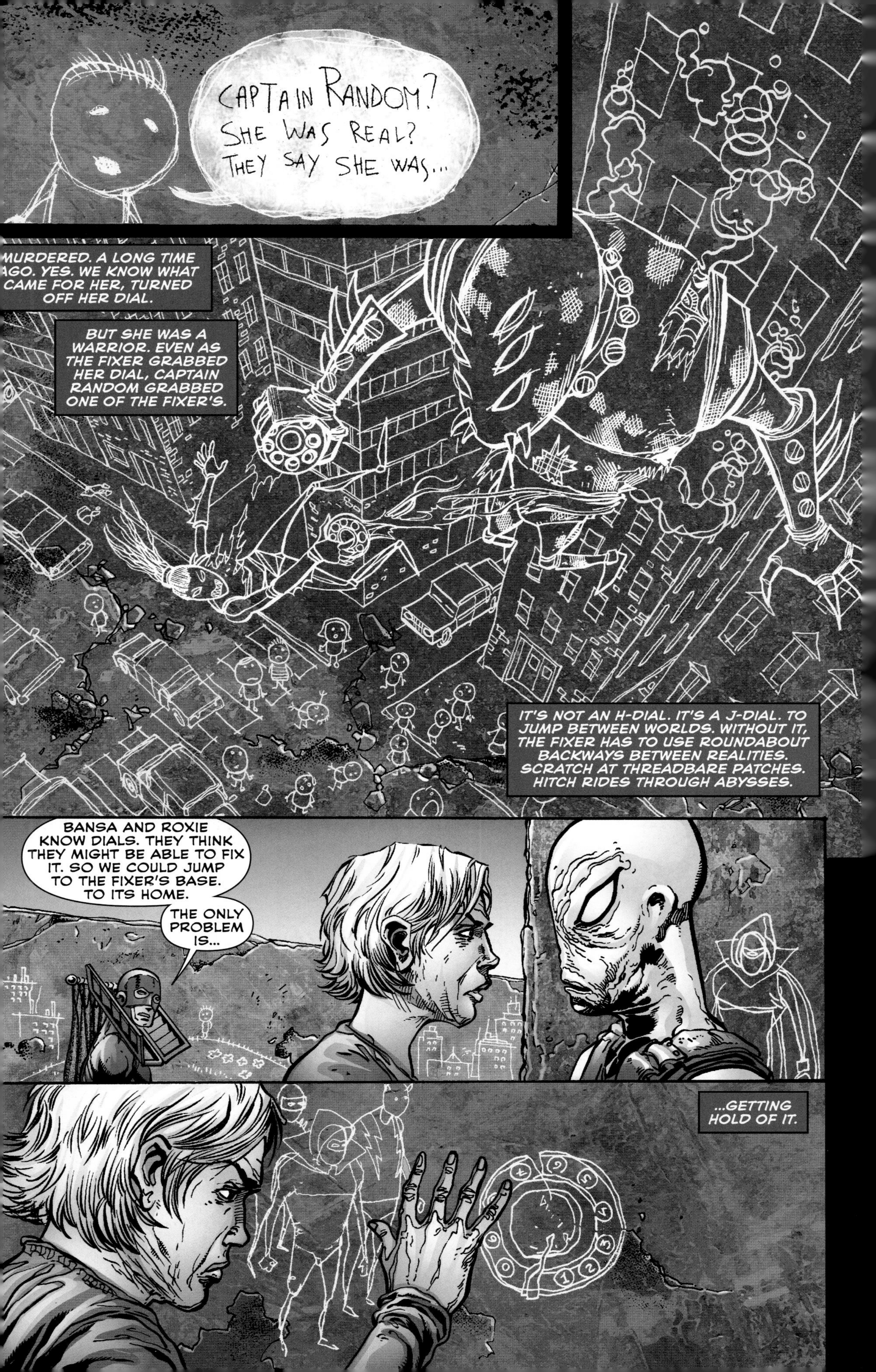
CAPTAIN RANDOM? SHE WAS REAL? THEY SAY SHE WAS...
MURDERED. A LONG TIME AGO. YES. WE KNOW WHAT CAME FOR HER, TURNED OFF HER DIAL.
BUT SHE WAS A WARRIOR. EVEN AS THE FIXER GRABBED HER DIAL, CAPTAIN RANDOM GRABBED ONE OF THE FIXER'S.
IT'S NOT AN H-DIAL. IT'S A J-DIAL. TO JUMP BETWEEN WORLDS. WITHOUT IT, THE FIXER HAS TO USE ROUNDABOUT BACKWAYS BETWEEN REALITIES. SCRATCH AT THREADBARE PATCHES. HITCH RIDES THROUGH ABYSSES.
BANSA AND ROXIE KNOW DIALS. THEY THINK THEY MIGHT BE ABLE TO FIX IT. SO WE COULD JUMP TO THE FIXER'S BASE. TO ITS HOME.
THE ONLY PROBLEM IS...
...GETTING HOLD OF IT.

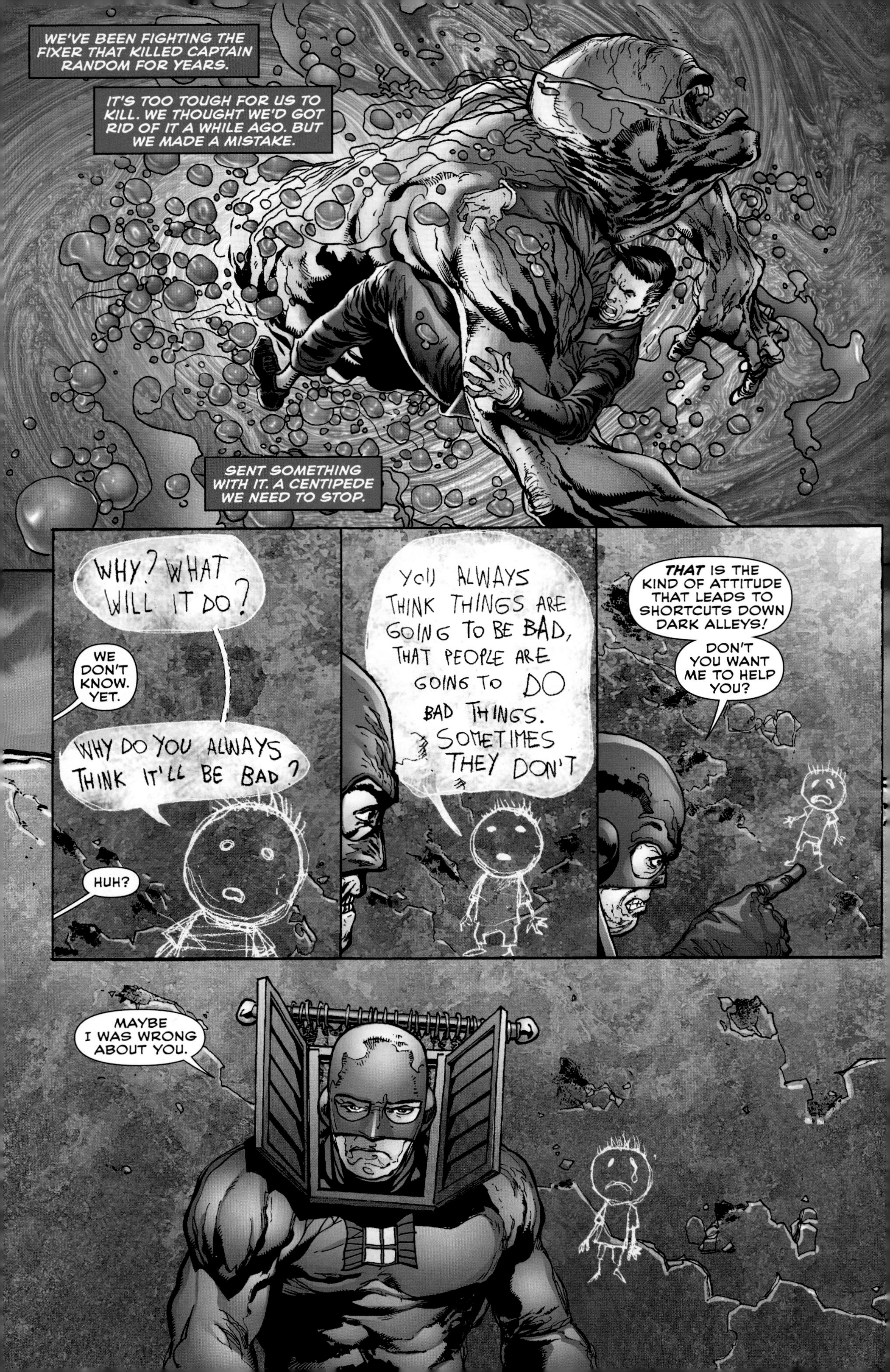
WE'VE BEEN FIGHTING THE FIXER THAT KILLED CAPTAIN RANDOM FOR YEARS.
IT'S TOO TOUGH FOR US TO KILL. WE THOUGHT WE'D GOT RID OF IT A WHILE AGO. BUT WE MADE A MISTAKE.
SENT SOMETHING WITH IT. A CENTIPEDE WE NEED TO STOP.
WHY? WHAT WILL IT DO?
WE DON'T KNOW. YET.
WHY DO YOU ALWAYS THINK IT'LL BE BAD?
HUH?
YOU ALWAYS THINK THINGS ARE GOING TO BE BAD, THAT PEOPLE ARE GOING TO DO BAD THINGS. SOMETIMES THEY DON'T
THAT IS THE KIND OF ATTITUDE THAT LEADS TO SHORTCUTS DOWN DARK ALLEYS!
DON'T YOU WANT ME TO HELP YOU?
MAYBE I WAS WRONG ABOUT YOU.

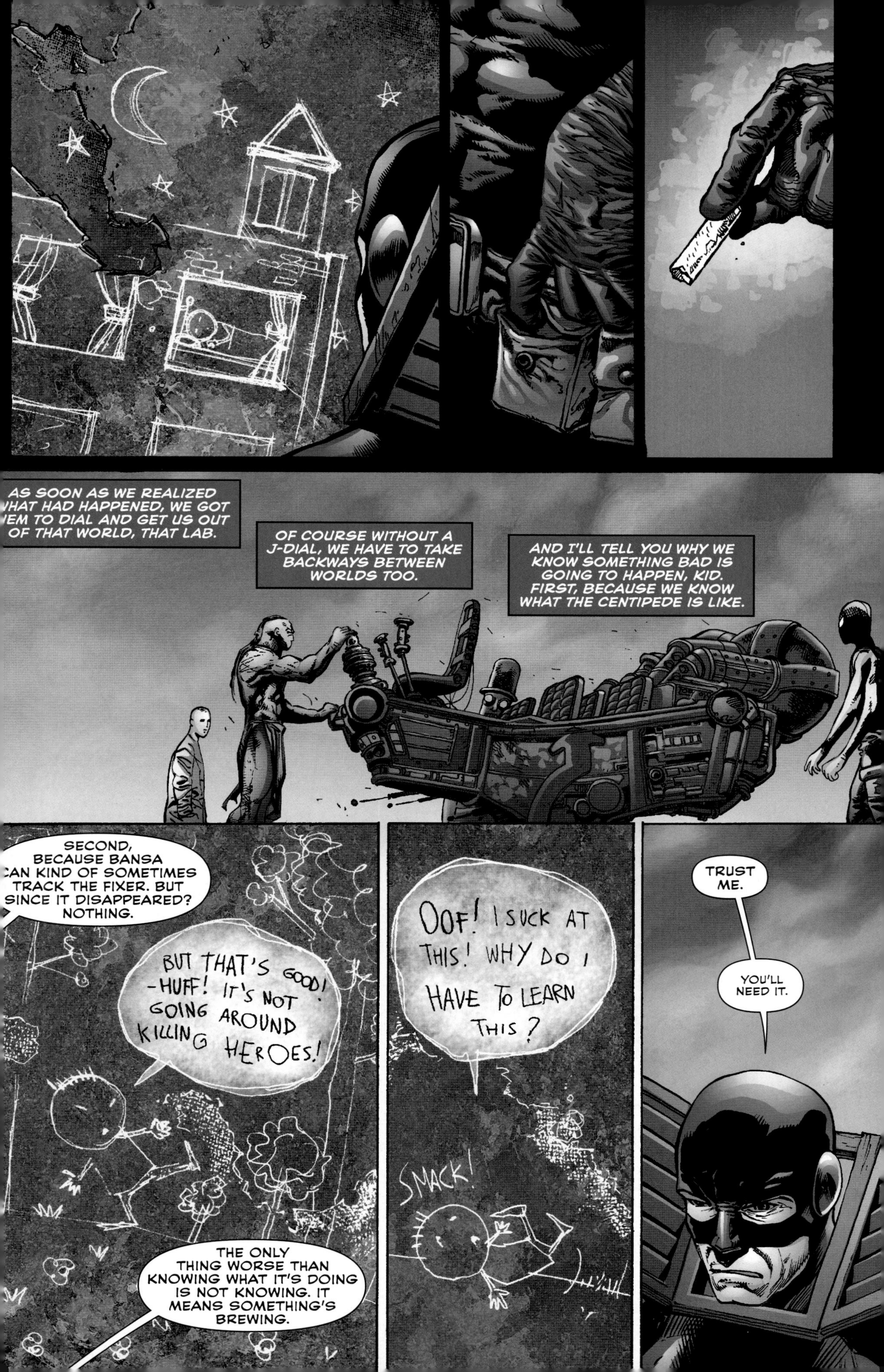
AS SOON AS WE REALIZED WHAT HAD HAPPENED, WE GOT 'EM TO DIAL AND GET US OUT OF THAT WORLD, THAT LAB.
OF COURSE WITHOUT A J-DIAL, WE HAVE TO TAKE BACKWAYS BETWEEN WORLDS TOO.
AND I'LL TELL YOU WHY WE KNOW SOMETHING BAD IS GOING TO HAPPEN, KID. FIRST, BECAUSE WE KNOW WHAT THE CENTIPEDE IS LIKE.
SECOND, BECAUSE BANSA CAN KIND OF SOMETIMES TRACK THE FIXER. BUT SINCE IT DISAPPEARED? NOTHING.
BUT THAT'S GOOD! -HUFF! IT'S NOT GOING AROUND KILLING HEROES!
THE ONLY THING WORSE THAN KNOWING WHAT IT'S DOING IS NOT KNOWING. IT MEANS SOMETHING'S BREWING.
OOF! I SUCK AT THIS! WHY DO I HAVE TO LEARN THIS?
SMACK!
TRUST ME.
YOU'LL NEED IT.

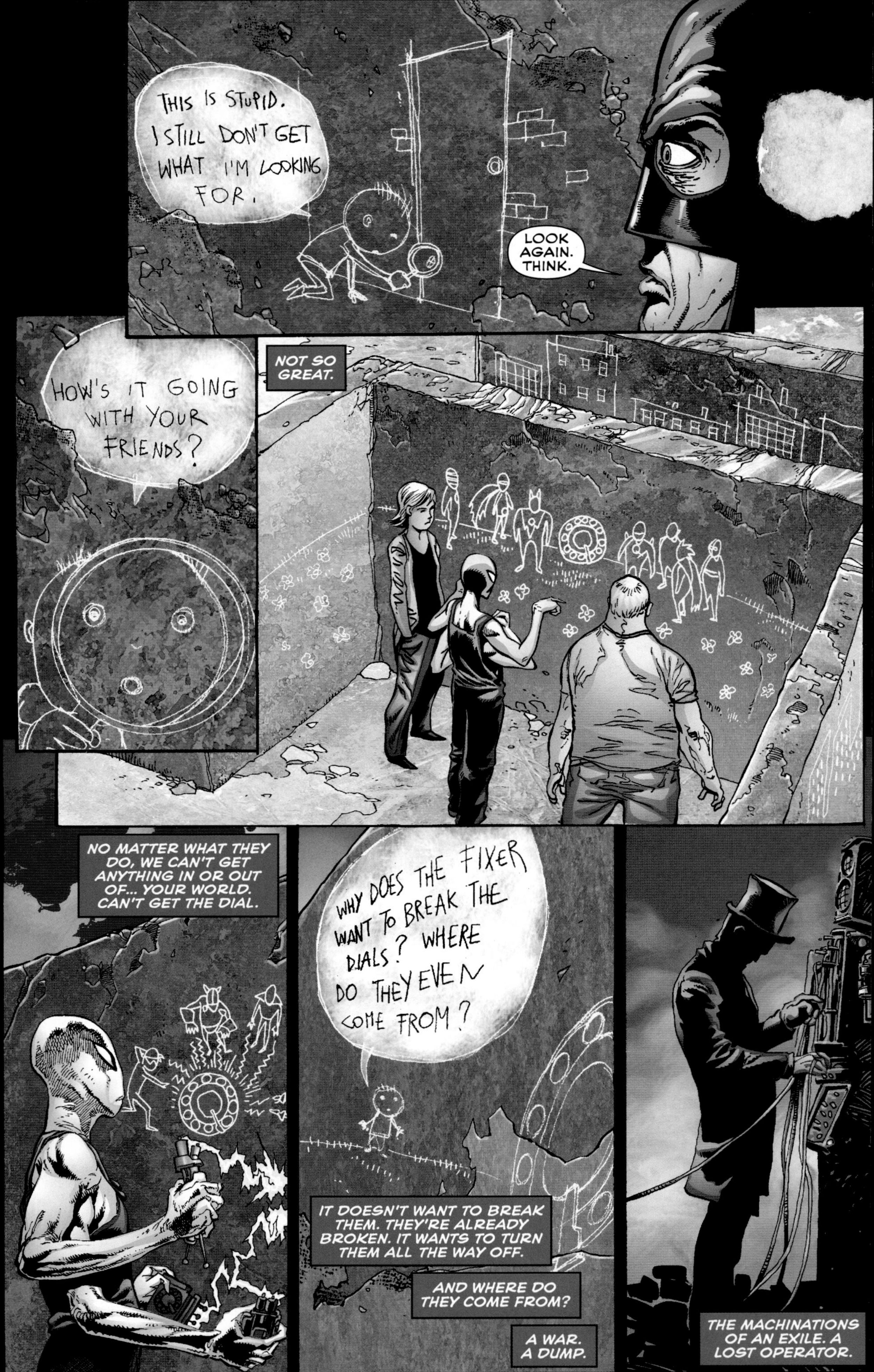
THIS IS STUPID. I STILL DON'T GET WHAT I'M LOOKING FOR.
LOOK AGAIN. THINK.
HOW'S IT GOING WITH YOUR FRIENDS?
NOT SO GREAT.
NO MATTER WHAT THEY DO, WE CAN'T GET ANYTHING IN OR OUT OF... YOUR WORLD. CAN'T GET THE DIAL.
WHY DOES THE FIXER WANT TO BREAK THE DIALS? WHERE DO THEY EVEN COME FROM?
IT DOESN'T WANT TO BREAK THEM. THEY'RE ALREADY BROKEN. IT WANTS TO TURN THEM ALL THE WAY OFF.
AND WHERE DO THEY COME FROM?
A WAR. A DUMP.
THE MACHINATIONS OF AN EXILE. A LOST OPERATOR.

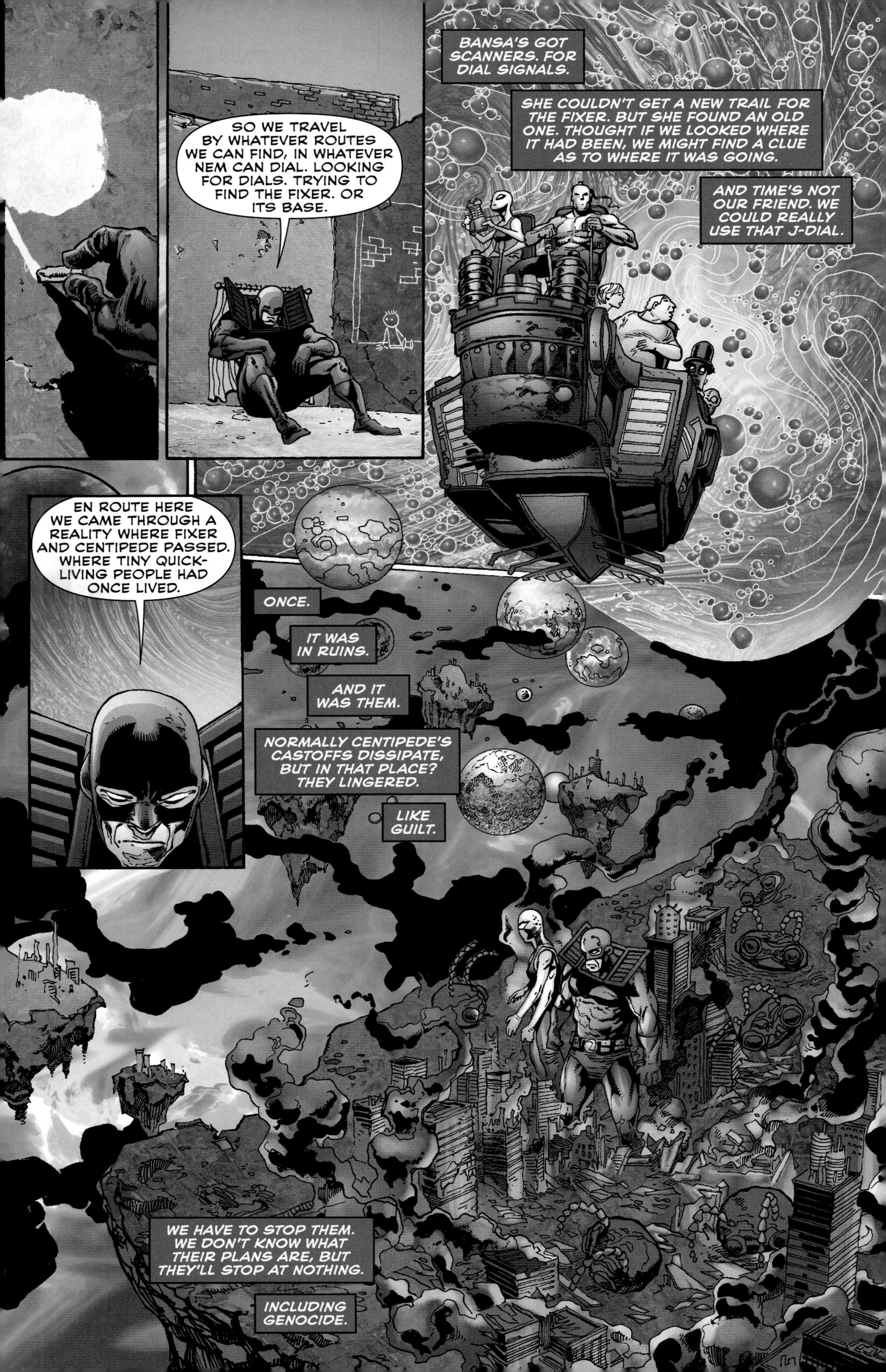

SO WE TRAVEL BY WHATEVER ROUTES WE CAN FIND, IN WHATEVER NEM CAN DIAL. LOOKING FOR DIALS. TRYING TO FIND THE FIXER. OR ITS BASE.
BANSA'S GOT SCANNERS. FOR DIAL SIGNALS.
SHE COULDN'T GET A NEW TRAIL FOR THE FIXER. BUT SHE FOUND AN OLD ONE. THOUGHT IF WE LOOKED WHERE IT HAD BEEN, WE MIGHT FIND A CLUE AS TO WHERE IT WAS GOING.
AND TIME'S NOT OUR FRIEND. WE COULD REALLY USE THAT J-DIAL.
EN ROUTE HERE WE CAME THROUGH A REALITY WHERE FIXER AND CENTIPEDE PASSED. WHERE TINY QUICK-LIVING PEOPLE HAD ONCE LIVED.
ONCE.
IT WAS IN RUINS.
AND IT WAS THEM.
NORMALLY CENTIPEDE'S CASTOFFS DISSIPATE, BUT IN THAT PLACE? THEY LINGERED.
LIKE GUILT.
WE HAVE TO STOP THEM. WE DON'T KNOW WHAT THEIR PLANS ARE, BUT THEY'LL STOP AT NOTHING.
INCLUDING GENOCIDE.

WHO ARE YOU ALL? WHY DO YOU DO THIS?

WE'RE ALL DIAL-TOUCHED. BANSA GATHERED US. WE NEED EACH OTHER.

LEARN ABOUT THE EXCHANGE, IT CHANGES YOU.

YAABA.

WHETHER YOU'RE A HUMAN FROM THE SAME ODD WORLD AS NELSON AND ROXIE, WHO FINDS AN H-DIAL IN THE A TREE...

NEM.

...A COGSMITH WHO FINDS A G-DIAL IN THE MACHINE WEBS, TO CALL UP RANDOM ARTIFACTS HE COULDN'T DREAM OF...

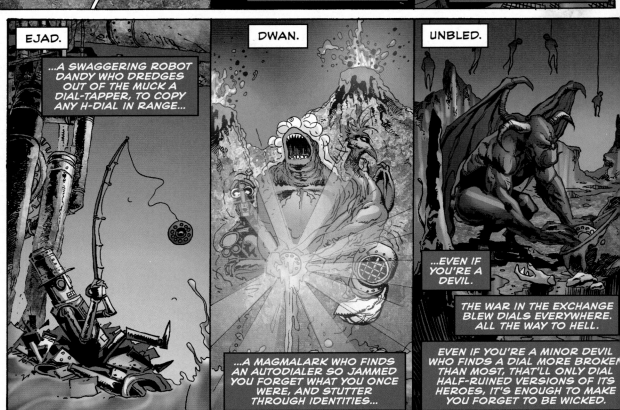

EJAD.

...A SWAGGERING ROBOT DANDY WHO DREDGES OUT OF THE MUCK A DIAL-TAPPER, TO COPY ANY H-DIAL IN RANGE...

DWAN.

...A MAGMALARK WHO FINDS AN AUTODIALER SO JAMMED YOU FORGET WHAT YOU ONCE WERE, AND STUTTER THROUGH IDENTITIES...

UNBLED.

...EVEN IF YOU'RE A DEVIL.

THE WAR IN THE EXCHANGE BLEW DIALS EVERYWHERE. ALL THE WAY TO HELL.

EVEN IF YOU'RE A MINOR DEVIL WHO FINDS A DIAL MORE BROKEN THAN MOST, THAT'LL ONLY DIAL HALF-RUINED VERSIONS OF ITS HEROES, IT'S ENOUGH TO MAKE YOU FORGET TO BE WICKED.

WE HAVE A MISSION.

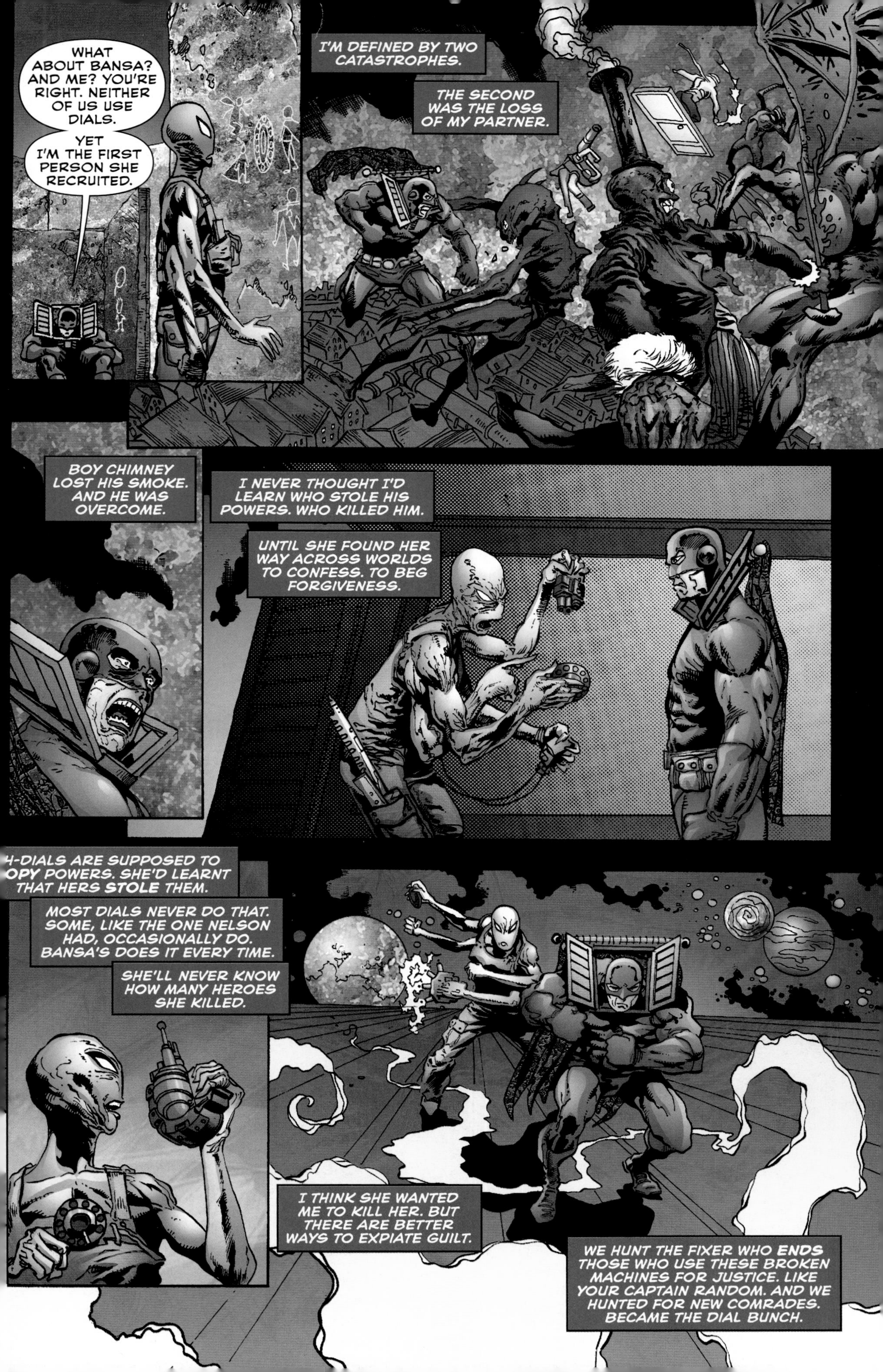
WHAT ABOUT BANSA? AND ME? YOU'RE RIGHT. NEITHER OF US USE DIALS.
YET I'M THE FIRST PERSON SHE RECRUITED.
I'M DEFINED BY TWO CATASTROPHES.
THE SECOND WAS THE LOSS OF MY PARTNER.
BOY CHIMNEY LOST HIS SMOKE. AND HE WAS OVERCOME.
I NEVER THOUGHT I'D LEARN WHO STOLE HIS POWERS. WHO KILLED HIM.
UNTIL SHE FOUND HER WAY ACROSS WORLDS TO CONFESS. TO BEG FORGIVENESS.
H-DIALS ARE SUPPOSED TO COPY POWERS. SHE'D LEARNT THAT HERS STOLE THEM.
MOST DIALS NEVER DO THAT. SOME, LIKE THE ONE NELSON HAD, OCCASIONALLY DO. BANSA'S DOES IT EVERY TIME.
SHE'LL NEVER KNOW HOW MANY HEROES SHE KILLED.
I THINK SHE WANTED ME TO KILL HER. BUT THERE ARE BETTER WAYS TO EXPIATE GUILT.
WE HUNT THE FIXER WHO ENDS THOSE WHO USE THESE BROKEN MACHINES FOR JUSTICE. LIKE YOUR CAPTAIN RANDOM. AND WE HUNTED FOR NEW COMRADES. BECAME THE DIAL BUNCH.

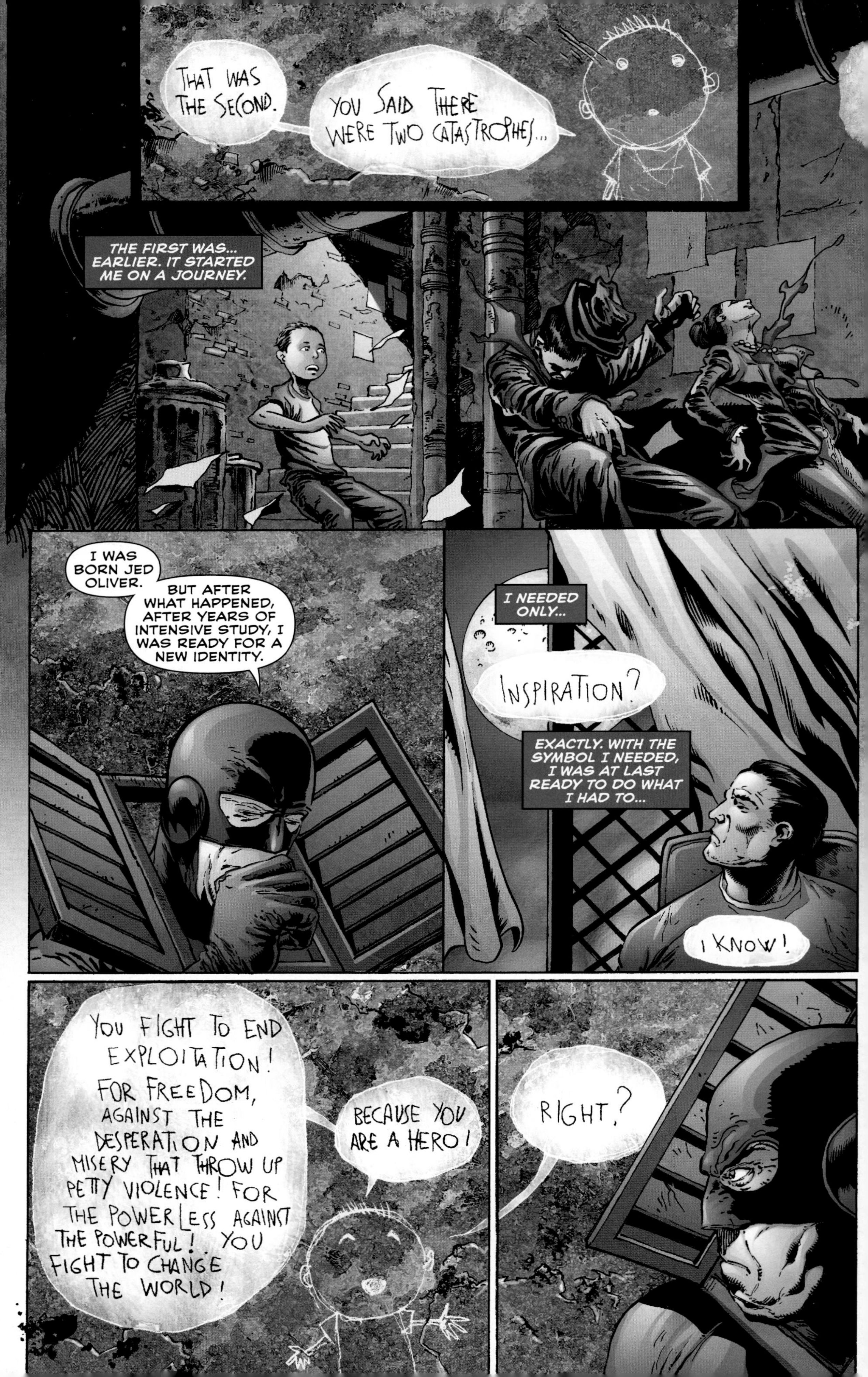
THAT WAS THE SECOND.
YOU SAID THERE WERE TWO CATASTROPHES...
THE FIRST WAS... EARLIER. IT STARTED ME ON A JOURNEY.
I WAS BORN JED OLIVER.
BUT AFTER WHAT HAPPENED, AFTER YEARS OF INTENSIVE STUDY, I WAS READY FOR A NEW IDENTITY.
I NEEDED ONLY...
INSPIRATION?
EXACTLY. WITH THE SYMBOL I NEEDED, I WAS AT LAST READY TO DO WHAT I HAD TO...
I KNOW!
YOU FIGHT TO END EXPLOITATION! FOR FREEDOM, AGAINST THE DESPERATION AND MISERY THAT THROW UP PETTY VIOLENCE! FOR THE POWERLESS AGAINST THE POWERFUL! YOU FIGHT TO CHANGE THE WORLD!
BECAUSE YOU ARE A HERO!
RIGHT?

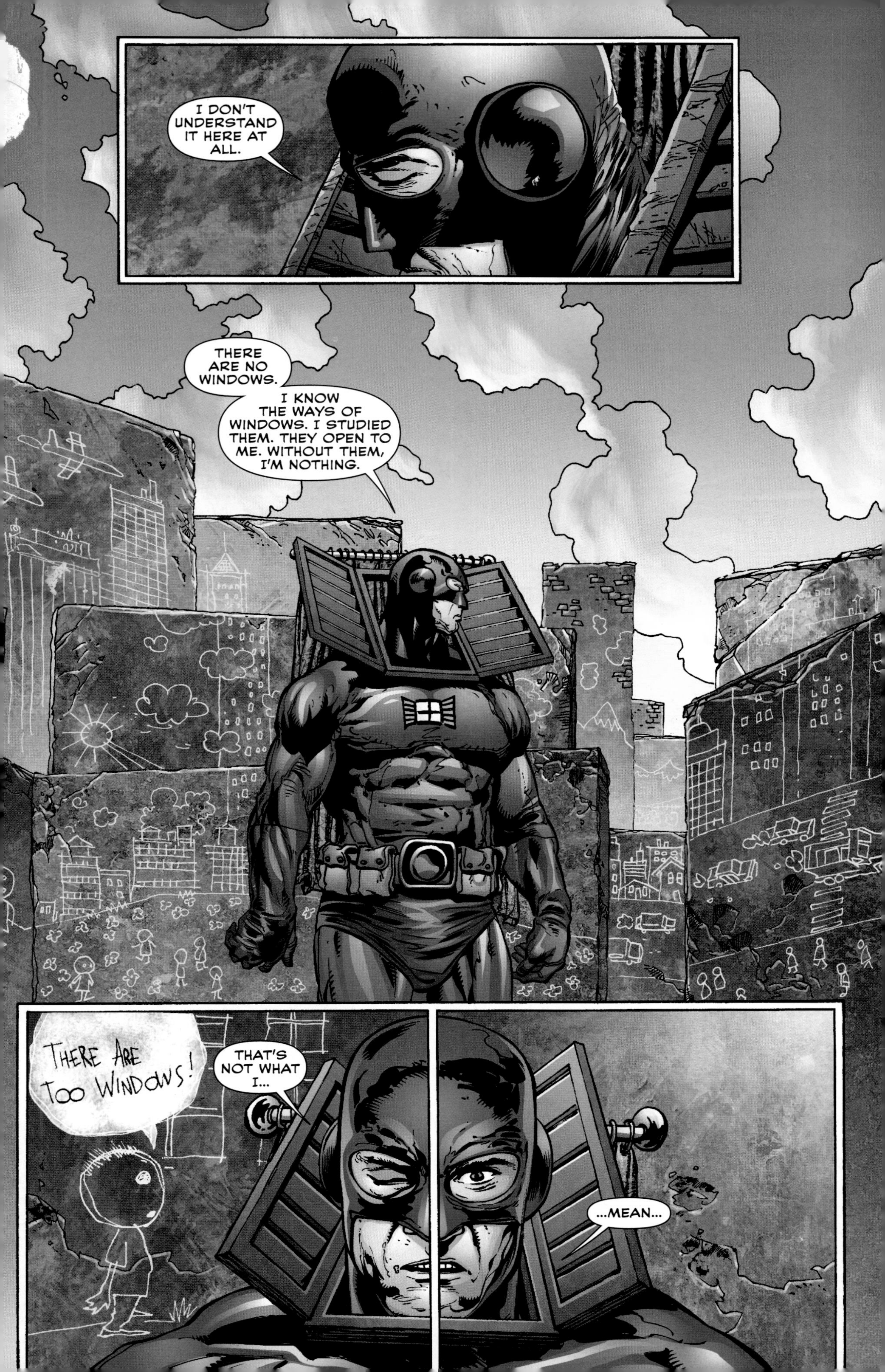
I DON'T UNDERSTAND IT HERE AT ALL.
THERE ARE NO WINDOWS.
I KNOW THE WAYS OF WINDOWS. I STUDIED THEM. THEY OPEN TO ME. WITHOUT THEM, I'M NOTHING.
THERE ARE TOO WINDOWS!
THAT'S NOT WHAT I...
...MEAN...

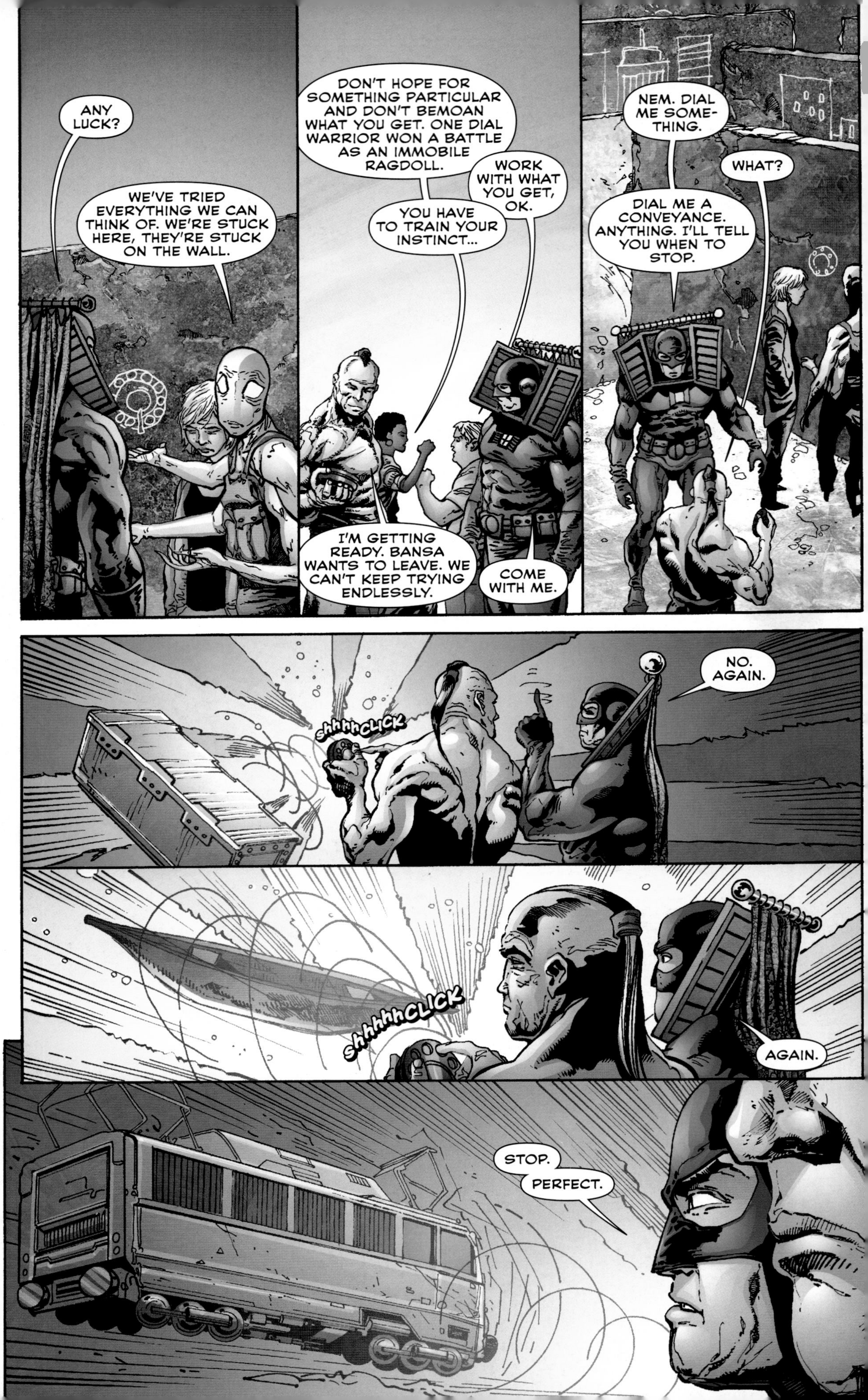
ANY LUCK?
WE'VE TRIED EVERYTHING WE CAN THINK OF. WE'RE STUCK HERE, THEY'RE STUCK ON THE WALL.
DON'T HOPE FOR SOMETHING PARTICULAR AND DON'T BEMOAN WHAT YOU GET. ONE DIAL WARRIOR WON A BATTLE AS AN IMMOBILE RAGDOLL.
YOU HAVE TO TRAIN YOUR INSTINCT...
WORK WITH WHAT YOU GET, OK.
I'M GETTING READY. BANSA WANTS TO LEAVE. WE CAN'T KEEP TRYING ENDLESSLY.
COME WITH ME.
NEM. DIAL ME SOME-THING.
WHAT?
DIAL ME A CONVEYANCE. ANYTHING. I'LL TELL YOU WHEN TO STOP.
shhhhCLICK
NO. AGAIN.
shhhhhCLICK
AGAIN.
STOP.
PERFECT.

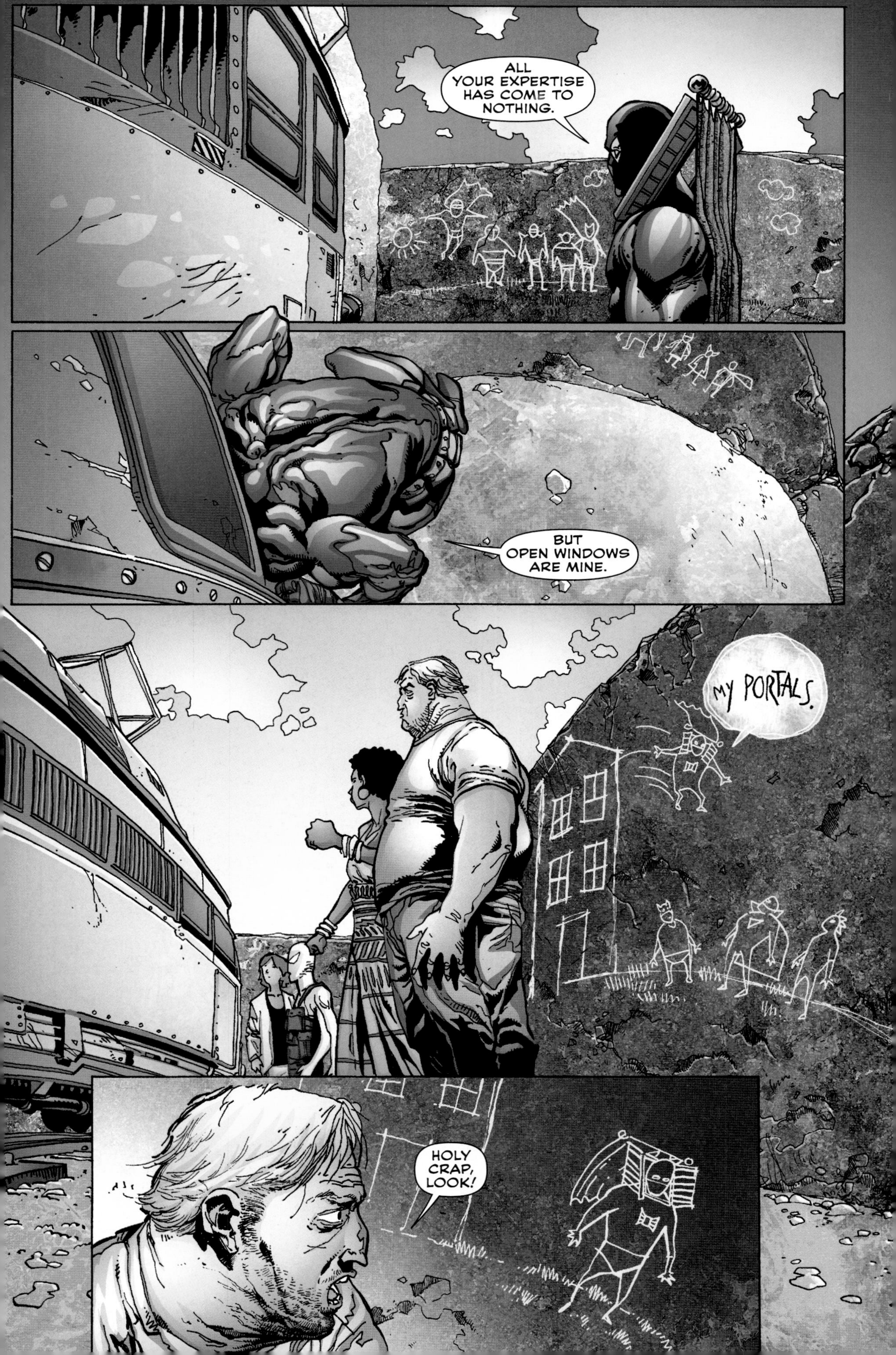
ALL YOUR EXPERTISE HAS COME TO NOTHING.
BUT OPEN WINDOWS ARE MINE.
MY PORTALS.
HOLY CRAP, LOOK!

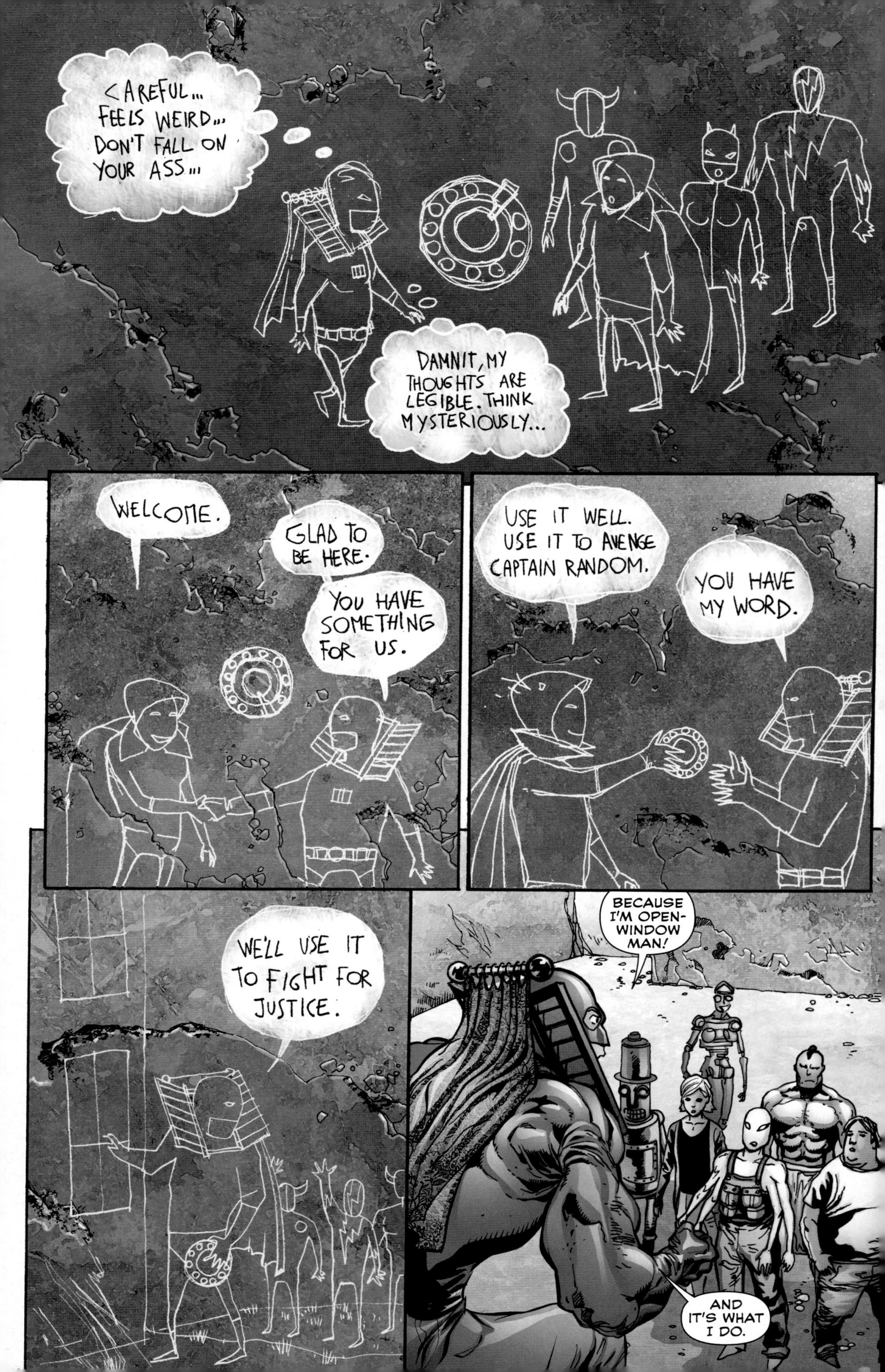
CAREFUL... FEELS WEIRD... DON'T FALL ON YOUR ASS...
DAMNIT, MY THOUGHTS ARE LEGIBLE. THINK MYSTERIOUSLY...
WELCOME.
GLAD TO BE HERE.
YOU HAVE SOMETHING FOR US.
USE IT WELL. USE IT TO AVENGE CAPTAIN RANDOM.
YOU HAVE MY WORD.
WE'LL USE IT TO FIGHT FOR JUSTICE.
BECAUSE I'M OPEN-WINDOW MAN!
AND IT'S WHAT I DO.

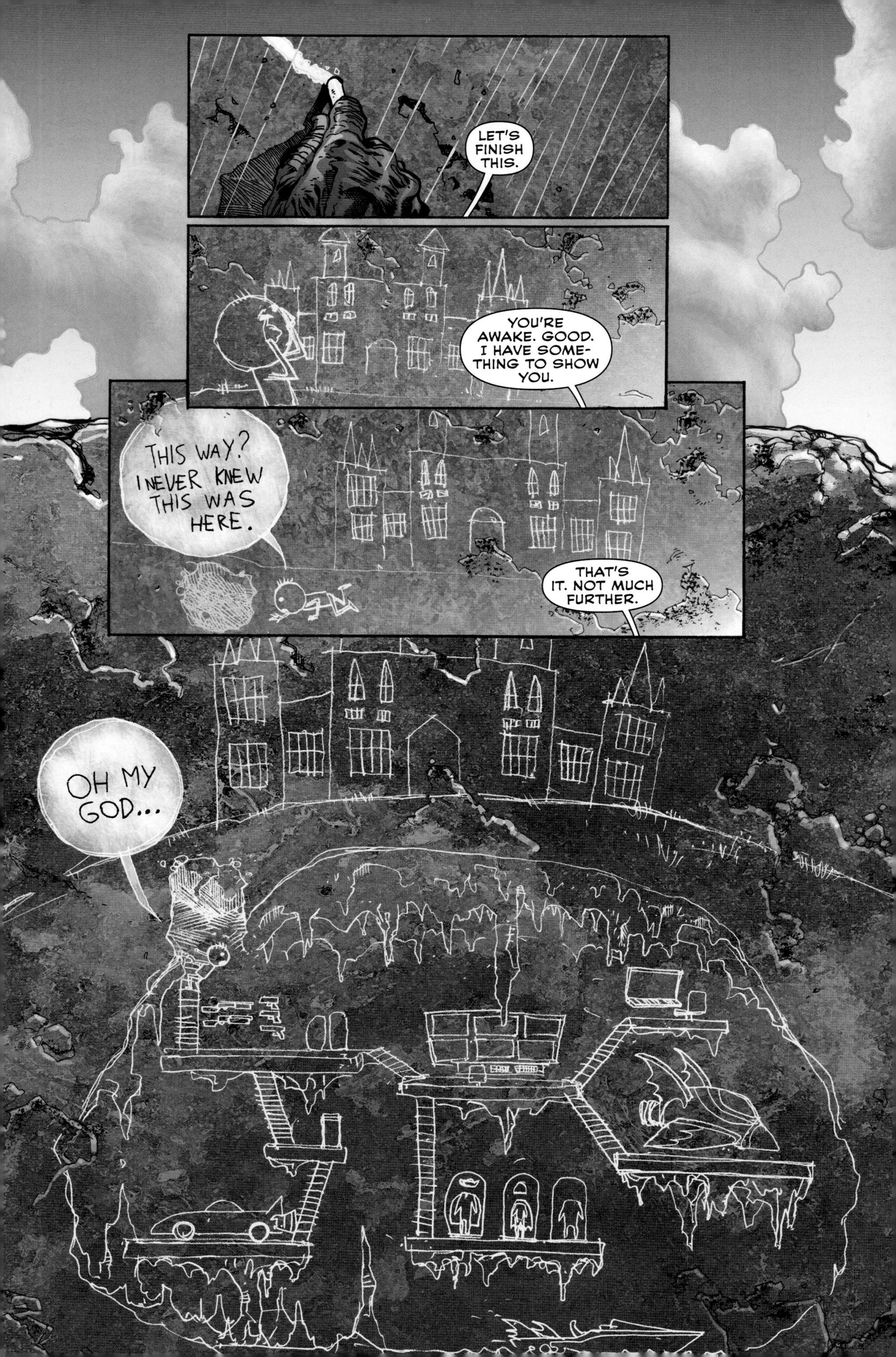
LET'S FINISH THIS.
YOU'RE AWAKE. GOOD. I HAVE SOME-THING TO SHOW YOU.
THIS WAY? I NEVER KNEW THIS WAS HERE.
THAT'S IT. NOT MUCH FURTHER.
OH MY GOD...

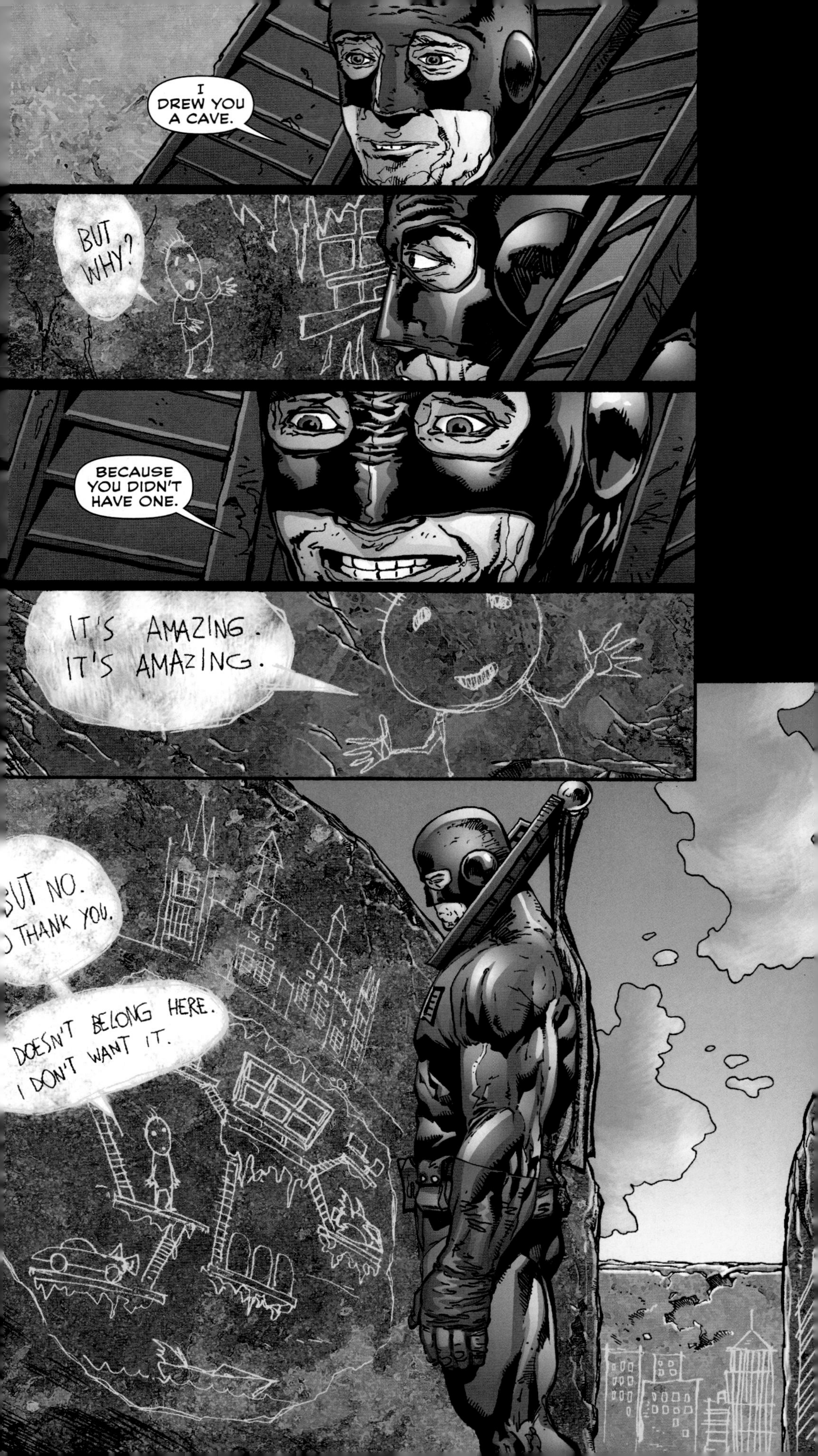
I DREW YOU A CAVE.
BUT WHY?
BECAUSE YOU DIDN'T HAVE ONE.
IT'S AMAZING. IT'S AMAZING.
UT NO. THANK YOU.
DOESN'T BELONG HERE. I DON'T WANT IT.

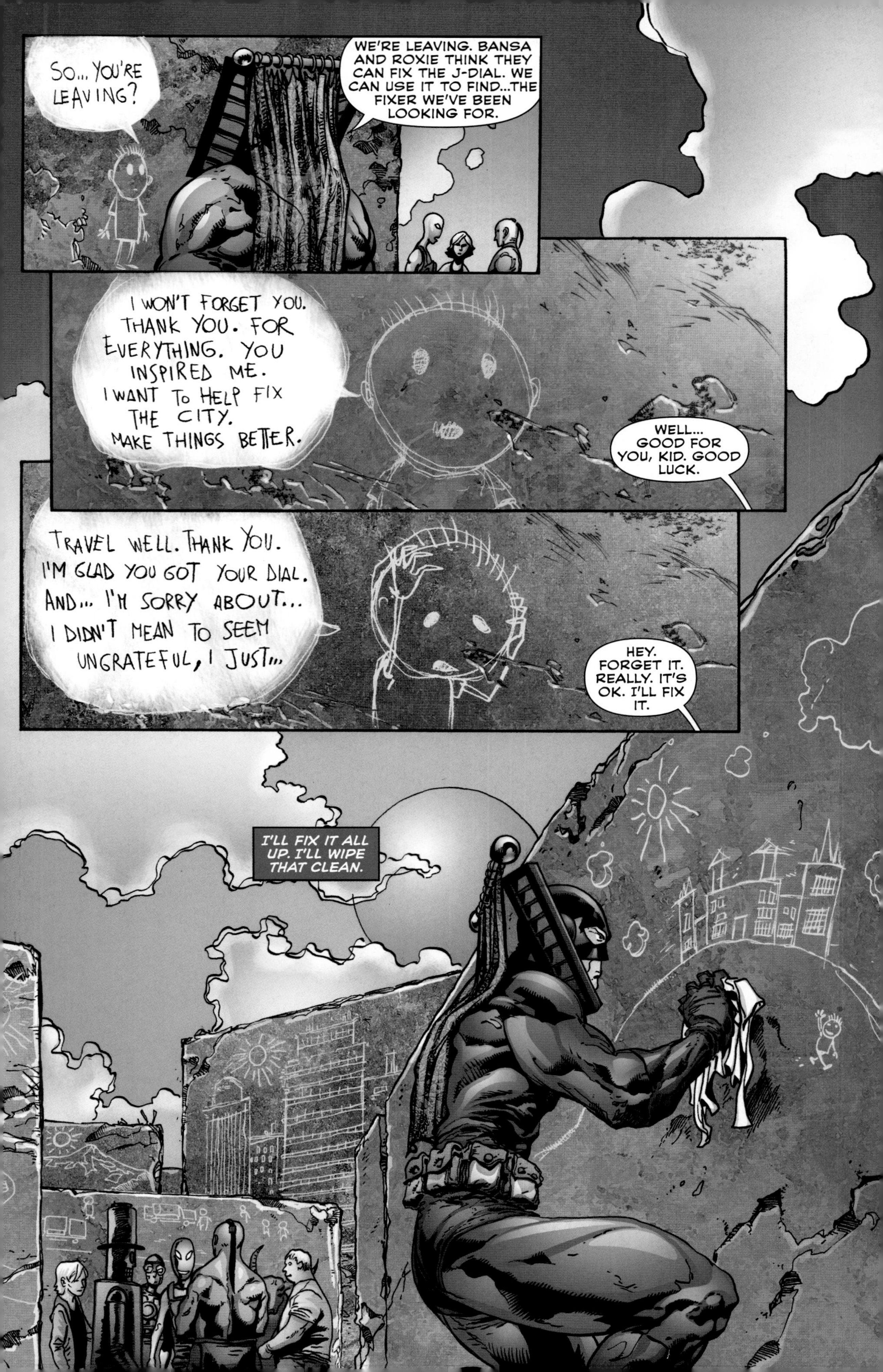

SO... YOU'RE LEAVING?
WE'RE LEAVING. BANSA AND ROXIE THINK THEY CAN FIX THE J-DIAL. WE CAN USE IT TO FIND...THE FIXER WE'VE BEEN LOOKING FOR.
I WON'T FORGET YOU. THANK YOU. FOR EVERYTHING. YOU INSPIRED ME. I WANT TO HELP FIX THE CITY. MAKE THINGS BETTER.
WELL... GOOD FOR YOU, KID. GOOD LUCK.
TRAVEL WELL. THANK YOU. I'M GLAD YOU GOT YOUR DIAL. AND... I'M SORRY ABOUT... I DIDN'T MEAN TO SEEM UNGRATEFUL, I JUST...
HEY. FORGET IT. REALLY. IT'S OK. I'LL FIX IT.
I'LL FIX IT ALL UP. I'LL WIPE THAT CLEAN.

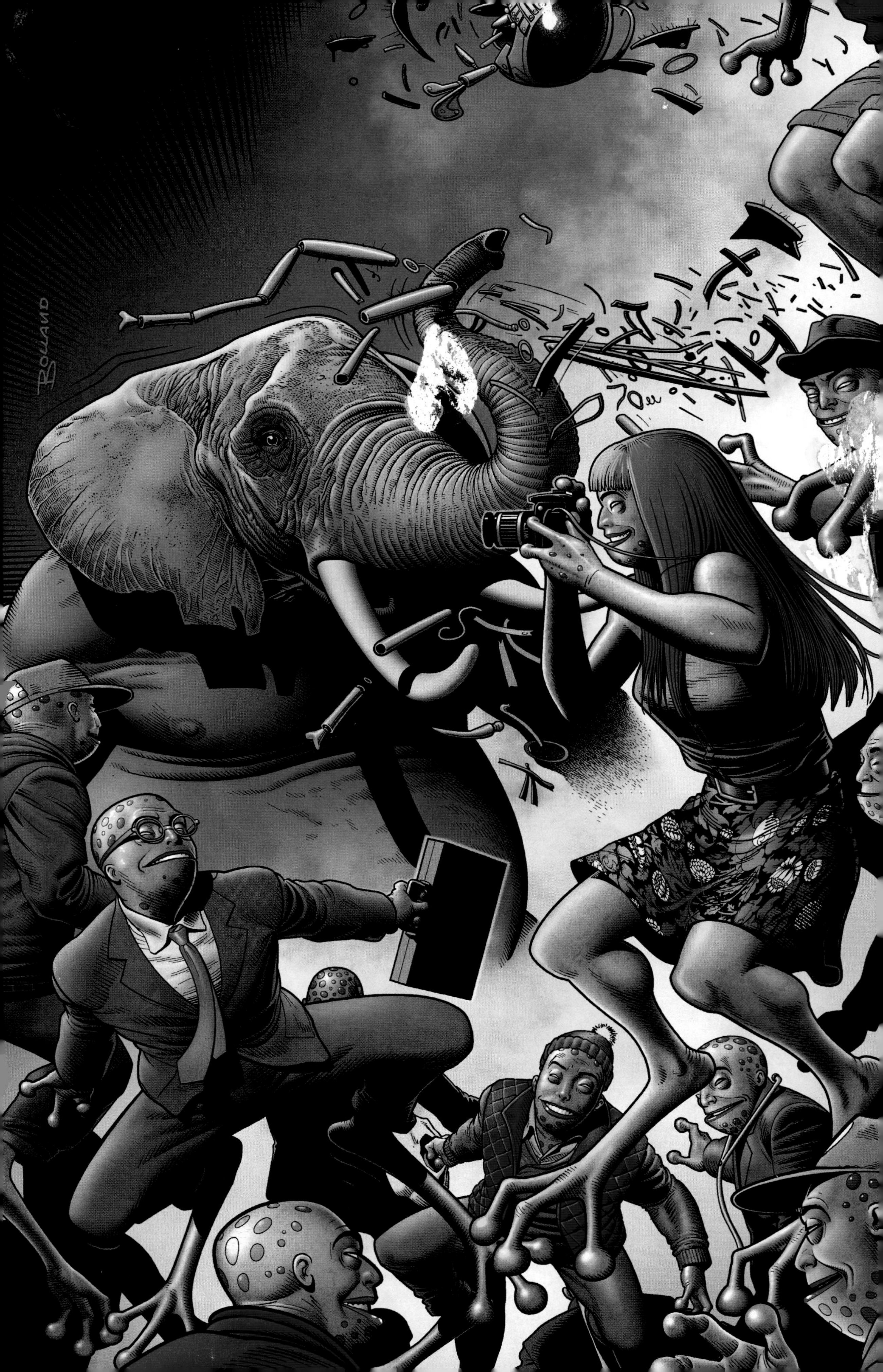
BOLLAND

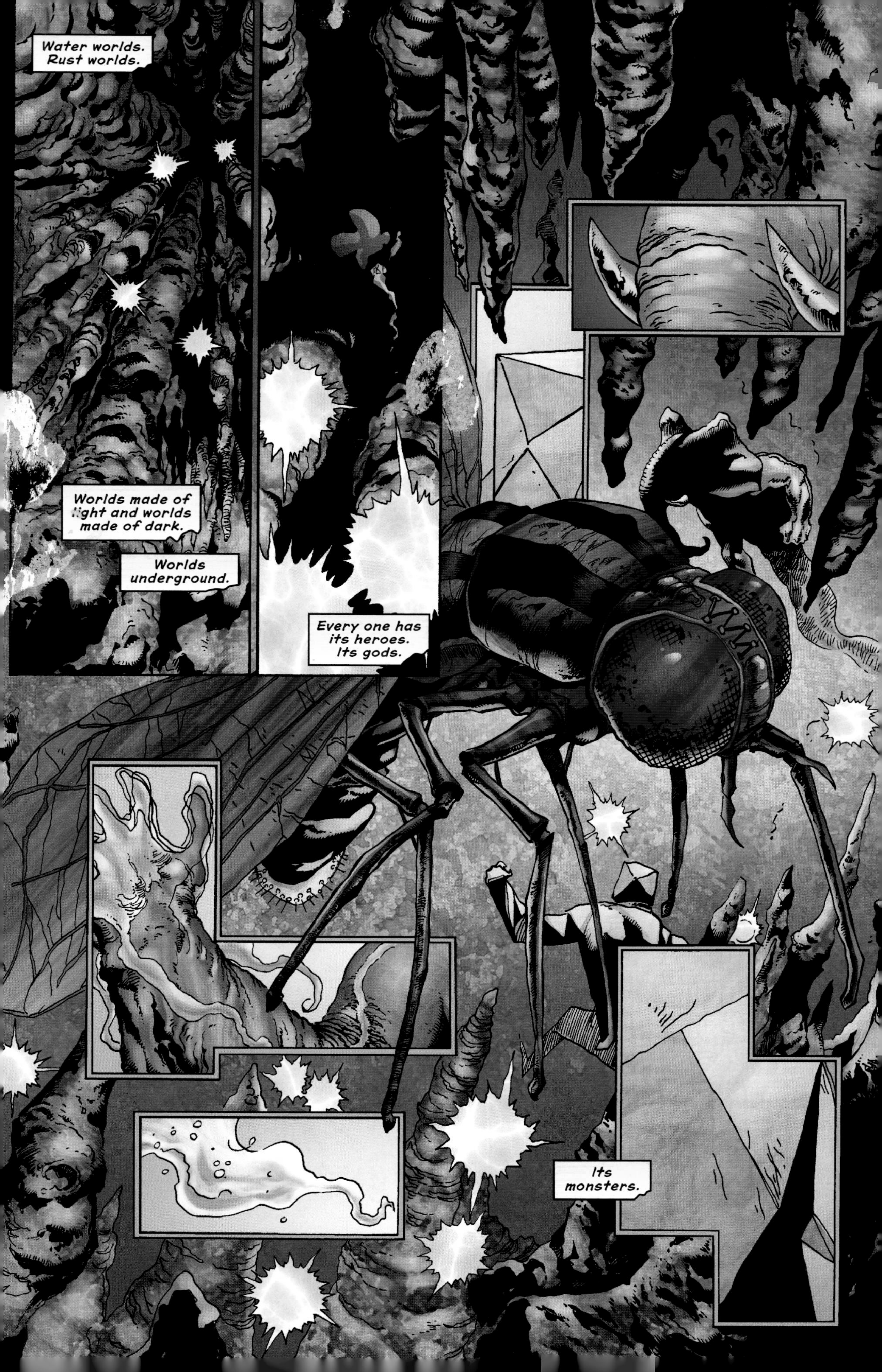
Water worlds. Rust worlds.
Worlds made of light and worlds made of dark.
Worlds underground.
Every one has its heroes. Its gods.
Its monsters.

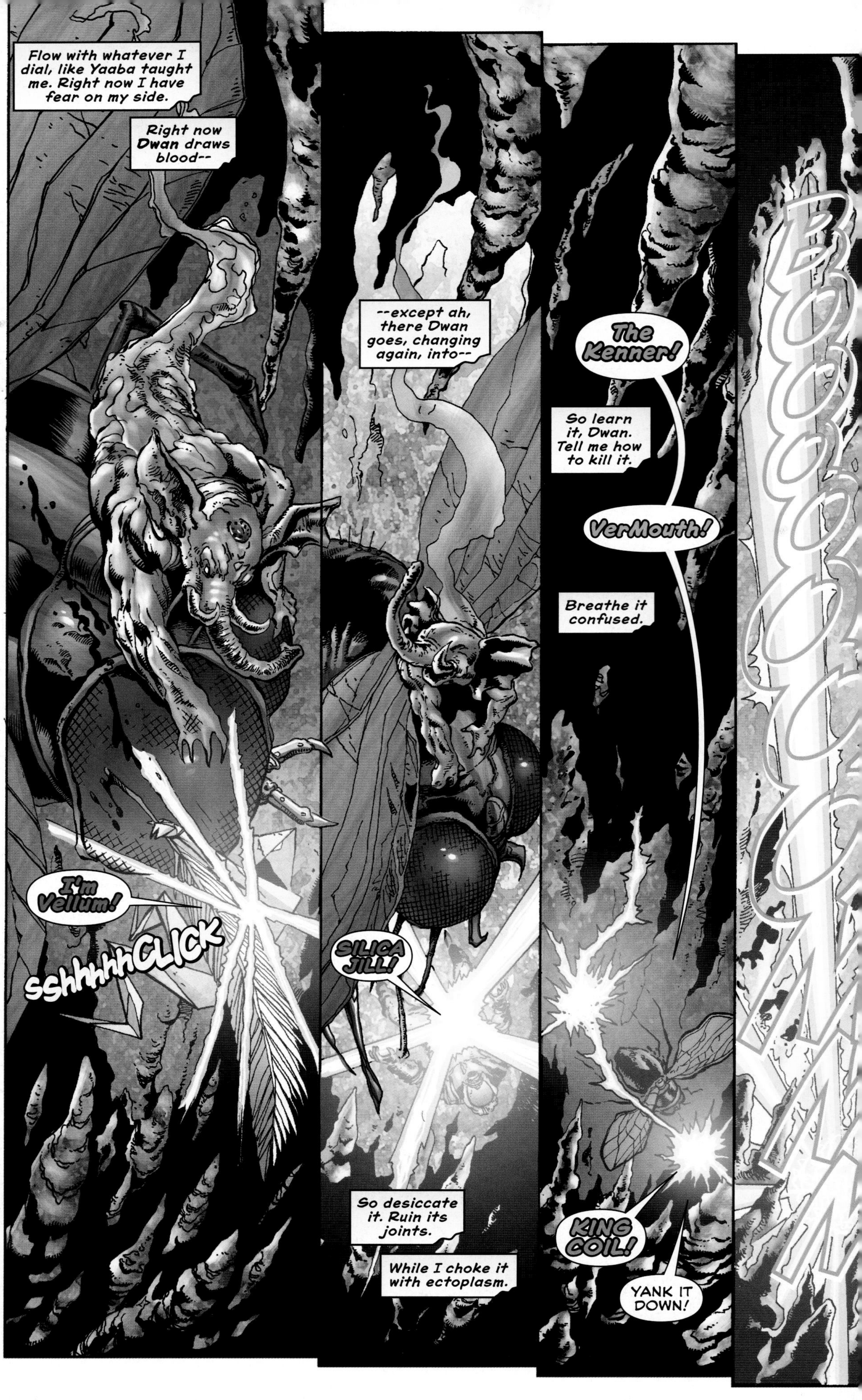
Flow with whatever I dial, like Yaaba taught me. Right now I have fear on my side.
Right now Dwan draws blood--
I'm Vellum!
sShhhhhCLICK
--except ah, there Dwan goes, changing again, into--
SILICA JILL!
So desiccate it. Ruin its joints.
While I choke it with ectoplasm.
The Kenner!
So learn it, Dwan. Tell me how to kill it.
VerMouth!
Breathe it confused.
KING COIL!
YANK IT DOWN!

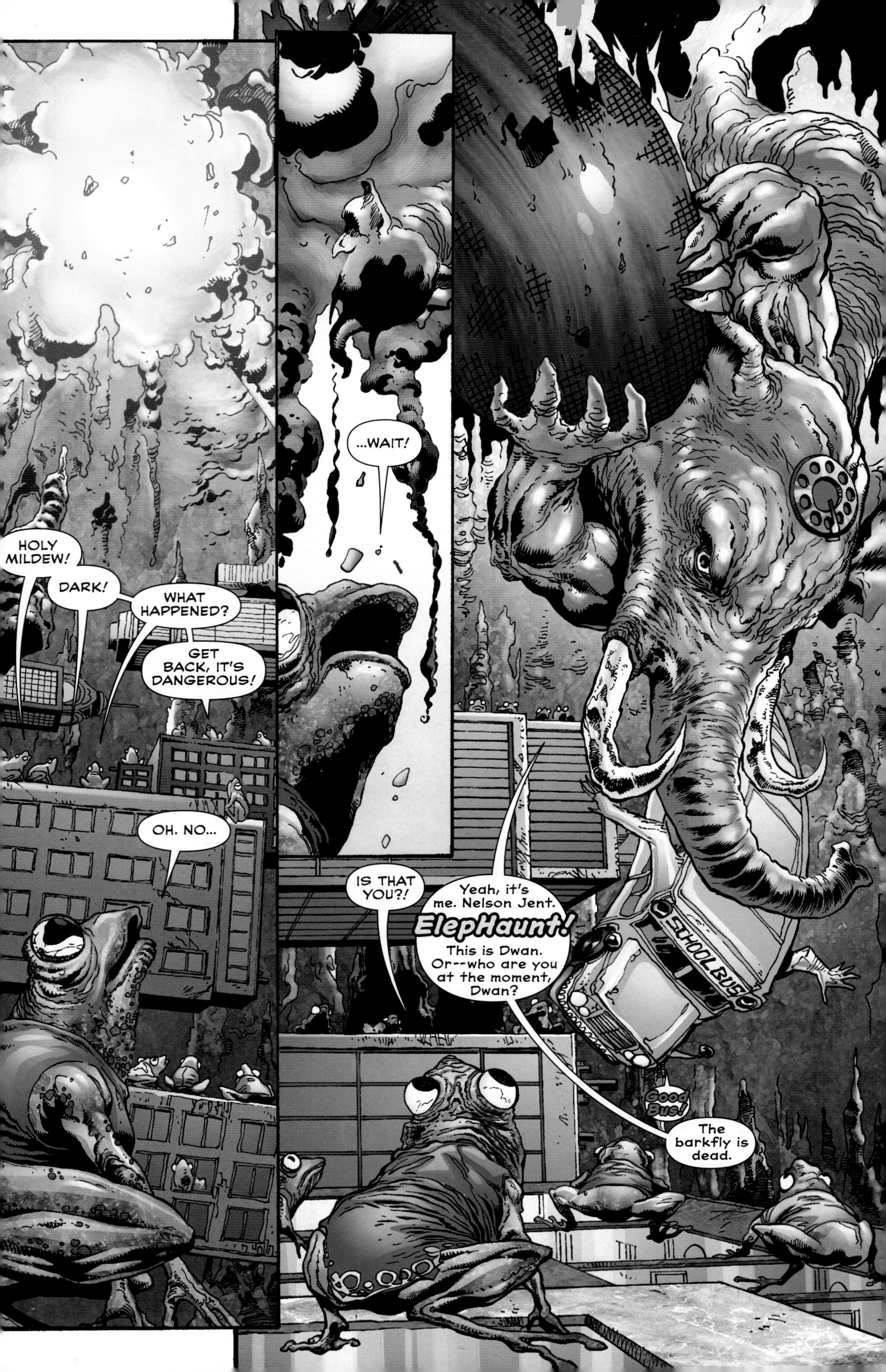
HOLY MILDEW!
DARK!
WHAT HAPPENED?
GET BACK, IT'S DANGEROUS!
OH. NO...
...WAIT!
IS THAT YOU?!
Yeah, it's me. Nelson Jent.
ElepHaunt!
This is Dwan. Or--who are you at the moment, Dwan?
SCHOOLBUS
Good Bus!
The barkfly is dead.

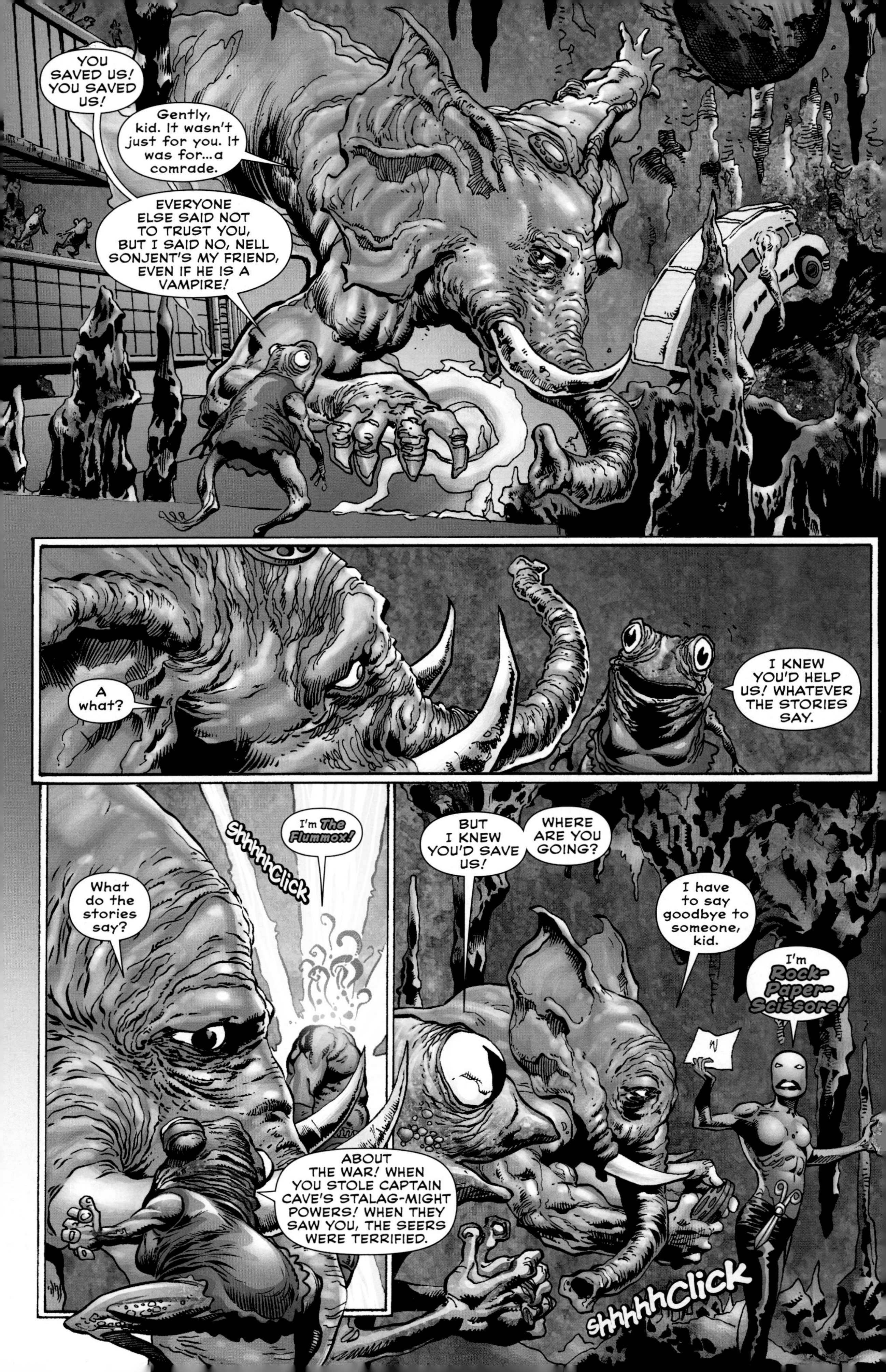
YOU SAVED US! YOU SAVED US!
Gently, kid. It wasn't just for you. It was for...a comrade.
EVERYONE ELSE SAID NOT TO TRUST YOU, BUT I SAID NO, NELL SONJENT'S MY FRIEND, EVEN IF HE IS A VAMPIRE!
A what?
I KNEW YOU'D HELP US! WHATEVER THE STORIES SAY.
What do the stories say?
ShhhhhClick
I'm The Flummox!
ABOUT THE WAR! WHEN YOU STOLE CAPTAIN CAVE'S STALAG-MIGHT POWERS! WHEN THEY SAW YOU, THE SEERS WERE TERRIFIED.
BUT I KNEW YOU'D SAVE US!
WHERE ARE YOU GOING?
I have to say goodbye to someone, kid.
I'm Rock-Paper-Scissors!
shhhhhClick

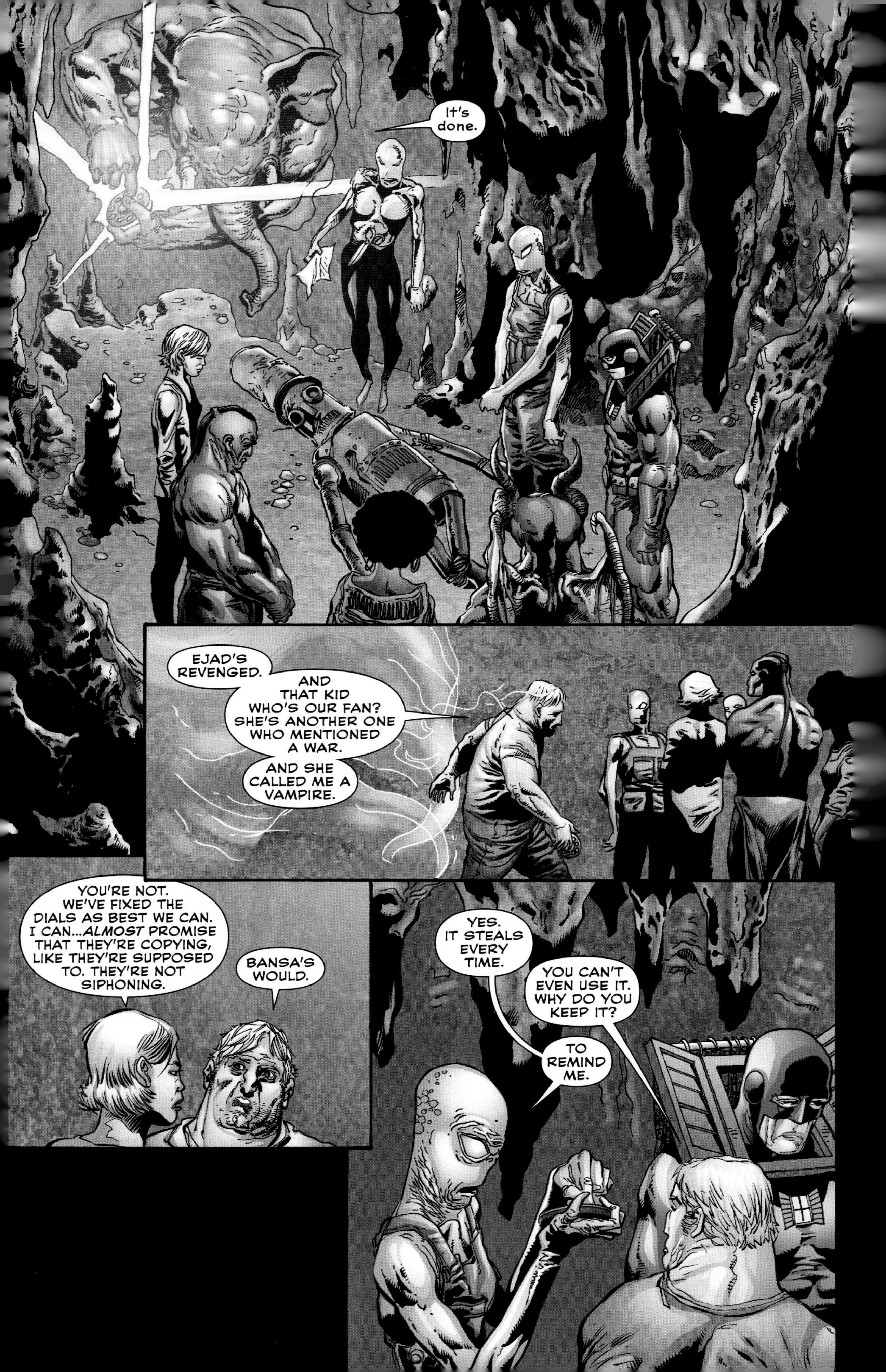
It's done.
EJAD'S REVENGED.
AND THAT KID WHO'S OUR FAN? SHE'S ANOTHER ONE WHO MENTIONED A WAR.
AND SHE CALLED ME A VAMPIRE.
YOU'RE NOT. WE'VE FIXED THE DIALS AS BEST WE CAN. I CAN...*ALMOST* PROMISE THAT THEY'RE COPYING, LIKE THEY'RE SUPPOSED TO. THEY'RE NOT SIPHONING.
BANSA'S WOULD.
YES. IT STEALS EVERY TIME.
YOU CAN'T EVEN USE IT. WHY DO YOU KEEP IT?
TO REMIND ME.

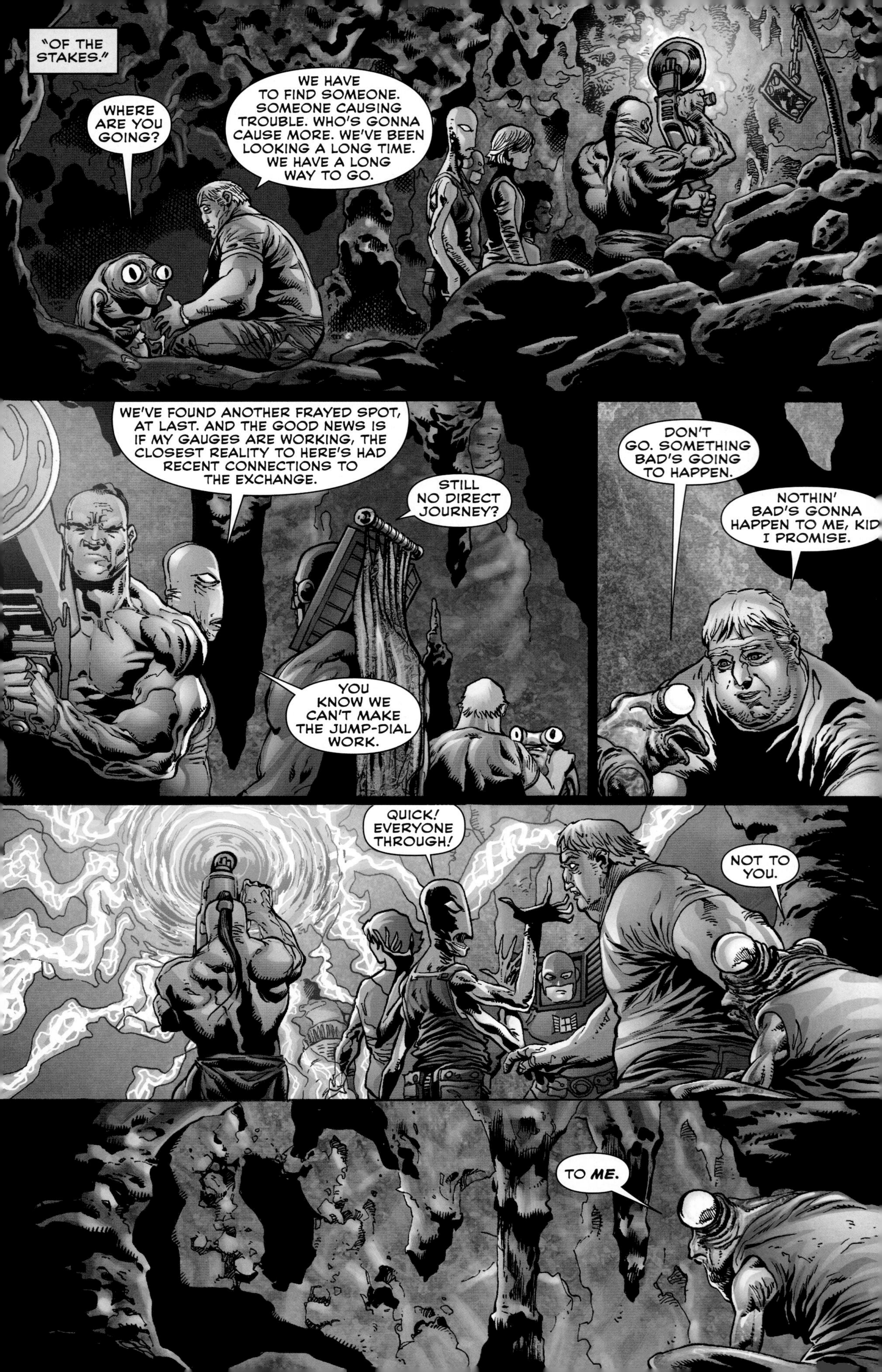
"OF THE STAKES."
WHERE ARE YOU GOING?
WE HAVE TO FIND SOMEONE. SOMEONE CAUSING TROUBLE. WHO'S GONNA CAUSE MORE. WE'VE BEEN LOOKING A LONG TIME. WE HAVE A LONG WAY TO GO.
WE'VE FOUND ANOTHER FRAYED SPOT, AT LAST. AND THE GOOD NEWS IS IF MY GAUGES ARE WORKING, THE CLOSEST REALITY TO HERE'S HAD RECENT CONNECTIONS TO THE EXCHANGE.
STILL NO DIRECT JOURNEY?
YOU KNOW WE CAN'T MAKE THE JUMP-DIAL WORK.
DON'T GO. SOMETHING BAD'S GOING TO HAPPEN.
NOTHIN' BAD'S GONNA HAPPEN TO ME, KID I PROMISE.
QUICK! EVERYONE THROUGH!
NOT TO YOU.
TO *ME*.

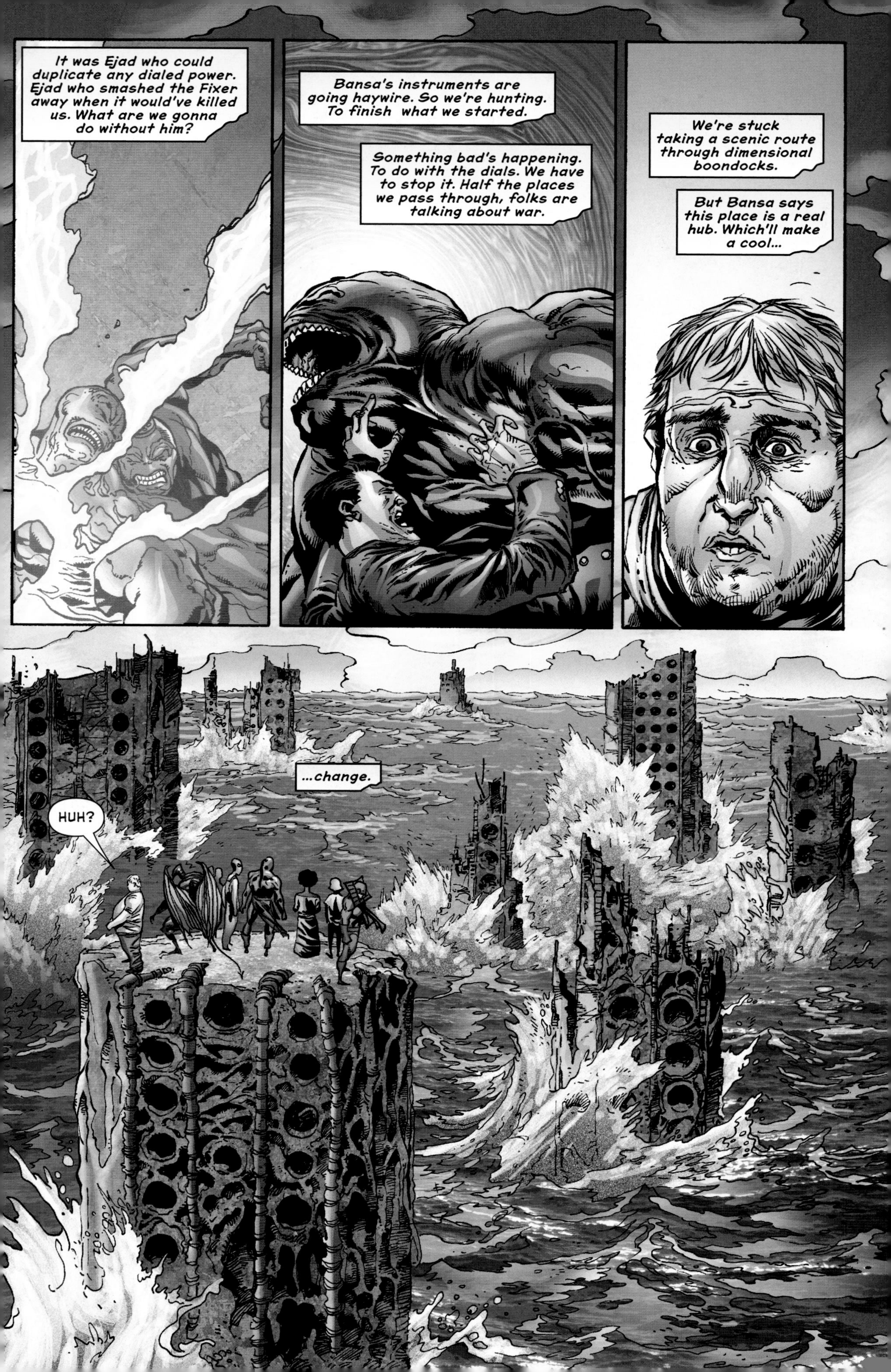
It was Ejad who could duplicate any dialed power. Ejad who smashed the Fixer away when it would've killed us. What are we gonna do without him?
Bansa's instruments are going haywire. So we're hunting. To finish what we started.
Something bad's happening. To do with the dials. We have to stop it. Half the places we pass through, folks are talking about war.
We're stuck taking a scenic route through dimensional boondocks.
But Bansa says this place is a real hub. Which'll make a cool...
...change.
HUH?

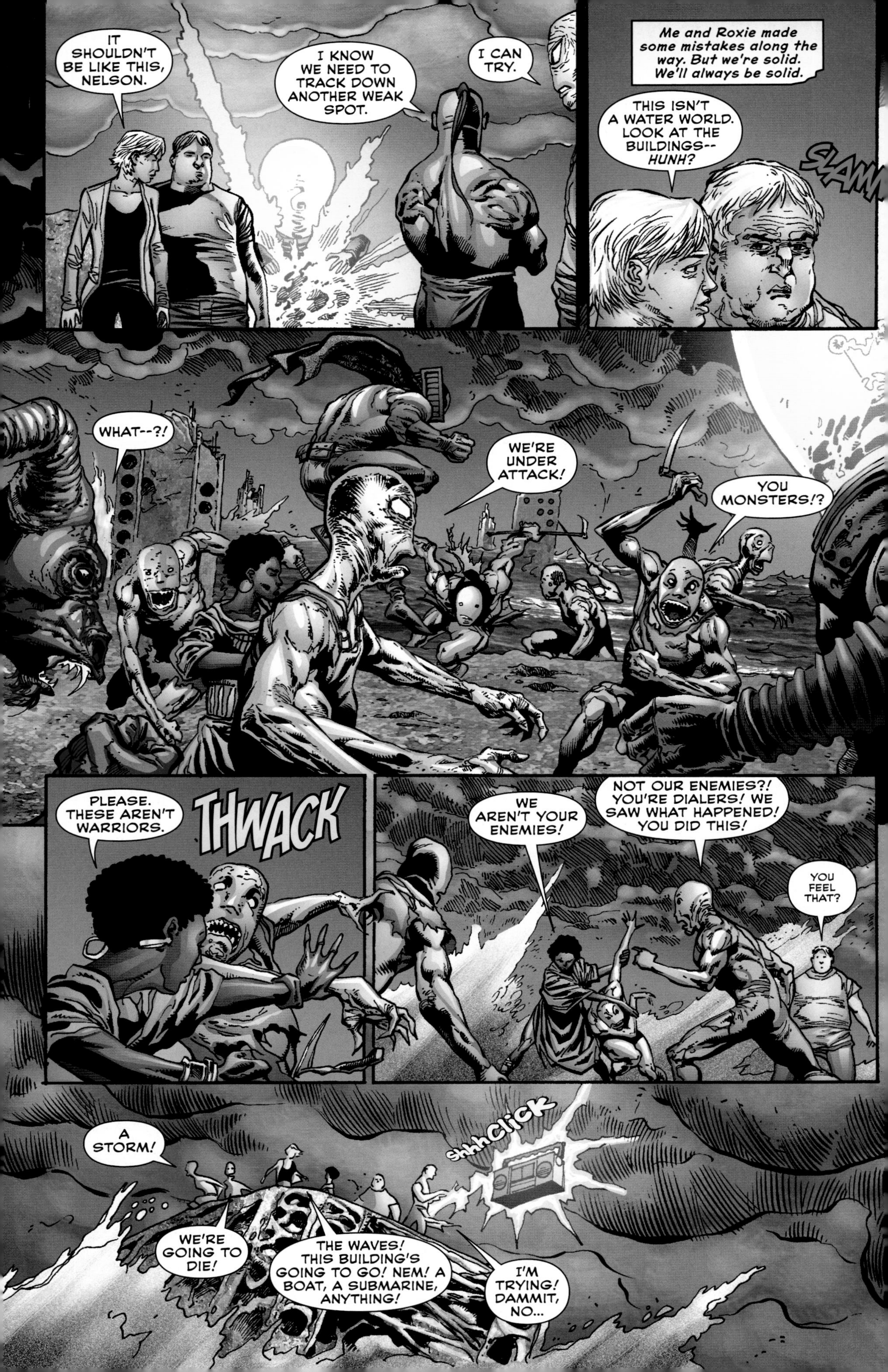
IT SHOULDN'T BE LIKE THIS, NELSON.
I KNOW WE NEED TO TRACK DOWN ANOTHER WEAK SPOT.
I CAN TRY.
Me and Roxie made some mistakes along the way. But we're solid. We'll always be solid.
THIS ISN'T A WATER WORLD. LOOK AT THE BUILDINGS-- HUNH?
SLAMM
WHAT--?!
WE'RE UNDER ATTACK!
YOU MONSTERS!?
PLEASE. THESE AREN'T WARRIORS.
THWACK
WE AREN'T YOUR ENEMIES!
NOT OUR ENEMIES?! YOU'RE DIALERS! WE SAW WHAT HAPPENED! YOU DID THIS!
YOU FEEL THAT?
A STORM!
shhhCLICK
WE'RE GOING TO DIE!
THE WAVES! THIS BUILDING'S GOING TO GO! NEM! A BOAT, A SUBMARINE, ANYTHING!
I'M TRYING! DAMMIT, NO...

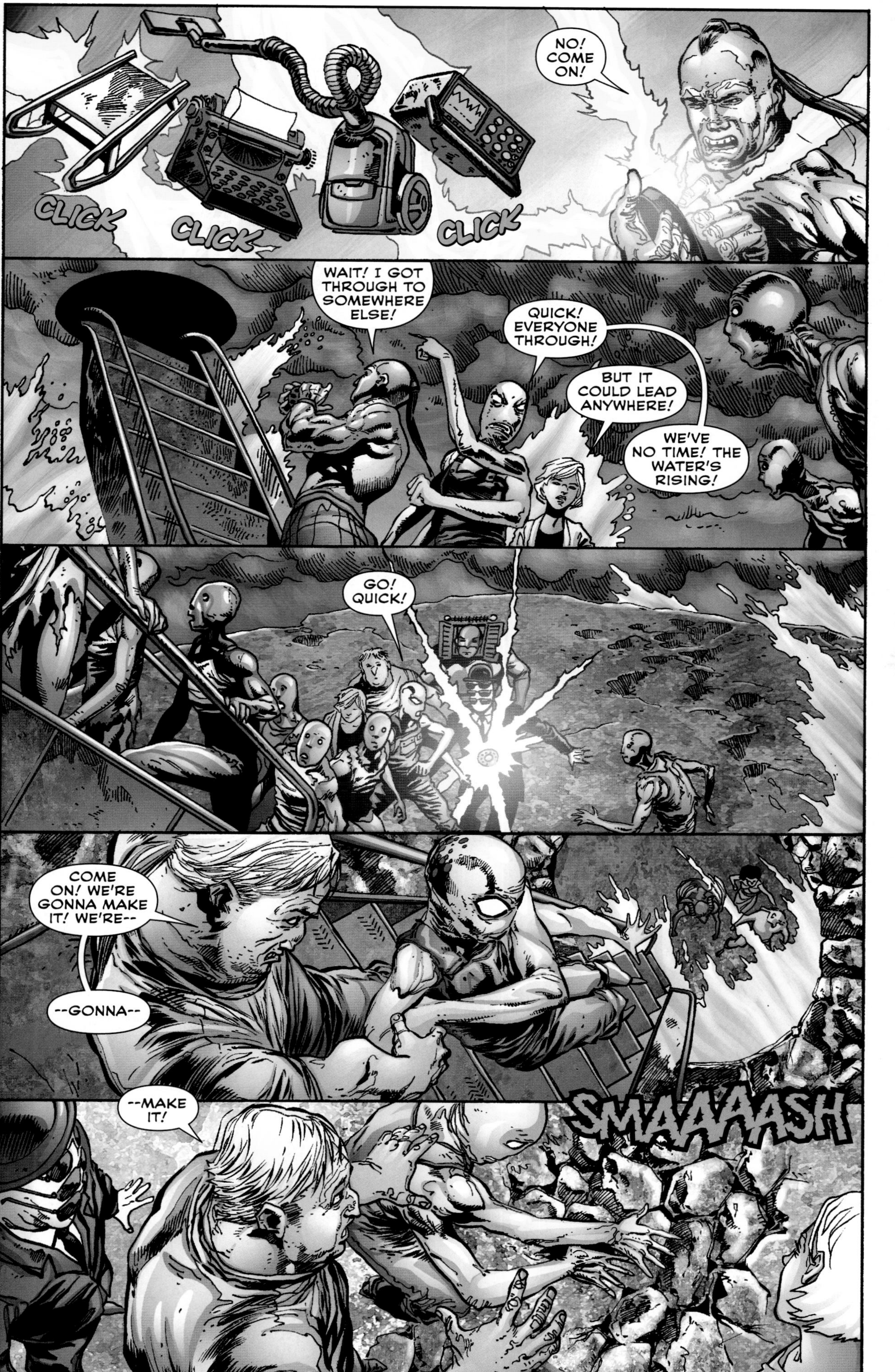

NO! COME ON!
CLICK
CLICK
CLICK
WAIT! I GOT THROUGH TO SOMEWHERE ELSE!
QUICK! EVERYONE THROUGH!
BUT IT COULD LEAD ANYWHERE!
WE'VE NO TIME! THE WATER'S RISING!
GO! QUICK!
COME ON! WE'RE GONNA MAKE IT! WE'RE--
--GONNA--
SMAAAAASH
--MAKE IT!

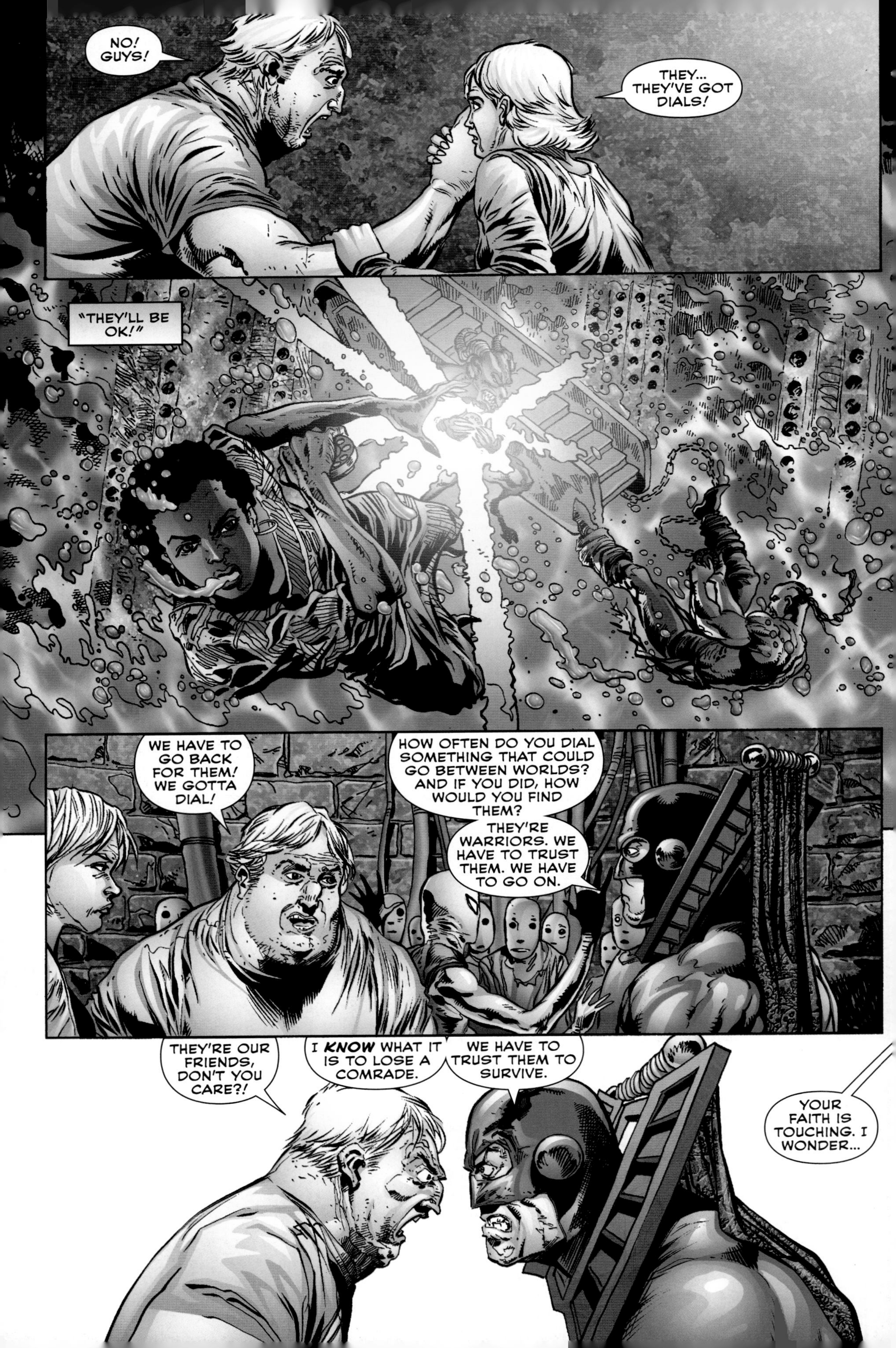
NO! GUYS!
THEY... THEY'VE GOT DIALS!
"THEY'LL BE OK!"
WE HAVE TO GO BACK FOR THEM! WE GOTTA DIAL!
HOW OFTEN DO YOU DIAL SOMETHING THAT COULD GO BETWEEN WORLDS? AND IF YOU DID, HOW WOULD YOU FIND THEM?
THEY'RE WARRIORS. WE HAVE TO TRUST THEM. WE HAVE TO GO ON.
THEY'RE OUR FRIENDS, DON'T YOU CARE?!
I **KNOW** WHAT IT IS TO LOSE A COMRADE.
WE HAVE TO TRUST THEM TO SURVIVE.
YOUR FAITH IS TOUCHING. I WONDER...

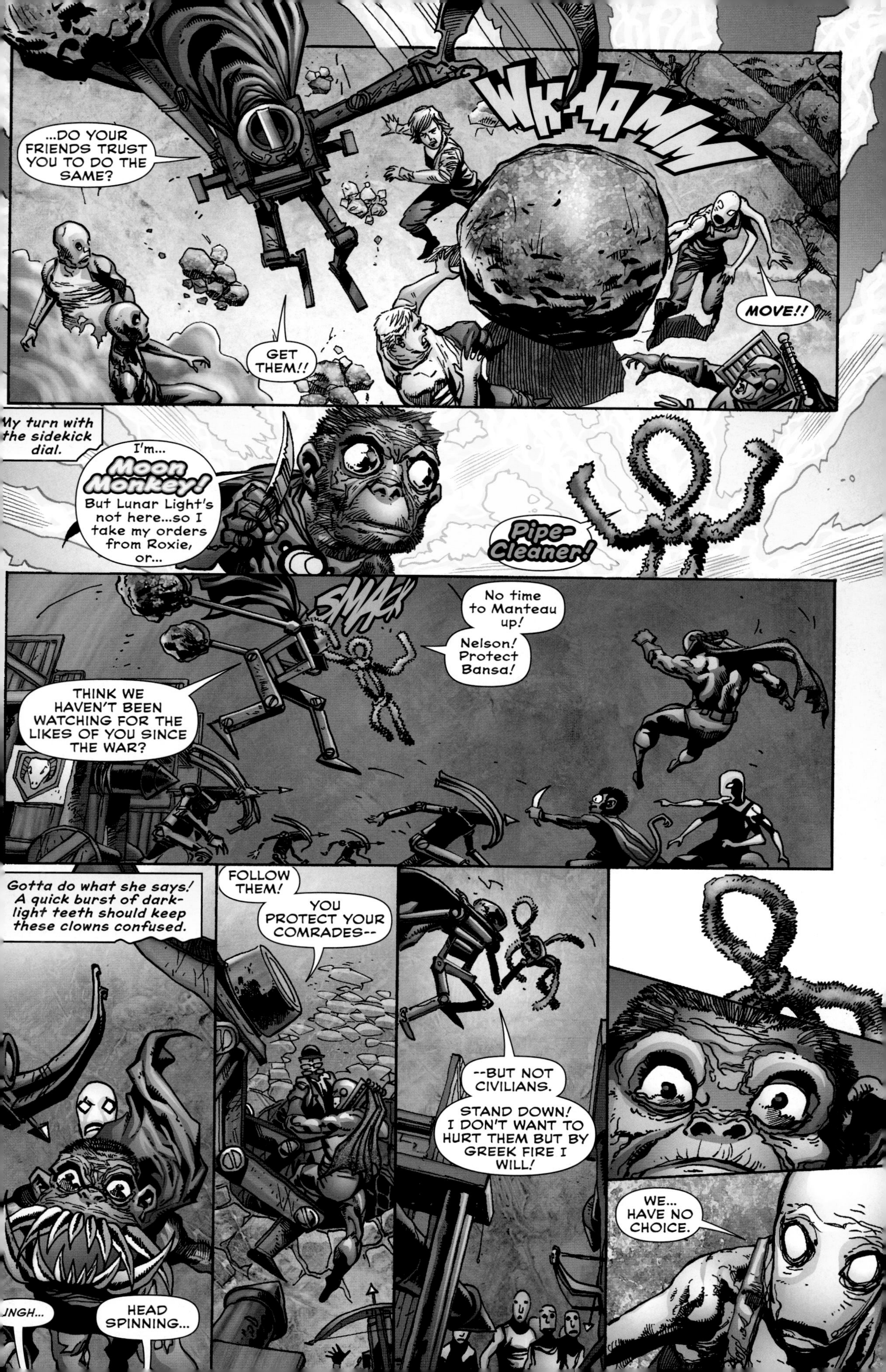
...DO YOUR FRIENDS TRUST YOU TO DO THE SAME?
WK-HAMM
GET THEM!!
MOVE!!
My turn with the sidekick dial.
I'm... Moon Monkey! But Lunar Light's not here...so I take my orders from Roxie, or...
Pipe-Cleaner!
SMACK
No time to Manteau up!
Nelson! Protect Bansa!
THINK WE HAVEN'T BEEN WATCHING FOR THE LIKES OF YOU SINCE THE WAR?
Gotta do what she says! A quick burst of dark-light teeth should keep these clowns confused.
FOLLOW THEM!
YOU PROTECT YOUR COMRADES--
--BUT NOT CIVILIANS.
STAND DOWN! I DON'T WANT TO HURT THEM BUT BY GREEK FIRE I WILL!
UNGH...
HEAD SPINNING...
WE... HAVE NO CHOICE.

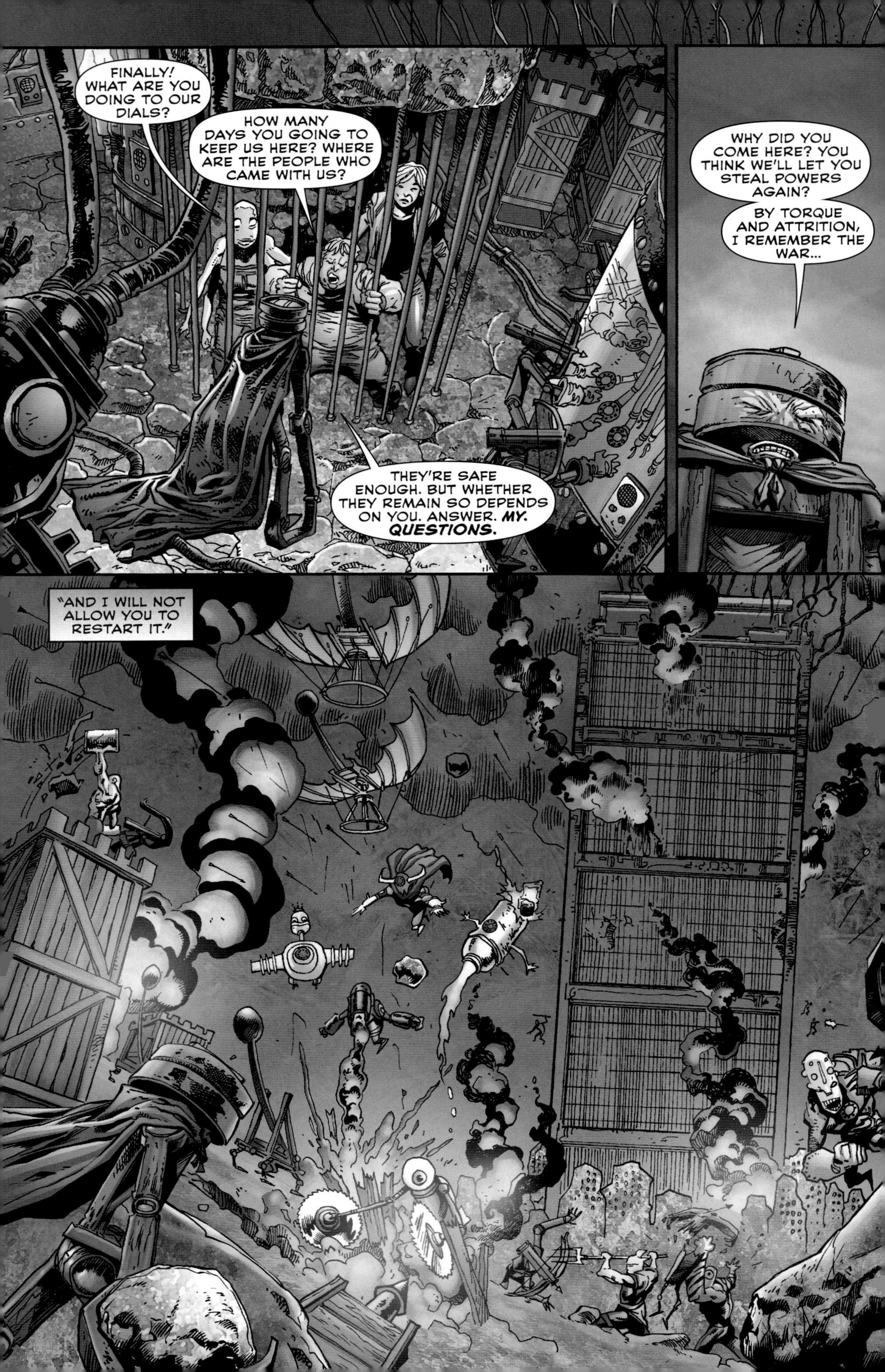
FINALLY! WHAT ARE YOU DOING TO OUR DIALS?
HOW MANY DAYS YOU GOING TO KEEP US HERE? WHERE ARE THE PEOPLE WHO CAME WITH US?
THEY'RE SAFE ENOUGH. BUT WHETHER THEY REMAIN SO DEPENDS ON YOU. ANSWER. MY. QUESTIONS.
WHY DID YOU COME HERE? YOU THINK WE'LL LET YOU STEAL POWERS AGAIN?
BY TORQUE AND ATTRITION, I REMEMBER THE WAR...
"AND I WILL NOT ALLOW YOU TO RESTART IT."

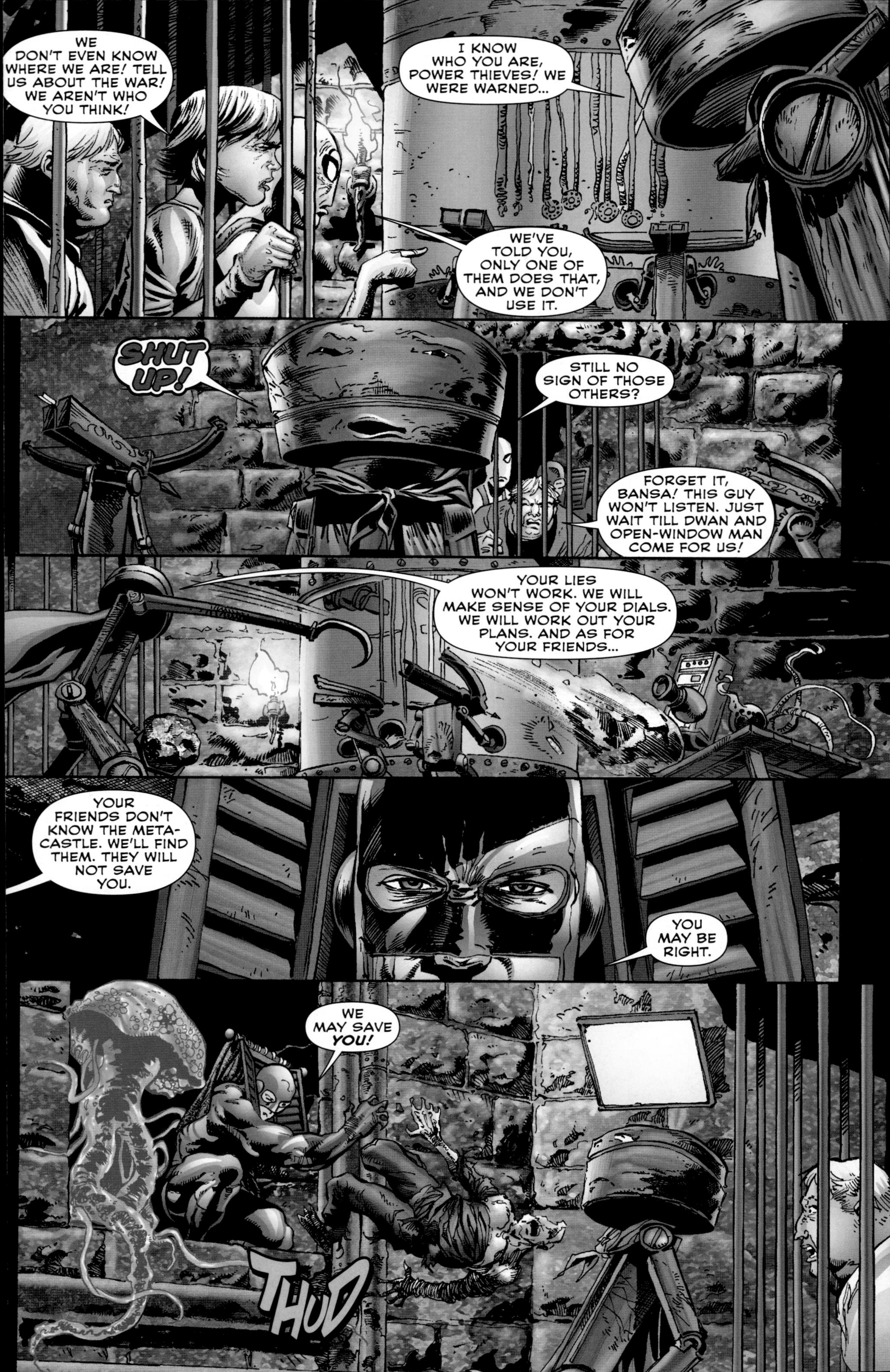
WE DON'T EVEN KNOW WHERE WE ARE! TELL US ABOUT THE WAR! WE AREN'T WHO YOU THINK!
I KNOW WHO YOU ARE, POWER THIEVES! WE WERE WARNED...
WE'VE TOLD YOU, ONLY ONE OF THEM DOES THAT, AND WE DON'T USE IT.
SHUT UP!
STILL NO SIGN OF THOSE OTHERS?
FORGET IT, BANSA! THIS GUY WON'T LISTEN. JUST WAIT TILL DWAN AND OPEN-WINDOW MAN COME FOR US!
YOUR LIES WON'T WORK. WE WILL MAKE SENSE OF YOUR DIALS. WE WILL WORK OUT YOUR PLANS. AND AS FOR YOUR FRIENDS...
YOUR FRIENDS DON'T KNOW THE META-CASTLE. WE'LL FIND THEM. THEY WILL NOT SAVE YOU.
YOU MAY BE RIGHT.
WE MAY SAVE *YOU!*
THUD

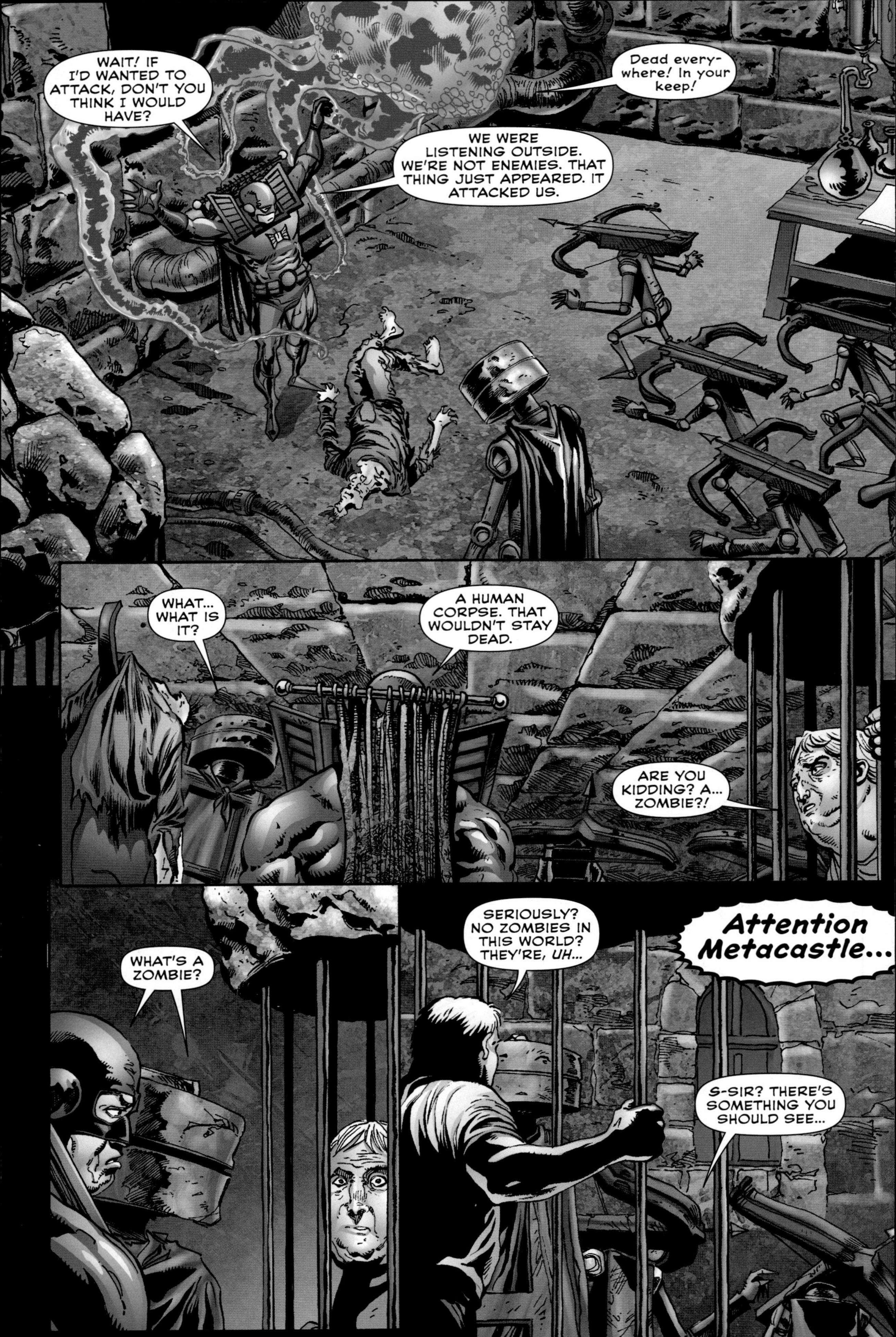
WAIT! IF I'D WANTED TO ATTACK, DON'T YOU THINK I WOULD HAVE?
Dead everywhere! In your keep!
WE WERE LISTENING OUTSIDE. WE'RE NOT ENEMIES. THAT THING JUST APPEARED. IT ATTACKED US.
WHAT... WHAT IS IT?
A HUMAN CORPSE. THAT WOULDN'T STAY DEAD.
ARE YOU KIDDING? A... ZOMBIE?!
WHAT'S A ZOMBIE?
SERIOUSLY? NO ZOMBIES IN THIS WORLD? THEY'RE, UH...
Attention Metacastle...
S-SIR? THERE'S SOMETHING YOU SHOULD SEE...

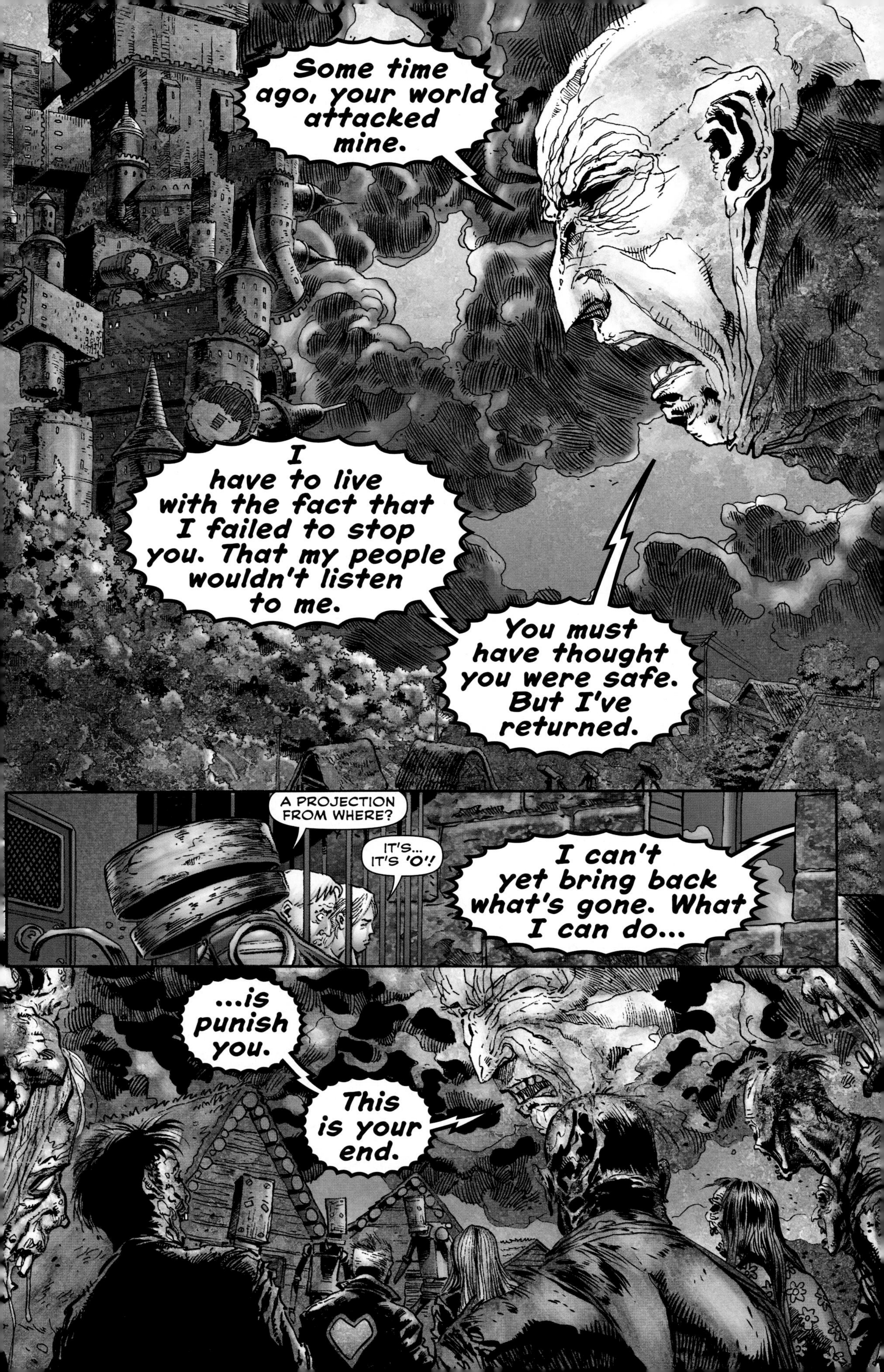
Some time ago, your world attacked mine.
I have to live with the fact that I failed to stop you. That my people wouldn't listen to me.
You must have thought you were safe. But I've returned.
A PROJECTION FROM WHERE?
IT'S... IT'S 'O'!
I can't yet bring back what's gone. What I can do...
...is punish you.
This is your end.

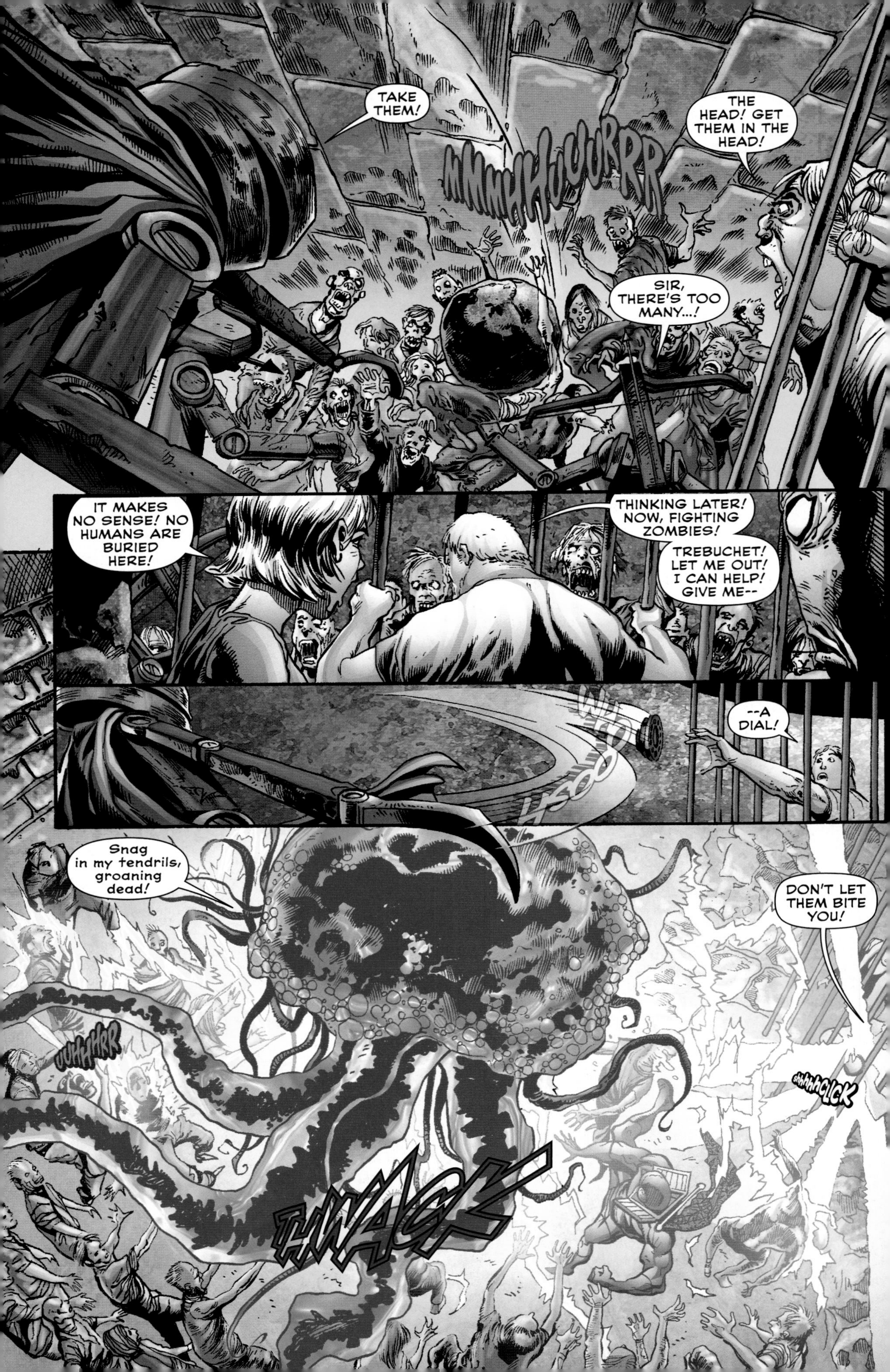
TAKE THEM!
THE HEAD! GET THEM IN THE HEAD!
MMMHUURRR
SIR, THERE'S TOO MANY...!
IT MAKES NO SENSE! NO HUMANS ARE BURIED HERE!
THINKING LATER! NOW, FIGHTING ZOMBIES!
TREBUCHET! LET ME OUT! I CAN HELP! GIVE ME--
--A DIAL!
Snag in my tendrils, groaning dead!
DON'T LET THEM BITE YOU!
UUHHHRR
shhhhCLICK
THWACK

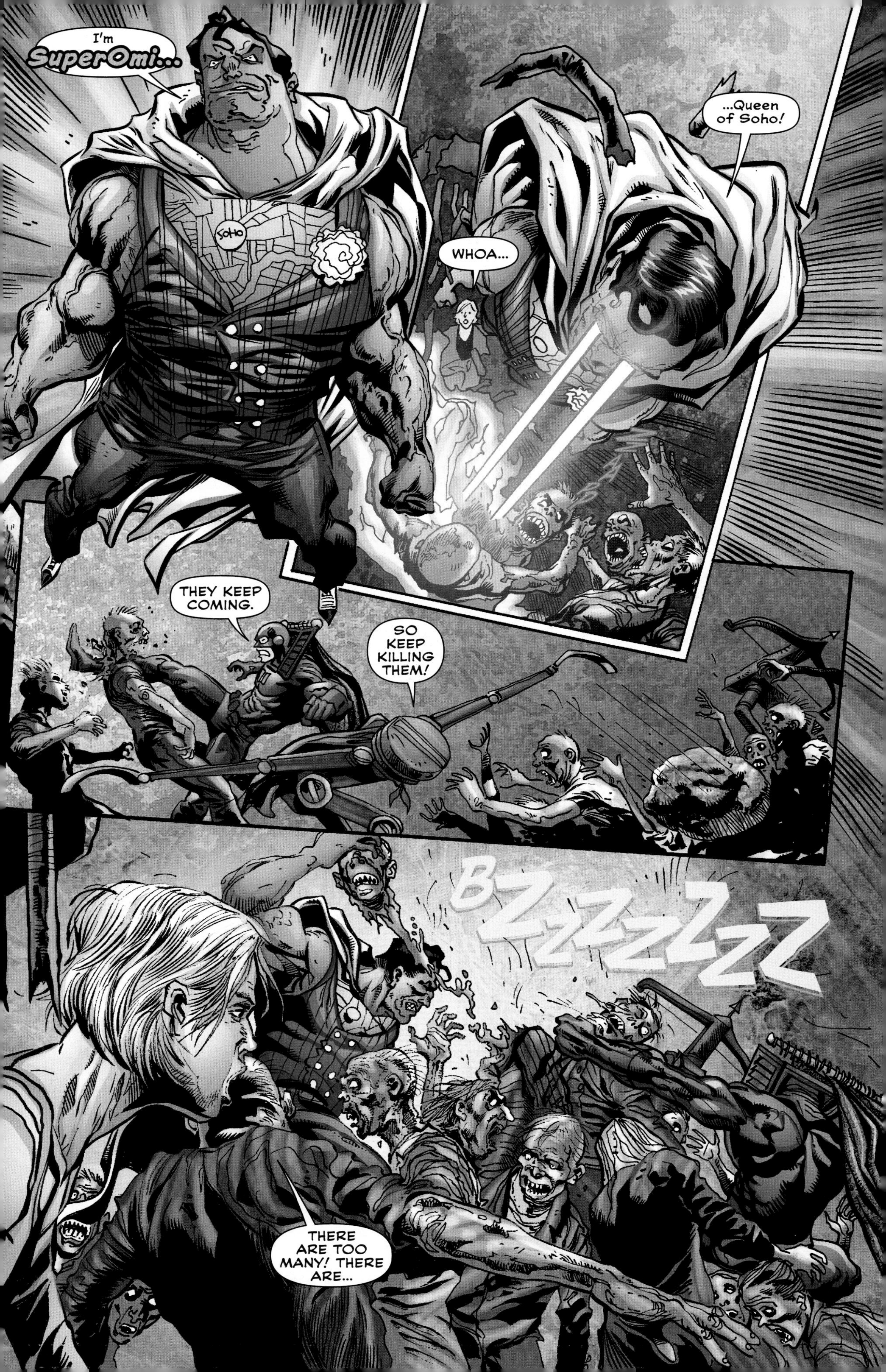

I'm SuperOmi...
...Queen of Soho!
WHOA...
SOHO
THEY KEEP COMING.
SO KEEP KILLING THEM!
BZZZZZZZ
THERE ARE TOO MANY! THERE ARE...

Blimey!

WHAT...?

...TOO MANY?

THOSE THINGS JUST DISAPPEARED.

WHERE DID THEY COME FROM IN THE FIRST PLACE? MAKES NO SENSE...

SURE IT DOES.

IT'S LIKE THE POWERS WE DIAL-TAPPED. FROM ANOTHER PLACE.

A FLOOD... THE LIVING DEAD... YOU SEE WHAT'S HAPPENING?

THE FIXER AND CENTIPEDE AREN'T OUR ONLY PROBLEMS. THE LOST OPER-ATOR'S BACK.

AND HE'S DIALING RANDOM APOCALYPSES.

MURDERER!

THIS TIME IT WENT WRONG. HE LOST THE CONNECTION.

BUT HE'LL TRY AGAIN.

HE'LL DO MORE THAN THAT! HE'LL DESTROY EVERY WORLD THAT FOUGHT IN THE DIAL WAR!

SOMETHING BAD'S GOING TO HAPPEN.

"HE COULD DIAL FIRE, ICE AGE, NUCLEAR DESTRUCTION. SOME ALIEN APOCALYPSE WE CAN'T IMAGINE."

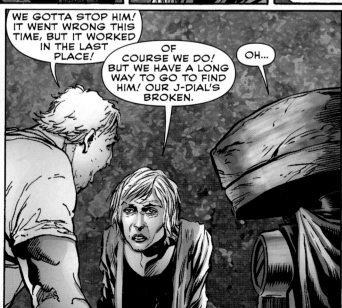

WE GOTTA STOP HIM! IT WENT WRONG THIS TIME, BUT IT WORKED IN THE LAST PLACE!

OF COURSE WE DO! BUT WE HAVE A LONG WAY TO GO TO FIND HIM! OUR J-DIAL'S BROKEN.

OH...

...WE FIXED THAT.

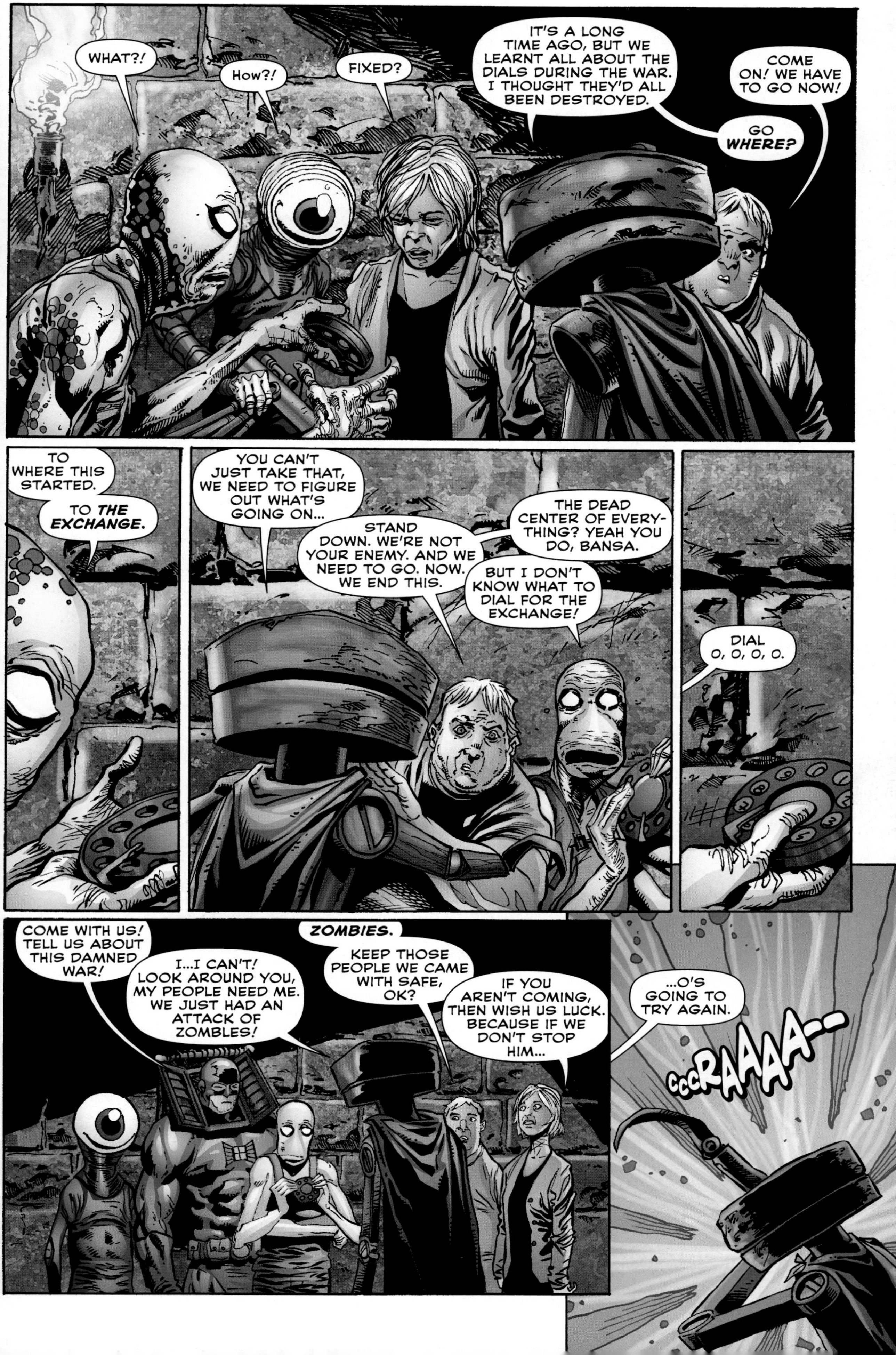
WHAT?!
How?!
FIXED?
IT'S A LONG TIME AGO, BUT WE LEARNT ALL ABOUT THE DIALS DURING THE WAR. I THOUGHT THEY'D ALL BEEN DESTROYED.
GO WHERE?
COME ON! WE HAVE TO GO NOW!
TO WHERE THIS STARTED.
TO THE EXCHANGE.
YOU CAN'T JUST TAKE THAT, WE NEED TO FIGURE OUT WHAT'S GOING ON...
STAND DOWN. WE'RE NOT YOUR ENEMY. AND WE NEED TO GO. NOW. WE END THIS.
THE DEAD CENTER OF EVERY-THING? YEAH YOU DO, BANSA.
BUT I DON'T KNOW WHAT TO DIAL FOR THE EXCHANGE!
DIAL 0, 0, 0, 0.
COME WITH US! TELL US ABOUT THIS DAMNED WAR!
I...I CAN'T! LOOK AROUND YOU, MY PEOPLE NEED ME. WE JUST HAD AN ATTACK OF ZOMBIES!
ZOMBIES.
KEEP THOSE PEOPLE WE CAME WITH SAFE, OK?
IF YOU AREN'T COMING, THEN WISH US LUCK. BECAUSE IF WE DON'T STOP HIM...
...O'S GOING TO TRY AGAIN.
cccRAAAA--

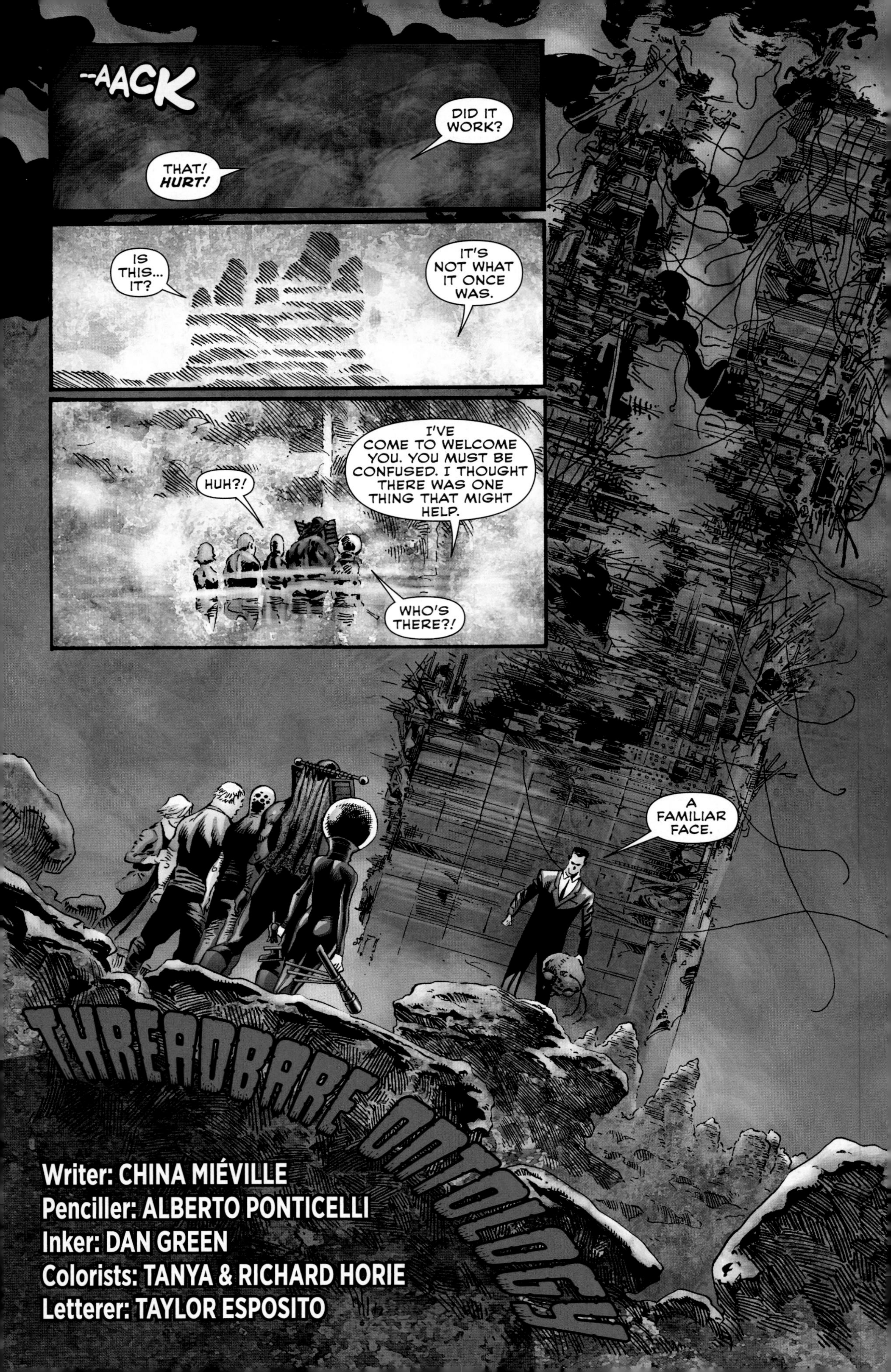
--AACK
DID IT WORK?
THAT! HURT!
IS THIS... IT?
IT'S NOT WHAT IT ONCE WAS.
HUH?!
I'VE COME TO WELCOME YOU. YOU MUST BE CONFUSED. I THOUGHT THERE WAS ONE THING THAT MIGHT HELP.
WHO'S THERE?!
A FAMILIAR FACE.
THREADBARE ONTOLOGY
Writer: CHINA MIÉVILLE
Penciller: ALBERTO PONTICELLI
Inker: DAN GREEN
Colorists: TANYA & RICHARD HORIE
Letterer: TAYLOR ESPOSITO

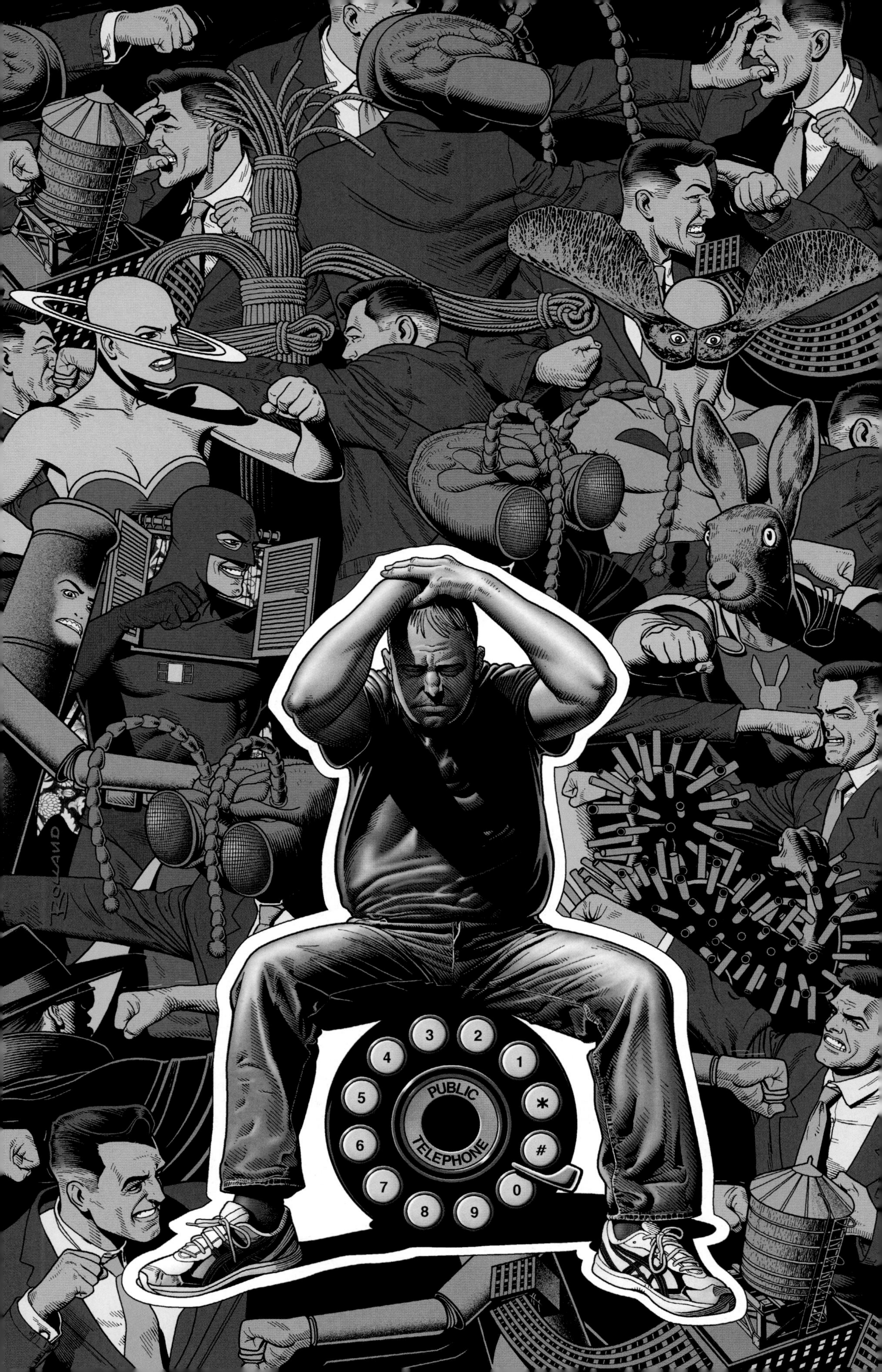
PUBLIC
TELEPHONE

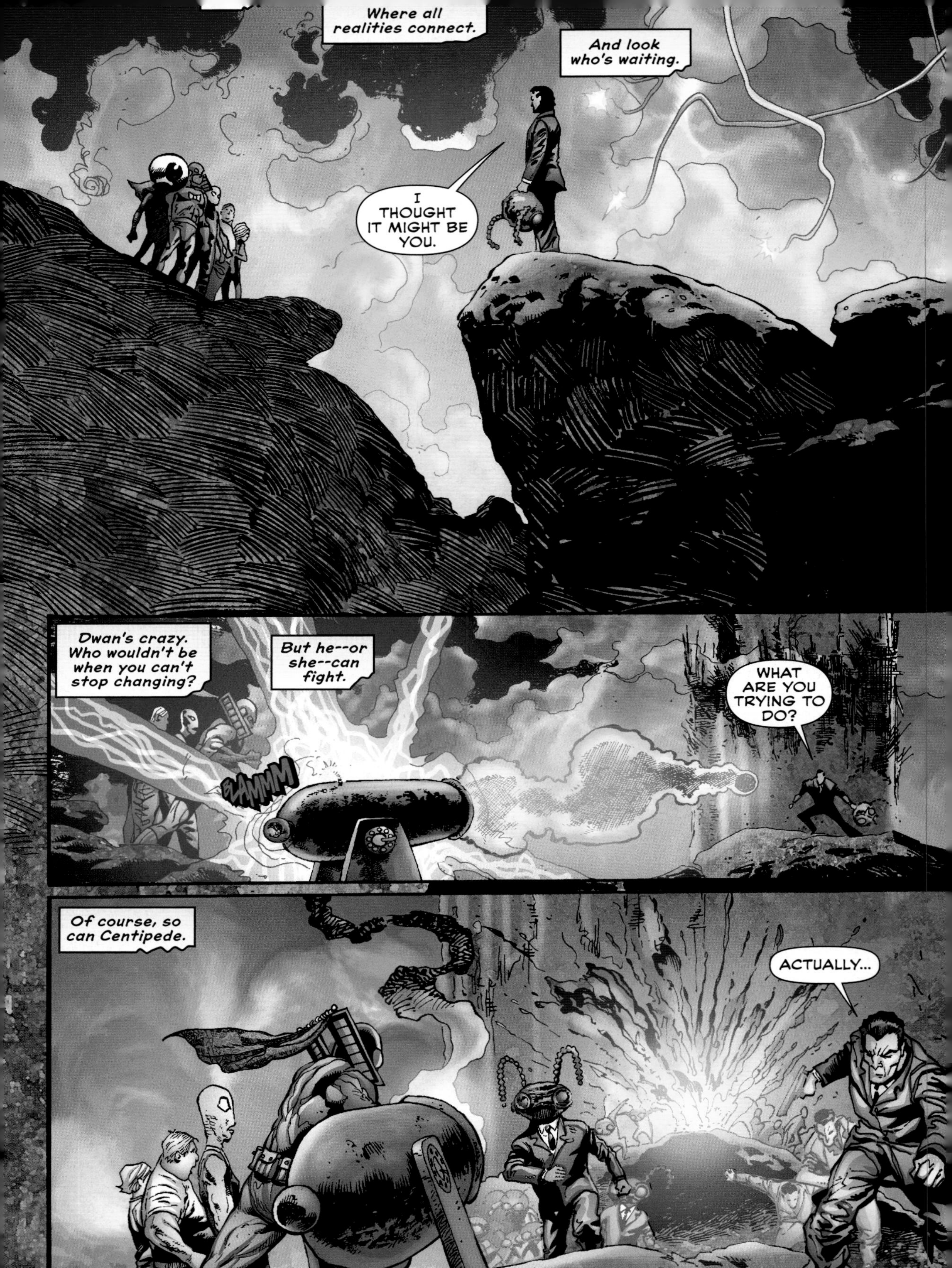
Where all realities connect.
And look who's waiting.
I THOUGHT IT MIGHT BE YOU.
Dwan's crazy. Who wouldn't be when you can't stop changing?
But he--or she--can fight.
BLAMMM
WHAT ARE YOU TRYING TO DO?
Of course, so can Centipede.
ACTUALLY...

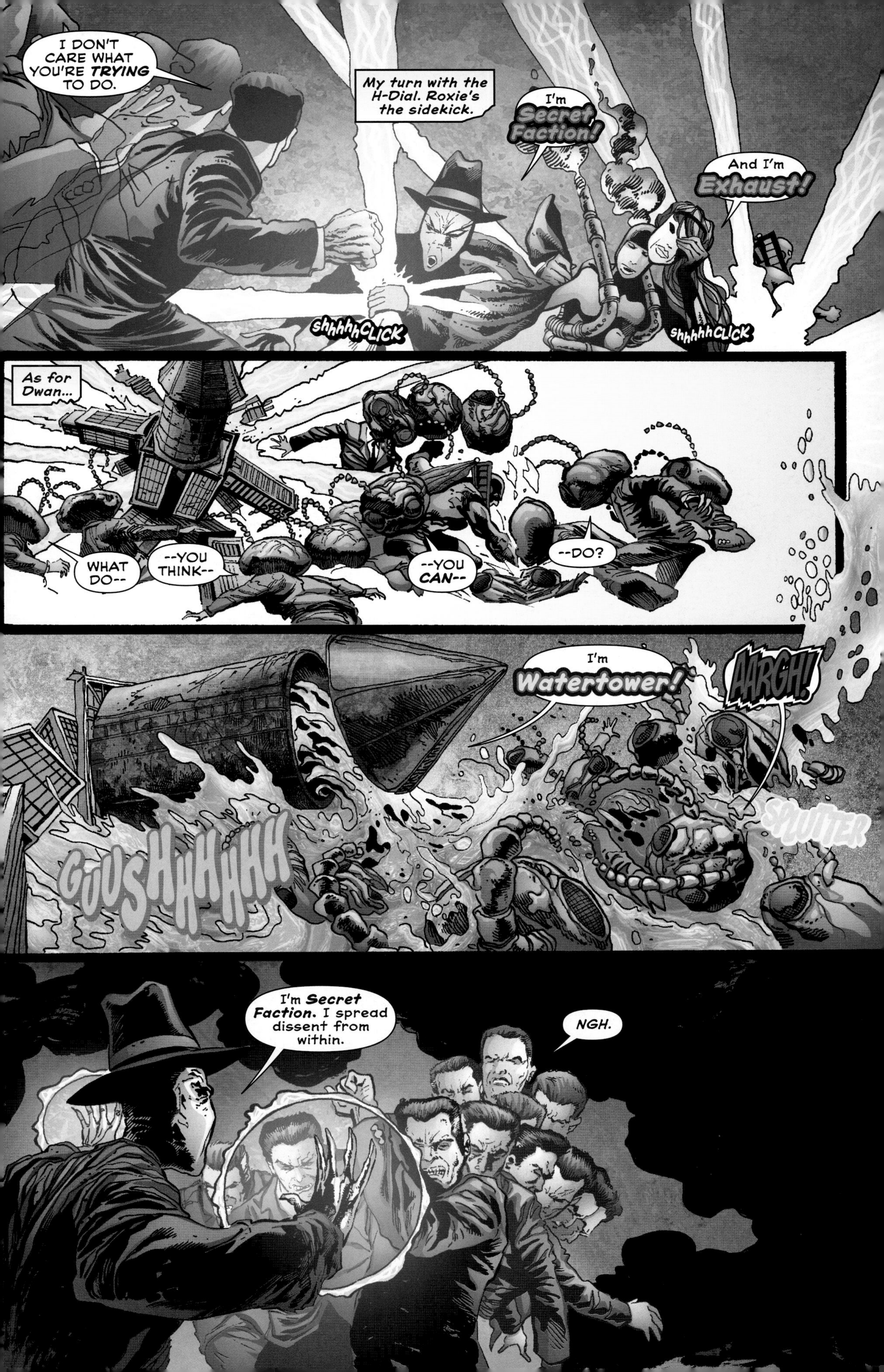
I DON'T CARE WHAT YOU'RE TRYING TO DO.
My turn with the H-Dial. Roxie's the sidekick.
I'm Secret Faction!
And I'm Exhaust!
shhhhhCLICK
shhhhhCLICK
As for Dwan...
WHAT DO--
--YOU THINK--
--YOU CAN--
--DO?
I'm Watertower!
AARGH!
SPLUTTER
GUUSHHHHHH
I'm Secret Faction. I spread dissent from within.
NGH.

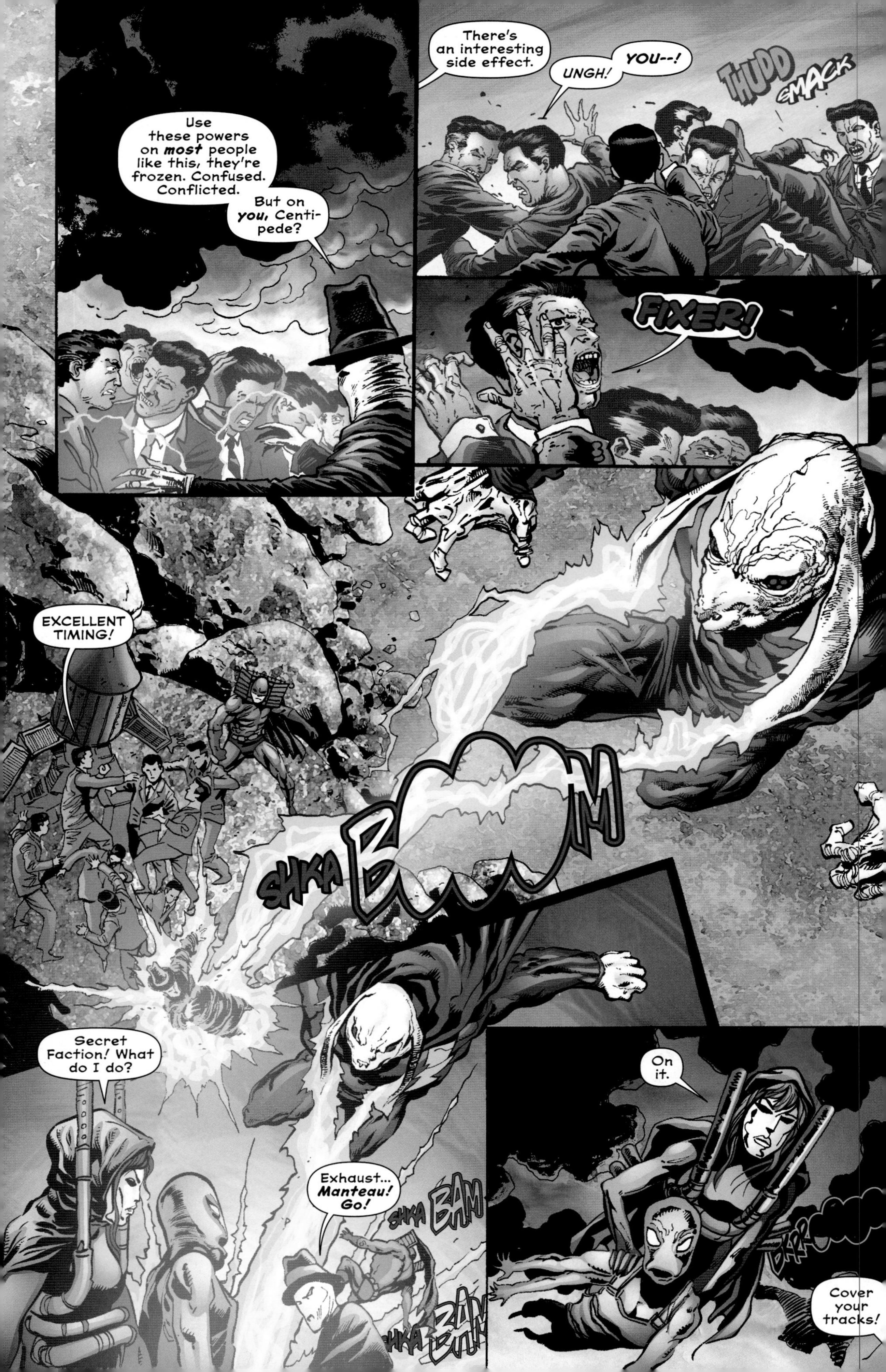

Use these powers on *most* people like this, they're frozen. Confused. Conflicted.
But on *you,* Centi-pede?
There's an interesting side effect.
UNGH!
YOU--!
THUDD
SMACK
FIXER!
EXCELLENT TIMING!
SHKA BOOOM
Secret Faction! What do I do?
Exhaust... *Manteau! Go!*
SHKA BAM
SHKA BAM
On it.
Cover your tracks!

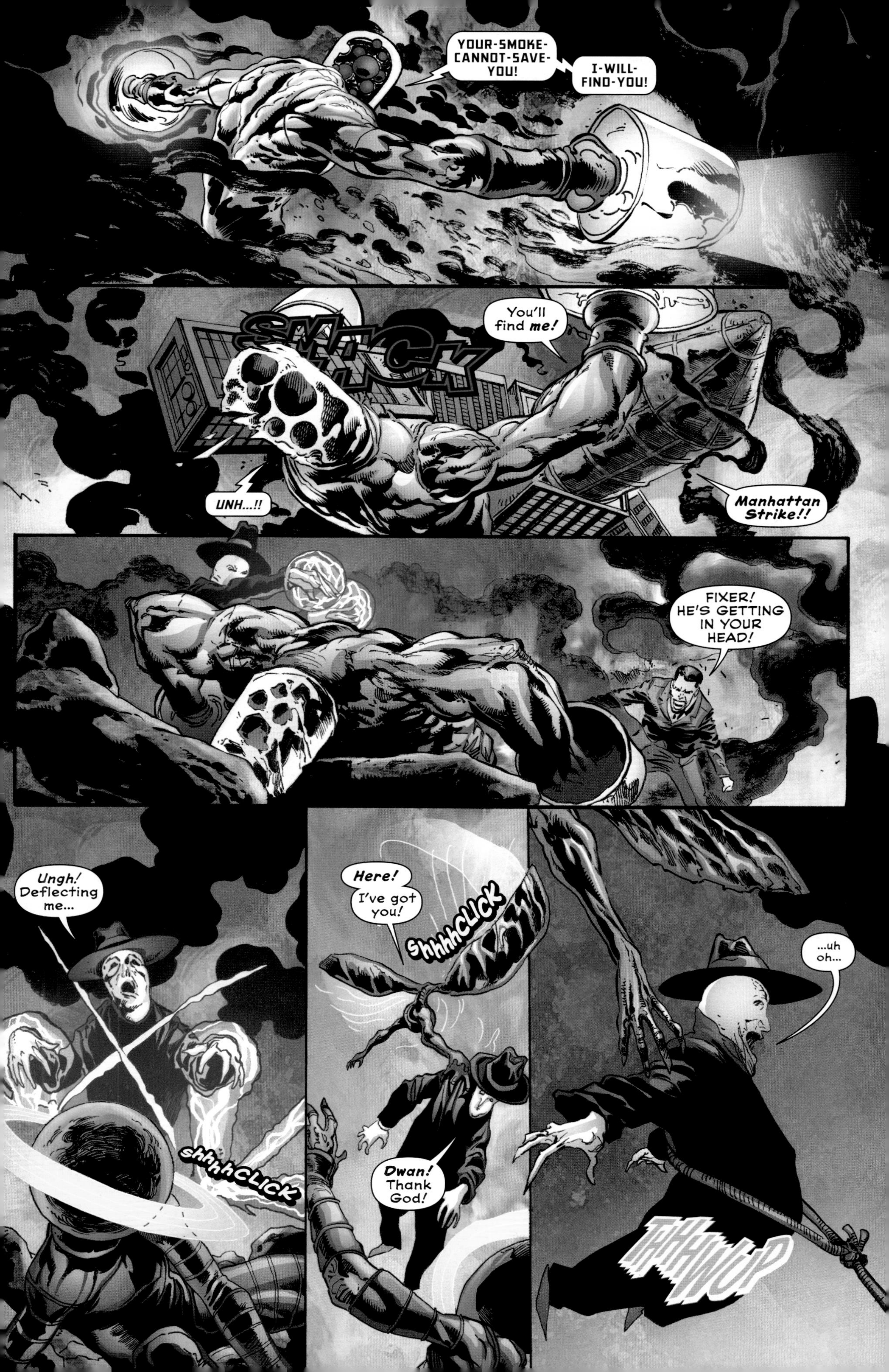
YOUR-SMOKE-CANNOT-SAVE-YOU!
I-WILL-FIND-YOU!
You'll find *me!*
UNH...!!
Manhattan Strike!!
FIXER! HE'S GETTING IN YOUR HEAD!
Ungh! Deflecting me...
shhhhCLICK
Here! I've got you!
ShhhhCLICK
Dwan! Thank God!
...uh oh...

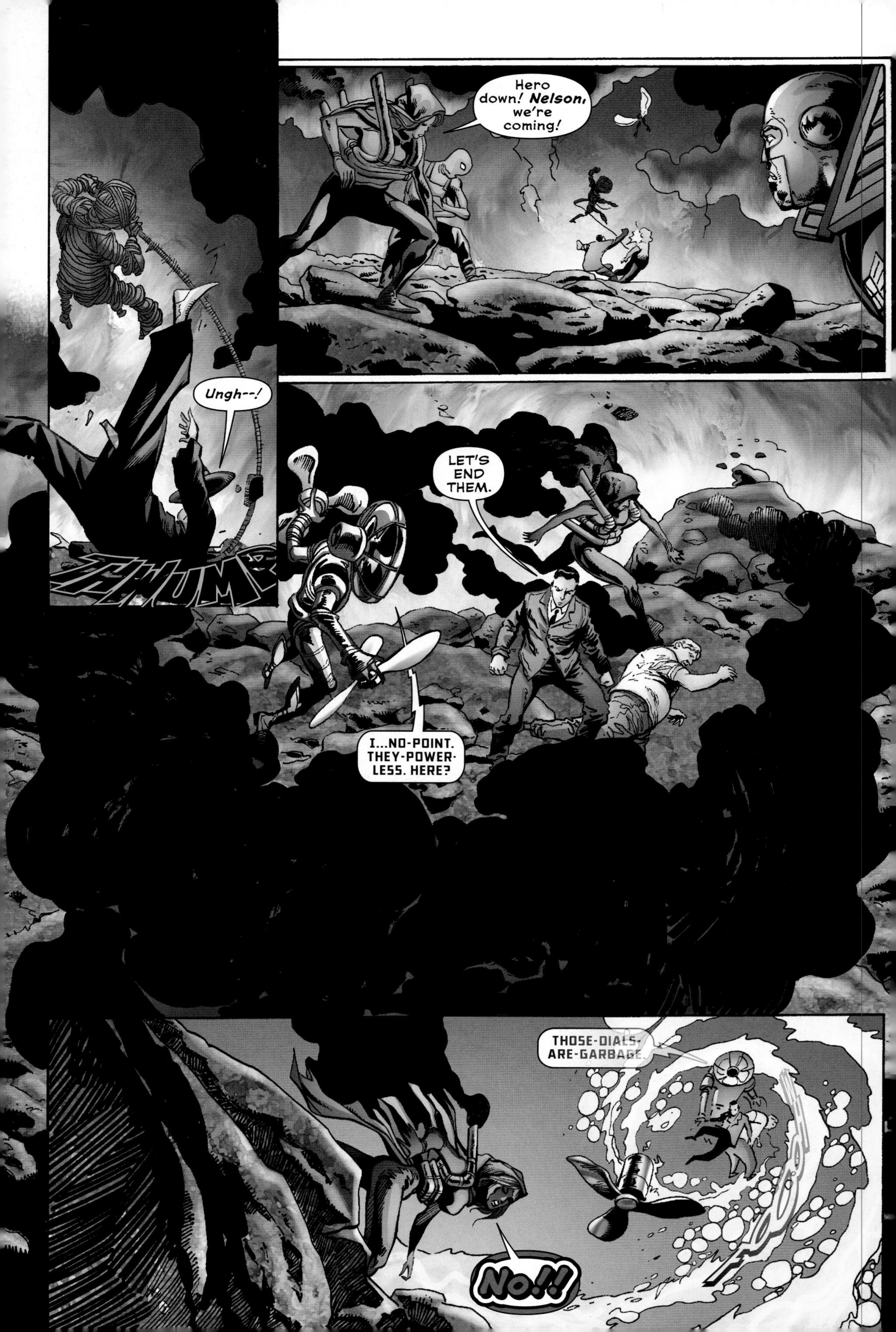
Hero down! Nelson, we're coming!
Ungh--!
THUMP
LET'S END THEM.
I...NO-POINT. THEY-POWER-LESS. HERE?
THOSE-DIALS-ARE-GARBAGE.
No!!

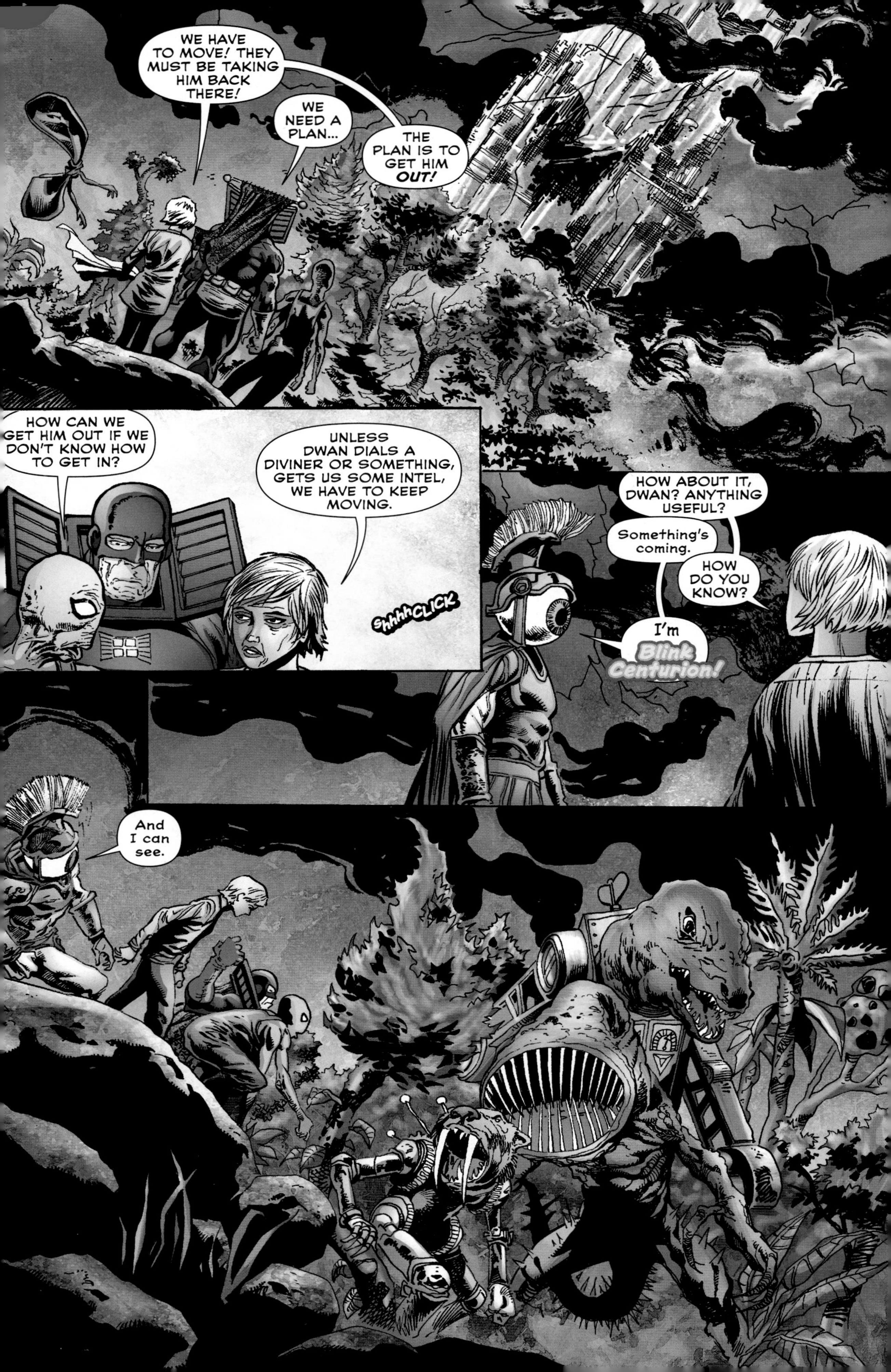
WE HAVE TO MOVE! THEY MUST BE TAKING HIM BACK THERE!
WE NEED A PLAN...
THE PLAN IS TO GET HIM OUT!
HOW CAN WE GET HIM OUT IF WE DON'T KNOW HOW TO GET IN?
UNLESS DWAN DIALS A DIVINER OR SOMETHING, GETS US SOME INTEL, WE HAVE TO KEEP MOVING.
SHHHHCLICK
HOW ABOUT IT, DWAN? ANYTHING USEFUL?
Something's coming.
HOW DO YOU KNOW?
I'm Blink Centurion!
And I can see.

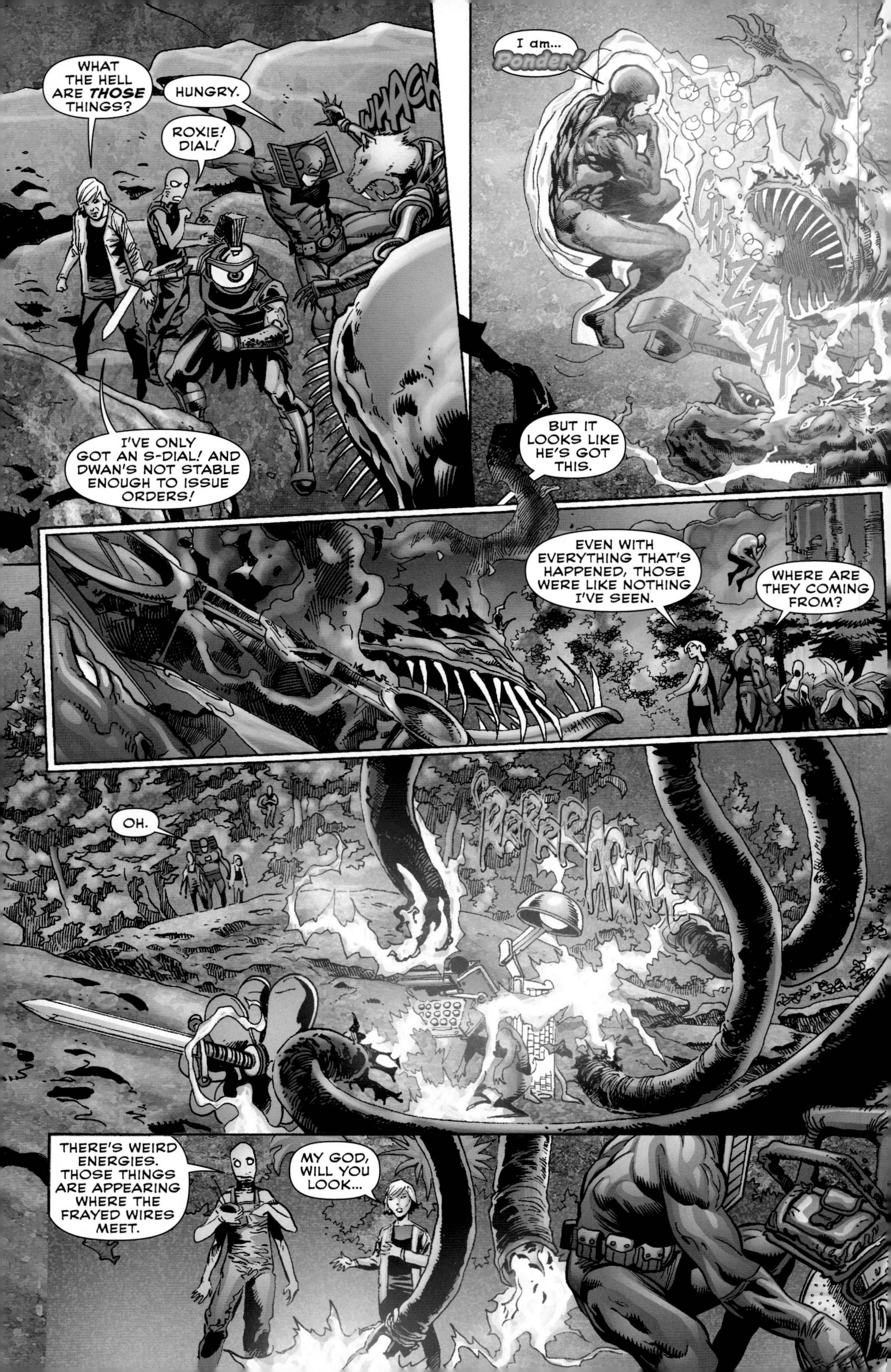
WHAT THE HELL ARE *THOSE* THINGS?
HUNGRY.
WHACK
ROXIE! DIAL!
I'VE ONLY GOT AN S-DIAL! AND DWAN'S NOT STABLE ENOUGH TO ISSUE ORDERS!
I am... Ponder!
BUT IT LOOKS LIKE HE'S GOT THIS.
EVEN WITH EVERYTHING THAT'S HAPPENED, THOSE WERE LIKE NOTHING I'VE SEEN.
WHERE ARE THEY COMING FROM?
OH.
THERE'S WEIRD ENERGIES. THOSE THINGS ARE APPEARING WHERE THE FRAYED WIRES MEET.
MY GOD, WILL YOU LOOK...

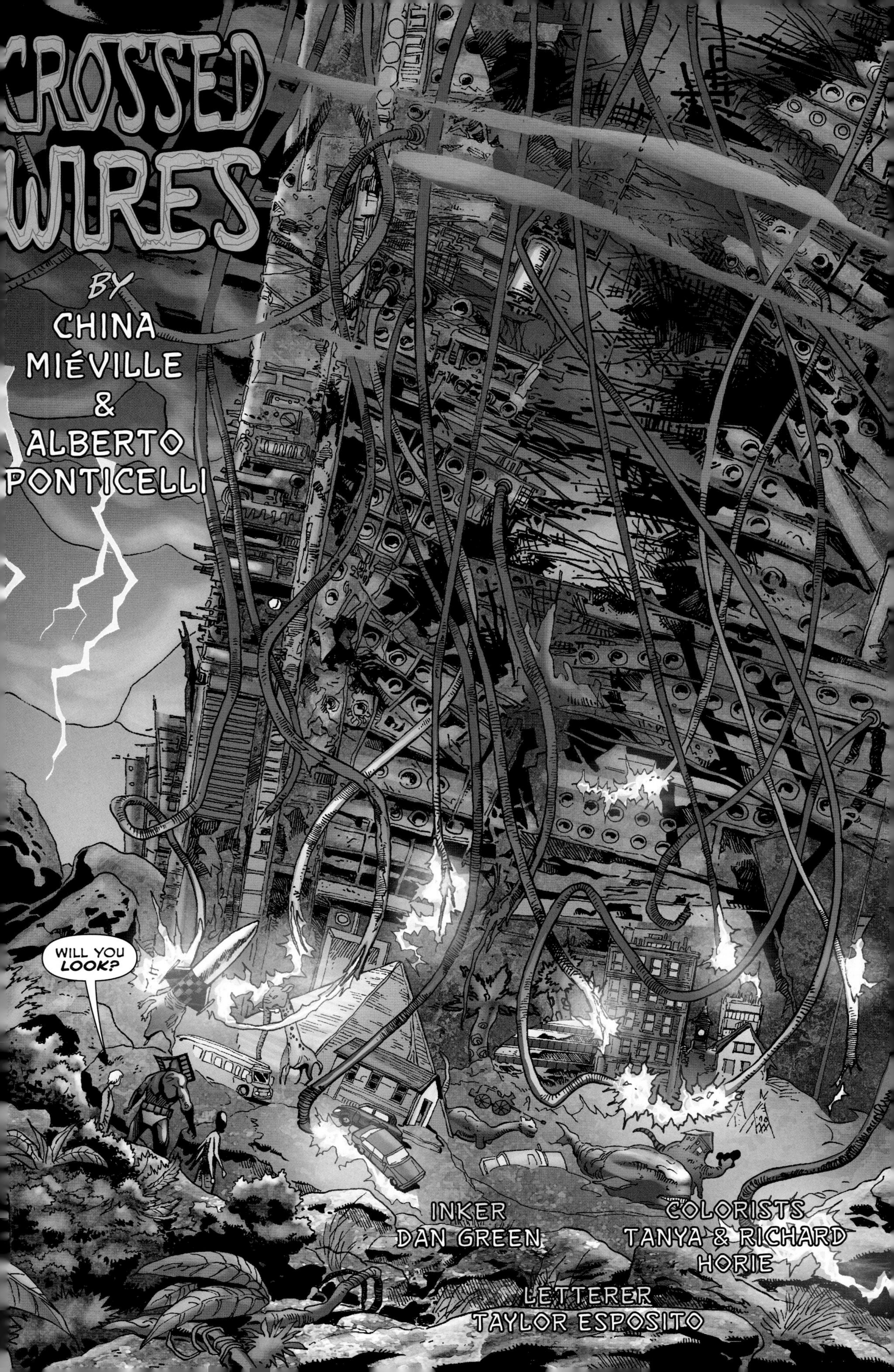
CROSSED WIRES
BY
CHINA MIÉVILLE
&
ALBERTO PONTICELLI
WILL YOU LOOK?
INKER
DAN GREEN
COLORISTS
TANYA & RICHARD HORIE
LETTERER
TAYLOR ESPOSITO

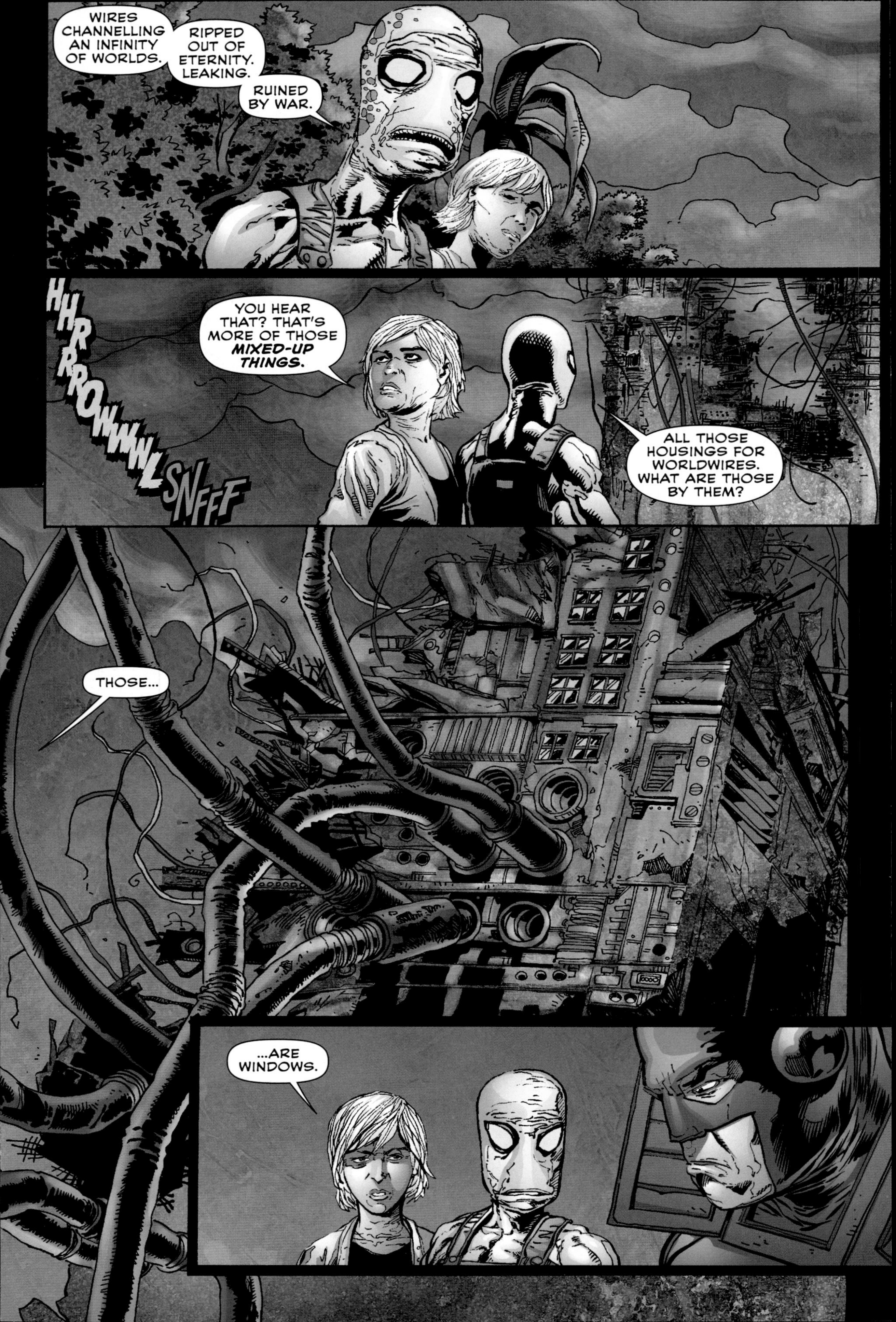
WIRES CHANNELLING AN INFINITY OF WORLDS.
RIPPED OUT OF ETERNITY. LEAKING.
RUINED BY WAR.
HHRRROWWWLSNFFF
YOU HEAR THAT? THAT'S MORE OF THOSE *MIXED-UP THINGS.*
ALL THOSE HOUSINGS FOR WORLDWIRES. WHAT ARE THOSE BY THEM?
THOSE...
...ARE WINDOWS.

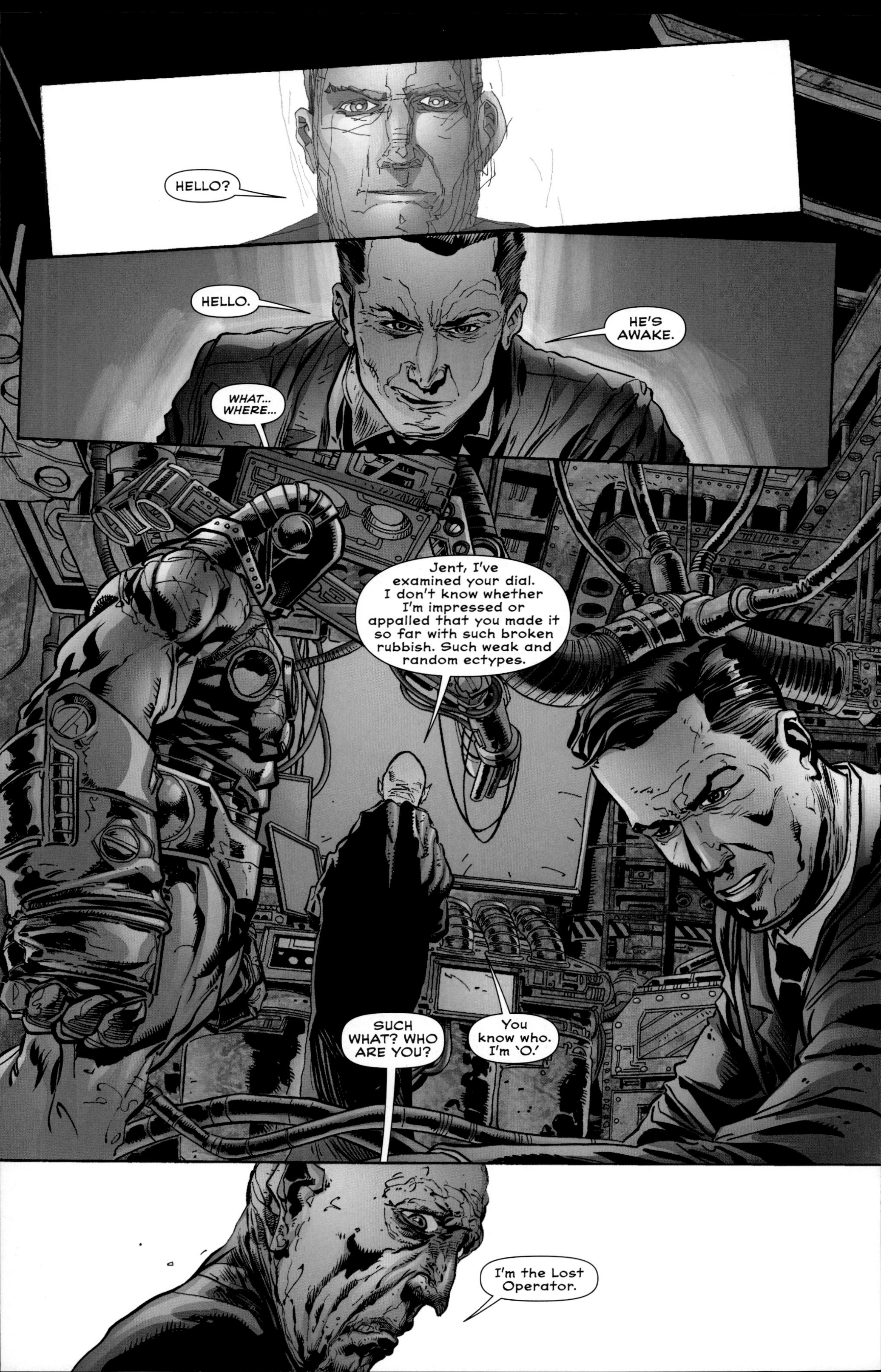
HELLO?
HELLO.
HE'S AWAKE.
WHAT... WHERE...
Jent, I've examined your dial. I don't know whether I'm impressed or appalled that you made it so far with such broken rubbish. Such weak and random ectypes.
SUCH WHAT? WHO ARE YOU?
You know who. I'm 'O.'
I'm the Lost Operator.

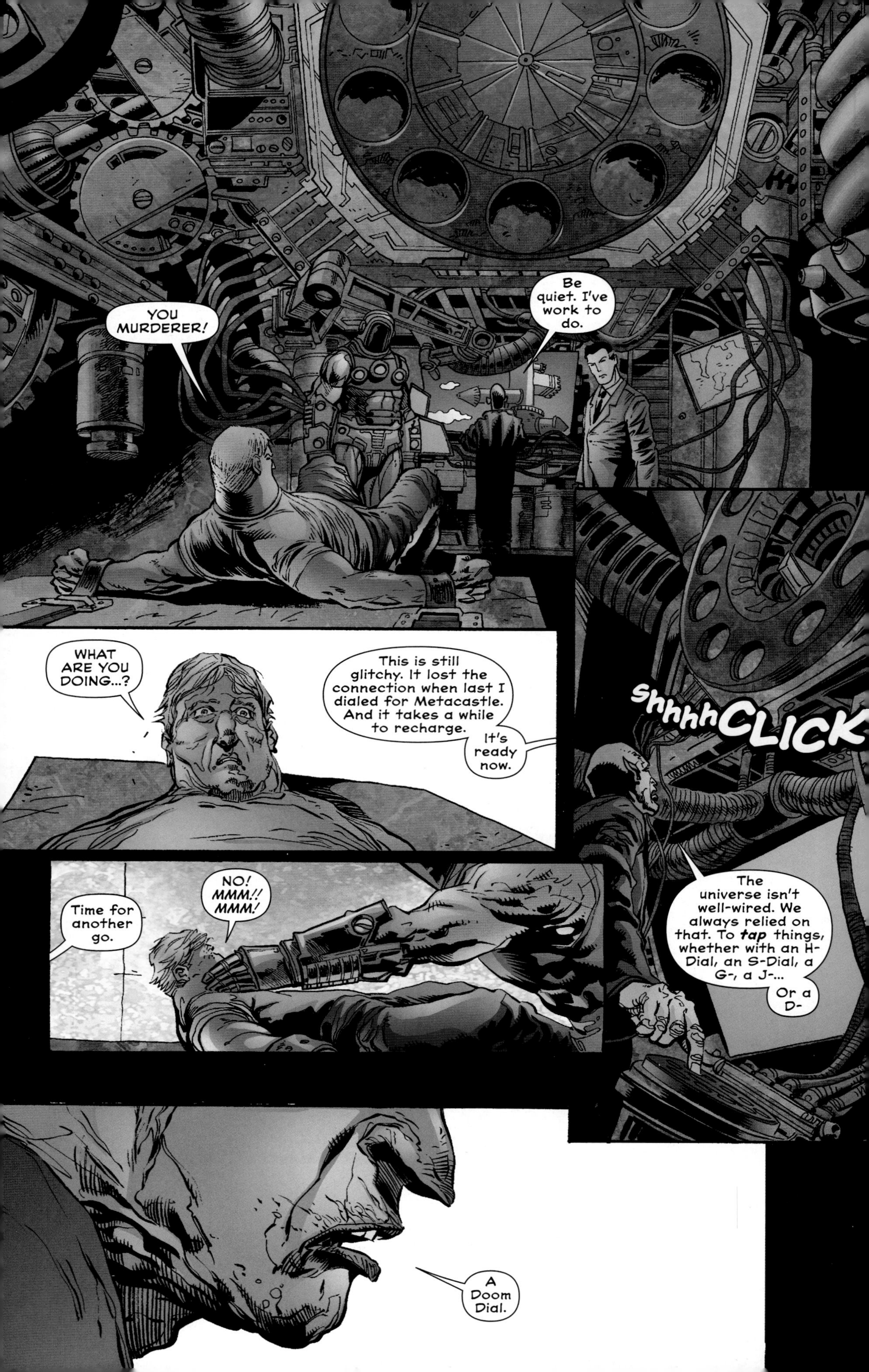

YOU MURDERER!
Be quiet. I've work to do.
WHAT ARE YOU DOING...?
This is still glitchy. It lost the connection when last I dialed for Metacastle. And it takes a while to recharge.
It's ready now.
Time for another go.
NO! MMM!! MMM!
ShhhhCLICK
The universe isn't well-wired. We always relied on that. To *tap* things, whether with an H-Dial, an S-Dial, a G-, a J-...
Or a D-
A Doom Dial.

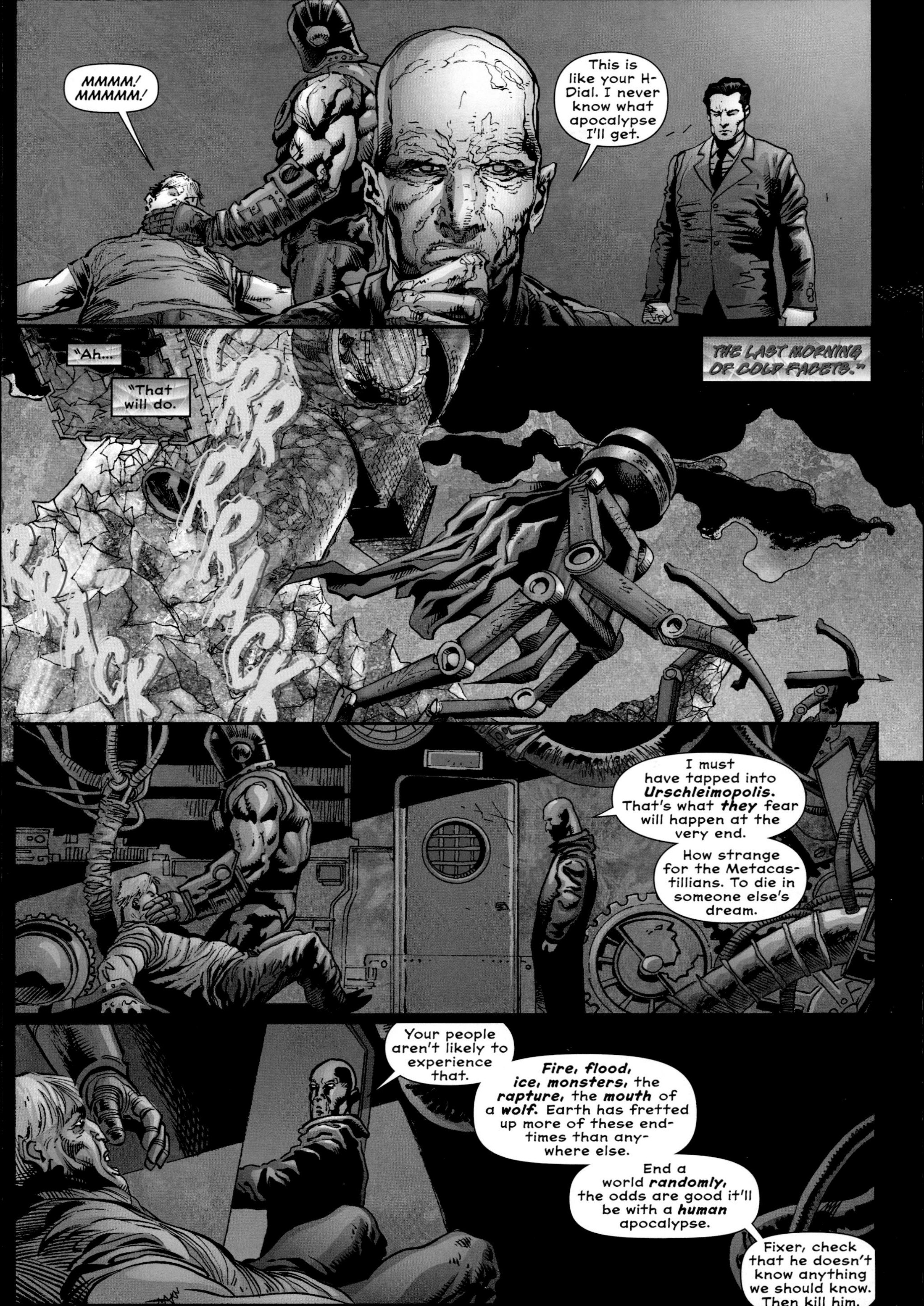
MMMM! MMMMM!
This is like your H-Dial. I never know what apocalypse I'll get.
"Ah...
"That will do.
THE LAST MORNING OF COLD FACETS."
CRRRACK
RRRACK
I must have tapped into *Urschleimopolis.* That's what *they* fear will happen at the very end.
How strange for the Metacastillians. To die in someone else's dream.
Your people aren't likely to experience that.
Fire, flood, ice, monsters, the *rapture,* the *mouth* of a *wolf.* Earth has fretted up more of these end-times than anywhere else.
End a world *randomly,* the odds are good it'll be with a *human* apocalypse.
Fixer, check that he doesn't know anything we should know. Then kill him.

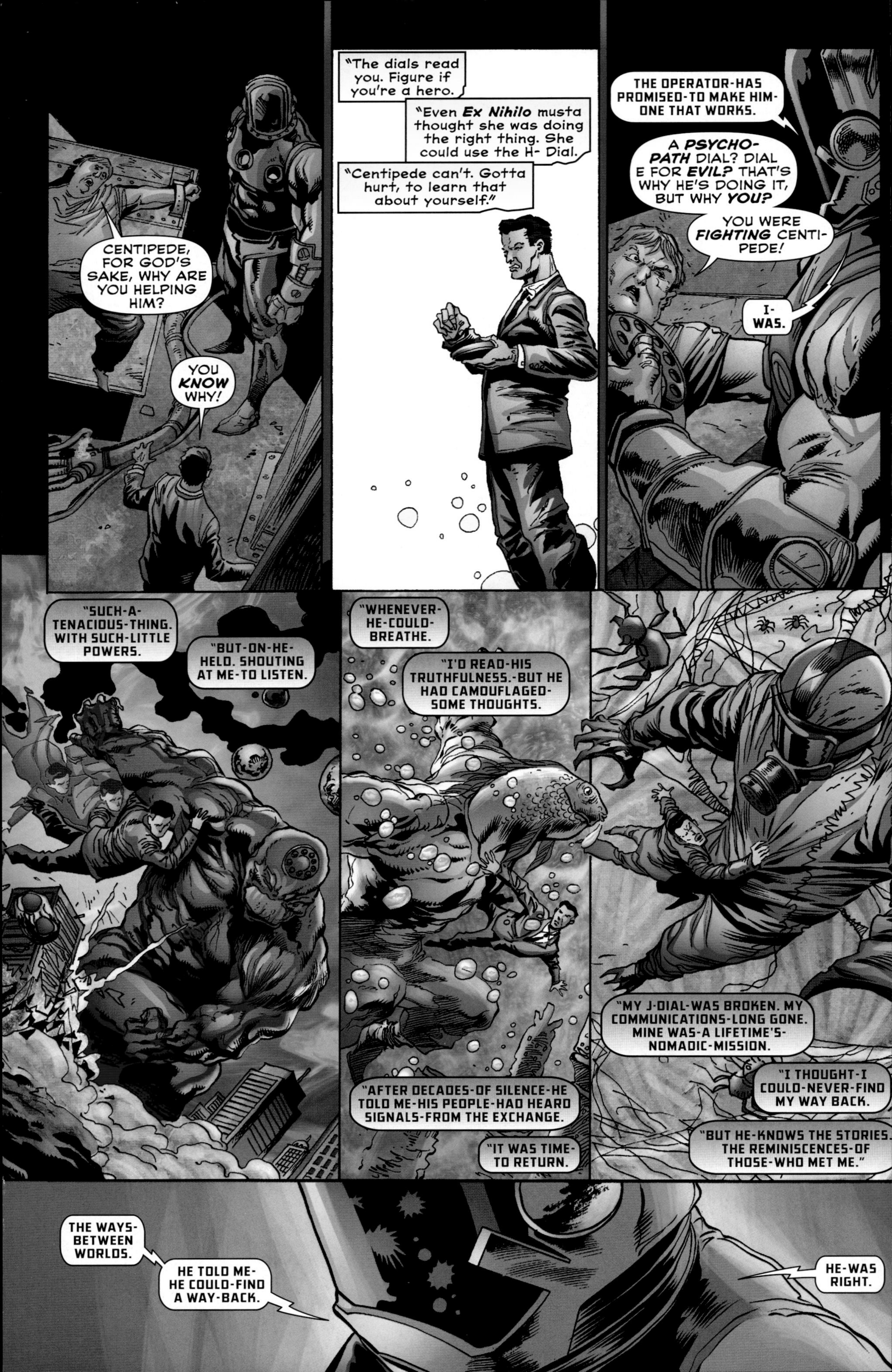
CENTIPEDE, FOR GOD'S SAKE, WHY ARE YOU HELPING HIM?
YOU KNOW WHY!
"The dials read you. Figure if you're a hero.
"Even Ex Nihilo musta thought she was doing the right thing. She could use the H- Dial.
"Centipede can't. Gotta hurt, to learn that about yourself."
THE OPERATOR-HAS PROMISED-TO MAKE HIM-ONE THAT WORKS.
A PSYCHO-PATH DIAL? DIAL E FOR EVIL? THAT'S WHY HE'S DOING IT, BUT WHY YOU?
YOU WERE FIGHTING CENTI-PEDE!
I-WAS.
"SUCH-A-TENACIOUS-THING. WITH SUCH-LITTLE POWERS.
"BUT-ON-HE-HELD. SHOUTING AT ME-TO LISTEN.
"WHENEVER-HE-COULD-BREATHE.
"I'D READ-HIS TRUTHFULNESS.-BUT HE HAD CAMOUFLAGED-SOME THOUGHTS.
"AFTER DECADES-OF SILENCE-HE TOLD ME-HIS PEOPLE-HAD HEARD SIGNALS-FROM THE EXCHANGE.
"IT WAS TIME-TO RETURN.
"MY J-DIAL-WAS BROKEN. MY COMMUNICATIONS-LONG GONE. MINE WAS-A LIFETIME'S-NOMADIC-MISSION.
"I THOUGHT-I COULD-NEVER-FIND MY WAY BACK.
"BUT HE-KNOWS THE STORIES. THE REMINISCENCES-OF THOSE-WHO MET ME."
THE WAYS-BETWEEN WORLDS.
HE TOLD ME-HE COULD-FIND A WAY-BACK.
HE-WAS RIGHT.

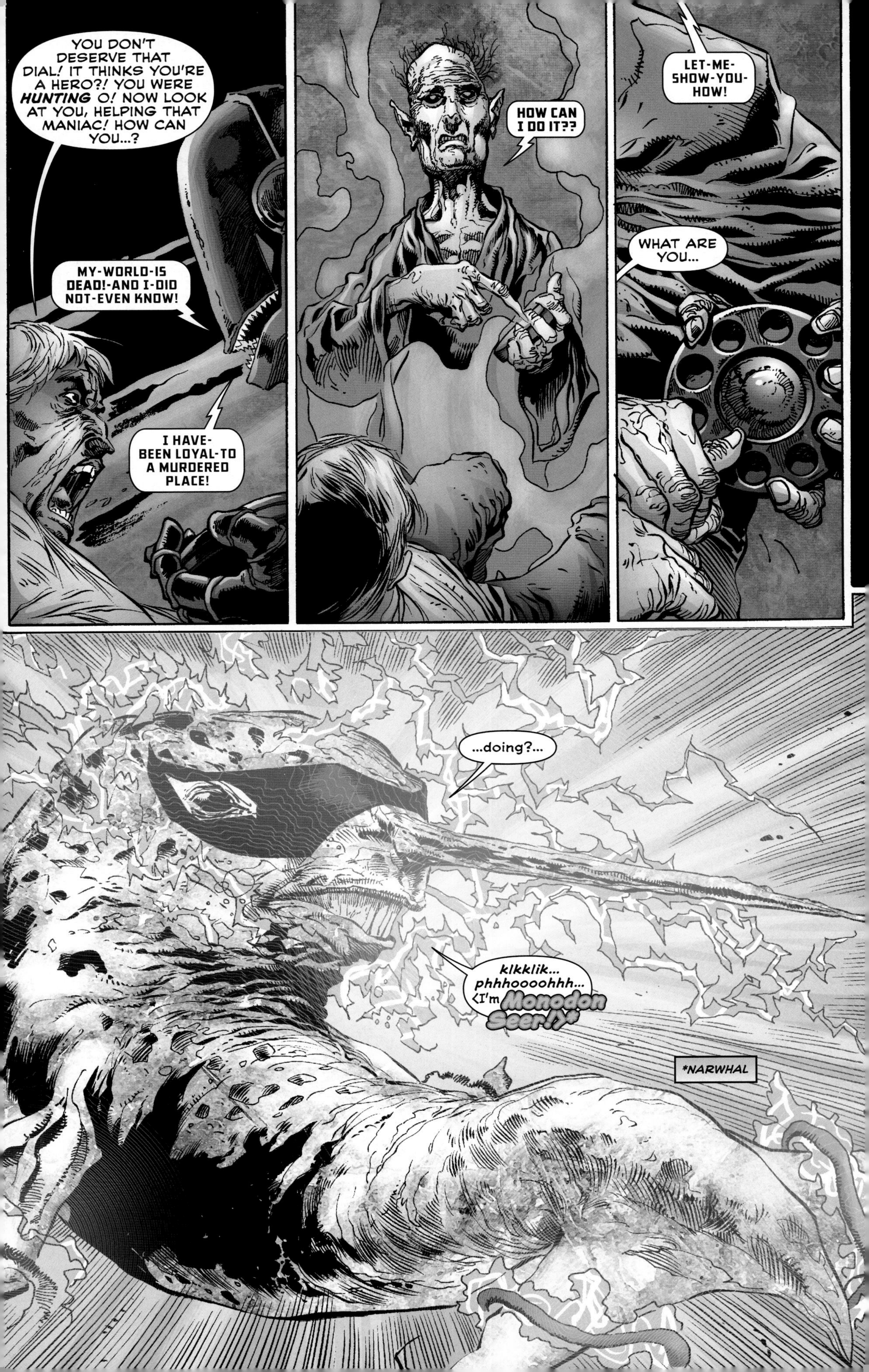
YOU DON'T DESERVE THAT DIAL! IT THINKS YOU'RE A HERO?! YOU WERE HUNTING O! NOW LOOK AT YOU, HELPING THAT MANIAC! HOW CAN YOU...?
MY-WORLD-IS DEAD!-AND I-DID NOT-EVEN KNOW!
I HAVE-BEEN LOYAL-TO A MURDERED PLACE!
HOW CAN I DO IT??
LET-ME-SHOW-YOU-HOW!
WHAT ARE YOU...
...doing?...
klkklik... phhhoooohhh... <I'm Monodon Seer!>*
*NARWHAL

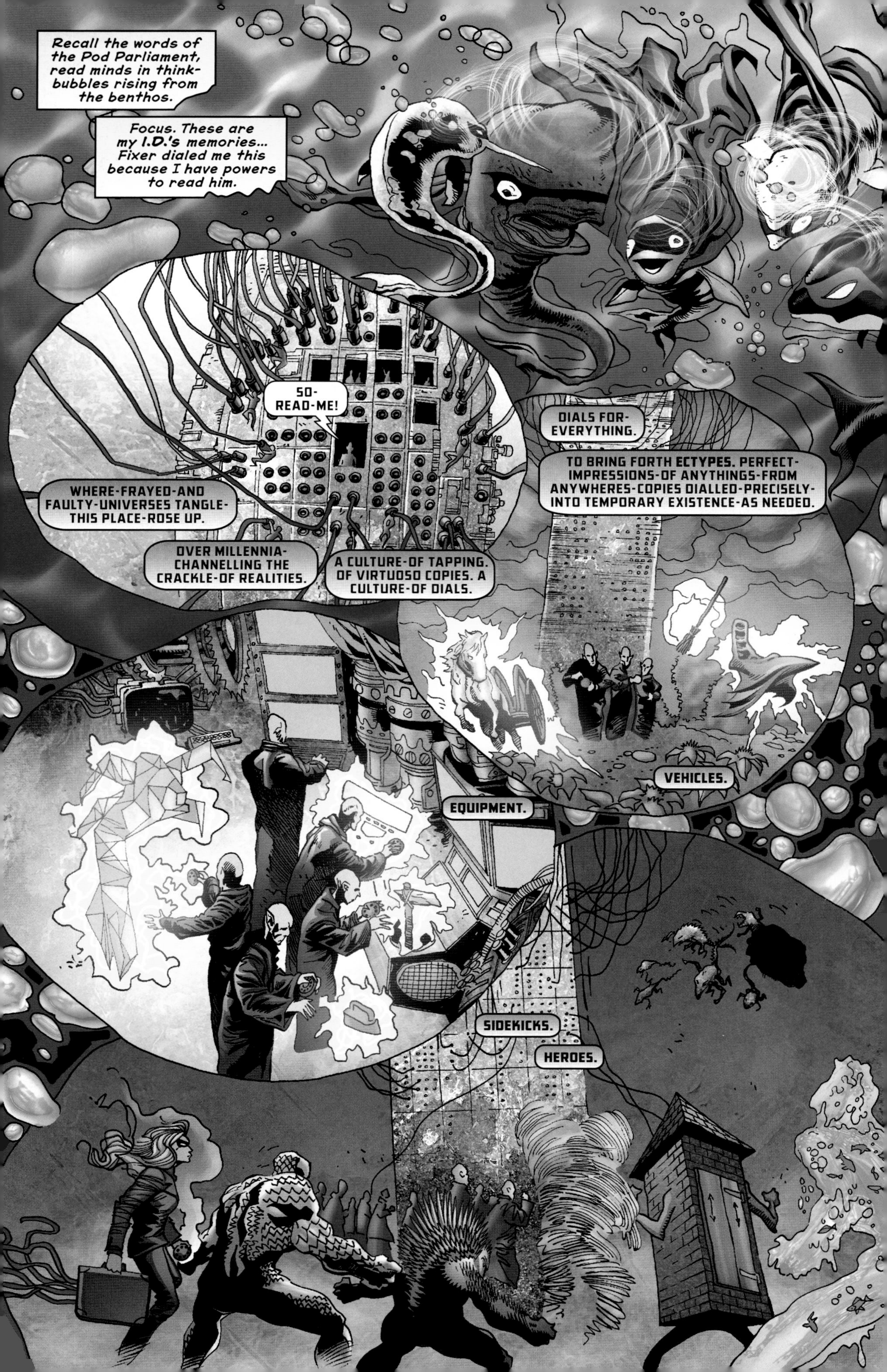
Recall the words of the Pod Parliament, read minds in think-bubbles rising from the benthos.
Focus. These are my I.D.'s memories... Fixer dialed me this because I have powers to read him.
SO-READ-ME!
WHERE-FRAYED-AND FAULTY-UNIVERSES TANGLE-THIS PLACE-ROSE UP.
OVER MILLENNIA-CHANNELLING THE CRACKLE-OF REALITIES.
A CULTURE-OF TAPPING. OF VIRTUOSO COPIES. A CULTURE-OF DIALS.
DIALS FOR-EVERYTHING.
TO BRING FORTH ECTYPES. PERFECT-IMPRESSIONS-OF ANYTHINGS-FROM ANYWHERES-COPIES DIALLED-PRECISELY-INTO TEMPORARY EXISTENCE-AS NEEDED.
VEHICLES.
EQUIPMENT.
SIDEKICKS.
HEROES.

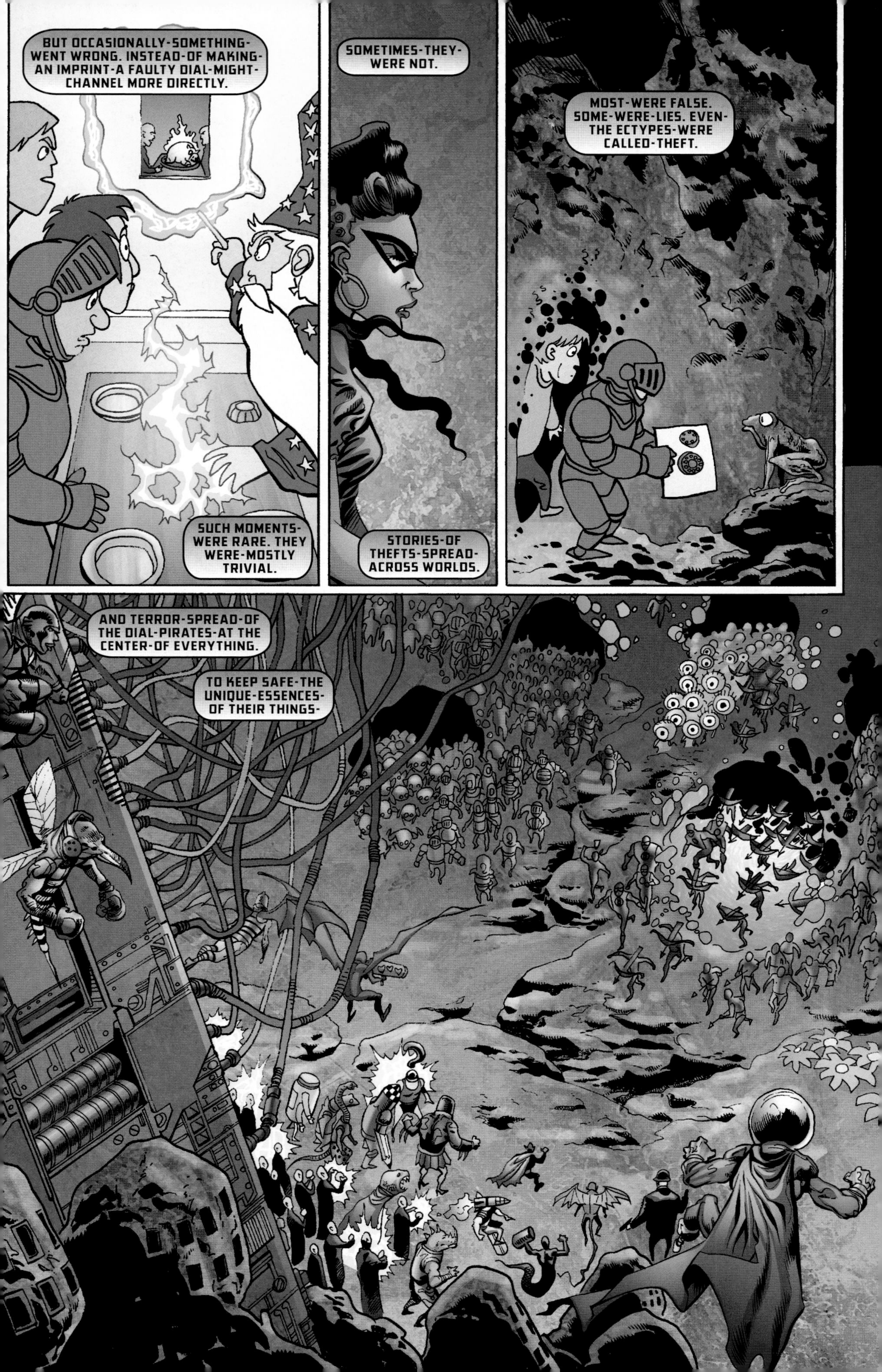
BUT OCCASIONALLY-SOMETHING-WENT WRONG. INSTEAD-OF MAKING-AN IMPRINT-A FAULTY DIAL-MIGHT-CHANNEL MORE DIRECTLY.
SUCH MOMENTS-WERE RARE. THEY WERE-MOSTLY TRIVIAL.
SOMETIMES-THEY-WERE NOT.
STORIES-OF THEFTS-SPREAD-ACROSS WORLDS.
MOST-WERE FALSE. SOME-WERE-LIES. EVEN-THE ECTYPES-WERE CALLED-THEFT.
AND TERROR-SPREAD-OF THE DIAL-PIRATES-AT THE CENTER-OF EVERYTHING.
TO KEEP SAFE-THE UNIQUE-ESSENCES-OF THEIR THINGS-

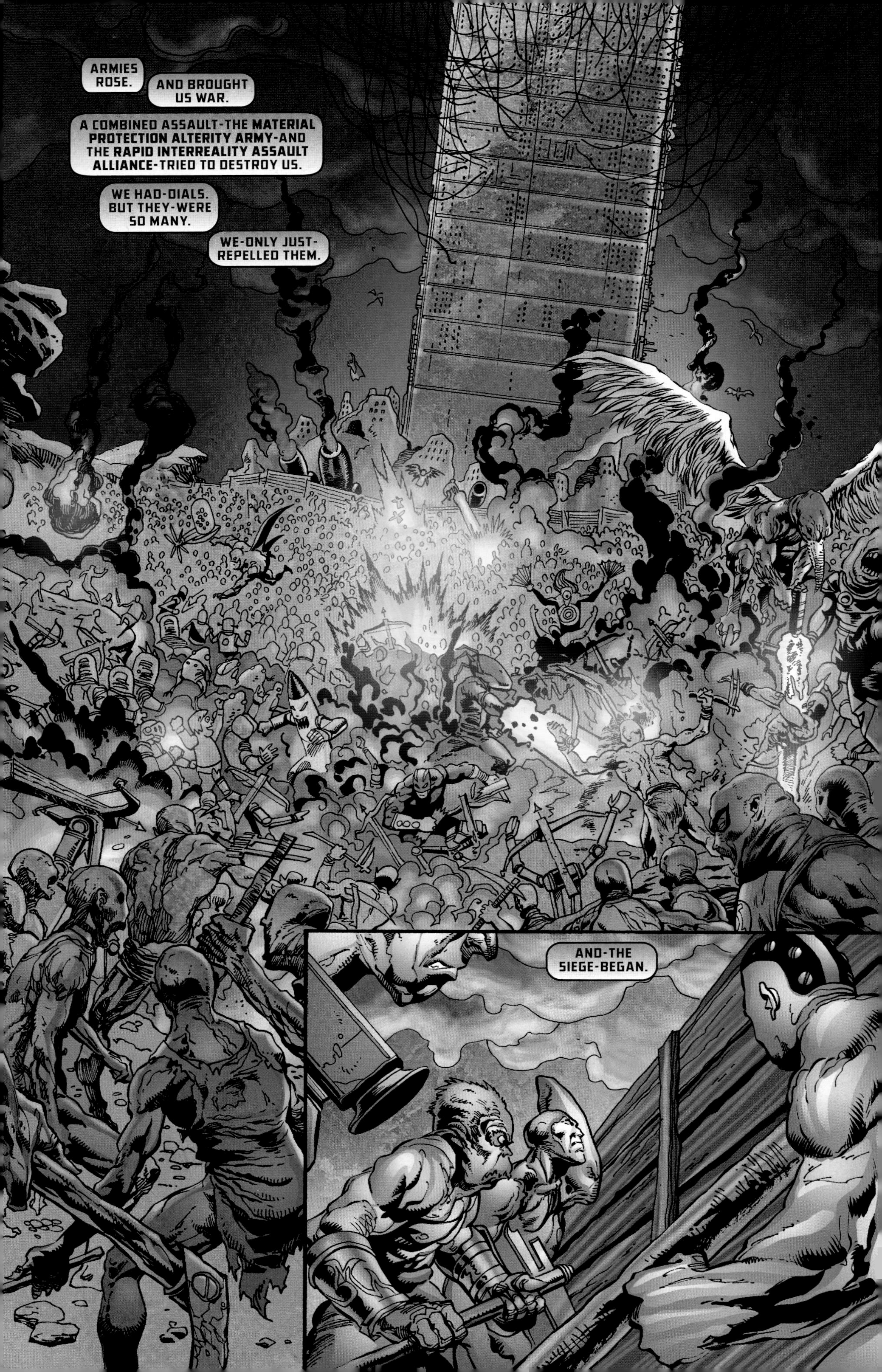
ARMIES ROSE.
AND BROUGHT US WAR.
A COMBINED ASSAULT-THE MATERIAL PROTECTION ALTERITY ARMY-AND THE RAPID INTERREALITY ASSAULT ALLIANCE-TRIED TO DESTROY US.
WE HAD-DIALS. BUT THEY-WERE SO MANY.
WE-ONLY JUST-REPELLED THEM.
AND-THE SIEGE-BEGAN.

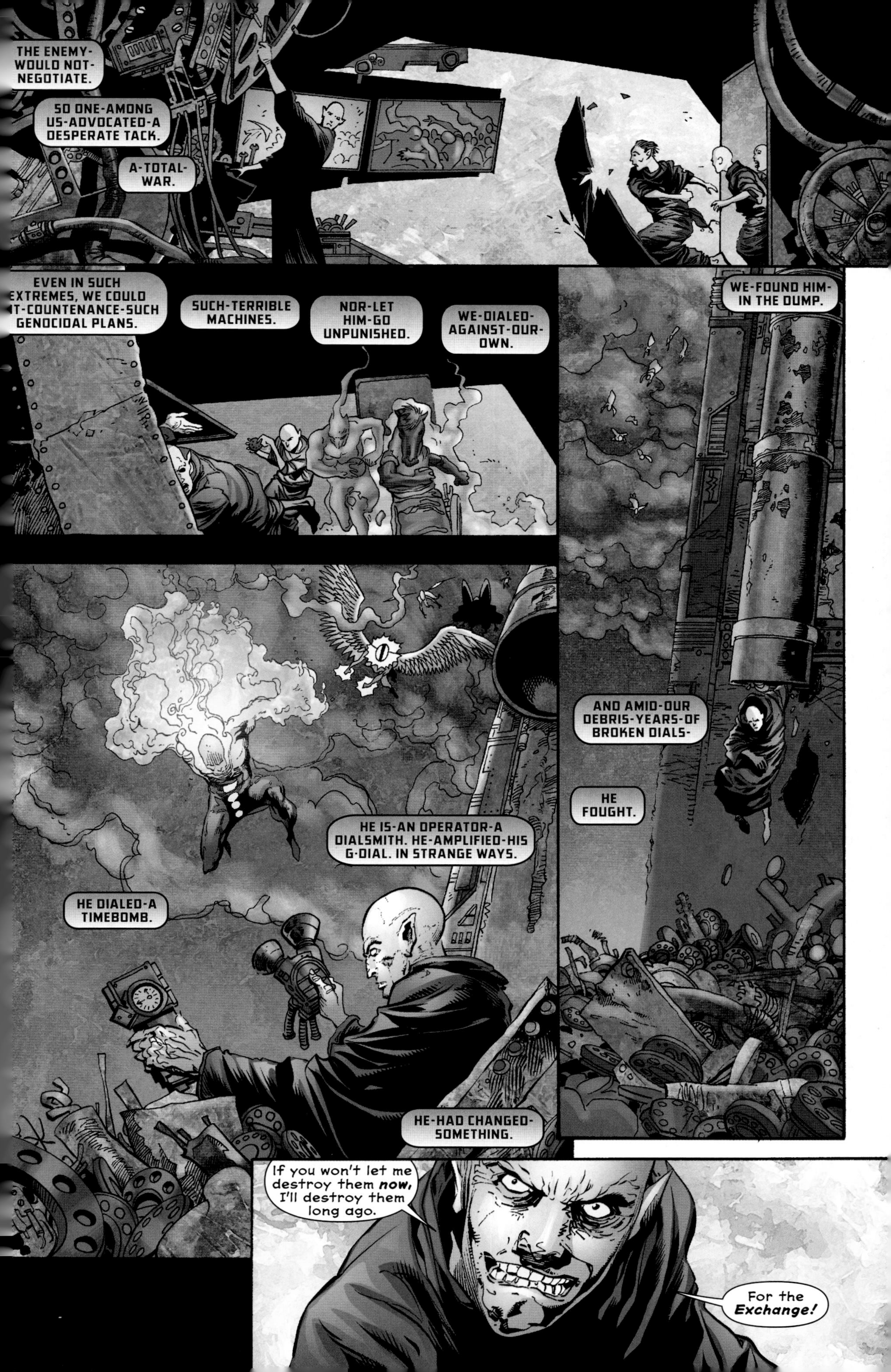
THE ENEMY-
WOULD NOT-
NEGOTIATE.
SO ONE-AMONG
US-ADVOCATED-A
DESPERATE TACK.
A-TOTAL-
WAR.
EVEN IN SUCH
EXTREMES, WE COULD
NT-COUNTENANCE-SUCH
GENOCIDAL PLANS.
SUCH-TERRIBLE
MACHINES.
NOR-LET
HIM-GO
UNPUNISHED.
WE-DIALED-
AGAINST-OUR-
OWN.
WE-FOUND HIM-
IN THE DUMP.
AND AMID-OUR
DEBRIS-YEARS-OF
BROKEN DIALS-
HE
FOUGHT.
HE IS-AN OPERATOR-A
DIALSMITH. HE-AMPLIFIED-HIS
G-DIAL. IN STRANGE WAYS.
HE DIALED-A
TIMEBOMB.
HE-HAD CHANGED-
SOMETHING.
If you won't let me
destroy them *now*,
I'll destroy them
long ago.
For the
Exchange!

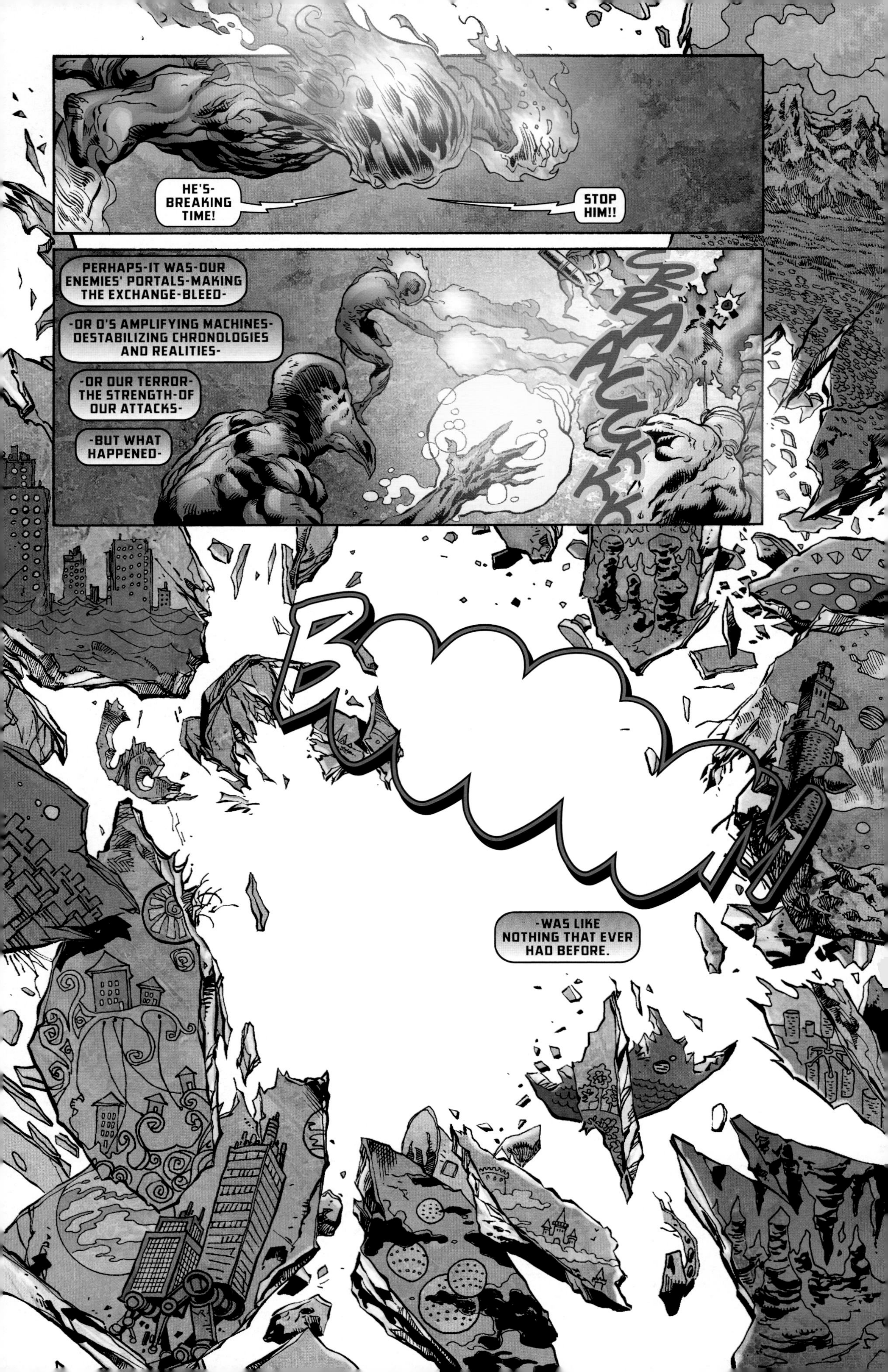
HE'S-
BREAKING
TIME!
STOP
HIM!!
PERHAPS-IT WAS-OUR
ENEMIES' PORTALS-MAKING
THE EXCHANGE-BLEED-
-OR O'S AMPLIFYING MACHINES-
DESTABILIZING CHRONOLOGIES
AND REALITIES-
-OR OUR TERROR-
THE STRENGTH-OF
OUR ATTACKS-
-BUT WHAT
HAPPENED-
CRRAACKKK
BOOOM
-WAS LIKE
NOTHING THAT EVER
HAD BEFORE.

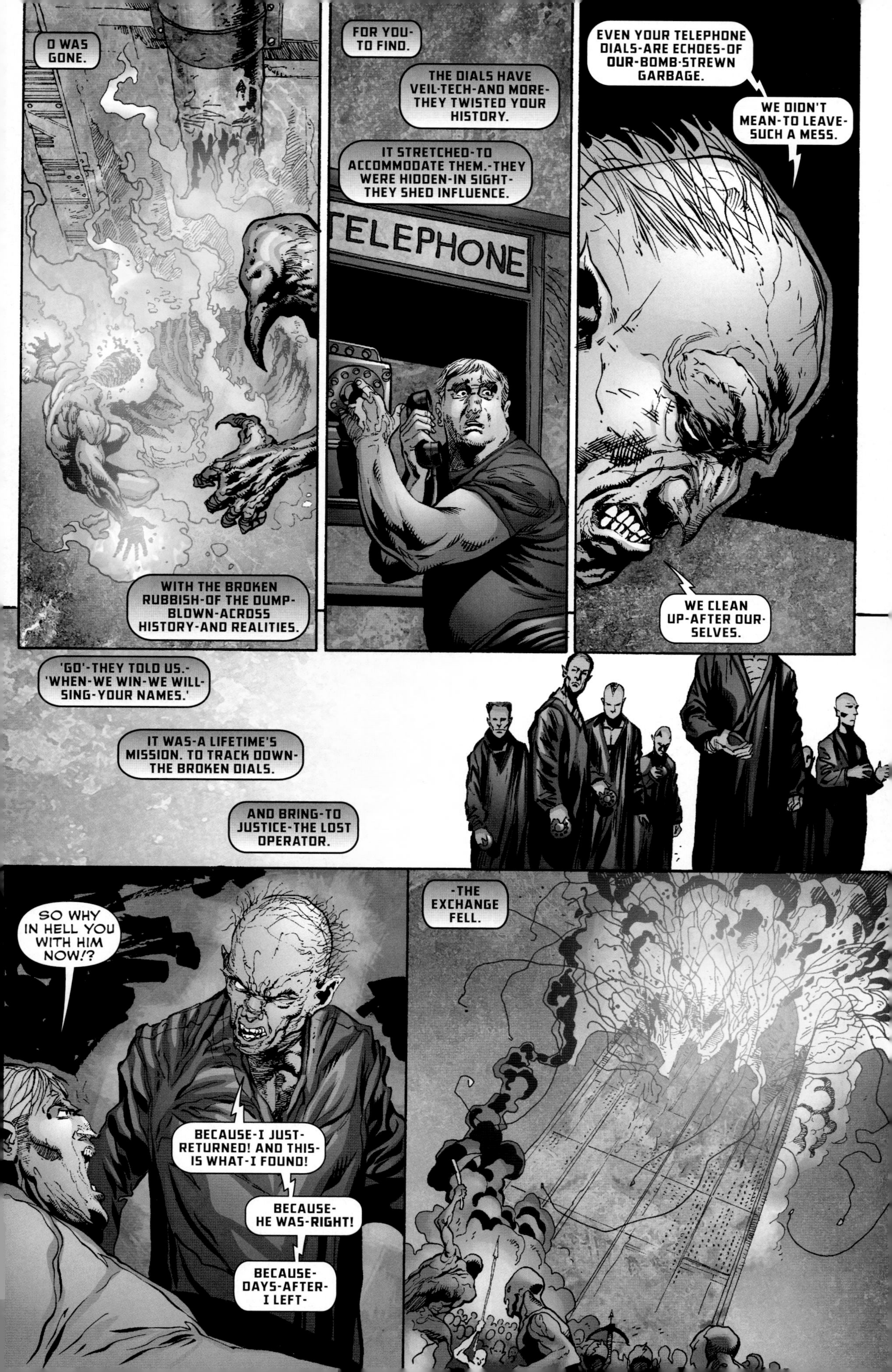
O WAS GONE.
WITH THE BROKEN RUBBISH-OF THE DUMP-BLOWN-ACROSS HISTORY-AND REALITIES.
FOR YOU-TO FIND.
THE DIALS HAVE VEIL-TECH-AND MORE-THEY TWISTED YOUR HISTORY.
IT STRETCHED-TO ACCOMMODATE THEM.-THEY WERE HIDDEN-IN SIGHT-THEY SHED INFLUENCE.
TELEPHONE
EVEN YOUR TELEPHONE DIALS-ARE ECHOES-OF OUR-BOMB-STREWN GARBAGE.
WE DIDN'T MEAN-TO LEAVE-SUCH A MESS.
WE CLEAN UP-AFTER OUR-SELVES.
'GO'-THEY TOLD US.-'WHEN-WE WIN-WE WILL-SING-YOUR NAMES.'
IT WAS-A LIFETIME'S MISSION. TO TRACK DOWN-THE BROKEN DIALS.
AND BRING-TO JUSTICE-THE LOST OPERATOR.
SO WHY IN HELL YOU WITH HIM NOW!?
BECAUSE-I JUST-RETURNED! AND THIS-IS WHAT-I FOUND!
BECAUSE-HE WAS-RIGHT!
BECAUSE-DAYS-AFTER-I LEFT-
-THE EXCHANGE FELL.

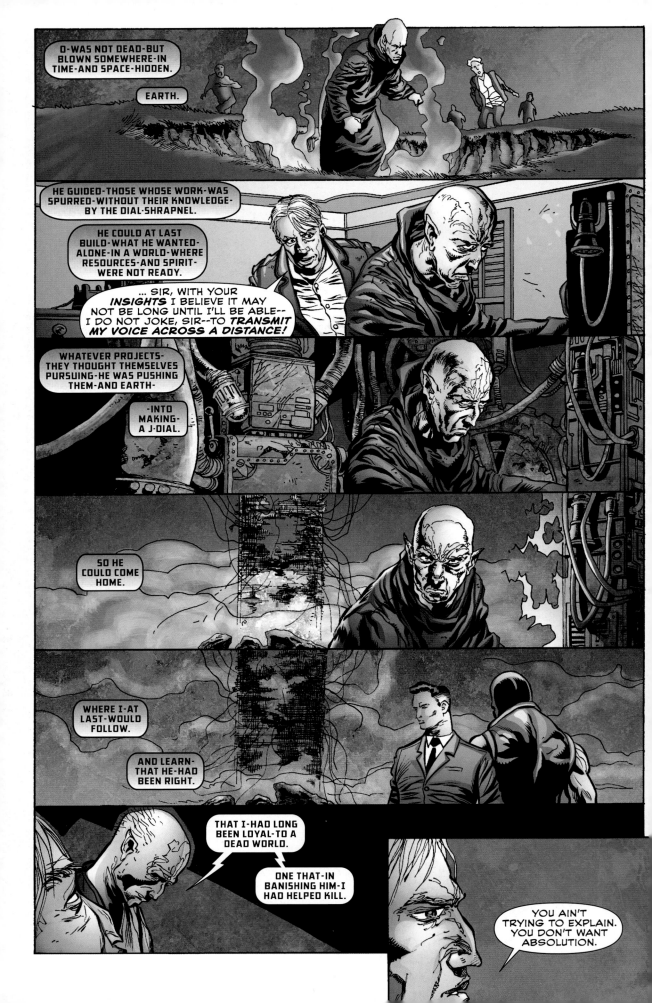

O-WAS NOT DEAD-BUT BLOWN SOMEWHERE-IN TIME-AND SPACE-HIDDEN.

EARTH.

HE GUIDED-THOSE WHOSE WORK-WAS SPURRED-WITHOUT THEIR KNOWLEDGE- BY THE DIAL-SHRAPNEL.

HE COULD AT LAST BUILD-WHAT HE WANTED- ALONE-IN A WORLD-WHERE RESOURCES-AND SPIRIT- WERE NOT READY.

... SIR, WITH YOUR *INSIGHTS* I BELIEVE IT MAY NOT BE LONG UNTIL I'LL BE ABLE-- I DO NOT JOKE, SIR--TO *TRANSMIT MY VOICE ACROSS A DISTANCE!*

WHATEVER PROJECTS- THEY THOUGHT THEMSELVES PURSUING-HE WAS PUSHING THEM-AND EARTH-

-INTO MAKING- A J-DIAL.

SO HE COULD COME HOME.

WHERE I-AT LAST-WOULD FOLLOW.

AND LEARN- THAT HE-HAD BEEN RIGHT.

THAT I-HAD LONG BEEN LOYAL-TO A DEAD WORLD.

ONE THAT-IN BANISHING HIM-I HAD HELPED KILL.

YOU AIN'T TRYING TO EXPLAIN. YOU DON'T WANT ABSOLUTION.

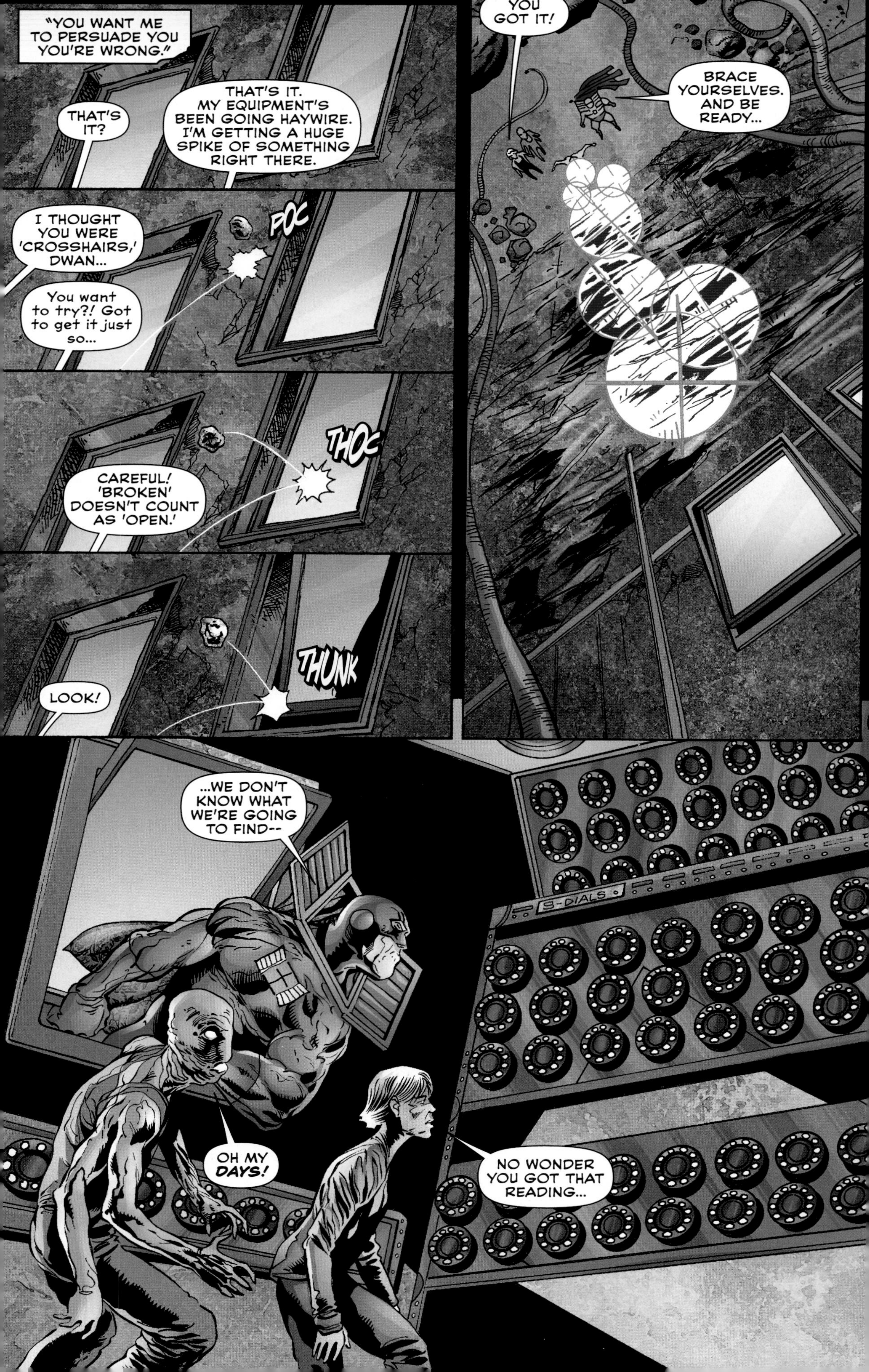

"YOU WANT ME TO PERSUADE YOU YOU'RE WRONG."
THAT'S IT?
THAT'S IT. MY EQUIPMENT'S BEEN GOING HAYWIRE. I'M GETTING A HUGE SPIKE OF SOMETHING RIGHT THERE.
I THOUGHT YOU WERE 'CROSSHAIRS,' DWAN...
POC
You want to try?! Got to get it just so...
THOC
CAREFUL! 'BROKEN' DOESN'T COUNT AS 'OPEN.'
THUNK
LOOK!
YOU GOT IT!
BRACE YOURSELVES. AND BE READY...
...WE DON'T KNOW WHAT WE'RE GOING TO FIND--
S-DIALS
OH MY DAYS!
NO WONDER YOU GOT THAT READING...

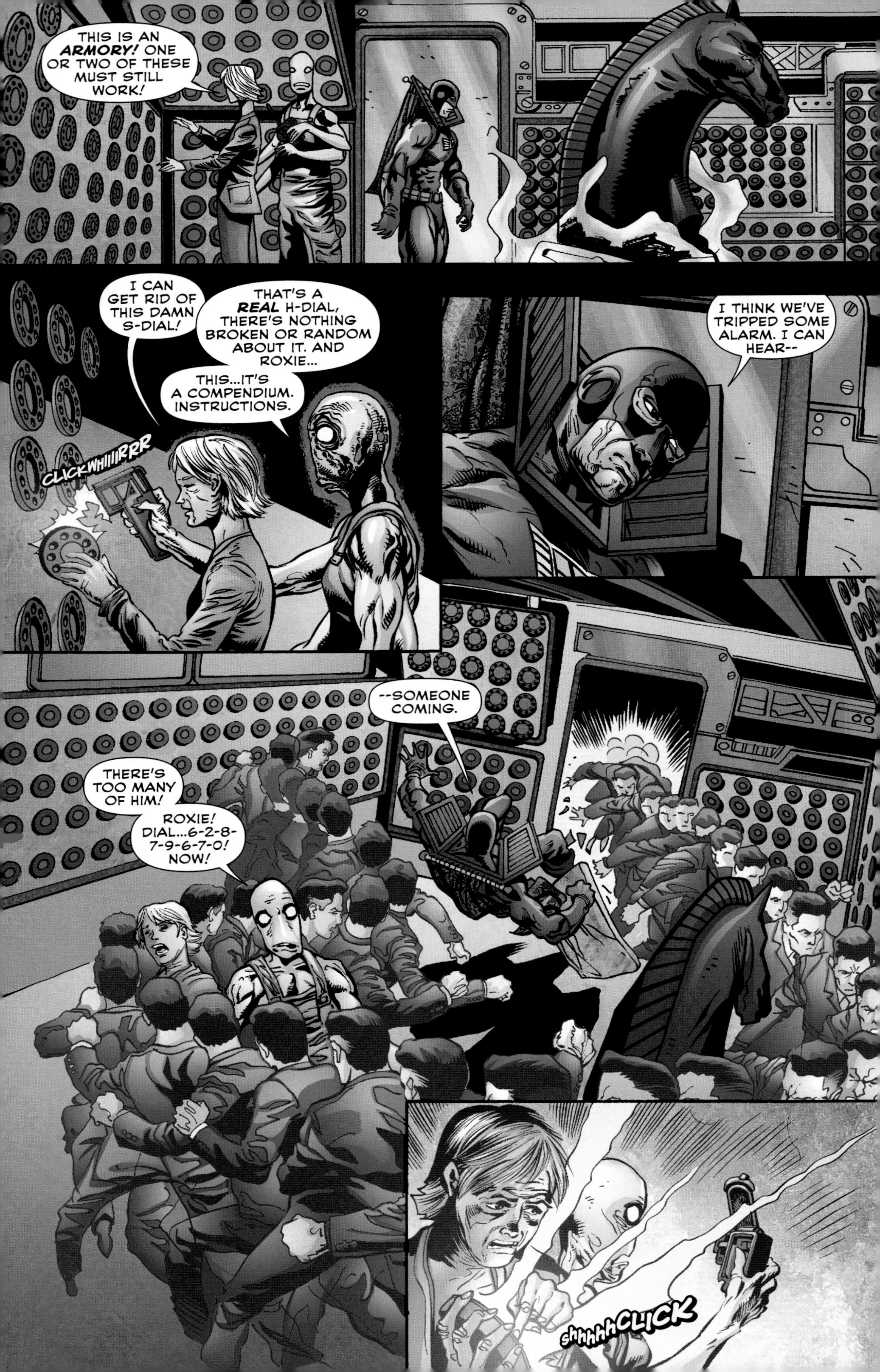
THIS IS AN ARMORY! ONE OR TWO OF THESE MUST STILL WORK!
I CAN GET RID OF THIS DAMN S-DIAL!
THAT'S A REAL H-DIAL, THERE'S NOTHING BROKEN OR RANDOM ABOUT IT. AND ROXIE...
THIS...IT'S A COMPENDIUM. INSTRUCTIONS.
CLICKWHIIIIRRR
I THINK WE'VE TRIPPED SOME ALARM. I CAN HEAR--
--SOMEONE COMING.
THERE'S TOO MANY OF HIM!
ROXIE! DIAL...6-2-8-7-9-6-7-0! NOW!
shhhhhCLICK

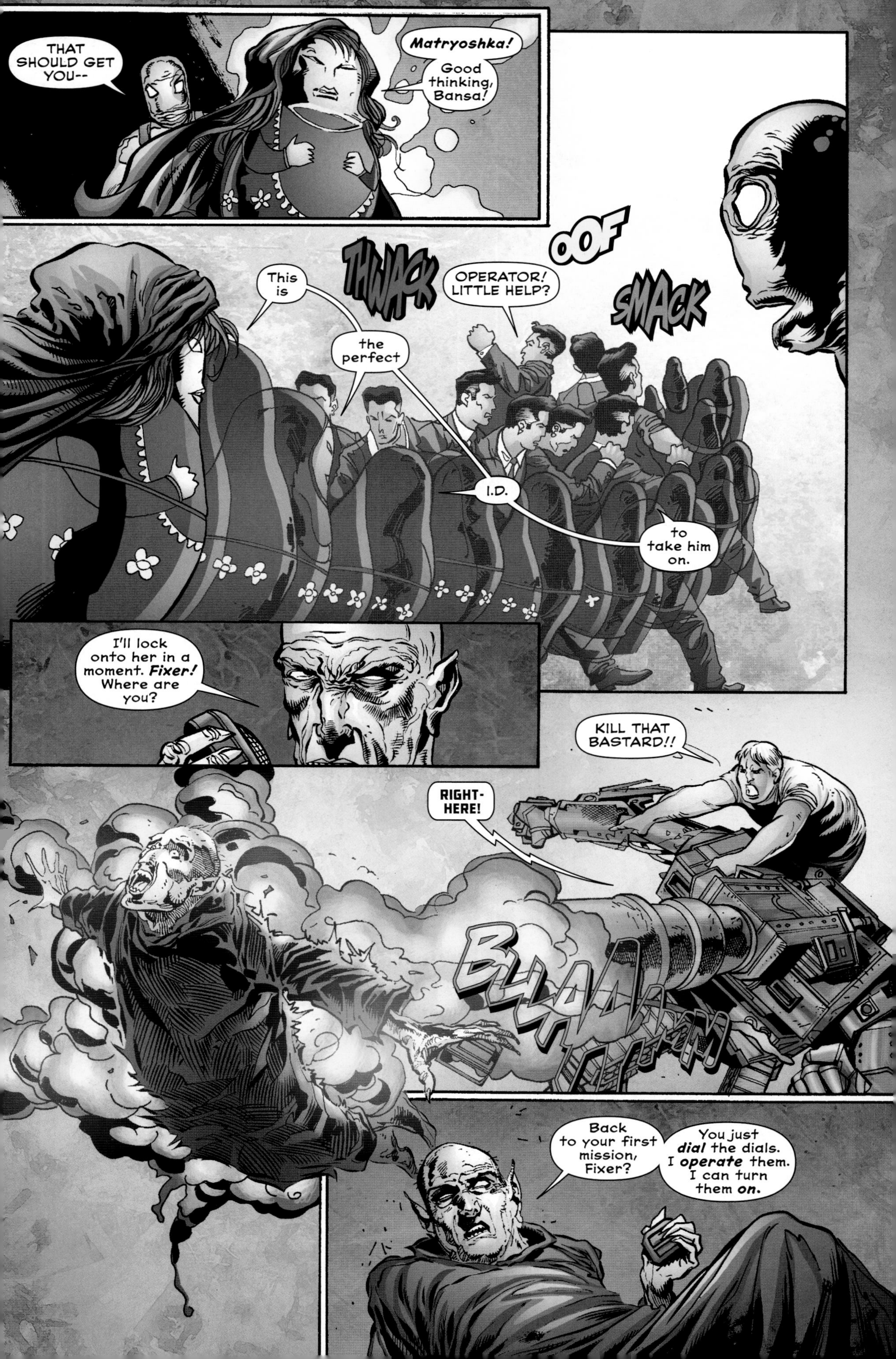
THAT SHOULD GET YOU--
Matryoshka!
Good thinking, Bansa!
This is
the perfect
I.D.
to take him on.
THWACK
OPERATOR! LITTLE HELP?
OOF
SMACK
I'll lock onto her in a moment. Fixer! Where are you?
KILL THAT BASTARD!!
RIGHT-HERE!
BLAAAMM
Back to your first mission, Fixer?
You just dial the dials. I operate them. I can turn them on.

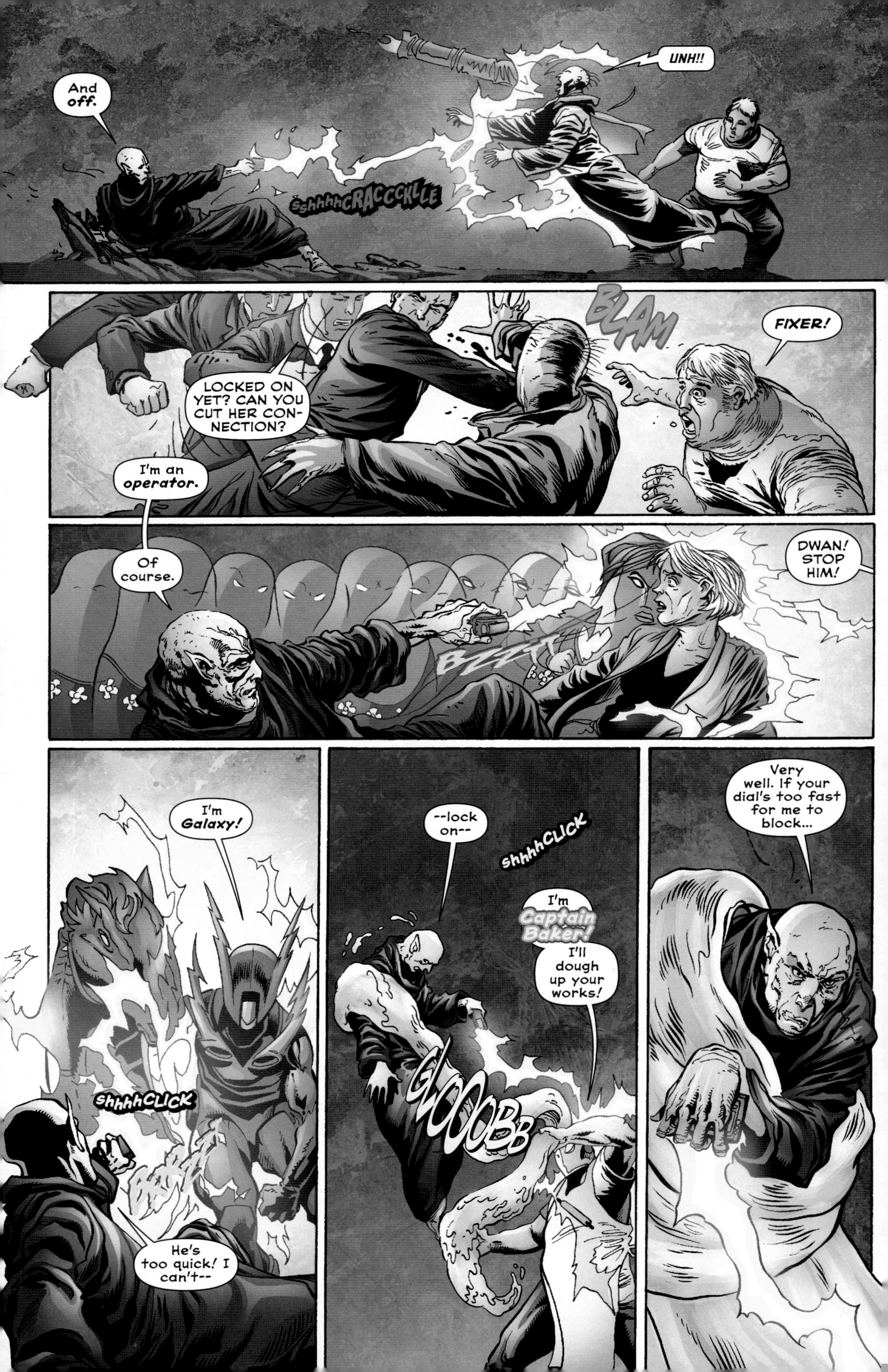
And off.
UNH!!
SshhhhCRACCCKLLE
BLAM
FIXER!
LOCKED ON YET? CAN YOU CUT HER CONNECTION?
I'm an operator.
Of course.
DWAN! STOP HIM!
BZZZT
I'm Galaxy!
ShhhhCLICK
He's too quick! I can't--
--lock on--
ShhhhCLICK
I'm Captain Baker! I'll dough up your works!
GLOOOBB
Very well. If your dial's too fast for me to block...

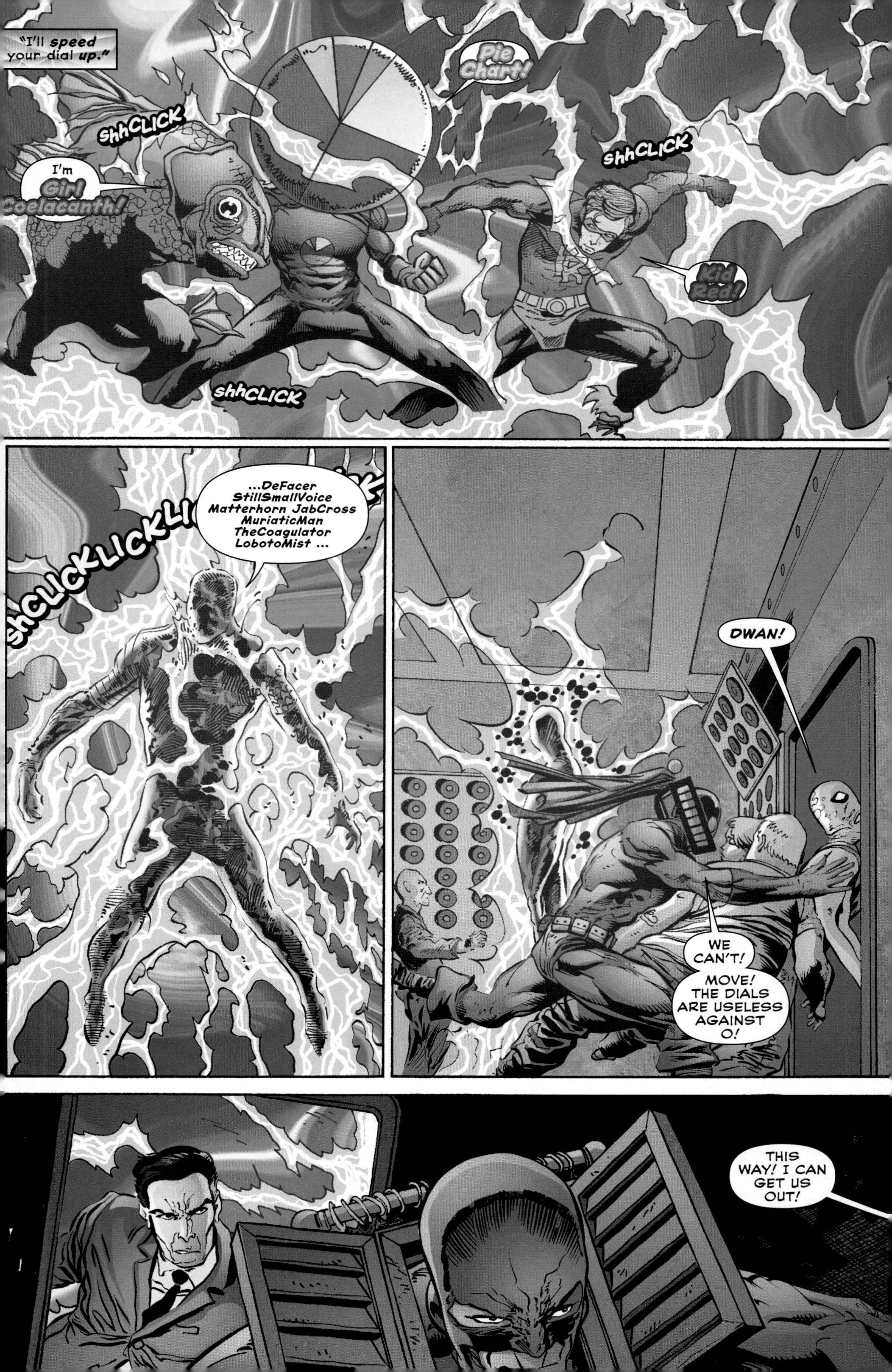
"I'll speed your dial up."
Pie Chart!
ShhCLICK
I'm Girl Coelacanth!
ShhCLICK
Kid Red!
shhCLICK
...DeFacer StillSmallVoice Matterhorn JabCross MuriaticMan TheCoagulator LobotoMist ...
shCLICKLICKLI
DWAN!
WE CAN'T!
MOVE! THE DIALS ARE USELESS AGAINST O!
THIS WAY! I CAN GET US OUT!

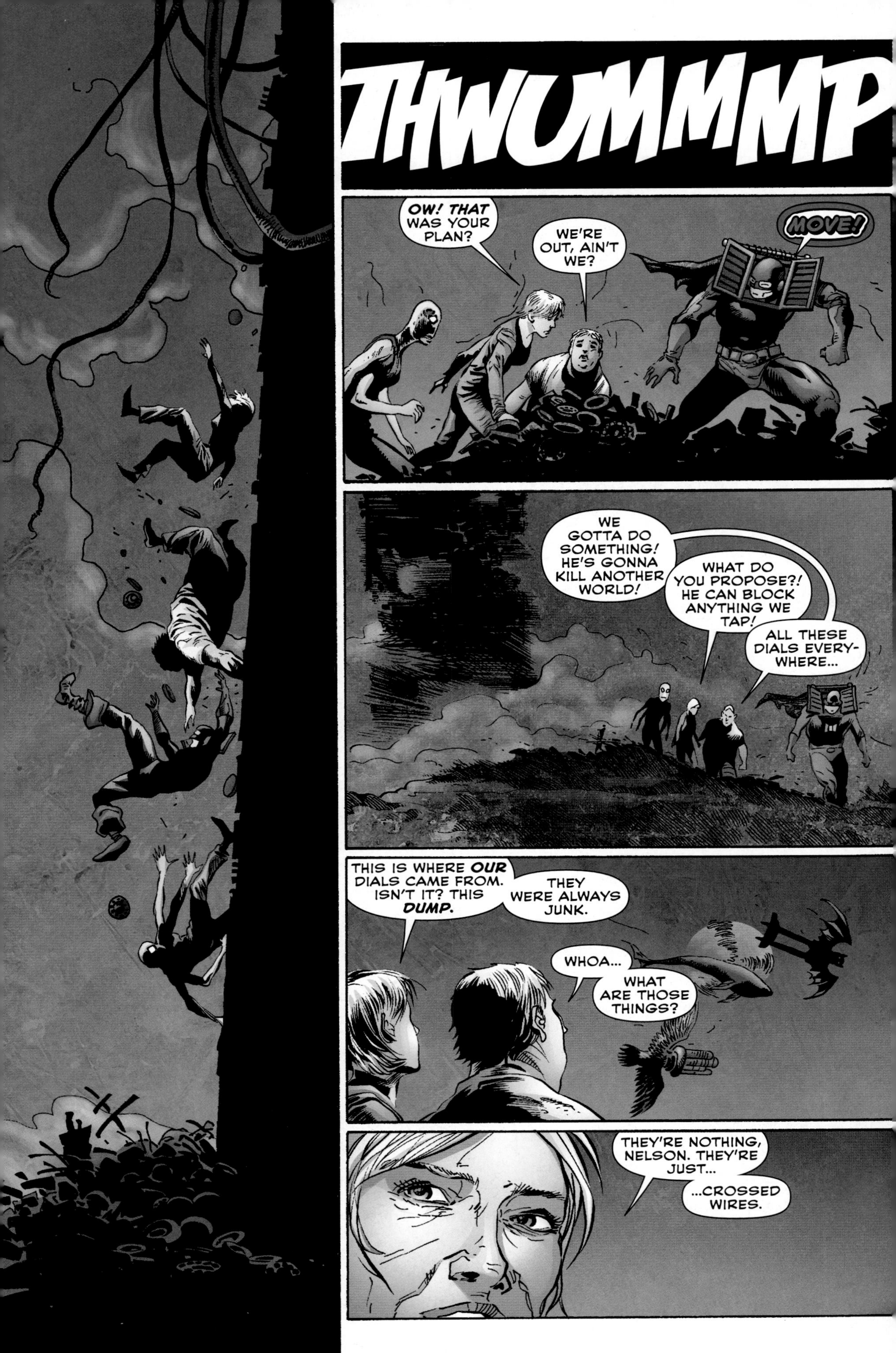
THWUMMMP
OW! THAT WAS YOUR PLAN?
WE'RE OUT, AIN'T WE?
MOVE!
WE GOTTA DO SOMETHING! HE'S GONNA KILL ANOTHER WORLD!
WHAT DO YOU PROPOSE?! HE CAN BLOCK ANYTHING WE TAP!
ALL THESE DIALS EVERY-WHERE...
THIS IS WHERE OUR DIALS CAME FROM. ISN'T IT? THIS DUMP.
THEY WERE ALWAYS JUNK.
WHOA...
WHAT ARE THOSE THINGS?
THEY'RE NOTHING, NELSON. THEY'RE JUST...
...CROSSED WIRES.

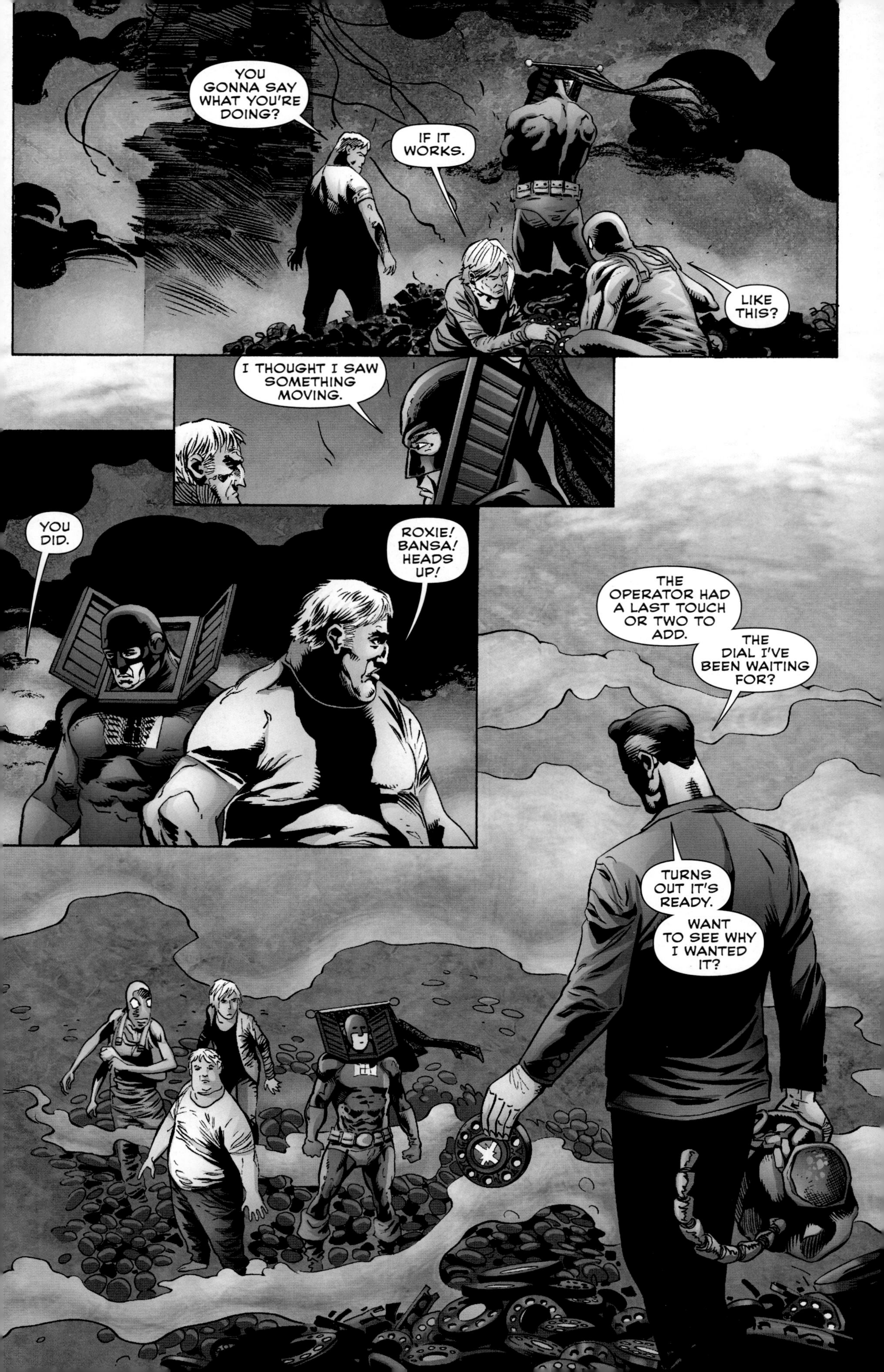
YOU GONNA SAY WHAT YOU'RE DOING?
IF IT WORKS.
LIKE THIS?
I THOUGHT I SAW SOMETHING MOVING.
YOU DID.
ROXIE! BANSA! HEADS UP!
THE OPERATOR HAD A LAST TOUCH OR TWO TO ADD.
THE DIAL I'VE BEEN WAITING FOR?
TURNS OUT IT'S READY.
WANT TO SEE WHY I WANTED IT?

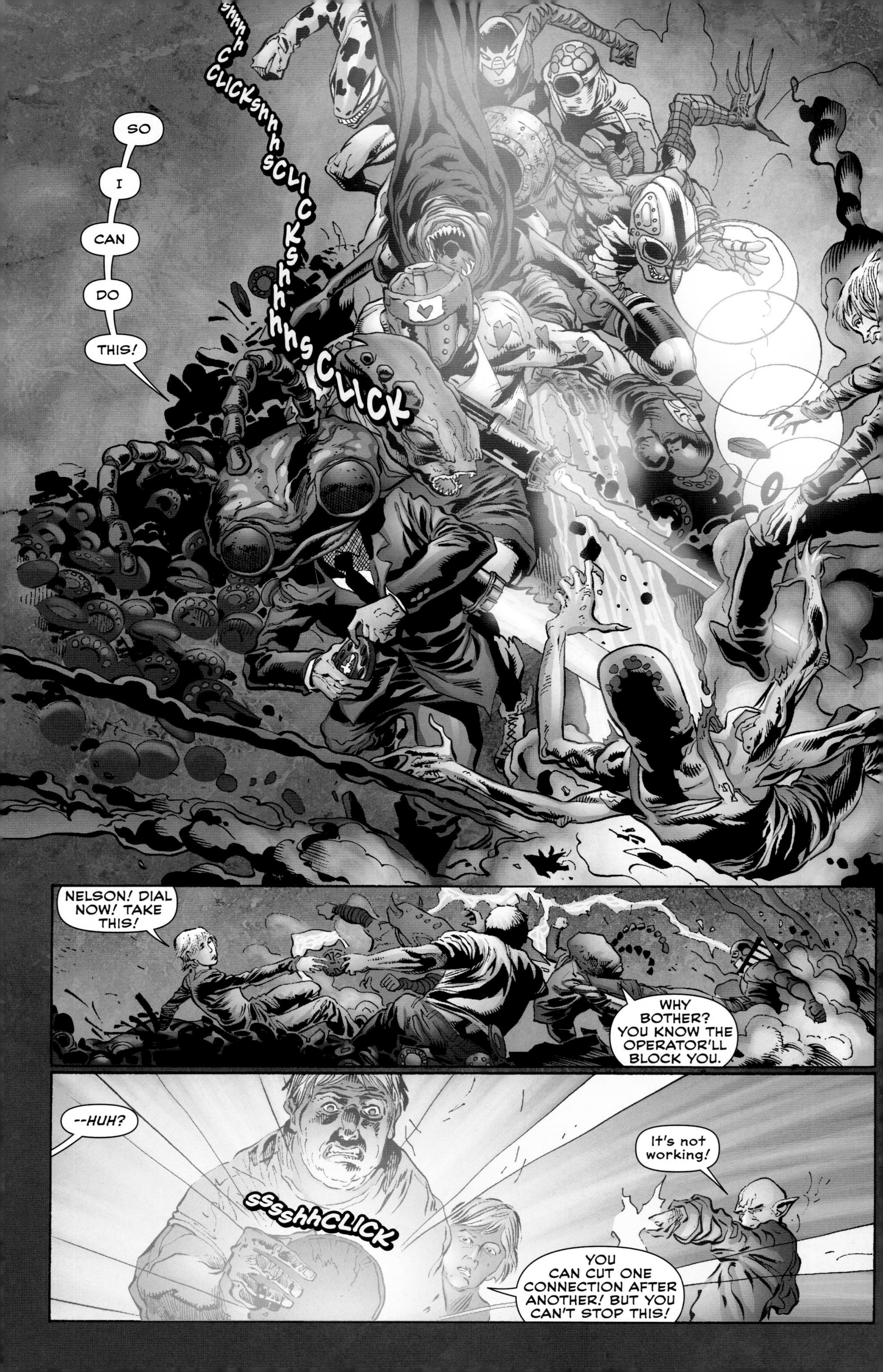
shhhh
C
CLICKshhhhsCLICKshhhhhsCLICK
SO I CAN DO THIS!
NELSON! DIAL NOW! TAKE THIS!
WHY BOTHER? YOU KNOW THE OPERATOR'LL BLOCK YOU.
--HUH?
sSsshhCLICK
It's not working!
YOU CAN CUT ONE CONNECTION AFTER ANOTHER! BUT YOU CAN'T STOP THIS!

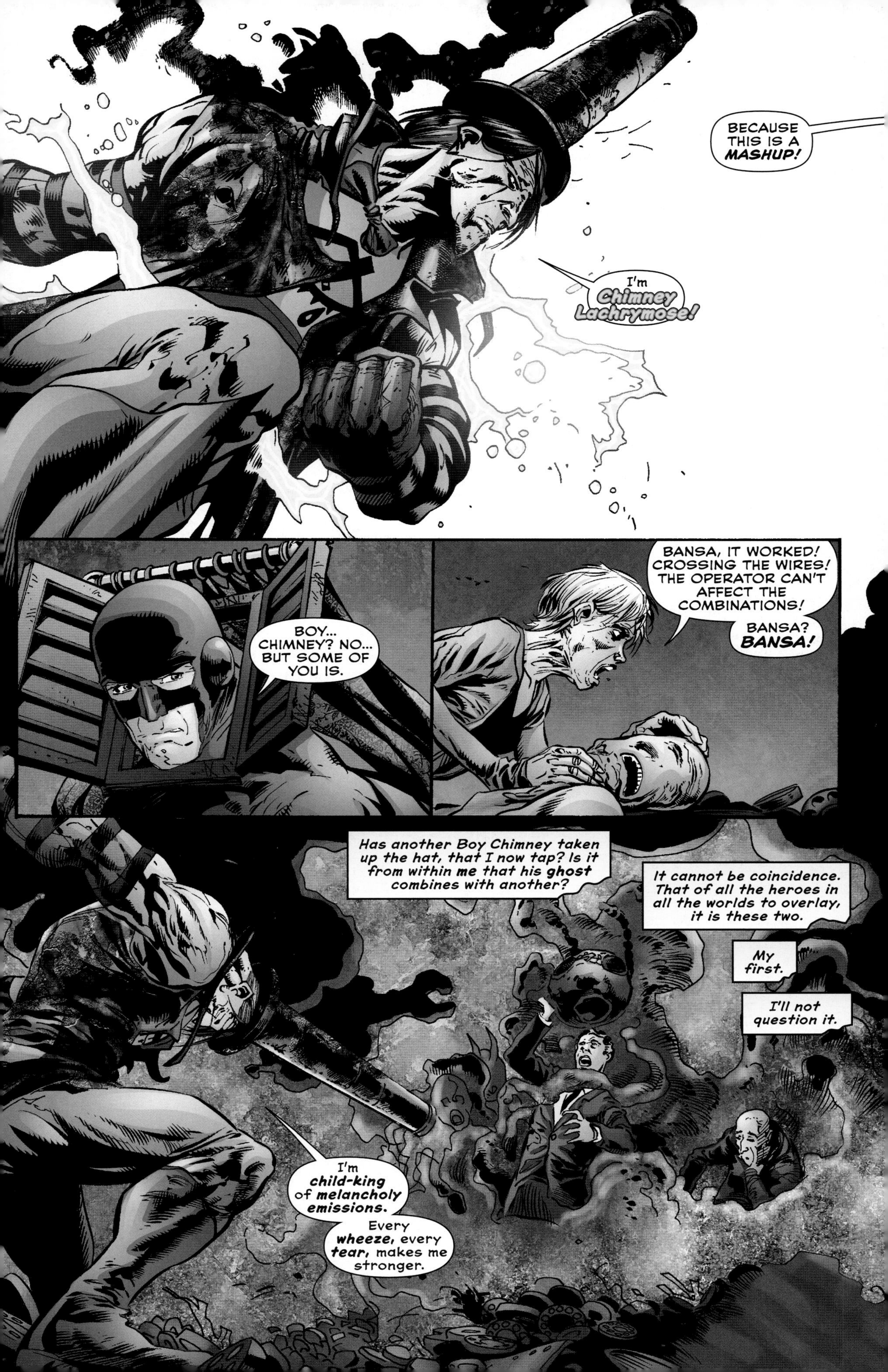
BECAUSE THIS IS A ***MASHUP!***
I'm ***Chimney Lachrymose!***
BOY... CHIMNEY? NO... BUT SOME OF YOU IS.
BANSA, IT WORKED! CROSSING THE WIRES! THE OPERATOR CAN'T AFFECT THE COMBINATIONS!
BANSA? ***BANSA!***
*Has another Boy Chimney taken up the hat, that I now tap? Is it from within **me** that his **ghost** combines with another?*
It cannot be coincidence. That of all the heroes in all the worlds to overlay, it is these two.
My first.
I'll not question it.
I'm **child-king** of **melancholy emissions.**
Every **wheeze**, every **tear**, makes me stronger.

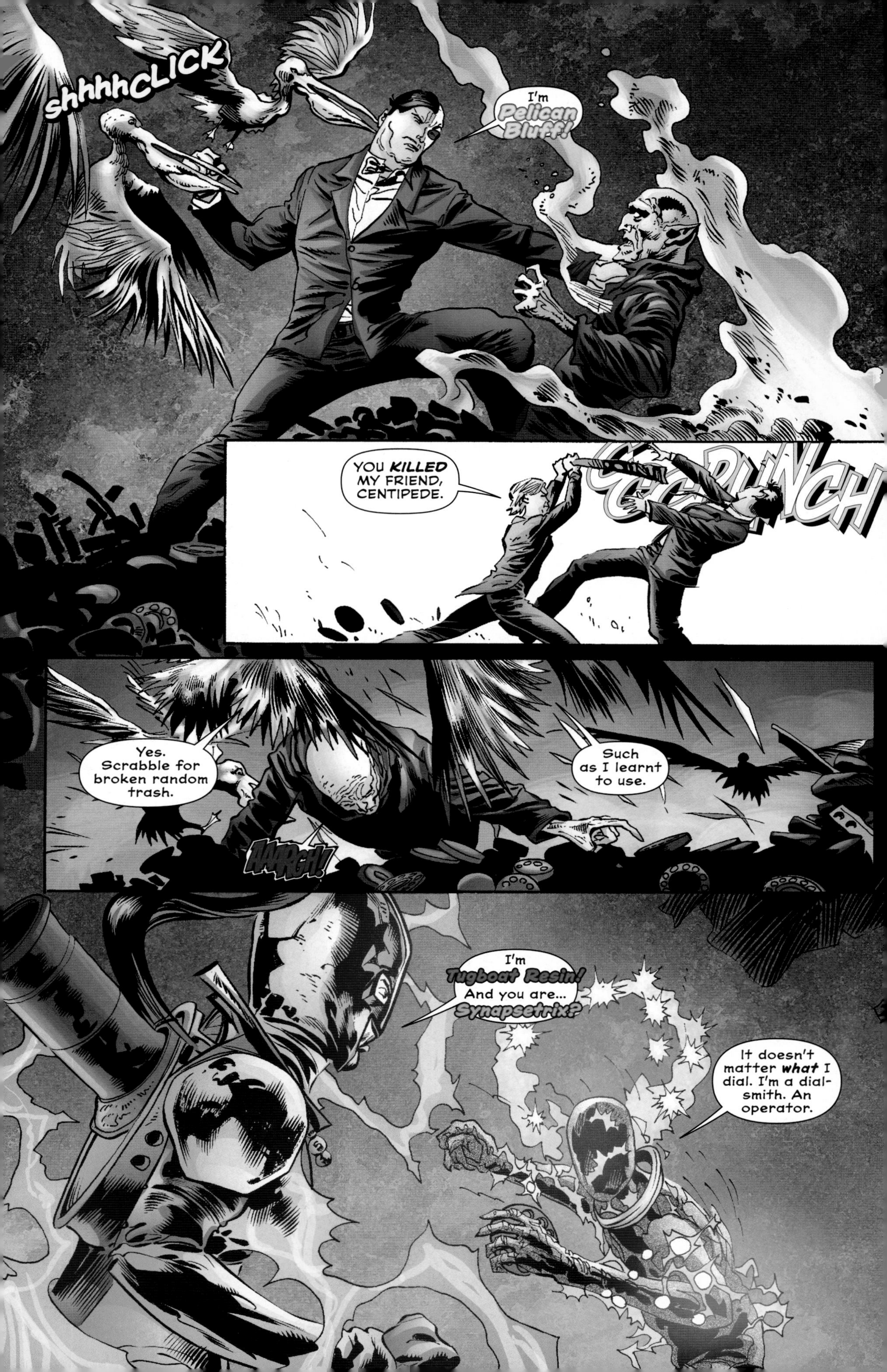

shhhhCLICK
I'm Pelican Bluff!
YOU KILLED MY FRIEND, CENTIPEDE.
CCCRUNCH
Yes. Scrabble for broken random trash.
Such as I learnt to use.
AAARGH!
I'm Tugboat Resin! And you are... Synapsetrix?
It doesn't matter what I dial. I'm a dial-smith. An operator.

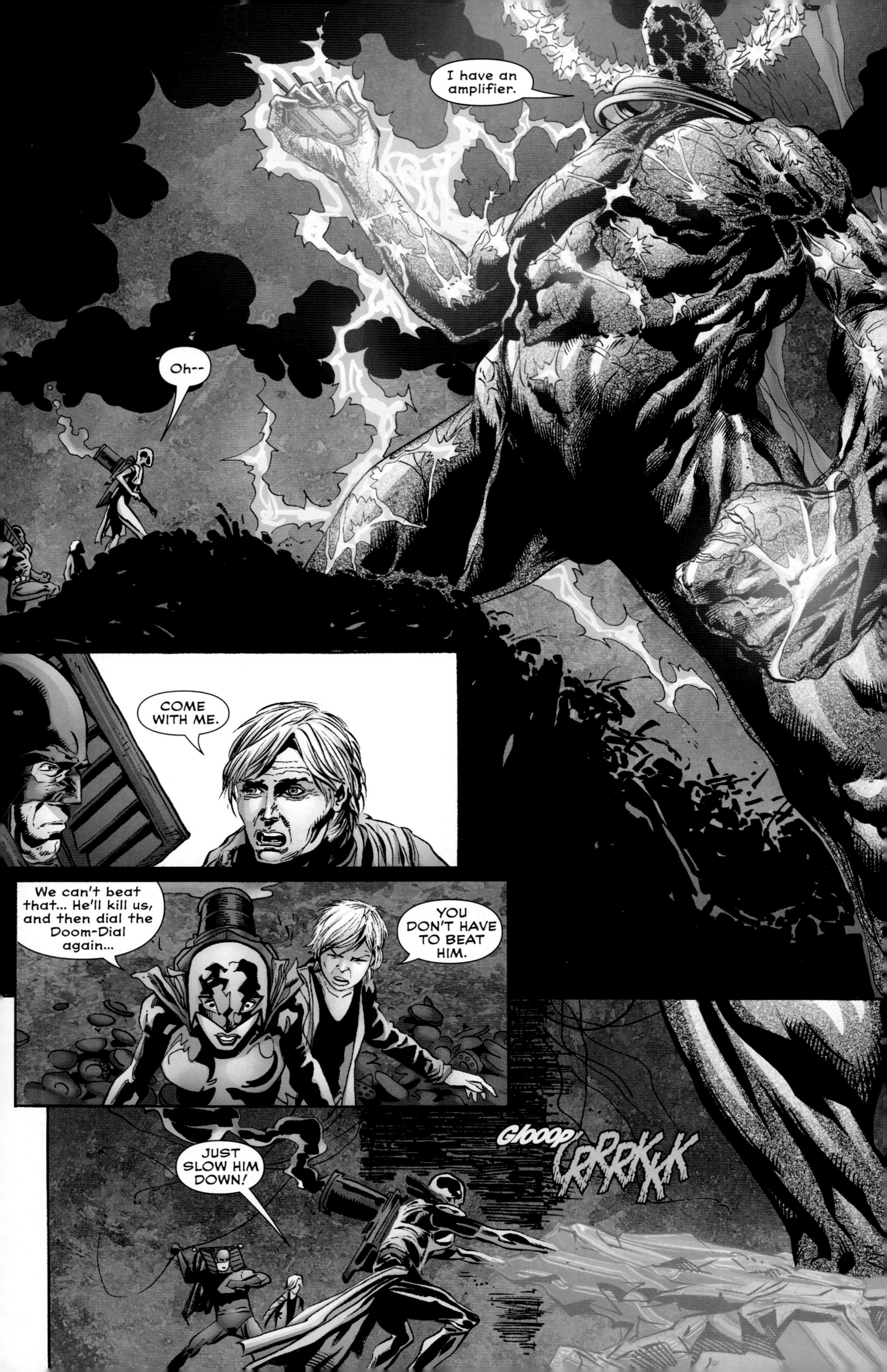

I have an amplifier.
Oh--
COME WITH ME.
We can't beat that... He'll kill us, and then dial the Doom-Dial again...
YOU DON'T HAVE TO BEAT HIM.
JUST SLOW HIM DOWN!
GLOOOP
CRRKKK

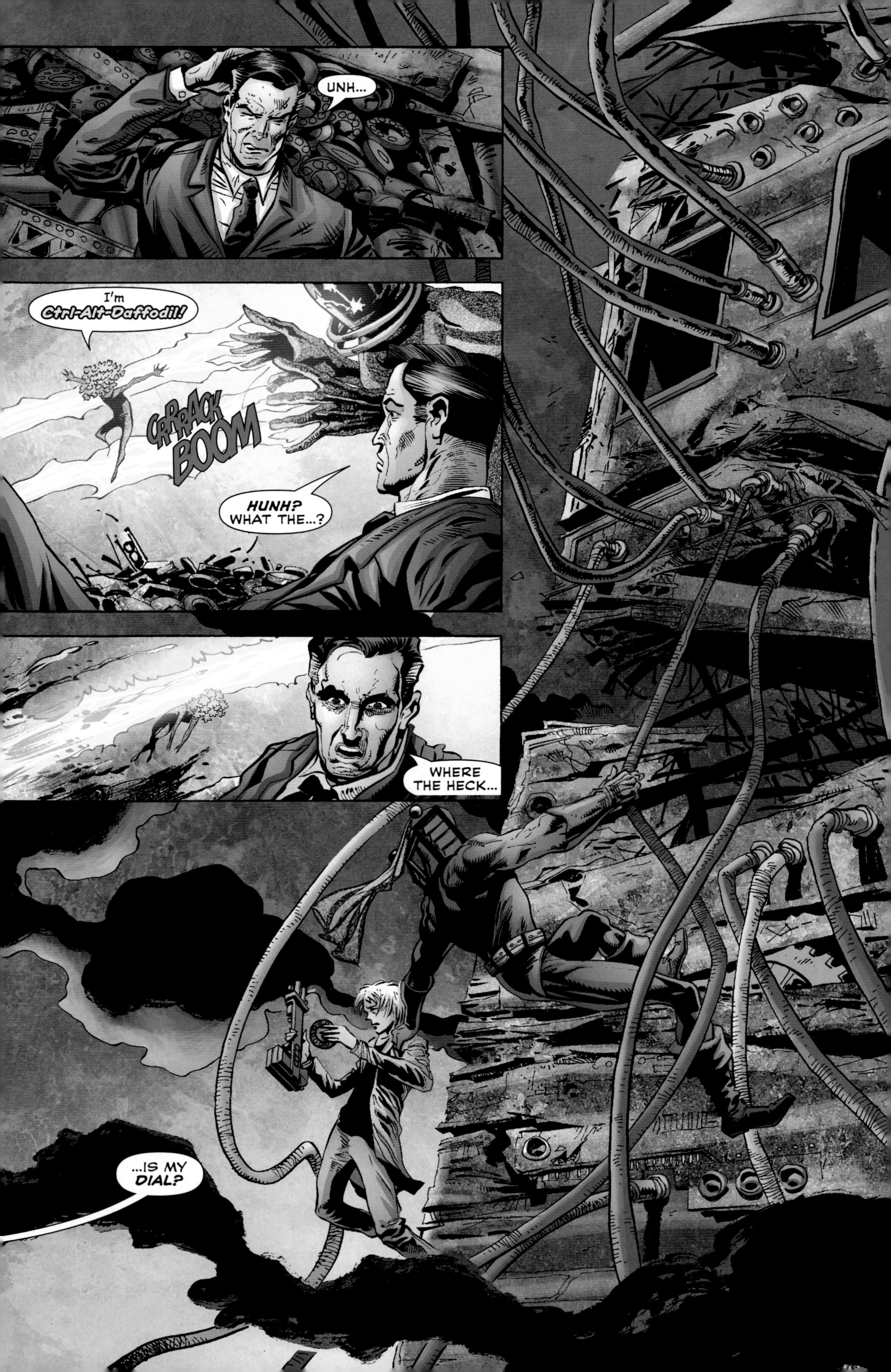
UNH...
I'm Ctrl-Alt-Daffodil!
CRRRACK BOOM
HUNH? WHAT THE...?
WHERE THE HECK...
...IS MY DIAL?

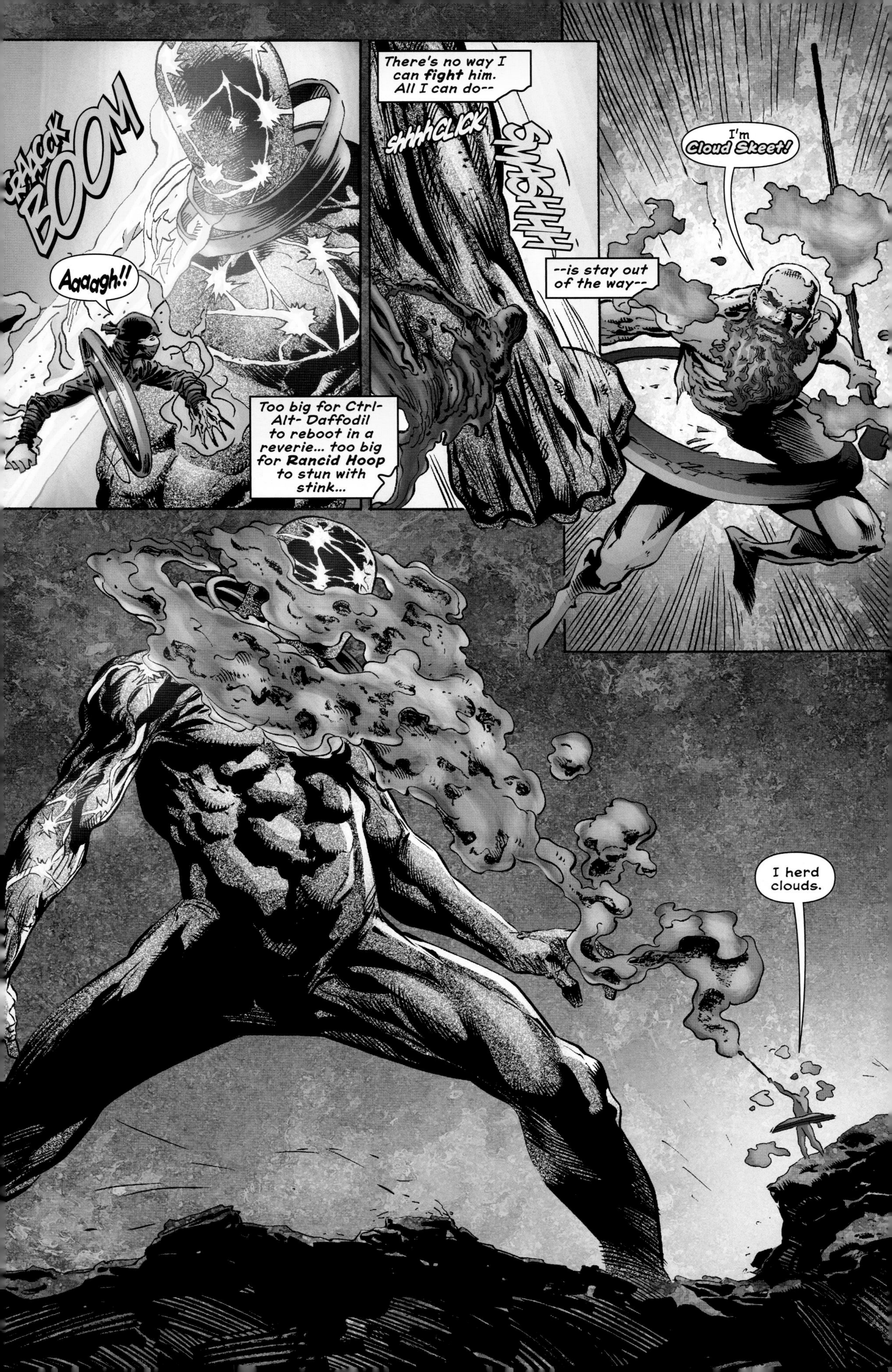

CRAACK BOOM
Aaaagh!!
Too big for Ctrl-Alt-Daffodil to reboot in a reverie... too big for Rancid Hoop to stun with stink...
There's no way I can fight him. All I can do--
SHHHHCLICK
SMASHHH
--is stay out of the way--
I'm Cloud Skeet!
I herd clouds.

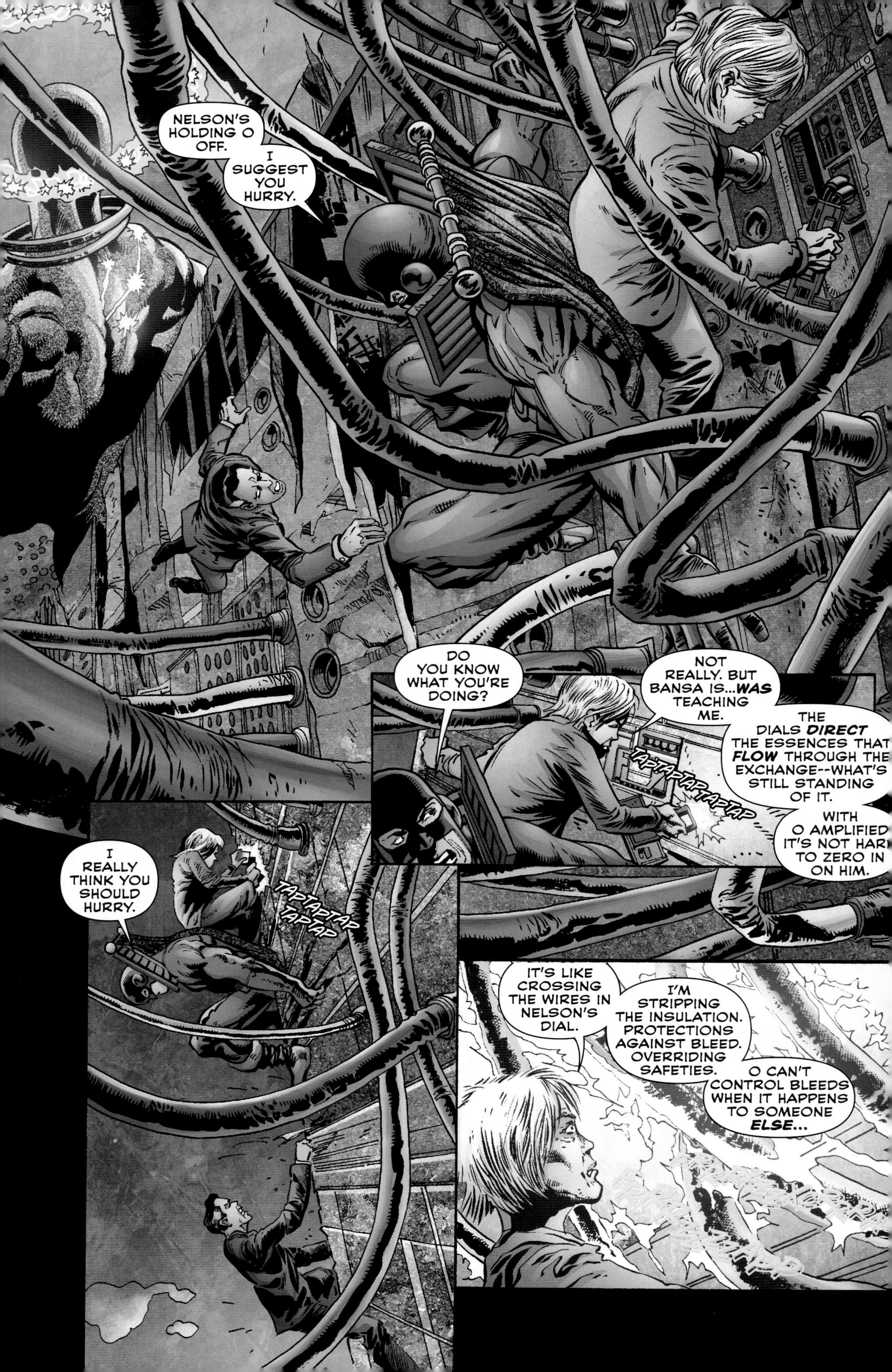
NELSON'S HOLDING O OFF.
I SUGGEST YOU HURRY.
DO YOU KNOW WHAT YOU'RE DOING?
NOT REALLY. BUT BANSA IS...WAS TEACHING ME.
THE DIALS DIRECT THE ESSENCES THAT FLOW THROUGH THE EXCHANGE--WHAT'S STILL STANDING OF IT.
TAPTAPTAPTAPTAP
WITH O AMPLIFIED IT'S NOT HAR TO ZERO IN ON HIM.
I REALLY THINK YOU SHOULD HURRY.
TAPTAPTAP TAPTAP
IT'S LIKE CROSSING THE WIRES IN NELSON'S DIAL.
I'M STRIPPING THE INSULATION. PROTECTIONS AGAINST BLEED. OVERRIDING SAFETIES.
O CAN'T CONTROL BLEEDS WHEN IT HAPPENS TO SOMEONE ELSE...

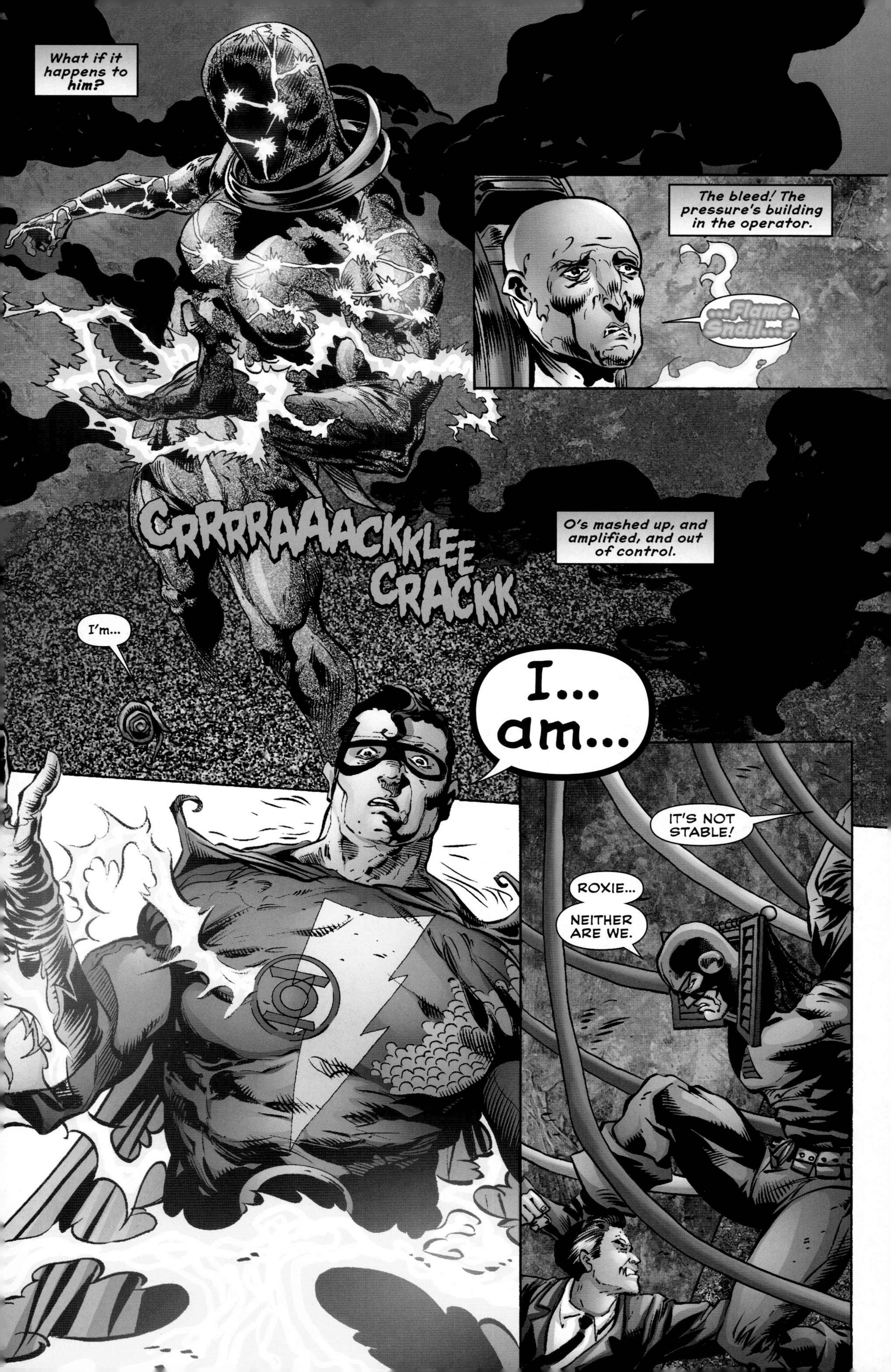
What if it happens to him?
The bleed! The pressure's building in the operator.
...Flame Snail...?
O's mashed up, and amplified, and out of control.
CRRRRAAACKKLEE CRACKK
I'm...
I... am...
IT'S NOT STABLE!
ROXIE...
NEITHER ARE WE.

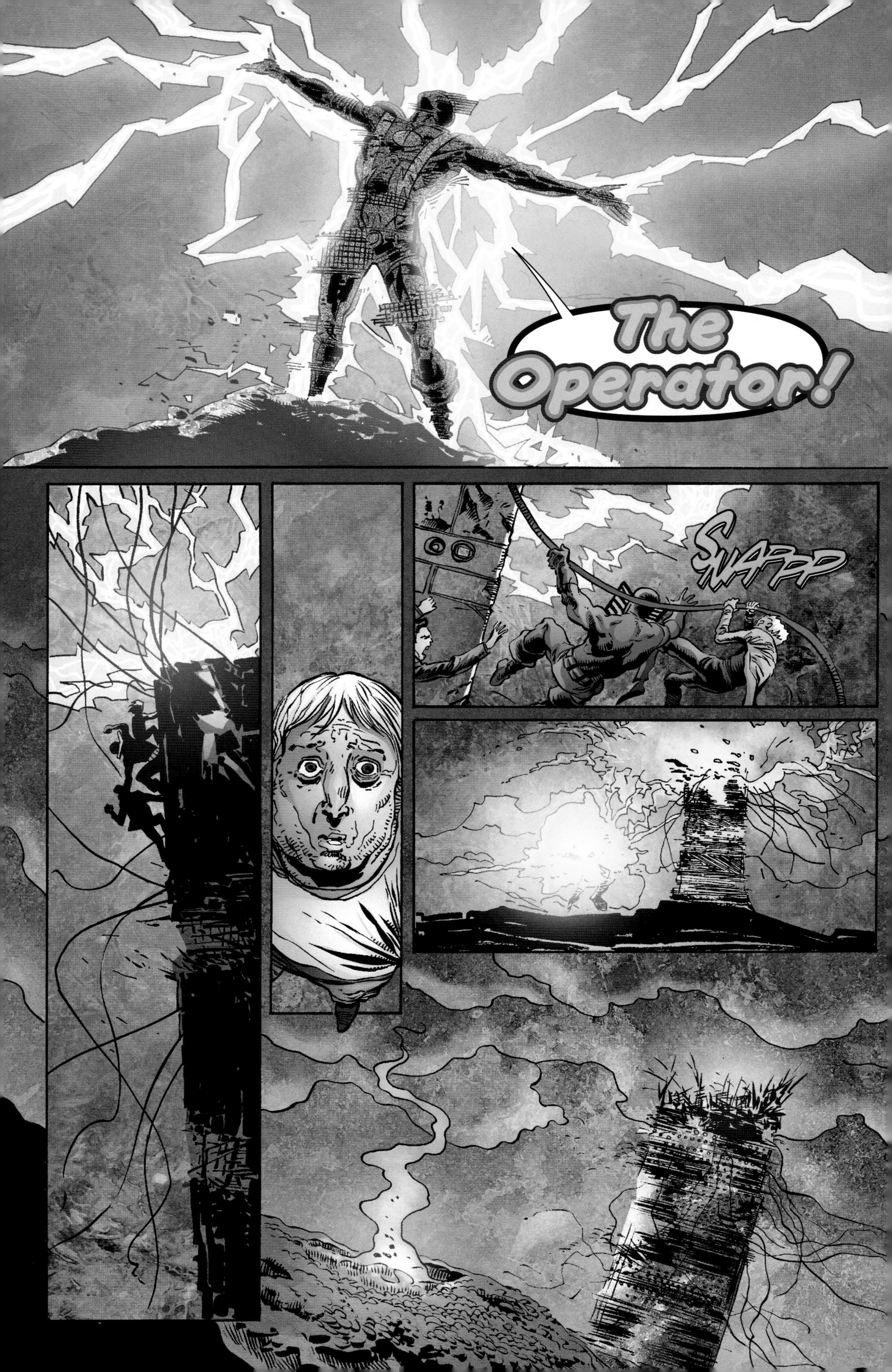
The Operator!
SNAPPP

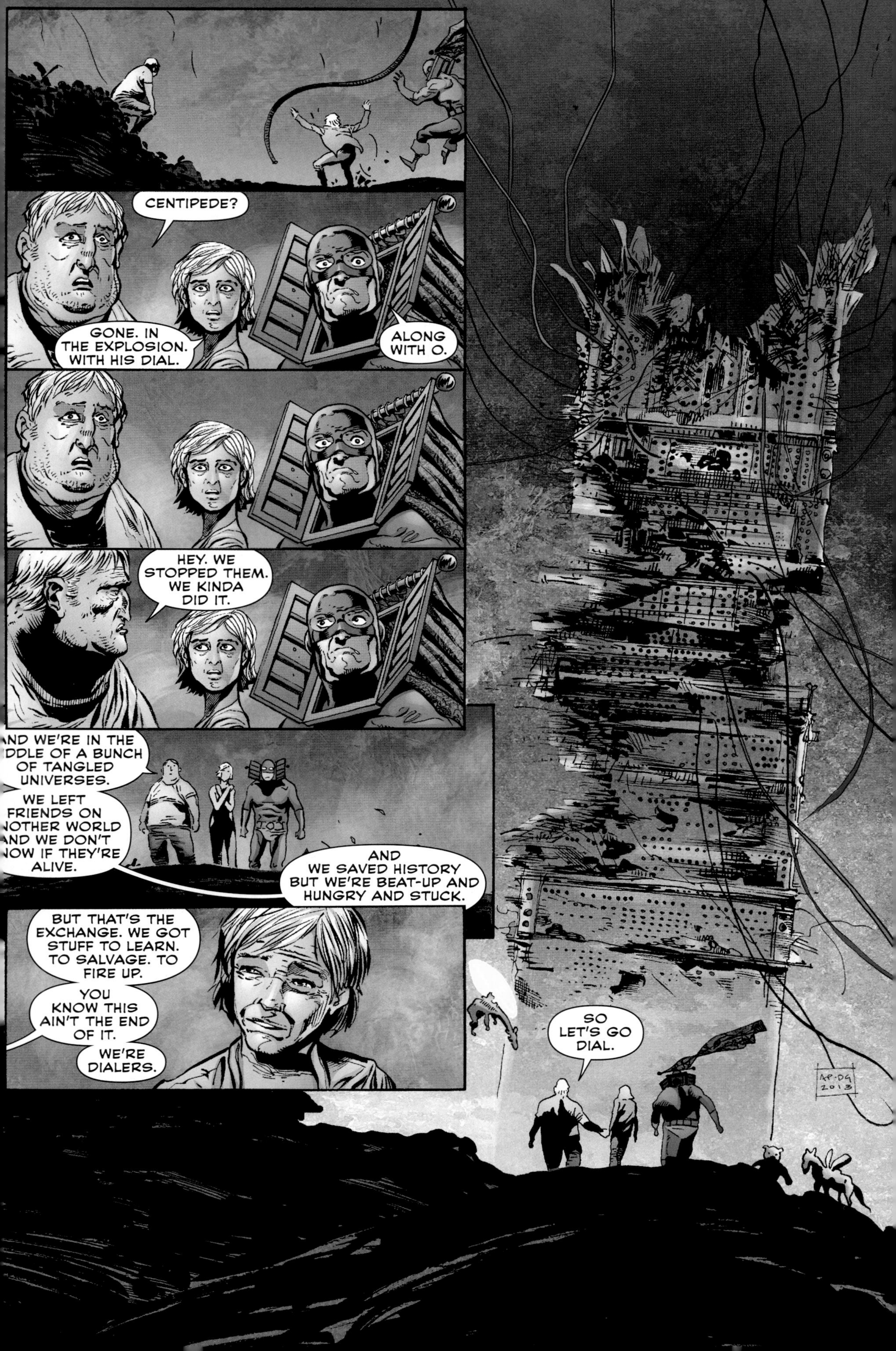
CENTIPEDE?
GONE. IN THE EXPLOSION. WITH HIS DIAL.
ALONG WITH O.
HEY. WE STOPPED THEM. WE KINDA DID IT.
AND WE'RE IN THE IDDLE OF A BUNCH OF TANGLED UNIVERSES.
WE LEFT FRIENDS ON NOTHER WORLD AND WE DON'T NOW IF THEY'RE ALIVE.
AND WE SAVED HISTORY BUT WE'RE BEAT-UP AND HUNGRY AND STUCK.
BUT THAT'S THE EXCHANGE. WE GOT STUFF TO LEARN. TO SALVAGE. TO FIRE UP.
YOU KNOW THIS AIN'T THE END OF IT.
WE'RE DIALERS.
SO LET'S GO DIAL.
AP·DG 2013

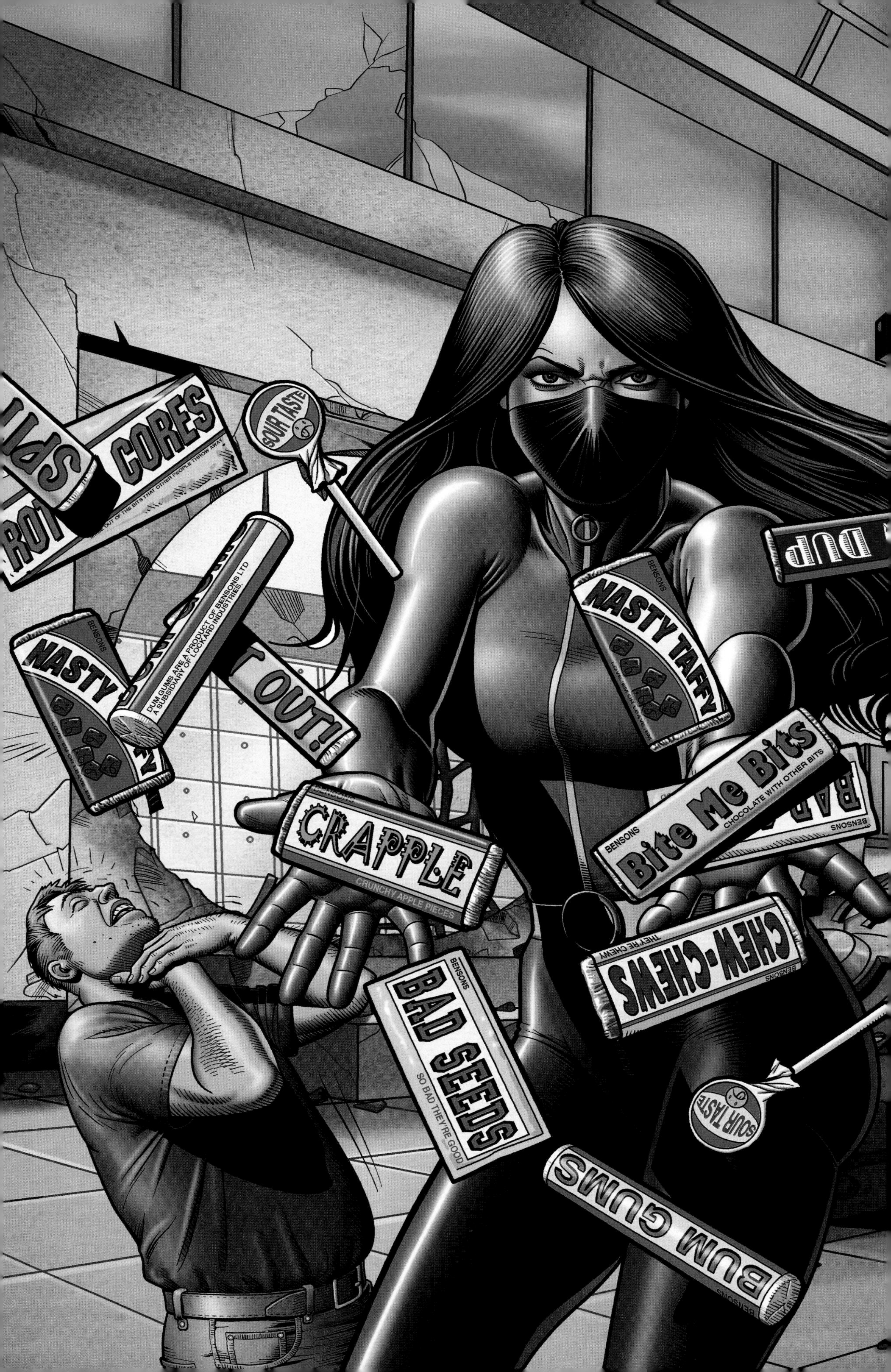
CORES
SOUR TASTE
BENSONS
NASTY
DUM GUMS ARE A PRODUCT OF BENSONS LTD
A SUBSIDIARY OF LOCKARD INDUSTRIES.
OUT!
BENSONS
NASTY TAFFY
BENSONS
CRAPPLE
CRUNCHY APPLE PIECES
BENSONS
Bite Me Bits
CHOCOLATE WITH OTHER BITS
BENSONS
CHEW-CHEWS
THEY'RE CHEWY
BENSONS
BAD SEEDS
SO BAD THEY'RE GOOD
SOUR TASTE
BUM GUMS
BENSONS

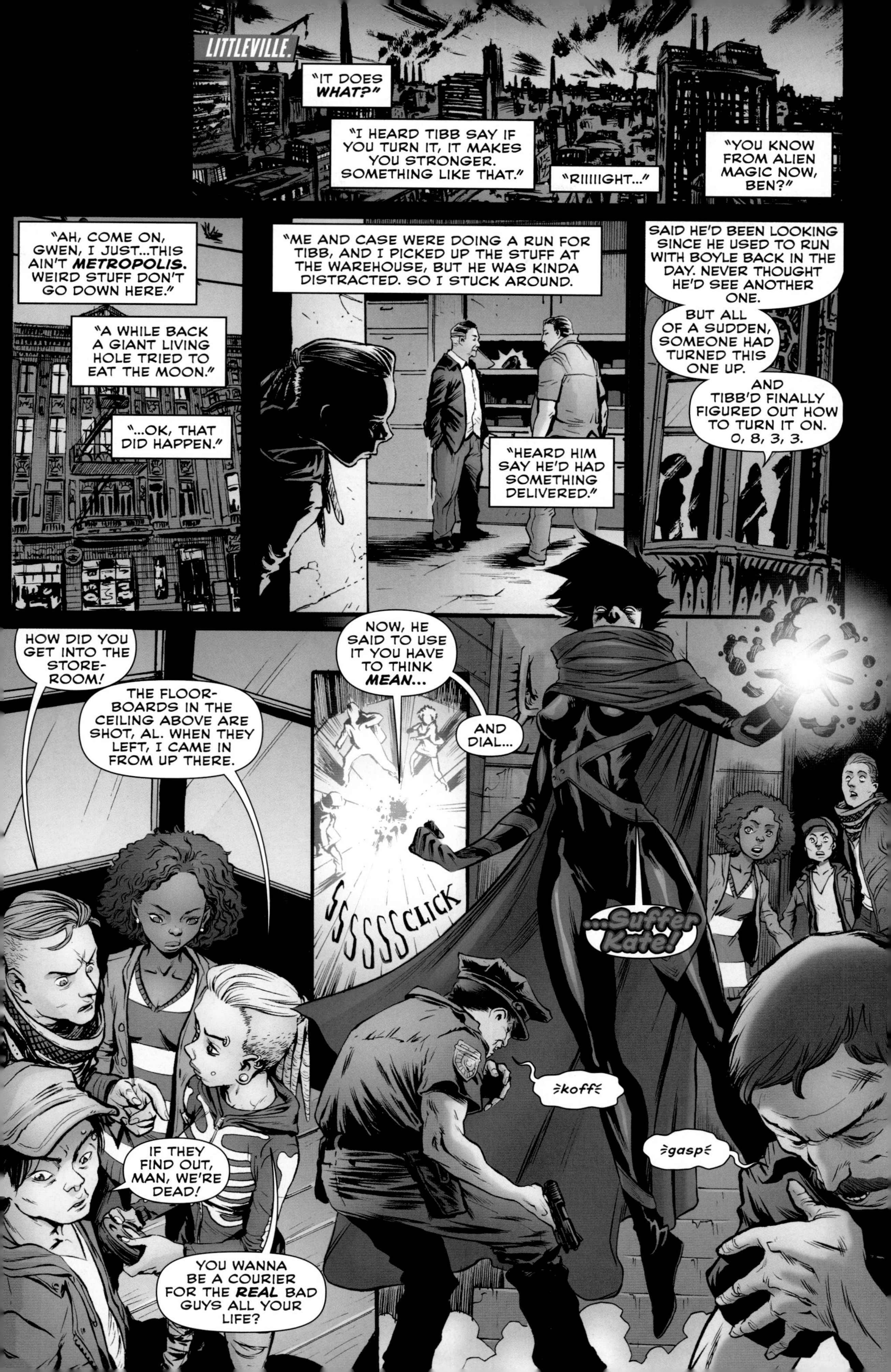
LITTLEVILLE.
"IT DOES WHAT?"
"I HEARD TIBB SAY IF YOU TURN IT, IT MAKES YOU STRONGER. SOMETHING LIKE THAT."
"RIIIIGHT..."
"YOU KNOW FROM ALIEN MAGIC NOW, BEN?"
"AH, COME ON, GWEN, I JUST...THIS AIN'T METROPOLIS. WEIRD STUFF DON'T GO DOWN HERE."
"A WHILE BACK A GIANT LIVING HOLE TRIED TO EAT THE MOON."
"...OK, THAT DID HAPPEN."
"ME AND CASE WERE DOING A RUN FOR TIBB, AND I PICKED UP THE STUFF AT THE WAREHOUSE, BUT HE WAS KINDA DISTRACTED. SO I STUCK AROUND.
"HEARD HIM SAY HE'D HAD SOMETHING DELIVERED."
SAID HE'D BEEN LOOKING SINCE HE USED TO RUN WITH BOYLE BACK IN THE DAY. NEVER THOUGHT HE'D SEE ANOTHER ONE.
BUT ALL OF A SUDDEN, SOMEONE HAD TURNED THIS ONE UP.
AND TIBB'D FINALLY FIGURED OUT HOW TO TURN IT ON. 0, 8, 3, 3.
HOW DID YOU GET INTO THE STORE-ROOM!
THE FLOOR-BOARDS IN THE CEILING ABOVE ARE SHOT, AL. WHEN THEY LEFT, I CAME IN FROM UP THERE.
NOW, HE SAID TO USE IT YOU HAVE TO THINK MEAN...
AND DIAL...
SSSSSSCLICK
...Suffer Kate!
koff
gasp
IF THEY FIND OUT, MAN, WE'RE DEAD!
YOU WANNA BE A COURIER FOR THE REAL BAD GUYS ALL YOUR LIFE?

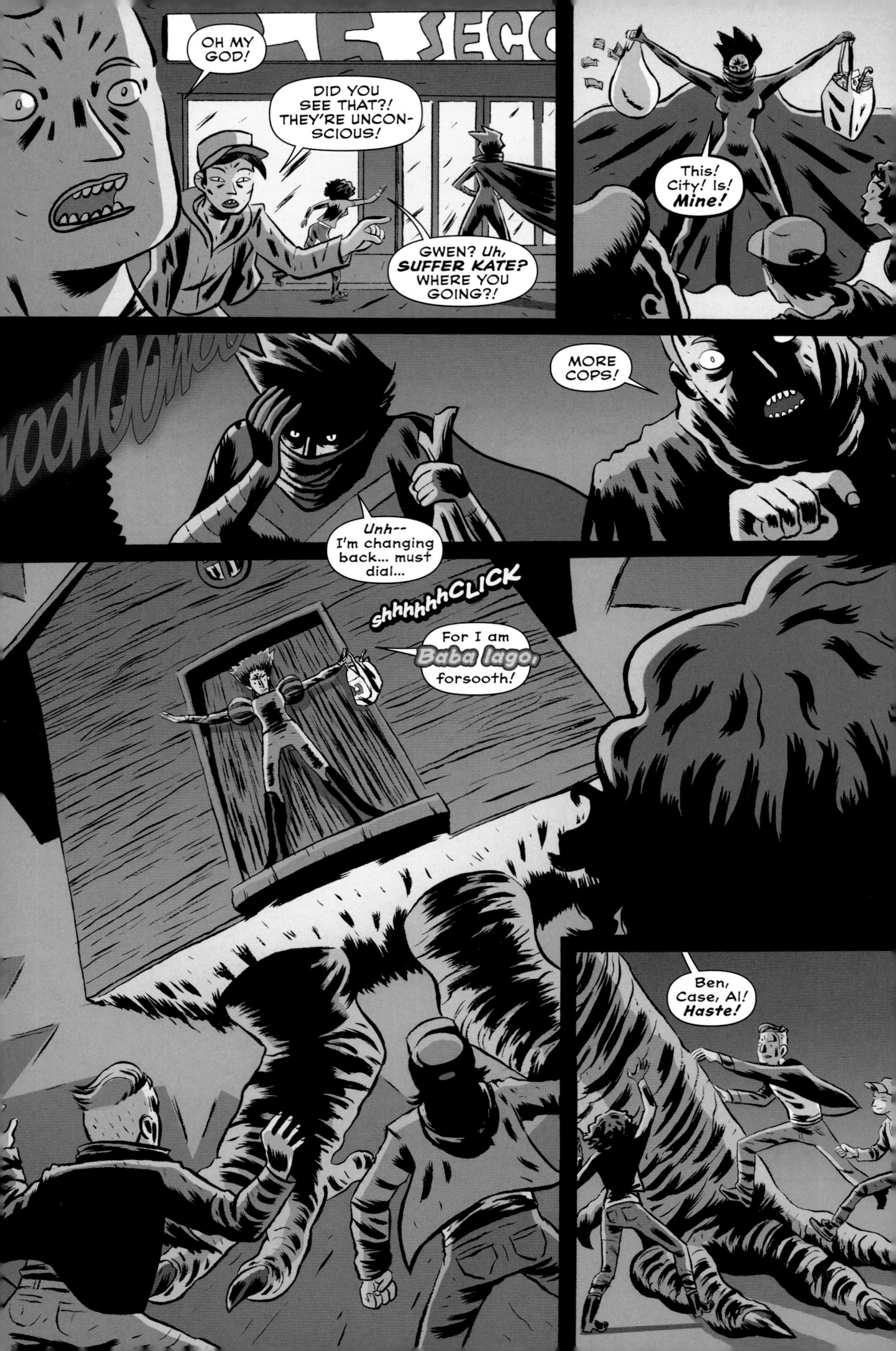
OH MY GOD!
DID YOU SEE THAT?! THEY'RE UNCONSCIOUS!
GWEN? Uh, SUFFER KATE? WHERE YOU GOING?!
This! City! Is! Mine!
MORE COPS!
Unh-- I'm changing back... must dial...
shhhhhhCLICK
For I am Baba Iago, forsooth!
Ben, Case, Al! Haste!

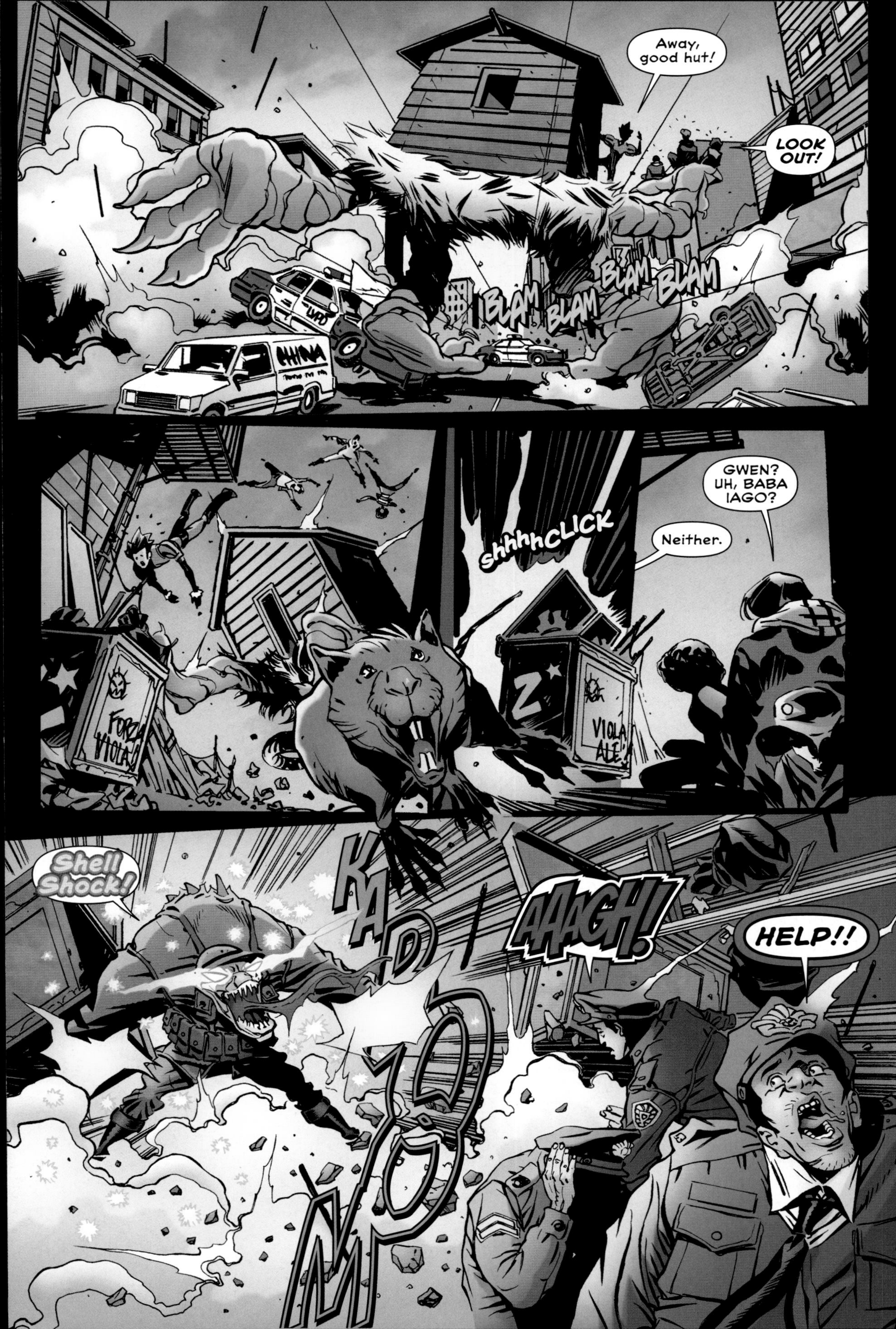
Away, good hut!
LOOK OUT!
BLAM
BLAM
BLAM
BLAM
LVPD
CHINA
FORZA VIOLA!
VIOLA ALE!
GWEN? UH, BABA IAGO?
Neither.
shhhhCLICK
Shell Shock!
KA
AAAGH!
HELP!!
BOOM

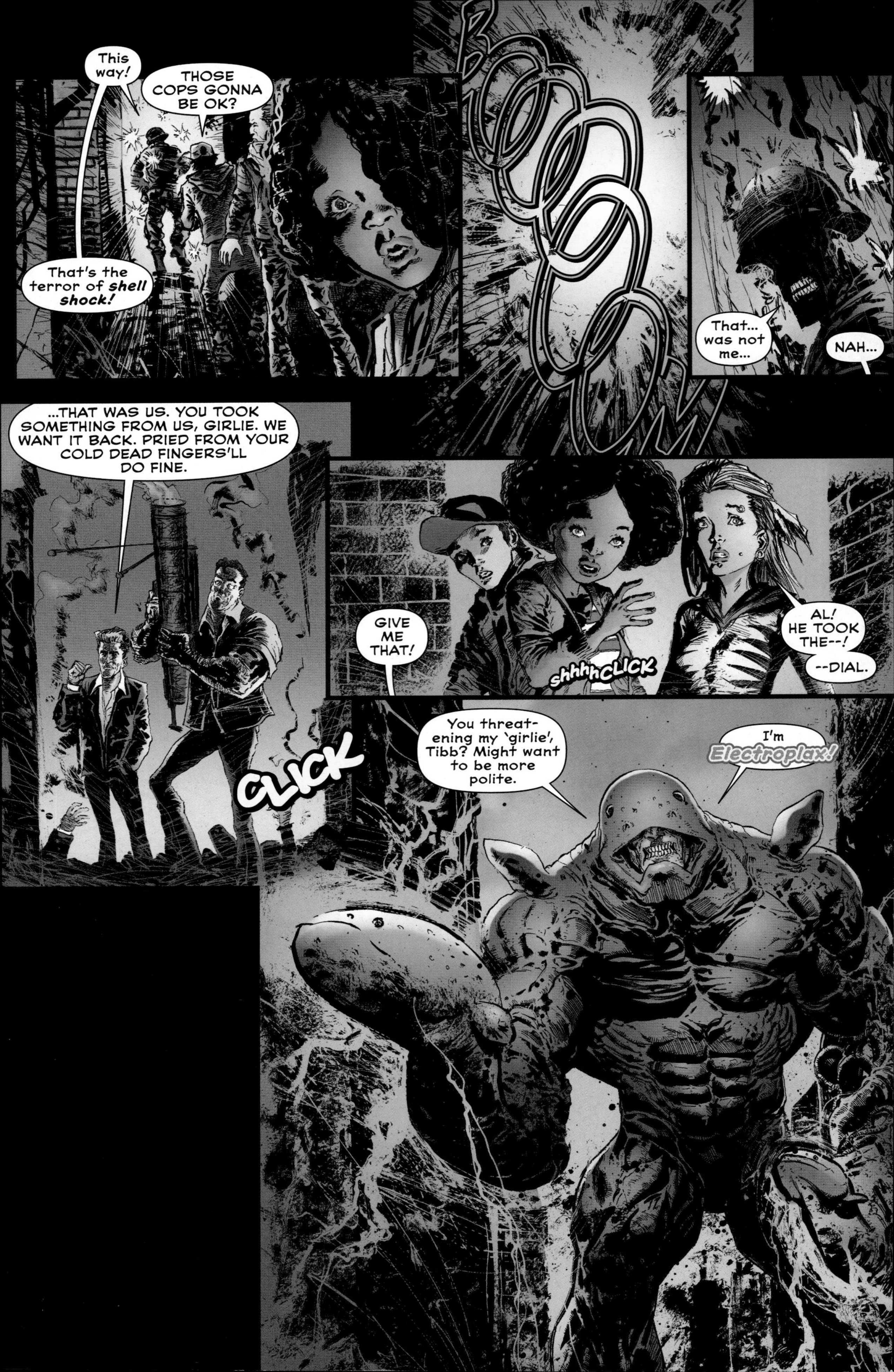

This way!
THOSE COPS GONNA BE OK?
That's the terror of **shell shock!**
BOOOOOOOM
That... was not me...
NAH...
...THAT WAS US. YOU TOOK SOMETHING FROM US, GIRLIE. WE WANT IT BACK. PRIED FROM YOUR COLD DEAD FINGERS'LL DO FINE.
GIVE ME THAT!
shhhhCLICK
AL! HE TOOK THE--!
--DIAL.
CLICK
You threat-ening my 'girlie', Tibb? Might want to be more polite.
I'm Electroplax!

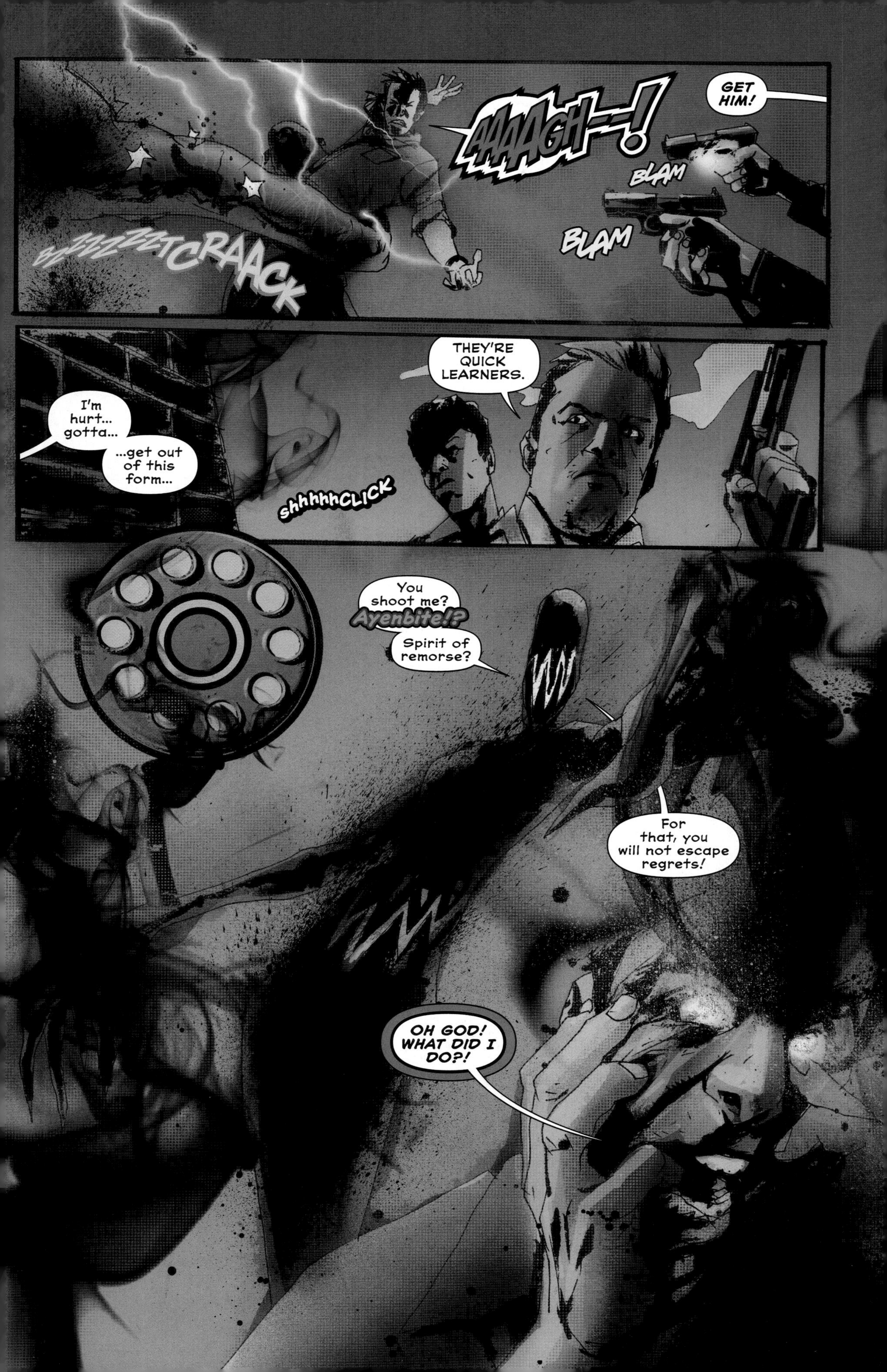
AAAAGH--!
GET HIM!
BLAM
BLAM
BZZZZZZTCRAACK
I'm hurt... gotta...
...get out of this form...
THEY'RE QUICK LEARNERS.
shhhhhCLICK
You shoot me?
Ayenbite!?
Spirit of remorse?
For that, you will not escape regrets!
OH GOD! WHAT DID I DO?!

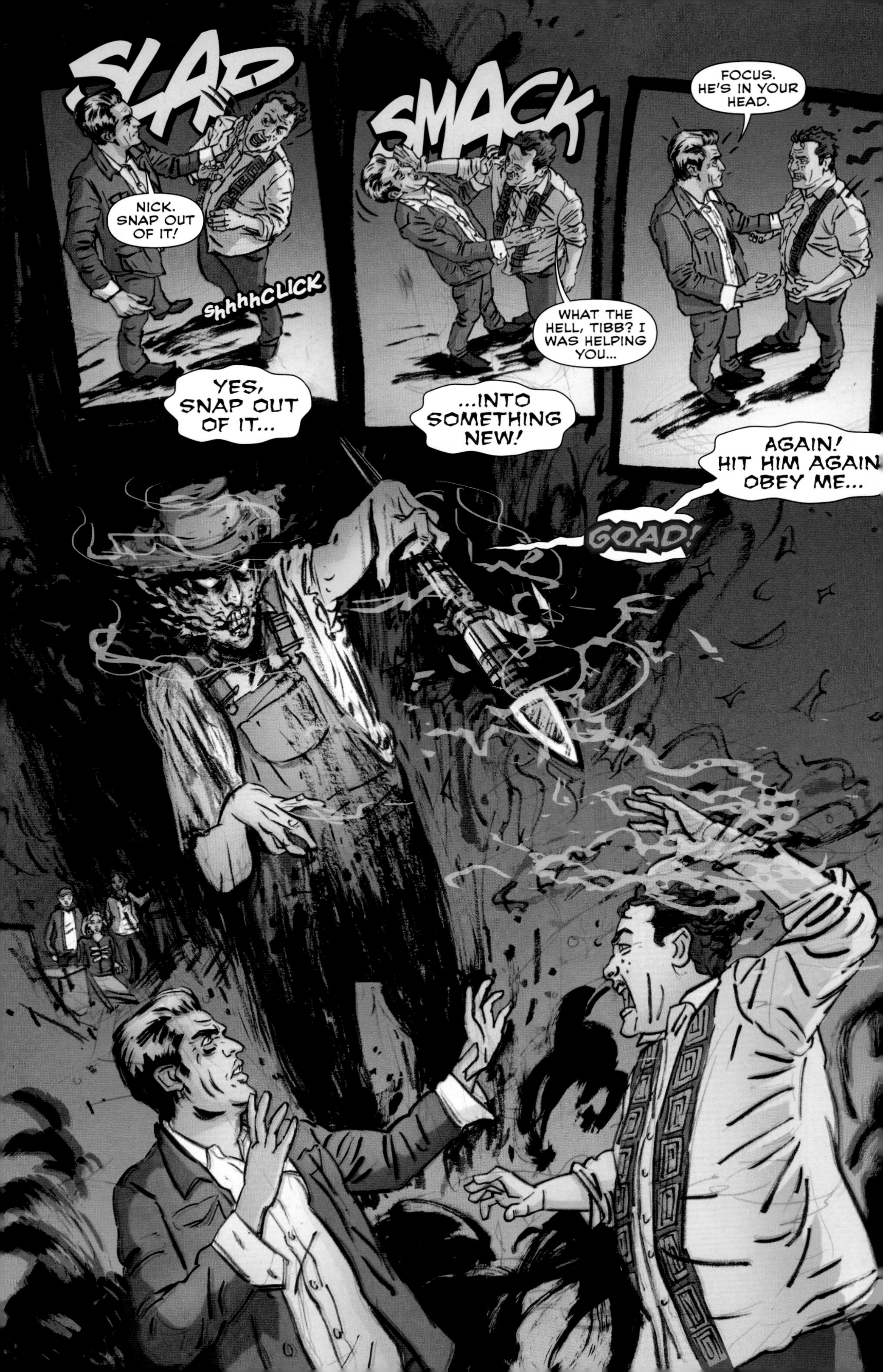
SLAP
NICK. SNAP OUT OF IT!
ShhhhCLICK
YES, SNAP OUT OF IT...
SMACK
WHAT THE HELL, TIBB? I WAS HELPING YOU...
...INTO SOMETHING NEW!
FOCUS. HE'S IN YOUR HEAD.
AGAIN! HIT HIM AGAIN OBEY ME...
GOAD!

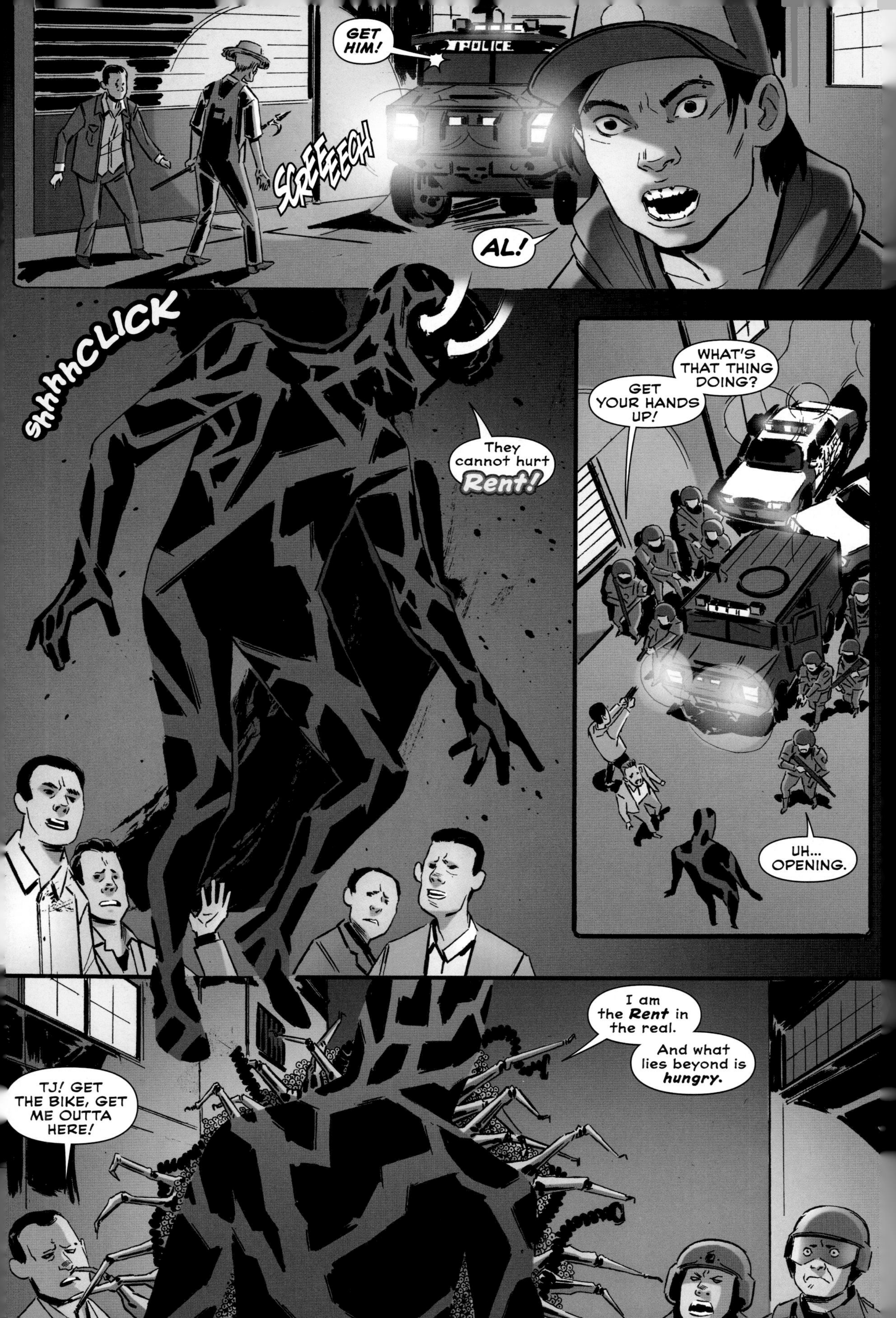
GET HIM!
SCREEEEECH
AL!
shhhhCLICK
They cannot hurt Rent!
WHAT'S THAT THING DOING?
GET YOUR HANDS UP!
UH... OPENING.
I am the Rent in the real.
And what lies beyond is hungry.
TJ! GET THE BIKE, GET ME OUTTA HERE!

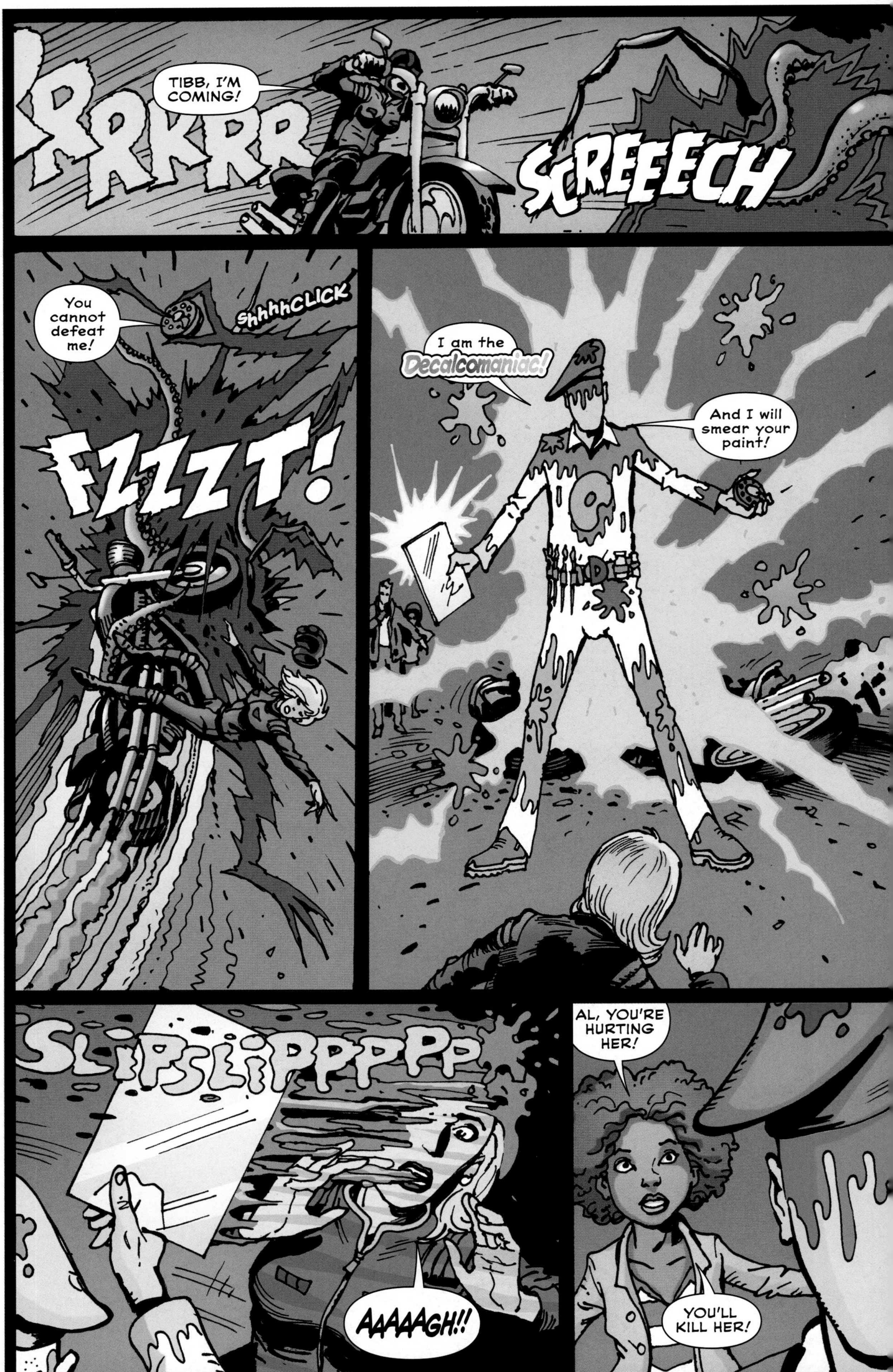
RRKRR
TIBB, I'M COMING!
SCREEECH
You cannot defeat me!
ShhhhCLICK
FZZZT!
I am the Decalcomaniac!
And I will smear your paint!
SLIPSLIPPPPP
AAAAAGH!!
AL, YOU'RE HURTING HER!
YOU'LL KILL HER!

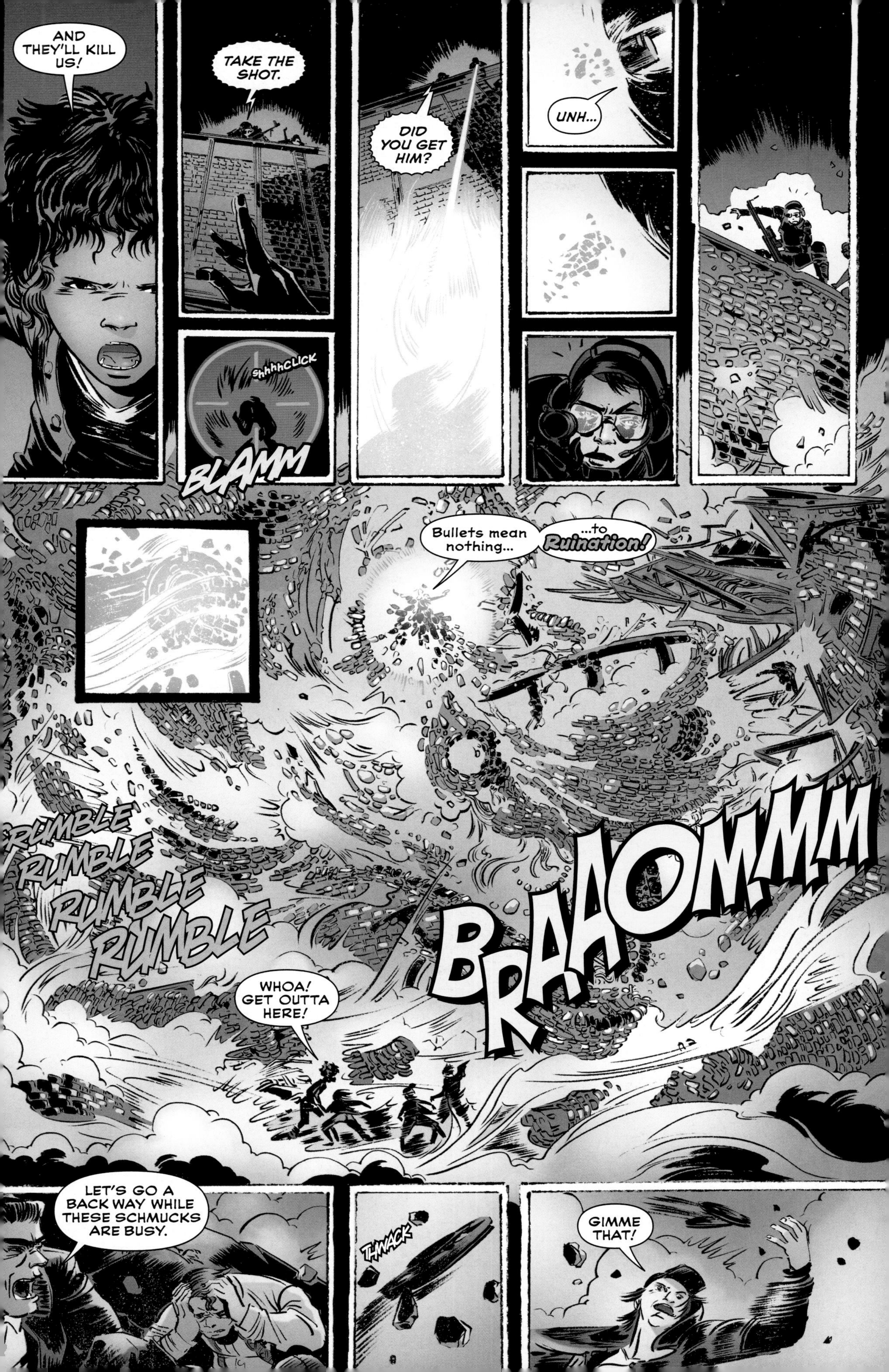
AND THEY'LL KILL US!
TAKE THE SHOT.
shhhhCLICK
BLAMM
DID YOU GET HIM?
UNH...
Bullets mean nothing...
...to Ruination!
RUMBLE RUMBLE RUMBLE RUMBLE
BRAAOMMM
WHOA! GET OUTTA HERE!
LET'S GO A BACK WAY WHILE THESE SCHMUCKS ARE BUSY.
THWACK
GIMME THAT!

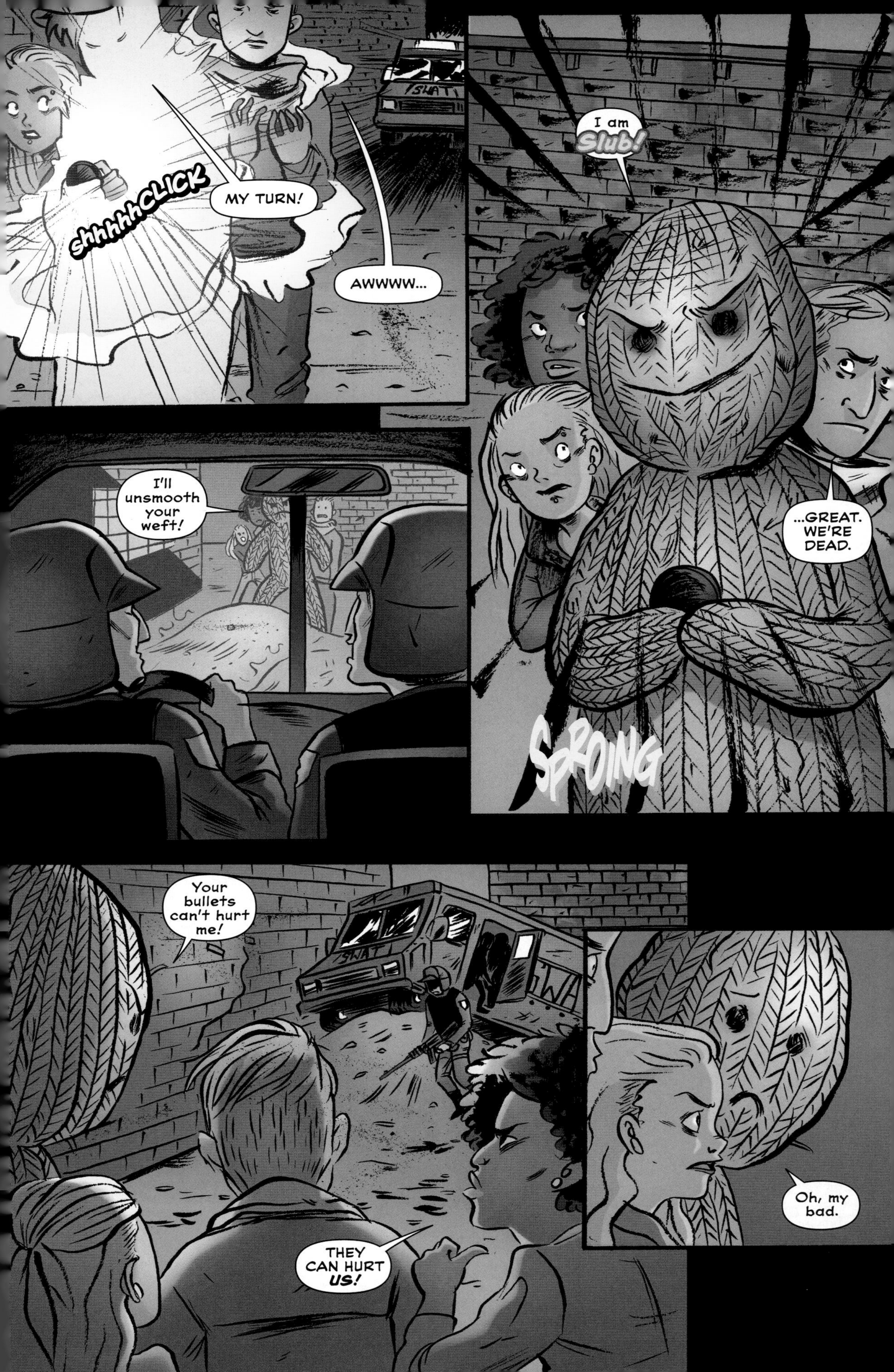
shhhhhCLICK
MY TURN!
AWWWW...
I am Slub!
...GREAT. WE'RE DEAD.
SPROING
I'll unsmooth your weft!
Your bullets can't hurt me!
THEY CAN HURT US!
Oh, my bad.

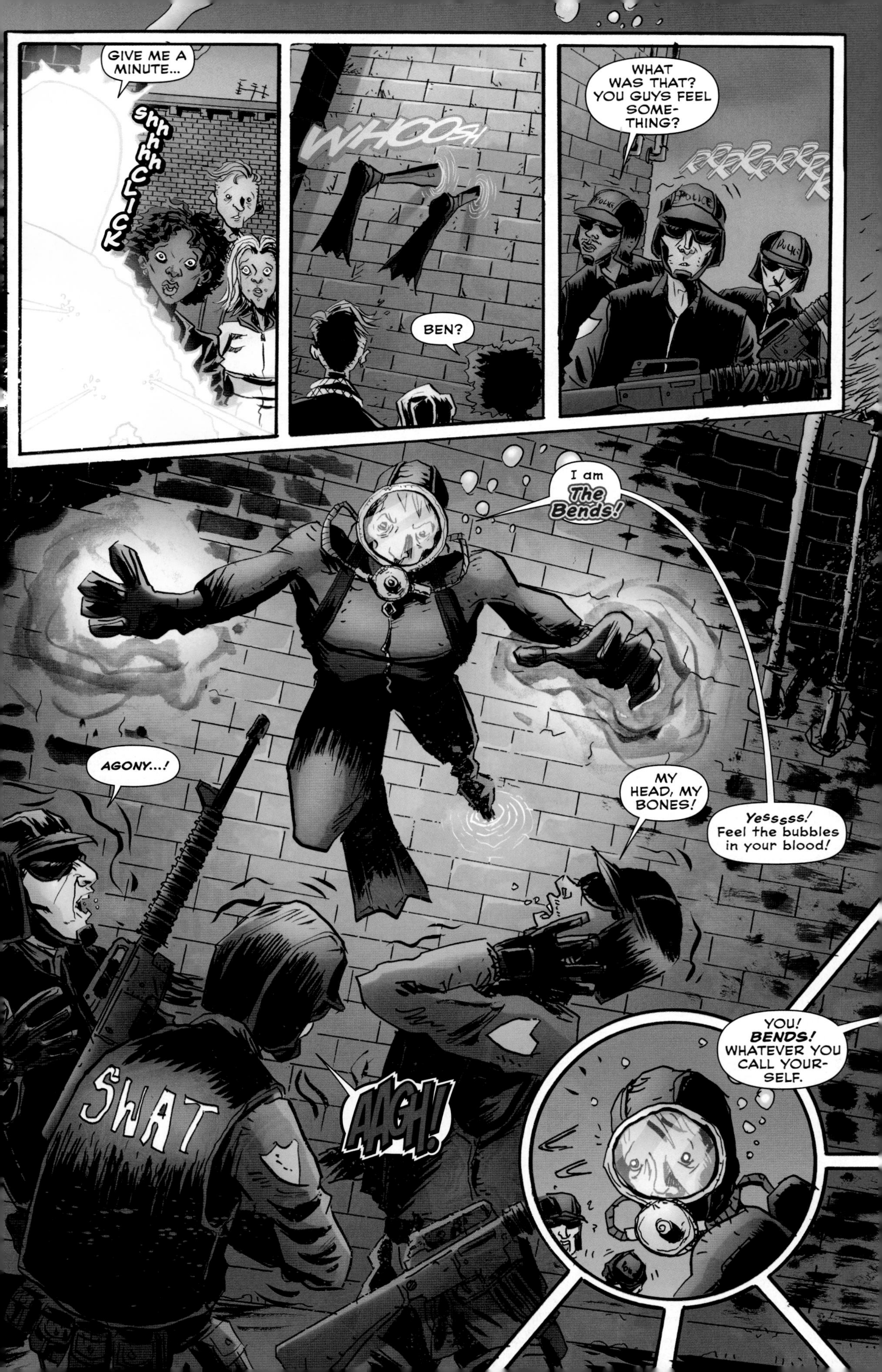
GIVE ME A MINUTE...
SHHHHCLICK
WHOOSH
BEN?
WHAT WAS THAT? YOU GUYS FEEL SOME-THING?
RRRRRRRRR
I am The Bends!
AGONY...!
MY HEAD, MY BONES!
Yessssss! Feel the bubbles in your blood!
SWAT
AAGH!
YOU! BENDS! WHATEVER YOU CALL YOUR-SELF.

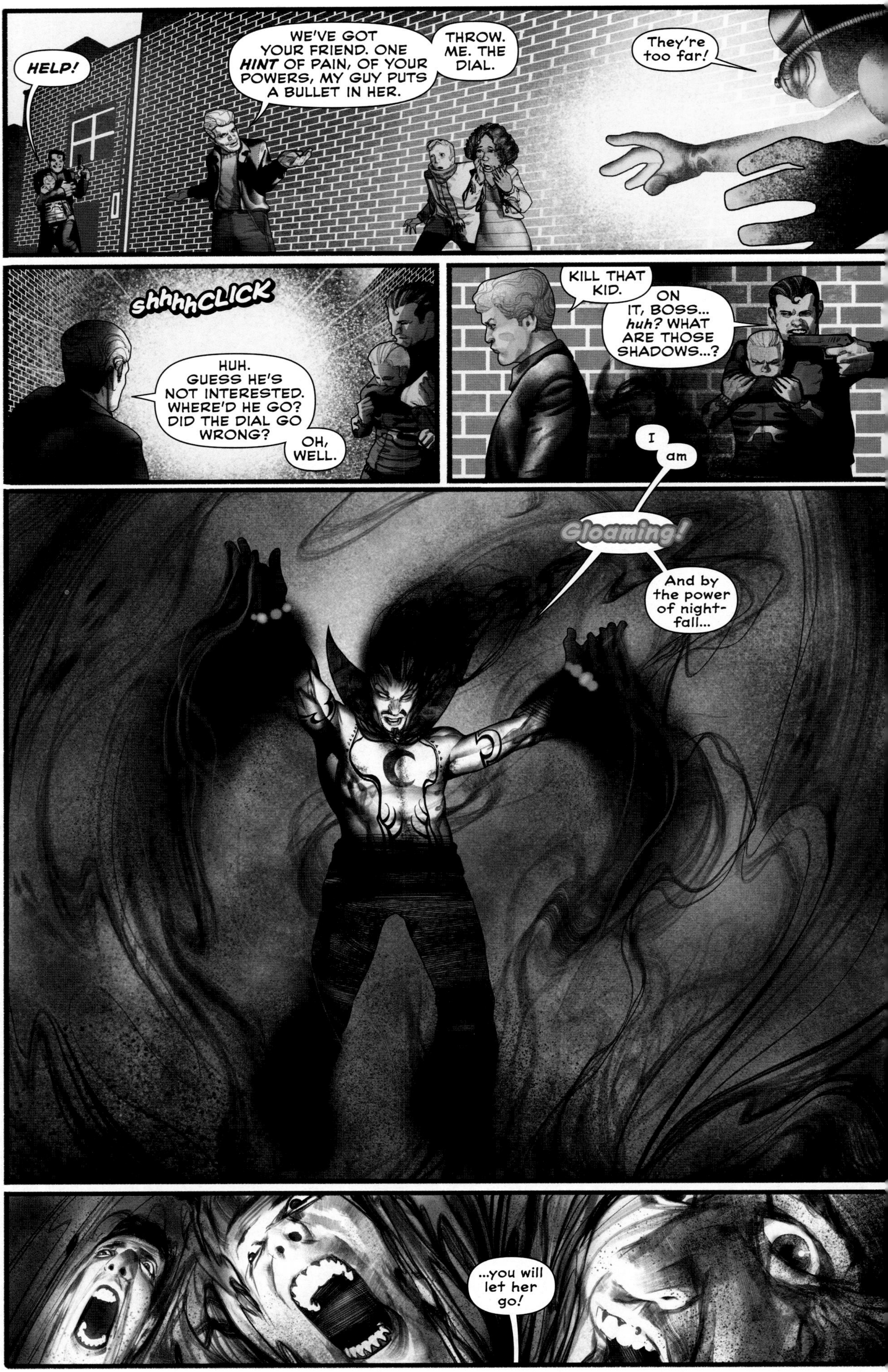

HELP!
WE'VE GOT YOUR FRIEND. ONE HINT OF PAIN, OF YOUR POWERS, MY GUY PUTS A BULLET IN HER.
THROW. ME. THE DIAL.
They're too far!
shhhhCLICK
HUH. GUESS HE'S NOT INTERESTED. WHERE'D HE GO? DID THE DIAL GO WRONG?
OH, WELL.
KILL THAT KID.
ON IT, BOSS... huh? WHAT ARE THOSE SHADOWS...?
I am
Gloaming!
And by the power of night-fall...
...you will let her go!

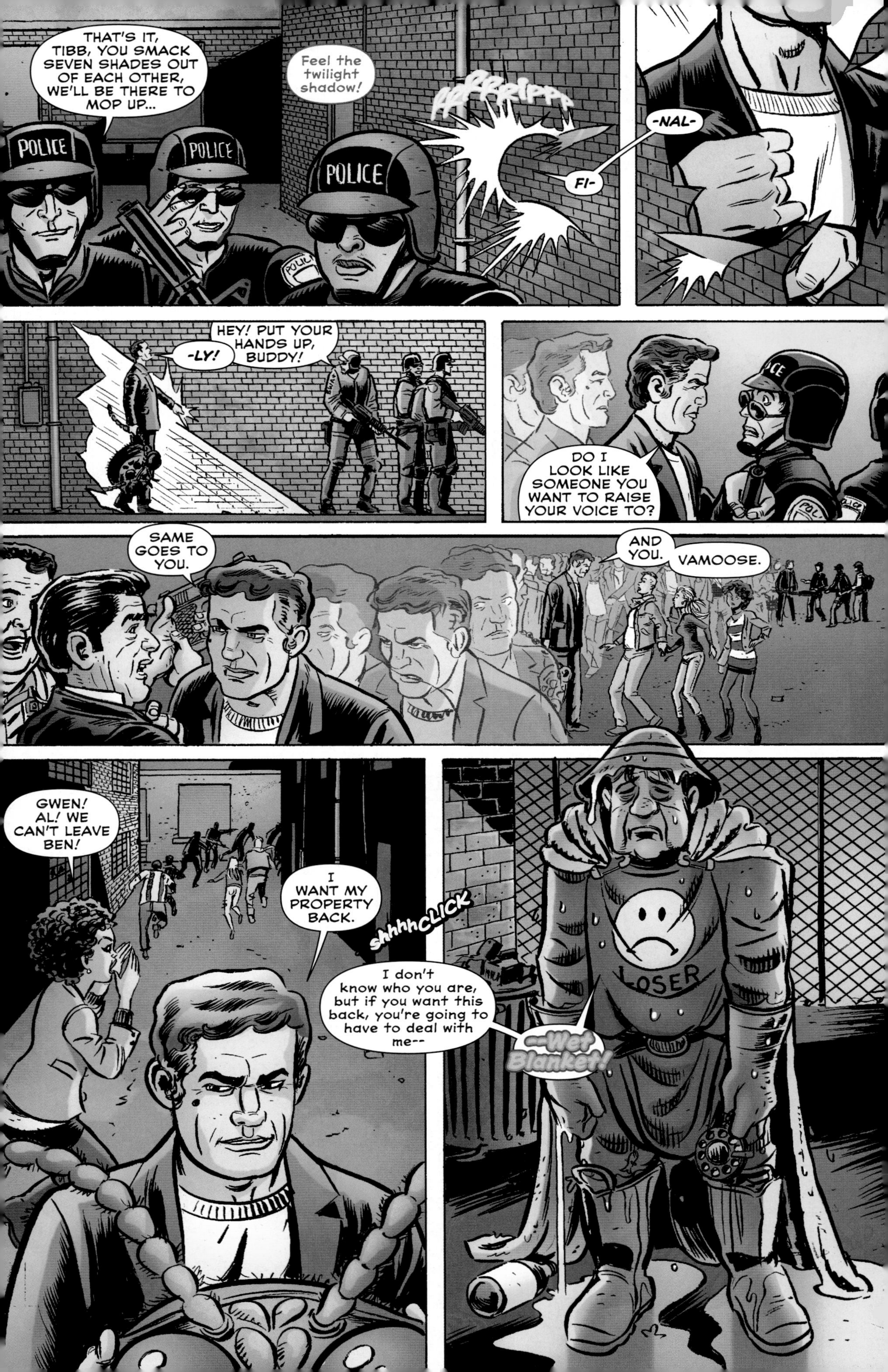
THAT'S IT, TIBB, YOU SMACK SEVEN SHADES OUT OF EACH OTHER, WE'LL BE THERE TO MOP UP...
POLICE
POLICE
Feel the twilight shadow!
POLICE
RRRRRIPPP
FI-
-NAL-
-LY!
HEY! PUT YOUR HANDS UP, BUDDY!
DO I LOOK LIKE SOMEONE YOU WANT TO RAISE YOUR VOICE TO?
SAME GOES TO YOU.
AND YOU.
VAMOOSE.
GWEN! AL! WE CAN'T LEAVE BEN!
I WANT MY PROPERTY BACK.
shhhhCLICK
I don't know who you are, but if you want this back, you're going to have to deal with me--
--Wet Blanket!
LOSER

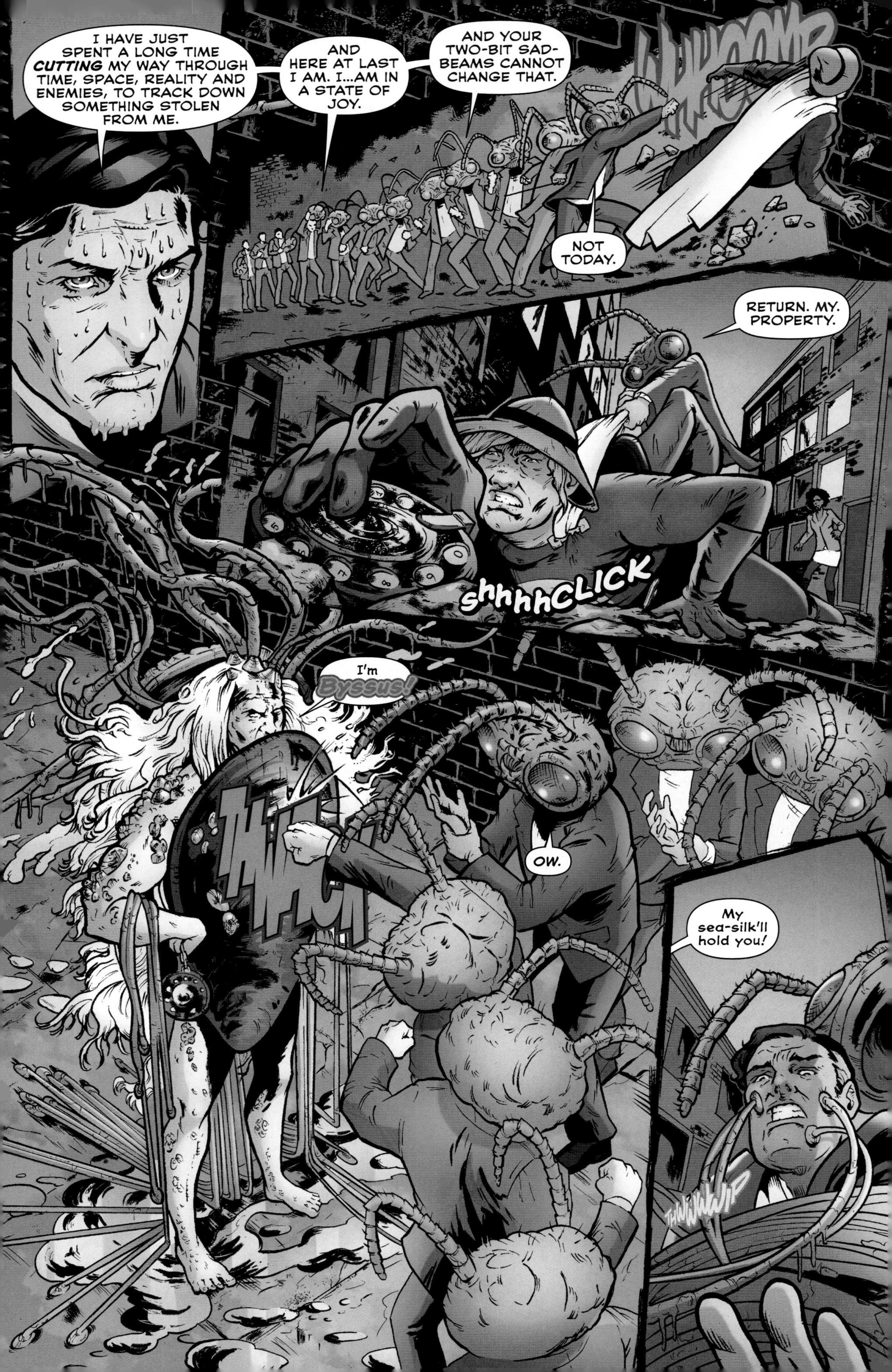
I HAVE JUST SPENT A LONG TIME *CUTTING* MY WAY THROUGH TIME, SPACE, REALITY AND ENEMIES, TO TRACK DOWN SOMETHING STOLEN FROM ME.
AND HERE AT LAST I AM. I...AM IN A STATE OF JOY.
AND YOUR TWO-BIT SAD-BEAMS CANNOT CHANGE THAT.
WHOOMP
NOT TODAY.
RETURN. MY. PROPERTY.
shhhhCLICK
I'm Byssus!
OW.
My sea-silk'll hold you!
THWWWWIP

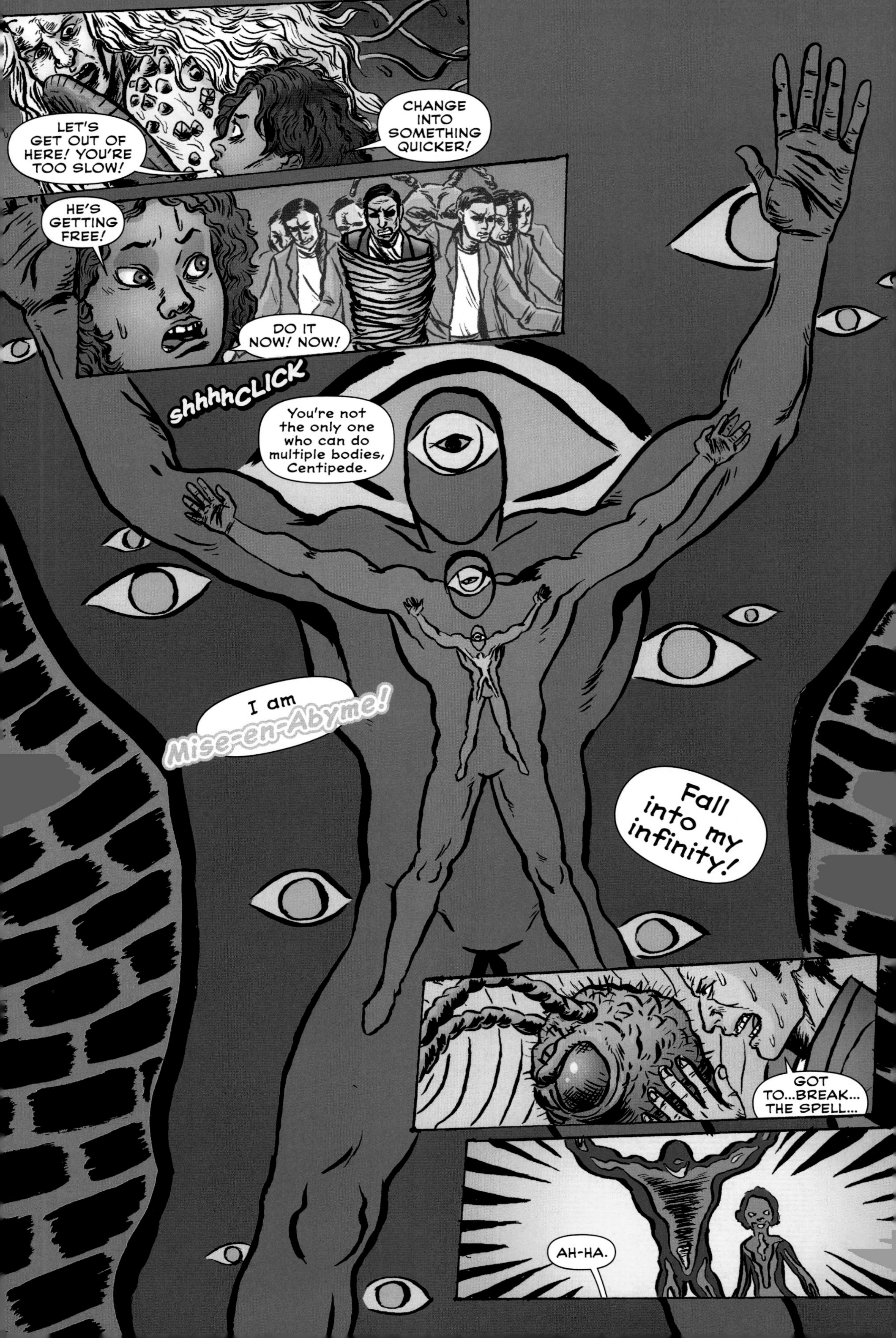
LET'S GET OUT OF HERE! YOU'RE TOO SLOW!
CHANGE INTO SOMETHING QUICKER!
HE'S GETTING FREE!
DO IT NOW! NOW!
shhhhCLICK
You're not the only one who can do multiple bodies, Centipede.
I am Mise-en-Abyme!
Fall into my infinity!
GOT TO...BREAK... THE SPELL...
AH-HA.

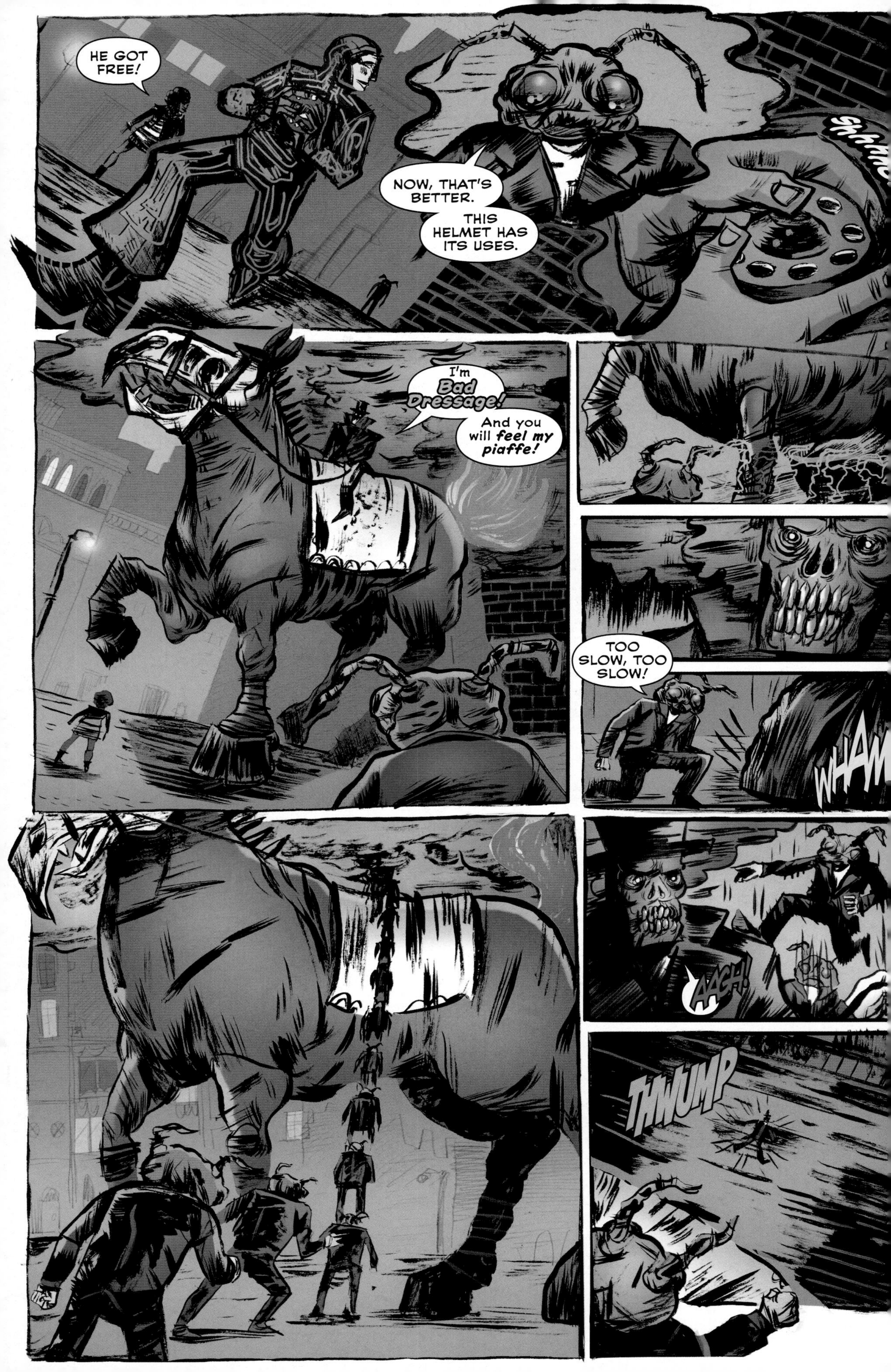
HE GOT FREE!
NOW, THAT'S BETTER.
THIS HELMET HAS ITS USES.
I'm Bad Dressage!
And you will feel my piaffe!
TOO SLOW, TOO SLOW!
WHAM
AACH!
THWUMP

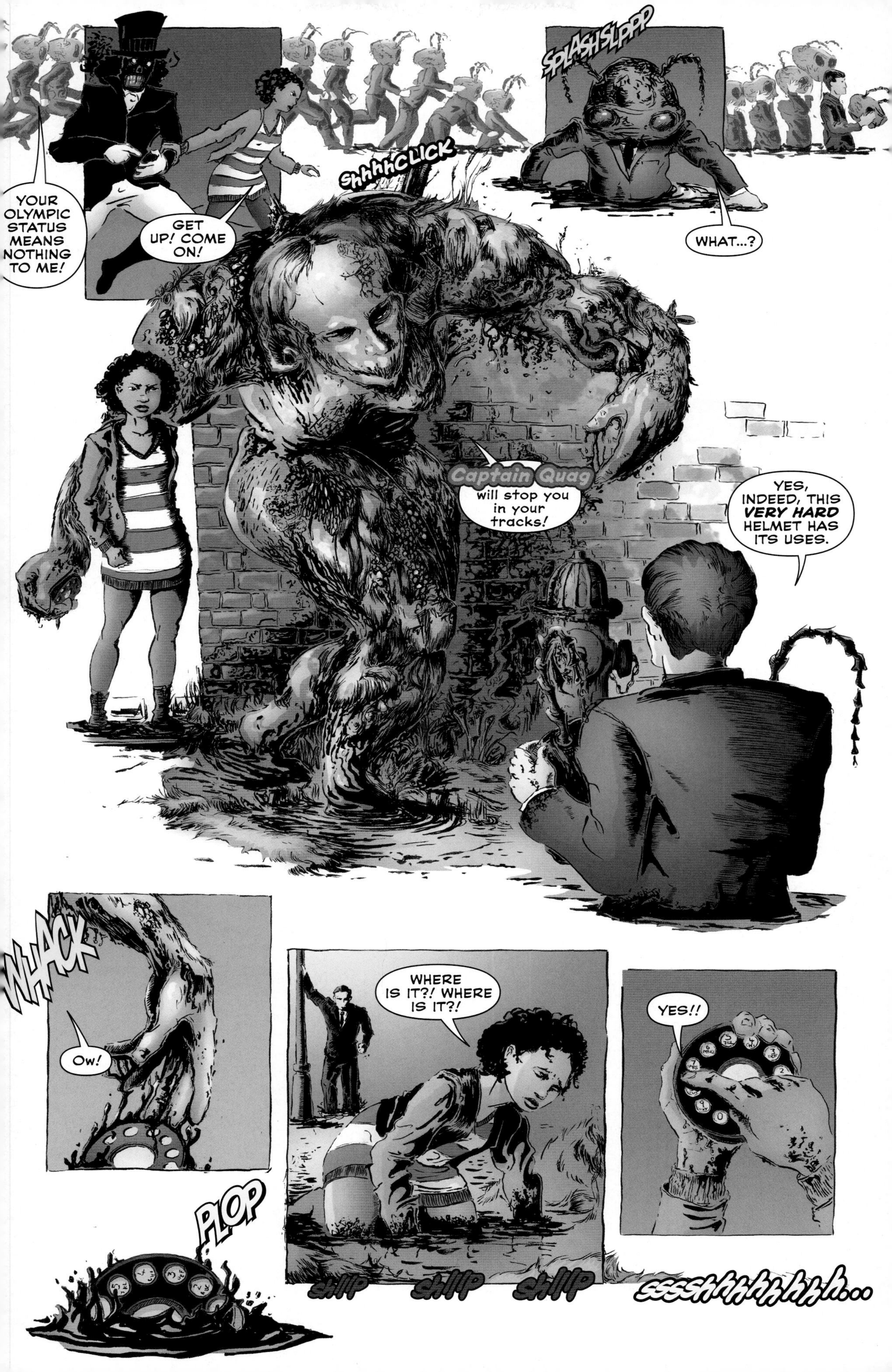
YOUR OLYMPIC STATUS MEANS NOTHING TO ME!
GET UP! COME ON!
SHHHHCLICK
SPLASHSLPPP
WHAT...?
Captain Quag will stop you in your tracks!
YES, INDEED, THIS VERY HARD HELMET HAS ITS USES.
WHACK
Ow!
PLOP
WHERE IS IT?! WHERE IS IT?!
SHLLP SHLLP SHLLP
YES!!
SSSSHHHHHHHH..

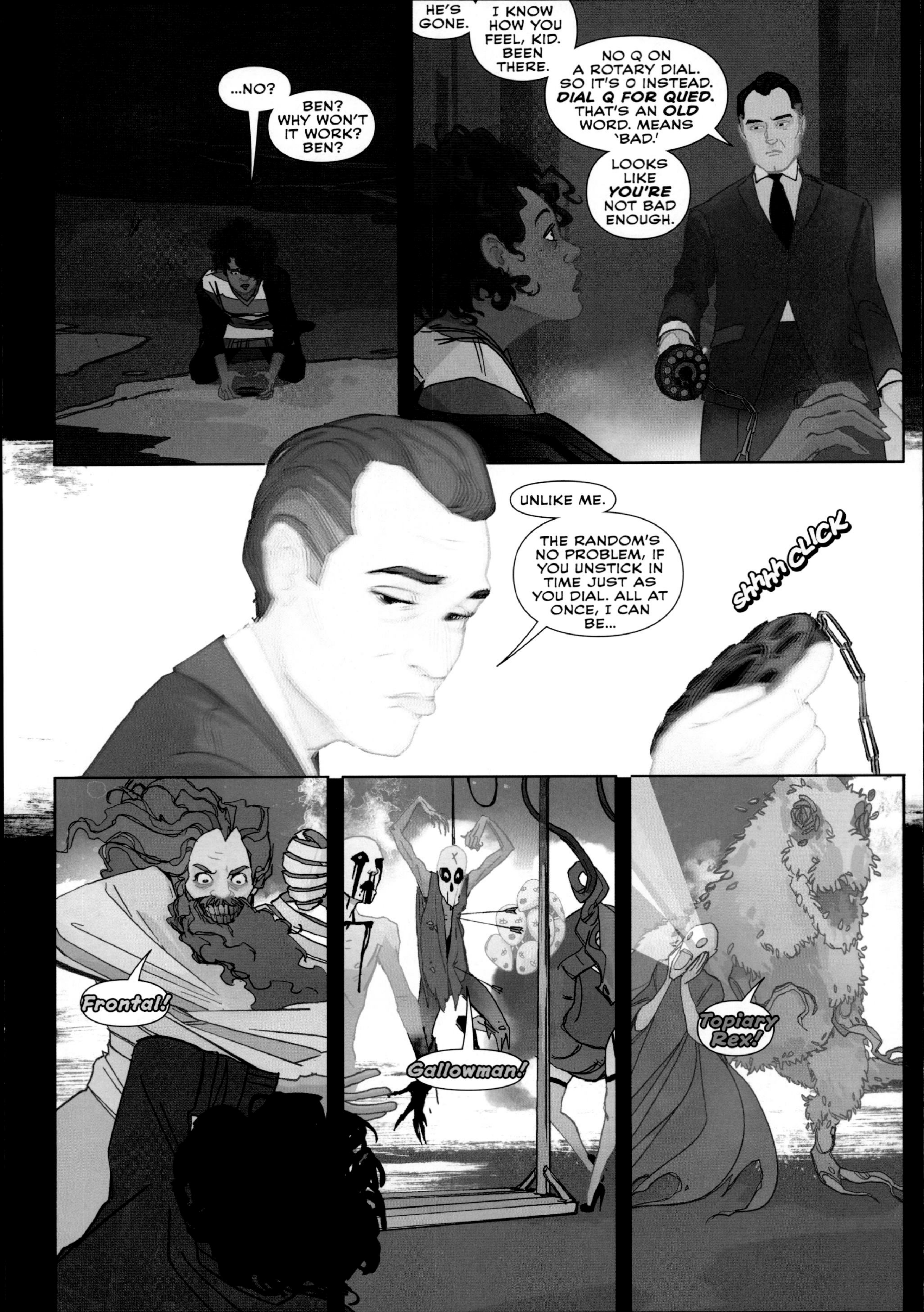
...NO?
BEN? WHY WON'T IT WORK? BEN?
HE'S GONE.
I KNOW HOW YOU FEEL, KID. BEEN THERE.
NO Q ON A ROTARY DIAL. SO IT'S 0 INSTEAD. **DIAL Q FOR QUED.** THAT'S AN **OLD** WORD. MEANS 'BAD.'
LOOKS LIKE **YOU'RE** NOT BAD ENOUGH.
UNLIKE ME.
THE RANDOM'S NO PROBLEM, IF YOU UNSTICK IN TIME JUST AS YOU DIAL. ALL AT ONCE, I CAN BE...
shhhh CLICK
Frontal!
Gallowman!
Topiary Rex!

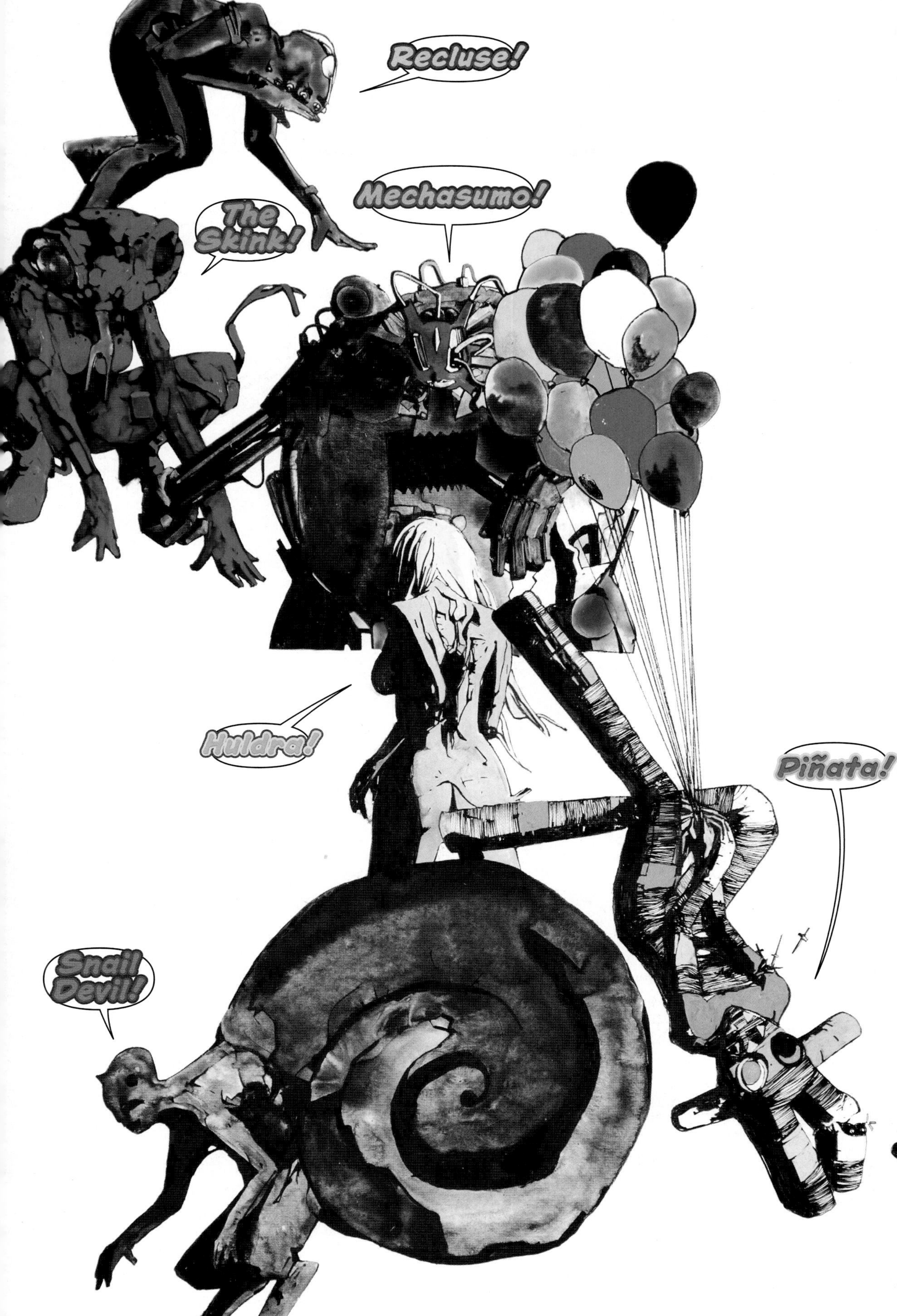
Recluse!
Mechasumo!
The Skink!
Huldra!
Piñata!
Snail Devil!

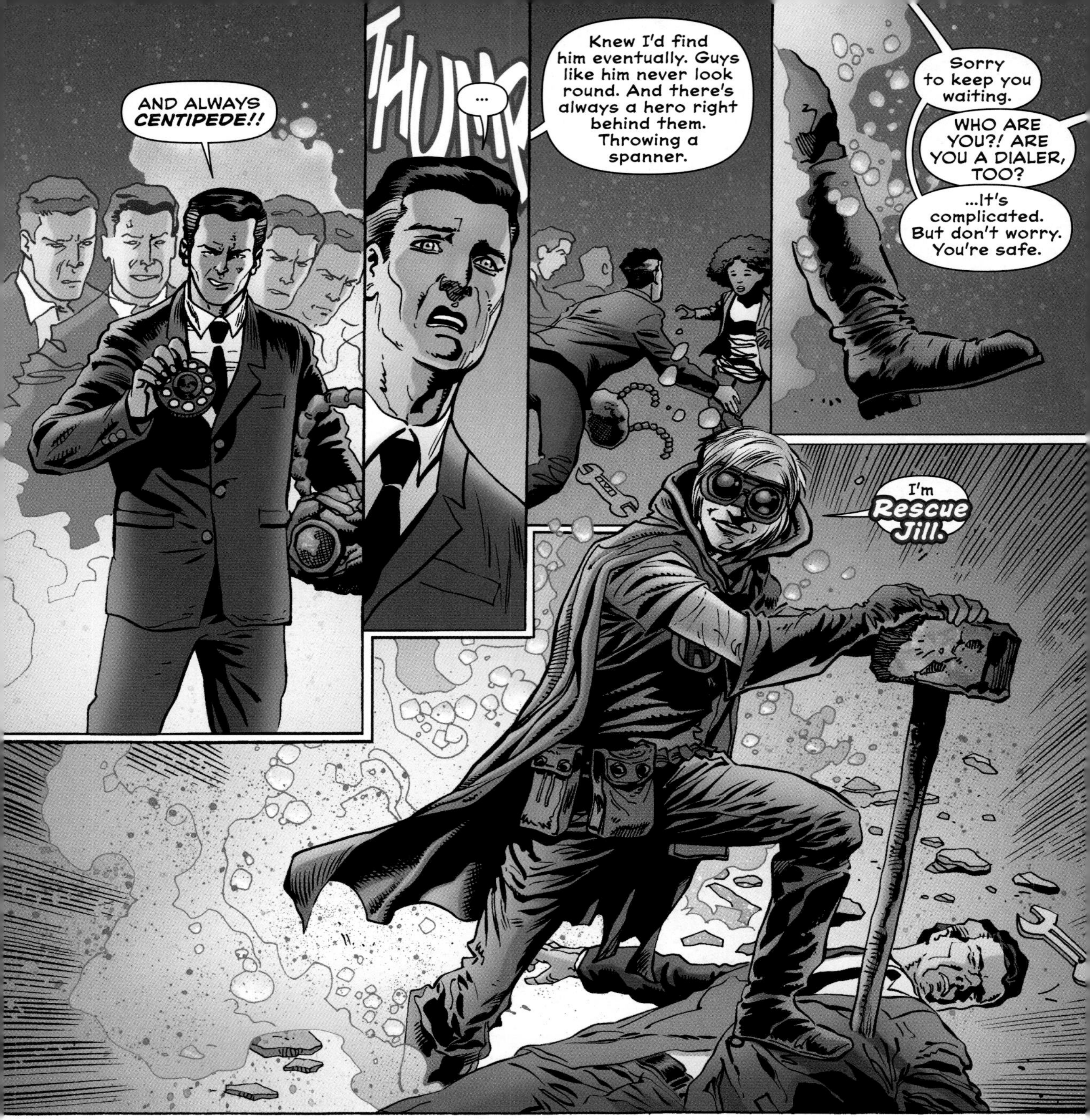

AND ALWAYS CENTIPEDE!!
THUMP
...
Knew I'd find him eventually. Guys like him never look round. And there's always a hero right behind them. Throwing a spanner.
Sorry to keep you waiting.
WHO ARE YOU?! ARE YOU A DIALER, TOO?
...It's complicated. But don't worry. You're safe.
I'm Rescue Jill.

DIAL Q FOR QUED

WRITTEN BY CHINA MIÉVILLE

ART BY

PAGE 1 - MATEUS SANTOLOUCO PAGE 2 - CARLA BERROCAL PAGE 3 - RICCARDO BURCHIELLI PAGE 4 - LIAM SHARP
PAGE 5 - JOCK PAGE 6 - TULA LOTAY PAGE 7 - MARLEY ZARCONE PAGE 8 - BRENDAN MCCARTHY PAGE 9 - EMMA RIOS
PAGE 10 - EMI LENOX PAGE 11 - JEFF LEMIRE PAGE 12 - FRAZER IRVING PAGE 13 - DAVID LAPHAM PAGE 14 - CARMEN CARNERO
PAGE 15 - SLOANE LEONG PAGE 16 - KELSEY WROTEN PAGE 17 - MICHELLE FARRAN PAGE 18 - ANNIE WU
PAGE 19 - ZAK SMITH PAGE 20 - ALBERTO PONTICELLI AND DAN GREEN

COLORS BY
EVA DE LA CRUZ w/
FRAZER IRVING (PAGE 12)
ANNIE WU (PAGE 18)
& ZAK SMITH (PAGE 19)

LETTERING BY
TAYLOR ESPOSITO

DIAL H
AFTERWORD BY CHINA MIÉVILLE

I wasn't very good at canon. Oh, I got better as I got older, but as a kid, I pieced together my comics knowledge like a mudlark, scobbing together whatever titles I could find in local shops and libraries — new copies, second-hand ones, beaten-up and ripped-to-shreds remnants — without any understanding of publisher or continuity. I'd cross-fertilize them with the various exciting bits and pieces I'd picked up, all the rumors and half-truths regarding superheroes.

This led to an idiosyncratic version of the DCU. Once, many years ago, as a very young child, I was delighted to discover a pile of comics in an attic. They featured a blond, orange-shirted superhero who could speak to fish. "Ah," I thought, settling down to read. "This must be this 'Superman' of whom I've heard so much." I was intrigued that so many of his adventures were maritime.

As the years passed, I got a bit more systematic, but I never lost the excitement at the sheer chaotic variety of costumes, monikers and powers I might find fighting for justice, every time I opened a comic. It was always a surprise. This addiction to the proliferation of the superheroic is something many of us never grow out of.

In fact, inventing superheroes is one of the basic games of childhood. Tie a towel around your neck and come up with a power set, all the abilities you think you'll need. Justify that hot mess as coherent by some ingenious, tendentious argument. Finally, give your wonder a name. (Electrical blast and tiger stripes? Electrotiger!) This is what we do. Like countless kids around the world, I was a martyr to superherogenesis.

And then, one early-eighties morning, I picked up, with my usual surrender to chance, a copy of what I now know to be NEW ADVENTURES OF SUPERBOY #30. Within which was a B-feature, a secondary story — something called "Dial H for Hero."

I pieced together the shtick of what it was I was reading. Some rather annoying boy called Chris King, had, because of some magic dial, been turned into "Mr. Opposite." In which guise, shameless in his purple-and-black outfit, he could make anything behave the opposite of how it should. Chris King had never had this epistemologically troubling power before, nor ever would again. He knew, though, the moment the ability arose in him, at utter random, what it was he could do and how. And he knew his superhero name.

That was how this worked.

After a while, I could breathe again. My heartbeat finally slowed. Thus began my devotion to the H-Dial.

***

Whatever the particularities of the H-Dial story — and it's appeared in titles since the 1960s — this basic norm, the surrender of the dialer to random powers, has remained the same. And no matter how much the storylines, particularly the original ones, played this for gags, for absurdities and thrills, for the simple joy of endless superpower invention, there were always a few troubling elements to the situation.

The DCU has long been a very crowded place. It brims with heroes. And pretty much all the obvious and useful powers have been taken. So if you have a title the very raison d'être of which is to come up with two, three, four or more new heroes every month, and you don't want to repeat yourself, there's a drive to more and more unlikely characters. Where does that leave you? Where does that leave the dialer? With the Human Starfish, is where. With the superbaby Mighty Moppet. With King Coil. A giant, animated, super-heroic coil. With coil powers. It was the '60s.

It's pretty standard these days to point out that putting on a mask, inventing a name and running around hitting people is a very odd thing to do. To put it charitably, it bespeaks identity issues. So what about when you don't even get to choose your superheroic identity? And it changes every day? And might reboot you as a starfish or a giant coil? What does that do to a crime-fighter?

And you think Batman needs therapy.

Perhaps most intriguing of all the questions the dial threw up was, "Where does it come from?" In a setting as baroque and as intimately explored as the DCU, it's almost beyond belief that this has never been answered. There've barely even been hints. It's unlikely that Dave Wood, who wrote the first scripts in HOUSE OF MYSTERY, wanted to do anything other than come up with a mechanism to invent endless heroes. But his brilliant success at this inexorably raised the question. What could possibly have led to the creation of this dial?

For a long time, DIAL H FOR HERO and its successors have been my comics obsessions. No other title, I've long explained to any of my poor friends who'll listen, combines childlike joy in superhero creation, a neo-surrealist faith in the aleatory, a post-Vertigo focus on the erosion of identity, and an opening into one of the few utter mysteries left in the history of the DCU.

Also King Coil.

For all these reasons, during the years when I would periodically chat with people from DC about the possibility of writing comics for them, after we had batted various ideas and titles around, I would conclude the conversation, every single time, increasingly plaintively, with "You should let me take on DIAL H."

I'd do my riff. I'd urge them to see that these areas needed to be investigated. I'd talk about fidelity to the inspired genius of the original idea, a respectful updating, humorous and goofy still, but serious, too, an investigation of lost and unstable souls. A realization of costs as well as benefits, of the terrible mechanisms at play. There could be, I would say, there had to be a slow creep of understanding, an origin story. Once there was an epic and epochal war. These dials came from somewhere, I'd say. I would whisper the phrase the Exchange. I would mutter about the lost Operator.

"You should let me take on DIAL H," I'd say. The DC people would smile politely. That would be that.

Until, very suddenly, they said yes.

DIAL H
CHARACTER DESIGNS BY MATEUS SANTOLOUCO

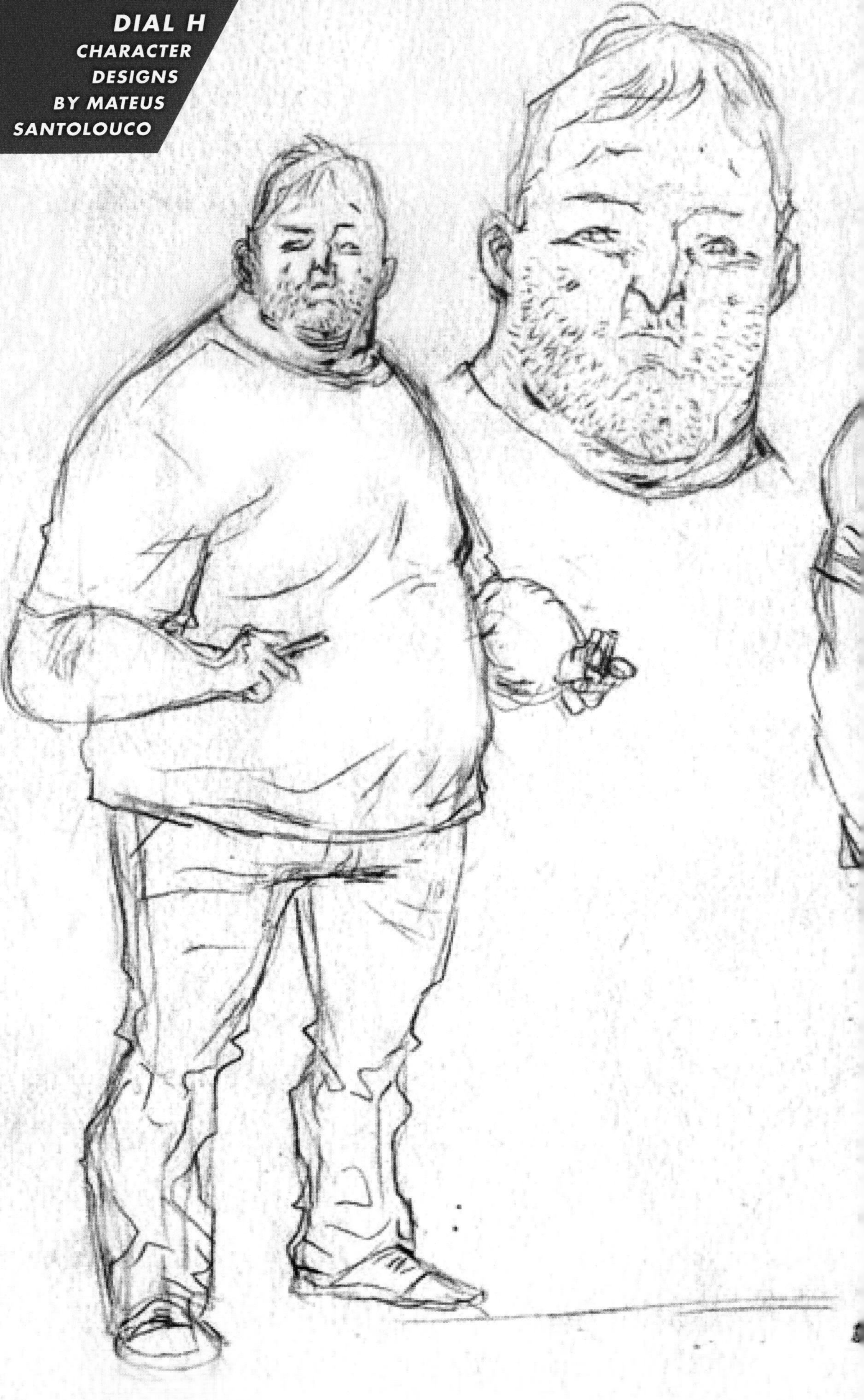

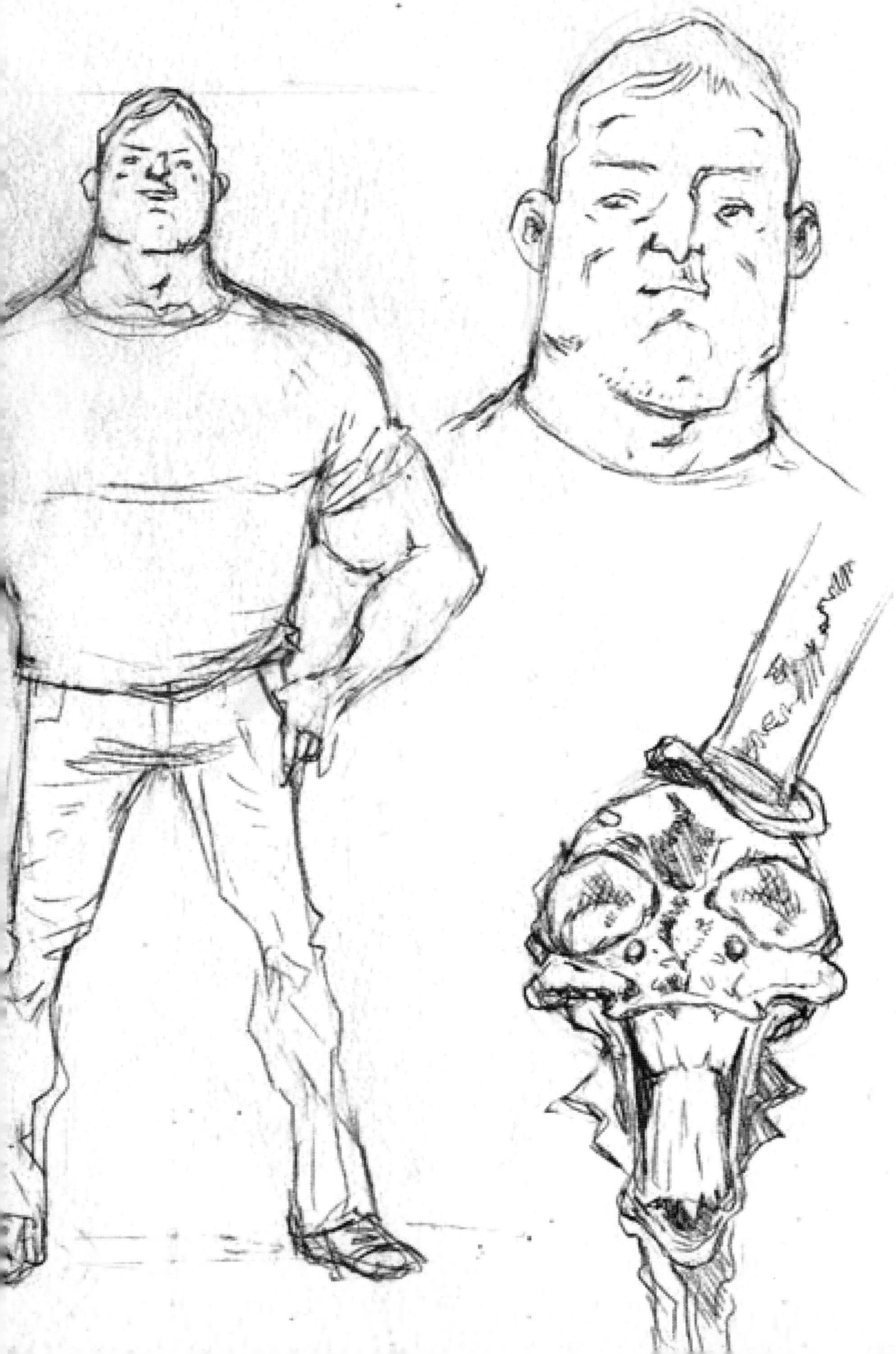

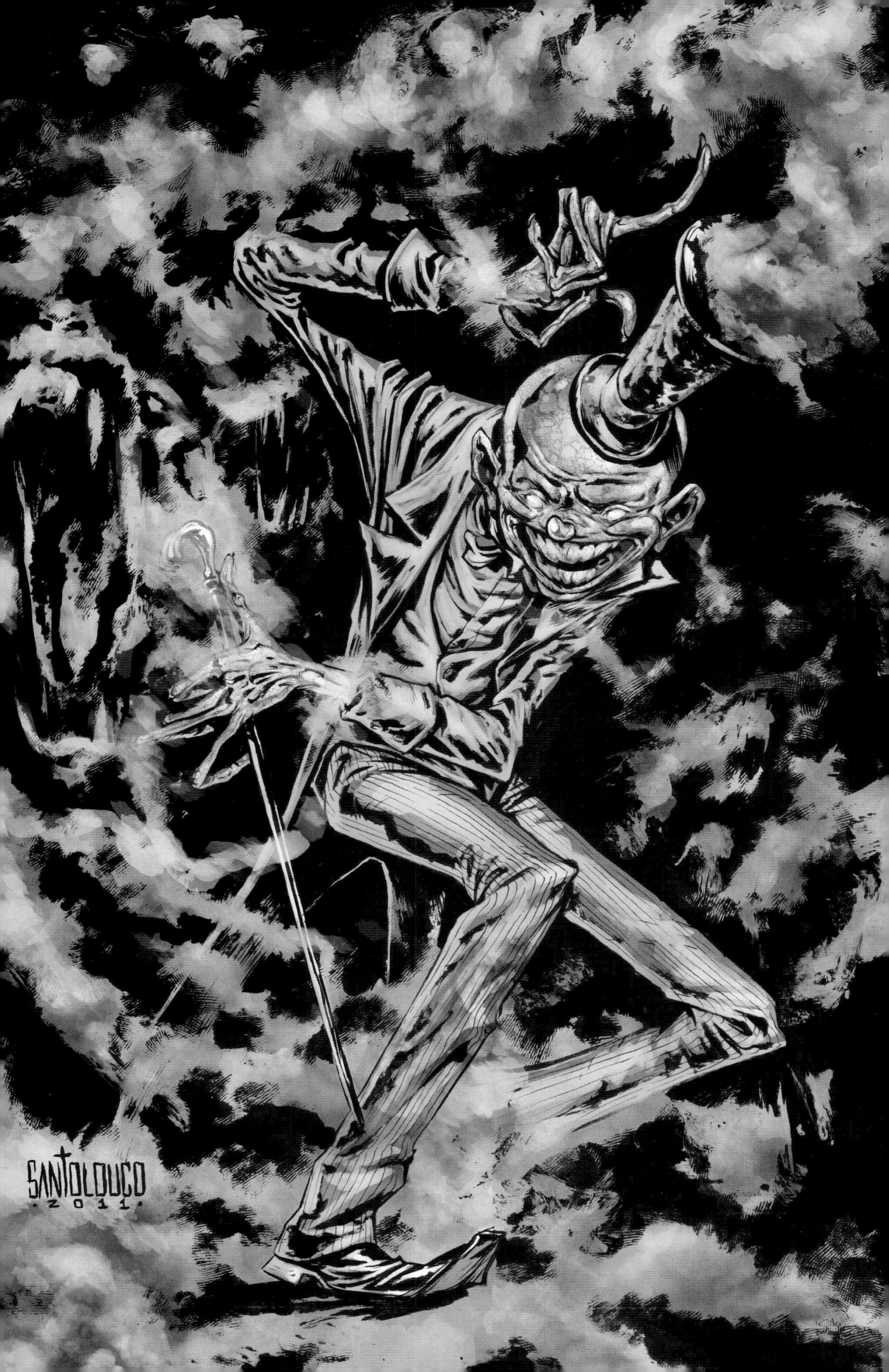
SANTOLOUCO
2011

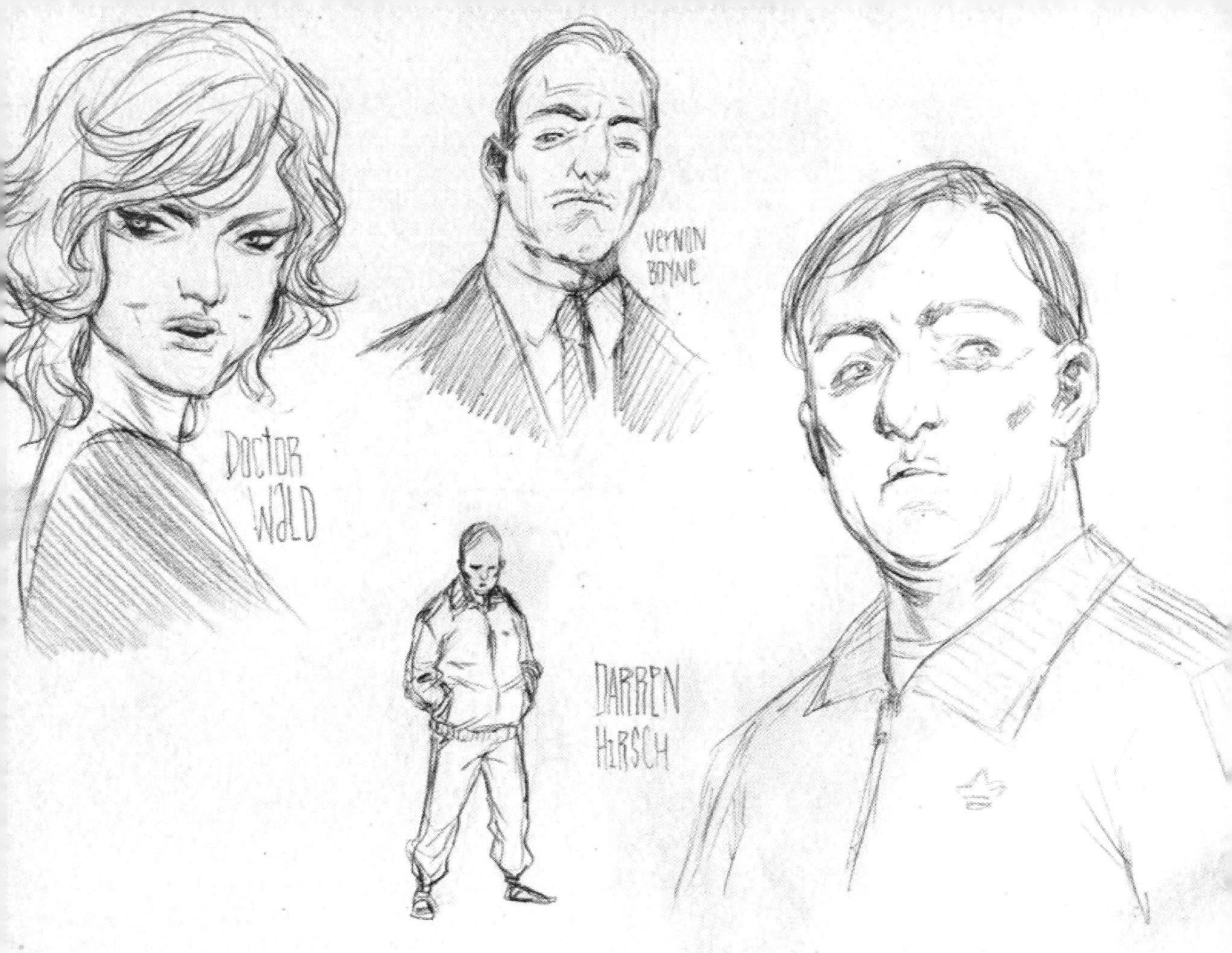
Doctor Wald
Vernon Boyne
Darren Hirsch

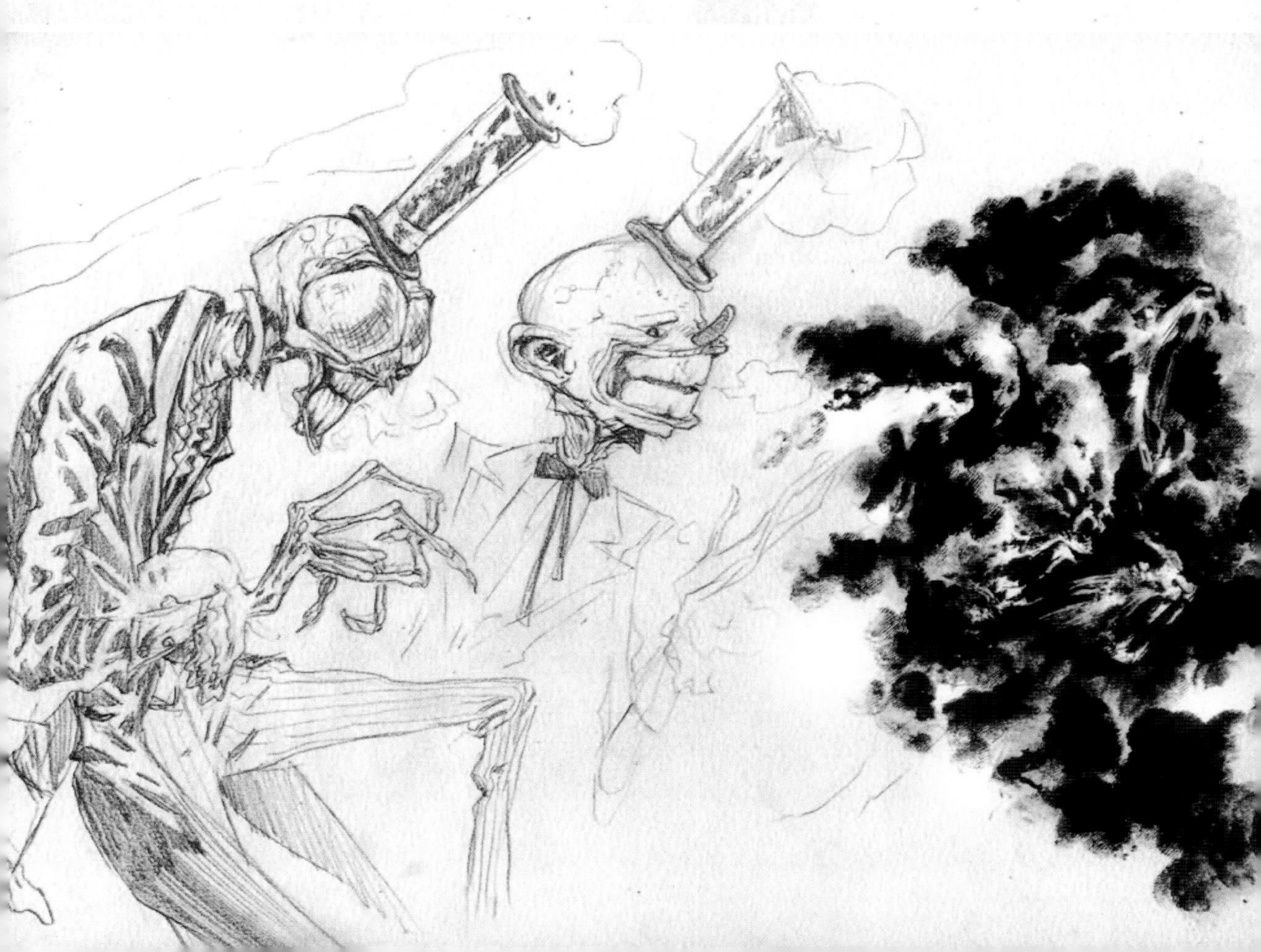

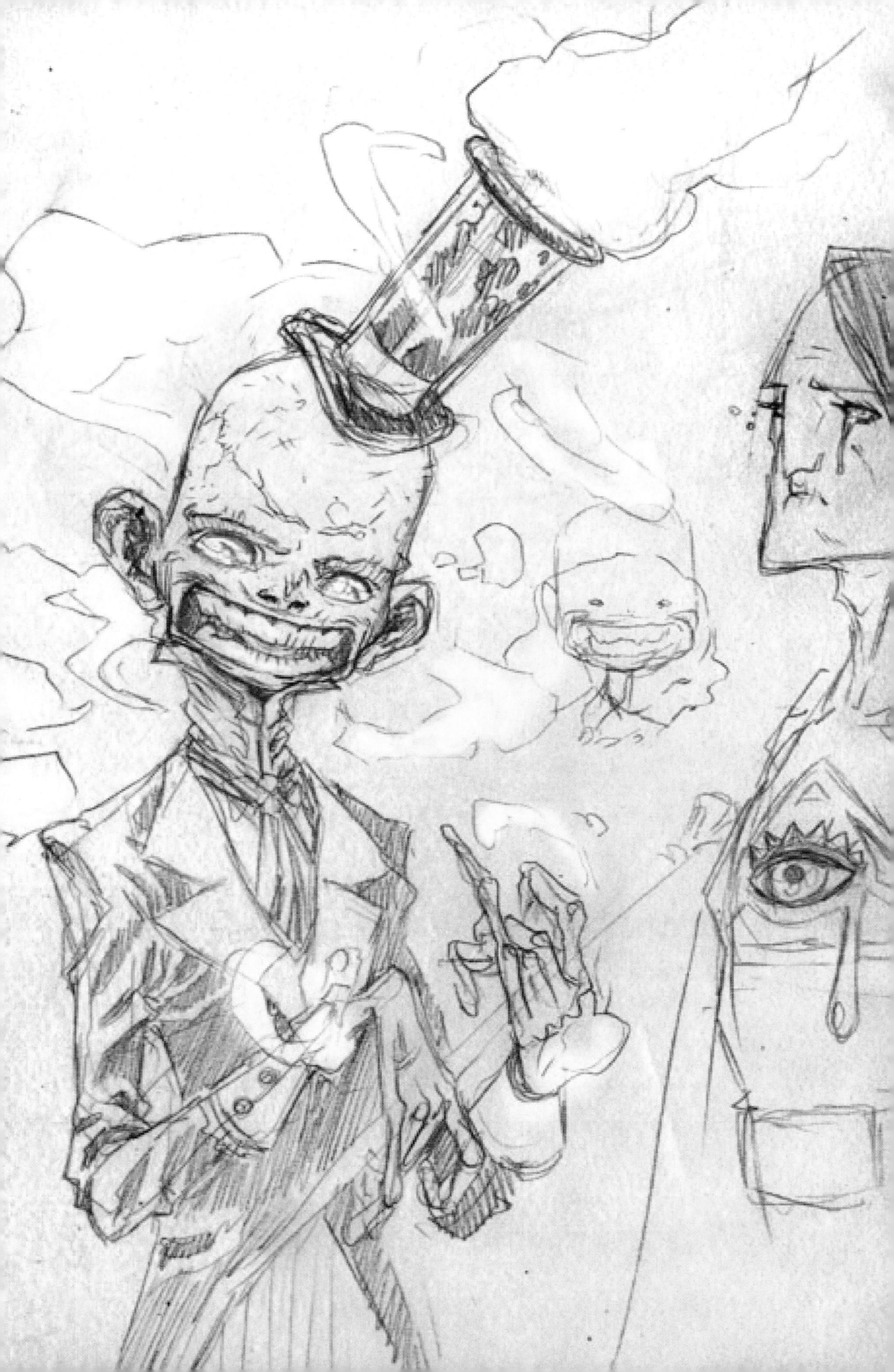

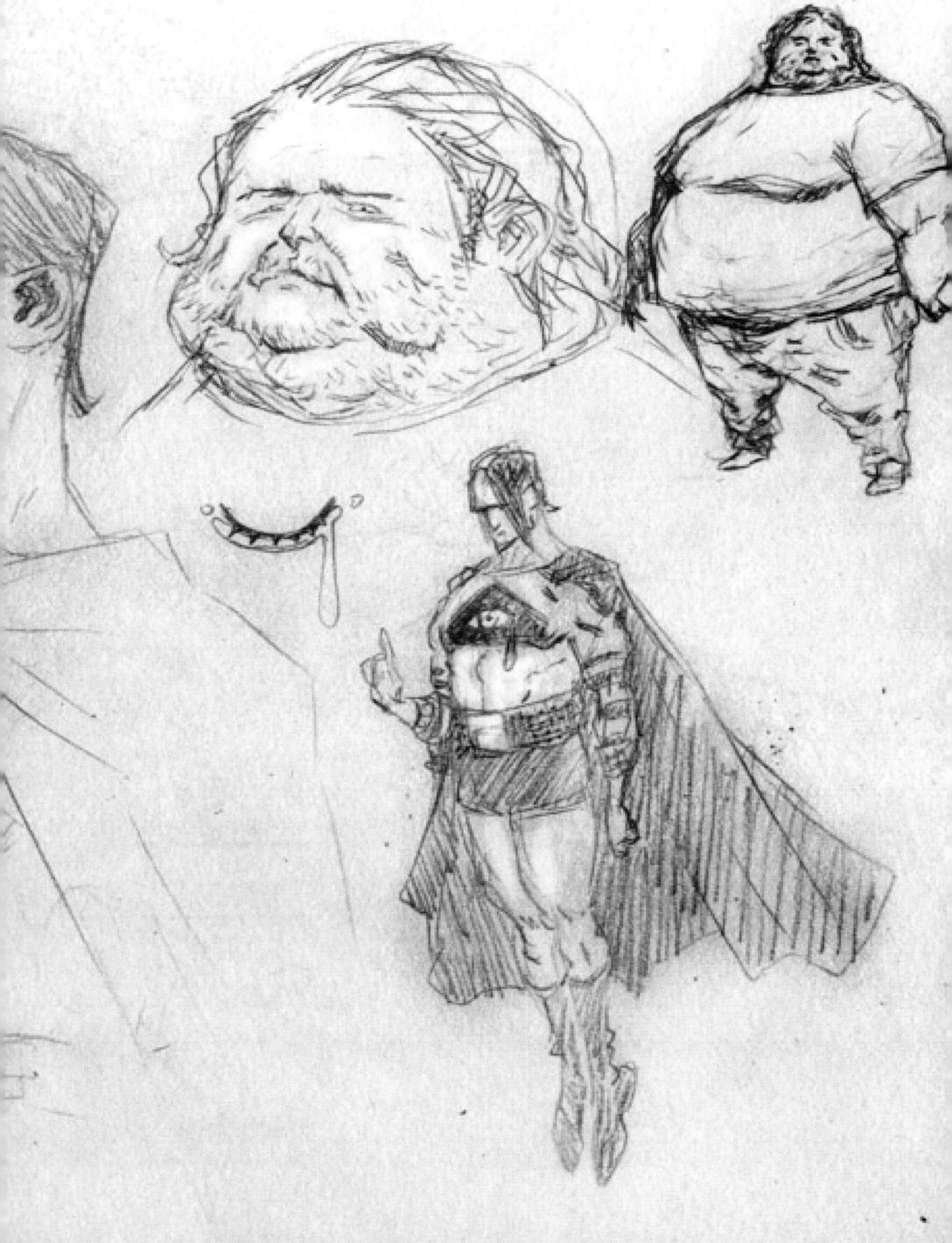

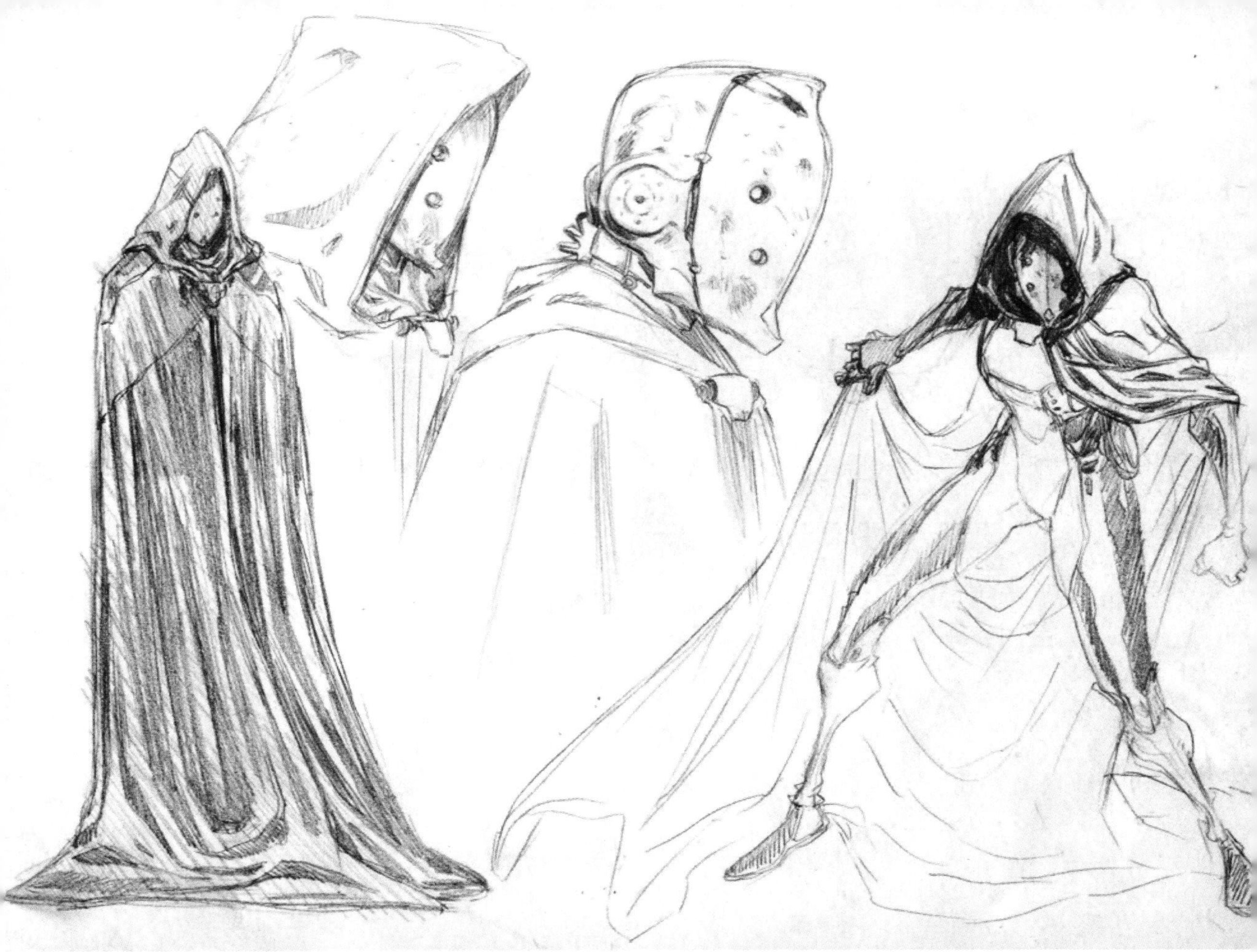

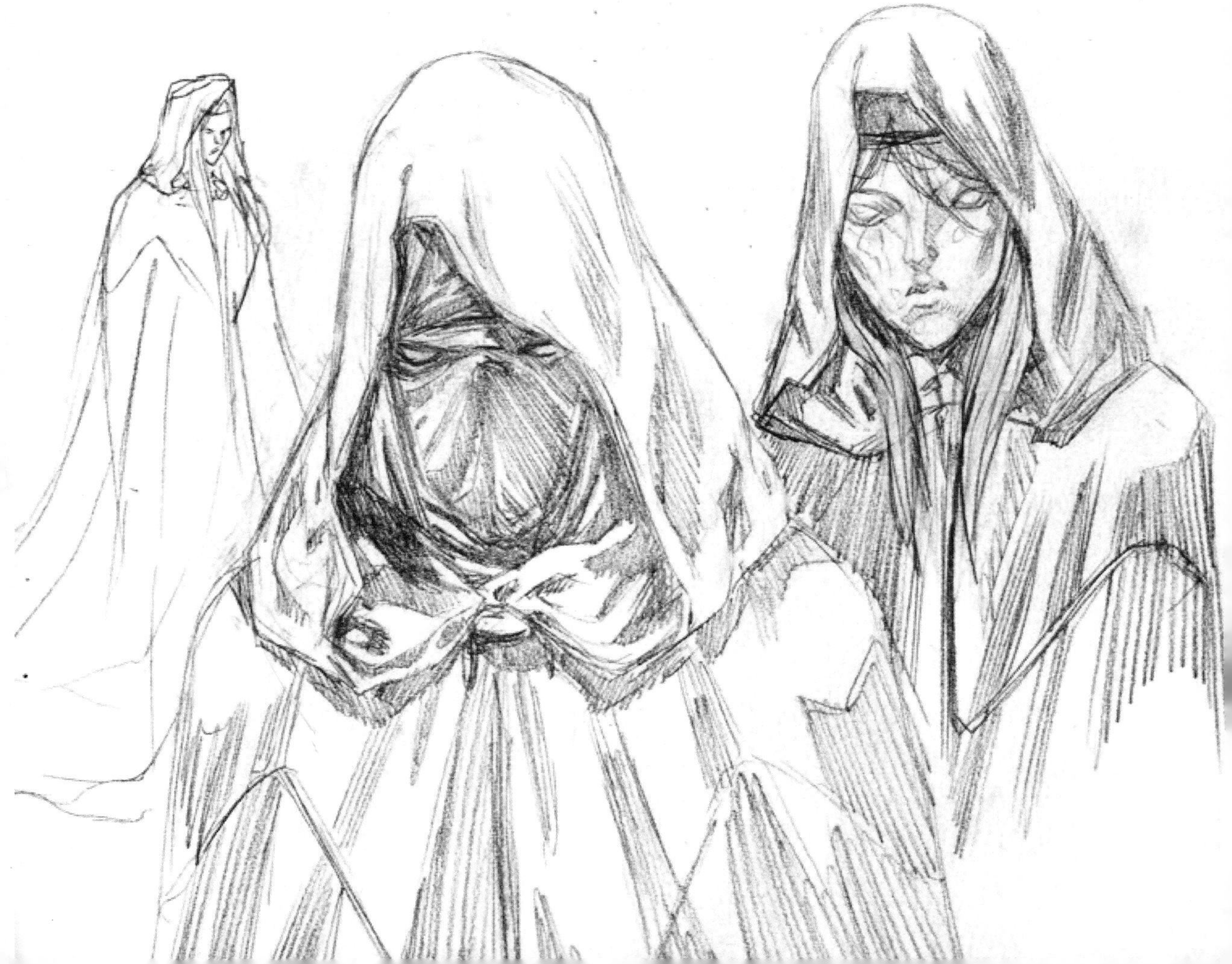

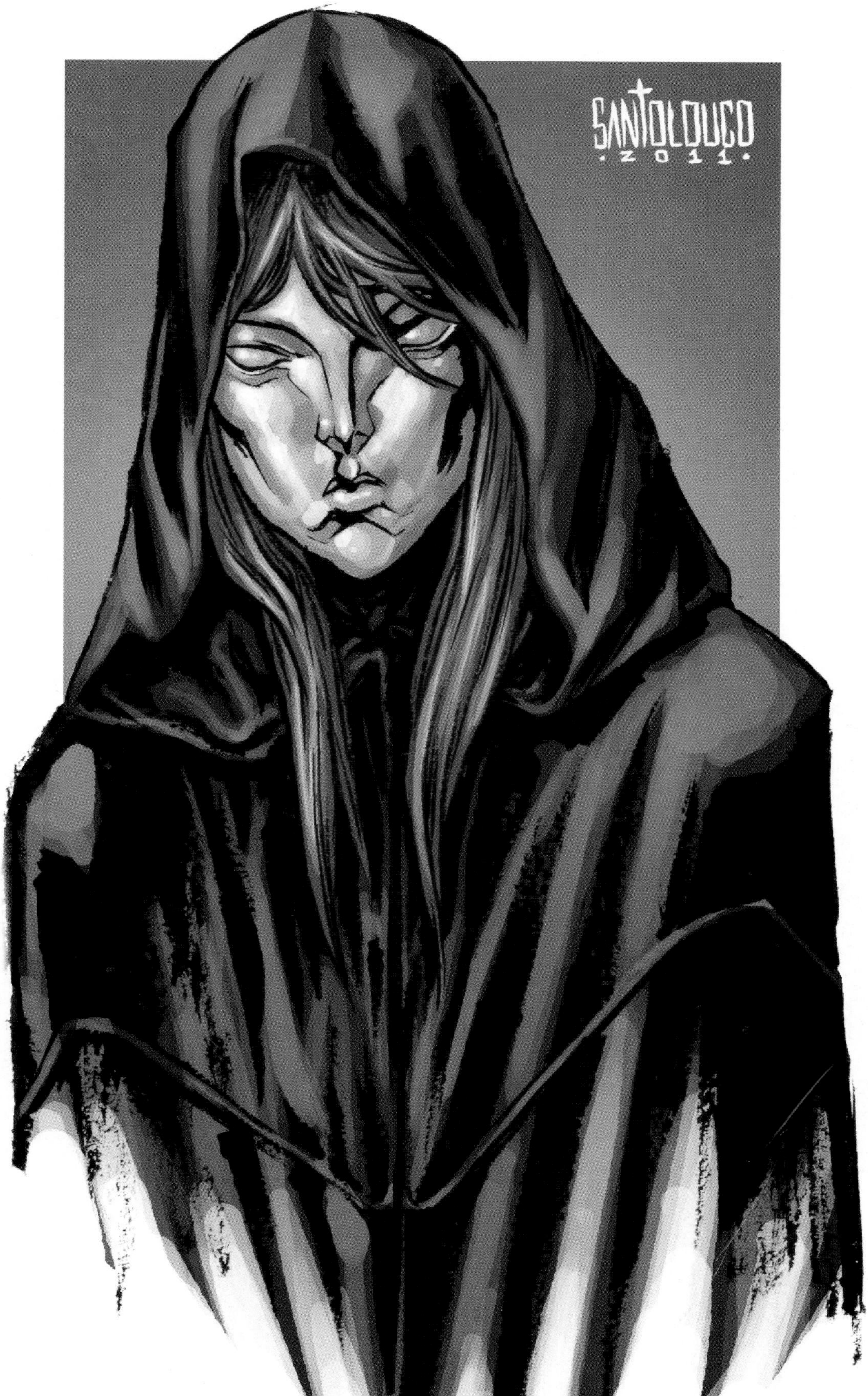
SANTOLOUCO
·2011·

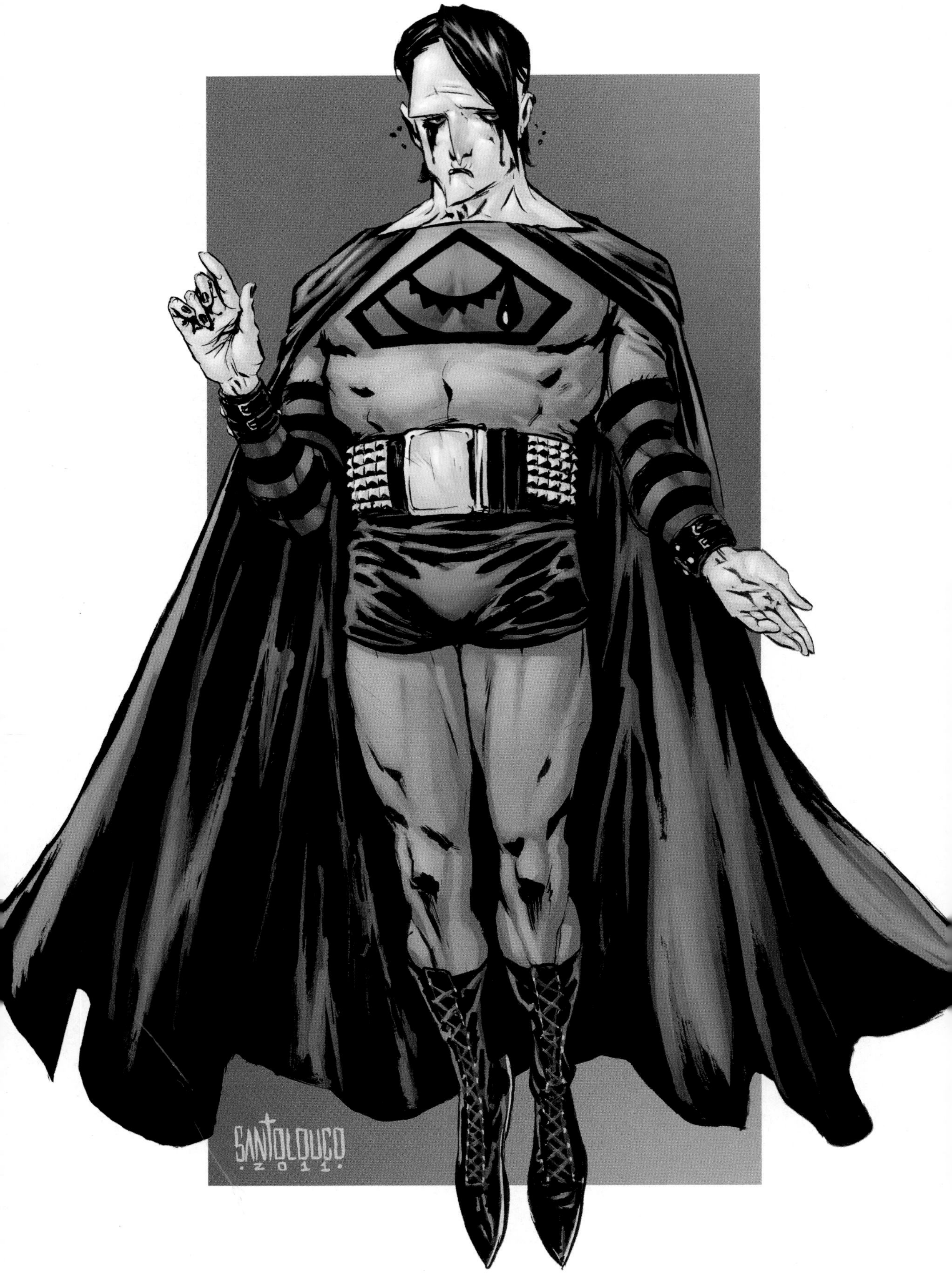
SANTOLOUCO
·2011·

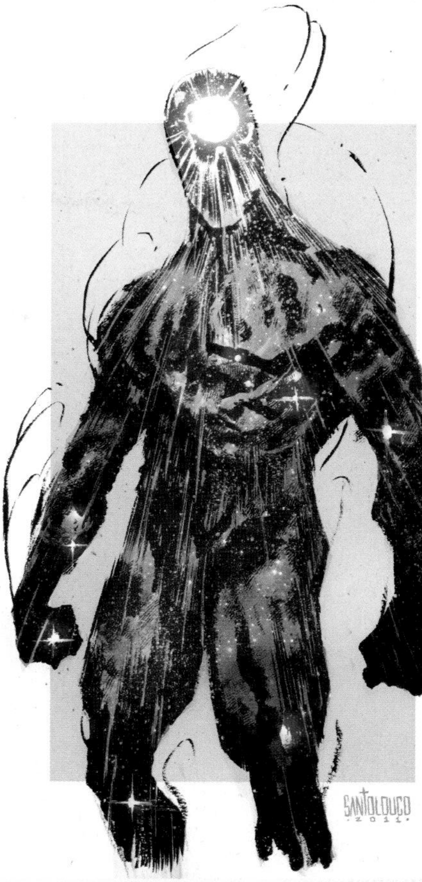
SANTOLOUCO
2011

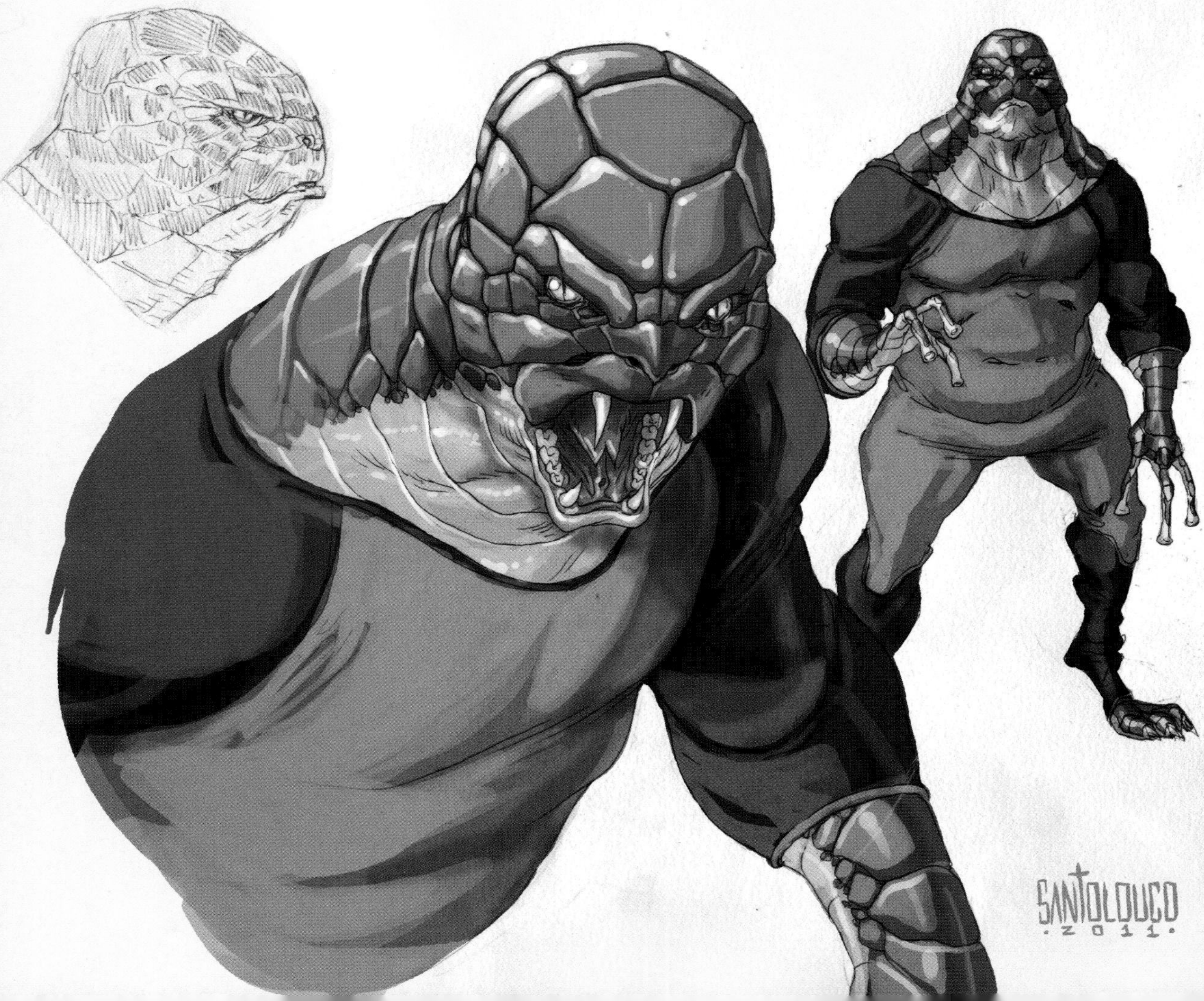
SANTOLOUCO
2011

DIAL H INTERIOR PAGE PENCILS BY ALBERTO PONTICELLI

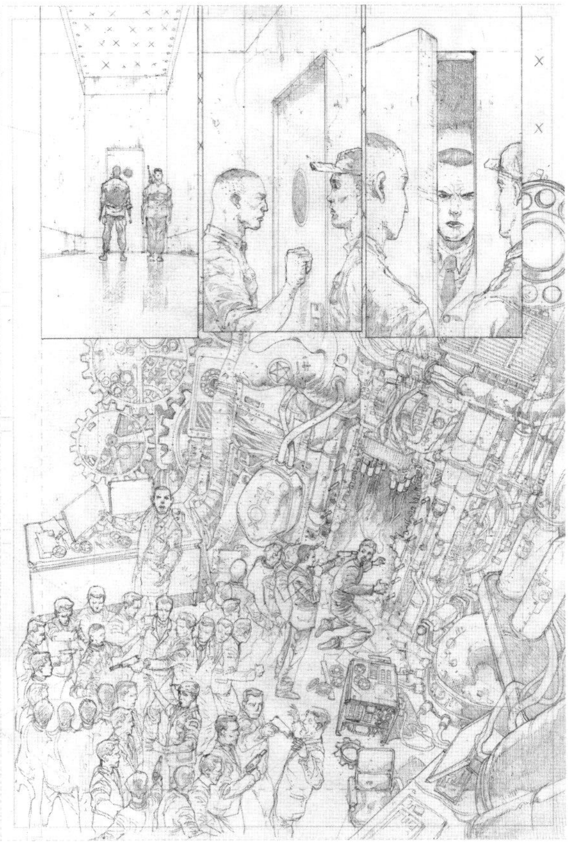

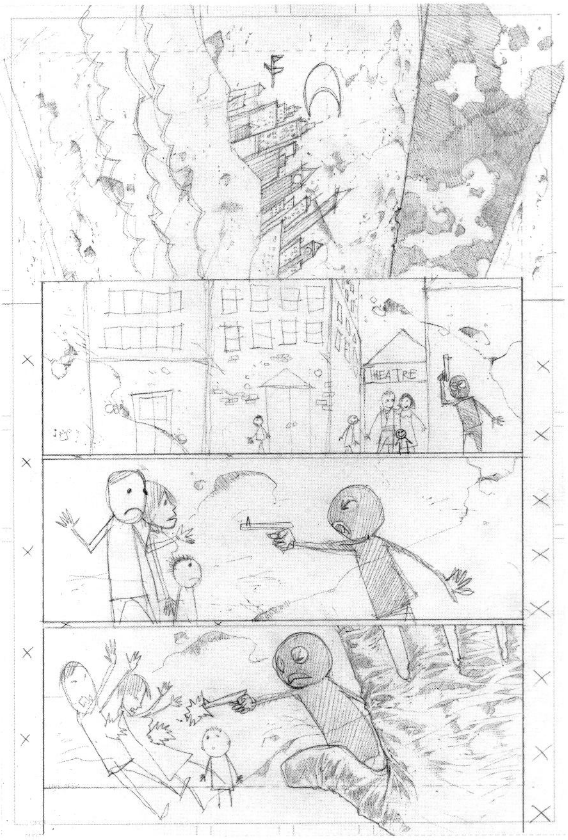
THEATRE

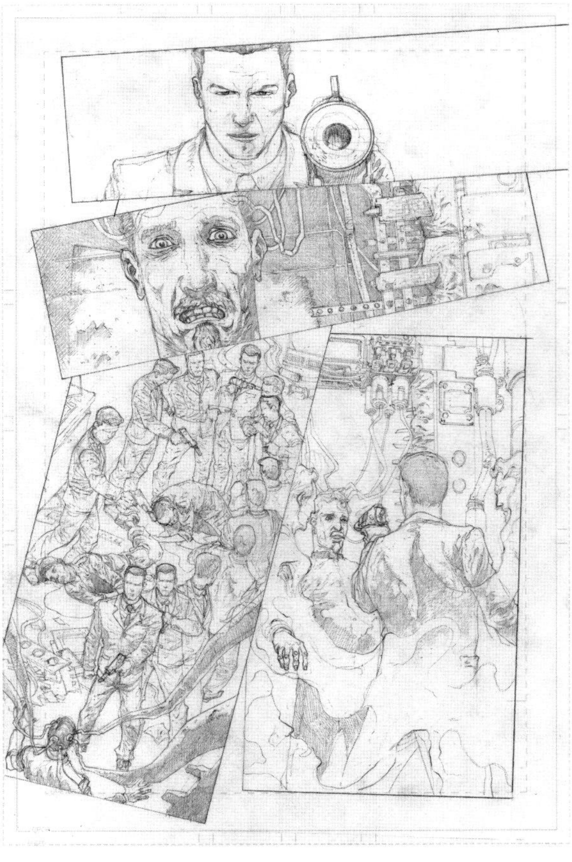

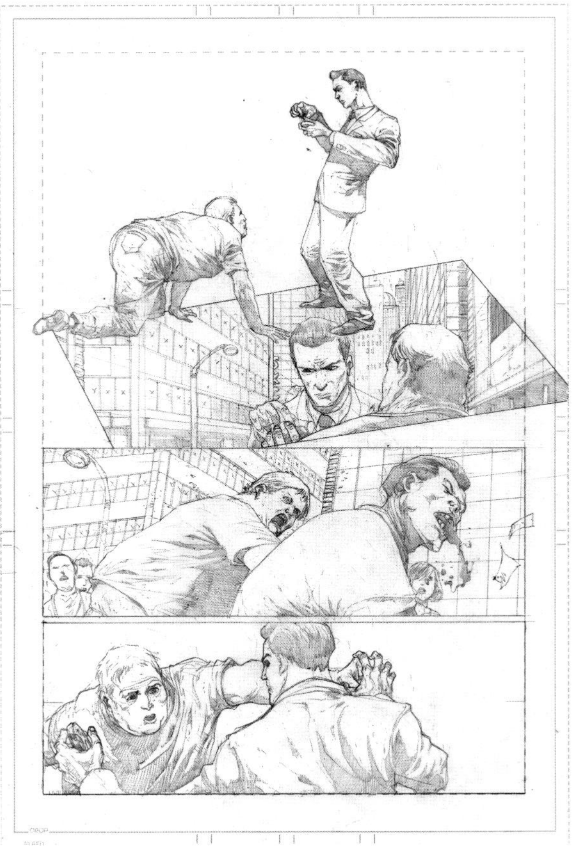

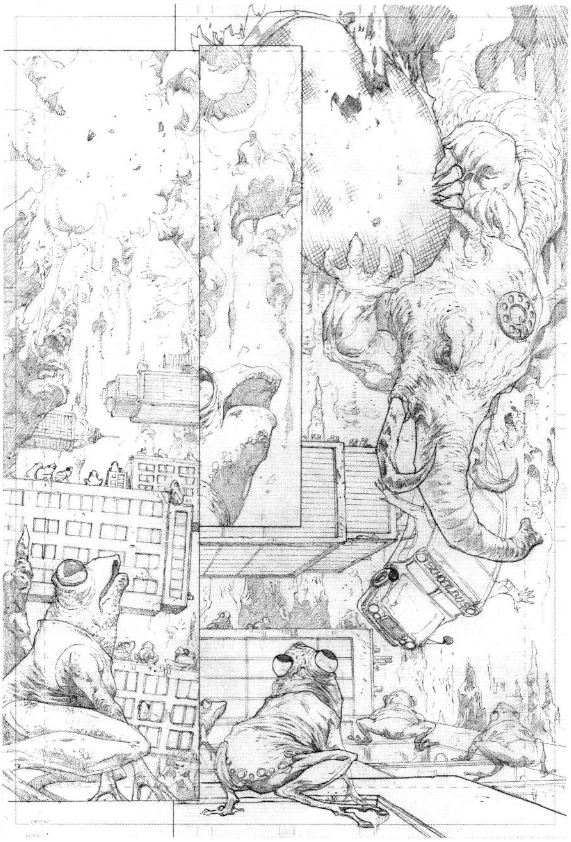
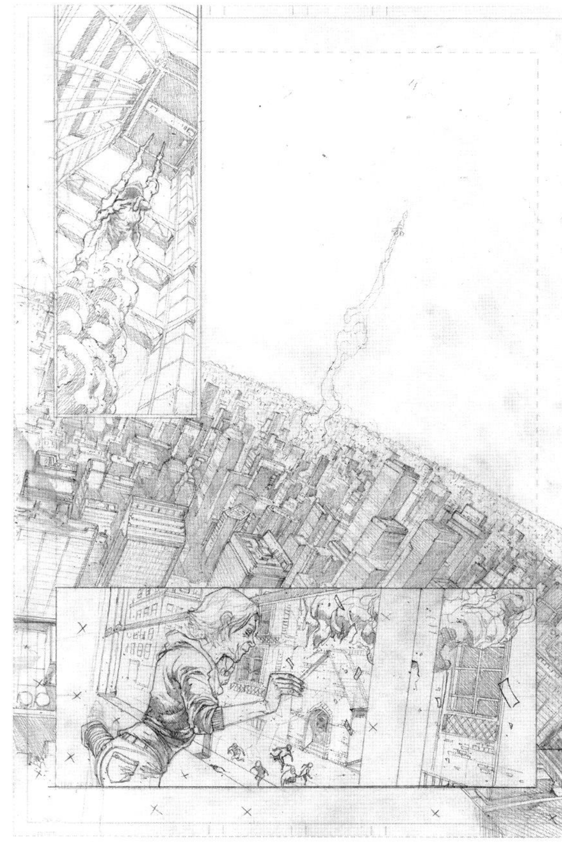
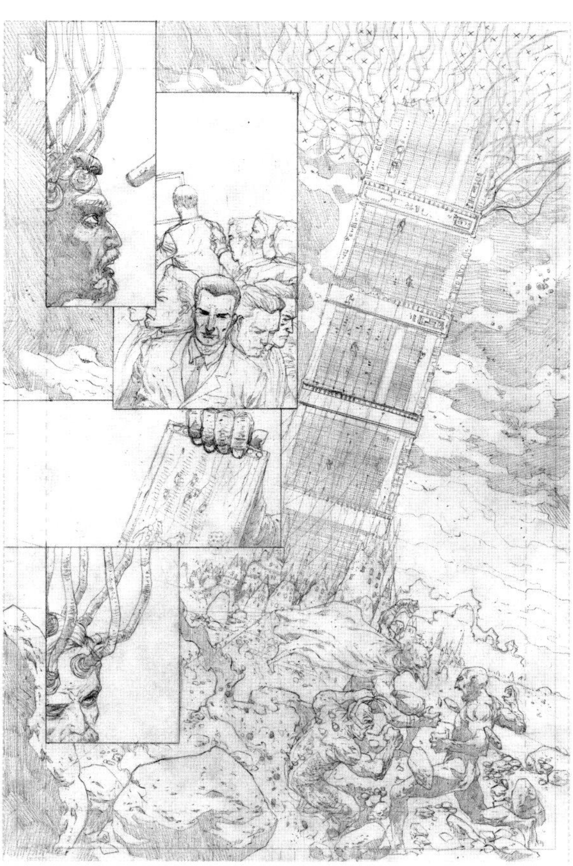
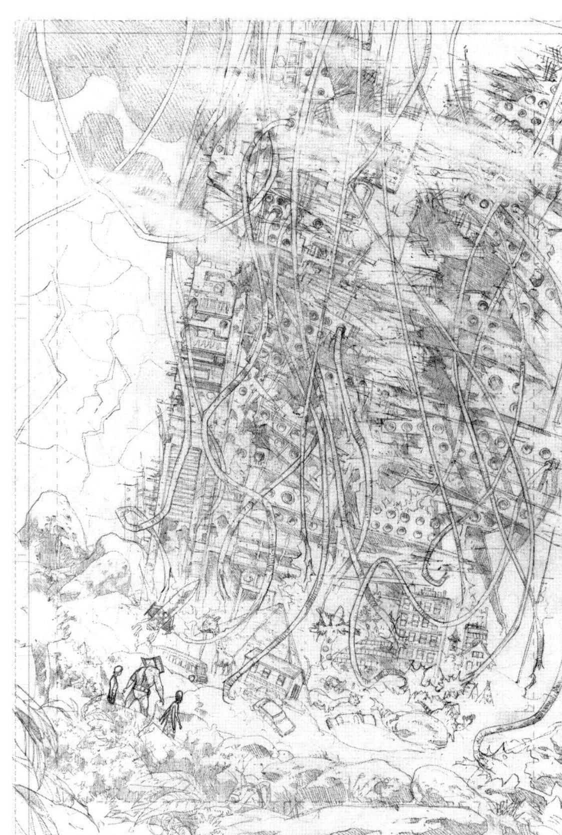

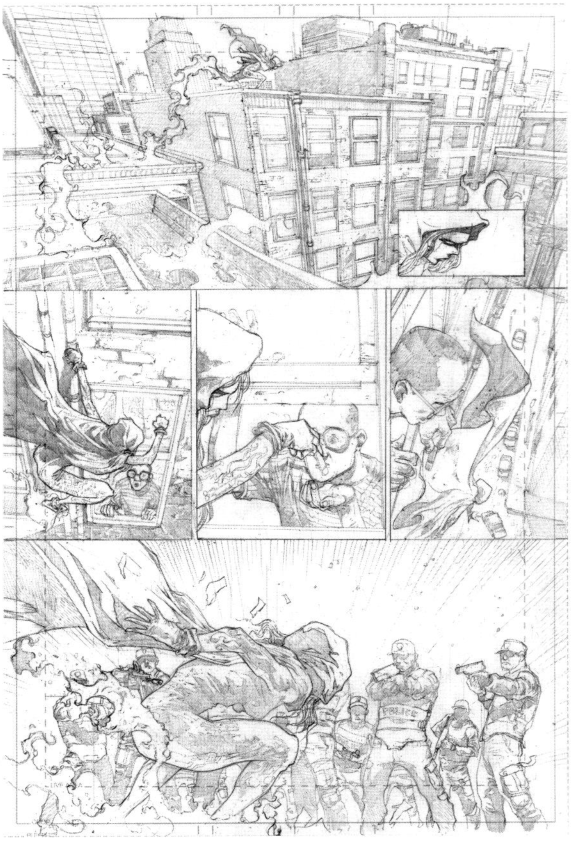
POLICE
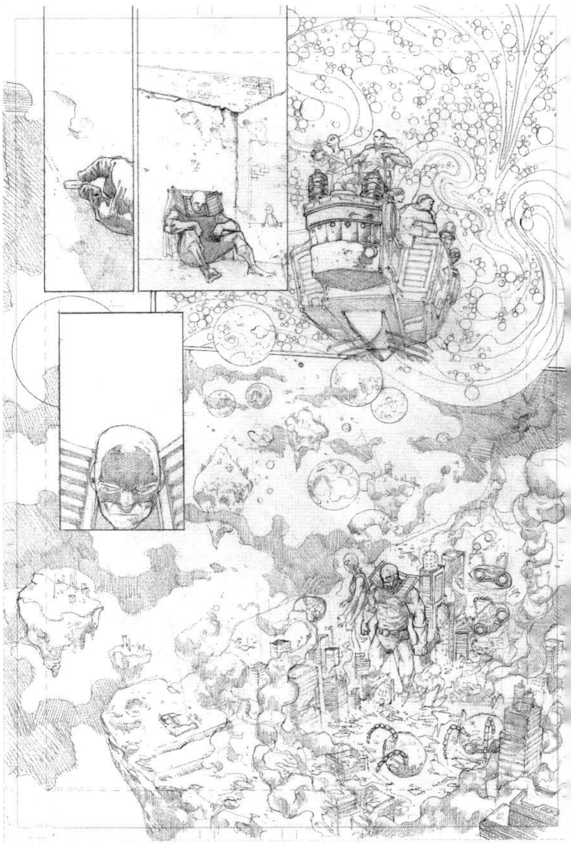
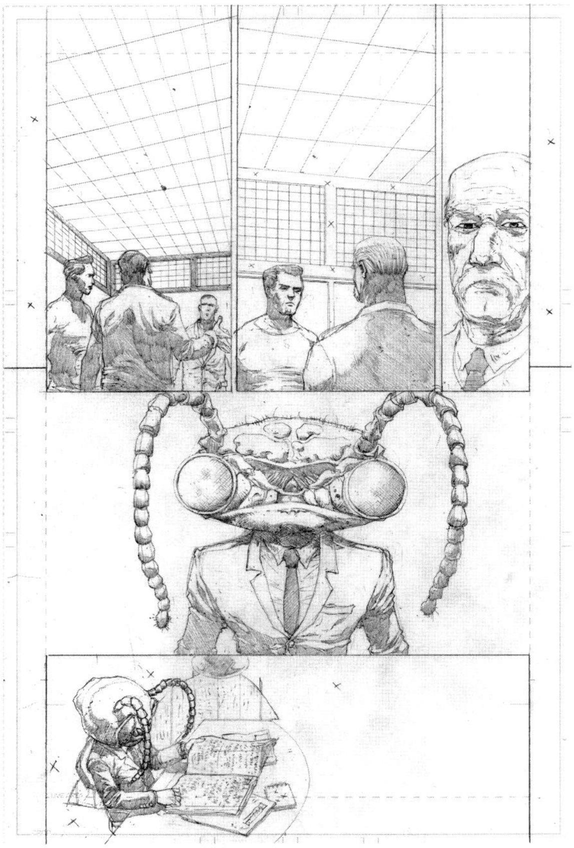
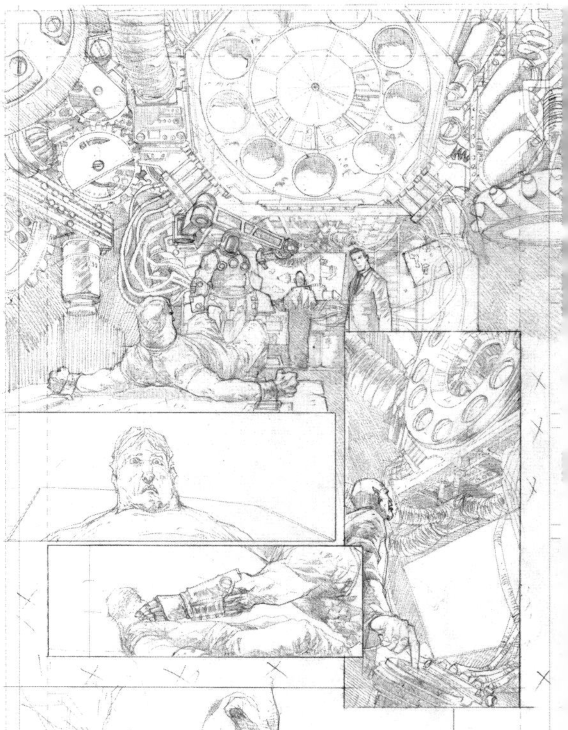

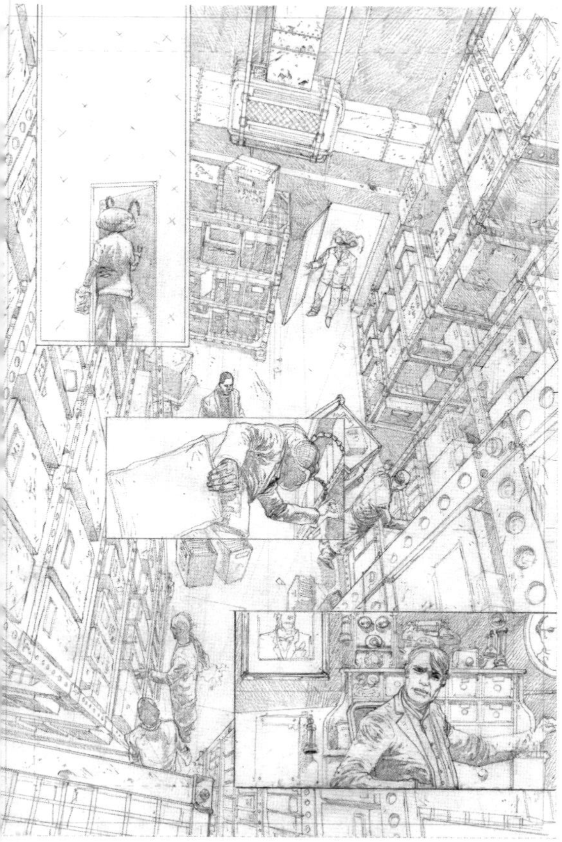

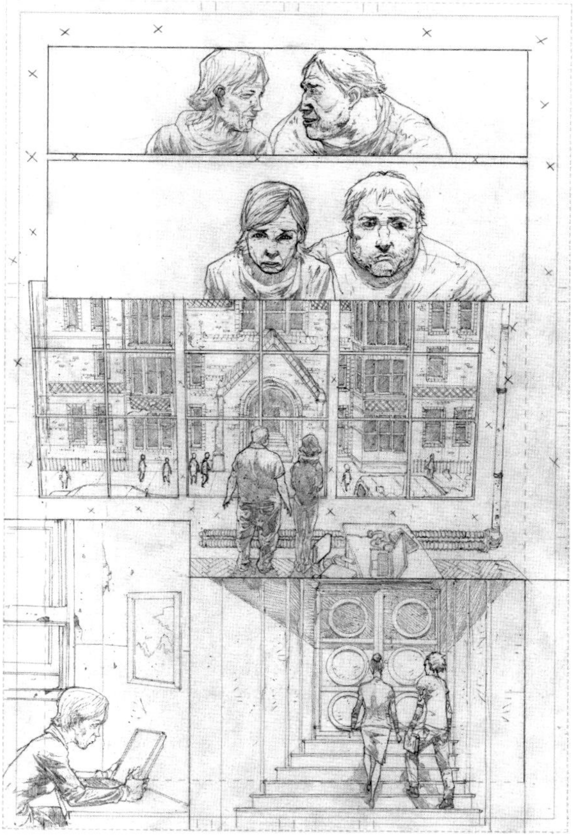

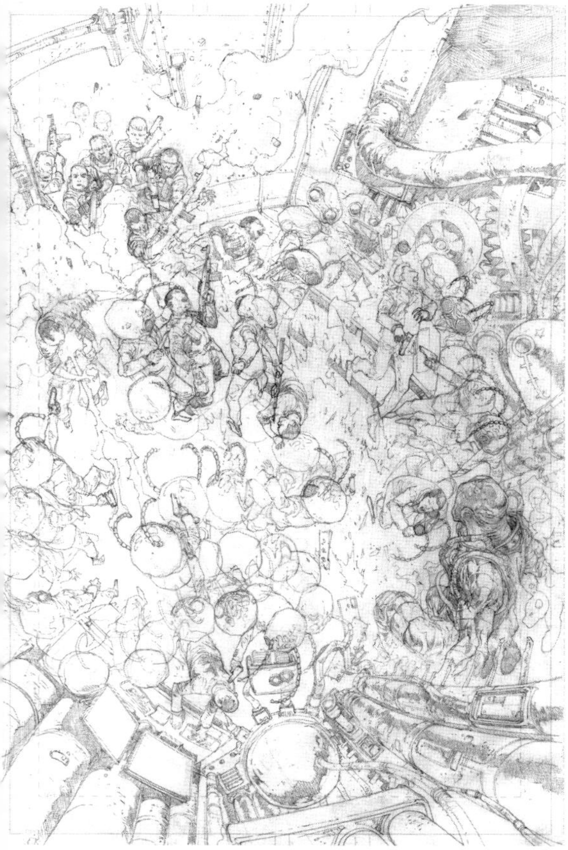

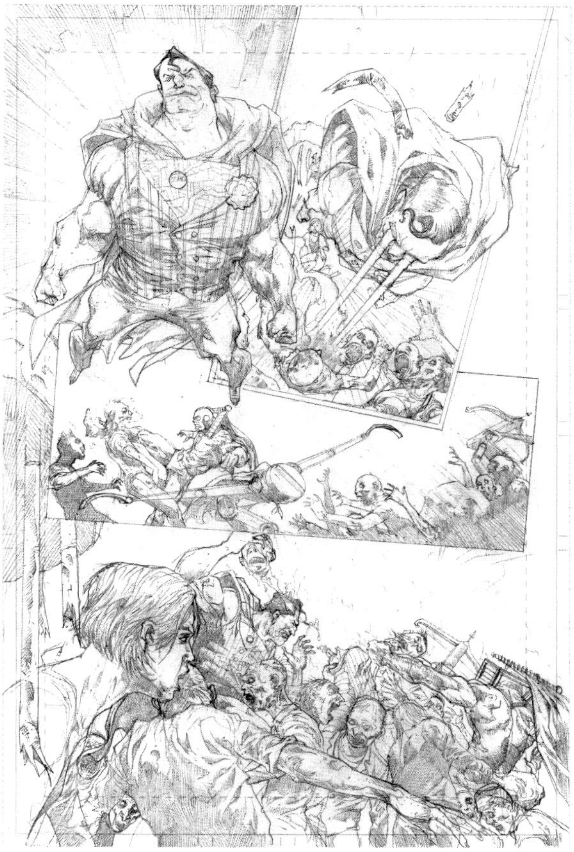

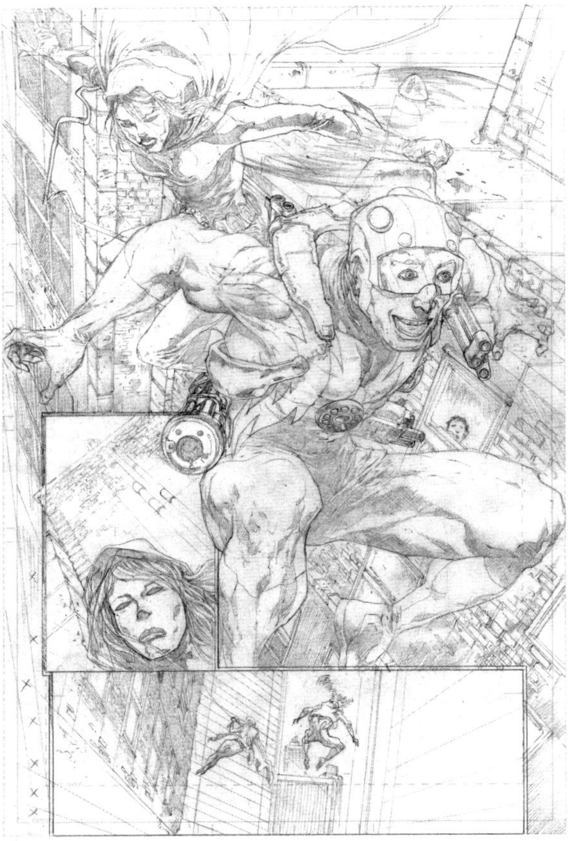
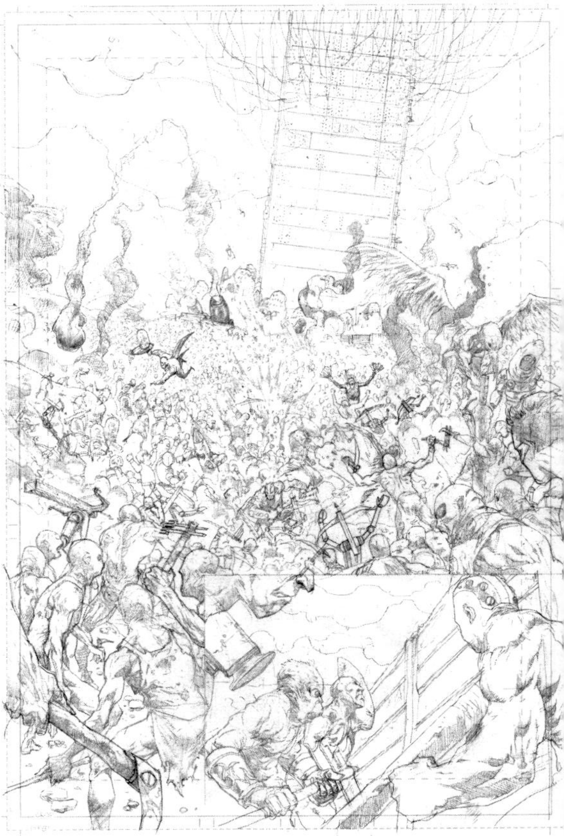
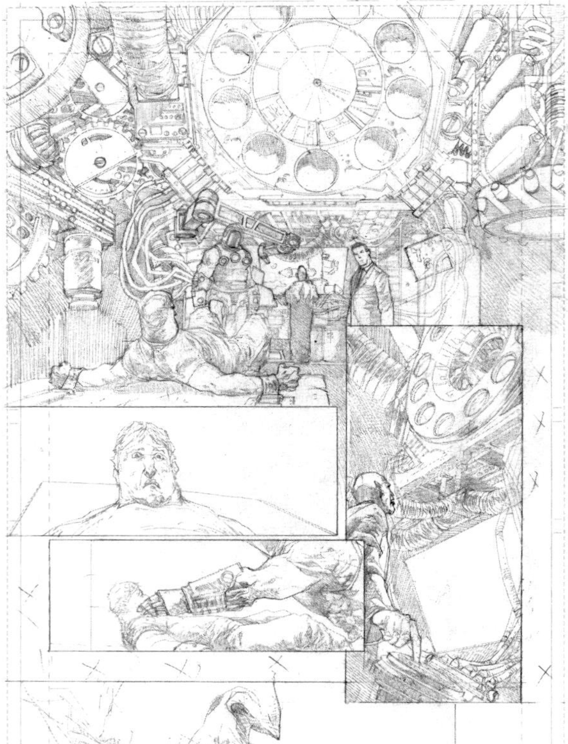
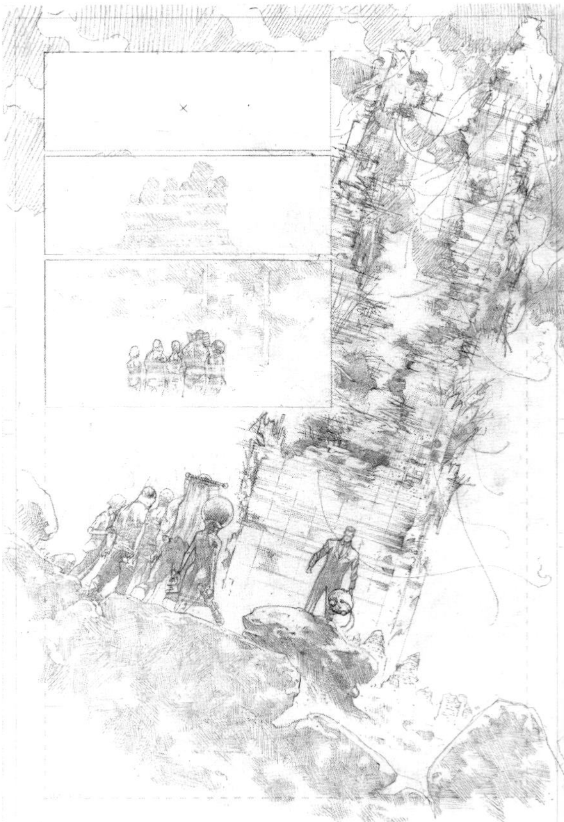